Charles

with love and best
wishes from Mum and Dad

Christmas 1999

FRA FILIPPO LIPPI

The Carmelite Painter

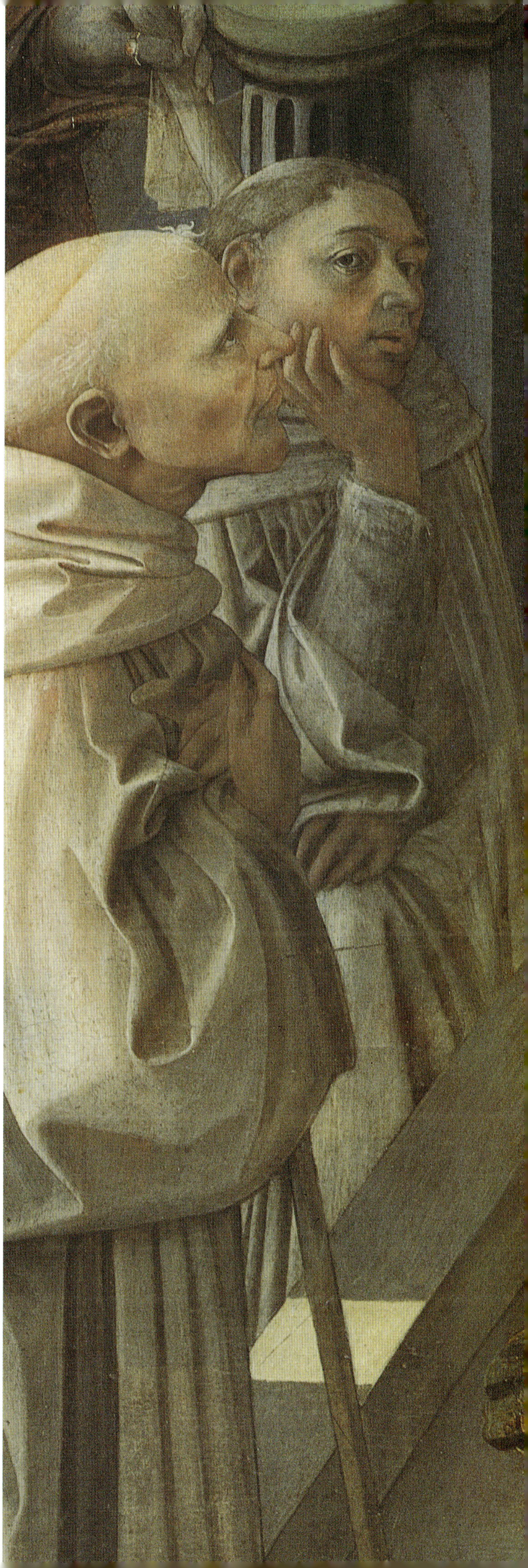

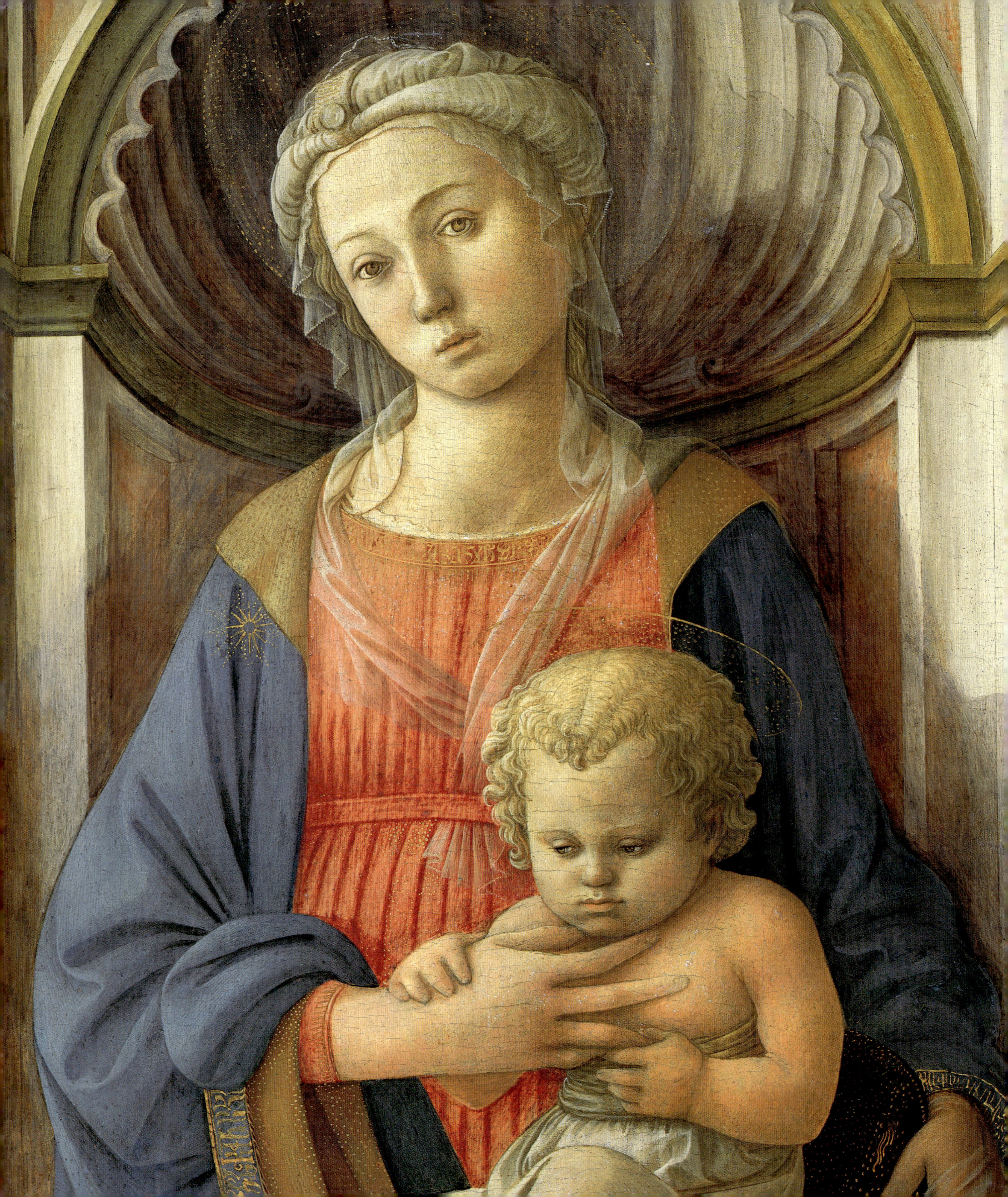

FRA FILIPPO LIPPI

The Carmelite Painter

MEGAN HOLMES

YALE UNIVERSITY PRESS
New Haven & London

Published with the assistance of the Getty Grant Program

Designed by Gillian Malpass

Printed in Singapore

Library of Congress Cataloging-in-Publication Data

Holmes, Megan, 1959–
Fra Filippo Lippi the Carmelite painter / Megan Holmes.
p. cm.
Includes bibliographical references and index.
ISBN 0-300-08104-9 (cloth : alk. paper)
1. Lippi, Filippo, ca. 1406–1469 – Criticism and interpretation.
2. Painting, Renaissance – Italy. I. Title.
ND623.L7H65 1999
759.5 – dc21 99-14918 CIP

A catalogue record for this book is available from
The British Library

Frontispiece Filippo Lippi, *Madonna and Child*, detail of fig. 133.

Page i Filippo Lippi, *Coronation of the Virgin*, detail of fig. 214, with self-portrait (right).

CONTENTS

facing page Filippo Lippi, Adoration of the Magi, detail of fig. 128.

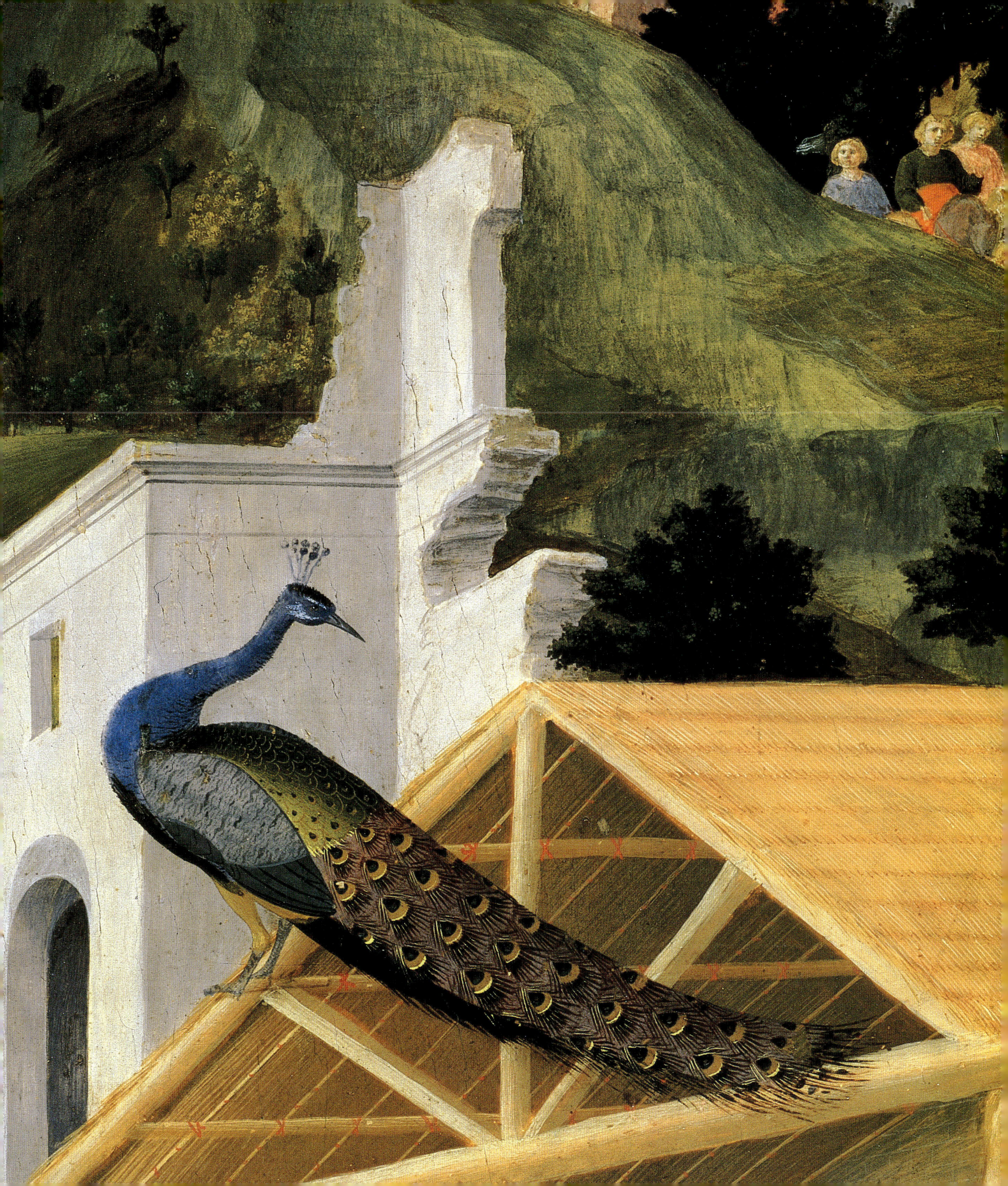

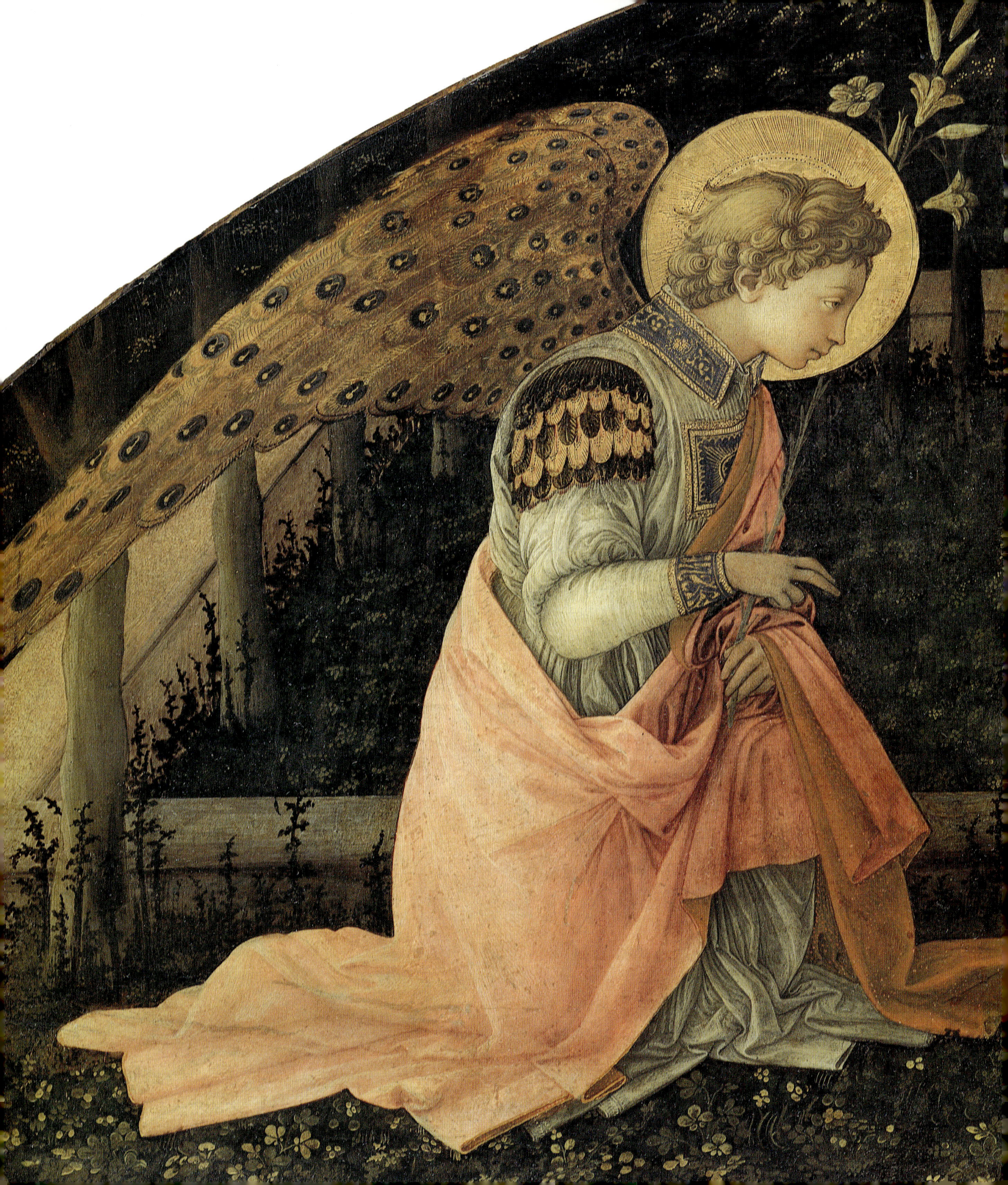

ACKNOWLEDGMENTS

THE INSPIRATION FOR THIS BOOK dates back to a paper presented in a graduate seminar, "Context and Form," at Harvard University taught by T. J. Clark in 1985. The project matured under the helpful guidance of my graduate advisers. James Ackerman gave me considerable latitude in defining the scope of the project and responded to my chapter submissions with helpful comments and editorial advice. John Shearman – with hundreds of post-its – provided a critical reading of the dissertation draft. His many suggestions were integrated into the dissertation and are now part of the fabric of the book.

I am indebted to many scholars for their contributions to this study. Stephen Campbell, Elizabeth Cropper, Charles Dempsey, Deborah Krohn, Patricia Rubin, and Eve Sanders read the text at various stages and gave excellent criticisms. I received helpful directives also from the readers for Yale University Press. William Hood, one of the readers, offered an insightful critique of my treatment of Renaissance monasticism that prompted me to tighten my argumentation and rethink certain sections. Kate Lowe and Saundra Weddle were generous in sharing their work on the Florentine nunnery Le Murate and reviewing Chapter 9 on Fra Filippo Lippi's altarpieces for Le Murate and Sant' Ambrogio. Antoinette Roesler-Friedenthal discussed her ideas about Fra Filippo Lippi's self-portrait in Spoleto with me. Kim Butler kindly checked my Latin translations. Jonathan Davies, Jonathan Nelson, and Brenda Preyer were generous in providing archival citations. Gino Corti and Michael Rocke assisted in deciphering Notarile documents from the Florentine Archives. Jeffrey Ruda met me and discussed his book on Fra Filippo Lippi prior to its publication. Eve Sanders provided vital computer software for the conversion of the text. I should like to thank also the curatorial staff of the National Gallery in London, the Alte Pinakothek in Munich (with special gratitude to Cornelia Syre), the Metropolitan Museum in New York, and the National Gallery of Art in Washington. Thanks also to the staff at the Archivio di Stato, the Kunsthistorisches Institut, and the Gabinetto Fotografico of the Florentine Soprintendenza per i Beni Artistici e Storici, the staff and scholars at the Villa I Tatti in Florence, Joyce de Vries, and Sue Capitani of Florida State University's Florence Program.

For providing a stimulating environment for the discussion of art history, visual representation, and critical theory, I owe many thanks to my fellow graduate students at Harvard University and in Florence, and later, during my two years teaching in Baltimore, to my colleagues and the graduate students at The Johns Hopkins University. Gillian Malpass, my editor at Yale University Press, provided invaluable advice and support throughout the various stages leading up to publication of this book. I should like to thank also the copy-editor, Katharine Ridler.

Patricia Rubin deserves my special thanks. Her rigorous standards in pursuing a history of Italian Renaissance art grounded in historical scholarship have been a model for my own work. First as a mentor, and later as a colleague and friend, she has been most generous with her support, constructive criticism, and lively humor. She read the dissertation and offered helpful suggestions, and reviewed an early draft of Chapter 6. She also put me in contact with Gillian Malpass of Yale University Press, which has led to the publication of this book.

And finally, I should like to single out and thank some important people in my personal life: Giovanni Minonne, for living with this project for so many years and for checking my Italian translations; Jack and Ann Holmes, for their support and their interest in my academic endeavors – with special thanks to Ann Holmes for her editorial assistance and persistence in those battles lost and won (Burckhardt, I fear, continues to "trumpet"); Lise Apatoff, without whose steady friendship the final editing of the manuscript would not have taken place; and Lia Francesca Minonne, who arrived on the scene during the last stages of this project, reordering my universe, and succeeding where all others had failed in teaching me the necessity of the short endnote.

This project has been generously supported by a number of fellowships. The original dissertation research was undertaken with a Harvard University travel grant, a Kress Foundation Institutional Fellowship, and a Kress Foundation Dissertation Fellowship. The book manuscript was completed during a fellowship year at the Villa I Tatti.

facing page Filippo Lippi, *Annunciation*, detail of fig. 223.

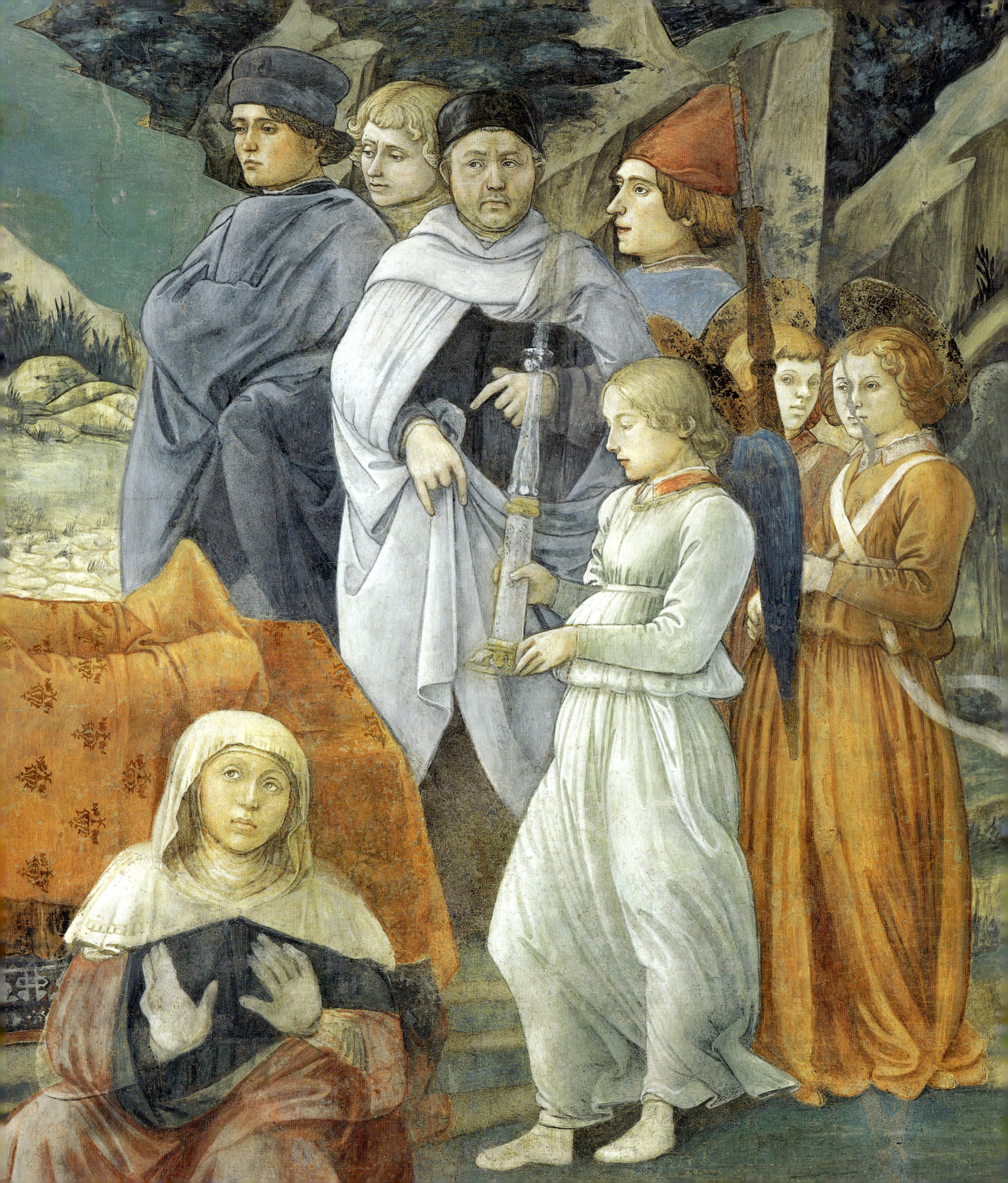

INTRODUCTION

THE FOLLOWING STORY IS TOLD about the *quattrocento* Florentine country parish priest, the Piovano Arlotto: "Among the neighbors of Piovano Arlotto, there was a father with a single young son, handsome and well-built, whose mother had died a few years earlier. The father remarried another woman, young and beautiful." The young man was neglected by his father and his new wife and reduced to wearing old tattered clothing. His friends came to his aid and contrived a scheme to redress the situation that involved making love with his stepmother. Once this amorous alliance was established, she became (not surprisingly) more attentive to his material needs. But one day,

> The father . . . discovered the son astride the woman. There was a great commotion which lasted many days and was heard by all in the neighborhood. But no one knew what they were fighting and shouting about day after day. One day, they were shouting so loudly that once again many neighbors hurried over, among them the Piovano Arlotto. . . .
>
> The Piovano knocked on the door. The father and son came down. . . .
>
> The Piovano asked, "What's the matter? Every day you've done nothing but shout for some time now."
>
> The father responded, "My Piovano, if you were to know, you'd say I have reason." But the situation being what it was, the father of the boy said, "Piovano, I can't tell you about it."
>
> The boy responded, "Piovano, I want to tell you about it. My father embraced my mother perhaps a thousand times while she was living, and now that I have embraced my stepmother a couple of times, this father of mine blows up a storm every day in the neighborhood."
>
> The Piovano said, "Don't make any more noise. To embrace, one with another, doesn't come about if not from charity. Each one of you take what gives you pleasure, be in peace and don't fight any more, for no one will come to know of your affair, and from now on, be the wiser.[1]

The question I wish to raise with this story is what or who determined the fixity of meaning in *quattrocento* Renaissance society? When did a physical embrace signify *carità* (charity) and when did it connote *adulterio* (adultery)? The Piovano Arlotto is able to absolve an incident of adultery into an excusable, even just act for a number of reasons acceptable to the Renaissance Florentine audience of the ribald anecdote, the *facezia*. For one thing, "at this time the Piovano was young" ("a quel tempo il Piovano era giovane"), and in the Arlotto stories, this is the standard means of excusing Arlotto's own sexual peccadillos and the way he makes humorous example out of those of others. Arlotto was also a privileged interpreter of the gray area between venal sin and holy virtue. The historical character Arlotto di Giovanni Mainardi, on whom the *facezie* are based, was well positioned within the Florentine social world. He was the son of an indebted member of an established family from the Mugello and a friend of many among the Florentine social elite.[2] As the more or less upright priest of San Cresci a Maciuoli, he was either "holier than thou" or reasonably and imaginatively less so. In addition, he had a remarkable talent – highly respected in the period – for running against mundane expectations in ingeniously asserting his extraordinary interpretation of situations.

This *facezia*, however, pivots on the contingency of meaning associated with a gesture like an embrace. The son used the term euphemistically, in defending – with carnivalized logic – his carnal relations with his stepmother. Arlotto sidestepped this reading, and transformed the embrace into a manifestation of the Christian virtue *carità*, before eradicating the sign entirely, when he reconstituted the then wiser family at the end of the tale. The embrace itself had certain conventional meanings, but its interpretation was contested by the various individuals who acted upon the symbol as it was generated and exchanged. The significance of any gesture, symbol, or act was dependent on a combination of the discursive codes and social practices which ascribed certain values to it and, of particular significance in *quattrocento* Florence, on the position of the individuals involved, their relationship to one another, and the context of the communication.

1 Filippo Lippi, *Dormition of the Virgin*, detail of fig. 159, with self-portrait.

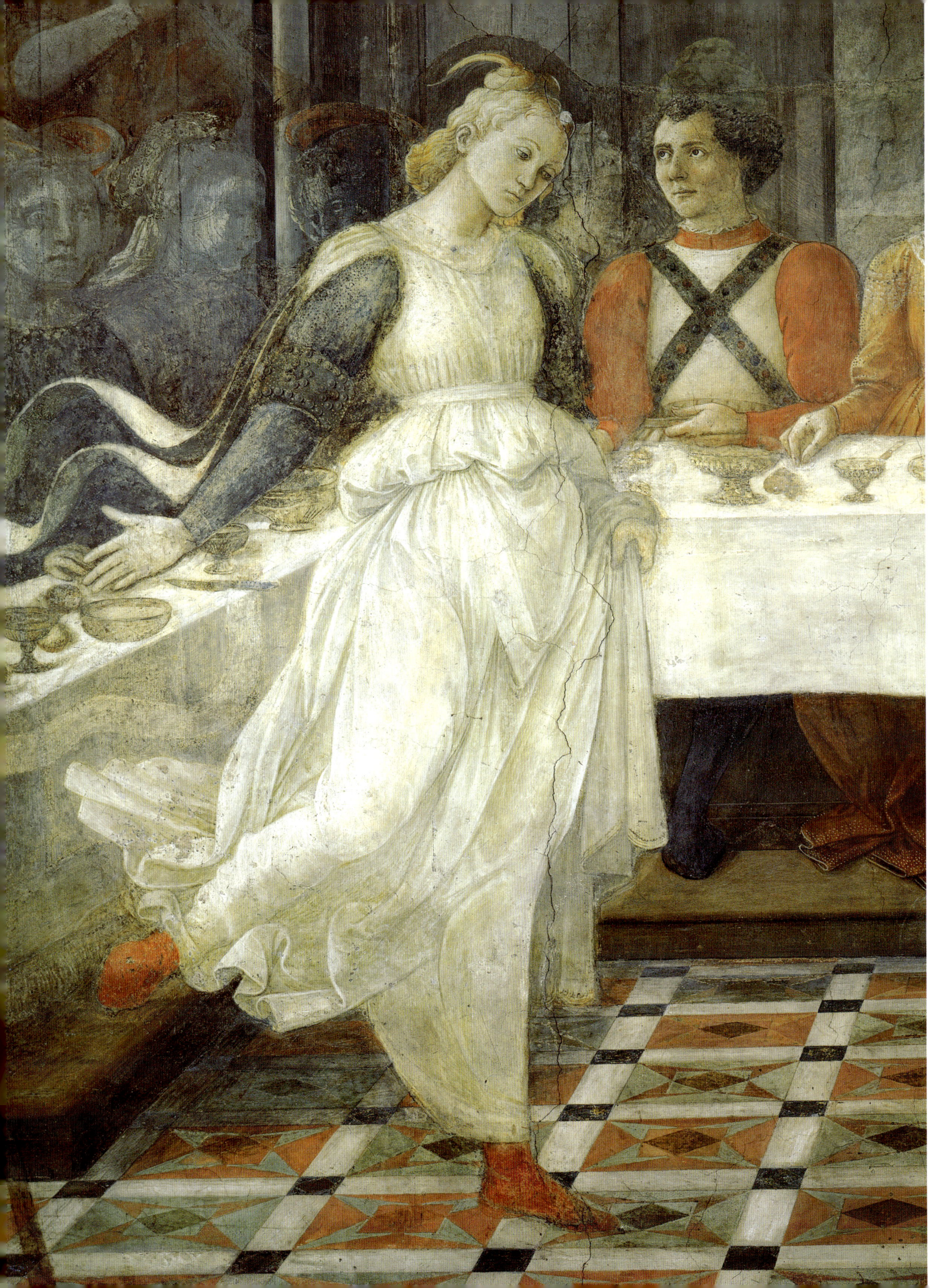

I have used this *facezia* to introduce my study of the *quattrocento* Florentine artist Fra Filippo Lippi because there is compelling common ground between the Arlotto character and Lippi. That shared terrain is the Florentine religious culture represented in the burlesque humor, the quotidian concerns, and the pragmatic negotiations in the *facezie*. The painter, like Arlotto, was a spirited interpreter of *quattrocento* Florentine religious life. Like Arlotto's, the social and discursive terrain in which Fra Filippo operated was defined by religious markers. He was a Carmelite friar and a beneficed priest, and was a maker of religious images. He, too, was involved in mobilizing conventional symbols and endowing them with a particular meaning within a specific religious discursive context. While Arlotto's most efficacious pulpit was the *osteria* table, Fra Filippo's principle communicative mode was the painted *tavola*. But some of the Florentines who commissioned Fra Filippo's altarpieces – like Giovanni and Piero de' Medici, Giovanni Benci, and Domenico Maringhi – made their way into the Arlotto stories as the Piovano's interlocutors or the butts of his *burle*. And many of the subjects that the painter tackled in his pictorial imagery were also treated by the Piovano – the antiquity of the Carmelites, the efficacy of images, the relationship between a religious representation and the sacred person or event signified, interpretations of the Christian mysteries and canonical events, and public participation in Christian rites. Not as socially distinguished or as conveniently fictive as the Arlotto character, Fra Filippo was at times a bold and humorous orchestrator of meaning within his environment, and at other times an agent, a transmitter of the designs of others.

The principal focus of this study is the religious context in which Fra Filippo Lippi lived his life and executed his paintings. I examine the range of meanings that were communicated through the religious pictorial imagery of Fra Filippo Lippi, and consider how these meanings were produced and experienced within *quattrocento* Florentine society. I suggest that there is a significant relationship between the experiences of the painter – a Carmelite friar who, after leaving the monastery, was constantly at odds with ecclesiastical authorities – and the images of the Virgin and Child, the Annunciation, the Nativity, the Coronation of the Virgin, and the Christian saints that he painted. There is also a necessary connection to be made between this artist and his works and Florentine society at a critical moment during the early Renaissance – a period poised between republican and Medicean rule, between the Schism and the Reformation, between a feudal and a capitalist economy.

Fra Filippo Lippi's unique status as a Carmelite "friar painter," with greater movement between the social spaces of the *claustrum* (cloister) and the *seculum* (secular society) than his fellow practitioners, afforded him the opportunity to explore critical issues within religious representation. My interest is to set Fra Filippo's painting within the context of Carmelite representational practices and in relation to other specific sites within Florentine religious culture. I focus on Lippi's artistic activities in the city of Florence or working for Florentine patrons, from the 1430s through the 1450s.[3] During this second quarter of the *quattrocento*, religious art was the principal site where new artistic conceptions and technologies came into collision with traditional practices and values. It is no coincidence that two monastic artists, Fra Filippo and his contemporary, the Observant Dominican Fra Angelico, were perceived to be among the most progressive painters working in the city at this time, dominating the upper end of the painting market.

My study turns on the role that religion played in early Renaissance society and culture. The scholarly debate over this question has progressed considerably since 1860 when Jacob Burckhardt trumpeted:

> These modern men, the representatives of the culture of Italy, were born with the same religious instincts as other medieval Europeans. But their powerful individuality made them in religion, as in other matters, altogether subjective, and the intense charm which the discovery of the inner and outer universe exercised upon them rendered them markedly worldly.[4]

Revisions of the Burckhardtian thesis have tended towards micro-histories which focus on individual communities, social groups, or institutions. These studies demonstrate Renaissance continuities with earlier religious practices, label as "religion" what Burckhardt had dismissed as pagan, magic, and superstition, and recover the histories of people other than his "intellectual giants."[5] In the past decade, additional correctives with a broader scope have come from historians and religious historians who have been influenced by anthropology and comparative religion. These new perspectives have helped to dim the aura that had hallowed Christianity as the principal religious system in a privileged, progressive Western civilization. Consequently, Christian rites, sacraments, and institutions have been subjected to a similar sort of scrutiny to that which Western scholars had traditionally turned upon non-Western, "primitive," and "third world" cultures.[6]

Historians have worked with several schemes in attempting to characterize the range of religious experiences particular to Renaissance society. They generally have recourse to a bifurcated model, contrasting "traditional" practices with "modern" ones, or the "magical" with the "religious," the "irrational" with the "rational." Natalie Zemon Davis presents a strong argument against the use of such categories. "Can we learn as much as we would like about the meaning, modes and uses of popular religion to peasants and city dwellers if we judge by [these] . . . standards?" She offers instead a conception of "popular religion" characterized by

> its willingness, first, to give organizational expression to "the internal articulations" of society and even to encourage such articulation . . . and, second, to give ritual expression to

2 Filippo Lippi, *Banquet of Herod*, detail of fig. 98.

a wide range of feelings and moods, from the cruel to the comic. . . . Also we have noted the possibilities of serious social criticism in rite or play which vigorously turns worldly values or hierarchies upside down.[7]

Even with Davis's enriching treatment, however, one is still caught up in a religious culture divided into its "high" and "low," or its "official" and "popular" manifestations, and a population designated as "dominant" or "oppressed." More recent studies in religion that focus on gender have demanded a re-thinking of the way in which relations are defined between different social groups.[8] The monolithic groupings have fragmented into complicated, dynamic configurations where social and economic positions are cut across by divisions of gender and race. The very process by which religion functioned ideologically, servicing the dominant elements within a society and contributing toward cultural hegemony, becomes an infinitely complicated one, with multiple sites, variant forms, and points of resistance.

In my study of the religious context of the life and art of Fra Filippo Lippi, I approach religion from two different perspectives. On the one hand, I consider Christianity as one among a number of competing ideologies in Western Europe during the early Renaissance. Christianity claimed as its principal prerogative the demarcation of the sacred in relation to the secular, and the intervention in the spiritual and moral life of the population. Christianity was embodied by a range of institutions with their respective regulatory codes, rituals, and doctrines, and was maintained by designated functionaries and participating publics. During the early Renaissance, this ideological system and its institutional forms were experiencing pressure from various quarters.

There were internal schisms within the Church itself: between Western and Eastern Orthodoxy, between the papacy and the proponents of the Conciliar movement, between the Roman Curia and local religious authorities, between the secular clergy and the monastic clergy, and between unsanctioned and sanctioned cults. The Church as a territorial state was under attack by a shifting alliance headed by the Imperial forces. Within individual communes and signorial states in Italy, the Church's jurisdiction was in competition with that of the local government and with established social and cultural practices. Canon law issues intersected with secular Roman judicial determinations. One of the key sites of collision was the very basis of the economy that fortified the Italian Renaissance territorial commune and signorial state. It was increasingly a moneyed economy in which exchange value was guaranteed by the gold florin. Mercantile ventures were funded by speculative capital and interest-accruing loans. The Church launched a powerful campaign against usurious practices, but the offenders were among the communities' most powerful members, who were themselves often political and social allies of the local Church functionaries.

Considering religion from this perspective, I pay careful attention to Fra Filippo Lippi's institutional religious affiliations and his professional religious activities. I take an interest in the religious concerns of his patrons and of the churches and monasteries where his paintings were displayed. I investigate the particular religious dogmas that inform the iconography of his paintings, speculate on the social function of the pictured doctrine, and consider how Lippi's various publics would have received the symbolic language of his religious paintings. I suggest how, in Lippi's work, certain terms governing religious representation were brought into relief and questioned by this most inventive artist during a key moment in Italian Renaissance history when the very status and authority of the Christian church were being debated within the city of Florence.

In dealing with issues related to Renaissance religion, I work with an open-ended conception of a historically specific, socially differentiated and gendered variant of the classic "homo religiosus." The overarching characteristic of this "religious person" is that he or she entertained beliefs in a transcendental reality, endowing the forces and entities of this cosmos with the capacity to influence the course of events in the natural world. This religious person also engaged in rituals of supplication, mollification, homage, and thanksgiving, which were necessary to ensure the efficacy of these transcendental powers over mundane happenings. The religious response, as I am describing it, is thus a historically specific recourse by the individuals and social aggregates within a community to interpret their immediate material reality in terms of a broader, transcendent cosmos which represents the "Really Real." This religious response is formulated, in part, out of the existential experience of living in the shadow of death, at the mercy of an unpredictable and uncontrollable nature with its storms, droughts, and pestilences, and cultural forces like wars, tyranny, and economic and social oppression – which, depending upon a person's social position, could be equally unpredictable, uncontrollable, and ideologically "naturalized."

In the individual chapters, I work toward defining what the Renaissance religious response entailed, relative to religious images. I discuss how religious sentiments were expressed in the pictorial imagery and in the facture of a painting. I look into what motivated a patron to commission a religious work of art and how different individuals incorporated images in their religious devotion. The religious images of Fra Filippo Lippi are considered as symbolic representations within a discursive field of symbolic exchange.

Caroline Walker Bynum has proposed a definition of the religious symbol which has some bearing upon my study. Influenced by the work of Paul Ricoeur, Victor Turner, and Clifford Geertz, she suggests that symbols are "polysemic," "reflecting not just a multiplicity of meanings but a multiplicity of relationships between meanings." She observes that a symbol's meaning "is not so much imparted as appropriated in a dialectical process whereby it becomes subjective reality for the one who uses the symbol."[9] Thus, Lippi's painted images can be seen to have functioned as religious symbols which signified diverse, complex meanings to their various audiences. The artist, in accordance with the designs of his patrons and certain constraints imposed upon him by the context in which the images were to be displayed, mobilized a symbolic language which itself was not stable. There were often competing, paradoxical, incompatible meanings posited within the pictorial syntax of the imagery. The individuals who beheld Lippi's images experienced the symbolic content in diverse ways, depending upon their individual (but nonetheless socially constituted) perspectives. Such a view offers the possibility that a *quattrocento* altarpiece or fresco may itself have been the site of and the stake in contested meaning. A Lippi *Coronation of the Virgin* or *Madonna and Child with Saints* may have played some role in the formulation and transformation of certain culturally held beliefs, and in the process, may have affected – in small and subtle ways – the dynamic constitution of the society itself.

In the first part of the book, "The Claustrum," I focus upon Fra Filippo Lippi as the Carmelite friar and painter. The approach I take to religion in this part of the study is predominantly one of mapping the artist's institutional religious affiliations and seeing how his experiences and way of envisioning the sacred were shaped by the doctrines, rules, rituals, and practices of the Carmelites of Santa Maria del Carmine in Florence. Here I am concerned with Lippi as the maker of religious images, looking at some of the factors that would have informed his artistic sensibilities and contributed to certain discreet meanings posited within the symbolic content of his paintings.

In Chapter 1, I provide a historiography of "the religious Fra Filippo Lippi," looking at how the principal biographers from Vasari to the present have addressed the painter's religious status and activities. This is followed by a brief documention of Fra Filippo Lippi's experiences and routine activities when he was cloistered in Santa Maria del Carmine, concluding with speculation about how he may have come to be a friar painter. In Chapter 2, I focus on the monastery of Santa Maria del Carmine. I explore a range of religious representations and manifestations of the sacred in the Carmine and other local Carmelite institutions from the late *duecento* to the mid-*quattrocento*. I also analyse the urban socio-political character of Florentine Carmelite religious rituals. In Chapter 3, I consider Fra Filippo Lippi as a "Carmelite painter" and look at the Carmelite iconography of three paintings attributed to the young friar. In Chapter 4, I look at the incidence of monastic artistic production in *quattrocento* Tuscany – how it was regulated, how it differed from secular artistic practices, and what kinds of representational solutions it generated.

The second part of the book, "The Seculum," addresses Fra Filippo Lippi's life and artistic production during his mature years, after he left Santa Maria del Carmine. In Chapter 5, I examine how Fra Filippo maintained his relationship with the Carmelite Order, moving with apparent ease between the *claustrum* and the *seculum*. I also explore his new religious affiliations following his appointments as rector of San Quirico at Legnaia and chaplain of San Niccolò de' Frieri and Santa Margherita in Prato. In Chapter 6, I look more generally at Fra Filippo Lippi's painting practice, considering the distinctive features of his pictorial production, his workshop organization, and patronage network. I then suggest, in Chapter 7, that Fra Filippo's experiences and perspective as a Carmelite friar left their mark upon certain of his mature paintings.

In the third and final part of the book, "Art and Religion in Fifteenth-Century Florence," my approach to religion becomes more diversified. I continue to locate the artist's perspective as the maker of the religious image, and introduce the patron's role in mobilizing the production and determining the imagery. I also consider the difficult matter of the reception of specific religious works of art in a pre-modern era in which public opinion was rarely recorded, and a critical discourse on art in its nascent stages. I bring into my discussion examples of the different kinds of experiences that *quattrocento* Florentines had with religious images, and try to situate Fra Filippo Lippi's paintings and their publics in relation to these recorded instances and didactic *exempla*. The two chapters in this section are "case studies" focusing on individual paintings – all from the 1440s – and interesting circumstances related to the context of their production, signification, and function. Each chapter addresses a different sphere of religious activity and experience in *quattrocento* Florence. Chapter 8 focuses on an altarpiece that Fra Filippo painted for the novitiate chapel of the Franciscan monastery Santa Croce, commissioned by Cosimo de' Medici. In Chapter 9, I examine two altarpieces that Lippi painted over roughly the same period, for the high altars of two Florentine Benedictine nunnery churches.

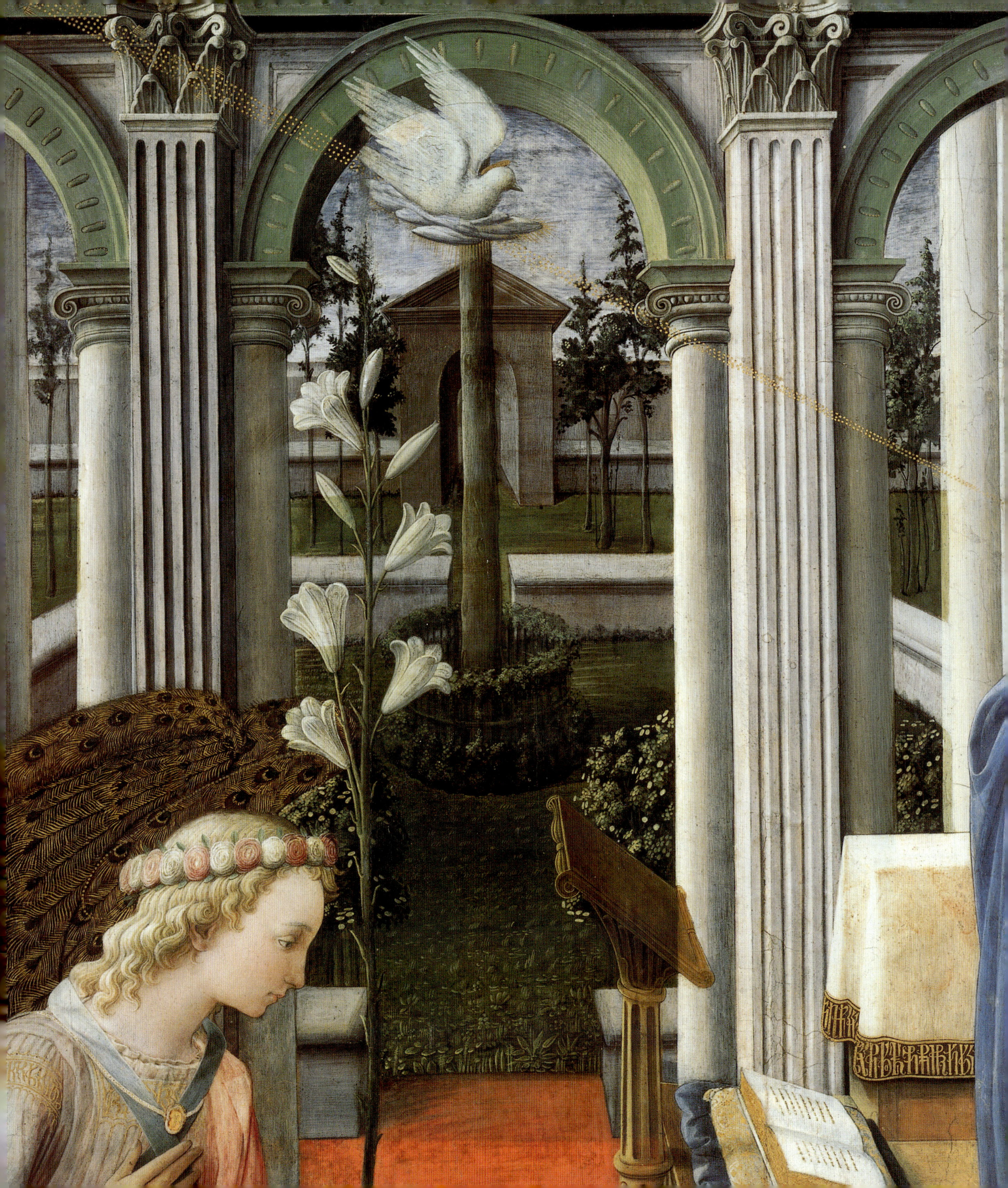

PART I

THE *CLAUSTRUM*

3 Filippo Lippi, *Annunciation*, detail of fig. 220.

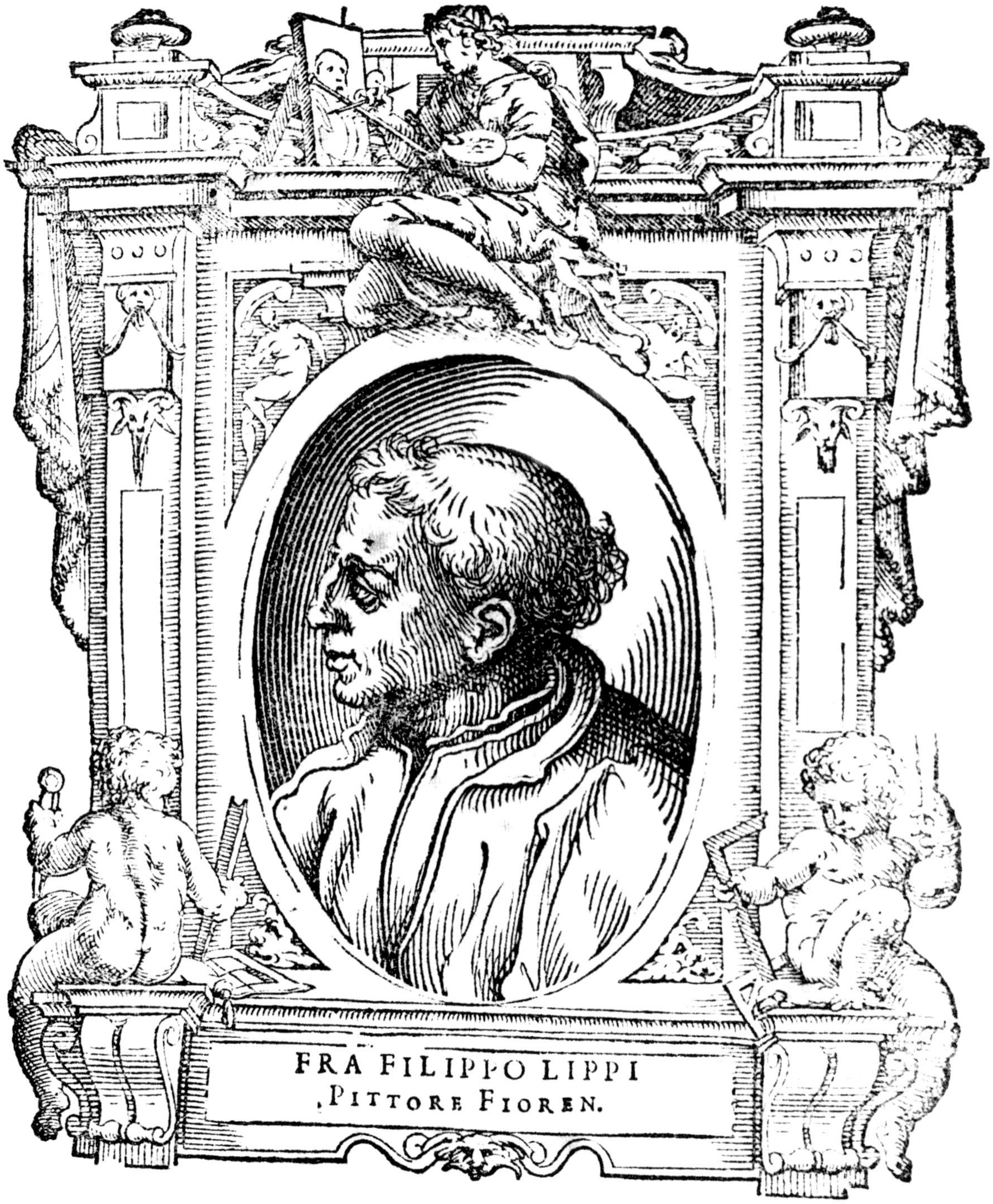

4 Giorgio Vasari, *Fra Filippo Lippi*, woodcut from *Ritratti de' più eccellenti pittori scultori et architetti contenuti nelle vite di M. Giorgio Vasari* (Florence, 1568).

CHAPTER ONE

FRA FILIPPO LIPPI *CARMELITANO*

THE LITERARY LIFE OF THE FRATE

GIORGIO VASARI, WRITING THE FIRST extended literary account of Fra Filippo Lippi in 1550, introduced a set of terms governing the painter's negotiation of the religious and secular spheres:

> On a pilaster in the church [of Santa Maria del Carmine] . . . he made a figure of San Marziale which brought him infinite fame, for it could bear comparison with the works that Masaccio had painted. Wherefore, hearing himself so greatly praised by the voices of all, at the age of seventeen, he boldly threw off his monastic habit, *even though he had already been ordained deacon; having little or no concern for this, he left the Order.*[1]

At first sight Vasari's account seems to offer a simple formula, based on a dichotomy between art and religion: in order to fulfill his promise as a painter, Lippi chose to leave the Carmelite Order. Unlike Vasari's treatment of Fra Angelico or Lorenzo Monaco, in his *Vita* of Lippi, there is an implicit incompatibility between the religious and the artistic calling.

In fact, the subtext of Vasari's *Vita* of Lippi is more complicated. Lippi occupies a special place in Vasari's *Le vite de' più eccellenti pittori, scultori ed architettori.* He is presented as one of the canonical artists in Vasari's lineage of the great Florentine painters, embodying the spirit of Masaccio ("many said that the spirit of Masaccio had entered into the body of Fra Filippo") and "extolled" and "imitated" by Michelangelo.[2] Lippi's *Vita*, despite the particularities of the artist's individual circumstances, conforms to a Vasarian model of "the progress of an excellent and famous painter." The treatment of Lippi's Carmelite experiences is strongly colored by this Vasarian narrative trope and the importance that Vasari accorded the Brancacci chapel in the historical development of Florentine art.[3]

Fra Filippo's monastery of Santa Maria del Carmine is cast as a sort of proto-Accademia where the young Lippi, who showed little inclination in theological studies, was encouraged to develop his artistic talents by the prior who "resolved to give him every opportunity and convenience for learning to paint."[4] Veritable master classes took place in the Brancacci chapel.

There the young artist ventured daily to practice his art by imitating the newly painted masterpieces of Masaccio, and "in company with many young men, who were ever drawing in it, he surpassed the others by a great measure in dexterity and knowledge."[5] The throwing-off of the monastic habit by the seventeen-year-old Lippi parallels the surpassing and rejection of the Master by other prodigious painters in Vasari's *Vite*.

Having broken his monastic vows and passed into the *seculum* (but inexplicably maintaining his title of Fra), Vasari's Filippo Lippi is no longer directly implicated in religious affairs. He matures under the powerful patronage of Cosimo de' Medici, Pope Eugenius IV, Carlo Marsuppini, and King Alfonso of Naples. Lippi's relationship with Cosimo de' Medici is particularly important to Vasari's economy of artistic production. It also exemplifies his conception of *amicizia* between patron and artist.[6] At first Cosimo tries to lock Lippi up in his palace, forcing the painter to give his full attention to a project Lippi had undertaken for him. But Lippi manages to escape down a rope of knotted sheets. After this episode, "Cosimo gave him liberty to go out when he pleased; . . . he strove to keep a hold on him for the future by kindness, and so he was served by Filippo with great readiness, and was wont to say that virtues of rare minds were celestial beings, and not slavish hacks."[7]

The artist-genius is thus disembodied into a celestial entity and fed on paternal kindness. But Lippi – the social, "bodied" being – nevertheless manages to surface in Vasari's account, appearing as an idiosyncratic individual with an excessive sensual appetite. Lippi proves to be "so amorous, that, if he saw any women who pleased him, and if they were to be won, he would give all his possessions to win them." His aim was "to have complete liberty for himself and his appetites."[8]

Vasari noted that "So greatly was he esteemed for his excellent gifts, that many circumstances in his life that were worthy of blame were passed over in consideration of the eminence of his great talents."[9] Some of these overlooked details are unveiled for the reader – particularly those pertaining to the artist's amorous philanderings – but certainly not all of them. Vasari gave the artist's sensual appetite free play, but not, at the height of the Counter Reformation, within the religious domain. Thus, the transgressive Carmelite friar and priest Filippo Lippi emerges as a layman, and his love, the nun Lucrezia Buti, appears as a novice or a boarder in the convent of Santa Margherita; and the vituperative Archbishop Antonino who petitioned Pope Callistus III to strip Lippi of his benefice, and Antonino's vicars who tossed Lippi into prison and recommended that he be excommunicated, are replaced by the benevolent Eugenius IV, willing to declare Filippo and Lucrezia "man and wife" (an offer Vasari's Lippi rejects).

But there is still a sense of unease regarding Lippi's moral character lurking within the *Vita*, a sort of faint imprint in the discursive account left by the historical Lippi, the transgressive friar. Lippi is given a fixed and unquestionable place in Vasari's Canon of Great Artists; Vasari also tells how Lippi's body came to rest in a tomb (fig. 147) commissioned by Lorenzo de' Medici, designed by Filippino Lippi, inscribed with a eulogy composed by Angelo Poliziano, and worthy of an *uomo illustro* within the *quattrocento* humanist tradition. But even as he laid the painter to rest within such encomiastic trappings, Vasari hinted that the artist's life might have been forfeited in a vendetta. There were rumors of a death by poison perpetrated by the aggrieved relatives of Lucrezia Buti – a kind of divine justice?

An attempt to redress Vasari's omissions and distortions has been partially carried out by nineteenth and twentieth-century archivists and art historians. Gaetano Milanesi presented the first comprehensive corrective in his annotated edition of Vasari's *Vite* (1878–81), complemented by a short piece, "Fra Filippo Lippi" (published earlier and then incorporated into the edition as a commentary following the Lippi *Vita*). Milanesi described his method quite simply: "to demonstrate by way of contemporary documents, or through reasonable conjectures, that these things in fact occurred."[10] He consulted notarial documents and the Carmine account books in an effort to chronicle and partially reconstruct Lippi's experiences as a Carmelite friar. After Lippi became a friar in 1421, Milanesi discovered that he had remained in Santa Maria del Carmine well past his seventeenth year. Lippi apparently retained his status as a Carmelite friar even after he left the convent to live in the *seculum*, probably in the 1430s, with the permission of the prior or provincial master. Milanesi speculated that the painter ultimately abandoned the cloister "so he could better turn over the profit from his painting for the support of some of his needy relatives."[11] He further conjectured that Lippi was also a priest, offering as evidence Lippi's benefice as rector of San Quirico at Legnaia, bestowed upon him in 1442 by Eugenius IV. He also recorded two other benefices that he believed the artist to have held – at San Niccolò de' Frieri in Florence and Santa Margherita in Prato.

Through Milanesi's efforts to include whatever information he could uncover that was relevant to the individual paintings cited by Vasari, we begin to get a sense of Lippi's contract negotiations with colleagues and patrons and the progress of his commissions. Some of these negotiations were tempestuous, with Lippi's probity brought into doubt. But Milanesi refrains from characterizing (or, for that matter, judging) the painter's behavior relative to his religious condition until he comes to the Lucrezia Buti affair.

"Most prominent among the more notable events in Fra Filippo Lippi's life, so full of strange adventures, is, without a doubt, that regarding Lucrezia Buti."[12] The documentation he uncovers has scandalous implications:

> By now it is clear that Lucrezia was a professed nun; that in 1456, having fled from the monastery and taken shelter in the house of Fra Filippo, there she gave birth to a son who was Filippino; and afterwards, repentant of her error or compelled by ecclesiastical authorities, she returned to Santa Margherita, renewing her monastic vows in 1459; and finally, in 1461 . . . along with her sister Spinetta, she was once again sheltered in the house of the friar.[13]

Attitudes toward love, cohabitation, and the family had changed substantially from the mid-sixteenth to the late nineteenth century, and in order for Milanesi to accept the conditions of the Fra Filippo–Lucrezia relationship (now acknowledged to be one between an apostate nun and an apostate friar), her consent had to be invented, and speculation about their marriage confirmed. In Vasari's account, during the Feast of the Assumption of the Virgin, Fra Filippo "led Lucrezia from the other nuns and took her away." She refused to leave the house of the painter "whether for fear or for other reasons."[14] But this suggestion of force and intimidation is absent from Milanesi's history. Putting in question the sincerity of his pledge to emend Vasari's colorful drama with "reasonable conjecture," Milanesi reconstructs the encounter between Lucrezia and Fra Filippo. Following Vasari, he has the incorrigible friar catch sight of the beautiful nun whom he then wishes to use as the model for the Virgin in the altarpiece he was making for the monastery of Santa Margherita where she was cloistered. But Lippi's presence within Santa Margherita and his contact with the nuns was then quite legitimate, since Milanesi identifies him as the official chaplain of the small Augustinian community.[15] Milanesi then posits an unhappy Lucrezia, committed to the nunnery along with her sister Spinetta by her elder brother Antonio who inherited the responsibility for a sizable family upon her father's death. Fra Filippo and Lucrezia are much in contact, particularly during her sittings for the altarpiece, and "little by little, a great trust was born between them: whereby it is natural that Lucrezia would not hesitate to confess to the friar how she was committed to the monastery and, against her will, made a nun."[16] She confesses to wanting to leave the cloister ("di gran cuore sarebbesi fuggita di là") and the smitten Lippi contrives a means of escape during the chaotic *festa* of the Assumption when the nuns join the public in the Pieve square to witness the unveiling of the miraculous relic of the Virgin's girdle. Lucrezia then lives in Fra Filippo's house in Prato for two years, along with her sister Spinetta. The nuns return to the monastery in 1459, but Lucrezia is back with Fra Filippo and their son Filippino by 1461. Milanesi then turns Lippi into the consummate family man, refuting Vasari's claim that Lippi refused the pope's offer to legitimize his relationship so that he could continue to philander.[17] Milanesi suggests that

> [The pope], moved by the warm recommendations of Cosimo [de' Medici], and perhaps because he was a great supporter of virtuous men, and also in consideration of the excellence of Fra Filippo Lippi in his painting, conceded, in order to remove every scandal, the possibility of having Lucrezia as his legitimate wife, releasing them both from their monastic vows, and granting the friar a dispensation from the restrictions of his Order.[18]

He goes on to discredit the rumor that Fra Filippo might have been poisoned by Lucrezia's siblings, because "he was no longer the seducer, but the husband of their sister."[19]

Milanesi's contribution to the documentation of Lippi's paintings (locations, provenances, production details, patrons, fuller descriptions, bibliography, iconography) is unparalleled. He also provided the factual basis for much of what we know about the painter's biography. But his professed objectivity collapses at certain points, under the pressure of nineteenth-century bourgeois morality. The broader implications of the "religious Lippi" – how the artist's religious status might have influenced the artist's work – were not at issue for Milanesi, so intent was he to clear up the "Lucrezia Buti Scandal." In Milanesi's telling, the "religious Lippi" left the Carmine under legitimate conditions with the approval of his superiors, and only came under ecclesiastical censure during the Lucrezia Buti affair when he was deprived of his benefices. But as his private moral conduct regarding Lucrezia was motivated by honest intentions, he was excused by the pope, released from his vows and his relationship with her was legitimized.

Vasari's *Vita*, with Milanesi's annotations, became the point of reference for subsequent studies dealing with the life and work of Fra Filippo Lippi. The question of Fra Filippo's religious condition was treated only in passing, usually to demonstrate the painter's strong "Renaissance" preference for worldly, secular, as opposed to religious, pursuits. There were also the occasional protestations over the artist's moral conduct.[20] It was the Carmelite scholar Padre Paolo Caioli who brought attention back to the question of Fra Filippo as a monastic Renaissance painter.

Caioli was the first to comb carefully the records of Lippi's monastery Santa Maria del Carmine and document the artist's religious activities in his article "Un altro sguardo sulla vita di fra Filippo Lippi" (1958).[21] His valuable archival work provided the basis for the brief biographical sketch of Fra Filippo's early life as a Carmelite that I give at the end of this chapter. Here, I shall merely point out Caioli's departures from the Vasari–Milanesi account and call attention to the critical position that informs his analysis.

The traditional scenario of the poor orphan abandoned on the Carmine doorstep by indigent relatives was revised by Caioli who proposed instead that Lippi's family had long-standing links with the monastery. Via dell'Ardiglione, where Vasari says Filippo's father had his house, is adjacent to the Carmine. Caioli cites a tradition claiming that Lippi's father was the gardener in the monastery, and suggests that one of the friars, Fra Niccolò Lippi, was a relative. While none of these assertions has any factual foundations, Caioli does convincingly demonstrate that Fra Filippo's older brother, Giovanni di Tommaso, was also a Carmelite in Santa Maria del Carmine.

Caioli takes the position that, far from being a misfit or a rebel, the young Carmelite Fra Filippo – as he emerges from the documentary record – participated in the standard activities of a Carmelite friar of the day. Fra Filippo's presence in the Carmine from 1421 to 1430 is attested and the fact that throughout this period he took part in religious processions to neighboring Carmelite convents in the Tuscan *provincia*. He was also active in the Confraternity of Sant'Agnese in the Carmine, which had mixed lay and religious membership.

Following the artist's return from Padua in 1434, Caioli speculates, he probably lived outside of the Carmine. Like Milanesi, Caioli assumes that Fra Filippo must have done so with permission from his superiors and maintained an amicable relationship with the Carmelites. Caioli then follows Lippi's life outside of the cloister through to his death, presenting a convincing argument for Lippi's having remained a friar throughout his life. He thus refutes Milanesi's contention that Lippi was released from his vows by the pope and that his union with Lucrezia Buti was legitimized – impossibilities had he remained a priest and friar. Caioli does not seem to have been inordinately troubled by the Lucrezia Buti affair, particularly as it occurred during the period when the friar had ranged farthest from the Carmelite fold.

The agenda for Caioli was clearly to recover a "Carmelite Lippi" for the historical record and prestige of his own Order. He presents Filippo Lippi as one whose profession was sincerely motivated ("sinceramento commosso"): "We would not want to maintain that even from the beginning he did not cultivate the religious life, but only that on occasion he considered intolerable the weight which is sweet to the soul truly given to God" but he does concede that "Perhaps this life completely given over to silence and meditation was not conducive to the lively, restless character of Fra Filippo."[22] Caioli sees a direct relationship between the reforming tendencies within the Carmelite Order – particularly those initiated by Angelo Mazzinghi – and Fra Filippo's gradual estrangement from the Order: "Fra Filippo was no longer able to feel at ease around a religious person of such great penitence."[23]

The reader is offered understanding rather than censure,

against a backdrop of a romanticized view of Renaissance Christianity and the Carmelite Observant reform movement. This general sense of understanding which saturates Caioli's account tends to blur and confuse his analysis of the transformation of Lippi's religious condition. The picture of Lippi, the restless and animated artist who was unsuited for the rigorous life of a Carmelite friar, and who consciously took a measured distance from the Order during his mature middle age, does not agree with the record of impetuousness and transgression that Caioli himself carefully documents during the painter's later years. After Milanesi's case for Lippi's moral salvation, we run up against Caioli leveling down the range, degree, and religious significance of Lippi's controversial activities after he left the Carmelite cloister, in the name of a detached Christian understanding.

In the most recent addition to the literature, Miklós Boskovits, writing for *Arte cristiana* in 1986, essentially follows Caioli's construction of an early religious period for the artist Lippi while he was still cloistered in Santa Maria del Carmine.[24] Boskovits's interest in the religious ambience in the Florentine Carmine was generated by a group of controversial paintings that Boskovits wanted to place securely within the early Lippi oeuvre. He begins the article with a discussion of these paintings – a fresco in the Carmine, the Trivulzio *Madonna of Humility*, the Empoli and Cini *Madonna and Child with Saints*, a *St. John the Evangelist* fragment, and the Fitzwilliam Museum triptych. He argues against a thesis put forth by Curtis Shell – that some of these works are from mid-century by a Lippi imitator – emphasizing the Carmelite subject matter of the Trivulzio, Carmine, and Empoli paintings and the stylistic continuity between this group and Lippi's documented early works. Boskovits then poses a question:

> It still remains to be seen whether, and to what degree, the fact that he was a Carmelite friar influenced the artistic development of Lippi. The religious condition has often been called upon to explain the peculiarities in the painting of Lorenzo Monaco and Beato Angelico. Instead, in the case of Fra Filippo – who, from the time of Vasari, has come to be considered the example of a failed religious calling (and perhaps precisely because of this, his attitude considered more typically Renaissance) – such factors usually are forgotten.[25]

He proceeds to explore the environment of the Carmine when Lippi lived within its walls, searching for causal factors that may have contributed to the stylistic character of the early works of the artist. If Lippi was not free to wander the streets of Florence and encounter the outstanding practicing artists of the time in their workshops, who, then, were the artists he could have known in the Carmine itself? Masaccio, Masolino, perhaps even Donatello and Brunelleschi (the last having designed the machinery used to transport Christ up to the rafters in the annual Carmine Ascension Day *sacra rappresentazione*). Lippi could have been exposed to northern European painting through contact with the German wool-weavers of the Confraternity of Santa Caterina who worshiped in the Carmine.[26]

Boskovits goes further, describing the religious environment within the Carmine itself: religious practices were much influenced by the Observant reform movement within the Order and the monastery *studium*, which supported the serious study of theology and philosophy.[27] While Caioli had suggested that this environment alienated the young artist and prompted his departure from the cloister, Boskovits argues that it had a strong influence on Fra Filippo's early work: "The atmosphere of seriousness and study in his environment and the scholastic culture of those who oversaw the early activities of the friar painter probably did not fail to influence the artistic vision of Fra Filippo."[28] Boskovits characterizes the pictorial style that emerged as a "robust," "pure," "almost provocative realism," a "vigorous vernacular."[29] And he considered this "realism" to be less inspired by a humanist, neo-classical, Albertian prescription for securing mimetic likeness than by the vivid immediacy of the religious vision preached by reformed Carmelites, Dominicans, and Franciscans in the early *quattrocento*. Lippi's early life is Boskovits's focus, so the eventual lapse into rather anti-social behavior is only alluded to, as a sort of inevitable awakening of an innocent "in an unknown world, marked by enticement and vengeance, responsibility and temptation."[30]

Boskovits's thesis is attractive, and some of his arguments will be taken up in greater detail in Chapter 3. I would not go as far as he does in setting up an "anti-humanist" pictorial realism – derived from the sermons of Giovanni Dominici and practised in the monasteries by *frate* painters and in the monastic churches by the likes of Masaccio – versus a "humanist" vision codified by Alberti, patronized by patricians and aristocrats, and realized by commercial or "court" artists like Gentile da Fabriano and Pisanello. The tangible immediacy of the Florentine humanists' invocation of the antique within the *quattrocento* urban environment seems to me to be of a similar order to the vivid, personal, and realistic manner in which the sacred was enacted throughout the city. The relationship between the two seems to be more dynamically integrated and less polarized – and could be clarified by a broader look at the historical process of *quattrocento* socio-religious transformations. There was significant commerce and exchange between the mendicant monasteries and the secular world of the Florentine patricians, including the humanists among them.[31]

Vasari, Milanesi, Caioli, and Boskovits all share, to some degree, the assumption that the cloistered life interfered with Lippi's ambition to run a professional painting practice. There is also the suggestion that the painter's character was not suited to the rigors of monastic life. We know from the experiences of Fra Angelico among others that it was indeed possible during the fifteenth century for a painter to work out of a monastery, balancing artistic activities with the daily routine of religious worship and responsibilities. The question I should like to pose is this: what was it about Filippo Lippi's particular painting production and his social relationships as a friar painter that rendered it impracticable or unsuitable or impossible to conduct his practice from within a Carmelite monastery? In addition, both Caioli and Boskovits oversimplify Lippi's transition from the cloister to the *seculum*, as though the painter were passing from a pristine cell of Carmelite obedience into a pre-capitalist urban morass. Their positions are underpinned by a series of oppositions: inside the convent/outside in secular society, early life/mature life, religious morality/secular immorality. These easy oppositions, with Fra Filippo's envisioned clear passages from one to the other, oversimplify his uneven, pragmatic, opportunistic, and conflictual negotiations through the ever-changing petty patronage networks and unstable structures of civil, mercantile, and religious *quattrocento* Florentine society. Over the course of this study, I shall attempt to document Fra Filippo Lippi's changing religious condition and demonstrate the contingencies that came to bear on his complex movement between the *claustrum* and the *seculum*, and his negotiations of the sacred.

On the surface, my concerns are more broadly historical than those expressed by the key figures cited above. By looking at how religion shaped the particular experiences and artistic production of Lippi throughout his life, I want to raise the question of what, in fact, was the function and significance of religion and the religious in *quattrocento* Florence. But my agenda also has a dimension that is polemically art historical. I want to examine the role of pictorial representation in securing, undermining, transforming this religious function in society, and to determine what part Lippi's paintings may have played.

Having established the historiographical tradition for the study of Lippi as a Carmelite painter, I shall now offer my own narrative account of his early associations with the Carmelite Order, staying as close as possible to the documentation.

FILIPPO LIPPI AND SANTA MARIA DEL CARMINE

Information regarding Lippi's entry into Santa Maria del Carmine comes, unconfirmed, from Vasari. In his *Vita* of Lippi, he narrates how, following the death of his father and mother, the orphan Filippo was placed in the monastery at the age of eight by his aunt Lapaccia who could not afford to support him.[32] There is another tradition that says that Lippi's father had been a gardener at Santa Maria del Carmine.[33]

The colorful specificity of the early biographic accounts must be toned down and somewhat modified in the light of the accumulated documentation. What emerges, interestingly, is a more extensive association between Santa Maria del Carmine and Filippo Lippi's family. His father, Tommaso di Lippo, was a butcher who owned part of a house on Borgo San Frediano near the Piazza de' Nerli.[34] He was an active member of the local Compagnia di San Frediano and was evidently acquainted with the friars of Santa Maria del Carmine, frequently serving as a witness to notarial transactions at the Carmine. He died some time after 1411.[35] Tommaso's widow, Antonia (whom Milanesi identifies as Tommaso's second wife and Filippo's stepmother[36]), was still alive in 1431 when she paid her annual dues to the Compagnia di Sant'Agnese located in the Carmine.[37] According to her *catasto* report of 1427–28 (written out for her by the prior of the Carmine), she was forty-two years old, without any taxable wealth. She was living with a daughter of Tommaso's in a rented house on the Piazza del Carmine that belonged to the Carmelite Fra Albizzo de' Nerli.[38] Filippo had an older brother, Giovanni, some three years his senior, who also became a *frate* in the Florentine Carmine.[39] It has been suggested that the lector at the Carmine, Fra Niccolò Lippi, was a paternal uncle of Fra Filippo Lippi.[40]

If Filippo Lippi was in fact committed to the Carmine at eight years of age by his indigent mother or by his aunt, he would have spent some six years as a *fanciullo* (young boy) in the monastery before beginning his novitiate at fourteen.[41] We know of these *fanciulli* in the religious houses primarily from the harsh criticism of monastic reformers who did not like to see monasteries serve as orphanages.[42] In the record books of the Carmine, *fanciulli* are virtually invisible. Their status in the convent was not legitimized in the Carmelite Rule or in the Constitutions, nor were they significant contributors toward the religious ministrations or maintenance of the convent. Their rare mentions in the convent books are always generic, never by their personal names.[43] It would appear that the boys were assigned to the care of one of the older *frati*, and that they helped in small tasks about the convent and participated in certain religious routines and festive activities.[44]

During Lippi's period as a *fanciullo* in the Carmine, he would have survived a devastating visitation of the plague in 1417, which lasted for eight months.[45] Monasteries were particularly hard hit on account of the close quarters and the communal nature of monastic life. According to the Carmelite *Necrologium*, twelve *frati* died that year, roughly a third of the total convent population (not counting the lay employees and *fanciulli*).[46]

The first record we have of Fra Filippo Lippi dates from June 18, 1421, when he took his vows. His profession followed a year spent as a novice in the convent. The Carmelites had one novitiate for the entire Tuscan *provincia*, located in the Florentine convent. Every Carmelite prior in Tuscany was responsible for recruiting two novices, "or at least one," each year, and subsidizing the one-florin clothing fee required for each.[47] If this dictum were actually followed, the number of novices from the Tuscan convents serving their year's novitiate in the Florentine Carmine would have ranged from ten to twenty.[48]

A master of the novices was appointed annually at the provincial chapter meeting along with the other convent administrators. Fra Filippo passed his year's novitiate under the guidance of Fra Giovanni Dominici. In 1417, we find Lippi's master mentioned with the following authority: "we designate Johannes Dominici lector Master and Instructor of the Novices in our convent in Florence with full authority over them, so that none should interfere, unless our Reverend Provincial [Prior] should wish it."[49] The duty of the master of the novices was to instruct the novices "as much in the Divine Offices as in good practices,"[50] with emphasis given to learning the Carmelite Rule and very elementary scriptural lessons. For those novices who had already had a grammar school education and were going to pursue a course in theology or in the arts in the Carmelite *studia*, the year marked a break in their scholarly pursuits and an indoctrination into the routines, prayers, and regulations particular to the Carmelite Order.[51] The novices lived apart in a separate dormitory where the master of the novices also had his cell, and had a more restricted diet than the professed *frati*.[52]

Fra Filippo professed in 1421, in a ceremony attended by "each and every friar of the chapter and convent," officiated by the prior of the Carmine, Fra Pietro di Francesco of Prato.[53] We have some record of his personal movements and activities after his profession, which reflect the standard curative procedures, administrative duties, and festive activities of the convent *frati* over the course of the Carmelite calendar. Fra Filippo was based in the Florentine Carmine from 1422 to 1432.[54] He participated in the religious processions to neighboring Tuscan convents prescribed on particular feast days in the Florentine Carmelite liturgical calendar.[55] In addition to these documented activities, it can be assumed that he participated in the daily religious devotional routines of the Florentine Carmelite *frati*.[56]

There is no record of Lippi's ordination as priest, which probably occurred sometime during the second half of the 1420s.[57] He would have moved up through the clerical ranks from acolyte, to subdeacon, to deacon, to priest. As a priest in the Carmine, his principal task would have been to assist in performing masses. Daily masses were held at the Carmine for the *frati*, and there was also a secondary group of masses that the *frati* were commissioned to sing at the various altars within the church and convent for the confraternities and for private patrons, living and deceased. The *frati* also sang masses outside the convent at the various oratories in the city and before altars in the other city churches. Fra Filippo is documented singing mass in the Carmine on one occasion – although at a later date than the period that I am concentrating on here.[58]

Lippi did not enter the *studium*. This need not be cast as dramatically as Vasari would have it, when he insists that Lippi was "dense in his knowledge of letters and poorly suited for learning."[59] It was typically only the *frati* from the wealthier patrician families, often bringing some form of prior education into the convent (and private wealth to pay for the additional expenses for books, travel, and the degree itself), who went on to obtain a degree in theology, philosophy, or the liberal arts in the Carmelite *studia*.[60] Only four or five *frati* a year attended the Florentine Carmelite *studium*, and Filippo Lippi and his brother Giovanni – orphaned sons of a butcher – were not among them.

Fra Filippo did not distinguish himself as a career administrator within the Order, as did the Dominican painter Fra Angelico. While most of the top administrative positions – prior, master of the novices, *soci*, and *definatori* – went to those patrician friars who had obtained degrees in the Carmelite *studia*, sub-priorships and sacristan positions were often held by *frati* of humble origin. Lippi's brother Giovanni was sub-prior at Lucca in 1424 and 1442, sub-prior at the Florentine convent in 1425 and 1441, and prior at Prato in 1433.[61] Lippi did hold one administrative position for a very brief period: he was elected sub-prior of the Sienese Carmine for a short term of ten months from November 7, 1428, to August 24, 1429.[62]

By the start of the following decade, Fra Filippo was actively engaged as a painter. An unusually informative list of the *frati* in the Carmine compiled in early January, 1431, includes "frate Filippo di Tommaso dipintore."[63] He is last mentioned as a vested friar of Santa Maria del Carmine the following year. He disappears from the record for the next two and a half years, resurfacing in Padua on July 1, 1434.[64] The circumstances of his departure and the conditions under which he lived and worked in Padua are not known, and many questions remain unanswered. (What kind of agreement did he negotiate with the Carmelites? Did he live in the Paduan Carmine? Is it mere coincidence that his Paduan stay corresponds with Cosimo de' Medici's exile from Florence, spent in Padua and Venice?)[65] What is apparent, however, is that in Padua he was engaged as a professional artist and was integrated into the community of painters in the city.[66] When he returned to Florence, at some point before 1437, it appears that he no longer lived within the cloistered environment of Santa Maria del Carmine.[67]

TRAINING AND EARLY ARTISTIC INFLUENCE

There is virtually no documentary information on Fra Filippo's artistic training and his early activities as a *frate dipintore* working out of the Florentine Carmine. Vasari describes him as an autodidact who learned to paint by going each day to the Brancacci chapel in the Carmine and imitating the work of Masaccio. Since Vasari, most scholars have sidestepped the question of how the young artist might have acquired his painting skills, concentrating instead on his stylistic lineage – as though the art historian's favorite indicator, "influence" itself, could have endowed the artist with practical tools.[68]

There are several possible ways in which Filippo Lippi could have received something akin to a professional apprenticeship that would have given him the facility that we see in his first documented works from the late 1430s. There are, however, two key conditions to this training. The first is that it would have to have taken place in Florence because Filippo Lippi was a vested member of the convent of Santa Maria del Carmine in Florence throughout this period. The second is that it would have to have been arranged with the consent of his Carmelite superiors. Any activity that would have taken the friar away from his daily cycle of religious devotion or necessitated his departure from the convent would have required the permission of the prior or sub-prior of Santa Maria del Carmine.

In reviewing the early chronology of Fra Filippo Lippi, the period following his profession as a Carmelite friar in 1421 seems to be the most reasonable time to posit an apprenticeship of sorts, when he could have learned the rudiments of painting more or less according to professional standards.

c. 1406–07	Filippo Lippi is born
c. 1414	He enters Santa Maria del Carmine as a *fanciullo*
c. 1420 June	He begins his novitiate in the Carmine
1421 June 18	He professes as a Carmelite
1422 Jan. to 1432 Jan.	He is listed among the friars of Santa Maria del Carmine most of these years and is documented as a participant in numerous processions
1428 Nov. 7 to 1429 Aug. 24	He serves as sub-prior in the Carmelite monastery in Siena
1431 Jan. 1	He is called "dipintore" in a Carmine account book
1434 Feb. 1	He is documented painting in Padua for the Santo

Between 1421 and 1431 (when he is first referred to as a painter), Fra Filippo passed from about his fifteenth to his twenty-fifth year, and the earlier age corresponds to the standard age of a new apprentice in a Florentine painter's shop.[69]

The first possibility regarding Fra Filippo's training that I shall explore has the most art-historical appeal. It involves adapting the Vasarian scenario to what we now know about the painting of the Brancacci chapel and the early life of Fra Filippo. Vasari described the young friar studying the "newly painted" frescoes in the Brancacci chapel. Masaccio and Masolino – whatever their relationship may have been or the precise chronology of their engagement in the Brancacci chapel – executed the frescoes between 1425 and 1428.[70] Fra Filippo was a friar in the Carmine at that time. Is it viable to suggest that he learned to paint from these masters over this three-year period? Carmelite interest in the fresco project could well have encouraged Lippi's superiors to agree to an unofficial apprenticeship.

This begs an important question: could such a particular tutelage – comprised of one on-site project, and a fresco one at that – have endowed Fra Filippo with the extreme facility that we see in the early, securely attributed panel paintings – the Tarquinia *Madonna and Child* (1437; fig. 6), the Metropolitan Museum and Turin polyptych (c. 1437), and the Barbadori altarpiece (1437–39; fig. 103)? In addition, there is a particular quality in the mature paintings of Fra Filippo which I think points to his not having received his initial training from a painter of the caliber of a Masaccio or Masolino. I shall try to explain.

In Lippi's documented paintings, there is a sort of overextension, a constant reaching out beyond that, which is at hand. This is immediately evident in his elaborate painting process, which is legible across the surface and through the pigment layers of his pictures, characterized by constant changes and reworkings. Scored marks in the gesso ground often do not make their way into the painted composition.[71] Forms exceed their brush contour lines or are redefined beneath voluminous drapery folds. A shadowy pentimento endows a figure with a third hand (see fig. 141).[72] Laboratory analysis of Lippi's panel paintings and recent restoration work on his frescos offer further evidence of Lippi's tendency to paint his way through pictorial problems. A Madonna's face is worked up from *terra verde* underpainting to a modelling layer of *bianca* and lake, only to be covered with *terra verde* and fleshtones anew.[73]

I am by no means suggesting that Lippi's painting technique was unsure or that the artist was lacking in technical ability. In fact, his technical expertise, evident particularly in the accomplished illusionist architectural designs in his fresco cycles in Prato and Spoleto, was of a very high level. I am trying to get at something else. Lippi was no patient, mechanical practitioner. He lacked a certain discipline that would permit him to accept his own limitations and those of the medium in which he was working. He was always pushing against the limits of what he could do in tempera, on panel, or on a wet plaster wall, chasing after complicated, not fully realized conceptions. It is as though there were a constant tension in his work between the design as it is fixed on the panel or wall and all the innovative possibilities which that design could offer. The forms appear infused with a potential energy, as though the figures and settings were always on the verge of animation and the lines, color, and metal leaf threaten to reorient themselves in different combinations.

This tension in Lippi's work suggests something about his artistic training. It points to a gap that may have existed, when he was learning to paint, between the technical, iconographical, and representational conventions in which he was trained, and his acute artistic perception (enriched and stimulated by the experience of watching Masaccio and Masolino at work in Santa Maria del Carmine) and awareness of Brunelleschi's and Donatello's architectural and sculptural innovations in Florence during the 1420s. The way that Lippi worked through compositional dilemmas in the very process of painting, which one sees in his mature work, may have evolved early as a means of bridging this gap between his technical means and his representational ambitions.

There is a second possibility regarding Fra Filippo's training, which places him in the milieu of the professional painters in the Carmine neighborhood and would have provided him with a thorough immersion in the art of painting. It centers on the Compagnia di Sant'Agnese. This Compagnia (which will be discussed in Chapter 2) was attached to Santa Maria del Carmine and was composed of laymen and women and a presiding Carmine friar. Lippi later became involved in the activities of this Compagnia and his brother Giovanni and his mother or

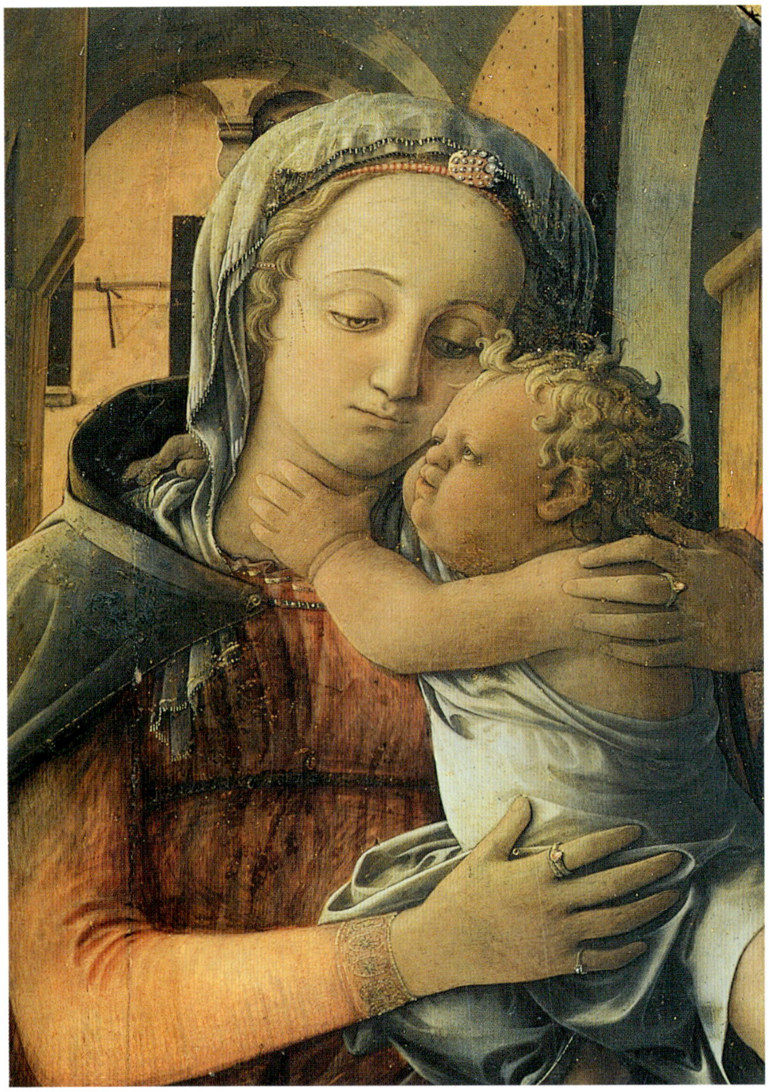

5 Filippo Lippi, Tarquinia *Madonna and Child*, detail of fig. 6.

stepmother Antonia were members.[74] It was a prominent *compagnia* in the Santo Spirito quarter of the city and, as the immediate neighborhood of Santa Maria del Carmine happened to be one where a high concentration of painters and artisans resided, the Compagnia also had many artist members.[75] It is possible that the Compagnia could have organized an arrangement between the convent and one of these painters, a sort of "extra-legal" arrangement among members. The young friar could have been granted permission by his superiors to spend a certain period of each day in the *bottega* of one of the painter members who worked in the neighboring San Frediano parish, with the Compagnia di Sant'Agnese acting as *mezzano*, insuring that the situation was satisfactory for all parties.[76] The Compagnia did, on occasion, oversee the private or commercial affairs of its members, usually in response to testament bequests.[77]

Following this scenario, the painter members or associates of the Compagnia who are possible candidates to have been the painting master of the young Fra Filippo Lippi are Stefano di Lorenzo Pucetti, Bicci di Lorenzo, and Piero di Chellino Chellini.[78] Bicci di Lorenzo, in particular, had a more extensive relationship with Santa Maria del Carmine. Antonio Billi claimed that he painted the Martyrs of the Church in the Carmine and both Bicci and his wife were buried in the church.[79] There is, however, very little sign in Lippi's work from the late 1430s (or in the controversial early paintings) that he was in any way indebted to Bicci di Lorenzo (see fig. 37). Stefano di Lorenzo Pucetti and Piero di Chellino Chellini were minor masters, and we know nothing about the character of their work. These factors would not necessarily rule them out, as I am suggesting that Fra Filippo was ultimately more influenced by the innovative artists who were working in his midst, and by the religious representational practices in the Carmine, than he was by the master who taught him how to paint.

The strongest argument against both of these first two hypotheses is the lack of precedent, particularly for the second, more formal arrangement proposed. Monastic artists – Fra Angelico being a contemporary example – were most frequently trained in the *seculum*, and practiced professionally before taking their vows.[80] This does not seem to have been the case with Lippi, in the light of the documentation and the sixteenth-century biographical material. However, a brief period of artistic flowering did sometimes occur within a monastery in the wake of a monastic artist who had been trained in the *seculum* before professing, who then taught his trade to others within the monastery. The group of Camaldolesi miniaturists (including Don Lorenzo Monaco) at Santa Maria degli Angeli during the late *trecento* is an example. This second model offers the simplest solution to the problem regarding the training of the young *frate* Filippo Lippi. And there appears to have been, in fact, another *frate dipintore* in Santa Maria del Carmine during the early *quattrocento*: Fra Arrigo d'Arrigo "de Alamania Superiori."[81]

It is not known when the German Carmelite Fra Arrigo d'Arrigo first entered the Florentine convent of Santa Maria del Carmine. He was present by 1418, and sang his first mass on January 22, 1420.[82] He rose within the Carmelite Tuscan ranks and occupied numerous official positions, ranging from sacristan, sub-prior and prior of various convents, to the prestigious posts of *socio*, *definatore*, and vicar of the Tuscan *provincia*.[83] The entry in the Carmine *Necrologium* commemorating his death on April 12, 1458, alludes to his involvement in manuscript production: "Fra Henrygus Henrygi of Germany, priest of well-known fame died in Florence. [continued in a later hand] He was prior and vicar of the Tuscan province; he bound and decorated books with the customary illuminations and other ornaments, and conferred many other benefits upon this convent. Died and buried."[84] The only apparent confirmation of his artistic activity that I have found in the convent books is the following entry dating from June 14, 1436:

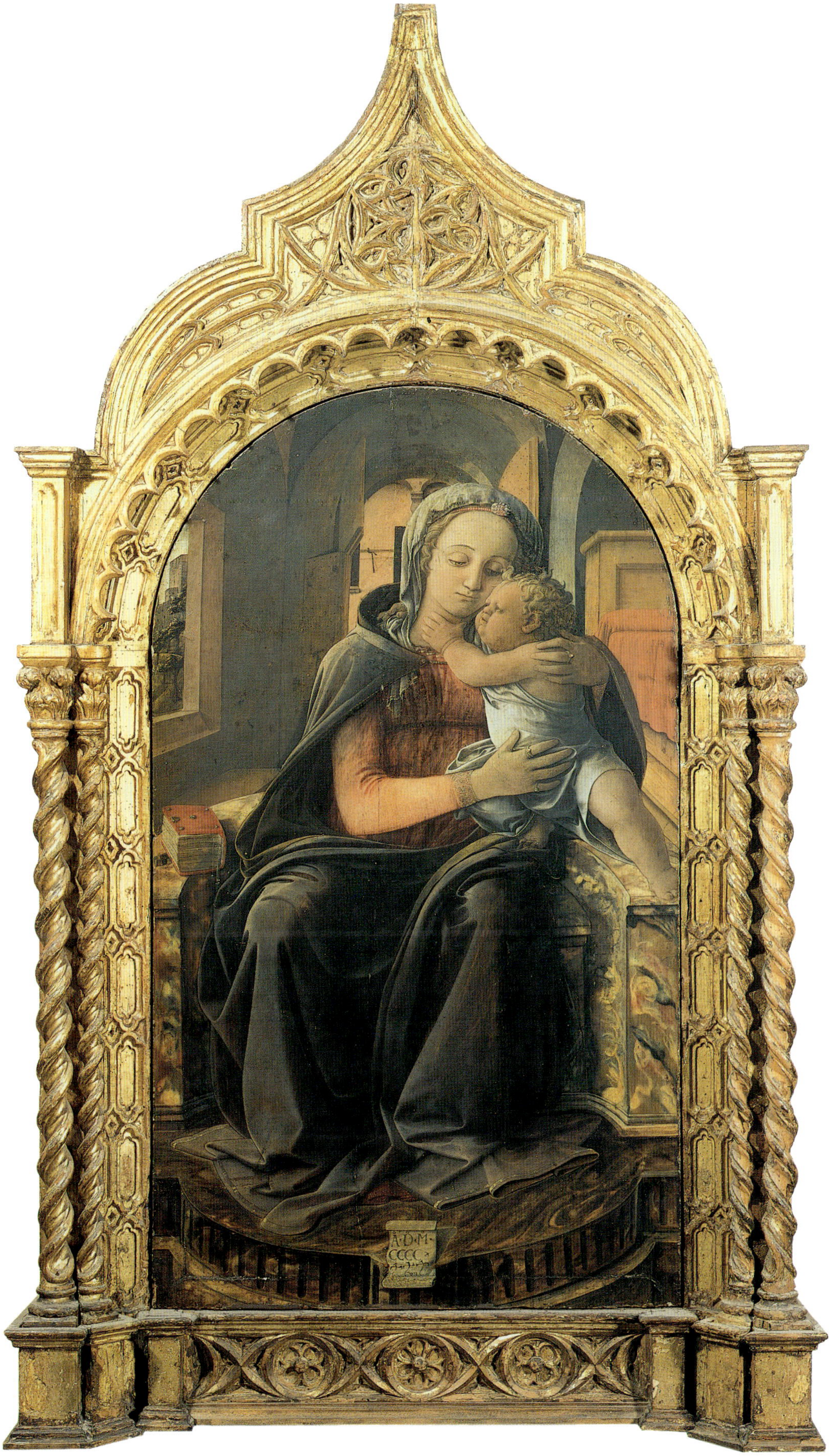

6 Filippo Lippi, Tarquinia *Madonna and Child*, 1437, Rome, Galleria Nazionale di Arte Antica (Palazzo Barberini).

Item on this day to the lector [for what he] gave to friar Arrigo for white cloth s.15

Item on this day to friar Arrigo for wood for the crucifix to remake it s.15

Item on this day to friar Arrigo for the painting of the wood of the crucifix s.6 [85]

Fra Arrigo would appear to be "remaking" ("fare di nuovo") a painted crucifix for the Carmine.[86] He was paid for wood and cloth (which would have been placed on top of the wood, beneath the gesso ground), and for "la dipintura del legno."

Fra Arrigo was present in Florence in 1418, 1425–26, and from 1429 at least through 1437. The period during the mid-20s overlaps with the beginning of the painting of the Brancacci chapel by Masolino and Masaccio. It is possible that the young Lippi's interest in painting could have been stimulated by this fresco activity in the convent church, in addition to Masaccio's painting of the *Sagra* in the cloister, and that he took up the study of painting with his fellow Carmelite, Fra Arrigo d'Arrigo, as a result. This scenario also helps to explain certain northern European characteristics in Lippi's mature painting style that have caught the fancy of a number of art historians.[87]

According to this scenario, Fra Arrigo d'Arrigo would have received some kind of training as a painter outside the Carmelite monastic milieu, possibly in his native Germany, and would have tutored the young Lippi in the rudiments of his craft. An interesting sidenote is that Lippi's only official Carmelite appointment, in 1428 as the sub-prior of the Sienese convent, came as a replacement for Fra Arrigo who had held the post for the preceding six months and returned to it in late August 1429 to mid-1430. Is it possible that he was engaged on an artistic project which Lippi took over during the ten months in which Fra Arrigo disappears from the records?

There are some factors, however, that work against the Fra Arrigo hypothesis. The first is that while the documents quoted above attest to Fra Arrigo's involvement in artistic production, they do not necessarily imply that he himself was doing the actual painting and illuminating. In addition, while Lippi did, on rare occasions, make his way into the Carmine and Compagnia di Sant'Agnese ledgers as "frate Filippo dipintore," Fra Arrigo was always referred to by his place of origin, "dalle Magnia" or "tedescho." And finally, Fra Arrigo's intermittent presence in Santa Maria del Carmine during the 1420s would not have provided Lippi with a continuous period – one that the Florentine guild statutes for lay painters ruled should be "no less than three years" – during which he could have learned the basics of painting from his fellow Carmelite.

But this all remains at the level of speculation. I shall turn now to more determinable matters, and look briefly at some of the artistic influences that gave breadth and dimension to Fra Filippo's representational ambitions. Keith Christiansen has described the innovative artists who worked within the Tuscan Carmelite ambience during the second and third decades of the *quattrocento* as a sort of avant-garde of early Renaissance painting.[88] The figure who looms largest is obviously Masaccio.

Masaccio's first Carmelite commission was probably the *Sagra*, which commemorated the consecration of Santa Maria del Carmine which took place on April 19, 1422. It was painted in the cloister of the convent some time after the event.[89] Masaccio's involvement in the Brancacci chapel (see figs. 60 and 66) occurred some time between 1425, when the scaffolding seems to have gone up in the chapel, and 1428, when the artist died in Rome. Masaccio was also engaged to paint a polyptych of the Madonna and Child with Saints for the Carmine in Pisa in 1426, for the chapel of Giuliano di Cosimo degli Scarsi da San Giusto (see fig. 200). Lippi would very probably have known this altarpiece, as the friars moved readily between the various convents of the Tuscan *provincia*.[90]

One cannot overemphasize the significance that the actual presence of Masaccio in the Carmine – painting day in and day out, in the cloister and in the Brancacci chapel – must have had on the young Carmelite painter. Lippi had no need to apply formally for permission from the convent prior to leave the premises in order to take in one of the most innovative artistic projects in the city, as it was unfolding before his eyes in his own monastery.

In Lippi's earliest documented works – the Tarquinia *Madonna and Child* (1437; fig. 6) and the Barbadori altarpiece (1437–39) (see fig. 103) – the influence of Masaccio is dramatically apparent. The corporeality of Lippi's figures comes out of Masaccio – their bulk, weight, cast shadows, and physical actions and reactions. And as with Masaccio, the mass of the bodies is matched by the psychological gravity of the figures represented. Through these means, both painters succeeded in representing sacred events in intensely human terms without their being in any way trivialized.[91]

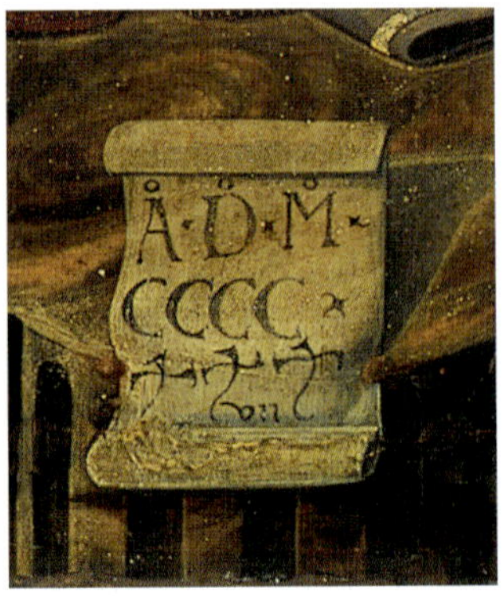

7 Filippo Lippi, Tarquinia *Madonna and Child*, detail of fig. 6.

From Masaccio's collaborator on the Brancacci chapel frescos, Masolino, Lippi took a less fundamental but nonetheless essential feature, the elegant and graceful carriage of his figures (see figs. 65 and 202). Lippi applied this *grazia* and *bellezza* to his female saints and angels. For, in marked contrast to Masaccio but closer to Donatello, Lippi endowed certain elements within his sacred cosmology with extremely idealized and very beautiful features.

Lippi must have been aware of Donatello's work in Florence dating from the 1410s and '20s. Many have noted the similarities between Lippi's Tarquinia *Madonna and Child* and Donatello's c. 1422 Pazzi *Madonna and Child* (see fig. 131) and the *Madonna of the Clouds*. And Lippi's San Lorenzo *Annunciation* (c. 1439; see fig. 104) most assuredly bears a debt to Donatello's Santa Croce *Cavalcanti Annunciation* (early 1430s; fig. 10) – early sixteenth-century sources even insist that Lippi painted a predella for the tabernacle, "at Donatello's request."[92] Donatello's pictorial reliefs, in particular, seem to have had resonance for the young Lippi: through them he came to know the dramatic economy and rhetorical phraseology of a proto-Albertian *istoria*. It was from the sculptor's complex cellular spatial constructions in his early *rilievo schiacciato* – such as the *Feast of Herod* (1423–27) – that Lippi's conception of pictorial space evolved. And finally, the architectural idiom that Lippi used throughout his work is a hybrid Donatello–Brunelleschi style, close to that found in the *Cavalcanti Annunciation* and in the more classical Parte Guelfa *St. Louis* niche for Orsanmichele.

Fra Filippo Lippi's relationship to the work of the Sienese painter Domenico di Bartolo is a difficult one to resolve. During the 1430s, the two painters worked in a very similar style, from which they both veered in the following decade. Domenico di Bartolo's *Madonna of Humility* (1433; fig. 11) and Filippo's Tarquinia *Madonna and Child*, in particular, share many features. There is the monumentality and preeminence of the physical body of the Virgin. Both paintings represent the Virgin and Child in a detached manner, caught up in their own intimate relation and concerns, which threatens to relegate the beholder to the position of a voyeur. Certain formal features, however, undermine this position – the porcelaneous, hard modeling of the figures which renders them "impenetrable," deflecting the intrusive gaze of the beholder, and the illusionist *cartoline* that unfold at the feet of the Virgin, designed for the beholder's eyes alone, thus orientating the viewer and rendering his/her "presence" within the pictorial space a legitimate one.

It is difficult to ascertain in which direction the influence flowed. Domenico was probably a little older than Filippo – born around the turn of the century and trained in a Sienese artistic ambience that included the powerful work of the sculptor Jacopo della Quercia. Vasari and Baldinucci both claimed that Domenico di Bartolo was the artist commissioned to paint the high altar of Santa Maria del Carmine in Florence, probably some time in the mid-1430s and recently associated with a panel by Domenico in Princeton (see fig. 34).[93] Fra Filippo would thus have had an intimate exposure to one work of Domenico's in his own convent church. He could also have encountered Domenico's work – and possibly have come to know the artist himself – during his ten months as the sub-prior of the Sienese Carmelite convent in 1428–29. However, it is more likely that the influence went in the opposite direction. Domenico's 1433 *Madonna of Humility* reveals what Carl Strehlke calls a "precocious assimilation of Florentine art – interpreted . . . with a distinctly Sienese accent."[94] His paintings from the early 1440s exhibit much less of a debt to Florentine painting, reflecting instead Sienese narrative traditions and a courtly style introduced into Sienese art by Gentile da Fabriano. It is thus probable that Fra Filippo Lippi was one of the elements within the Florentine artistic scene that Domenico di Bartolo absorbed during his early flirtation with Masacciesque pictorial realism. The two young artists could have entered into a brief artistic dialogue when their interests converged.

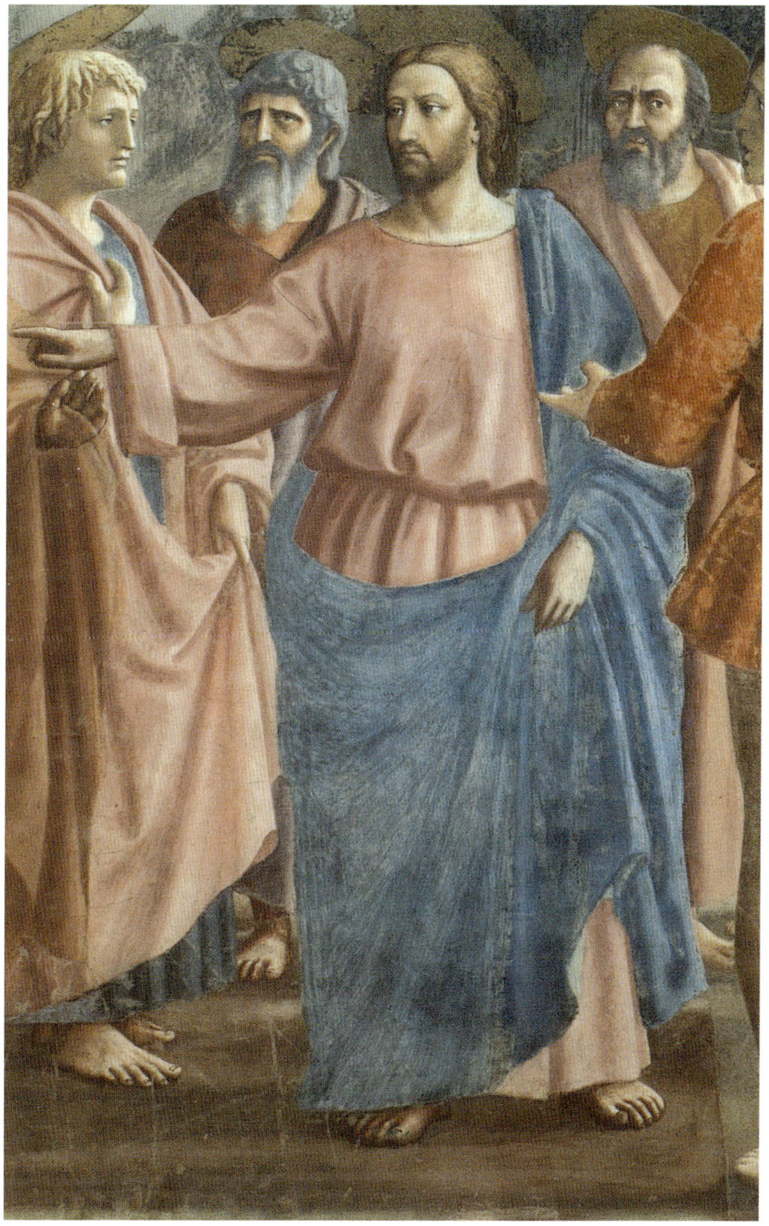

8 Masaccio, *Tribute Money*, detail of fig. 60.

Fra Filippo Lippi's circulation among the Tuscan Carmelite convents on special feast days would have exposed him to other

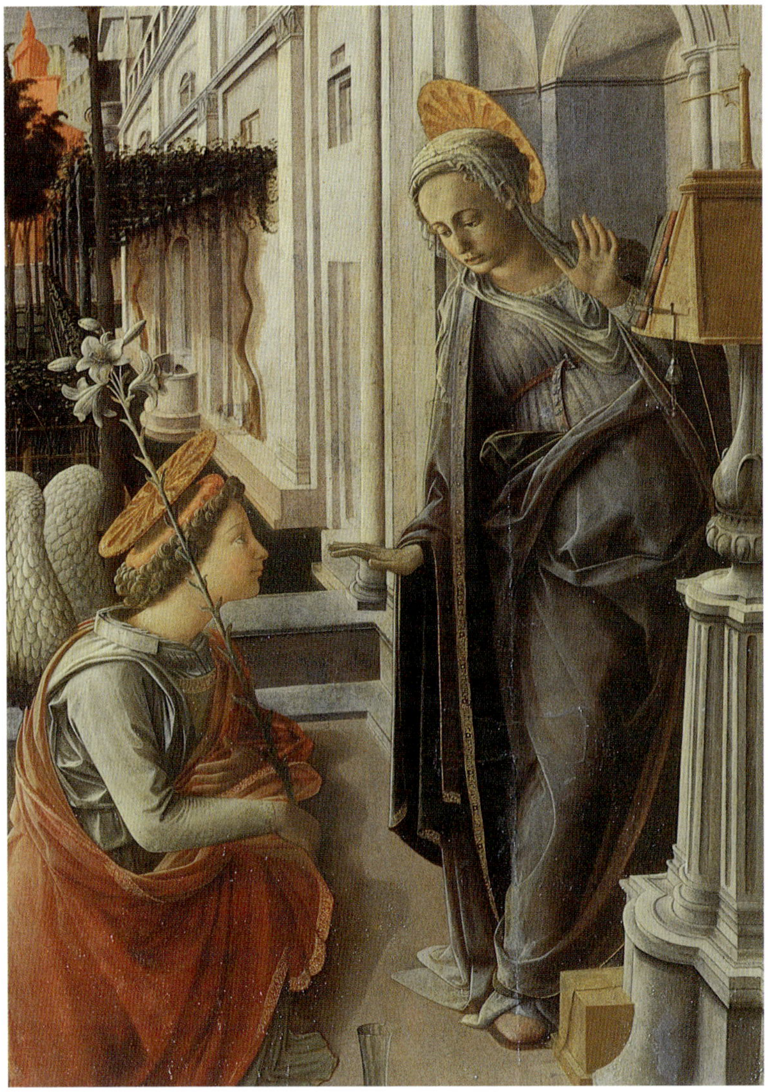

9 Filippo Lippi, *Annunciation*, detail of fig. 104.

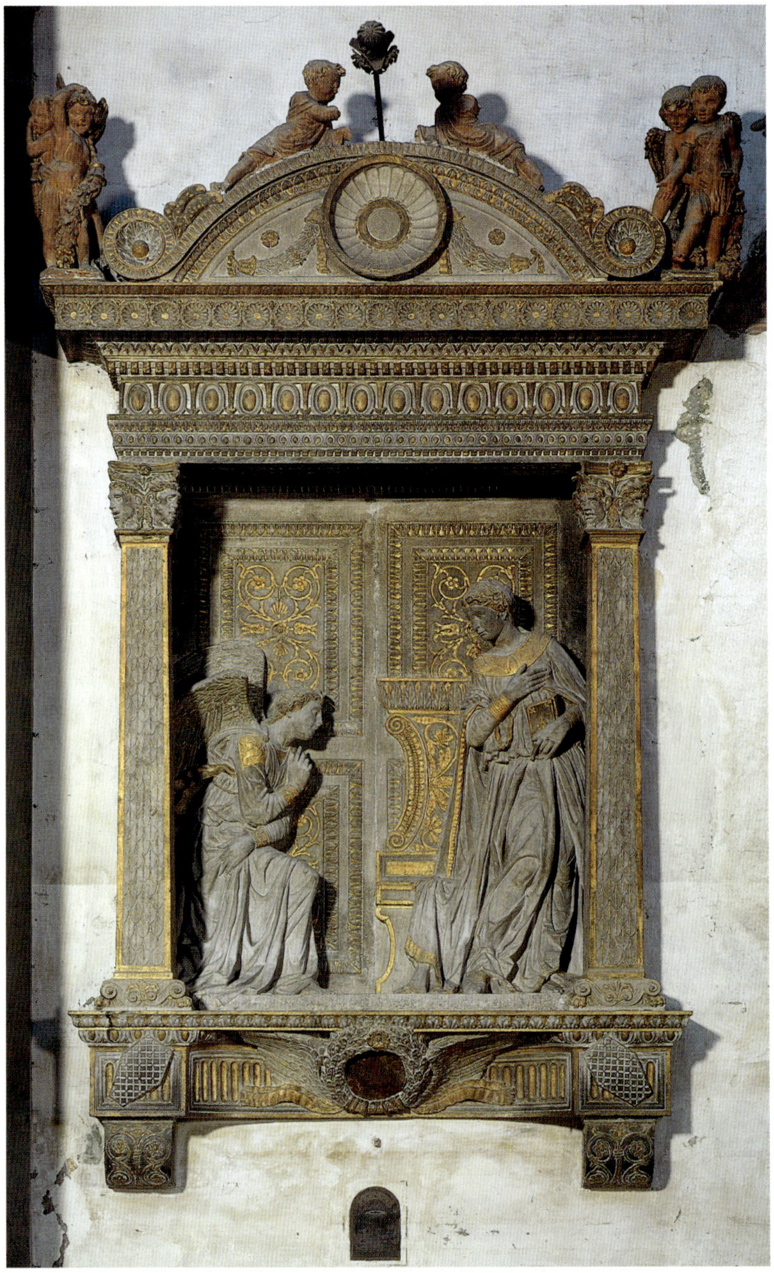

10 Donatello, *Cavalcanti Annunciation*, early 1430s, Florence, Santa Croce.

influential works of art. I have already mentioned Masaccio's altarpiece in the Carmelite church in Pisa. In Siena, Lippi would have seen Pietro Lorenzetti's polyptych for the high altar of the Carmelite convent church (fig. 20)[95] and the new altarpiece for the chapel of the Corpus Christi in the same church commissioned by the Arte della Lana and painted by Sassetta. His ten months in Siena in 1428–29 would have given him some exposure to the broader developments in contemporary Sienese art (the recent work there by Gentile da Fabriano, the paintings of Domenico di Bartolo and Sassetta, and Jacopo della Quercia's sculpture).

By 1434, Fra Filippo Lippi was in Padua and his activities as a *frate dipintore* appear to have been more heavily determined by his professional artistic, rather than his Carmelite religious, interests. In concluding this chapter, I should like to emphasize that we do not know which painter taught Lippi his particular technique of composing images and laying down brushstrokes; we do not know the formal means according to which Lippi acquired a pictorial idiom or the precise character of that early idiom – and this is a pity. However, the master's side was not the only site where a young painter's visual sensibilities were awakened. Nor were pictorial conventions the only representational structures that would have informed the painter's developing artistic conceptions. Fra Filippo's own convent, Santa Maria del Carmine, exposed him to a rich range of sacred images, rituals, and dramatic enactments, in addition to several miraculous manifestations of sacred presence. These were spectacles implicated within religious traditions, social negotiations, and historical processes that offered themselves up to the painter's imagination.

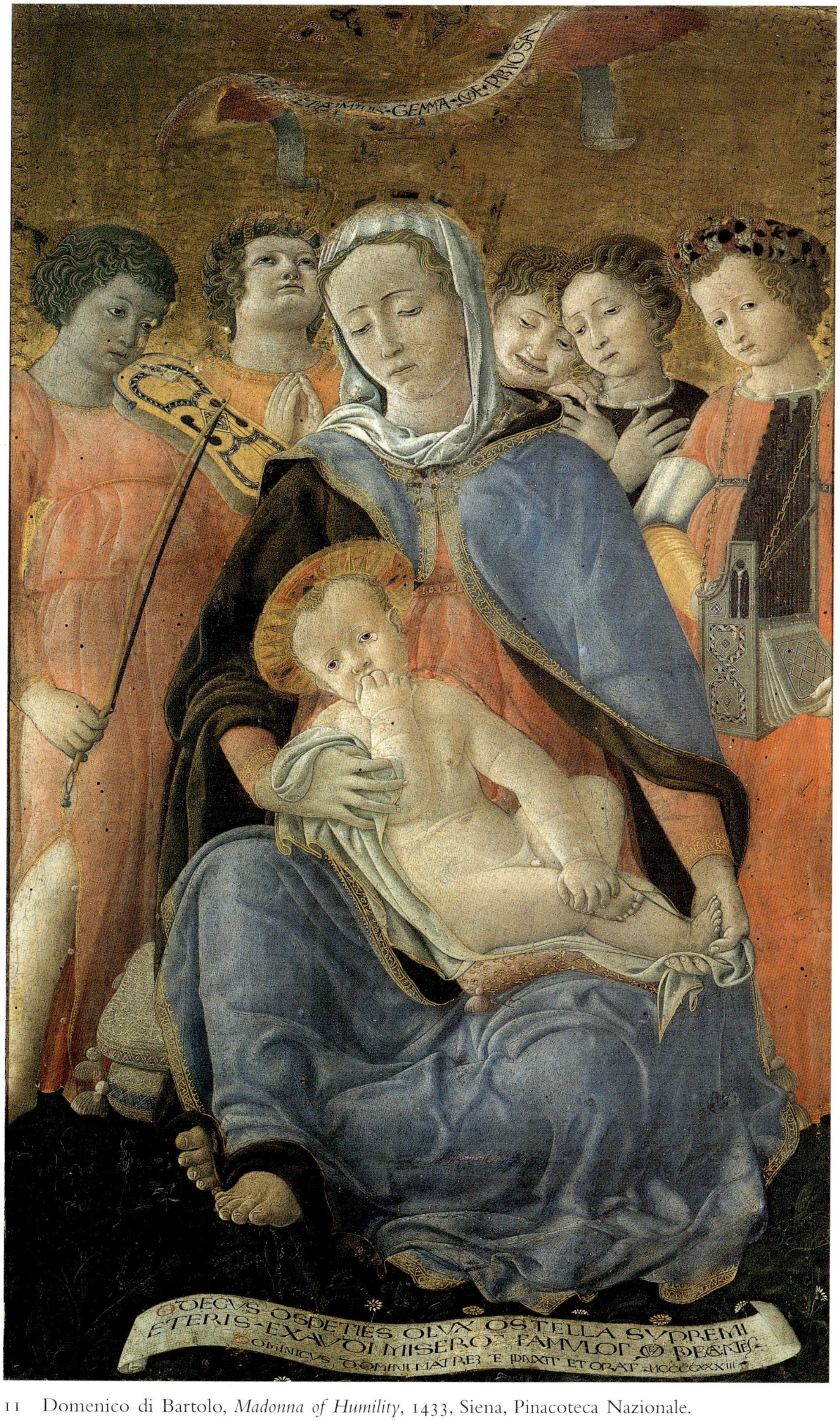

11 Domenico di Bartolo, *Madonna of Humility*, 1433, Siena, Pinacoteca Nazionale.

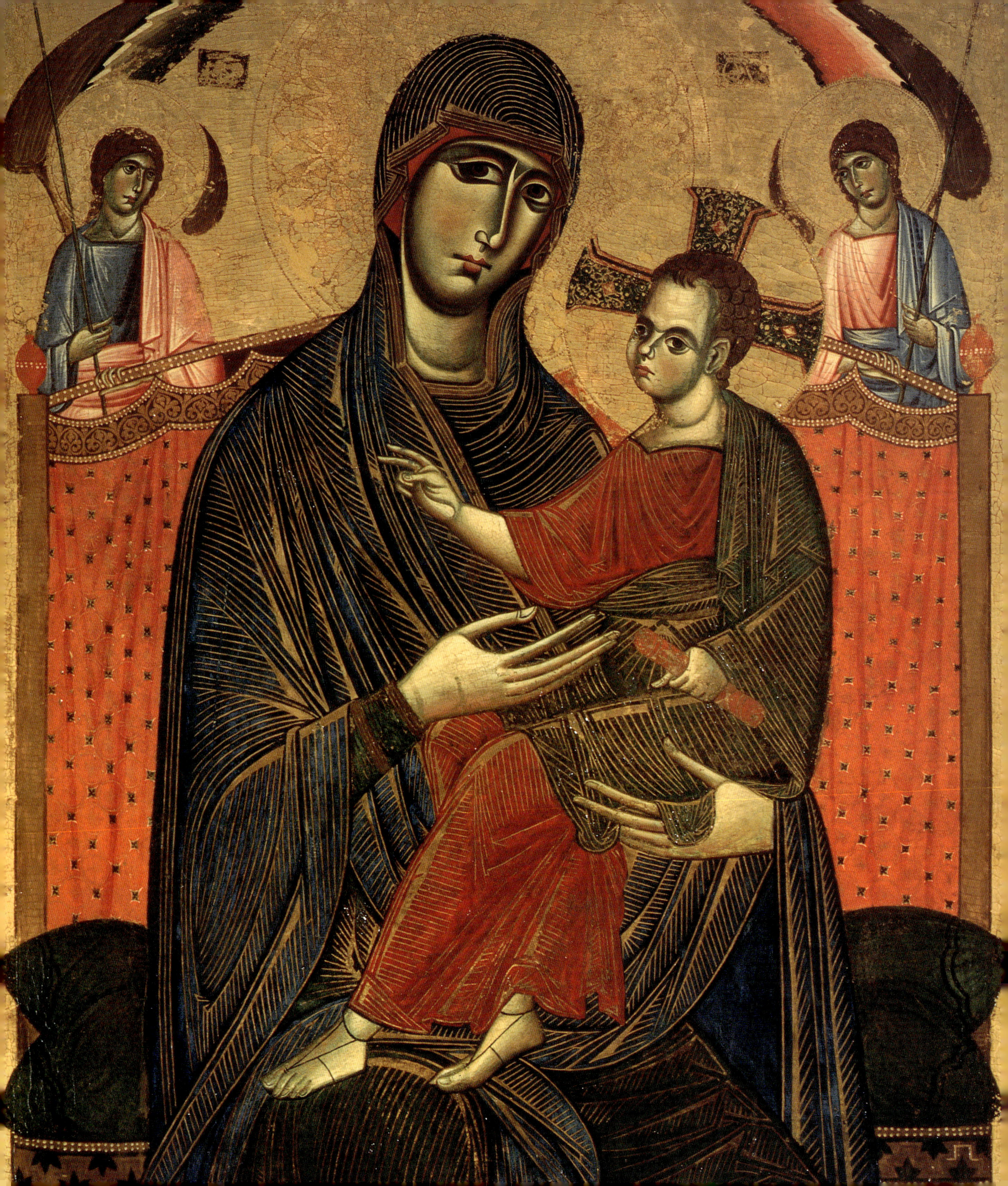

CHAPTER TWO

SANTA MARIA DEL CARMINE AND VISUAL REPRESENTATION

THE FLORENTINE CARMELITE MONASTERY Santa Maria del Carmine as the fluid socio-religious ambience in which Fra Filippo Lippi passed formative years should assert its relevance in a study of the artist as something more than mere background or framing. The Carmine was one of the primary sites where a new pictorial realism was being realized in the city of Florence during the second and third decades of the *quattrocento*, in Masaccio's *Sagra*, the Brancacci chapel frescos, Domenico di Bartolo's high altar image, Lippi's own blend of naturalism, and the spectacular Ascension Day *sacra rappresentazione*. How was the environment in the Carmine itself generative and why did the religious art take on the form it did? The situation becomes even more vivid if one opens the inquiry to other representational modes and abandons the singularly art historical perspective.

The Florentine Carmelites were very self-consciously producing their own history. Significant events – the consecration of the convent church in 1422, the preaching miracle of Fra Angelo Mazzinghi (c. 1438), the miraculous intervention of Beato Andrea Corsini in the Florentine victory at Anghiari in 1440 – were instantly taken up by the Carmelite chapter and fashioned into discursive accounts. Fra Pietro da Castagna wrote the posthumous Anghiari miracle into a celebratory *Vita* of the fourteenth-century Andrea Corsini. Fra Angelo Mazzinghi's sermon was commemorated in a "mysterious image" that hung on a pilaster in the convent church. In the case of the consecration of the church, one might say that the highly ritualistic, public, and publicized ceremony was itself an enactment carefully produced by the Carmelites. Even so, it was quickly reproduced in fresco by Masaccio above a portal in the convent cloister. The Carmelite painter Fra Filippo Lippi, too, was involved in this history-making process. Three paintings attributed to the young *frate* have distinct Carmelite imagery – and two of them present their Carmelite messages in none-too-subtle terms. Fra Filippo was also personally involved in the celebrations of Beato Andrea Corsini.

It is thus important to try to pin down more precisely just what this Carmelite agenda was, and how the Carmelites engaged the services of pictorial imagery in working it out. In the process, I shall gradually construct an image of the Carmine which is not merely background, so that when I eventually turn to the question of the Carmelite Lippi in subsequent chapters, the socio-religious context of Lippi's early artistic production can be understood in much of its complexity and subtlety. I begin with a brief description of Santa Maria del Carmine, and then examine the visual culture in the Carmine from the late *duecento* to the early decades of the *quattrocento*. Increasing specificity will be brought to the discussion as I approach the epoch in which Fra Filippo Lippi himself was a friar in the convent.

SANTA MARIA DEL CARMINE

During the late Middle Ages and early Renaissance, the Florentine Carmelite convent Santa Maria del Carmine was simultaneously a site of monastic enclosure, walled off from the urban surroundings in the parish of San Frediano, and a magnetic center of popular devotion, attracting the laity – woolworkers, silkweavers, shoemakers, spice merchants, bankers alike – from one of the poorer sections of the city. This was the curious paradox at the heart of late medieval mendicant monasticism: it was predicated upon both the process of retreat from the urban environment and a basic dependence upon it. The clergy functioned as a separate, trained, and privileged social group that maintained the designated consecrated spaces in Western Christendom and insured that sacred manifestations, ritual enactments, and signs of the sacred were correctly observed.

Mendicant monasteries offered the possibility of a "sacred preserve" within a changing urban scene dominated by the interests of the presiding oligarchies. Richard Trexler describes the task of the monastic clergy: to "provide and maintain a consecrated

12 Florentine, "Madonna del Popolo," detail of fig. 18.

center that could withstand the varied transformations the city underwent," to "tap the multiplicity of powers in the divine realm," and to intercede on behalf of the urban laity.[1] The city, meanwhile, supplied the economic base necessary for those mendicant "consecrated centers." While the relationship was healthily symbiotic and generated a rich urban religious culture, the interaction between the monastic and the lay spheres gave rise to numerous problems and conflicts, the most colorful of which are sensationally represented in the pages of Boccaccio.

In the convent of Santa Maria del Carmine, the paradoxical flight from, and dependency upon, the urban environment was played out in two significant ways. There was an ever-present tension between the interests of the convent and those of the lay public that participated in the religious services and formed the economic base of the convent. This tension functioned dialectically, shaping the physical environment and the religious activities that took place in the Carmelite church and convent. The second manifestation of this paradox was embedded within the Carmelite discursive accounts of their own history. During the course of the *trecento* and *quattrocento*, at the very moment in which the Order was becoming firmly enmeshed in the urban fabric of Western Christendom, Carmelites strove to recover a memory of the distant past when the Order was eremitical and centered in the Holy Land.

Santa Maria del Carmine was founded in 1268.[2] The foundation coincided with the gradual migration of the Carmelites to the West, away from their hermetic sanctuaries in the besieged Holy Land, away from the slopes of Mount Carmel where the Order had sprung up in the ruins of the ancient Fountain of Elijah. The first Western convents were established in Cyprus, Sicily, and England during the early decades of the thirteenth century. The first Tuscan house was set up in Pisa in 1248, followed by Siena (1256) and Florence (1267). The foundation of Santa Maria del Carmine coincided with a wave of mendicant

13 "Catena View of Florence," detail of fig. 206, showing Santa Maria del Carmine.

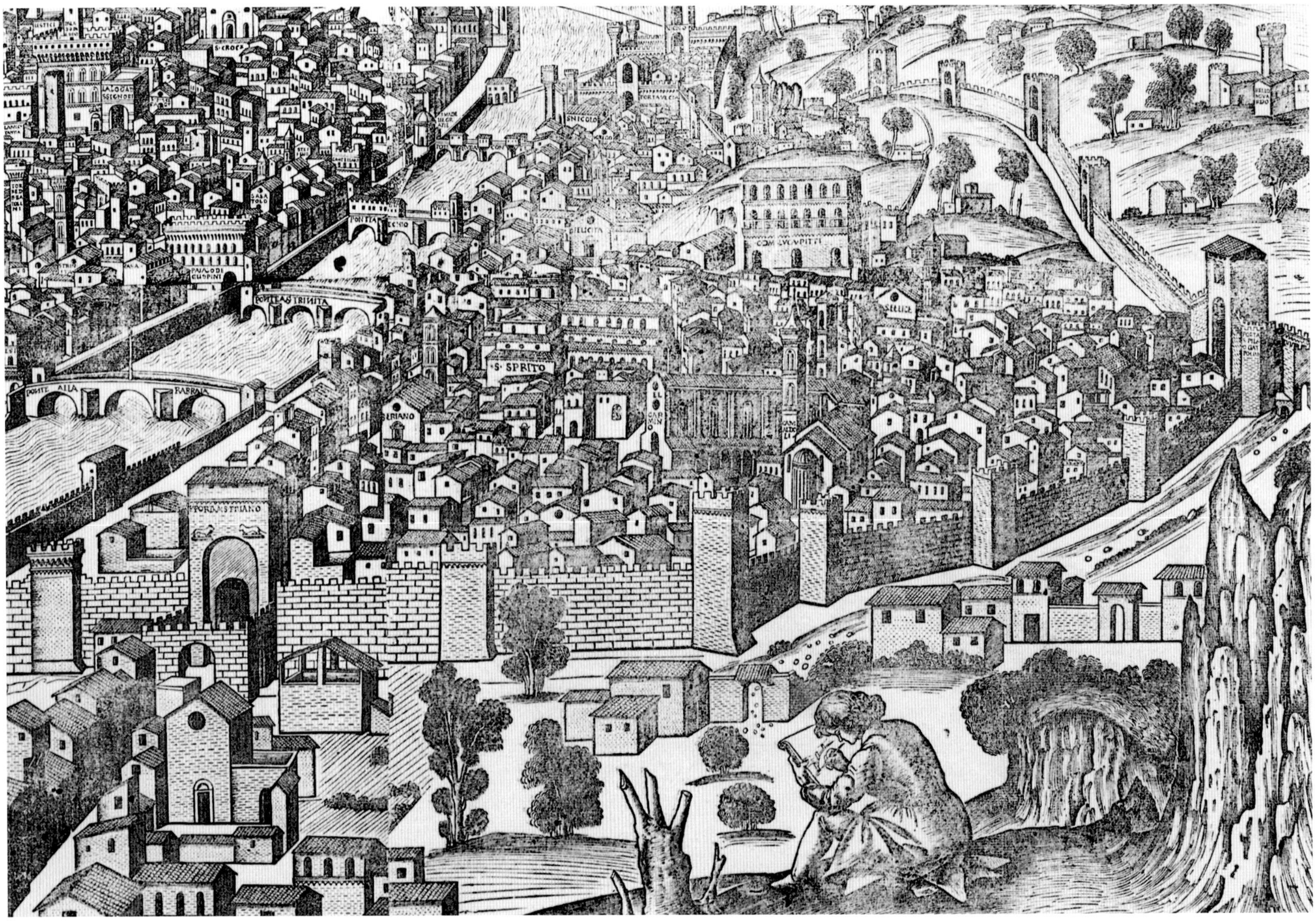

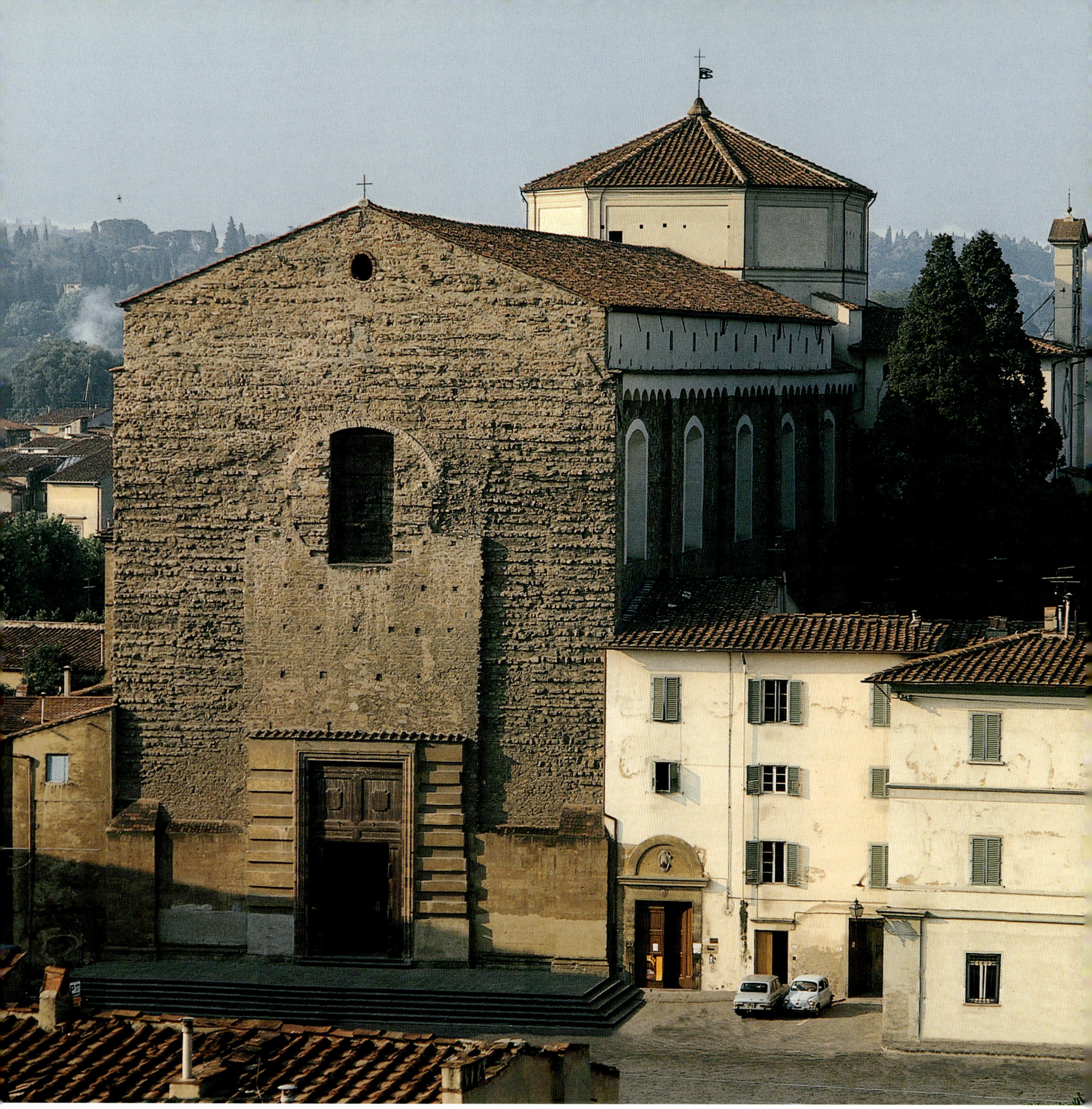

14 Santa Maria del Carmine, Florence.

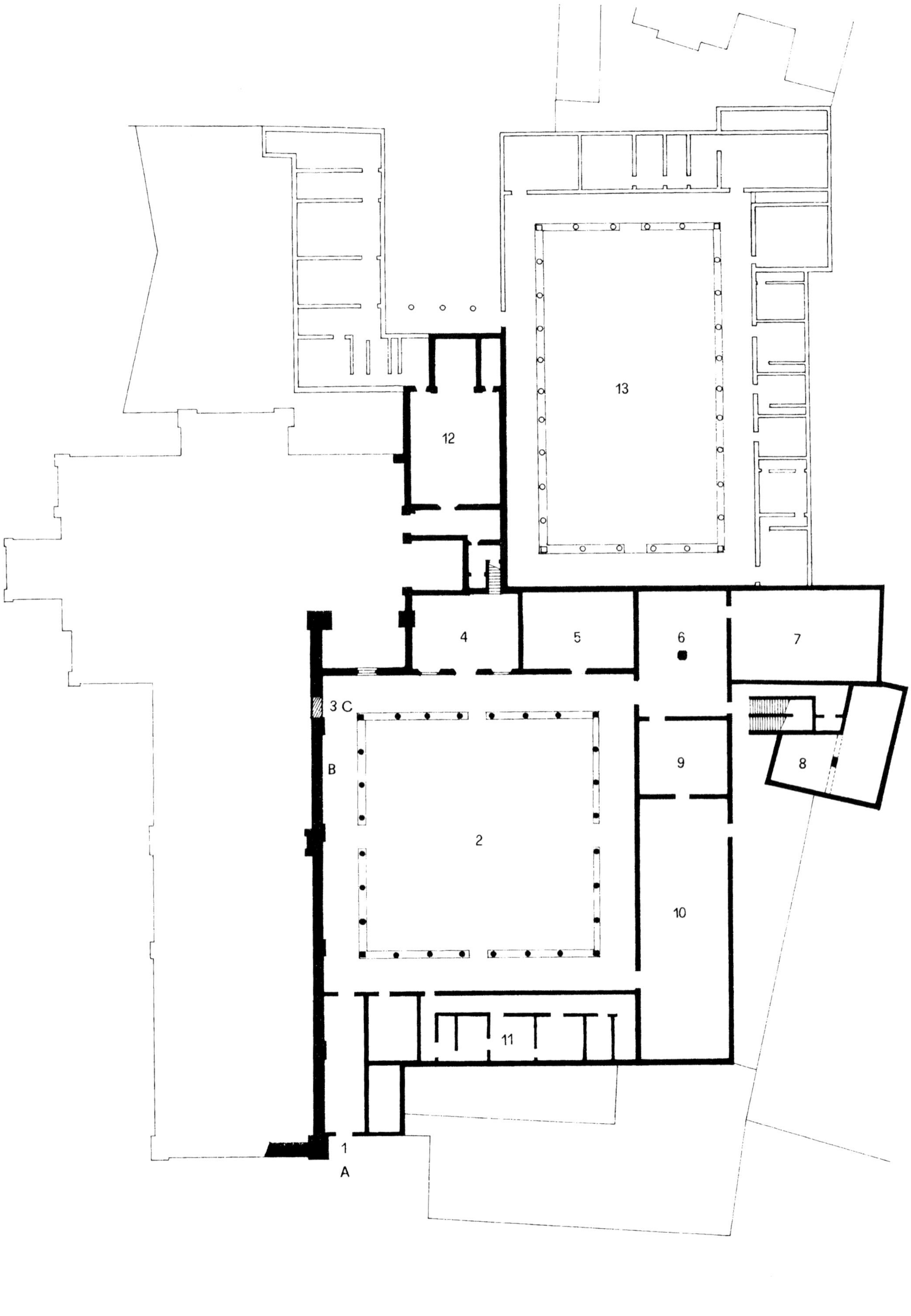
13
12
4
5
6
7
3 C
B
9
8
2
10
11
1
A

15 (*facing page*) Convent of Santa Maria del Carmine, Florence, reconstructed plan, early fifteenth century (after Giovannini and Vitolo) [Drawing: Yasin Visram].

GROUND LEVEL

1 "Porta del Martello" – the door leading from the Piazza into the convent
2 Cloister
3 Doorway leading into the church during the fifteenth century (precise location unknown)
4 Chapter house
5 Refectory
6 "Sala della Colonna"
7 Infirmary
8 Kitchen, storerooms, shops
9–10 Possible location of the Studium
11 Dormitory ("del buonriposo"): foresteria; rooms of the Provinciale
12 Sacristy
13 New cloister and convent buildings (1469–91)

SECOND FLOOR

4–5 Dormitory ("vecchio"): the novices dormitory and the library
9–10 Dormitory ("nuovo")
11 Dormitory ("del buonriposo")

A *Annunciation* fresco (no longer extant) above the Porta del Martello attributed to Filippo Lippi
B Original location of Filippo Lippi's fresco *Confirmation of the Carmelite Rule*
C Masaccio's *Sagra* (no longer extant) above the doorway leading into the church (precise location unknown)

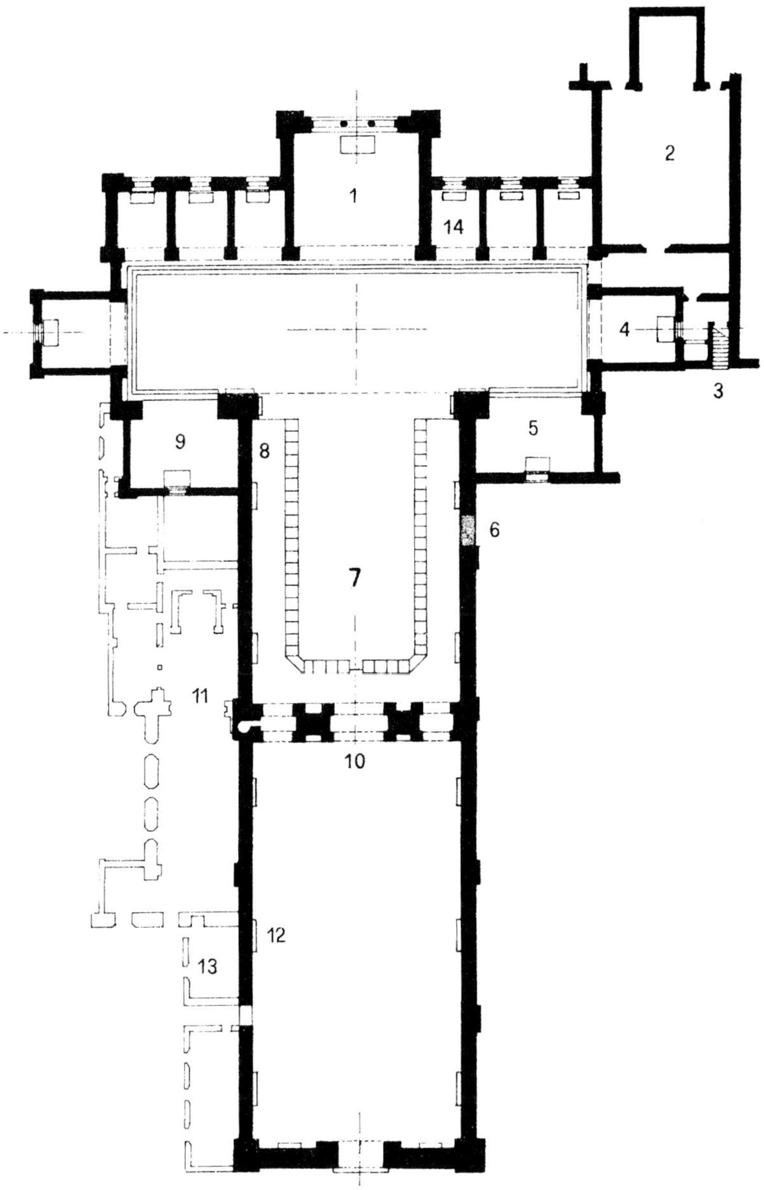

16 Church of Santa Maria del Carmine, Florence, reconstructed plan, early fifteenth century (after *Ricostruzione grafica delle fasi storiche della Chiesa del Carmine, Firenze* and *Il luogo teatrale*, scheda 1.18) [Drawing: Yasin Visram].

1 Main chapel; dedicated to Santa Maria del Carmine; patrons: Soderini (crypt below: Compagnia di San Niccolò di Bari)
2 Sacristy; chapel dedicated to St. Cecilia; patrons: Serragli
3 Stairway leading to the chapter house
4 Brancacci chapel; dedicated to St. Peter; patrons: Brancacci
5 Chapel of the Passion; patrons: Nerli
6 Doorway leading to the cloister in the fifteenth century (precise location unknown)
7 Friars' choir (precise configuration unknown)
8 Tomb of Fra Andrea Corsini
9 Chapel of St. Jerome; patrons: Pugliesi
10 Choir screen with four chapels including:
Chapel of St. Alberto of Trapani; patron: Paolo Dieciaiuti
Chapel of St. Angelo of Sicily; patrons: Carmelites
(precise locations unknown)
11 Oratory of the Compagnia di Sant'Alberto
12 Altar of the Compagnia di Sant'Agnese (or possibly the third altar on the left side of the nave)
13 Meeting place of the Compagnia di Sant'Agnese
14 Location of the painted image of Beato Angelo Mazzinghi on a pilaster in the Manetti chapel

monastic foundations in Florence – led by the Franciscans at San Gallo (1218) and Santa Croce (1228), followed by the Dominicans at Santa Maria Novella (1221), the Augustinians at Santo Spirito (1250), the Servites at SS. Annunziata (c. 1250), and the Umiliati at Ognissanti (1251).

When construction commenced on the church and convent of Santa Maria del Carmine in 1268, the property was situated just outside the city walls, near the well-frequented road to Pisa. In 1284, the city walls were extended and came to embrace not only the Carmine (within the Oltrarno *sesto*) but also the other three major mendicant churches that had also been erected at the periphery of the city, Santa Maria Novella, Santa Croce, and SS. Annunziata. This realignment of the city perimeters provided the Carmine with a ready source of patronage in the lay people from the parishes of San Frediano and San Felice in Piazza. The convent also drew many of its friars from this area, and the Carmelites quickly gained the support of local ecclesiastical officials and prominent patricians.[3]

Why were Florentines enthusiastic over the latest mendicant arrivals in town? The Carmelites' entry into the ranks of the approved mendicant orders in other parts of the West had been received with no such extended warm welcome, and the Oltrarno *sesto* of Florence already supported a major Augustinian foundation at Santo Spirito and the Camaldolese San Salvatore.[4] If the Florentine Carmine evolved out of a generative tension between Carmelite and lay interests, as I have suggested, it is somewhat easier to understand the advantage a Florentine settlement afforded the Carmelites than it is to make sense of the reverse attraction that the Carmelites held for the city. Florence was experiencing an economic and demographic boom during the second half of the *duecento*, and the city conveniently lay mid-way along the road between Rome and the south of Italy and lower Germany where the Order was beginning to take root. Carmelite houses had already been set up in Pisa and Siena. The Carmelites' ready reception in the city of Florence was conditioned in part by the politics of religious patronage and in part by the immediate and efficacious religious services the Carmelites were able to offer the local laity.

It appears that from the start the Carmelites fostered a particular variety of Marian worship that strongly appealed to the local laity.[5] The Carmelites claimed a privileged relationship to the Virgin: their Order was dedicated to the Virgin of Mount Carmel, and she functioned as the chief *padrona*. In the *quattrocento* the Carmelites even insisted that during her lifetime, the Virgin had visited the Carmelite hermits who lived on Mount Carmel. It seems that by a very early date, the Florentine Carmelite oratory housed the miracle-working image known as the "Madonna del Popolo" (fig. 12). A confraternity that took the name Compagnia di Santa Maria del Carmine was formed even before construction on the new convent church was under way.[6]

The convent in Florence was a relatively small monastic establishment (fig. 15). In 1301, the friars numbered twenty-six, increasing to forty-one by 1324, and peaking during the period just preceding the plague, which claimed the lives of thirty-six friars. In the early *quattrocento*, there were some thirty-five friars and ten novices.[7] The Florentine convent was the central monastery of the Tuscan Carmelite *provincia* which also included Carmelite foundations in Pisa, Siena, Lucca, Pistoia, Prato, Montecatini, Arezzo, and Lastra a Signa. The Carmine administration consisted of a prior, a sub-prior, and a sacristan, elected anually at the provincial chapter meeting, and a master of the novices. There was also a convent procurator who was in charge of the bookkeeping. The Carmine *studium* was overseen by the regent and a staff of *magistri* and *instruttori*. Continuity was provided by the provincial prior – usually appointed for life – who was based in the Florentine Carmine and was often also the regent of the *studium*. Laymen were hired to do the cooking, gardening, laundry, and to administer the friars' important weekly shave and tonsure.

The religious activities in the Carmine followed certain set routines, mandated by the Rule and Constitutions of the Order, but they were shaped also by specific events in the life of the city. Some activities – such as the Divine Offices – engaged only the friars, while others involved the laity as well. The Carmine liturgical calendar was unique, tailored specifically to the particular conditions of the convent.[8] It was based in part on the liturgy of the Holy Sepulcher in Jerusalem and included the feasts of certain early bishops of Jerusalem and early Christian martyrs from the Holy Land, a testimony to the Eastern origins of the Carmelite Order. Carmelite feasts were celebrated alongside those recognized in the Roman liturgy. Italian, Tuscan, and local Florentine saints were recognized with special observances, as well as saints who were associated with local cities and the Carmelite convents in the area.[9]

The convent friars participated in a daily cycle of worship that involved the recitation of the Divine Offices seven times a day, from Matins to the Night Office. Days were organized into *feste* and *ferie*, with the liturgy changing according to the annual festive calendar. The conventual side of life in the Carmine was complemented by a more public face in which the convent grounds – particularly the church – and services were utilized by the local laity for masses, burials, the endowment of private chapels and altars, confession, devotion, and many other religious and social activities.

The convent buildings (fig. 15) included a dormitory with a special wing for the novices, a refectory, kitchen, infirmary, workshops, visitors' quarters, garden, and in the early *quattrocento* a barber shop. The friars' religious activities predicated – in addition to the choir of the church where the Divine Offices and daily masses were sung – a sacristy, chapter house, a cloister, and a library. The last became the center of a *studium* founded in 1324 after the Carmelites, following the example of the other major mendicant orders, began to devote more time and attention to theological studies.

The convent church (fig. 16) was built along standard Gothic lines – "T"-shaped, with a long aisle-less nave leading to a transept lined with chapels. Additional altars were set up against the walls of the nave and beneath the arches of the stone choir screen that divided the nave about mid-way, known as the *ponte*.[10] The chapels were endowed by the major patrician families of the neighborhood: the Manetti, Lanfredini, Bonsi, Brancacci, Nerli, del Pugliese, Serragli, Soderini, Giamboni, Zampalocchi, Ferrucci, Biuzi, Forte, and Abadinghi.[11]

By the early *quattrocento*, the Soderini had emerged as the principal patrons of Santa Maria del Carmine. They were the patrons of the *cappella maggiore* and high altar dedicated to the Virgin and they donated alms for the principal feasts of the Annunciation, the Assumption of the Virgin, and on occasion provided the Pascal lamb for the Easter feast.[12] The Soderini were also numbered among the Carmine *frati*.[13] Two other notable patrons of the Carmine in the early *quattrocento* were the Nerli and the Brancacci. The Nerli patronized the chapel of the Passion, which was of particular significance to the Carmine friars because many of the Carmelites were buried there. During the early *quattrocento*, Fra Albizzo d'Azolino de' Nerli – both Carmelite and Nerli – paid for convent feasts in honor of the Crucifixion. The Brancacci were active contributors to Carmelite feast day celebrations and were in the process of decorating their family chapel.

There were a number of confraternities which were active in Santa Maria del Carmine. The oldest was the Compagnia di Santa Maria delle Laudi (or di Sant'Agnese), which was founded in 1264.[14] The Compagnia obtained the foot of St. Agnes in 1281, and this relic was stored above its altar along the left wall of the nave of the church. The Compagnia organized the annual Ascension Day *sacra rappresentazione* (which will be discussed later in this chapter) and subsidized a number of feasts each year and sang the lauds daily in the church. The confraternity was composed of lay men and women and at least one *frate* from the convent.[15] Fra Filippo Lippi, his brother Fra Giovanni, and his mother Antonia were all involved with the Compagnia.[16] Another active confraternity was the Compagnia di San Niccolò di Bari, founded in 1334, which had its chapel in the crypt of the church beneath the choir. In 1419, the Compagnia di Sant'Alberto was formed and, fifteen years later, the Compagnia di Santa Caterina, composed of German weavers.[17]

CARMELITE VISUAL IMAGERY

From the mid-thirteenth century when Carmelite activity was first documented, until the end of the fourteenth century, the Virgin occupied a central position in Carmelite worship as the *patrona* of the Order in the Holy Land and was represented predominantly as the "Virgin of Mount Carmel."[18] By 1229, the hermits on Mount Carmel had built a small church dedicated to the Virgin and in a papal bull of 1252, Innocent IV referred to the Carmelites as the friars of "S. Maria de Monte Carmeli." Their liturgy gave particular emphasis to the Virgin's feast days, and Carmelite prayers like the *Flos Carmeli* celebrated the Virgin in appealing poetic metaphor.[19] The Carmelites themselves maintained that the Virgin personally escorted each Carmelite friar to Paradise on the Saturday after his death (see fig. 181).[20]

Following the example of the brothers of Mount Carmel, Carmelite churches founded in the Holy Land and in the West were frequently dedicated to the Virgin of Mount Carmel. In Western Europe, there seems to have been a practice of transporting images of the Virgin from the Holy Land and setting them up as the focus of devotion in the new Carmelite establishments. The mid-thirteenth-century Byzantine *Virgin and Child* in the Sienese Carmine (fig. 17) probably made its way to the West in this fashion.[21] It is not known whether these images were icons in the traditional Byzantine sense, based upon a prototypical image of the Virgin of Mount Carmel, but they certainly must have functioned like icons in the West, impressing devotees with their resemblance to celebrated icons in Western Christendom, with their oriental look and an otherness which

17 Byzantine, *Virgin and Child*, c. 1250, Siena, San Niccolò al Carmine.

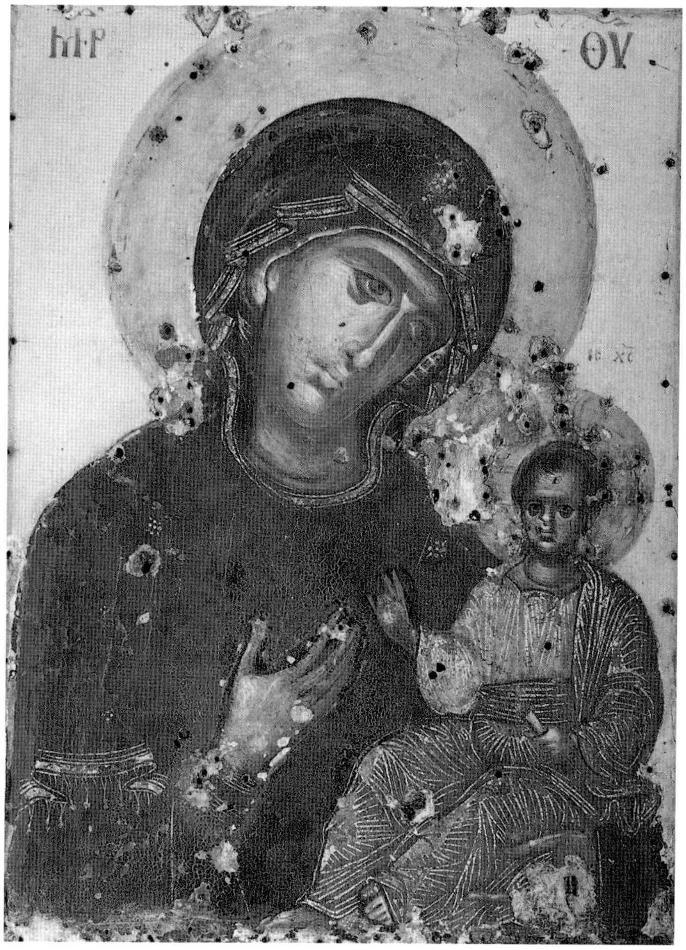

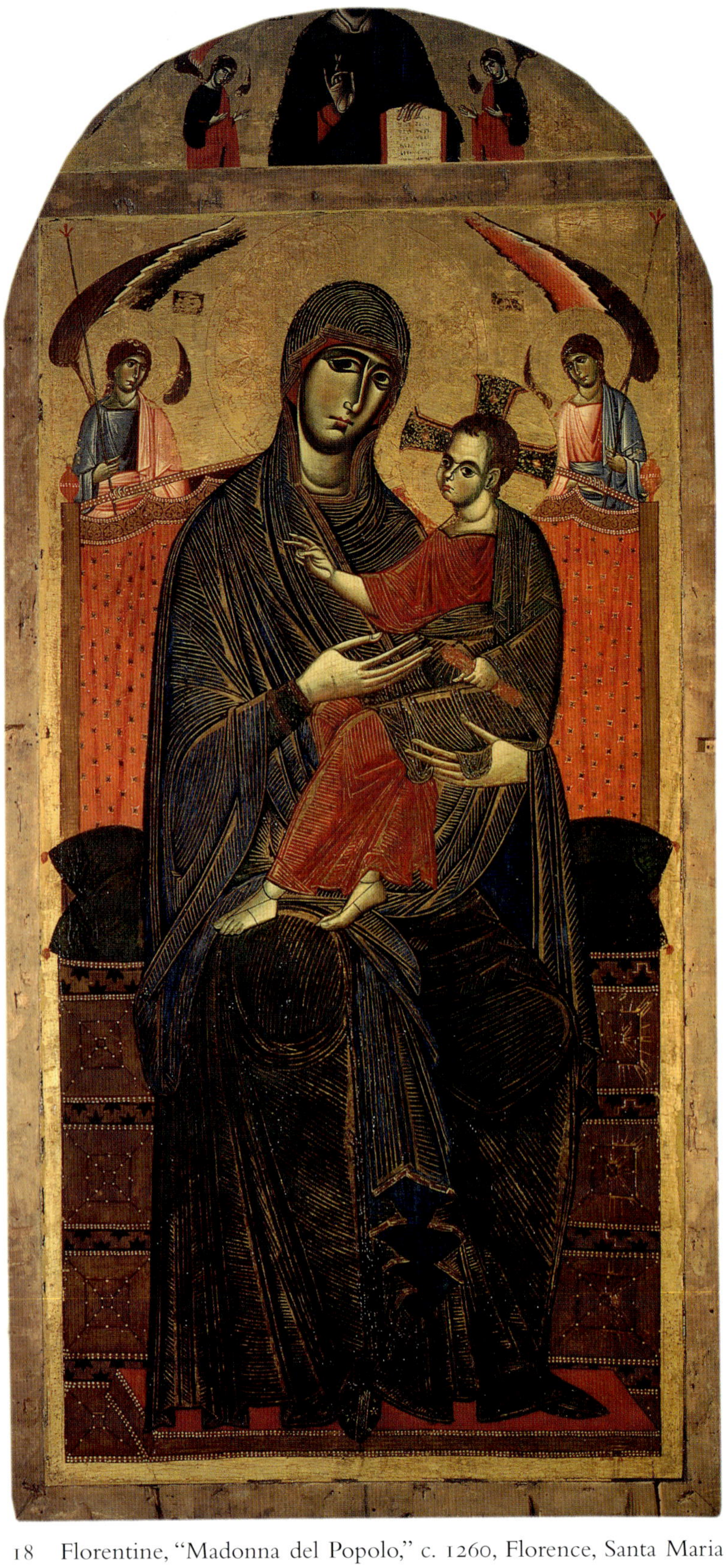

18 Florentine, "Madonna del Popolo," c. 1260, Florence, Santa Maria del Carmine, Brancacci chapel.

could have been construed as ancient, authentic, and authoritative. Carmelite convents in the West also forged the important link with the Carmelite's eastern *loci sancti* through a manipulation of symbols. A convent would be founded in the name of Santa Maria del Carmine, and a symbolic image – a new painting, often in a Byzantine style – of the patron of the Order and titular saint of the convent would be placed above an altar in the church. Full or half-length Madonna and Child images painted in a Byzantine style were to be found in the Carmelite churches in Florence, Lastra a Signa, Siena, Naples, and in Santa Maria in Traspontina in Rome.[22]

Marian devotion in Santa Maria del Carmine in Florence was focused upon the "Madonna del Popolo" (fig. 18). This monumental painting offered a full-length rendering of the Madonna and Child enthroned with angels, against a gold ground, with Christ blessing in the gable above. Modern scholars consider it to be a thirteenth-century Florentine work, attributing it to the "St. Agatha Master" or someone within the orbit of Coppo di Marcovaldo.[23] The style is consistent with that found in paintings executed in Florence during the 1260s and 1270s, when a strong Byzantine influence prevailed in Tuscan art. And it was also at this time that the convent of Santa Maria del Carmine in Florence was founded.[24] In scale, it is comparable to the *Maestà* by Guido da Siena and a precursor of the larger Madonna and Child compositions that Duccio, Cimabue, and Giotto evolved.

The first references to the "Madonna del Popolo," dating from the early *quattrocento*, indicate that it was a popular local cult object. Richa, citing a contemporary source, related that the spoils taken in the Florentine victory against Pisa in 1406 were presented to the "Madonna del Popolo" by the victors after they passed into the city through the San Frediano gate.[25] A second reference is found in a *Vita* of the fourteenth-century Carmelite saint Andrea Corsini, written by the Carmelite Fra Pietro da Castagna (c. 1440):

> And at that time, namely the year of the Lord 1300, in the church of the sacred Order of the Carmelites, there was an icon or a panel of the Mother of God, which in the vulgar speech was known as "Our Lady of the People," to which people out of devotion flocked to obtain grace, particularly women unable to conceive.[26]

As time passed and a new iconography of the Virgin prevailed within Carmelite representation, the "Madonna del Popolo" came to be noted for its antiquity and "maniera greca."[27] Giuseppe Richa considered it to be "extremely old, revealing everywhere the Greek style," suggesting that "it could have been carried from the Levant by those many painters who came to Florence or by the Florentines who went there for commercial reasons."[28] Gradually, there was a convergence of the *duecento* Florentine painting with its referent (eastern Madonna del Carmine), and the picture came to be considered a Byzantine icon.[29]

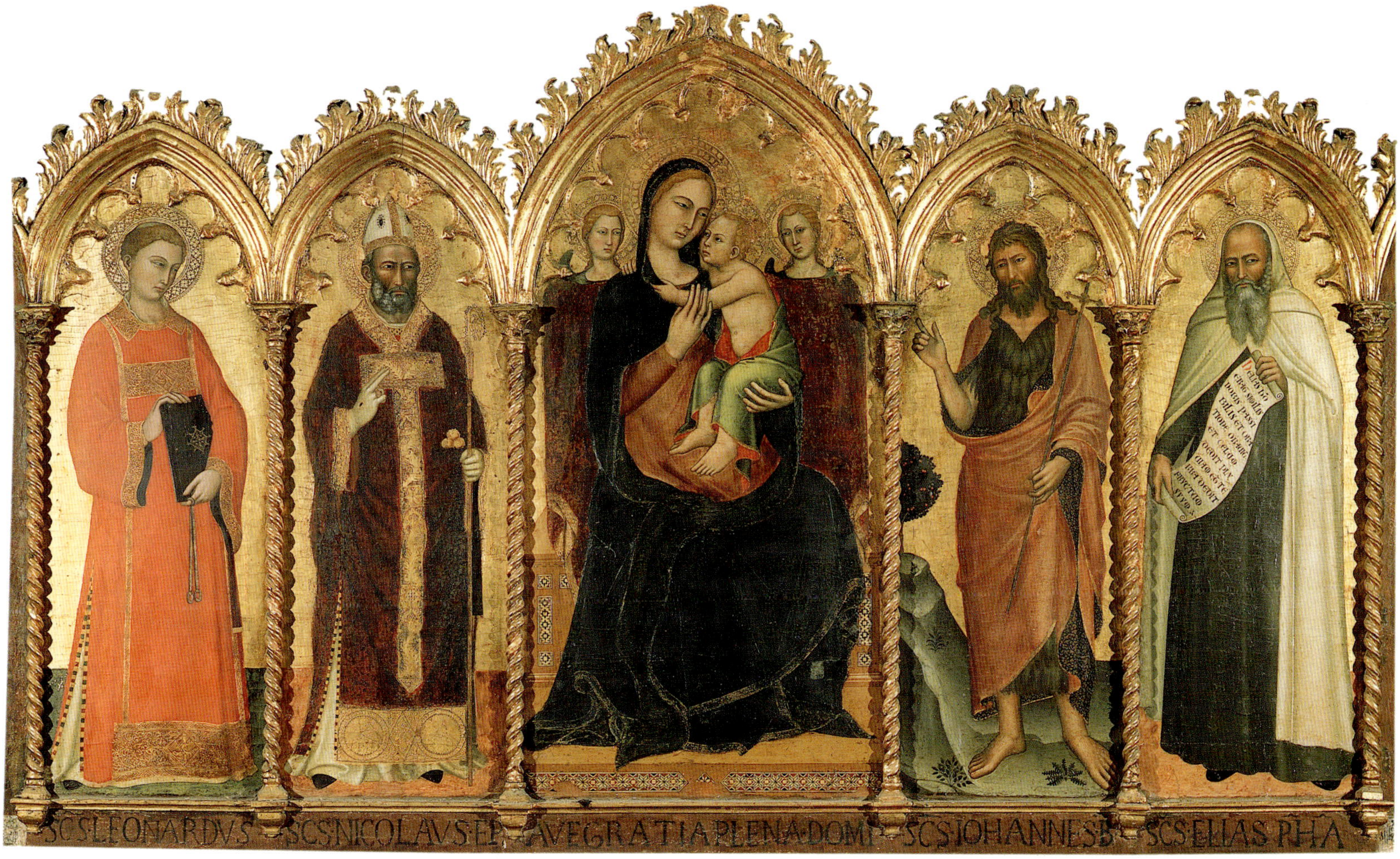

19 Andrea di Bonaiuto (attr.), *Madonna and Child with Sts. Leonard, Nicholas, John the Baptist, and Elijah*, early 1360s, Florence, Santa Maria del Carmine.

The strong Marian emphasis of *duecento* Carmelite imagery was gradually elaborated with a more expansive Carmelite visual doctrine. This is well exemplified in a small polyptych in Santa Maria del Carmine attributed to Andrea di Bonaiuto (fig. 19), dating from the early 1360s. The polyptych embodies a controversial Carmelite claim in the figure of the Old Testament prophet Elijah, who has made his way into the right-hand, lateral panel with the *titolo* "Sanctus Elias Propheta."

Elijah was a familiar figure in contemporary religious representation. He was presented as a precursor to John the Baptist and a prefiguration of Christ, interpreted through the narratives in the biblical Book of Kings. He was shown bearded ("a hairy man," II Kings 1:8) and robed, tucked into a gold-ground pinnacle of an altarpiece or a quatrefoil embedded in the illusionistic frame of a narrative fresco – spaces reserved for Old Testament premonitions of the coming of the new Christian order. However, Elijah as he appears in the Carmine polyptych – endowed with a halo and wearing the Carmelite habit with the black robe and white hooded cloak (fig. 29) – refers specifically to the prophet Elijah claimed by the Carmelites as "fundator," "Noster princeps," "professor," "Sanctus Padre."[30] The scroll that "Sanctus Elias" holds alludes to this role: "Helias ho[mo] erat similas nobis passibilis et oratione oravit et celum dedit pluviam et terra dedit fructum suum" ("Elijah was a man of like passions with us and he prayed fervently. And the heavens gave rain and the earth brought forth her fruit"). It is taken from the New Testament Epistle of St. James (5:17–18) and identifies Elijah as a Carmelite ("of like passions with us") and as a model for the intense and efficacious prayer practiced by the Carmelites.[31]

The Carmine altarpiece contains an abridged version of an extravagant claim about the origins of the Carmelite Order that had been fully expounded in the large polyptych above the high altar of the Sienese Carmine painted by Pietro Lorenzetti in 1327–29 (fig. 20).[32] In the Siena altarpiece, Saint Elijah appears in the central panel to the right of the Virgin (fig. 21). He turns toward the Christ Child and presents the text from the Book of Kings that refers to his victory over the false prophets of Baal on Mount Carmel. Opposite Elijah stands St. Nicholas, the titular saint of the Sienese Carmine. A second Old Testament prophet, Elijah's disciple Elisha, is represented as a saint in the lateral panel to the left of St. Nicholas (fig. 28). Elisha is

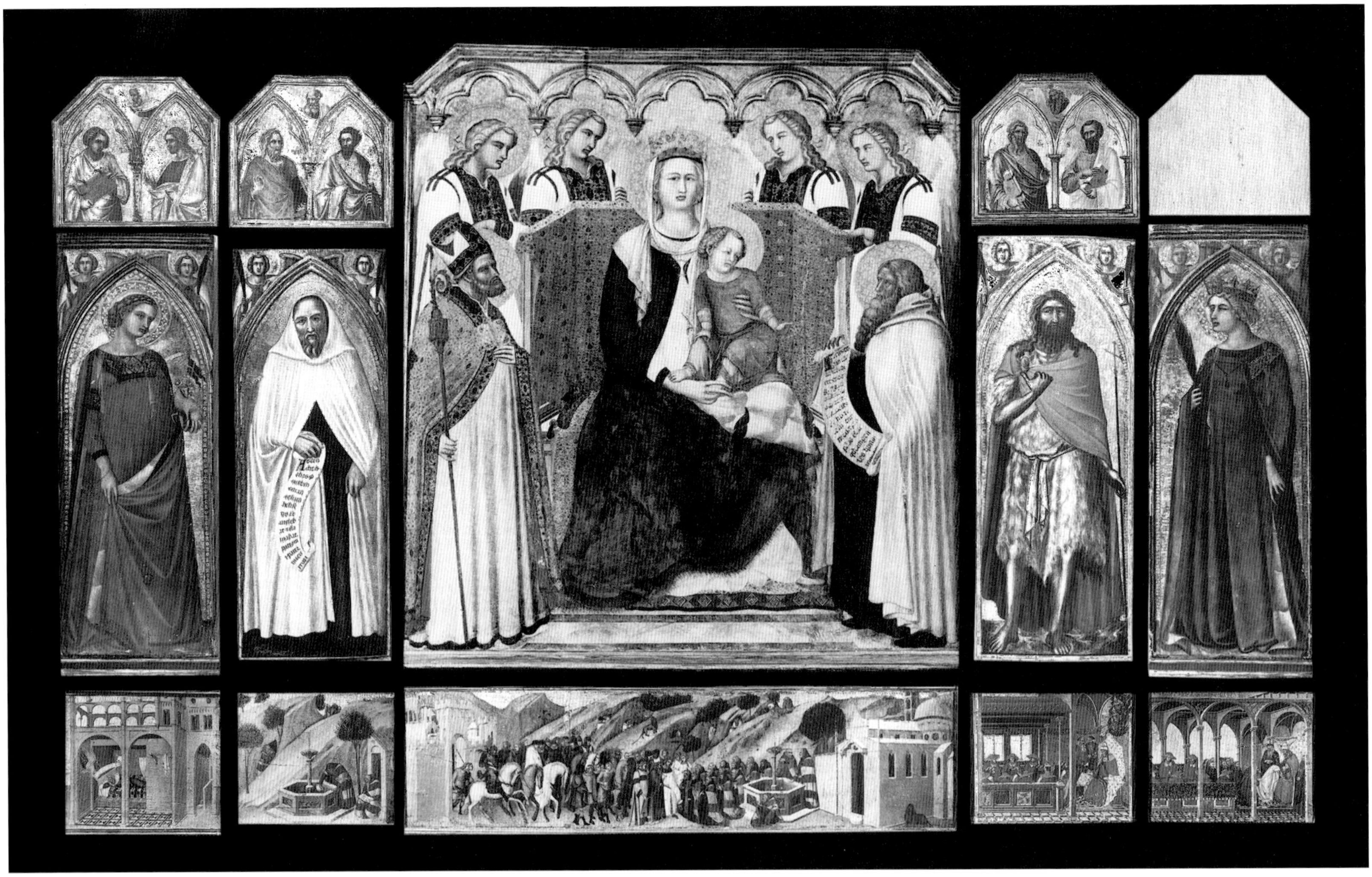

20 Pietro Lorenzetti, photomontage by Joanna Cannon of the polyptych for the high altar of San Niccolò al Carmine, Siena, 1327–29.

counter-balanced on the other side of the polyptych by the prophet and saint, John the Baptist. The outer wings contain images of Sts. Catherine and Agnes. The five scenes in the predella depict events in the history of the Carmelite Order: *The Annunciation to Sobac, Hermits at the Fountain of Elijah, St. Albert Presents the Rule to the Carmelites, The Pope Issues a Bull to a Carmelite Delegation*, and *The Approval of the New Carmelite Habit by Pope Honorius IV* (figs. 22a–e and 23–27). Joanna Cannon has demonstrated how Lorenzetti's altarpiece provides a visual analogue for the contemporary effort by Carmelite writers, such as John Baconthorpe and John of Cheminot, to plot the early history of the Order based upon "the Elian tradition."[33]

The effort to clarify this history began in the late thirteenth century, as the tangible details of Mount Carmel and the Holy Land began to grow dim in the memory of the friars established in Western Europe. The Order had moved west during the course of the thirteenth century, when the hermetic and monastic life became increasingly more difficult and dangerous in the face of Saracen attacks. In the process of relocating and adapting to the conditions of Western monasticism, the Order received permission to modify the Rule, and also transformed the liturgy along Dominican lines. Understandably, a crisis of identity set in. The Carmelites had to "Westernize," but they also had to represent themselves to the European public as distinct from the many other monastic orders to secure the patronage necessary for their survival in the West. The first Carmelite written attempt to explain the origins of the Order emerged as a redress to the problem that "certain recent friars of the Order did not know how to reply truthfully when asked from whom and how our Order came into being."[34] Thus, in the Constitutions of 1281, the Elian tradition was set down:

> We therefore affirm, to witness the truth, that beginning with the prophets Elijah and Elisha, pious dwellers on Mount Carmel, the holy fathers of both the Old and the New Testament, deeply in love with the solitude on the mountain, unquestionably lived there, in a manner deserving praise, near the Spring of Elijah, in holy penitence, continued uninterruptedly in holy succession.[35]

By the early fourteenth century, the Carmelites had self-

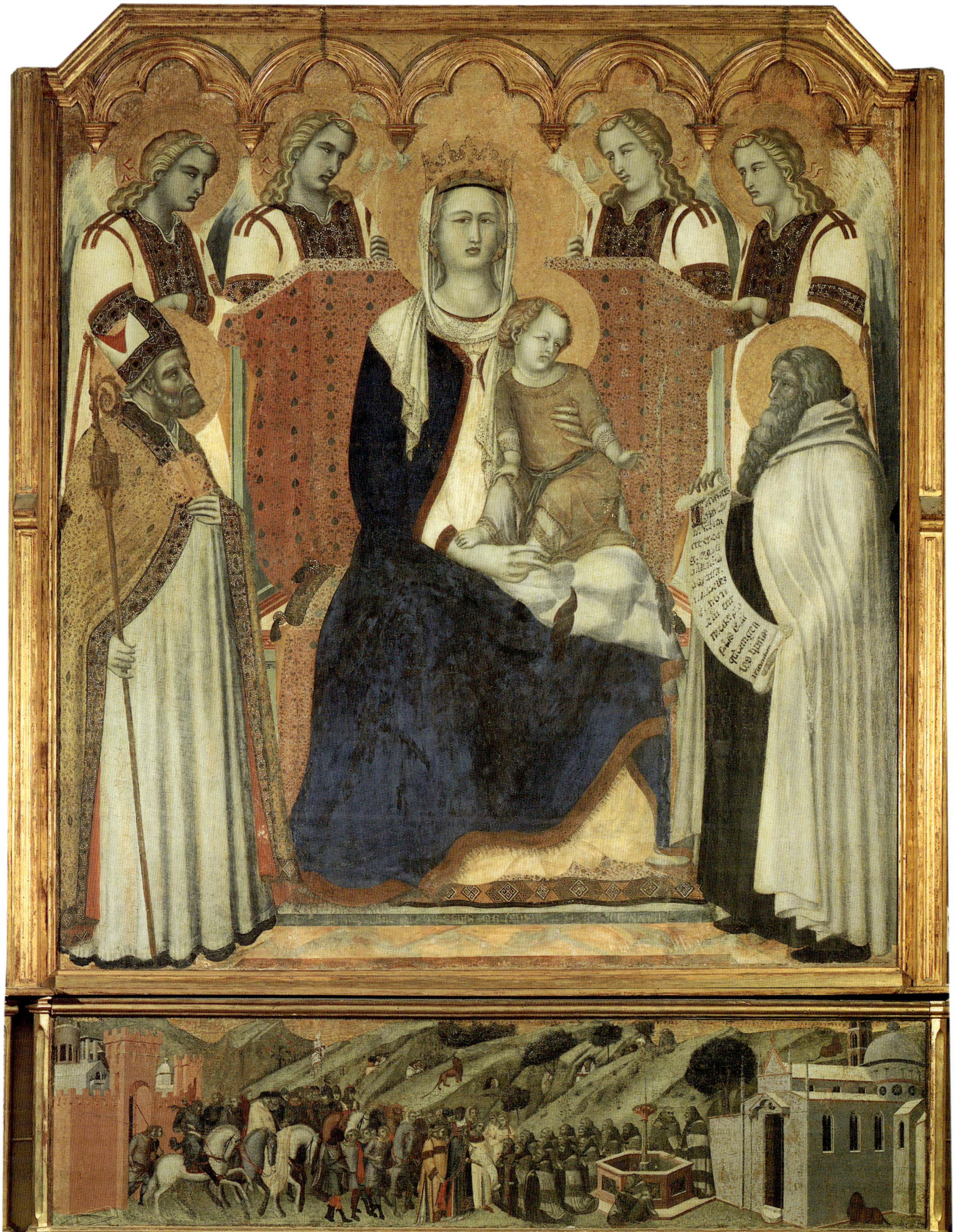

21 Pietro Lorenzetti, polyptych for the high altar of San Niccolò al Carmine, Siena, 1327–29, central panel, Siena, Pinacoteca Nazionale.

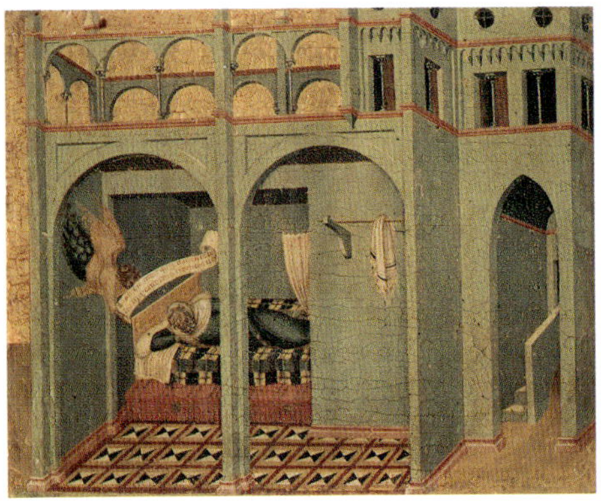
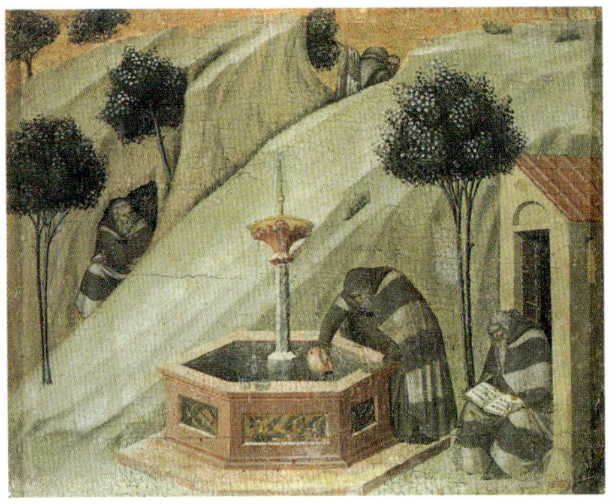
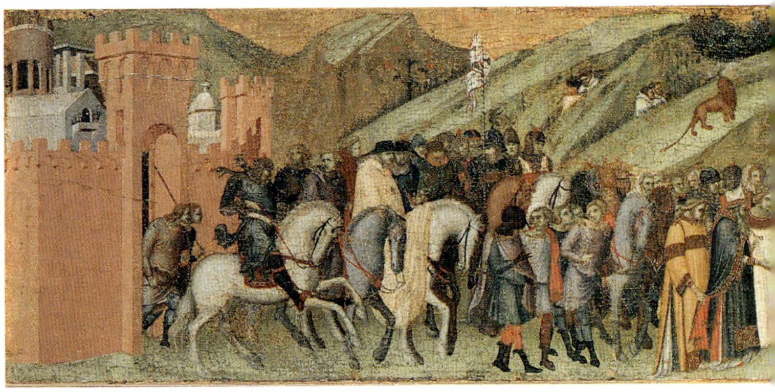

22a–e Pietro Lorenzetti, predella of the polyptych for the high altar of San Niccolò al Carmine, Siena, 1327–29, Siena, Pinacoteca Nazionale.

consciously cleansed their liturgy of Dominican features and returned to their original liturgy of the Holy Sepulcher used by the Church in Jerusalem, which included very particular rites for the major feasts that took place in that city.[36] At the same time, an expansive chronicling of the past was undertaken. The Fountain of Elijah on Mount Carmel became much more than a geographic locus or a metaphorical source, while Elijah, Elisha, and the "Children of the Prophets" were no longer mere Old Testament prototypes of the Carmelite hermetic calling, but were secured as progenitors. The history began in the tenth century BC with the dream of Elijah's father, Sobac, in which men dressed in white predicted that his son would have many followers (as illustrated by Lorenzetti in the predella of his altarpiece [fig. 23]). Then followed the life of Elijah, derived from the Book of Kings, and that of his disciples Elisha, Jonah, Abdiah, and others. The "Carmelite" hermits were thus present in the Holy Land during the miraculous events that surrounded the advent of Christ. They had a convent in Jerusalem near the Golden Gate where Joachim and Anne lived and where the Virgin was born.[37] The friars listened to the preaching of the Baptist outside the Golden Gate. By the fifteenth century, this part of the story had been elaborated. The general prior of the Order, Fra Giovanni Grossi, wrote (c. 1420) that the Virgin herself had visited the hermits on Mount Carmel.[38] A painted polyptych from the Carmelite church in Frankfurt from the end of the century shows St. Anne and her daughters, among them the Virgin carrying the Christ Child, at the Carmelite oratory by the Fountain of Elijah on Mount Carmel (fig. 57).[39] In the Brancacci chapel in the Florentine Carmine, the Carmelites emphasized that only they, among the monastic clergy, could

23 Pietro Lorenzetti, *The Annunciation to Sobac*, predella of the polyptych for the high altar of San Niccolò al Carmine, Siena, 1327–29, Siena, Pinacoteca Nazionale.

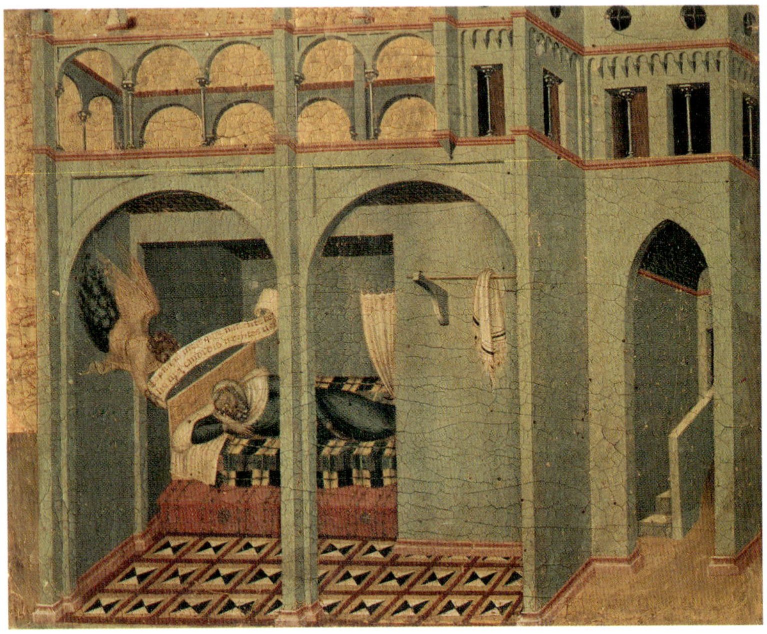

24 Pietro Lorenzetti, *Hermits at the Fountain of Elijah*, predella of the polyptych for the high altar of San Niccolò al Carmine, Siena, 1327–29, Siena, Pinacoteca Nazionale.

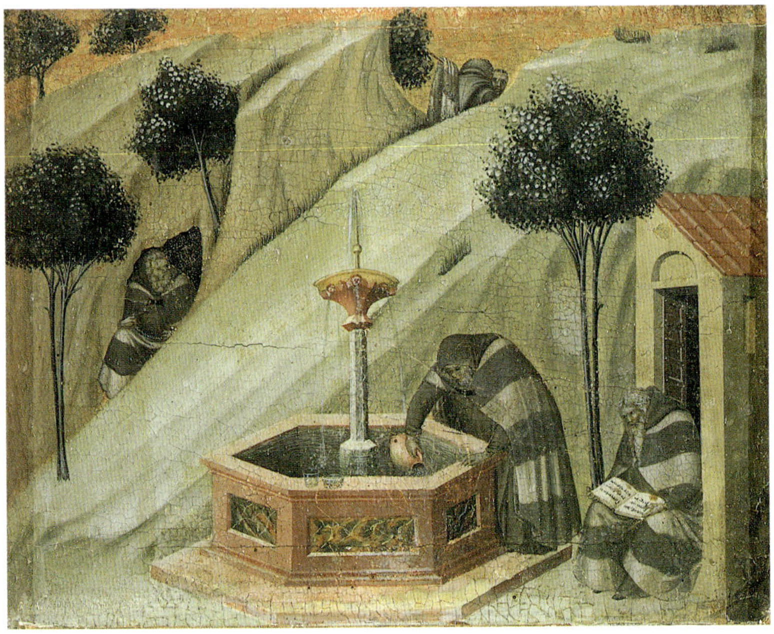

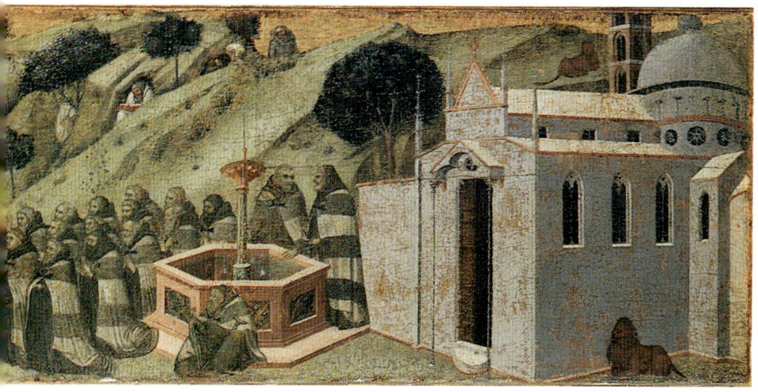

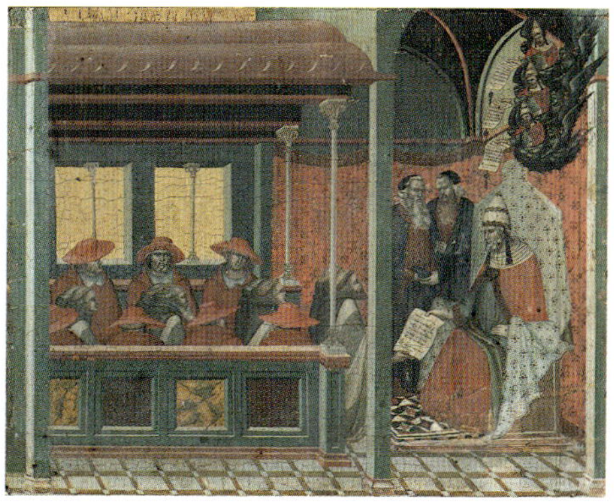

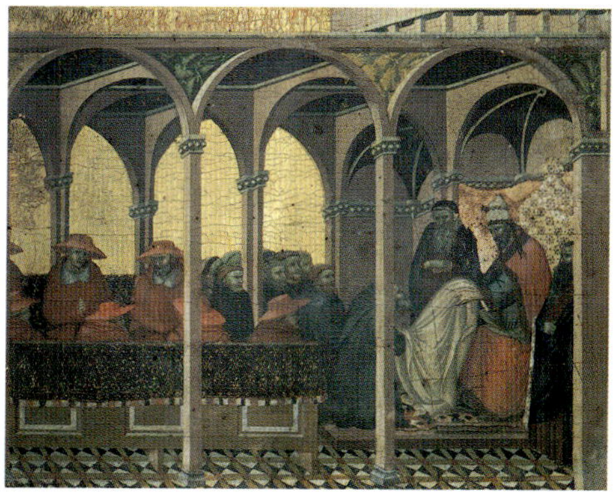

have been witnesses of St. Peter *in cathedra* (see fig. 66) and St. Peter preaching (see fig. 65).

One of Lorenzetti's predella scenes, *Hermits at the Fountain of Elijah* (see fig. 24), refers in a general way to the hermetic life on Mount Carmel that lasted over a thousand years. This epoch began with the construction of the primitive oratory dedicated to the Virgin, and culminated in the organization of the hermits into a cenobitical community that was recognized in the early thirteenth century by the head of Western Christendom, the pope. Hermits congregate around the Fountain of Elijah and the oratory, wearing the striated Carmelite habit (modeled after the cloak of Elijah, scorched as he ascended to heaven in a chariot of fire, and retrieved by his disciple Elisha).

The long central predella of Lorenzetti's altarpiece and the subsequent two scenes represent the modern documented history of the Order. The central scene, *St. Albert Presents the Rule to the Carmelites* (fig. 27), functions as a fulcrum in the organization of both the altarpiece and the contemporary histories of the Order. It marks the point at which the Carmelite narration passes from story to history, from *leggenda* to *historia*, and supports the entire edifice of Carmelite doctrine, giving it an official sanction within the institution of the Roman Church. Some time between 1206 and 1214, Albert, Patriarch of Jerusalem, traveled to Mount Carmel and presented the hermits with a Rule. The Rule was accepted by Pope Honorius III in 1226 with a papal bull. Having come under the pope's jurisdiction, the Carmelites received permission to construct convents near cities and modify their Rule, in accordance with the different demands of urban monasticism. A further papal dispensation allowed for the alteration of the Carmelite habit (apparently

25 Pietro Lorenzetti, *The Pope Issues a Bull to a Carmelite Delegation*, predella of the polyptych for the high altar of San Niccolò al Carmine, Siena, 1327–29, Siena, Pinacoteca Nazionale.

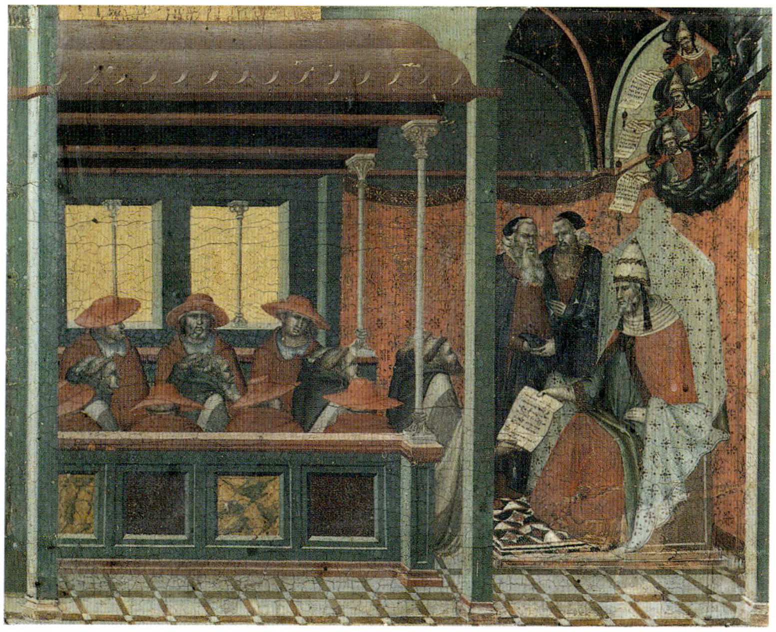

26 Pietro Lorenzetti, *Approval of the New Carmelite Habit by Pope Honorius IV*, predella of the polyptych for the high altar of San Niccolò al Carmine, Siena, 1327–29, Siena, Pinacoteca Nazionale.

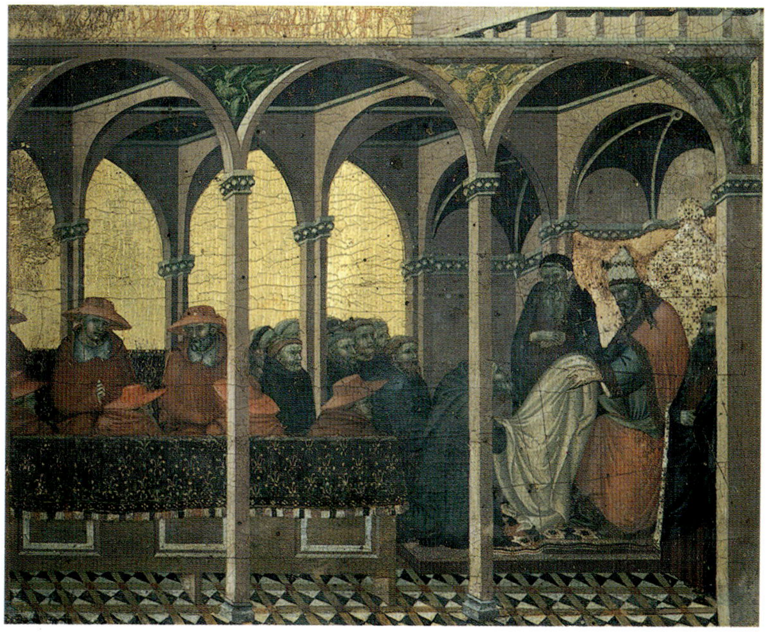

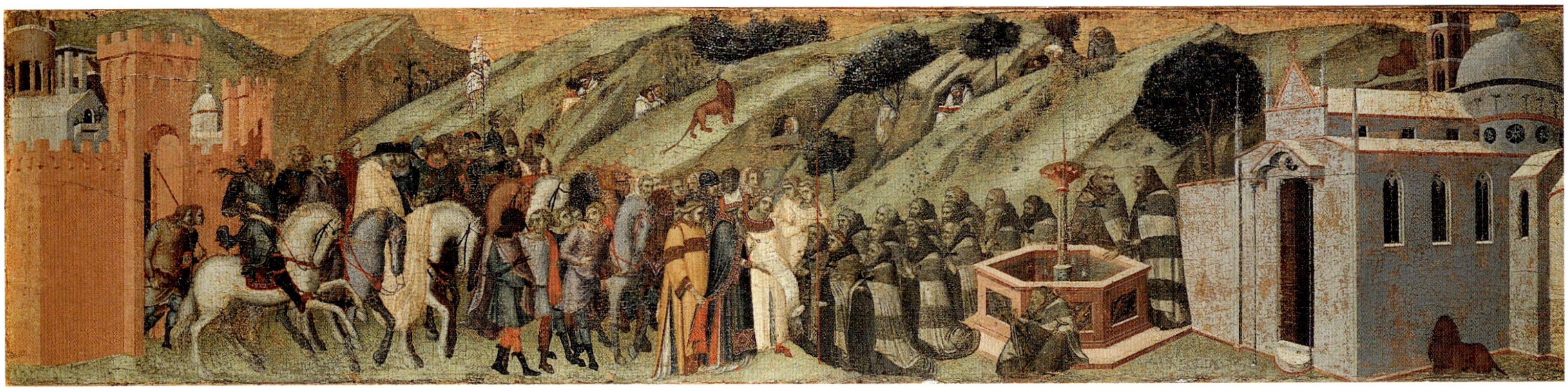

27 Pietro Lorenzetti, *St. Albert Presents the Rule to the Carmelites*, central predella scene of the polyptych for the high altar of San Niccolò al Carmine, Siena, 1327–29, Siena, Pinacoteca Nazionale.

the object of ridicule in the Western university *studia*), exchanging the black and white horizontally striped outer cape for a simple white one.[40] An important bull was passed in 1326 by Pope John XXII, which confirmed the Carmelites' mendicant rights along the lines of the Dominicans and Franciscans. The papal confirmations of the Carmelite Rule, and permission to change the traditional habit, are the subjects of Pietro Lorenzetti's final two predella scenes (figs. 25 and 26).

This Carmelite campaign "to witness the truth" about the origins of their Order by no means went uncontested. In one of the first notices documenting the Carmelites' presence on Mount Carmel – Jacobus de Vitry's *Historia orientalis*, dating from the second quarter of the thirteenth century – the writer explains that the Carmelite hermits had arrived in the East during the Crusades, and elected to remain behind, settling beside the Fountain of Elijah on Mount Carmel.[41] The denunciations against the Carmelite claims appear to have begun in earnest by the late *trecento*, provoking a Carmelite public defense of the Elian tradition in 1374.[42] In the mid-*quattrocento*, the Dominican Archbishop of Florence, Antonino, pointedly made his entry on the Carmelites in his chronicle *Historiarum Domini* under the year 1285, around the time that Pope Honorius IV granted the friars permission to change their habit. He insisted that the Order had been formed only shortly before this date by the Christian hermits living on Mount Carmel, who followed the Rule of St. Basil. He dismissed the Elian tradition, insisting that, "it appears neither in the Holy Scriptures nor in authentic accounts."[43] In *quattrocento* Florence, this learned theologian (who was also a member of a rival mendicant order) was not the only one to challenge the Carmelites over the questionable antiquity of their Order. The subject also made its way into the popular *facezie* literature, where it was scrutinized skeptically by the shrewd Piovano Arlotto.

> One morning, the Piovano Arlotto was in the Carmelite church, listening to the sermon of a friar who was young and more windy than learned. And, preaching on a subject on which he had become rather mixed up (that passage where the messengers from Judea asked St. John the Baptist who he was), the friar turned to the Piovano and said: "Who are you? Are you Elijah? Are you Jeremiah?" etc. And the Piovano, as these words were repeated innumerable times, lost patience. Unable to hold back his laughter, he answered the friar loudly, "I am neither Elijah nor Jeremiah, but the Piovano Arlotto; maybe you don't recognize me!" This riposte made all who were listening to the sermon laugh.[44]

The importance of Lorenzetti's altarpiece in establishing a Tuscan pictorial language for the Carmelite story can be seen in Andrea di Bonaiuto's Carmine polyptych. The figure of Elijah (see fig. 29) in the Carmine painting closely resembles Lorenzetti's Elisha (see fig. 28). The Florentine painter was faced with the task of representing what was still, in the 1360s, a relatively new iconography – a Carmelite prophet saint disposed in the lateral panel of a polyptych. Lorenzetti's Elisha offered the painter such a model. Both figures are presented frontally and fully occupy the arched polyptych panel to such an extent that the slight strip of gold visible between the white robe and the edge of the panel disappears at the bottom as frame and figure abut. An unabashed Carmelite presence. Both figures have their hoods drawn over their heads – a conventional reference to the hermetic life, but also, in Carmelite guidelines, an attitude of reverence within the convent and a "public face" to be worn outside the convent. Both images represent the prophets as elderly men with receding hairlines, creased brows, and long white beards. Lorenzetti's Elisha, rather than his Elijah, served as a prototype because the latter was too bound up in the primary iconographic formulation of the Sienese altarpiece: Elijah as Carmelite founder, progenitor, precursor is integrated into the large central panel of the polyptych and interacts directly with the Christ Child. Lorenzetti's Elisha, like the Florentine artist's Elijah, played an important yet secondary role in the iconography of the altarpiece and was, therefore, relegated to a side panel. The Elijah in the Florentine altarpiece occupies the outer right panel, acting as a sort of Carmelite bracket or context for the congregation of saints depicted. There is also a diachronic

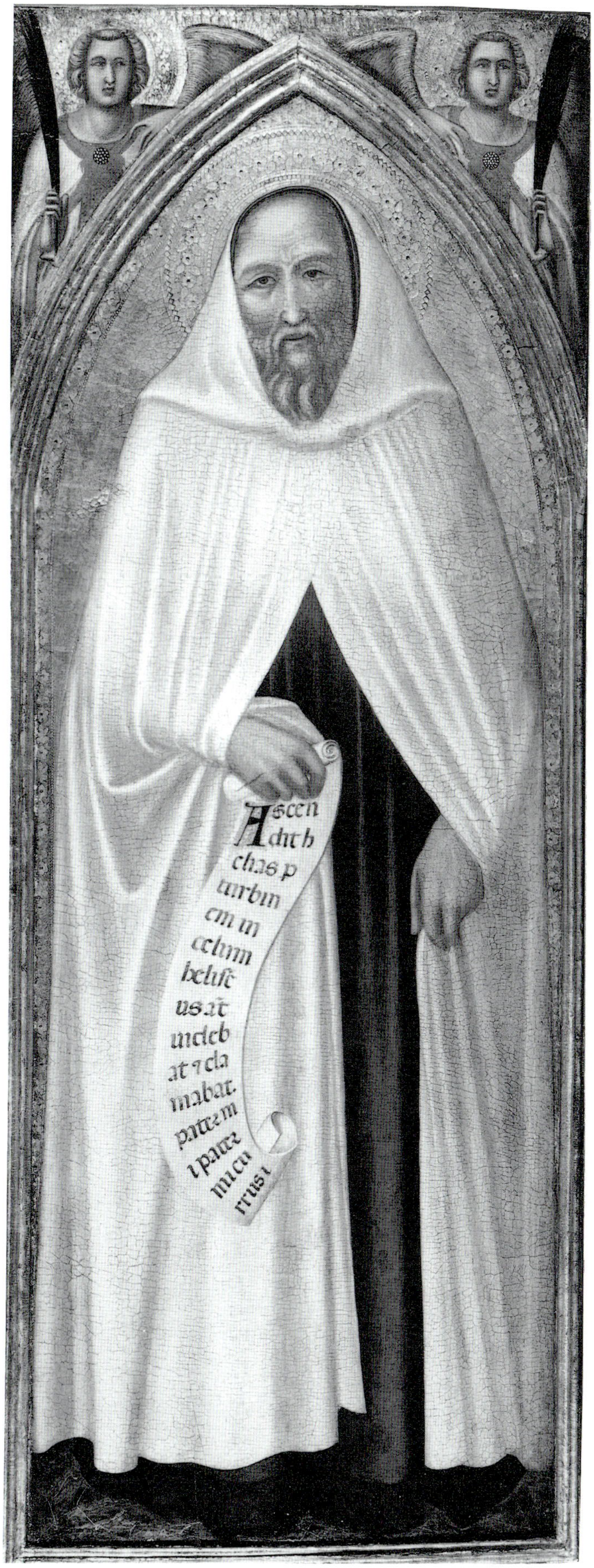

28 Pietro Lorenzetti, *Prophet Elisha*, lateral panel from the polyptych for the high altar of San Niccolò al Carmine, Siena, 1327–29, Pasadena, Norton Simon Museum.

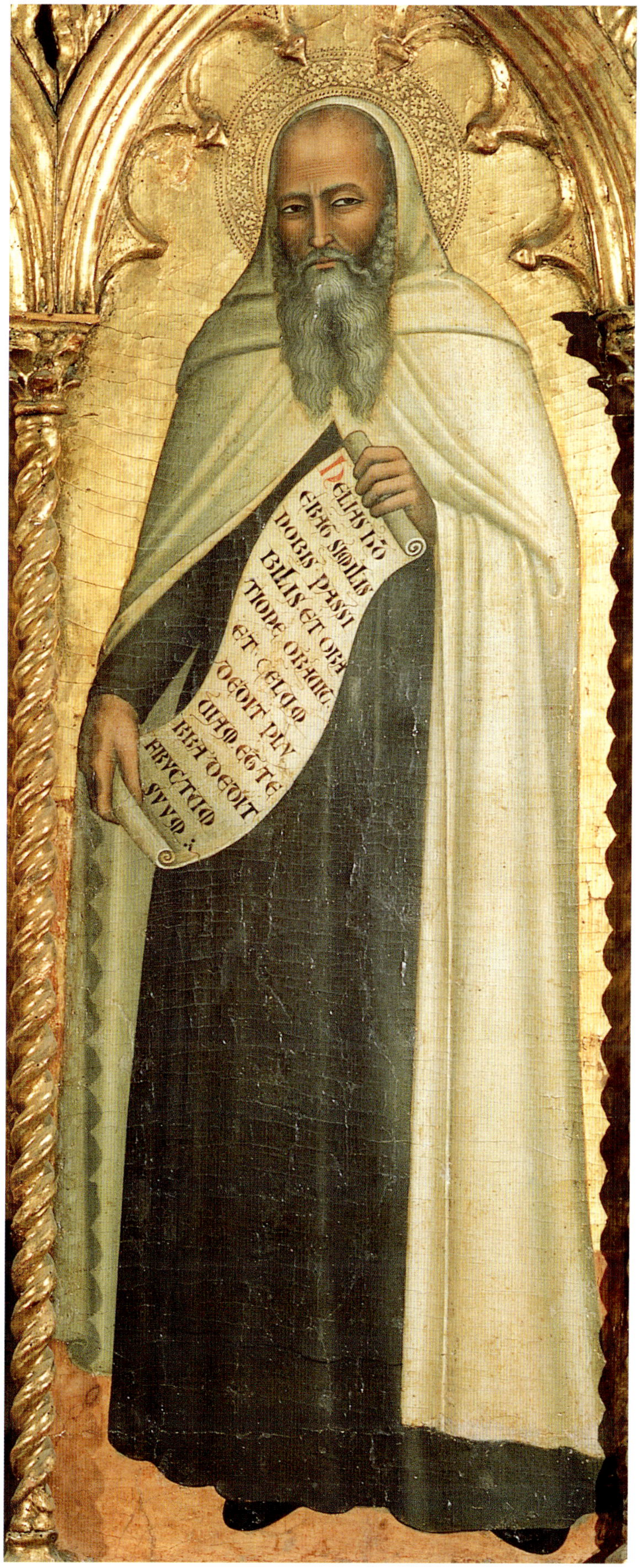

29 Andrea di Bonaiuto (attr.), *Elijah*, lateral panel from the *Madonna and Child with Sts. Leonard, Nicholas, John the Baptist, and Elijah*, early 1360s, Florence, Santa Maria del Carmine.

dynamic in play: moving from right to left, from the outside of the altarpiece toward the center, Elijah literally precedes and prefigures John the Baptist who appears in the panel next to him. The Baptist – both saint and prophet, like Elijah, and embodying "the spirit and power of Elijah" (Luke 1:17) – points his finger at the Christ Child ("Ecco Agnus Dei"), who is a short distance away across the gold-frame divide in the center panel.

While the figure of Elijah in the Florentine Carmine altarpiece is removed syntactically from the central focus of the iconographic message, he is the only figure that directly engages the attention of the devotee. The other saints and the Christ Child all gaze at cross purposes or focus on nothing visible or comprehensible to the viewer. Elijah looks out and makes eye contact. In addition, his frontal stance (again unique among the figures in the altarpiece) is a formal means of facilitating a direct engagement with the viewer. So too is the clear, legible text that he holds, which encourages the viewer to pause and read. In this way, the Carmelite context of the devotee's engagement with the altarpiece is given sharp emphasis, and Saint Elijah offers himself as the most accessible, immediate intercessor.

The polyptych may have been commissioned for the chapel of St. Nicholas of Bari that was situated beneath the choir of the church, founded in 1334 by the Compagnia di San Niccolò. That the polyptych was associated with an altar dedicated to St. Nicholas seems likely, given the place of precedence held by that saint to the right of the Virgin and Child, and the first record we have of the painting, though dating from the late nineteenth century, describes it in the chapel of the Compagnia.[45] It is significant that by the 1360s, "Sanctus Elias Propheta," represented as patron and founder of the Carmelite Order, had appeared in a work which had probably been commissioned by the laity for an altar in Santa Maria del Carmine. What initially had been a polemical iconographic statement expounded by the Order in the Lorenzetti polyptych, became a ready reference for the laity who worshipped in the Florentine Carmelite church.

After 1350, Saint Elijah images in Carmelite habit appeared unapologetically in Carmelite representations.[46] In the Florentine area there are several examples known. An early inventory of the Carmelite church of Santa Maria delle Selve in Lastra a Signa includes "a triptych with a Virgin Annunciate in the center and in the wings two Prophets in the Carmelite habit," and another polyptych which sounds similar in conception to that in the Carmine, "with the Virgin in the central compartment and in the wings St. Elijah, St. Sebastian, St. Peter and St. Paul."[47] A miniature from a *trecento* choral book in Washington, *Christ and the Virgin Enthroned with Forty Saints* (fig. 30), which may have belonged to the Compagnia di Sant'Agnese of Santa Maria del Carmine, shows the Carmelite prophet saints Elijah and Elisha given the privileged place at the foot of the cross.[48]

By the early *quattrocento* Elijah and Elisha were accompanied by additional Carmelite "sancti" in visual images. Carmelite compendia covering the history of the Order began to single out certain ancient hermits and early friars of Mount Carmel

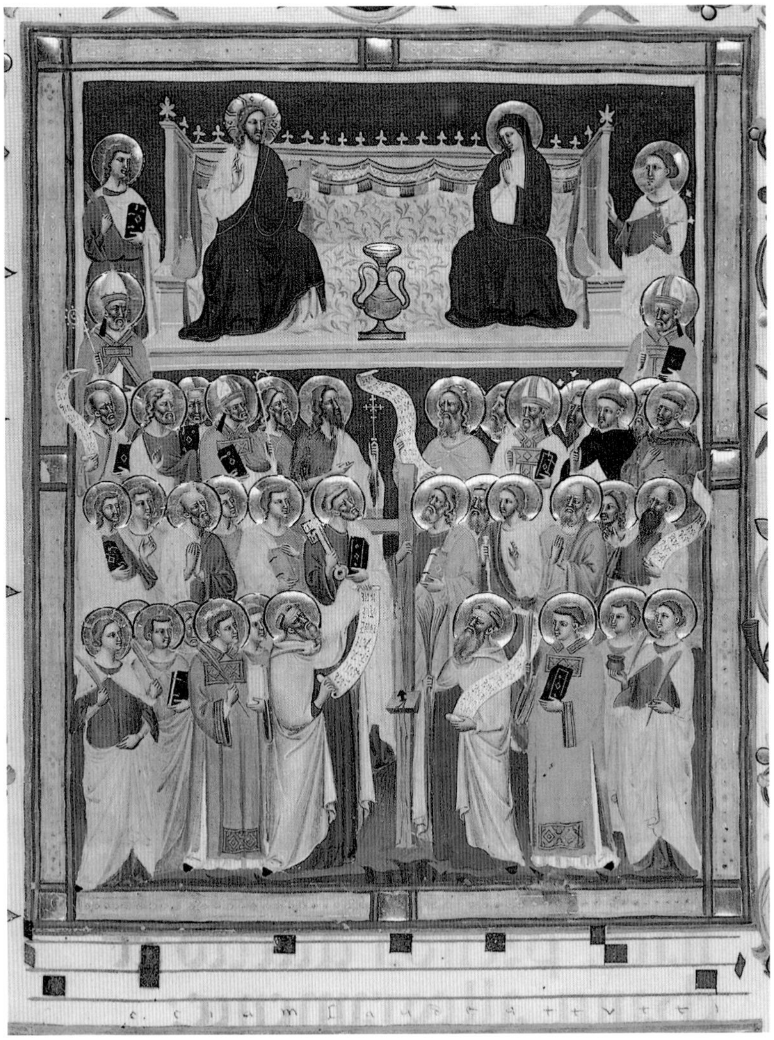

30 Master of the Dominican Effigies, *Christ and the Virgin Enthroned with Forty Saints*, c. 1340, illumination, Washington, National Gallery of Art, Rosenwald Collection.

and to elaborate some of the miraculous events associated with them. These included Bertold, Simon Stock, Angelo, Enoch, and Alberto. The treatment they received was cursory, as the objective was to establish an unbroken Carmelite lineage rather than produce a Carmelite "Golden Legend." Elijah and Elisha alone – the founders of the Order and figures already equipped with unassailable and detailed histories in the Old Testament Book of Kings – were written about more expansively and, as we have seen, were even designated "Sancti." By the turn of the century, however, two of the early Carmelite friars – Fra Angelo of Licata and Fra Alberto degli Abati da Trapani – began to be venerated as *beati* within the Order.

Fra Angelo was said to have been born in Jerusalem in 1185 and to have lived on Mount Carmel for many years.[49] Toward the end of his life he had a vision in which he was instructed by Christ to travel to Sicily. From there, he journeyed to Rome, where he presented relics from the Holy Land to the pope and emperor. He also visited the Lateran church where he is supposed to have met Sts. Francis and Dominic, who happened to be in the city at the time. He was martyred in Licata in Sicily in 1225.

Fra Angelo's cult blossomed in the *quattrocento*. His life was glossed over in Giovanni Grossi's *Viridarium* (c. 1420), but he was given a full descriptive *vita* in the 1440s by a writer masquerading as his contemporary and dear companion "Enoch." An Office was established in 1457, to be celebrated on Angelo's feast day, May 5, and all Carmelite convents were ordered to observe it. The cult of "Sant'Angelo" was confirmed verbally by Pius II in 1459.

Fra Alberto degli Abati, on the other hand, born a century after Angelo, was a native Sicilian of patrician birth.[50] He died in his bed in 1306, in the Carmelite monastery in Messina. Sicily was the background against which he performed model routine cenobitical activities. According to his *Vita*, he practiced a life of prayer, study, and work in the monastery of Messina. He administered the sacraments to the laity of Messina and tended his spiritual flock with miraculous deeds. He converted non-believers and helped to prevent famine through sermon and prayer when the city of Messina was under siege. Alberto served as an attractive example of the new Carmelite cenobitical monasticism.

After Fra Alberto's death, his cult grew steadily. It was initially concentrated primarily in Sicily, but by the end of the *trecento*, the Order was promoting the cult throughout Western Europe. In 1375, the general chapter considered petitioning the pope for his canonization. In 1395, the first extensive *vita* of Alberto was written and in 1411 a liturgical office was established. The cult was officially recognized by Pope Callistus III in 1457 and confirmed by Sixtus IV in 1478.

What is striking about these two Carmelite cult figures is that both were associated with Sicily. The veneration of Angelo and Alberto effectively performed the symbolic function of bridging the great divide between the early history of the Order, which took place in the Holy Land, and the modern condition of the Order – officially sanctioned and well documented – in the West. By the late fourteenth century, when the cults of Angelo and Alberto were gaining ground, the Carmelite monasteries in the Holy Land had long since been abandoned, and the site on Mount Carmel was described as in ruins in contemporary pilgrims' guides. It became necessary for the Order to construct a more immediate and emotionally engaging symbolic universe for its members and the lay public upon which it was dependent. Sicily had, in fact, been among the first locations in the West where the Carmelites had settled. Hence, Sicily, poised mid-way between the Levant and northern Europe, was an ideal middle ground in which to effect this symbolic transplantation of the Order from East to West, from hermetic to cenobitical monasticism. And it was in Sicily that the Old Testament prophets Elijah and Elisha bowed to a new Carmelite Order populated with Carmelite saints and *beati*.

The cult of Alberto was promoted much more extensively than that of Angelo in the Florentine Carmelite milieu. By 1391, the convent was in possession of certain relics of Alberto.[51] His feast day was celebrated annually on August 7 in the Florentine Carmine and in 1422 there is reference in the convent account books to a procession ("procecione di San Alberto").[52] A lay Compagnia di Sant'Alberto was established in the Carmine by 1419, when members were granted permission through the agency of Fra Albizzo de' Nerli to erect a small oratory ("una chasa con altare dentro") in the cemetery of the Florentine convent. There was a second altar dedicated to Alberto beneath the arches of the *ponte* in the nave of the church, founded by Paolo di Lorenzo Dieciaiuti, probably a few decades after that of the Compagnia di Sant'Alberto. Both altars were equipped with images of Alberto at unknown dates.[53] The convent of Santa Maria delle Selve in Lastra a Signa (Le Selve) had a chapel dedicated to Alberto by at least 1484, when Filippo Strozzi had a painting of Sts. Lawrence and Alberto installed above an altar located in a chapel "sotto il pozzo." There was also a niche containing a statue of Alberto in the choir.[54]

A polyptych attributed to Lippo d'Andrea (fig. 31), with a representation of St. Alberto in the left lateral panel (fig. 32), seems to have been a product of this cult worship of the Sicilian Carmelite in the early *quattrocento* in the Florentine environs.[55] The date "1420" on the frame of the altarpiece is most significant, for it was in that very year that the Carmelite general chapter, meeting at Montpellier, declared that "in every convent an image of Beato Alberto with rays should be painted."[56] At least one of the altars in the Carmine and at Le Selve should have been fitted with such an image at that time, and it is possible that the polyptych was commissioned with such an intention in mind.[57] The Order had maintained a line of caution at the general chapter meeting, referring to Alberto as "Beato," and prescribing that he be represented with rays rather than a saint's halo. In the Florentine Carmelite ambience, however, the Sicilian holy man was accorded the status of "Santo" in the feast day and confraternity celebrations – and, evidently, also in artistic representation.[58]

The 1420 date of the polyptch also is of interest because the character of the artistic decoration in Santa Maria del Carmine shifted dramatically at just about that date. The altarpiece, with its gold-ground, arched, compartmentalized panels and static figures with their Giottesque eyes and swarthy faces – features that endow the altarpiece with a late *trecento* feeling – is not inconsistent with the artistic style manifest in the private chapels and altars found in the nave, the transept, and the arches of the *tramezzo* of the church and also in the sacristy. These chapels were founded in the second half of the *trecento* and their decoration continued into the early *quattrocento*.[59] An artist alternatively identified as Spinello Aretino, Lorenzo di Bicci, or Lippo d'Andrea frescoed scenes from the life of St. Cecilia in the sacristy chapel (still extant; see fig. 146), shortly after 1390. There is speculation that the same artist was responsible for the frescos of the life of the Baptist in the Manetti chapel, which were lost in

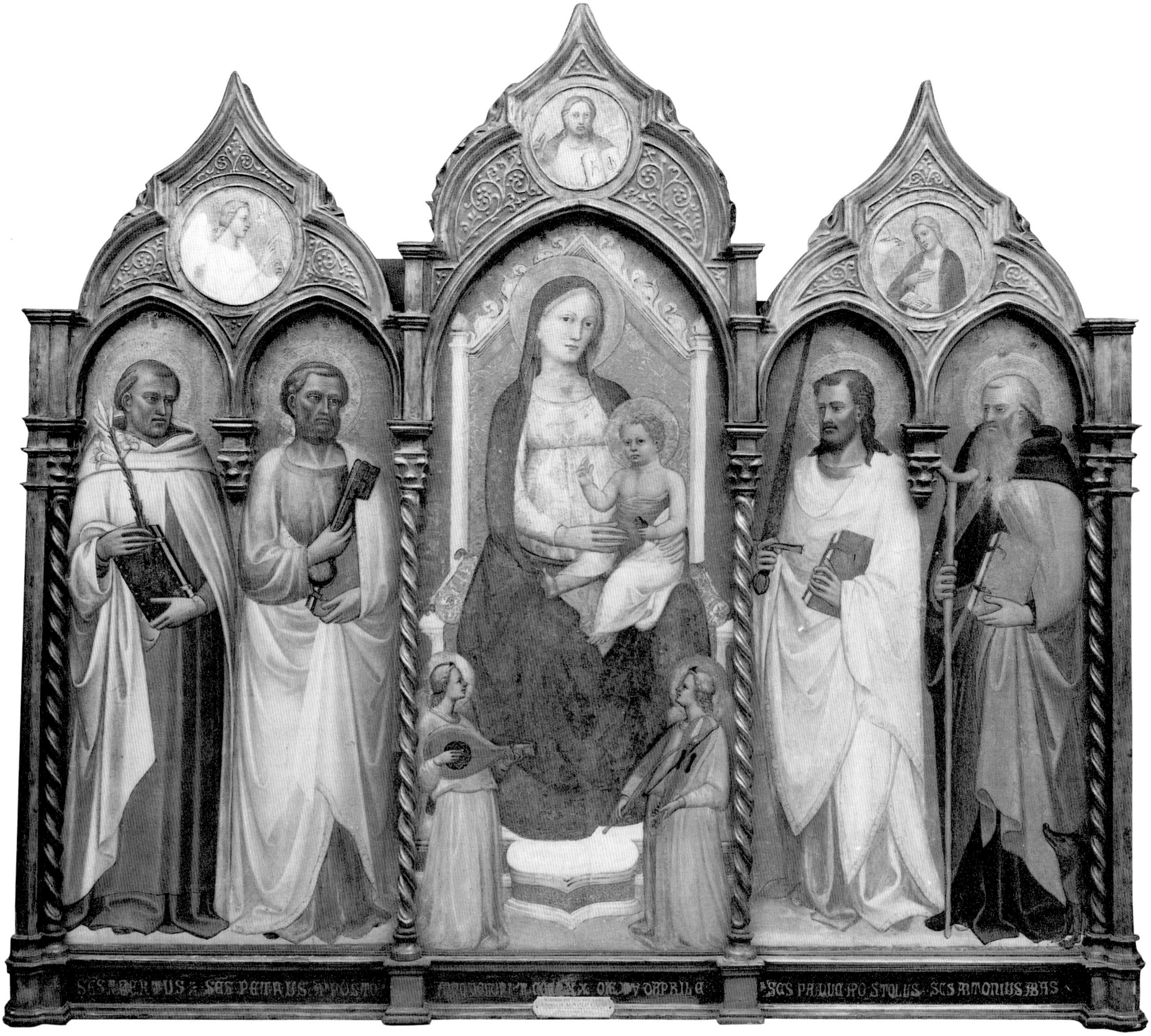

31 Lippo d'Andrea (attr.), *Madonna and Child with Sts. Alberto of Trapani, Peter, Paul, and Anthony Abbot*, 1420, New Haven, Yale University Art Gallery, University purchase from James Jackson Jarves.

the 1771 fire. Lorenzo Monaco painted an altarpiece for the Ardinghelli chapel between 1398 and 1400. A "Lippo" (considered to be Lippo d'Andrea) frescoed the Nerli chapel of the Passion in 1402, from which Passion scenes and a fragment representing the Carmelite St. Cyril (fig. 33) have been recovered.[60] Gherardo Starnina executed frescos from the life of St. Jerome in the Pugliese chapel in 1404. Dating from the same year as the polyptych are "i chrocifisi di chiesa," probably painted by Stefano di Lorenzo Pucetti.[61] There are also frescoed lunettes depicting a half-length *Madonna and Child* and a *Pietà with Two Carmelites* in the sacristy attributed to Lippo d'Andrea, which must date from about that time.

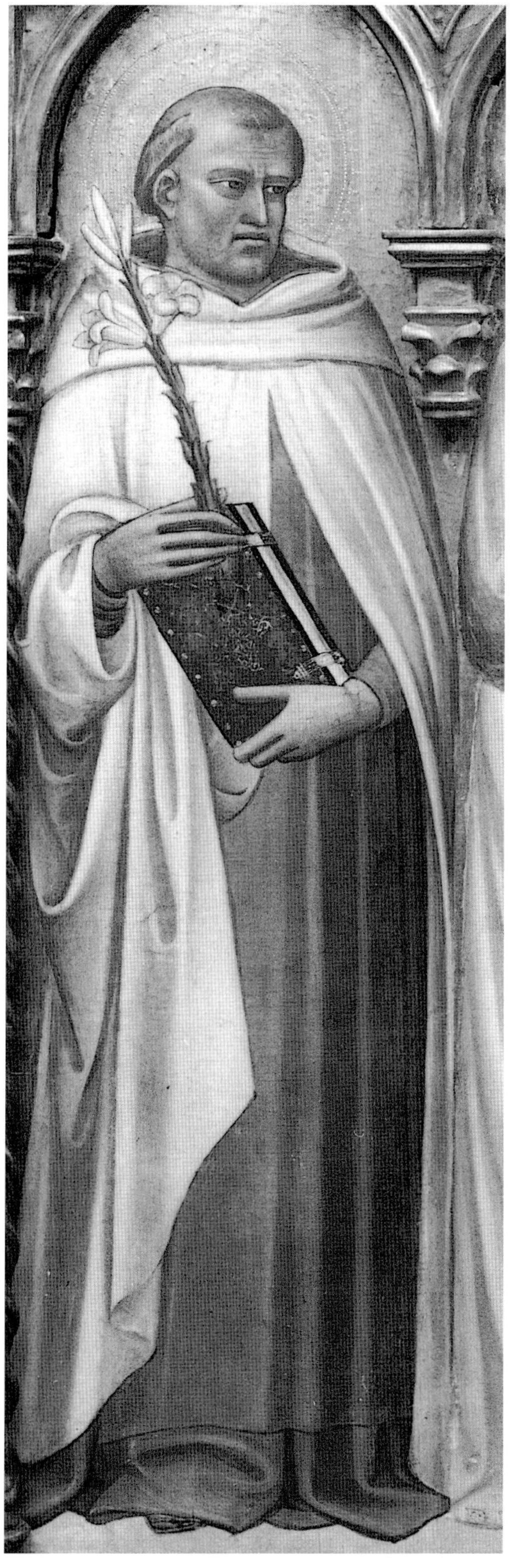

32 Lippo d'Andrea (attr.), *St. Alberto of Trapani*, detail of fig. 31.

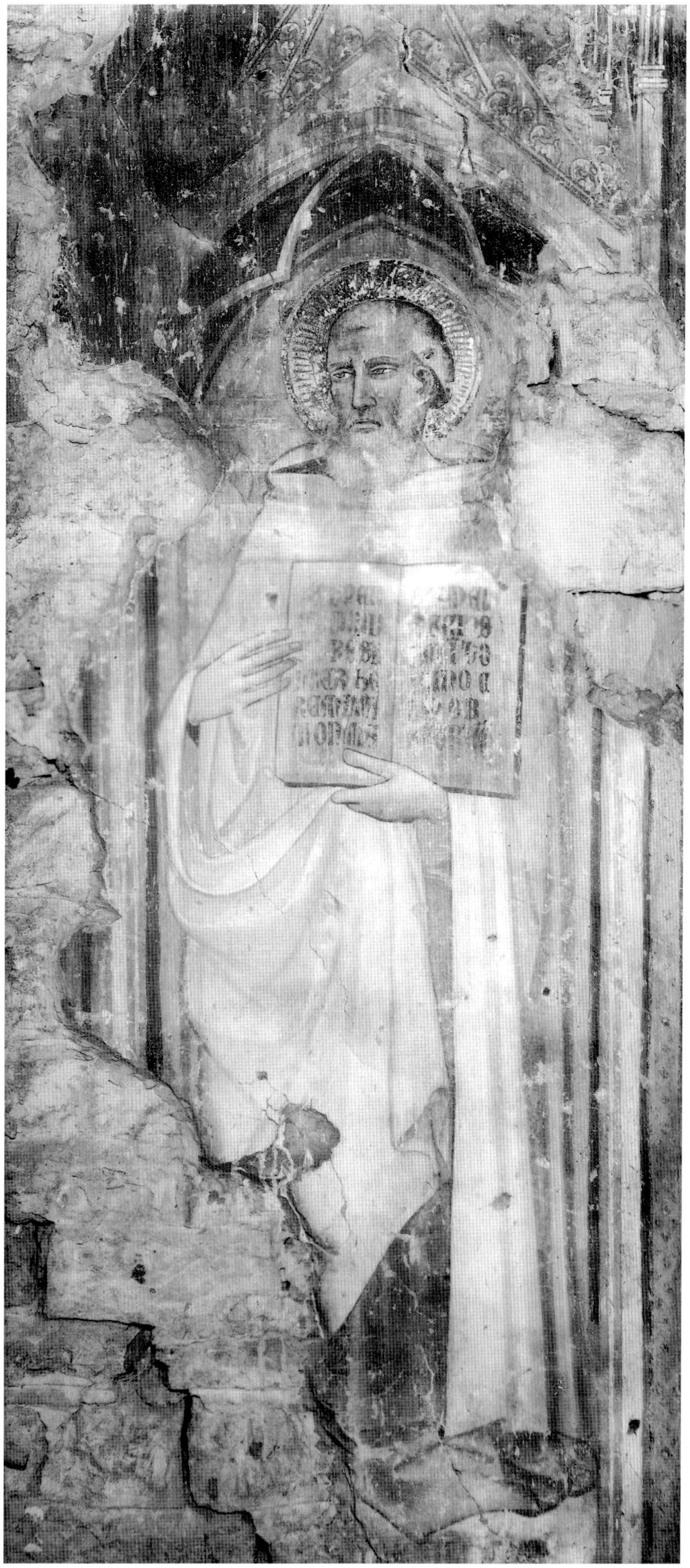

33 Lippo d'Andrea (attr.), *St. Cyril*, 1402, fresco fragment from the Chapel of the Passion in Santa Maria del Carmine, Florence.

The artistic mode of Lippo d'Andrea evolved out of the work of the very artists who had been painting in the Carmine at the turn of the century. The style of the polyptych was retrospective and would have served to reaffirm the religious attitudes and values encoded in the styles of the earlier works. It reflected a particular type of religious art being produced by several Florentine artists at the time for the growing number of altars made accessible to private patronage in the monastic and parish churches in the city. These painters included Niccolò di Pietro Gerini and his son Lorenzo di Niccolò, Giovanni del Ponte, Giovanni Toscani, and Bicci di Lorenzo who worked well into the mid-century, producing gold-ground, arched and pinnacled, compartmentalized polyptychs.

But something was underfoot in the Carmine. If the polyptych was indeed painted for Santa Maria del Carmine, within five years of its execution, its *retardataire* character would have appeared even more retrospective than at the time of its execution. Some time after 1422, Masaccio was invited to paint the

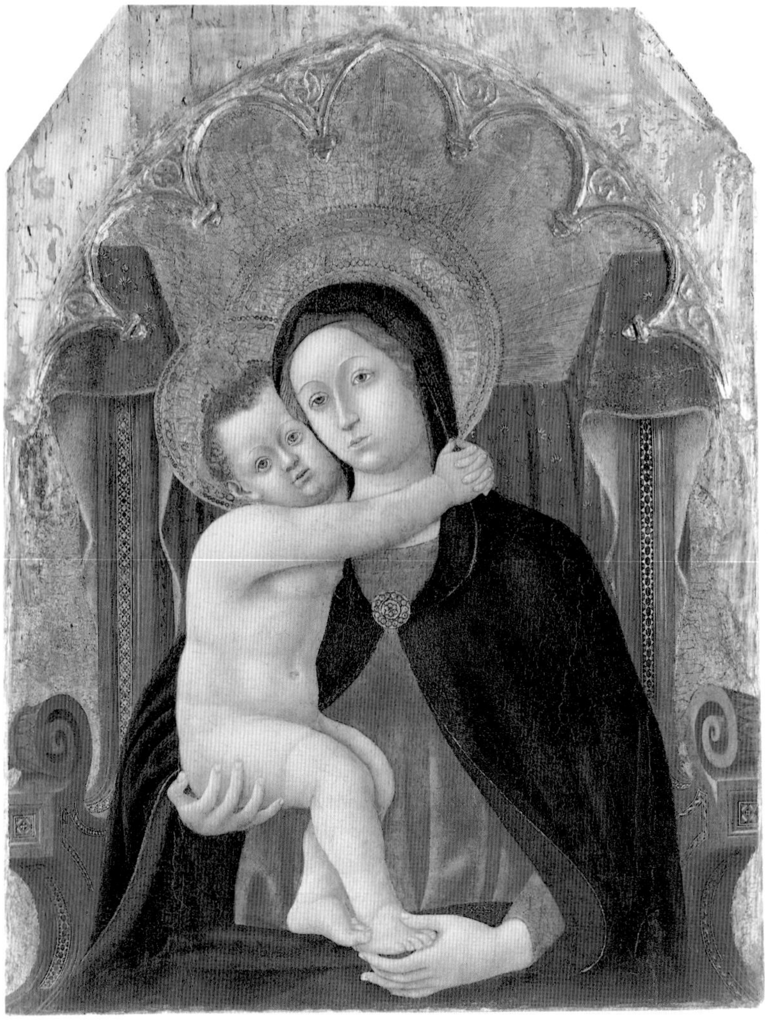

34 Domenico di Bartolo, *Madonna and Child*, c. 1435, Princeton, The Art Museum, Princeton University, Bequest of Dan Fellows Platt, Class of 1895.

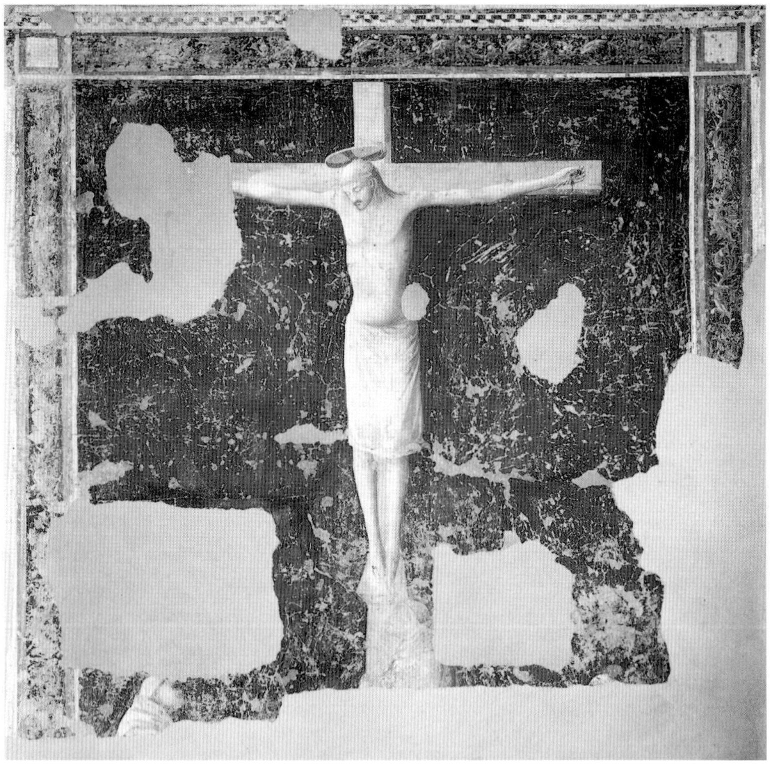

35 Florentine, *Crucifixion with Carmelites*, 1430s, detached fresco from the chapter house, Florence, Santa Maria del Carmine.

"Sagra," commemorating the consecration of the church. This marked a watershed in the artistic decoration of the Carmine. Over the next decade, the Carmine itself was a principal site of the major artistic revolution that was erupting in the city of Florence. Masolino and Masaccio were employed in the Brancacci chapel from about 1425 to 1428. In 1420, Tommaso Soderini's patronage rights to the high altar were confirmed and, if Vasari is correct, the innovative Sienese painter Domenico di Bartolo was engaged to paint the altarpiece, probably in the mid-1430s, possibly associated with a panel now in Princeton (fig. 34). A damaged fresco of the crucified Christ adored by Carmelite friars (fig. 35) was recently recovered in the chapter house, painted by an unidentified artist early in the second quarter of the fifteenth century, exhibiting a sensitivity to the effects of light in the rendering of the body of Christ and to the mechanics of foreshortening in the halo.[62] Fra Filippo Lippi's early artistic endeavors date from this time, including two attributed works that represent the Carmelite "Saints" Alberto and Angelo in a radically different stylistic manner.

MASACCIO'S *SAGRA*

The church and convent of Santa Maria del Carmine were formally consecrated by the Archbishop of Florence on April 19, 1422.[63] Sometime afterwards, the painter Masaccio was commissioned to represent the event, the "Sagra."[64]

The consecration of the Carmine and its commemoration in fresco were not isolated happenings in the city of Florence. In fact, there were a spate of important ecclesiastical consecrations in Florence during the first half of the *quattrocento*, including the Cathedral Santa Maria del Fiore (1436), the two major mendicant foundations Santa Maria Novella (1420) and Santa Croce (1442), and the church attached to the Hospital of Santa Maria Nuova, Sant'Egidio (1420). The latter consecration was commemorated in fresco by Bicci di Lorenzo (see fig. 37).

A copy of an undated (but presumably contemporary) account of the consecration of Santa Maria del Carmine describes the ceremony:

> For the everlasting memory of the event: All those present who will read this will know how, by the grace and mercy of God, on the Sunday after Easter, that is, April 19th of the year 1422, with the permission of Pope Martin V, obtained by the honorable Signor Francesco di Tommaso Soderini of Florence (which bull is now in our possession) *with the great rejoicing of the entire city and* with the participation of the populace, of both sexes, our entire convent church in Florence was most solemnly consecrated, and in addition, the altar of the Main Chapel and the altar of the Chapel of the Passion of our Lord Jesus Christ where the bodies of our friars repose and are buried.
>
> On the first of which [i.e. the altar of the Main Chapel] were placed these saints' relics, that is, [those] of Bartholomew the Apostle, Thomas the Apostle, Mark the Evangelist, and of S. Anterius, Pope and Martyr. On the second [i.e. the altar of the Chapel of the Passion], in truth, [were] these saints' relics: [those] of Barnabas the Apostle, Laurence and Pancrazio and also of Pope Clement and the martyr Sebastian.
>
> [The church was consecrated] by the most reverend in Christ, Father Signor Amerigo de' Corsini of Florence, the worthy first Archbishop of Florence, devotedly and solemnly assisted by the Lord Bishops, that is the most reverend in Christ Father and Signor Antonio del Fede of Florence of our Order, eminent Doctor of the sacred scriptures and, by the grace of God, the well-deserving Bishop of Soana, and by the most reverend Lord and Father, Signor Benozzo de' Federighi of Florence, by the grace of God, most worthy Bishop of Fiesole. Each of these said bishops, by special concession, piously conceded an indulgence of forty days, valid *in perpetuum* for the sins of those who, confessed and penitent, devoutly visit the church on that day, that is, the first Sunday after Easter or on any one of the days in the octave.
>
> Glory be to the highest Trinity and to the One true God the Father, the Son and the Holy Spirit, before whom, the most Holy Virgin Mary, Mother of God and patroness of our Order, and all the Saints always intercede for us.[65]

Some time after the consecration, Masaccio was commissioned to record the event in a *terra verde* fresco above the door leading from the Carmine cloister into the church.[66] The fresco was either destroyed or covered over around 1612, and the only record of its appearance we have derives from several descriptions and eight drawings thought to be copies after the lost fresco – dating, for the most part, from the sixteenth century.[67] The richest source is Vasari's account:

> It came to pass . . . that the said Church of the Carmine was consecrated; and Masaccio, in memory of this, painted the consecration just as it took place, with terra-verde and in chiaroscuro, over the door that leads into the convent, within the cloister. And he portrayed therein an infinite number of citizens in mantles and hoods, who are following the procession, among whom he painted Filippo di Ser Brunellesco in wooden shoes, Donatello, Masolino da Panicale, who had been his master, Antonio Brancacci, who caused him to paint the chapel, Niccolò da Uzzano, Giovanni di Bicci de' Medici, and Bartolommeo Valori. . . . He also painted there Lorenzo Ridolfi, who was at that time the ambassador of the Florentine Republic in Venice; and not only did he portray there the aforesaid gentlemen from the life, but also the door of the convent and the porter with the keys in his hand. This work, truly, shows great perfection, for Masaccio was so successful in placing these people, five or six to a file, on the level of that piazza, and in making them diminish to the eye with proportion and judgment, that it is indeed a marvel, and above all because we can recognize there the wisdom that he showed in making those men, as if they were alive, not all of one size, but with a certain discretion which distinguishes those who are short and stout from those who are tall and slender; while they are all standing with their feet firmly on one level, and so well foreshortened along the files that they would not be otherwise in nature.[68]

The eight drawings depict various combinations of figure groupings.[69] These figures are thought to represent the Florentine citizens in procession, alluded to by Vasari and the other writers in their descriptions of Masaccio's *Sagra*. Four of the drawings repeat compositions that are found in the drawing in Folkestone (fig. 36), which is the most extensive and detailed.

A strange omission in Vasari's description and in the other sixteenth-century evocations of Masaccio's *Sagra* is an elaboration of what one would assume to have been the central subject itself – the consecration of the church. The Carmelite account of the event, quoted earlier, indicates that the consecration was performed by the Archbishop of Florence, with the assistance of two other bishops. It also tells us that in addition to the church and convent, two specific altars were consecrated – the high altar and the altar of the chapel of the Passion. And yet Manetti described "the piazza del Carmine with many figures," and the Libro di Antonio Billi and Codice Magliabechiano refer to "a procession."[70] While Vasari identified the scene as "tutta la sagra come ella fu," involving a procession, the details he provides give little information about how the event was pictured. The drawings, emerging out of a sixteenth-century Florentine artistic milieu,

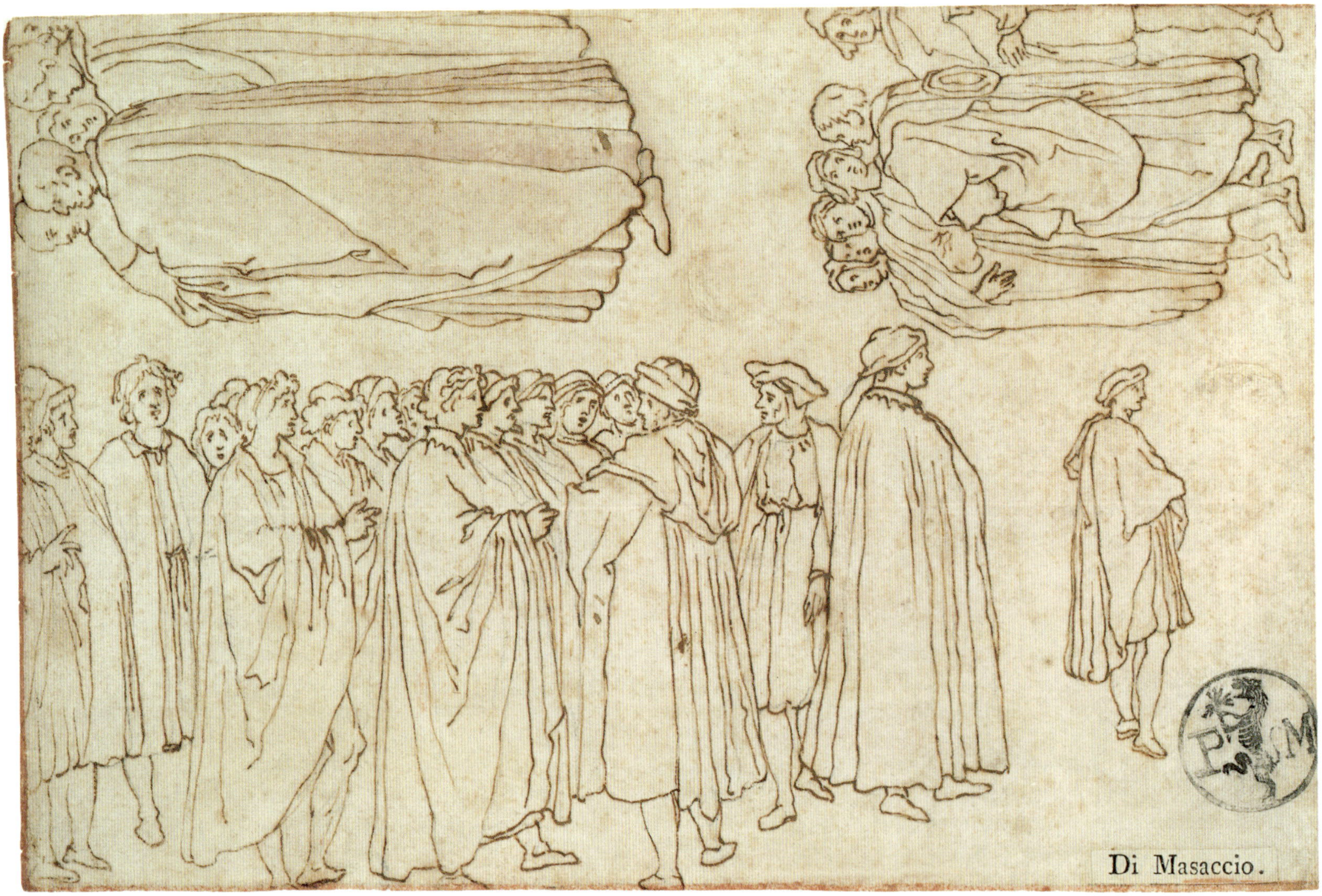

36 Florentine, drawing after Masaccio's *Sagra*, late sixteenth century, Folkestone (Kent), Folkestone Museum.

reflect similar preoccupations to those of Vasari. They reproduce only fragments of the overall composition, all of which explore the disposition and differentiation of the figure groupings.[71]

The consecration of a church was, in fact, a long drawn-out affair. According to Carmelite practices, it had the status of a religious feast day, followed a set liturgy, and, as a *totum duplex*, was observed for an entire octave (eight-day period). The dedication ceremony itself was a lengthy service involving the recitation of offices, a mass, the sprinkling of holy water, and a series of processions through the church, the convent, and outside in the piazza (some of which were performed by the friars only and others by the friars and the public). The convent's relics were displayed, and in addition to the church and convent, specific altars could be consecrated.[72] Hence, the "Sagra" was a fairly elaborate ritual, transpiring over an extended period of time, across diverse spaces, composed of a succession of religious rites, and engaging high religious officials, the convent friars, and their guests. In representing such an event, there was a call for dramatic and narrative economy.

From the sixteenth-century descriptions of the fresco, it seems that it was the procession involving the public in the piazza outside of the church that was chosen for commemoration. Masaccio's *Sagra* may thus have represented the consecration of the church and convent as the gathering of "the entire city and with the participation of the populace."[73] The "subject" of the fresco was, therefore, as much the consecration as it was the civic pageantry surrounding the event, explicated through the differentiation of the mass of people into individuated religious dignitaries, convent friars and patrons, and city office holders.

A comparison of what we know of Masaccio's *Sagra* with a fresco of a similar subject – Bicci di Lorenzo's *Martin V Confirming the Consecration of S. Egidio* (fig. 37), painted roughly at the same time for the facade of Sant'Egidio – may help to explain why the representation of the Carmelite consecration may have been given this emphasis.[74] Bicci di Lorenzo's fresco

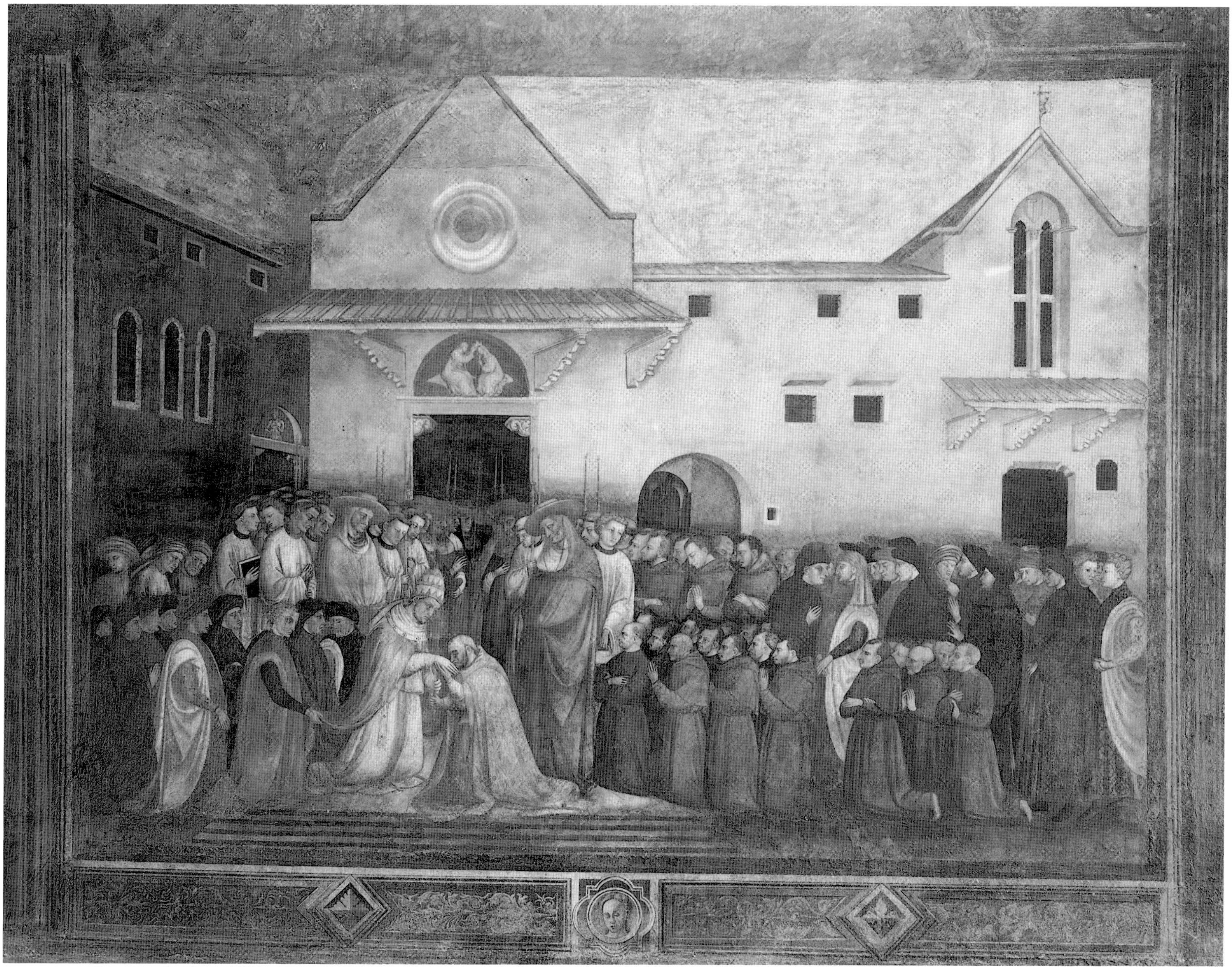

37 Bicci di Lorenzo, *Pope Martin V Confirming the Consecration of Sant'Egidio*, c. 1424, detached fresco from the facade of Sant'Egidio, now in the Ospedale di Santa Maria Nuova, Florence.

also depicted the festivities surrounding the consecration of a Florentine church. The newly completed church of Sant'Egidio (connected with the Hospital of Santa Maria Nuova) had been consecrated on September 9, 1420, by the Cardinal of Bologna.[75] Later that day, Pope Martin V confirmed the consecration. He was on his way out of Florence after an eighteen-month stay. He dismounted at Sant'Egidio briefly, before leaving the city through the Porta San Pier Gattolino for Rome.

Bicci di Lorenzo represented a congested congregation in the piazza in front of the church of Sant'Egidio. He followed a traditional *trecento* means of differentiating *il popolo* into standard social types, identifiable by dress conventions. A pope is distinguished by his tiara, pallium, and gloves; an important ecclesiastical official (the rector of the Hospital of Santa Maria Nuova) by his tonsure and rich robes; the cardinals by their tell-tale hats and red cloaks; the officiating clergy by their tonsures and tunicles; the *conversi* who worked in the hospital by their tonsures and quasi-monastic habits;[76] and the Florentine male patriciate by their secular attire consisting of à la mode, colorful brocaded tunics (*gonelle* and *pellande*) and cloaks (*mantelli*), and a variety of stylish hat-drapings (*cappucci*).[77]

Obviously, some of these generalized types would have been read as specific individuals by contemporary viewers familiar with the consecration – the pope as Martin V, the principal car-

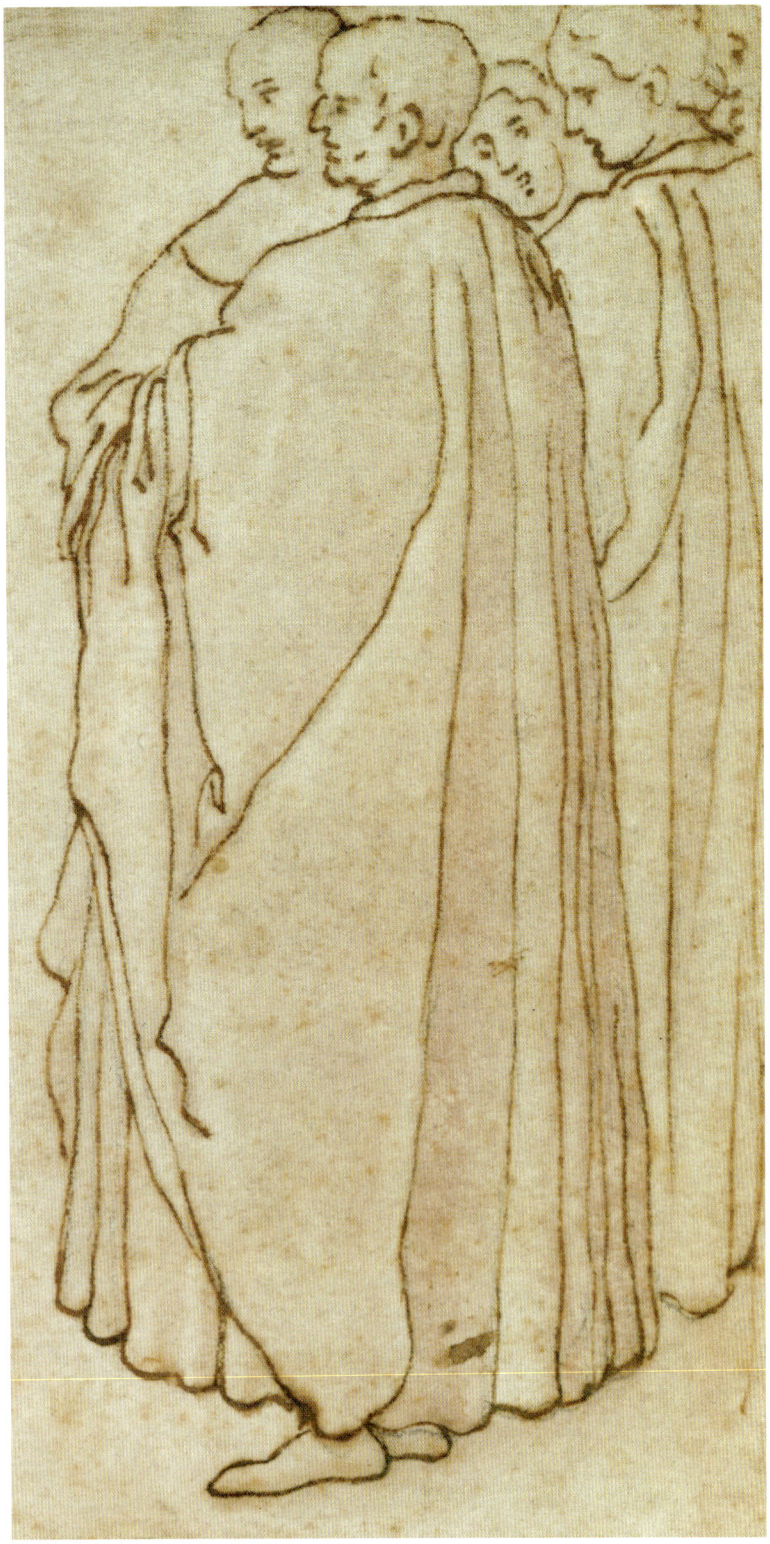

38 Florentine, drawing after Masaccio's *Sagra*, detail of fig. 36.

dinal standing to the right of the pope as the Cardinal of Bologna, the richly robed ecclesiastic kneeling and kissing Martin's gloved hand as the rector of Santa Maria Nuova, Michele di Frusino da Panzano.[78] Perhaps a Florentine audience

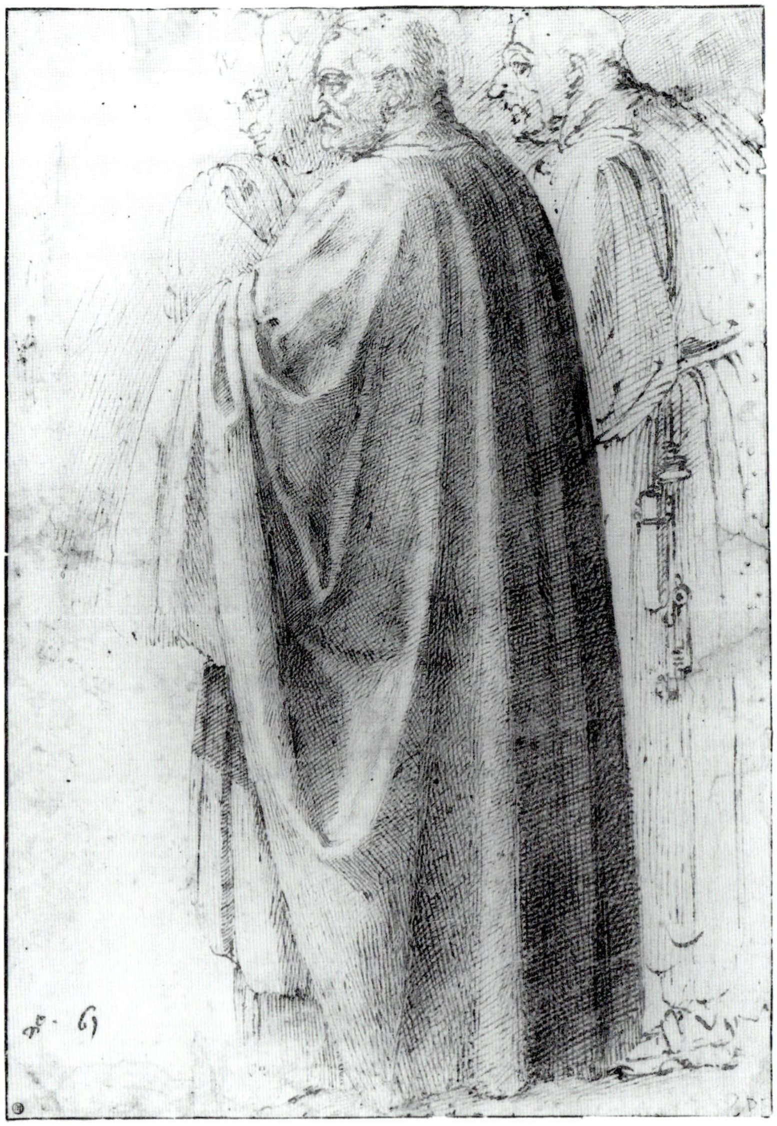

39 Michelangelo, drawing after Masaccio's *Sagra*, c. 1490–95, Vienna, Albertina (Inv. 116, recto).

would also have been able to identify the eight patricians who had been assigned by the *comune* to escort the pope out of the city, shown kneeling in attendance behind the pope in the fresco: Lorenzo Ridolfi, Matteo Castellani, Palla Strozzi, Rinaldo degli Albizzi, Carlo Federighi, Gherardo Canigiani, Filippo Giugni, and Giovanni di Bicci de' Medici.[79] But these identifications would have been made by "symbolic" interpretation – the process whereby a particular sign is the culturally accepted means of conveying a certain meaning.[80] In Bicci's fresco, a figure sporting a red, broad-rimmed hat and red robe signified "cardinal" to those who knew the code, which, in turn, could trigger a reference to the Cardinal of Bologna by viewers who could recall the specific ecclesiastic who had consecrated Sant'Egidio on September 9, 1420.

In Masaccio's *Sagra*, costume conventions, too, would have been an important key in interpreting the fresco. Vasari described "an infinite number of citizens in mantles and hoods" and the sixteenth-century drawings after the *Sagra* reveal laymen dressed in ceremonial attire very similar to that represented in Bicci's Sant'Egidio fresco. In the Casa Buonarroti and Folkestone drawings (fig. 36), a friar can be identified at the left of a group of figures by his hood and habit. Vasari also mentioned a figure in clogs ("zoccoli") and the convent porter with his keys.

It is evident, however, that Masaccio relied on another means of articulating the mass participation at the Carmelite consecration ceremony, one that could have prompted the viewers of the fresco to attend closely to each of the figures in procession (or at least those in the front line). Vasari noted that certain figures in Masaccio's *Sagra* were painted "from the life."[81] The drawing by Michelangelo after the fresco (fig. 39) offers additional evidence that many features were highly differentiated in the original, prompting Michelangelo to playful caricature. We gain some idea of Masaccio's portrait technique from the Brancacci chapel fresco *St. Peter in Cathedra in Antioch* (see fig. 40), where contemporary Carmelites and Florentines are integrated among the generic types who witness St. Peter's miracles. Hence, in contrast with Bicci di Lorenzo's fresco of *Martin V Confirming the Consecration of S. Egidio*, where differentiation in the figures was arbitrary and functioned as a means of enlivening the crowd through *varietà*, the precise identity of the participants in Masaccio's *Sagra* could have been secured by recognizing the particularized features of the figures. In semiotic terms, the portraits could have signified "iconically," where the painted likeness was intrinsically associated with the subject depicted, through what has been termed a process of identity.[82] The viewers of the fresco could have pieced together a composite meaning by attending to the features of each of the participants represented, recognizing familiar faces, and understanding the importance of the consecration of the church through the homage paid to the Carmelites by the pointed presence of specific Florentine citizens.

This dynamic engagement with the figures in procession propelled the beholder into a mode of looking very different from that required when viewing Bicci di Lorenzo's diagrammatic rendition. Rather than considering the fresco to represent the consecration by virtue of a series of equations between sign and referent, the viewer of Masaccio's *Sagra* would have experienced a more immediate simulation, as if thrust into the Piazza del Carmine, encouraged to mingle with the crowd and recognize fellow Florentines.

I should like to suggest that this dramatization of viewing that I have described in relation to Masaccio's *Sagra*, and the diffusion of the narrative of the consecration onto the processional activities of specific Florentine *grandi*, may have arisen from the absence of a resonant, dramatic centerpiece to the consecration festivities. Once again, Bicci di Lorenzo's fresco offers a useful point of contrast. While Masaccio seems to have represented a procession, which by its very nature has multiple points of focus and signifies synchronically, Bicci depicted a single, climactic

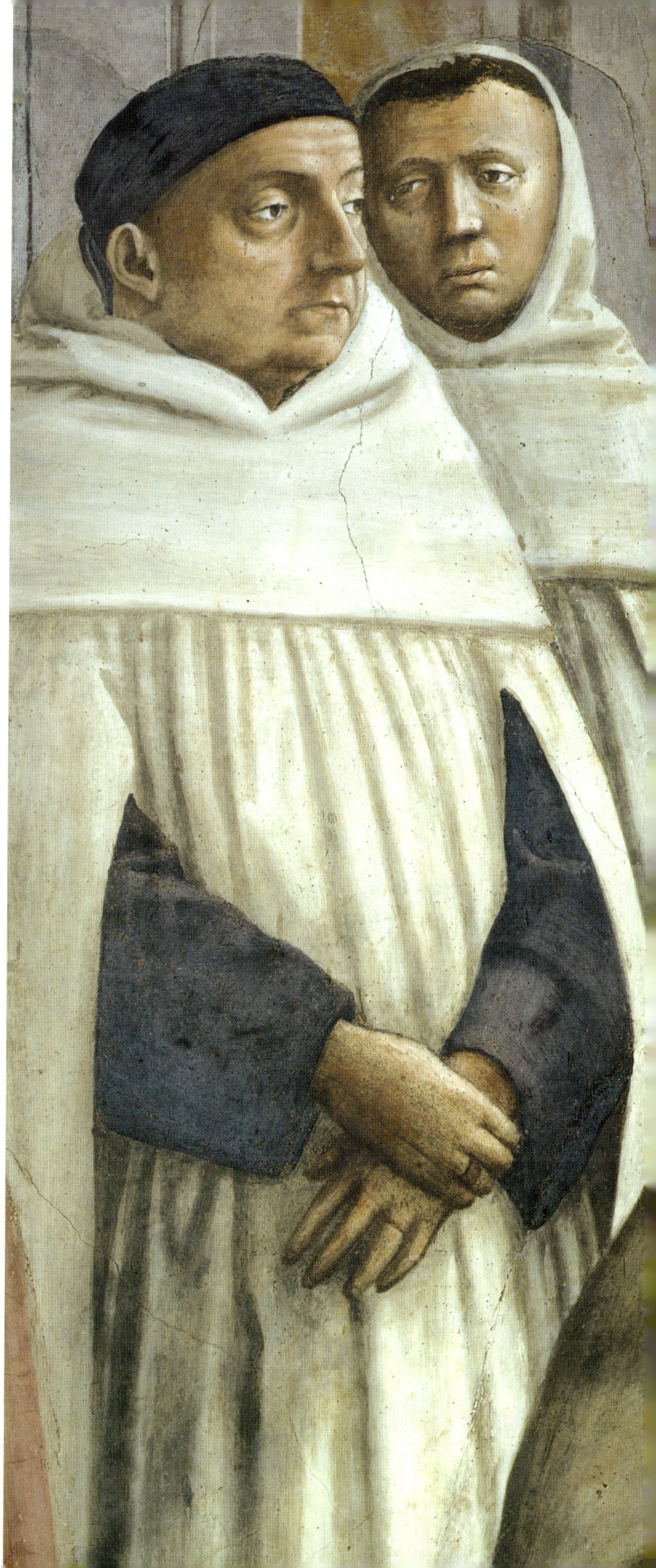

40 Masaccio, *St. Peter in Cathedra in Antioch*, detail of fig. 66.

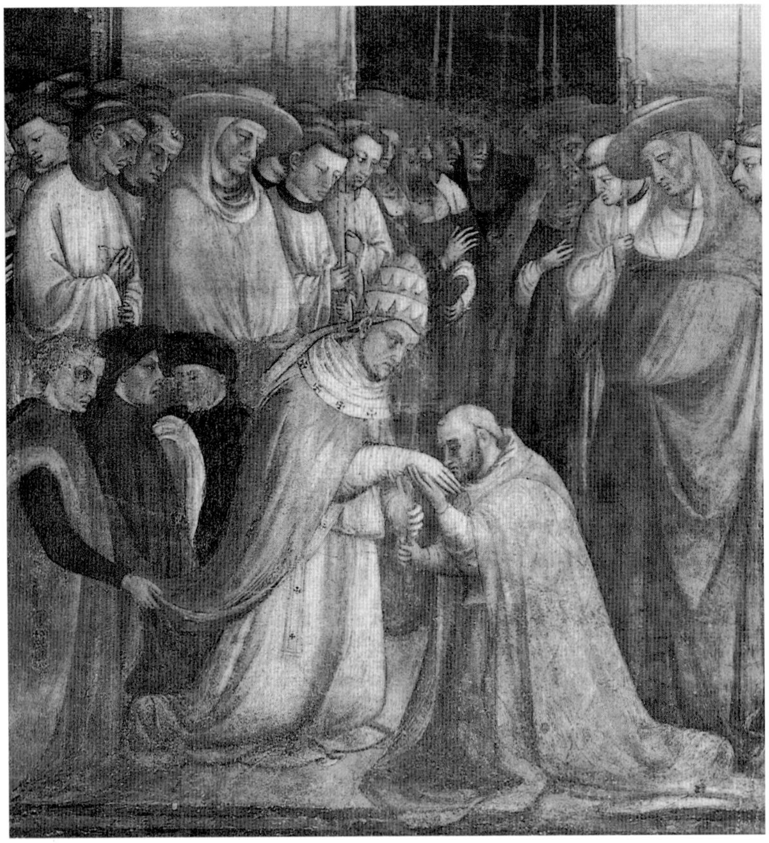

41 Bicci di Lorenzo, *Pope Martin V Confirming the Consecration of Sant'Egidio*, detail of fig. 37, with Pope Martin V and the hospital rector, Michele di Frusino da Panzano.

moment – Martin V blessing the consecration of the church, offering his gloved hand to the kneeling rector of Santa Maria Nuova (fig. 41). This papal blessing had provided the extended consecration rites of Sant'Egidio with a clear high point, a memorable freeze-frame in an octave of festivities that had begun at Vespers on September 8 and concluded at Vespers on the 16th.[83] And it was this moment that was chosen for commemoration in fresco on the church facade that faced the piazza.[84]

There is some indication that the Carmelites of Santa Maria del Carmine, too, had hoped to have Martin V himself preside over their consecration ceremonies. When the pope had arrived in Florence on February 26, 1418, it marked the first time for more than 150 years that a pope had set foot in the city. Martin's election at the Council of Constance in 1417 was perceived as heralding the definitive end of the Schism and the restoration of the papacy to Rome.[85] During the eighteen months that Martin resided in Florence, he and his cardinals continually performed religious rituals before the Florentine public. On Holy Thursday in 1418, the pope pronounced the excommunication of all heretics, schismatics, and simonists in the Piazza Santa Maria Novella. He personally blessed the olive branches at Santa Maria Novella and led the procession on Easter Sunday. He presented the city with a golden rose. Benedictions, indulgences, and benefices were liberally bestowed. While the Florentine *comune* was not completely in accord with the territorial claims of the pope and the political implications of the return of the papacy to Rome, the pope's actions as the spiritual head of the newly reunited Christian Church had profound implications for the Florentines. The pope's benedictions, orations, and indulgences served to reconsecrate the city itself, to reinscribe Florentine religious rites, sacred spaces, and secular life in a new, revitalized Christian Church.

The Carmelites, of course, participated in Martin's visit. Along with the other mendicant houses, Santa Maria del Carmine played host to one of the pope's cardinals, accommodating the Cardinal of Lodi.[86] He, in return, patronized the convent generously during his stay.[87] The pope's choir came to sing in the church, and the Ascension Day celebrations at the Carmine were attended by many of the high ecclesiastic authorities.[88] In addition, the Carmelites, as friars and keepers of the sacred, constituted an important presence within ritual celebrations and processions. When Martin entered the city through the Porta San Gallo, they were among "all the orders of friars with their relics and banners" that an eyewitness recounted were present to greet the pope.[89] Indeed, every time the city mobilized to honor the pope or participate in one of his initiatives, the diarists recorded the presence of "tutte le Regole de' frati" alongside the important city office holders.[90]

The Dominicans of Santa Maria Novella were particularly favored by the pope's stay. Martin resided in their convent, using the chapter house as his official papal chapel. Toward the end of his stay, on the first of September, 1420, Martin presided over the consecration of the church and convent of Santa Maria Novella performed by Cardinal Orsini.[91] This consecration, like that of Santa Maria del Carmine two years later, was more a symbolic than a functional act, involving the blessing of a mendicant establishment that had come into its prime during the long period of the Schism and the papacy's absence from Italy.[92]

There is evidence that the Carmelites and their principal patron were pushing to have Santa Maria del Carmine consecrated during Martin V's stay in Florence. On March 20, 1420, Francesco di Tommaso Soderini presented the pope with a request for permission to have the church, convent, and the high altar (of which he was the patron) of Santa Maria del Carmine consecrated. Martin granted Soderini his wish with a *breve* delivered on April 13 (back-dated to March 20).[93]

For reasons unknown, the consecration of Santa Maria del Carmine did not take place until two years later, in 1422, long after Martin had left the city with his cardinals.[94] The consecration occurred on April 19, the first Sunday after Easter. While the Carmelite Ordinal indicates that the Easter octave was a customary time to schedule a consecration, this date also coincided with civic celebrations of great importance in Florence that year.[95] Following the capitulation of Pisa to the Florentines in 1406 and the purchase of Porto Pisano from the Genovesi in 1421, the Florentine government encouraged the construction of a merchant fleet that would enable Florence to compete with

Venice and Genoa in Mediterranean trade.[96] The diarist Paolo Petribuoni informs us that on the preceding Friday and Saturday, and on the Monday after, the city was given over to public festivities celebrating the send-off of the first of the Florentine light galleys:

> On the 17th and the 18th and the 20th of April, 1422, that is, Friday and Saturday and Monday . . . a solemn procession was made through the whole territory, particularly on Monday the 20th of April, with all of the relics and the orders of friars and priests with the crosses of the churches. . . . And this was because on Monday . . . the first light armed galley was to leave from Pisa that would go to Alexandria. And on this day the trial runs off Corsica began.[97]

While this may seem worlds away from the consecration of Santa Maria del Carmine, religious and civic ceremonies were frequently interwoven around critical political events. Furthermore, at least one Carmine patron, Felice Brancacci, was immediately involved in these affairs.

This brings us back to the question of the identity of the figures depicted in procession in Masaccio's *Sagra*. The process of identification based on likeness would have been relatively novel for Masaccio's contemporaries. Those familiar with the convent, its patrons, and the city's *grandi* would have had little trouble in recognizing who was who. By Vasari's day, however, the participants were no longer recognizable and must have been known through verbal tradition.[98]

Vasari gave a series of names – Donatello, Brunelleschi, and Masolino; Antonio Brancacci, Niccolò da Uzzano, Giovanni di Bicci de' Medici, Bartolomeo Valori, and Lorenzo Ridolfi; and the Carmine porter. The trio of *quattrocento* artists can be dismissed outright. This kind of homage paid to contemporary artistic personalities seems to have emerged only in the late fifteenth century; it was only foreshadowed, at most, in signature self-portraits inserted unobtrusively into earlier paintings.[99] In place of "Antonio" Brancacci (d. 1390, whom Vasari considered to have been Masaccio's patron in the Brancacci chapel), one can substitute Felice Brancacci, who is the more likely candidate for the patron of the Brancacci chapel frescos.[100] Felice would have earned a place in the *Sagra* crowd on the basis of his concurrent patronage of Santa Maria del Carmine and his communal activities.[101] He had also been recently appointed by the newly established Sea Consuls as one of the two Florentine ambassadors designated to sail aboard a light galley to Egypt and negotiate trading rights with the Sultan. Felice embarked in July and remained in Egypt until early the following year.[102]

It is possible that the other Florentines whom Vasari mentions had been present at the consecration in their capacity as high office holders and power brokers and were represented in the fresco to demonstrate that the event had been significant enough to merit the participation of the city officials and principal citizens.[103] One of them, Niccolò da Uzzano, can be tied to the maritime interests of the *comune*. He was one of the six Sea Consuls who had supervised the construction of the first Florentine galley fleet and selected Felice Brancacci as ambassador. He was apparently also a particular friend of the Carmelite patron, Francesco di Tommaso Soderini.[104]

There were other important personalities present at the consecration of Santa Maria del Carmine not included in Vasari's list, particularly Francesco di Tommaso Soderini, the principal patron of the Carmine at the time,[105] and the officiating ecclesiastics and Carmelites. From the Carmelite description of the event, we know that the Florentine Archbishop, Amerigo Corsini, presided over the consecration, along with the Bishop of Fiesole, Benozzo Federighi, and the Carmelite Bishop of Soana, Fra Antonio de Fede. The prior of the convent, Fra Pietro di Francesco da Prato, and the sub-prior, Fra Mariano di Luca da Siena – a celebrated preacher – would surely have been distinguished Carmelite presences at the ceremony, as well as the regent of the Florentine Carmelite *studium*, Rev. Mag. Fra Matteo d'Antonio, and Fra Albizzo de' Nerli, who was a generous patron of his own convent. In the Folkestone (see fig. 38) and Casa Buonarroti drawings we see that at least one friar was represented, but it is curious that no traces of the three bishops or the eminent Carmelites made their way into the written accounts and drawings. In addition to these ecclesiastics and friars, another telling absence is that of the female contingents of the "populus utriusque sexus" who are said to have participated in the procession. Some of these omissions must be attributed to the particular preoccupations of the sixteenth-century writers and artists who left records of the fresco. Others may point to a marked interest on the part of the patrons in chronicling the male patrician participation in the Carmelite religious rite. Then, too, the *Sagra*, like many subsequent famous history paintings, was implicated in the rapid turning of the wheel of fortune: within a decade after it was painted, two eminent Carmine patrons – Francesco Soderini and Felice Brancacci – who surely must have been portrayed in the fresco, had fallen from public grace.[106]

The Carmelite account books are silent regarding the payment for the *Sagra* fresco. This suggests that the patron was not the convent but, rather, a layman. The fact that the fresco was in the convent cloister need not work against such a thesis, as laymen often patronized chapel and wall decorations in monastic cloisters. Keith Christiansen has made a convincing case for how the two frescos in the cloister – the *Sagra* and an episode from early Carmelite history attributed to Fra Filippo Lippi (see fig. 59) – combined with the Brancacci chapel frescos to present a coherent panoramic display of Carmelite ascendancy, from ancient to modern times.[107] Thus, we can see that the convent friars and private patrons together worked toward articulating this Carmelite history, and that the lay patronage base of the convent had an important place in this history, worthy itself of representation.

One candidate for the patron of Masaccio's *Sagra* is Francesco Soderini.[108] He had taken an active part in soliciting the pope's sanction for the consecration and was recognized for having done so in the Carmelites' own account of the ceremony, where it notes that the consecration was "procured by the honorable *domicello* Francesco di Tommaso Soderini." The papal bull granting permission for the consecration was addressed to Francesco himself and paid homage to his family's pious investment in the *cappella maggiore* of Santa Maria del Carmine: "the high altar which your good father himself founded to God with his bequest, and had constructed the elevated vault to its height and the paintings [which are] praised for their sumptuousness rather than mediocrity."[109] It is possible that Soderini secured the services of Masaccio, who was working on an altarpiece for the Pisan Carmelite church in 1426 and in the Brancacci chapel around the same time. Another possibility is that Felice Brancacci commissioned the *Sagra*. He was personally involved in the civic celebrations that bracketed the Carmine consecration and, in addition, certainly had relations with Masaccio when the latter decorated his family chapel in the Carmine.

The dating of Masaccio's *Sagra* need not be affixed tightly to the date of the consecration itself. According to standard liturgical practices, the anniversary of the consecration was to be celebrated each year on the first Sunday after Easter.[110] And, in fact, the Carmelite account books indicate that a special feast was observed for at least two years following the consecration, recording the "purchases made for the *Sagra*" in 1423, and "the festive meal of the convent . . . for the consecration" in 1424.[111]

Masaccio's *Sagra* would thus have been an element in a formalized retrospective commemoration of the consecration. This transition from history making into remembrance followed conventional liturgical practices and may even have had precedents in pictorial representation.[112] But Masaccio's *Sagra* must have radically transformed the nature of the commemoration, implanting in the place of "religious time" a particularized rendering of "historical time." This new history painting was born out of a collaborative venture of the Florentine Carmelites, their lay patrons, and Masaccio. The Florentine Carmelites were determined to write themselves into the history of their Order at the precise moment in which that history was being worked out in all of its specificity and the Western identity of the Order redefined. The patrons of the Carmelites sought the special protection of the Virgin of Mount Carmel and the Carmelite saints for themselves and their families, making a conspicuous public demonstration of their piety and influence in matters sacred. The painting style of Masaccio developed in the service of these representational needs. His spare, rhetorical narratives read through the dramatic carriage and interaction of figures, and his mastery at securing portrait likenesses brought to his painting all of the specificity of time, place, and participation that the Carmelites and their patrons required.

I have not been able to do full justice to the complicated subject of Masaccio's fugitive *Sagra*. What I am positing here is a stratification of incidents, traces, and explanations that cumulatively provide some idea of the circumstances out of which the fresco emerged. My aim is to integrate the *Sagra* into the survey of changing Florentine Carmelite practices and representational strategies developed in this chapter. The *Sagra* marked a key moment in this transformation. The fresco embodied a very self-conscious Carmelite attitude toward history making, and attested to the vital integration of the friars and their convent in the religious life of the city. It also represented the historical process under way in early *quattrocento* Florence, involving the reconsecration of the local religious scene and the changing modality of the sacred: the Carmine was becoming a site where events of great religious and civic significance took place. These events were recorded in representations which then served as points of reference in a new history – a modern Florentine Carmelite chronicle in which specific personalities (religious and lay) were emphasized and the Carmine and Carmelite context of contemporary events was delineated.

THE ASCENSION DAY *SACRA RAPPRESENTAZIONE*

Every year in the month of May, on the feast of the Ascension of Christ, the Confraternity of Sant'Agnese staged a *sacra rappresentazione* of the Ascension in the church of Santa Maria del Carmine. There is no better way to introduce the *sacra rappresentazione* than to reproduce the spectacle as seen through the observant eyes of a foreigner: the Russian Bishop Abraham of Suzdal, who had accompanied the Metropolitan of the Eastern Church to the Council of Florence in 1439, recorded in his *Journey*:

> This is the other wonderful thing I saw in the famed city of Florence. In the Church of the Ascension of our Lord and Savior Jesus Christ, on the Thursday of the sixth week after Easter, the Latins, by ancient tradition, celebrate the Ascension of our Lord who went to Heaven in his glory on the fortieth day after the Resurrection. This is what I saw.
>
> The church is 80 *sagenes* long from the front wall to the altar and 20 *sagenes* wide; in this church . . . there is a stone rood screen 20 *sagenes* long, on stone pillars 4 *sagenes* high. And on this rood screen on the left one sees a stone castle, wonderfully decorated with towers and ramparts, which represents the Holy City of Jerusalem; opposite the city against the wall rises a hill, 1½ *sagenes* high, raised up, to which there lead steps two hand-spans high; the hill is draped all around with red cloth.
>
> High above this is a wooden structure about 4 *sagenes* square and 8 *sagenes* high, beautifully painted underneath and on the sides. In the middle of the upper part of this structure is a large round opening, 2 *sagenes* in diameter, draped with a blue curtain, on which the sun, the moon and the surrounding stars are painted: a representation of the first celestial sphere. At the appointed time this drape is lifted, that is, the doors of Heaven are opened, and above is seen a man,

with a crown on his head, just like God the Father; he is supported in such a wondrous fashion over the doors of Heaven, lowering his gaze down over the Mount of Olives, where his divine Son, the Holy Virgin, and the Apostles are gathered, and blessing them with his hand. He seems, as he hovers in the air, not to be supported by anything. Around him is a throng of little children who represent angels with pipes and lutes and lots of tiny bells, and in their midst numerous tiny candles. And beside the Heavenly Father and the children, is fixed, against the opening which represents Heaven, a paper disc, whose lower edge touches that of the opening: on it are painted life-size angels. From the opening of Heaven down to the Mount of Olives run seven fine strong cords with ingenious iron pulleys. From these a young man, representing Christ in the act of ascending to the Father, is pulled up. Above the altar, beneath the roof of the church, in the same wall as the altar, is a stone chamber, measuring 3 *sagenes* on all sides; on the side open to the church it is hung with a red curtain on which is seen a crown in a circle, which without ceasing moves to right and left. Everything is marvellously organised, and nothing has ever been seen like it.

At the ninth hour people gather from everywhere in this church to witness the wonderful performance. When the church is full and silence reigns, all eyes are raised to the rood screen and what is arranged there. Then four young children, resembling angels in their head-dress and clothes, each with a flowering branch in his hand, appear on the rood screen; then one appears dressed like the Son of God made man, who sets out for the city representing Jerusalem, while the Angels precede him. He enters Jerusalem, and a short time later he comes out again with two actors who play the parts of the Holy Virgin and Mary Magdalene, represented by young men dressed as women. Then the Son of God goes back towards Jerusalem, and leads out Peter, the first of the Apostles, and after him come the other Apostles and he goes towards the Mount of Olives with his Holy Mother, and the Apostles, still preceded by the four Angels. The Apostles are all barefoot and dressed as we see them painted in holy pictures: some have beards, others are beardless, just as they were in reality.

When Christ approaches the Mount of Olives, he stops and looks back towards Jerusalem, while his Mother and Mary Magdalene stand to his right. The Apostle Peter, after throwing himself at Jesus' feet and receiving his blessing, takes himself to his place; and the remaining young men do likewise and place themselves on the right or on the left of Jesus, each in his place. When they have all positioned themselves in this fashion, Jesus distributes various gifts to them. He gives the Apostle Andrew a net with the words: You will be a fisher of men; to another he gives a book, to a third a sword with which he says: No harm will come to you from it if you use it in my name.

Then Jesus comes back to the Mount of Olives and goes to the step at the foot of the mountain while his Mother and Mary Magdalene remain on his right, and the Apostles remain at the foot of the mountain in their places. Then Jesus says: Since everything that was ordained has been fulfilled, I go to my Father and yours, to my God and yours; and he goes away to the top of the mountain where the apparatus with the ropes is prepared. The Apostles lean on one another and weep and say mournfully: Lord do not leave us, for we are like orphans. But Jesus answers: Weep not, I will not leave you like orphans. I go to my Father and will ask him to send you the Spirit of Consolation, the Spirit of Truth, which will teach you everything. For, if I do not go, the Comforter will not come to you.

After these and other words, a peal of thunder is heard, Christ appears on the Mount, and all turn their eyes upwards to see Heaven open and God the Father floating above, suspended in the air in wondrous fashion, in a great light, which comes from innumerable lamps; the little boys, who represent the heavenly Powers, move around him to the sounds of deafening music and sweet singing; the big painted angels on the discs move in the shape of a circle so that they seem to be alive. From Heaven where God the Father is there descends on the seven ropes an exceedingly beautiful and cleverly constructed *nuvola*: it is round and surrounded by swiftly turning discs. To the right and to the left are two children dressed as angels, with golden wings. When the *nuvola* is half-way down, Jesus takes two great golden keys and says to Peter: You are Peter and on this rock I shall build my church and the gates of Hell shall not prevail against it. And I shall give you the keys of the kingdom of Heaven and all that you shall bind on earth shall also be bound in Heaven and all that you shall unbind on earth shall also be unbound in heaven. And when he has blessed him and handed him the keys, he goes up with the help of the seven ropes in the direction of the *nuvola*, blessing Mary and the Apostles with his hand.

It is a marvellous sight and without equal: the ropes are set in motion by means of a very clever pulley-system, so that the person who represents Jesus seems really to go up by himself, and he reaches a great height without wobbling. The pulley-system is invisible.

The Holy Virgin and Apostles, seeing him depart, shed tears. When he approaches the *nuvola*, this envelops him from head to foot, the two Angels bow before him on the left and the right, and in the same instant the *nuvola* is lit up by a multitude of lights which shed their splendour everywhere.

But Jesus goes higher and higher, accompanied by the two Angels, and soon he steps out next to God the Father, the music ceases and it grows dark. Then the Virgin and the Apostles look up to the chamber above the altar: the curtain is drawn back from the place which represents upper Heaven, and there is light again.[113]

The two characteristics of the *sacra rappresentazione* that I want to explore here are the way in which the Carmine *frati* and the local laity combined their resources to produce a spectacle on such a scale that it figured in the annual religious calendar of the city at large, and the extent to which the Ascension drama registered certain over-determinations (or slippages) in the relationship between the religious representation and the sacred event that it claimed to represent.

The Ascension of Christ was a Christian mystery and a feast of particular significance to the Carmelite Order. The departure to the heavens of the Carmelite founder Elijah in a chariot of fire was considered to have prefigured the Ascension.[114] Along with other mysteries and martyrdoms that took place within or in the vicinity of Jerusalem, the Ascension also figured prominently in the Carmelite liturgy based on the Rite of the Holy Sepulcher. This Rite, given to the Carmelites in the early thirteenth century by Albert, Patriarch of Jerusalem, was designed for use in the patriarch's domain. Those feasts that commemorated events that had transpired within the city of Jerusalem were celebrated with processions to the actual holy sites.[115] The Carmelite liturgy retained the procedures prescribed in the Rite for the processions on the feasts of the Ascension and the Assumption.[116] Thus the impetus for a realistic dramatization of the Ascension with simulated effects may have come from the Carmelite liturgy. It is also consistent with the Carmelite tendency in the *trecento* and *quattrocento* to reproduce in discursive form the events in the early history of their Order that had taken place in the Holy Land.

It is not known precisely when the Ascension Day celebrations took on such significance in Santa Maria del Carmine and came to be dramatized in a *sacra rappresentazione*. By the last decades of the *trecento*, some sort of dramatization was presented, complete with a levitation device.[117] However, the presentation seems to have taken on the grand, spectacular dimensions conveyed in Bishop Abraham's description (and in a second account provided by Vasari) by the early 1420s.[118] It was around this time that Brunelleschi is thought to have been engaged to design the lighting and the complicated hoist for the play.[119] In 1425, Masolino is recorded painting the clouds and angels which were part of the scenery for the heavens.[120]

By the early *quattrocento*, the convent of Santa Maria del Carmine and the Confraternity of Sant'Agnese were lavishing extraordinary amounts of money on the feast. The Confraternity seems to have paid for the staging of the *sacra rappresentazione*, while the convent footed the bill for the banquet. On average, the convent expenses for the month of May, during which the feast occurred, were at least double those of other months. In 1419, the year Pope Martin V was in town, musicians were hired and 150 people dined at the Carmine, including members of the Signoria and Mercanzia, and cardinals and bishops.[121]

The Confraternity had the heavier responsibilities of setting up the *sacra rappresentazione*, for which preparations went on throughout the year.[122] Artists, engineers, blacksmiths, musicians, actors, tailors, and wigmakers, among others, were engaged. Funds were paid out of the Confraternity coffers but on occasion the *comune* seems to have assisted in the financing, and the Confraternity also solicited donations for the play.[123] In January, 1440, the Confraternity accepted a total of l.38 s.14 d.2 from the "people who have made donations for the festival of the Ascension in 1440." Among the individuals listed are "frate Filippo dipintore" (along with sixteen other Carmelite friars) and "Ser Pagolo di Lorenzo," who was the *capitano* of the Confraternity that year, and who acted as Lippi's notary during this period.[124]

Through a combined effort of the convent and the Confraternity, the Carmine Ascension Day celebration became a major event in the Florentine calendar during the *quattrocento*. It took its place alongside the processions and dramatizations in which large sectors of the city populace participated – those held on St. John's day, Epiphany, the Feast of the Annunciation, Pentecost, and Easter. The public character of the event becomes even clearer when one observes how, toward the end of the century, the major overhauling and adjustments of the staging of the Ascension Day *sacra rappresentazione* occurred around important visits of foreign dignitaries to the city.[125]

I want to return to Bishop Abraham of Suzdal's account and look more closely at the language he used to describe the dramatization of the Ascension mystery.[126] Abraham, in the mode of contemporary travelogues, gives very specific information about the physical setting of the play, elaborating measurements, contours, and materials. This literalness carries over to his description of the way in which the drama itself was performed.

It is helpful if we think for a moment of the religious representational practices in the Eastern Church with which Abraham would have been familiar. The painted icons in the Russian Church were based on venerated archetypes. The status and potency of an image depended upon its relationship to an archetype, which in turn claimed a special, authoritative relationship to the sacred being represented. The form and content of the religious imagery within the Eastern and Western Churches at the time were sufficiently different to prompt one of the Greek patriarchs at the Council of Florence to remark "When I enter a Latin church, I can pray to none of the saints depicted there because I recognize none of them. Although I do recognize Christ, I cannot even pray to him because I do not recognize the manner in which he is being depicted."[127]

It is perhaps on account of a similar challange to recognize the visual language of religious representation that Abraham of Suzdal was so attentive to the means by which the illusion of the Ascension was secured in the theatrical performance in the nave of the church of Santa Maria del Carmine: "a stone castle, wonderfully decorated with towers and ramparts, which *represents* the Holy City of Jerusalem . . . a large round opening . . . draped with a blue curtain, on which the sun, the moon and the surrounding stars are painted: a *representation* of the first celestial sphere. . . . little children who *represent* angels . . . two actors *who play the parts* of the Holy Virgin and Mary Magdalene, *represented* by young men dressed as women" (my italics). There are moments, however, when he relaxes his scrutiny of the mechanics of the mimetic enactment and slips into a description of the play as the Christian mystery itself. There are no longer boys and men, but angels, Jesus, the Virgin, and the Apostles. But this narrative mode is unstable, and an illusion that is too "miraculous" or "marvellous" can readily throw the account back to the mode documenting the means of representation.

The levitation device in particular distracts Bishop Abraham, undoubtedly because the Brunelleschi invention did not reveal its workings to the curious viewer who refused to suspend disbelief and participate in the fiction. ("The ropes are set in motion by means of a clever pulley-system, so that the person who represents Jesus seems really to go up by himself, and he reaches a great height without wobbling.") Hence, rather bizarre disjunctures occur in the descriptive account: "Jesus . . . goes away to the top of the mountain where the apparatus with the ropes is prepared," and then, "he goes up with the help of the seven ropes in the direction of the *nuvola*, blessing Mary and the Apostles with his hand." Perhaps the most telling passage is where Abraham registers a need to ground this mimetic enactment of the Ascension of Christ in an authoritative "truthful" mode of religious representation with which he is familiar. Before launching into the long description of the Ascension play as the sacred story in the second half of his text, he notes "the Apostles are all barefoot and dressed as we see them painted in holy pictures: some have beards, others are beardless, just as they were in reality." Painting – presumably Byzantine painting – becomes the mediating point of reference.

Cyrilla Barr's and Nerida Newbigin's careful reading of the account books of the Compagnia di Sant'Agnese provide further information regarding the props and the costumes worn by the individuals in the play. Wigs and beards were made from the hair of horse and oxtails, while the Magdalene's wig was constructed out of two pounds of hemp rope in 1438. According to an inventory of 1467, the actor representing God the Father wore a mask.[128] These details of costuming provoke certain questions about the relative stability of the illusion of likeness created in the *sacra rappresentazione*. While the 500 clay lamps used for the illumination of Paradise would have reinforced the illusion of heavenly splendor, the cultural convention prohibiting female participants in the play that necessitated a male Magdalene, supporting a wig of hemp, would have demanded a break in the illusion.

Bishop Abraham was not the only observer of the Ascension play to focus on the mechanics of the mimetic representation. Paolo di Matteo Petribuoni, writing about the *sacra rappresentazione* in 1422, noted:

> a living man instead of Our Lord went up into Heaven. He was pulled from the arches [of the *ponte*] to the platform and reached the roof, going straight upward. All episodes were represented in the likeness of [the life of] Our Lady, of St. Mary Magdalene and of the twelve Apostles. This festival was considered to be very beautiful on account of the many devices around the *nuvola*, so that when the *nuvola* came down and united with Christ ascending, then many candles burst at once into light, reflecting also on other figures of angels . . .[129]

With the benefit of Brunelleschi's elaborate technology of illusionism, the *sacra rappresentazione* of 1422 provoked even a Florentine to emphasize repeatedly that this was indeed a "festa," that men acted in the "similitudine" of sacred personages, and that the effects were achieved through "ingegni."[130] This was also the case in the late *trecento*, when the performance was much simpler (although still guaranteeing a trip to the rafters for the man representing Jesus). In his seventy-second novella, Franco Sacchetti lightly ironized the relationship between the Christian mystery and the dramatic, spectacular reenactment.

> On the day of the Ascension, in [the church of] the Order of the Carmelites in Florence who celebrate the feast, one of my friends, seeing Our Lord going up toward the roof on a rope, and going very slowly, [heard] someone saying:
>
> "He's going so slowly that He won't reach the roof today." And [my friend] said, "If He didn't go any faster, he is still on his way."[131]

With a deft touch, Sacchetti set up an amusing comparison between "nostro Signore" rising to the roof of the Carmine, playing out the religious drama in human dimensions, and the actual passage of Christ from this world to the other, with its unfathomable implications. The irony is doubly inflected since Sacchetti inserted this account at the end of a diatribe against the clergy and their penchant for gimmicks, the novel, and the superficial – all at the expense of a more profound religious faith. A friar had claimed that the Lord "n'andasse così veloce e ratto." How did the Lord ascend to Heaven? What did the Apostles look like, and on whose authority? Am I to trust this illusion of likeness that I see before my eyes? These were some of the questions raised by the Carmine *sacra rappresentazione* of the Ascension.

THE CARMELITE OBSERVANCE, VENERABLE CARMELITES, AND MIRACULOUS EVENTS

At some date during the 1430s, the Carmelite Fra Angelo Mazzinghi was preaching before a crowd on the feast of St. Lawrence, and the following event was said to have occurred:

> The venerable friar Angelo was seen by a great number of trustworthy people, to whom he was preaching with great confidence, inflamed and alight with compassion and love. He gave an excellent sermon, preaching about martyrdom and the glory and the crowns with which martyrs are presented in the eternal life. And at this point, this servant of God was so impassioned that the entire crowd was overcome with amazement. He was so afire that they visibly saw two angels

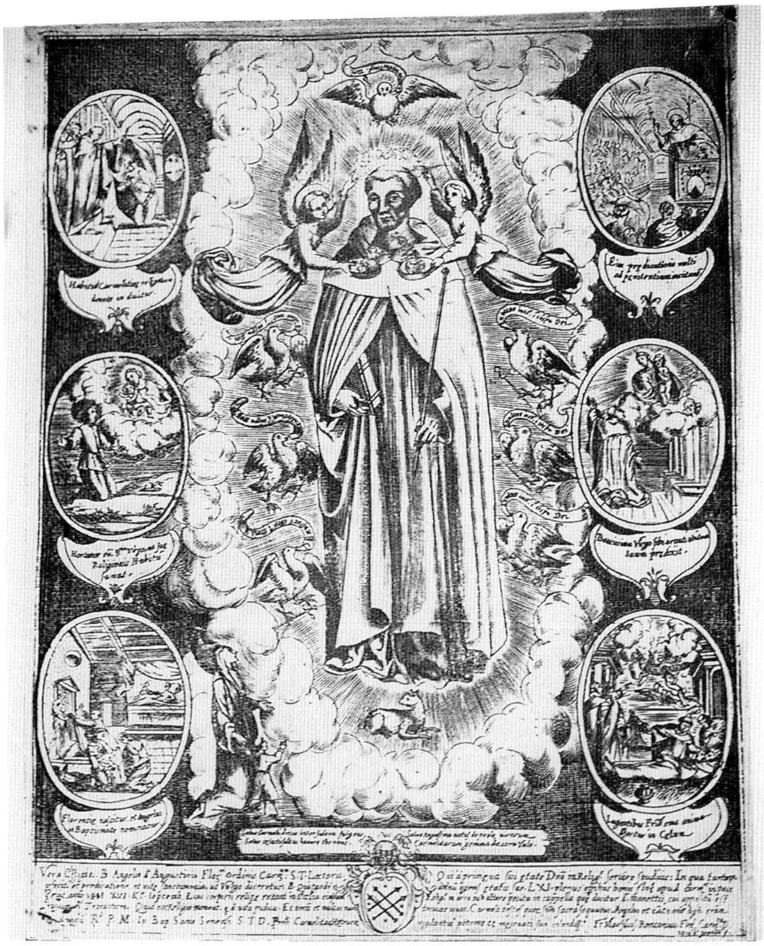

42 Fra Marsilio Ronconi, *Beato Angelo Mazzinghi*, engraving, 1641.

> standing before him, one on the right and one on the left, holding two golden vessels. And from the mouth of the above-mentioned father, there issued forth roses and flowers which fell into the said vessels. And the said angels gathered those roses and made crowns which they placed on the head of Beato *frate* Angelo. And over his white cloak was seen a pallium lined in violet. And this was observed by a great multitude.[132]

The miracle is described by the Carmelite Nicola Calciuri in his *Vita fratrum del Sancto Monte Carmelo* in a section entitled "The Nine Visions of the Order," written in 1461. Some time after the fact, a painting was made to commemorate the event and was hung on a pilaster in the chapel to the right of the main chapel in the transept of Santa Maria del Carmine.[133] Unfortunately, the painting no longer exists, a casualty of the devastating 1771 fire that swept through the church. Various descriptions and prints (fig. 42), however, provide some idea of its appearance:

> The figure of . . . [Beato Angelo Mazzinghi] can be seen in a mysterious image . . . where the above-mentioned father is painted full-length with celestial rays around his head, with his face turned toward Heaven, with a book in his right hand, and a red scepter in his left, surrounded by seven white doves with red beaks and feet, three on each side, each with one of their feet resting on a red cross. Then another [dove] without a cross, in the act of flying with wings extended and rays around its head, which represents the Holy Spirit with its seven gifts, and proclaims through the air these words: *Let the just man rejoice before God*. Under the feet of this blessed Father there is a very meek lamb lying and two celestial angels crown this earthly creature with a garland of roses and with vessels woven with wands or rushes; they catch at his [Beato Angelo's] breast the roses that fall from his mouth, because . . . instead of words [which are] invisible, real bouquets of roses and very beautiful lilies were sometimes seen to issue forth from his mouth as he preached.[134]

At the time of this "miracle," Fra Angelo d'Agostino Mazzinghi (1377–1438) was the most important figure associated with the Carmelite Observant movement at Santa Maria delle Selve in Lastra a Signa, some fifteen kilometers west of Florence.[135] In 1413, the founder of the Observant movement, Fra Jacopo Alberti, had been given permission to transform Le Selve into a reformed house through the institution of Constitutions that rehabilitated certain features of the "primitive" Carmelite Rule.[136] The early Carmelite emphasis on prayer, stricter enclosure, silence, minimal contact with the laity, and a simple diet without meat was revived. Le Selve was regarded with a particular reverence by the other convents in the Tuscan *provincia*, with a special grace conferred each year upon it at the provincial chapter meeting.[137] Fra Jacopo Alberti served as prior at Le Selve from 1413 to 1417. When he died in 1426, the friars from Santa Maria del Carmine traveled to Le Selve to attend the burial of the author of the Observant reforms. Filippo Lippi (around twenty years old at the time) was among them.[138]

Fra Angelo Mazzinghi was prior at Le Selve from 1417 to 1429, at which time he became the convent superior.[139] His obituary in the Carmine *Necrologium* puts his activity at Le Selve in relation to his other noteworthy attributes: "A venerable man of the greatest virtue and excellent doctrine, a teacher of judgment, achieving great fame and holiness in his life, and a most famous preacher, who was the first son at the inception of the Observance at Le Selve."[140] His contribution was manifold, extending to different sites of Carmelite and Carmine activity, to the hermitage of Le Selve as well as to the urban Carmine. He was one of the few friars on the Florentine Carmelite scene with a patrician background,[141] and this gave him a privileged economic position relative to the other friars, and greater influence with patrons and ecclesiastical and civic authorities.[142] As noted in his obituary, Fra Angelo was also a "predicator famosissimus" and was chosen by the provincial chapter to preach the Lenten sermons in Florence from 1432 to 1438. And it was during one of his sermons on the feast of St. Lawrence that the flowers were seen spilling forth miraculously from his mouth.

The Carmelite Observance was influenced by the reform movements within the other mendicant orders during the late *trecento* and early *quattrocento*. But the Observant movement within the Carmelite Order also emerged out of the fourteenth-century Carmelite search for a distinct identity and history. As the Carmelite Elian "fonte" on Mount Carmel became more and more remote and inaccessible, a need arose for a new spiritual center closer to home. Sicily had taken on such a role in the burgeoning Carmelite hagiography during the thirteenth and fourteenth centuries, serving as the backdrop for a new, inspired, cenobitical Carmelite religiosity in the West, complete with miracles and martyrdom. But the Carmelite "doctrine of origin" – if one can use the expression – persisted with further elaborations into the *quattrocento*. The hermitage on Mount Carmel was described in great detail by Calciuri in 1461, complete with measurements (taken from pilgrims' guides to the Holy Land) and the eremitical daily practices of the "Children of the Prophets." This picture of Carmelites in the Holy Land paradoxically became more and more vivid in the literary and visual representations as the Carmelite presence in, and contact with, the actual physical sites in the Middle East diminished. Evidently, these representations performed the important symbolic function of keeping the historic, "mythic" spiritual center and place of origin present. It became necessary to enact the Carmelite experiences in the Holy Land in Western Europe in order that the important myth should continue to function for the *frati*.

I should like to suggest that the transformation of the minor provincial convent of Le Selve into a center of Observant Carmelite reform involved such an enactment of the hermetic Carmelite life associated with the followers of the prophet Elijah on Mount Carmel. Le Selve – meaning literally "The Woods" – was tucked into the hills above Lastra a Signa (figs. 43 and 44). There, Carmelite *frati* could practice their religion with the same fervor and simplicity as had their desert forefathers. The corollary to this, and the second part of my argument, is that this renewal of the Carmelite spiritual center – transplanted from the Holy Land to the Tuscan *provincia* – then permitted the Tuscan urban convents to carry on the mediations between the religious and the lay spheres necessary to the survival of the Order in the West. This seems to be the explanation for the simultaneous tightening up and relaxation of Carmelite practices located in different convents within the same Tuscan *provincia*. For, shortly after the Observance was instituted at Le Selve, the Carmelite Rule was further relaxed for the rest of the Order. In 1432, the general prior of the Carmelite Order approached Pope Eugenius IV with a request to mitigate further the Carmelite Rule.[143] Three years later, Eugenius complied with a bull that permitted the Carmelites to eat meat three times a week and move about the convent enclosure at liberty.[144] It is this strange combination

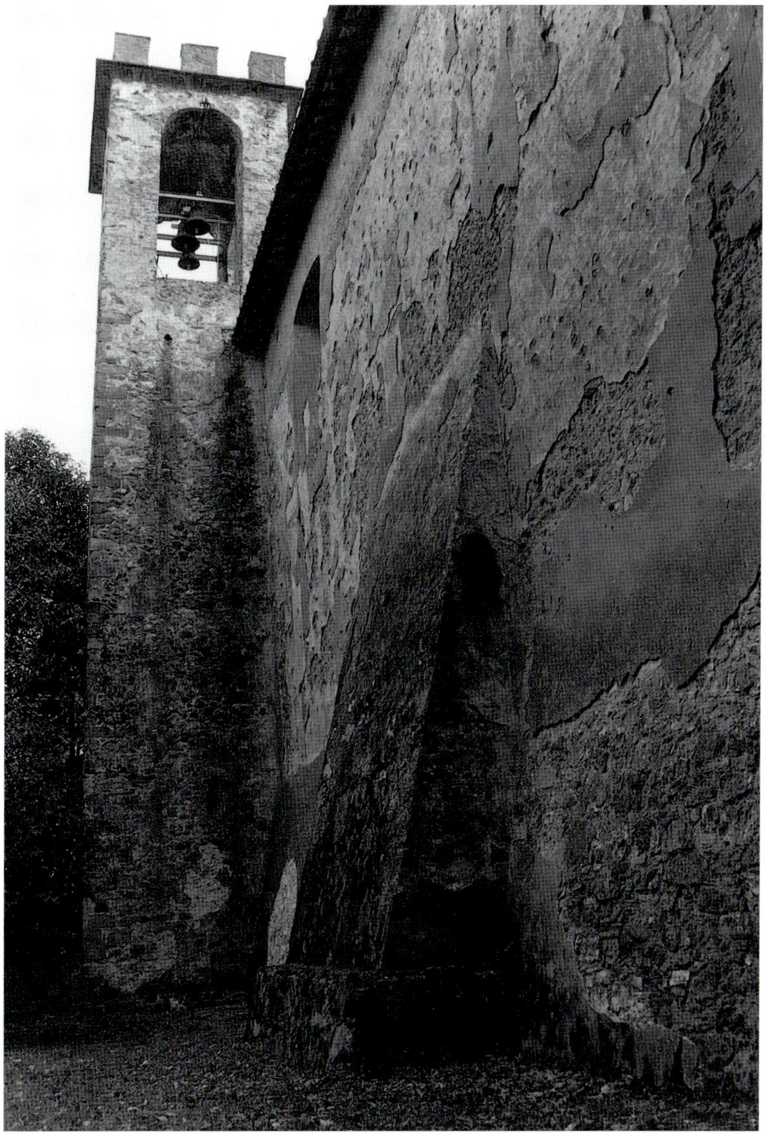

44 The tower of the church of Santa Maria delle Selve, Lastra a Signa (Province of Florence).

43 View of Santa Maria delle Selve, Lastra a Signa (Province of Florence).

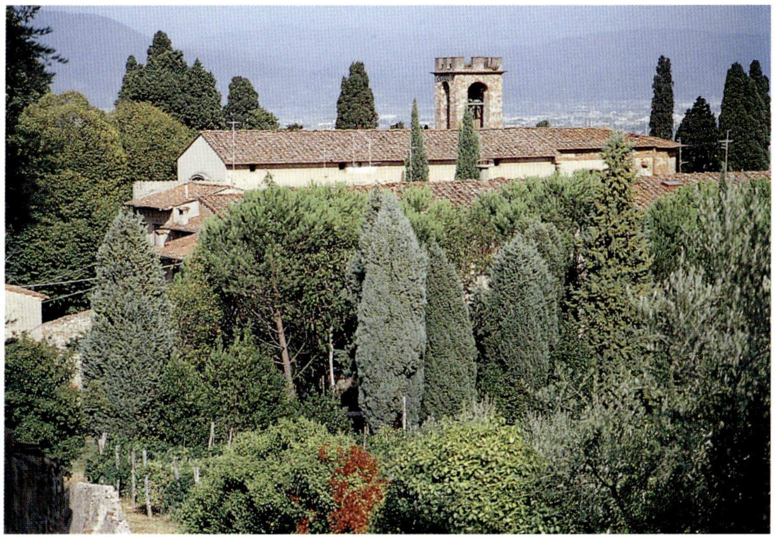

of mitigating revision and strict reform, tendencies that seemed to coexist without tension or contention, that distinguished the Carmelite reform movement during the early *quattrocento* from those of other monastic orders.

The *frati* of Santa Maria del Carmine were making a concerted effort to involve the entire city of Florence in the religious life of the convent – to attract worshipers, friars, participants in feast day celebrations and processions from well beyond the confines of the local parish of San Frediano, traditionally the source of human and material resources for the Carmine. And at the very same time that the Carmine *frati* were actively courting the Florentine public, contributing time, space, and the services of Carmelite friars to accommodate both the pious bequests of testators and the devotional needs of living patrons and confraternities, the brethren at Le Selve devoted themselves to a program of study and worship.

This dichotomy extended to the religious representations displayed within each convent. At Le Selve, the conception of the Carmelite Order that had crystallized late in the *trecento* continued to dominate. When the friars of Le Selve commissioned a tabernacle from the Florentine painter Neri di Bicci in 1454, they devised an iconographic program close in spirit to that of Lorenzetti's Siena Carmine polyptych of 1329 (see figs. 20–27) and Fra Filippo Riboti's *Decem libros de institutione et peculiaribus gestis religiosorum Carmelitarum* (c. 1370). The tabernacle neatly encompassed the three Carmelite visual traditions discussed in this chapter: Santa Maria del Carmine as the patron of the Order, Elijah as Carmelite saint and founder, and new Carmelite saints in the West. Neri noted in his *Ricordanze*:

> I have undertaken to paint and gild . . . a tabernacle with wings . . . in which I have to make a small panel to contain a Madonna and Child, of less than half-length, painted in the Greek manner and very old; on the [inside of the] wings I have to make on one side St. Elijah and St. Alberto and on the other, St. Elisha and St. Angelo of Jerusalem; and on the said small panel of Our Lady, a God the Father with many seraphim . . . and on the outside of the doors, a Virgin Annunciate and the angel.[145]

Neri was to take a pre-existing "Madonna panel" – not only "alla greca," which in *quattrocento* terminology could mean simply "not modern" and hence *trecento*, but "molto anticha" – and frame the Marian image with the context of the recently elaborated history of the Carmelite Order. Unfortunately, the tabernacle disappeared at the end of the nineteenth century, so one cannot examine first hand the artist's synthesis.[146] However, from the *Ricordanze* description, it is possible to envision how the closing of the tabernacle doors enacted the Mystery of the Incarnation, while the opening of the doors revealed the principal patron of the Order, the Madonna with the Christ Child in her arms, painted as she had been by Luke long ago in Eastern lands. The outer parameters of the open tabernacle were defined by the Old Testament Carmelite founder and the first disciple, "Saints" Elijah and Elisha, and flanking the Virgin were the only two Carmelites whose cults had gained widespread acceptance outside the Order, "Saints" Alberto and Angelo.[147]

In contrast with this painting commissioned by the friars of Le Selve, visual representations in the Florentine Carmine reflected upon the contemporary Carmelite scene and notable personalities. Masaccio's *Sagra* and the "mysterious image of Beato Angelo Mazzinghi" commemorated recent events,[148] while other works, like the *Confirmation of the Carmelite Rule* (see fig. 59) frescoed in the cloister and attributed to Filippo Lippi, and Masaccio's *St. Peter in Cathedra in Antioch* and Masolino's *St. Peter Preaching* (see figs. 66 and 65) in the Brancacci chapel, interpreted earlier happenings with reference to the present Carmelite condition.

This self-conscious, self-important attitude toward Carmelite recent history and current events in the Florentine Carmine produced an expectation of a sacred manifestation within the Carmelite environs. Even as the cults of the twelfth and thirteenth-century Carmelites St. Alberto and St. Angelo were gaining ground, close attention was being paid to the pious activities of contemporary Florentine Carmelites. A letter written soon after the death of the Carmelite Maestro Albizzo de' Nerli in 1428,[149] reveals something of this atmosphere of *meraviglia* and expectation:

> During his life he always rose for Matins and afterwards he remained in the church for two hours. And when he returned to his cell, many friars affirm that they saw a light before him which accompanied him to his cell. The friars asked him what it was and, making them promise not to speak of it during his life, he said that it was the Angel Raphael who was accompanying him. . . . Four days before his death, a friar who was in the church saw from afar a great burst of light and a very beautiful youth speaking with the master. He took courage and went closer, and when he was nearby he heard [Fra Albizzo] saying: "Always thanks be to you God because it is your pleasure to call me to you." And the friar asked him what happened. He responded: "Soon I will die and I will go to rest."

Four days later,

> during the singing of the Mass of the Madonna . . . kneeling and singing together with the novices, and with great devotion . . . he was heard saying "Into your hands, O God, I commend my Spirit," and he died. In this way it is believed that his spirit went to Paradise. Many people saw a great burst of light above the church around the twelfth hour, which remained there until the said father died. And it is believed by all that his spirit went to Paradise accompanied by that light.[150]

Some ten years later, flowers were seen issuing forth from the mouth of Fra Angelo Mazzinghi as he was preaching and were gathered up by attendant angels. The *Annali de' Carmelitani* list other miracles and acts of intercession performed by Fra Angelo during the 1430s.[151] In 1437, the Virgin herself is supposed to have revealed to Fra Angelo his coming death and on August 17 the following year he died in the monastery of Santa Lucia, with eyes fixed on the image of the crucifix held before him. Certain friars reported seeing his soul carried up to heaven by angels.[152] People flocked to see his body, which was transported to the church of the Carmine. A woman brought her son suffering from dropsy before the tomb of Fra Angelo, and he was miraculously cured.[153] And the "mysterious image" was painted and hung on a column in the choir of Santa Maria del Carmine.[154]

Evidently, there was great expectation that either Maestro Albizzo de' Nerli or the "first son" of the Observant reform, Fra Angelo Mazzinghi, would generate miraculous happenings and popular cults at Santa Maria del Carmine with their passing from this world to the next. As it happened, when miraculous events in the Carmine were finally brought to the attention of the Florentine Archiepiscopacy and Pope Eugenius IV in 1440, they did not directly involve either of these two contemporary Carmelites of patrician birth. Instead, they were focused on a Carmelite whose aura of sanctity had had more time to mature – Fra Andrea Corsini, who had died in 1374, after a twenty-five-year tenure as Bishop of Fiesole. But this is material for Chapter 5, since Lippi himself played a small, but nonetheless interesting, role in this celebration and affirmation of the cult of Beato Andrea. What I want to emphasize here is the atmosphere of anticipation and expectation prevalent in Santa Maria del Carmine during the third and fourth decades of the *quattrocento*. How would this have affected the way in which people perceived and conceived of sacred subjects? How did it influence what they saw when they turned their eyes upon Fra Angelo preaching, the "Madonna del Popolo," or Masaccio's *St. Peter Healing with his Shadow*? What kinds of spaces, colors, and shapes did they visualize to accompany a preacher's narration; or, alternatively, what narratives did they construct to match a figurative image? For it was within this environment of the sacred made manifest that Fra Filippo Lippi's vision of the sacred became concrete, taking on a particular pictorial form. It is compelling to postulate a Carmine style of imaging, in the third and fourth decades of the *quattrocento* in Florence, that was forged out of the combined interests of the Carmelite friars and the convent's lay patrons. Across a range of representational modes, genres, technologies, and executions, the imaging in the Carmine participated in a "style" that had a strong mimetic and performative component. The Carmine sacred terrain was being mapped out with resonant, tangible, local, and contemporary references.

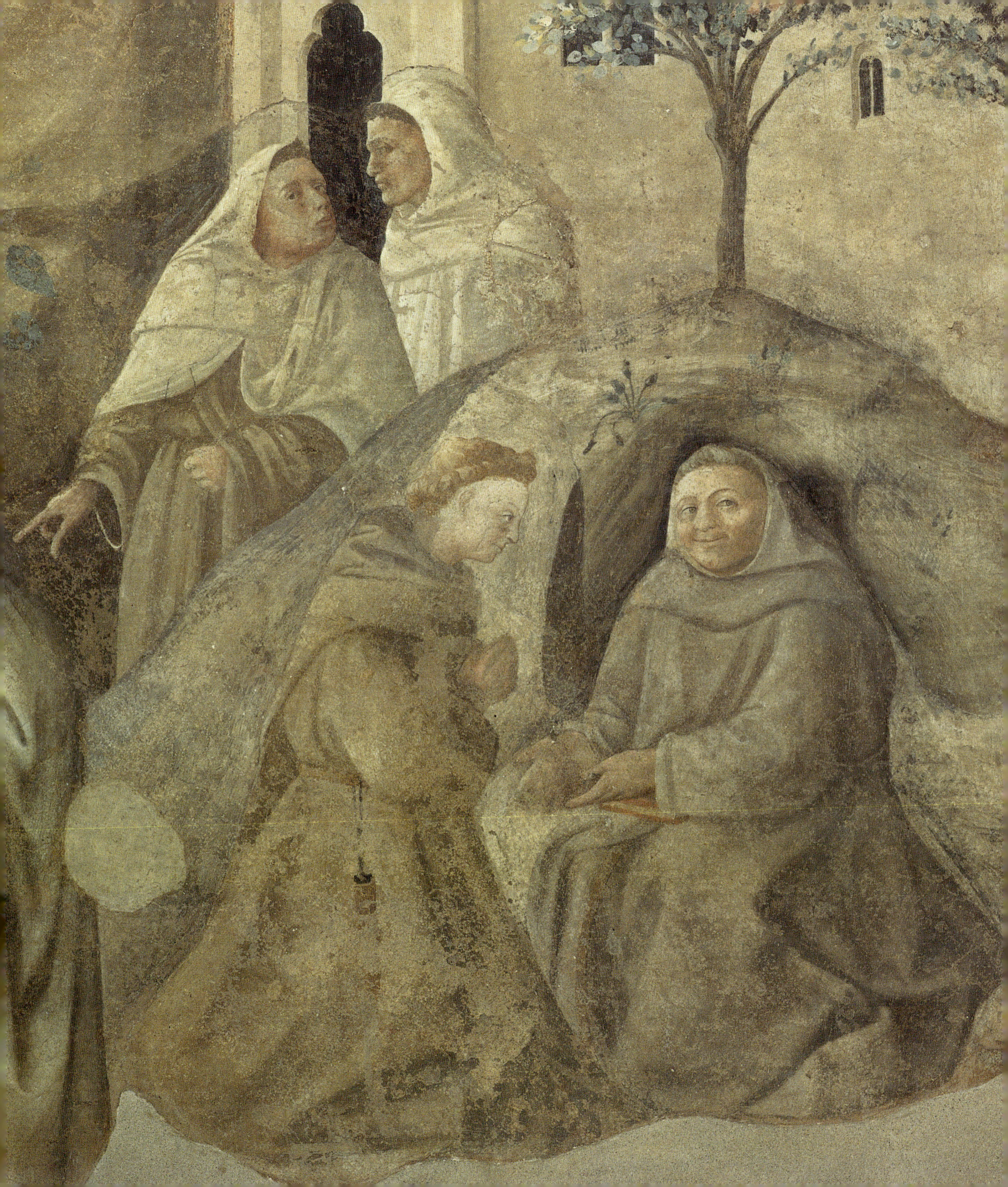

CHAPTER THREE

"FRA FILIPPO DIPINTORE" AND THE EARLY CARMELITE PAINTINGS

There are three paintings attributed to the young Fra Filippo Lippi that display an overt Carmelite iconography – the Empoli *Madonna and Child with Saints and Angels*, the Trivulzio *Madonna of Humility*, and the *Confirmation of the Carmelite Rule*. In this chapter I shall look carefully at these works and analyse the Carmelite content of each. These paintings, however, have not been unanimously accepted as Lippi's. I shall therefore also address the thorny matter of authorship as I work toward defining "Fra Filippo Lippi, the Carmelite painter."

The "early Lippi hand" has been a hybrid construction from the start. During the mid-1930s, both Mario Salmi and Bernard Berenson tackled the problem of identifying Lippi's early work prior to the dated Tarquinia *Madonna and Child* (1437) and they came up with two different oeuvres. Berenson set the stage in his ground-breaking essay "Fra Angelico, Fra Filippo Lippi e la cronologia," in which he demonstrated conclusively that Fra Filippo began painting under the influence of Masaccio and not Fra Angelico, and that his paintings that reflect the style of Fra Angelico date from a later period (around the mid-1440s).[1] With the Masacciesque Tarquinia *Madonna and Child* (see fig. 6) and Barbadori altarpiece (1437–9) (see fig. 103) thus established as the first "autograph" Lippi works, art historians were able to anticipate an earlier Lippi hand, less sure and dependent on Masaccio as a guiding light. Salmi attributed to the young artist the fresco fragment that had come to light in the Carmine cloister in 1860 (see fig. 58), the Trivulzio *Madonna of Humility* (see fig. 53), the Empoli *Madonna and Child with Saints and Angels* (see fig. 51), and a *Madonna and Child with Saints* at Chantilly.[2] Berenson looked for a more subtle and fully developed Masacciesque early Lippi. He pointed to a triptych in Cambridge with the Madonna and Child and a donor with Saints John the Baptist and Ansanus (fig. 46).[3] He rejected the attribution to Lippi of the Carmine fresco and the Empoli picture, identifying them as the work of Domenico Veneziano and Pesellino, respectively.[4] In 1949, a small *Madonna and Child with Saints and Donor* (fig. 47) in the Cini Collection in Venice came to the attention of scholars and, by virtue of its close similarity to the Cambridge painting, it was at once classified as "early Lippi."[5] These two groups, composed of five works in all, have been at the center of the dispute over the "early Lippi hand": first, the Carmine fresco, the Trivulzio *Madonna of Humility*, and the Empoli *Madonna and Child with Saints and Angels* and, second, the Cambridge triptych and the Cini *Madonna and Child with Saints*. Recently proposed as additions to the second group are a small panel of *St. John the Evangelist* (fig. 48) and an altarpiece fragment with Saint Catherine of Alexandria and an Evangelist in Lyon.[6]

Those art historians who accept all these works as belonging to Filippo Lippi (Marchini, Boskovits, and Berti and Paolucci) construct Lippi's artistic development as follows: a pre-Paduan juvenile period from about 1430 to 1434, during which the uneven and naive Empoli, Trivulzio, and Carmine images were painted, followed by a maturation period from the middle of the decade to 1437, during which the artist executed the Cambridge and Cini panels.[7] Curtis Shell rejected outright the first group of images, ascribing them to a "Prato Master" whom he considered a Lippi imitator painting in the 1440s.[8] Keith Christiansen also had reservations concerning this first group. He imagined a lost, quite accomplished early Lippi work that was the inspiration for Domenico di Bartolo's *Madonna of Humility* (1433; see fig. 11), and that was painted in a manner close to the refined style of the *St. John the Evangelist* panel, around 1432. If the Carmine fresco and the Empoli and Trivulzio panels are to be considered Lippi's, he felt that they must date from the previous decade (1421–32) when the painter was significantly less facile.[9] Jeffrey Ruda supports this latter view in his 1993 monograph on Lippi. While he finds the stylistic divergence between the two "early Lippi" groupings problematic, he concludes that they are "arguably the work of a single 'hand,' but a hand that seems to have been directed by two minds."[10] He pushes back

45 Filippo Lippi, *Confirmation of the Carmelite Rule*, detail of fig. 59, with four Carmelites in a desert hermitage.

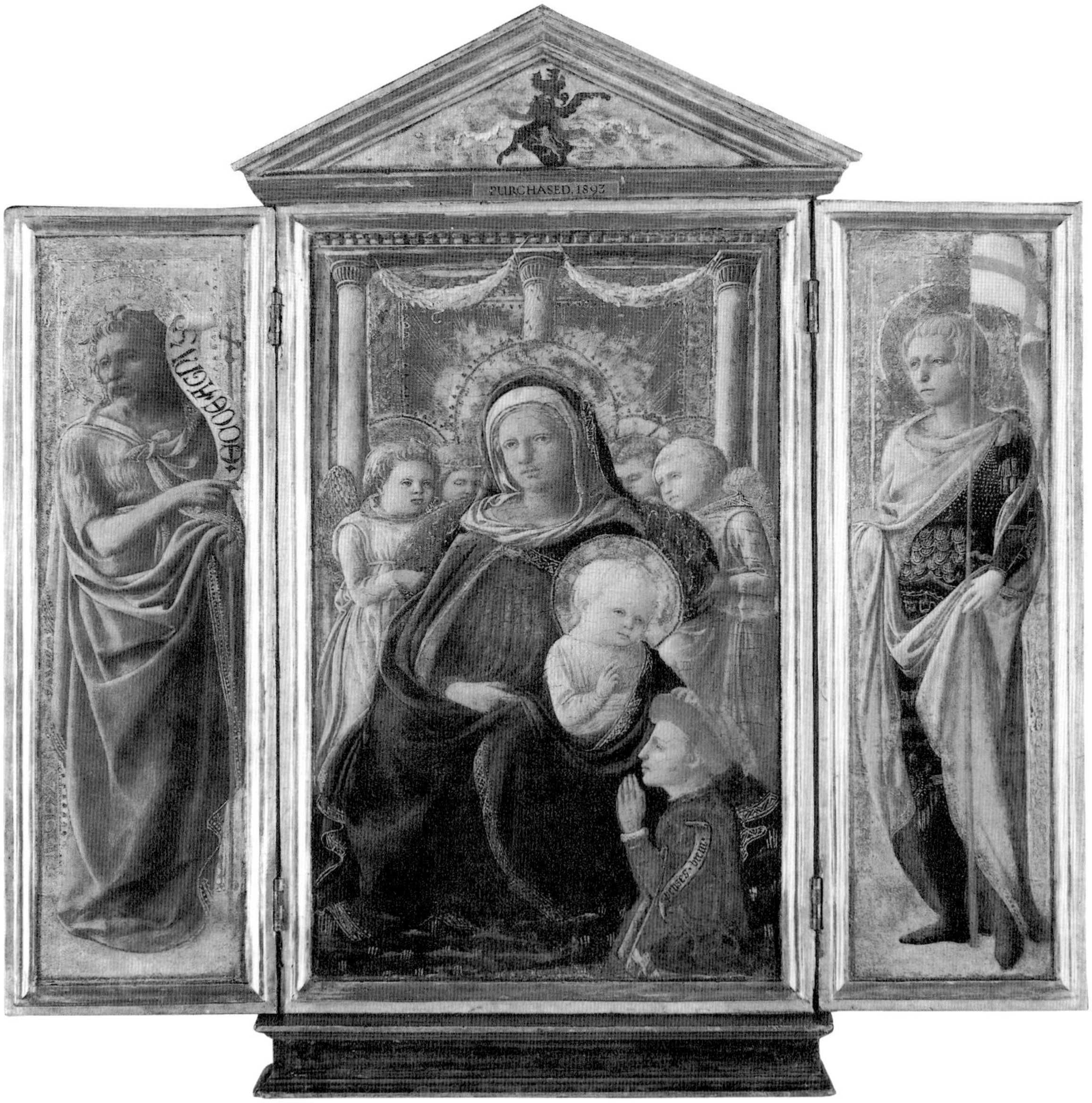

46 Filippo Lippi, *Madonna and Child with Donor and Sts. John the Baptist and (?) Ansanus*, c. 1435, Cambridge, Fitzwilliam Museum.

all of them to the mid- to late 1420s, suggesting that the earlier group (the Carmine fresco, the Trivulzio *Madonna of Humility*, and the Empoli panel) were executed under the influence of Masaccio's activity in the Carmine, while the second group he considers reflective of a subsequent exposure to the International Gothic style. Ruda then proposes an additional body of works for the early to mid-1430s.[11]

The three paintings that constitute the first grouping of "early Lippi works" described above have Carmelite subjects. This obviously makes their attribution to Fra Filippo particularly appealing for my purposes. I shall try, however, to keep the question of authorship somewhat open as I explore the Carmelite imagery in each of the paintings.

* * *

THE EMPOLI *MADONNA AND CHILD WITH SAINTS AND ANGELS*

The Empoli panel (fig. 51) takes off from a type of small-scale devotional image made popular by Bernardo Daddi in the previous century, with saints and angels stacked on either side of the Virgin and Child enthroned.[12] It is, however, considerably more animated than *trecento* renditions. An angel kneels down Annunciation-style before the little Christ Child (who is more head and halo than body) and offers him a (now barely discernible) flower. Angels play music. Saints displaying their attributes gather round. Bartholomew and Michael are most prominently placed, visible in full-figure in the foreground. St. Michael performs the important eye-catching gaze out of the pictorial space at the viewer, offering himself as the vehicle through which the devotee can enter into the other, pictured realm.

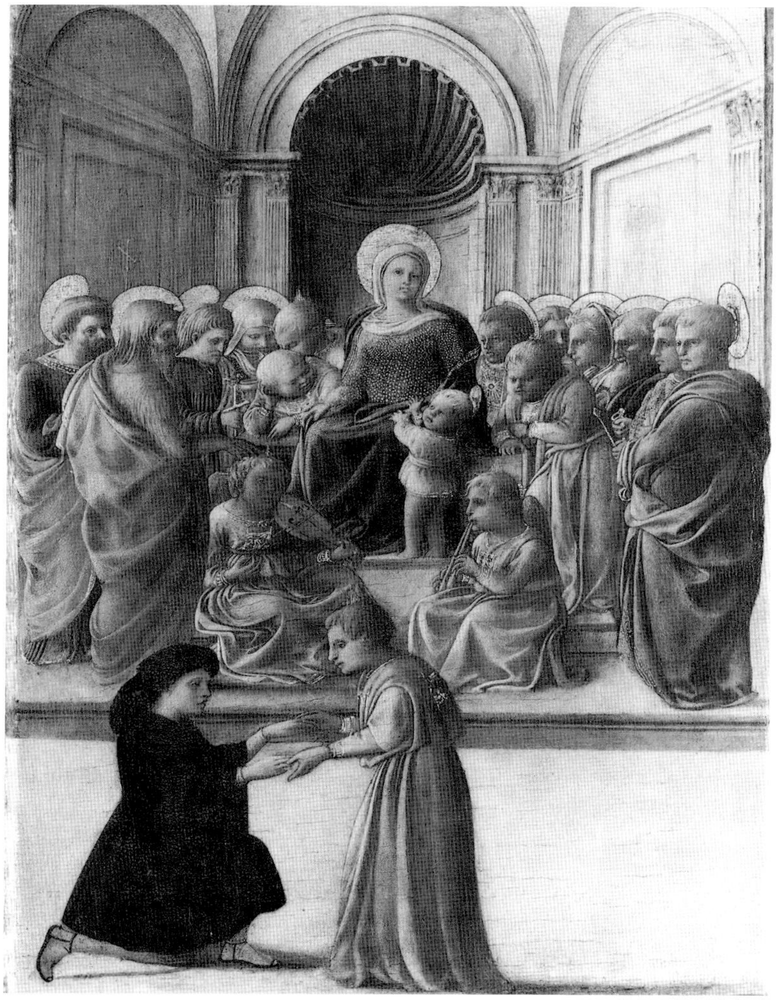

47 Filippo Lippi, *Madonna and Child with Saints, Angels, and Donor*, c. 1435, Venice, Vittorio Cini Collection.

This is an uneven picture, with moments of brilliant insight and some extremely weak passages. The compositional scheme is ingenious and striking. It is reminiscent of some of Fra Angelico's early stepped compositions. The artist has striven to convey the illusion of pictorial space.[13] The arrangement of the figures is plotted carefully to give the impression that angels and saints are assembled in a continuous circle around the enthroned Virgin. But this is an illusion contrived for the viewer's eye. According to the rational construction of the picture space, the figures are assembled in two groups – one in the relative foreground, composed of Sts. Michael and Bartholomew and the two music-making angels, and a second group in the background, on the upper steps and dais, composed of St. Alberto and the angels who form an arc around the Virgin's throne. Now that the picture has been restored and the original framing configuration been made more apparent, it is possible to envision how the frame with the three arches – the outer two slanting inward – was intended to give the impression of a three-dimensional tabernacle front that "casts" the upper regions of the pictured background in shadow.

Also satisfying in the painting are the raking light and cast shadows, the sense of space created by the red cloth above the throne, and the arbitrary fall of the framing boss, slicing through the halo of an angel and counteracted by the angel's upturned gaze.[14] Certain modeling passages are also delicate and marvelous, such as the folds of St. Bartholomew's cape and the wonderful bird-wings of the angel in the left foreground.[15] Less adept are the angel wings scratched into the gold leaf (in one case, the incised lines of a misconceived wing are visible beneath the painted wings). Hands are a disaster, and most successful when hidden. The throne doesn't make sense: one doesn't know where the seat begins and the back separates from the arms. And there is no dramatic economy to lend some order to the many things that are happening in the picture. It is as though the painter had succeeded in gathering the figures together in a common pictorial space and then failed to bring them under control. The aim, it appears, was to concentrate attention on the Virgin, the Christ Child, and the viewer, but it is not realized

48 Filippo Lippi, *St. John the Evangelist*, c. 1435, Princeton, The Barbara Piasecka Johnson Collection.

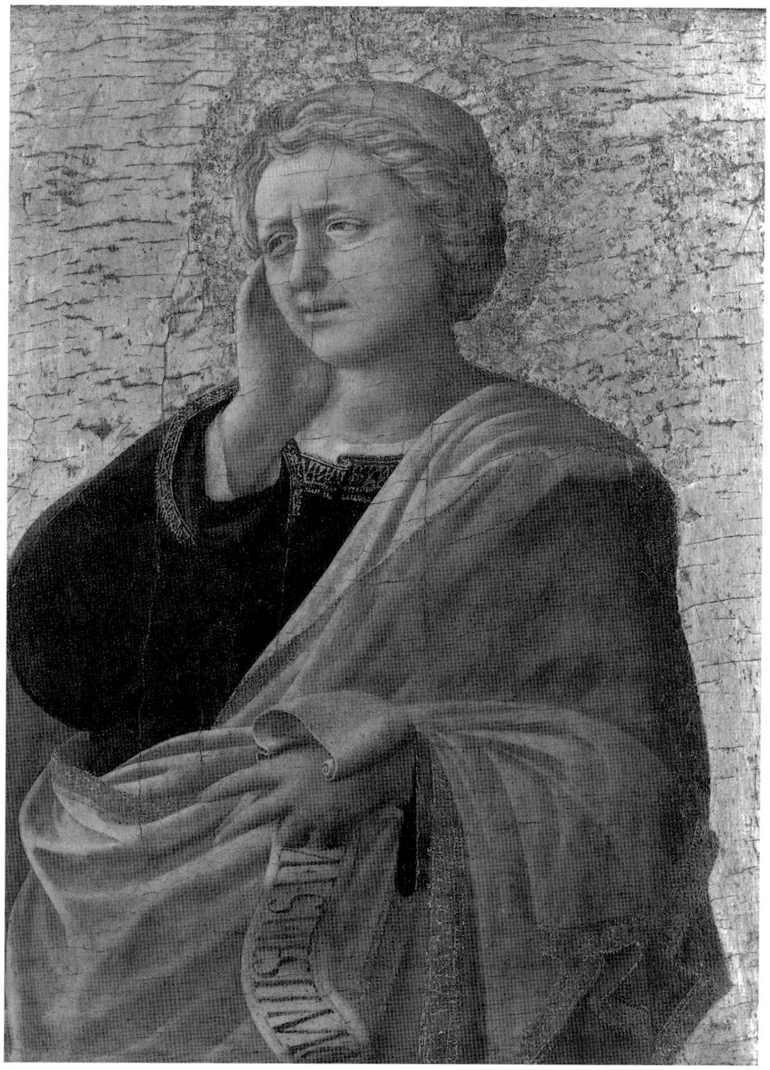

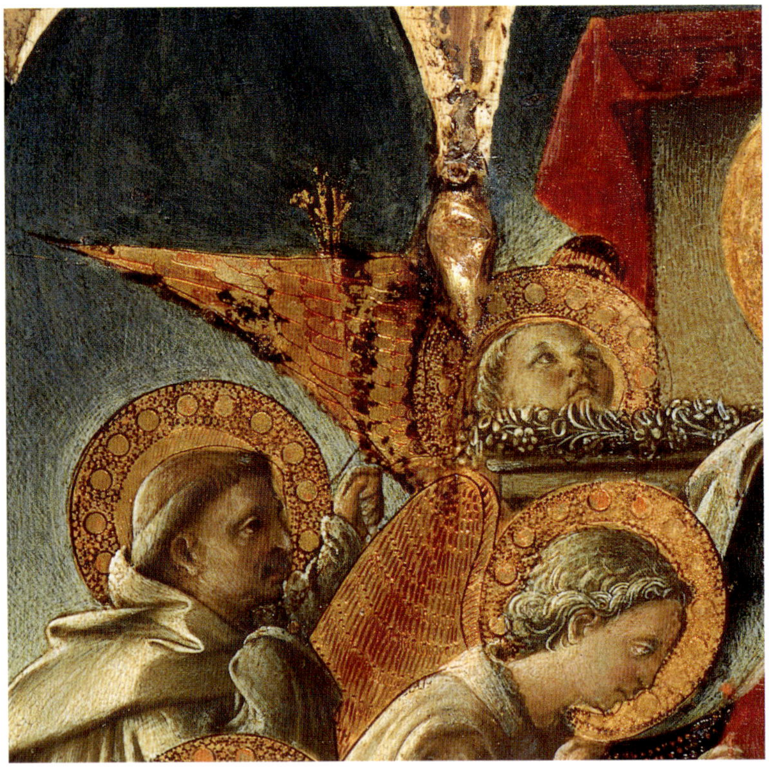

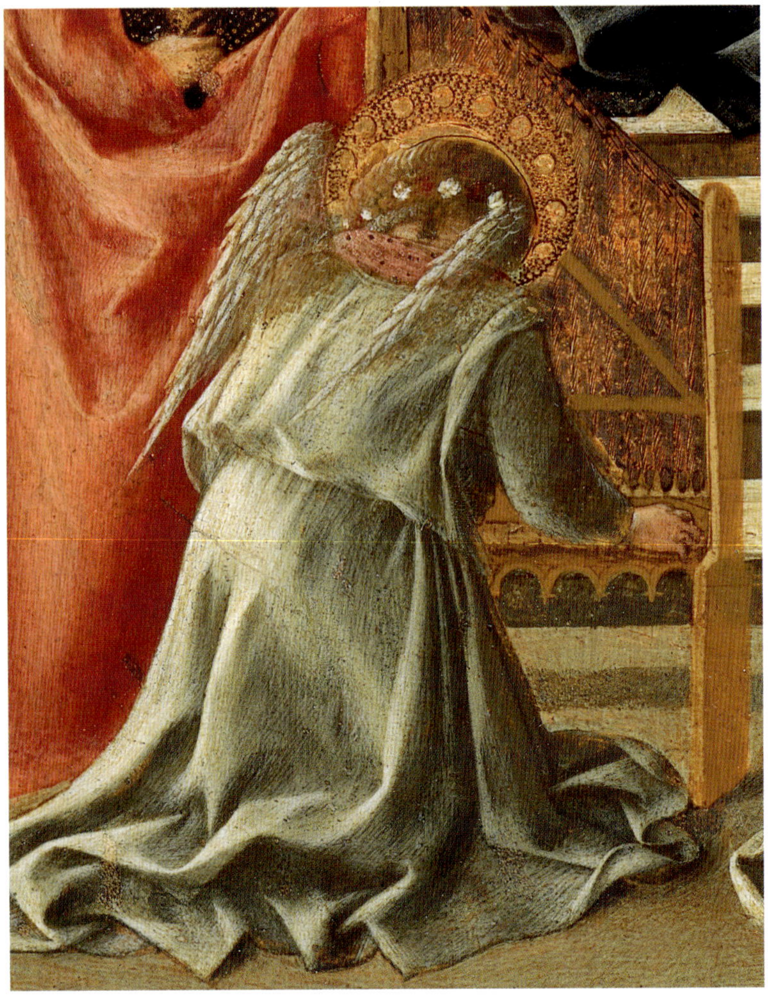

in the execution. The picture has many of the Lippi hallmarks in embryonic form – the pleated folds of the angel's robe as it falls to the ground in the left foreground, the simulated stone carving, accented with highlights, that seems too lively, the inclusion of a figure that looks out at the viewer, the overlapping and subsequent cancellation of figures, and an interest in the relationship between the frame, the pictorial space, and the viewer's space. However, the overall effect is that of a not too accomplished youthful work.

It is the presence of St. Alberto of Trapani which places the picture immediately within a Carmelite milieu.[16] St. Alberto, as described in the previous chapter, was a thirteenth-century Sicilian Carmelite who, by the early fifteenth century, was venerated in Sicily and in Carmelite churches throughout Europe.[17] The Carmelite general chapter ordered that Alberto's feast day be celebrated in 1411, and in 1420 each Carmelite chapter was instructed to display an image of Alberto within the convent. Relics of Alberto belonged to the Florentine Carmine, and a confraternity dedicated to him was formed there in 1419. Within this atmosphere of the burgeoning cult the Empoli devotional image was commissioned and painted.[18]

St. Alberto is clearly not the principal saint represented: Sts. Michael and Bartholomew, positioned in the foreground space, take precedence in the hierarchic presentation. Alberto, however, is given particular attention by the artist. Holding his lily high, he alone of the three saints depicted lifts his eyes to the Virgin in special devotion. And the Virgin, staring off to the left, seems to be looking at his lily.[19] The position of St. Alberto, beside the angel offering a flower to the Christ Child, also gives him some access to the inner sanctum where the Virgin and Child are situated. This is a privilege denied the other saints, who stand at the bottom of the stairs at a distance from the Virgin and Child. Another telling Carmelite – or more appropriately, Carmine – characteristic of the work is the evident influence of Masaccio's Brancacci chapel frescos. The figure of St. Bartholomew bears a marked resemblance to Masaccio's figure of St. Peter distributing alms, and there is an additional similarity to Masaccio's general modeling and treatment of light. The artist of the Empoli panel was also looking closely at other works by Masaccio. The two angels in the foreground with their backs to the viewer are very similar to the angels in the central panel of Masaccio's 1422 San Giovenale triptych (see fig. 52), particularly in the figure positions and in the modeling of the lower skirts of their robes.[20]

Whoever commissioned the work would seem to have been patrons of the Carmine, perhaps members of the Compagnia di Sant'Alberto, with a particular devotion to Sts. Michael and Bartholomew. I place this work very early in Fra Filippo Lippi's painting practice – and the dating depends upon when Lippi

49 and 50 Filippo Lippi, *Madonna and Child with Saints and Angels*, details of fig. 51.

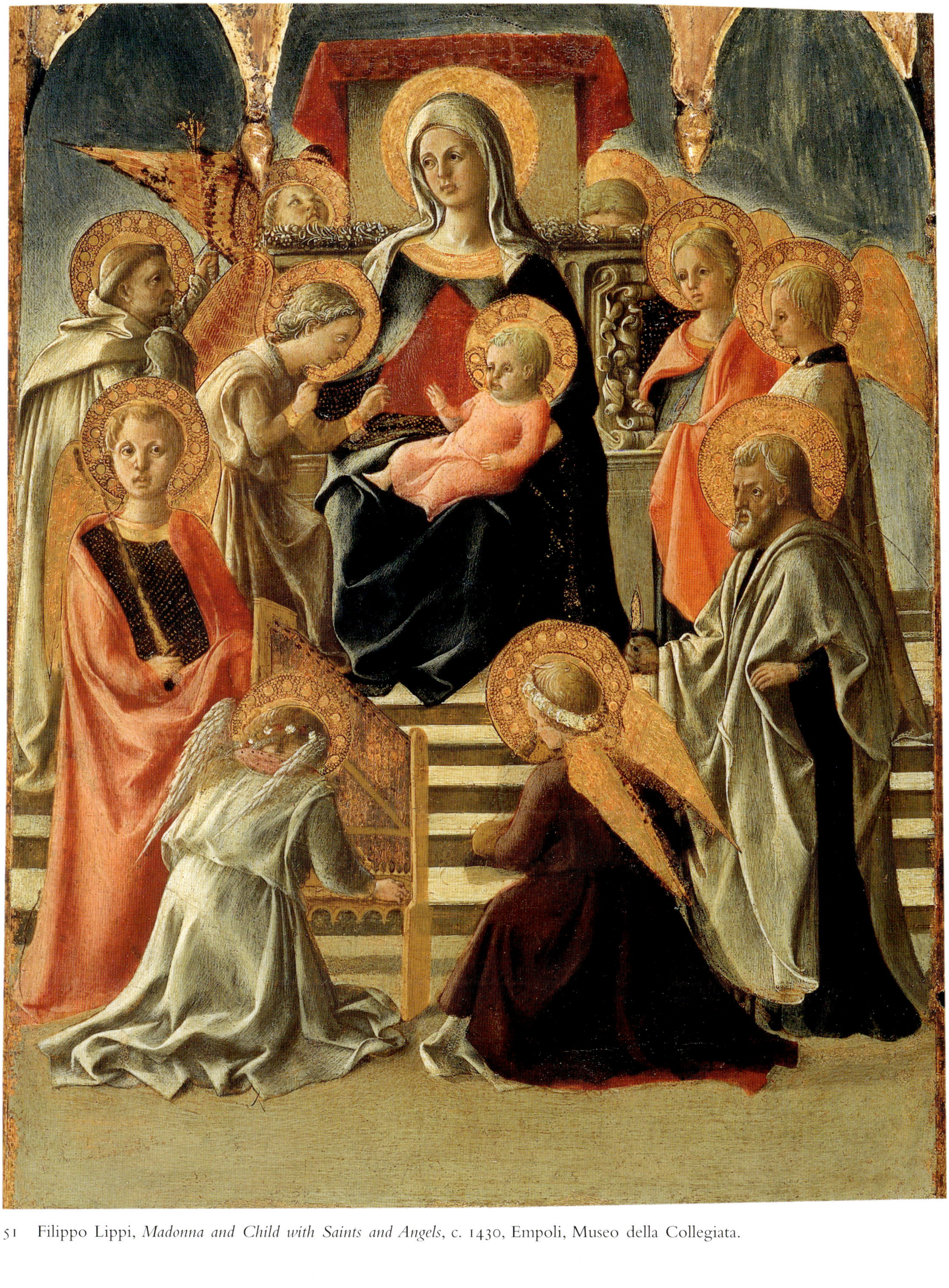

51 Filippo Lippi, *Madonna and Child with Saints and Angels*, c. 1430, Empoli, Museo della Collegiata.

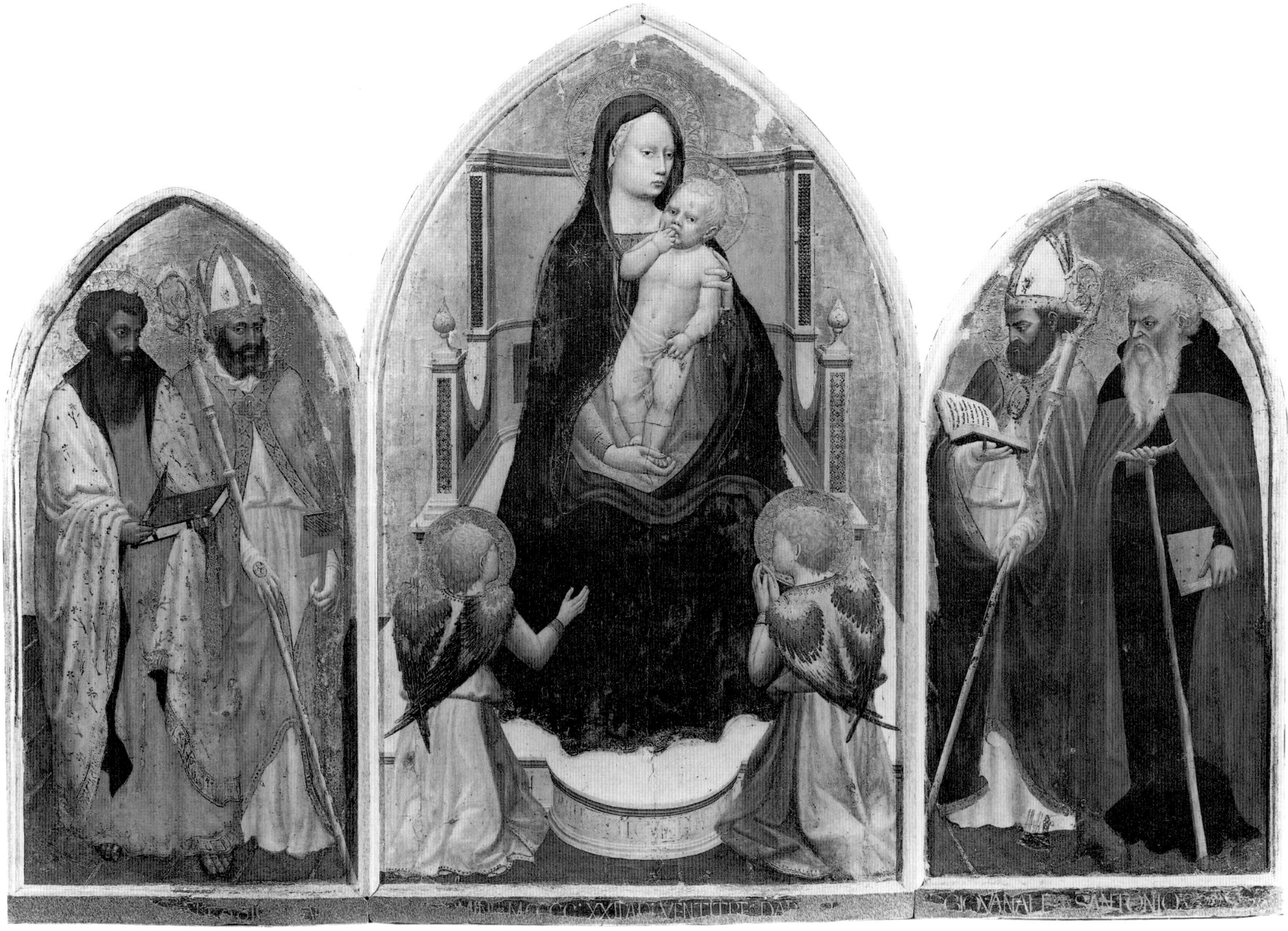

52 Masaccio, San Giovenale triptych, 1422, Cascia (Reggello), San Giovenale.

began to paint: some time between 1424 (three years after his profession as a Carmelite) and January, 1431, when Lippi is referred to as "dipintore" for the first time in the Carmine books. The evident debt to Masaccio's work in the Brancacci chapel suggests a date after 1427–28.

THE TRIVULZIO *MADONNA OF HUMILITY*

St. Alberto appears again in the Trivulzio *Madonna of Humility* (fig. 53), along with St. Angelo of Licata, an elderly female saint, and six youths dressed in white, all encircling the Virgin and Child.[21] The large gable-shaped panel seems to have been intended as an altarpiece – again, following a *trecento* model like the "Giottino" *Lamentation* in the Uffizi and the Umbro-Tuscan early fourteenth-century *Lamentation* in Pistoia. The picture space is compressed, and the pediment shape seems to exert a pressure upon the eleven figures, forcing them to sit, kneel, and crouch close together in the cramped, shallow space. Flowering plants grow in the small opening in the center foreground – a pink rose, a red rose, and what may be lily of the valley. The painting is not in very good condition, having suffered significant paint loss, particularly along the horizontal seams of the three wooden planks and at the edges where a later framing element was once superimposed on the panel. There is extensive damage running across the center of the picture, through the head of the Christ Child, the face of the child at the left and the hands of St. Alberto, which consequently have little to do with the lily he is supposed to be clutching.

In fact, the picture surface is so abraded that it is difficult to detect the continuity of the artist's hand, much less confirm the identity of that hand as that of the young Lippi. The facial mod-

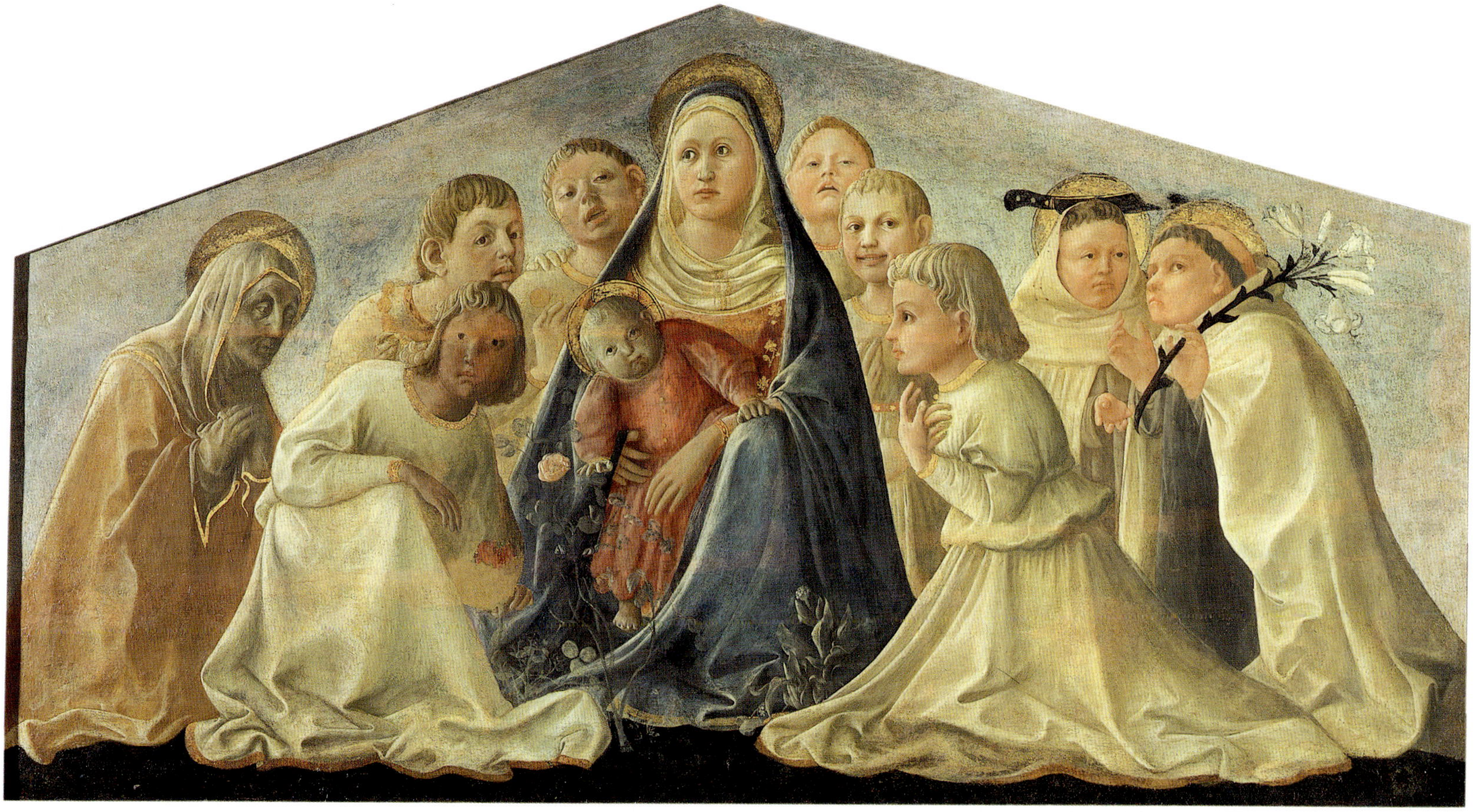

53 Filippo Lippi, *Madonna of Humility* (the Trivulzio *Madonna*), c. 1430–34, Milan, Castello Sforzesco.

eling seems too broad and the features too large and frozen into fixed expressions for Lippi. However, some areas are reminiscent of Lippi's mature style – the transparency of the female saint's veil and the shimmering highlights picked up in her orange cloak, the delicate pattern on the Virgin's veil and dress, the strange hydrocephalic physiognomy of the Christ Child's head, the classic Lippi sausage-fingers and toes, and the treatment of the middle child on the left who looks out, resting his hand on the shoulder of his companion. There is the extensive use of white highlight so familiar in early Lippi, the painted black line defining the profile of the child kneeling to the right of the Virgin, and the intense engagement between the painted figures and the viewer, secured through their direct gazes out of the picture. And, finally, there is the peculiar and self-conscious exhibit of *difficultà* seen in the foreshortened faces of the children at the back, and somewhat more perversely, in St. Angelo's halo visible through the perforation in the hilt of the knife resting in his scalp.

The combination of the early Filippo Lippi manner, the presence of the two Carmelite "saints" and the Florentine provenance of the picture (it passed from the Florentine Rinuccini family to the Trivulzio collection in 1831) have encouraged art historians to place the picture in the ambience of Santa Maria del Carmine in the late 1420s or early 1430s. There was an altar dedicated to St. Alberto in an oratory belonging to the Compagnia di Sant'Alberto in the cemetery to the left of the church, founded in 1419,[22] and an image of St. Alberto above this altar by at least 1495.[23] A second altar dedicated to St. Alberto was established beneath one of the arches of the *ponte* in the church of Santa Maria del Carmine by Paolo di Lorenzo Dieciaiuti (1405–c. 1473) at an unknown date.[24] This patron was personally acquainted with Fra Filippo Lippi, serving as his notary in the 1440s and 1450s. There is reference to an image above this altar when the *ponte* was taken down in 1568.[25] There was also an altar dedicated to St. Angelo di Licata beneath one of the arches of the *ponte*, founded by the friars of the convent, once again at an unknown date.[26] It would be most attractive to associate the Trivulzio *Madonna of Humility* with any one of these three Carmine altars.

It has been suggested that the painting was intended for the altar in the oratory of the Compagnia di Sant'Alberto which had *fanciulli* (young boys) as members.[27] If one accepts this proposal, some of the more uncomfortable, awkward aspects of the image begin to seem like very ingenious innovations. The squat proportions of the painting and the juvenile emotivity expressed by the saints and children depicted would thus be explained by the fact that one of its primary audiences was the body of *fanciulli* members of the Confraternity of St. Alberto.

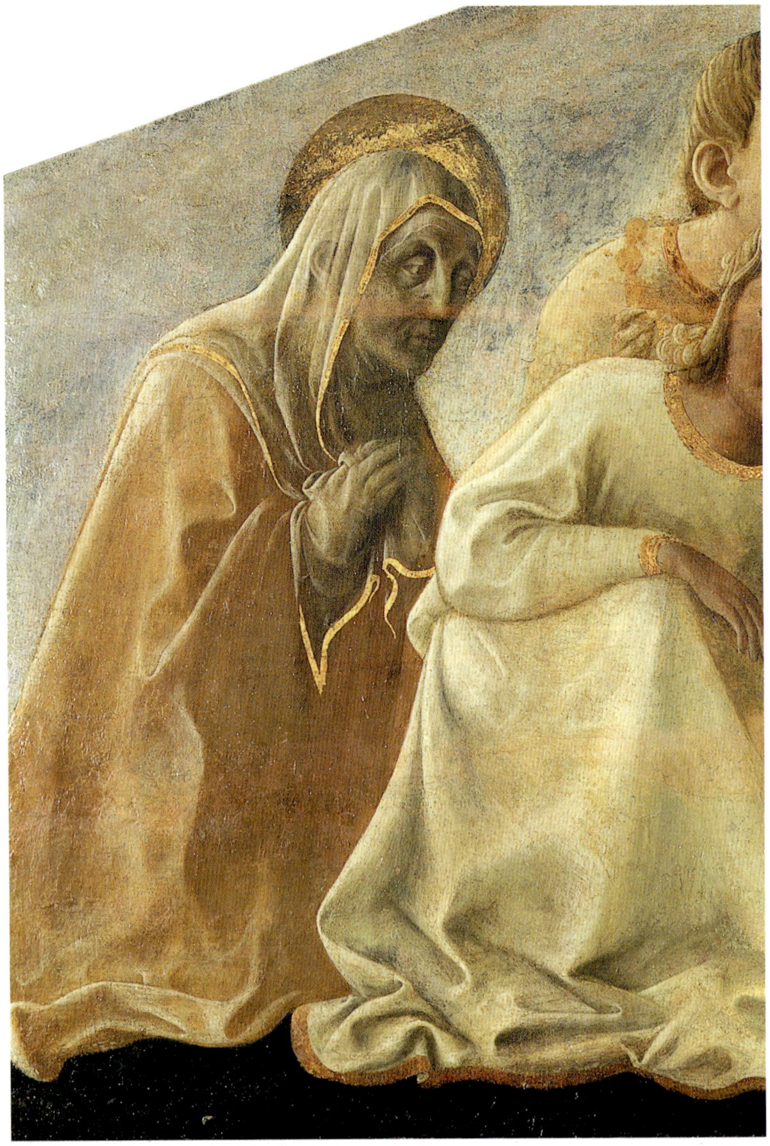

54 Filippo Lippi, *Madonna of Humility*, detail of fig. 53, with St. Anne.

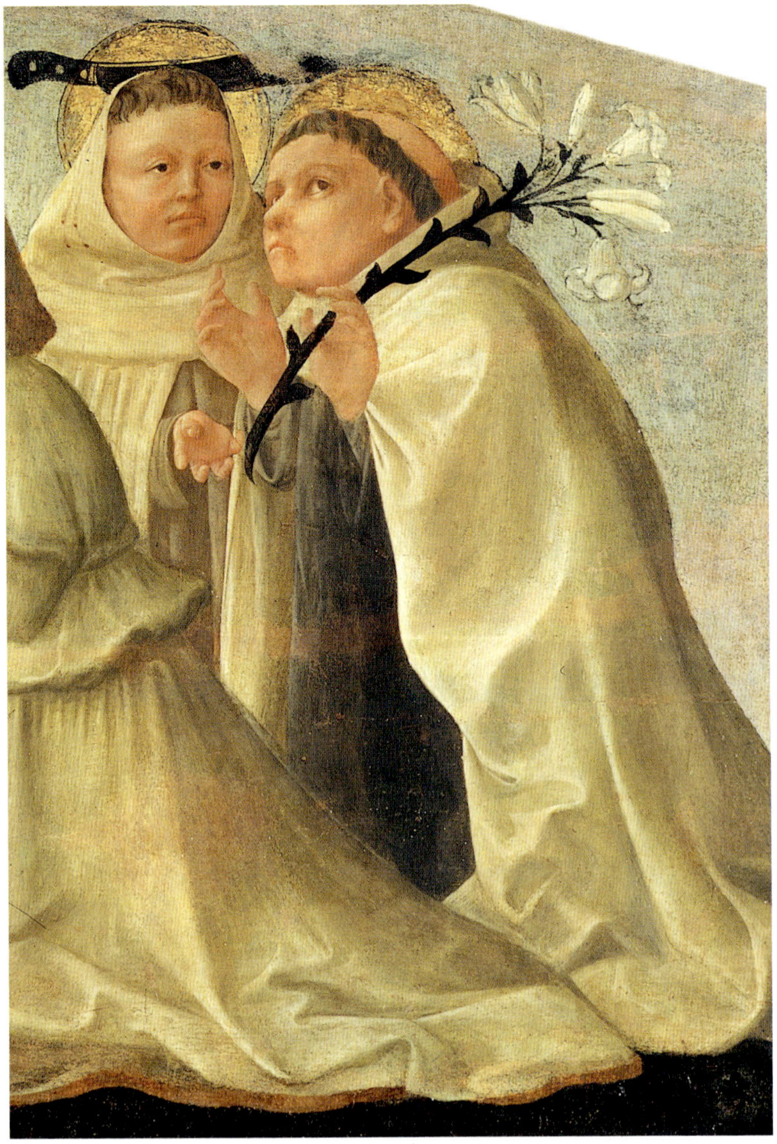

55 Filippo Lippi, *Madonna of Humility*, detail of fig. 53, with Sts. Angelo and Alberto.

The six children who gather round the Virgin and Child could thus be representatives of this confraternity.

The prospect of an altarpiece that included representations – not necessarily portraits but idealized representations – of the young boys who belonged to the Compagnia di Sant'Alberto is not completely out of line with the representational practices in the Carmine at the time. In Masaccio's *St. Peter in Cathedra in Antioch* (see fig. 66) and Masolino's *St. Peter Preaching* (see fig. 65) in the Brancacci chapel, contemporary Carmelites and laymen are included as witnesses. These scenes were painted on wall spaces, however. A representation above an altar – therefore much more directly involved in the mass – was governed by a stricter decorum than images placed in other spaces within the church and convent. If the *Madonna of Humility* does represent such *fanciulli*, then the artist succeeded in getting around the problem of depicting contemporary figures in such intimate proximity to holy figures in an altarpiece without recourse to traditional conventions, like the *Madonna della Misericordia* or diminutive supplicating donor figures, by playing with certain visual and cultural associations. Little boys are *innocenti*; they are angelic, like angels. At first glance one automatically endows the *fanciulli* with their sweet, open faces and their tunics of white and gold with the very wings and halos which are so surprisingly absent at second glance. Both Carmelite and Carmine beholders would have had ready references for these little boys like angels. In the Ascension play held each year in Santa Maria del Carmine, there were "little children who represent angels."[28] In Carmelite literature, the early desert followers of the Carmelite founder Elijah – the "Children of the Prophets" – were compared to angels: in their "joyfulness and humility . . . modesty and obedience . . . they didn't seem to be men but angels."[29]

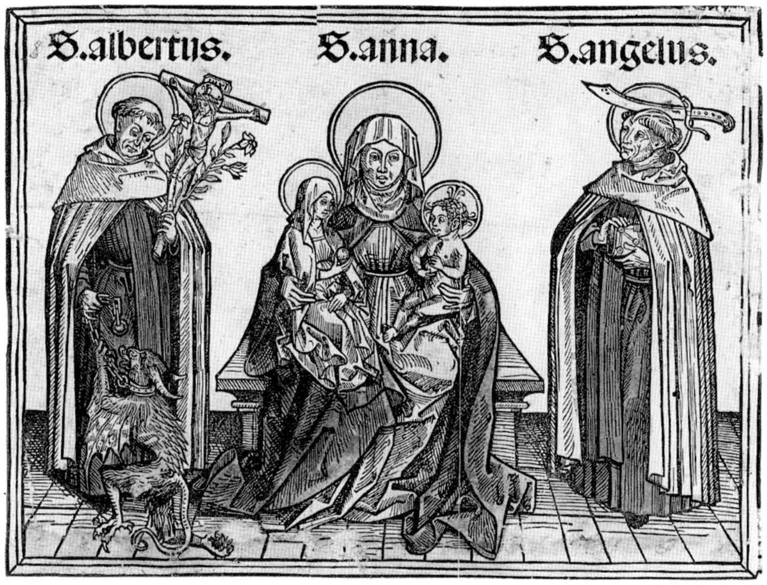

56 German, *St. Anne with the Virgin and Child and Sts. Alberto and Angelo*, c. 1500, woodcut, Bamberg, Staatsbibliothek (VI.Aa.26).

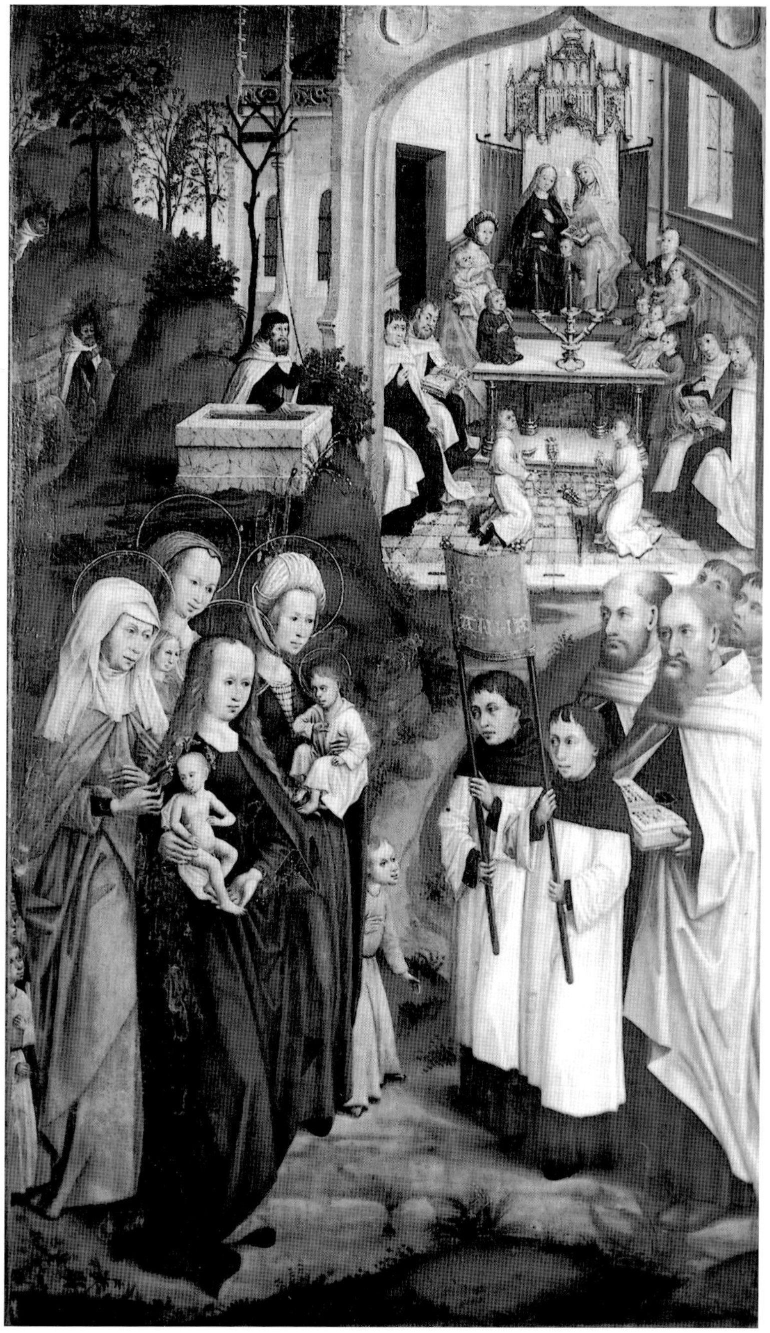

57 Flemish, *St. Anne with the Three Marys and their Children Visiting the Carmelite Oratory by the Fountain of Elijah on Mt. Carmel*, c. 1490, detail from the St. Anne polyptych, Frankfort am Main, Historisches Museum.

Upon closer examination, the Carmelite iconography in the Trivulzio *Madonna of Humility* turns out to be more extensive than the mere presence of the two Carmelite *beati*. The flower imagery and the presence of St. Anne both have Carmelite resonance. The carefully rendered and differentiated flowering plants that grow out of the earth at the feet of the Virgin reflect a Carmelite tradition of associating the Virgin and the Prophet Elijah with flowers and vines, symbolizing the insemination and flowering of the Carmelite Order. A famous example – and one that would have been known to a Carmelite in the early *quattrocento* – is found in the first two lines of Simon Stock's prayer to the Virgin: "Flos Carmeli, Vitis florigera" (Flower of Carmel, Flowering vine).[30] Some thirty-five years after the Trivulzio *Madonna* was painted, Nicola Calciuri, a Sicilian Carmelite cloistered at Santa Maria del Carmine, developed an elaborate cycle of sermons using a floral scheme of seven roses and their three leaves, "Li Fioriti dello sancto Monte Carmelo."[31]

The identity of the female saint at the left has been disputed, but I see no reason not to associate her with the aged St. Anne, the Virgin's mother.[32] There is a German woodcut of c. 1500 (fig. 56) associated with the Carmelites of Bamberg which depicts the Virgin and Child with Sts. Anne, Angelo, and Alberto together, following a more traditional iconographic convention where the diminutive Virgin sits on her mother's lap.[33] St. Anne was of particular significance to the Carmelites who were chiefly responsible for the propagation of her cult. The feast of St. Anne was accorded a *duplex* in the Ordinal of Sibert de Beka (1312). According to Carmelite legend, St. Anne's parents had lived on Mount Carmel. Her mother, Emerentiana, brought the young Anne to the Carmelite hermits when seeking advice about whether Anne should marry. These claims are wonderfully illustrated in the polyptych *The Legend of St. Anne* (c. 1490), originally in a chapel dedicated to St. Anne in the Carmelite church in Frankfurt. In one of the panels, Emerentiana is shown presenting St. Anne to the Carmelite hermits, while in another (fig. 57), Anne and her daughters – the apocryphal three Marys – with their babes in arm, are shown visiting the Carmelites on Mount Carmel.[34] By the mid-*trecento*, the Carmelites were claiming to have been on hand during the miraculous events surrounding the birth of the Virgin. They claimed to have founded a convent dedicated to St. Anne during the first century

AD on the very site where the Virgin had been born. They had a second convent in Jerusalem just outside the Golden Gate, where St. Anne met her husband Joachim upon his return to the city, often considered to be the site of the Virgin's immaculate conception.[35] St. Anne, as the mother of the Virgin, would also have had a special appeal to the *fanciulli* members of the Compagnia di Sant'Alberto.[36]

The Trivulzio *Madonna of Humility* seems to come out of a well-informed Carmelite ambience. It represents Carmelite issues that were of particular concern to the Order from about 1420 to 1460. In addition, like the Empoli panel, the Trivulzio painting bears a strong debt to Masaccio. The pyramidal composition of the Virgin and Child, with the elderly St. Anne nearby, is reminiscent of Masaccio's *Virgin and Child with St. Anne*, while the modeling of the pleats at the lower edge of the robes worn by the saints and children is similar to that found in the angels' robes of the San Giovenale triptych (see fig. 52).[37] The poor condition of the painting makes it difficult to determine confidently its authorship, but the Carmelite iconography and the strong influence of Masaccio point to the young friar. If one accepts as Fra Filippo's the other two paintings that are stylistically similar – the Empoli *Madonna and Child with Saints and Angels* and the Carmine *Confirmation of the Carmelite Rule* – then it would follow that this panel too was painted by the young Carmelite.

THE *CONFIRMATION OF THE CARMELITE RULE*

In Vasari's life of Lippi, he notes that at Santa Maria del Carmine the painter "wrought in terra-verde in the cloister close to the Consecration painted by Masaccio, a Pope confirming the Rule of the Carmelites."[38] A fresco considered to be the one described by Vasari was discovered in 1860, beneath a layer of plaster along the wall in the cloister of the convent (fig. 58).[39]

58 View of the cloister (remodelled in 1598–1612), Florence, Santa Maria del Carmine (photograph taken before the removal of Filippo Lippi's fresco in 1939).

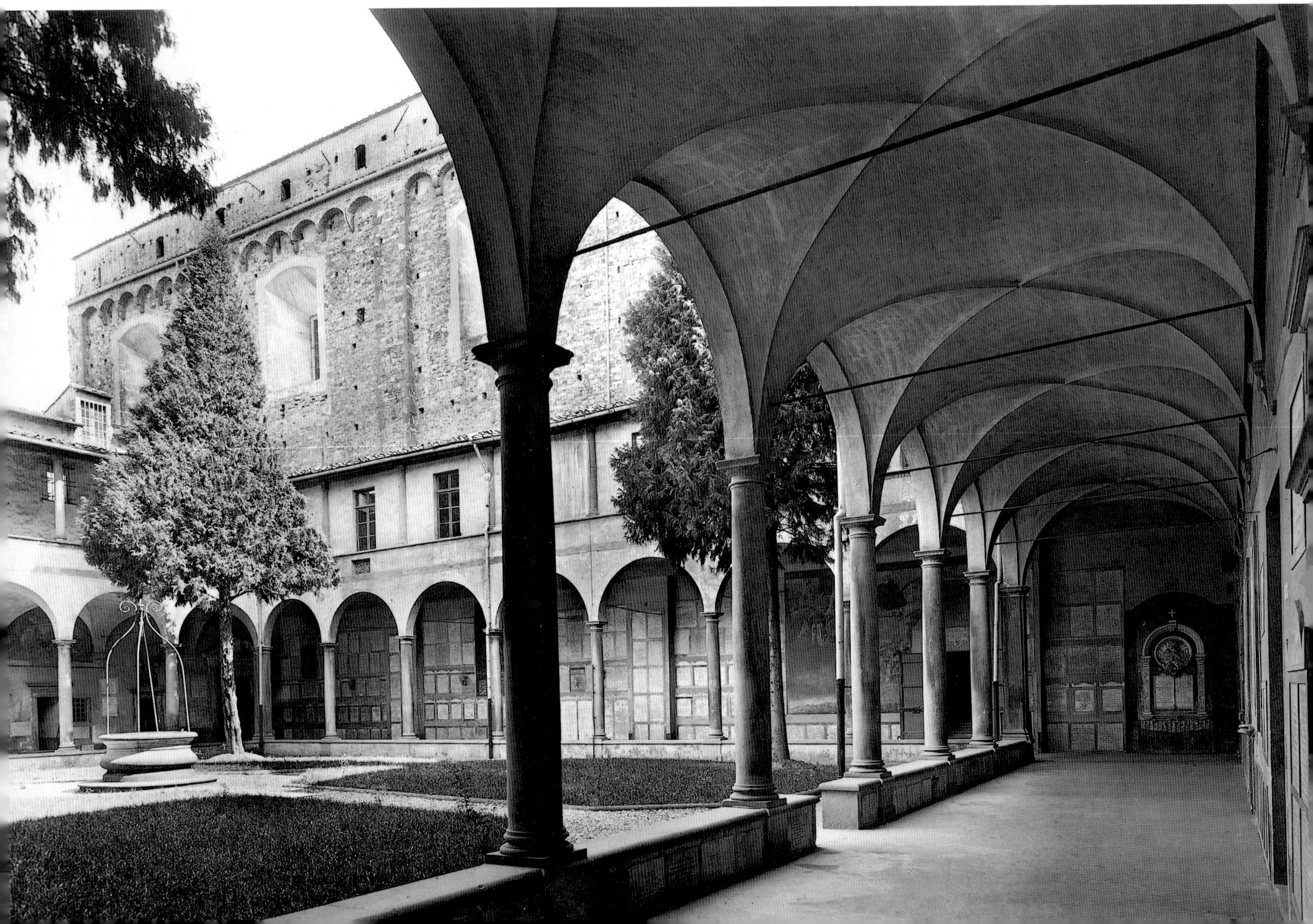

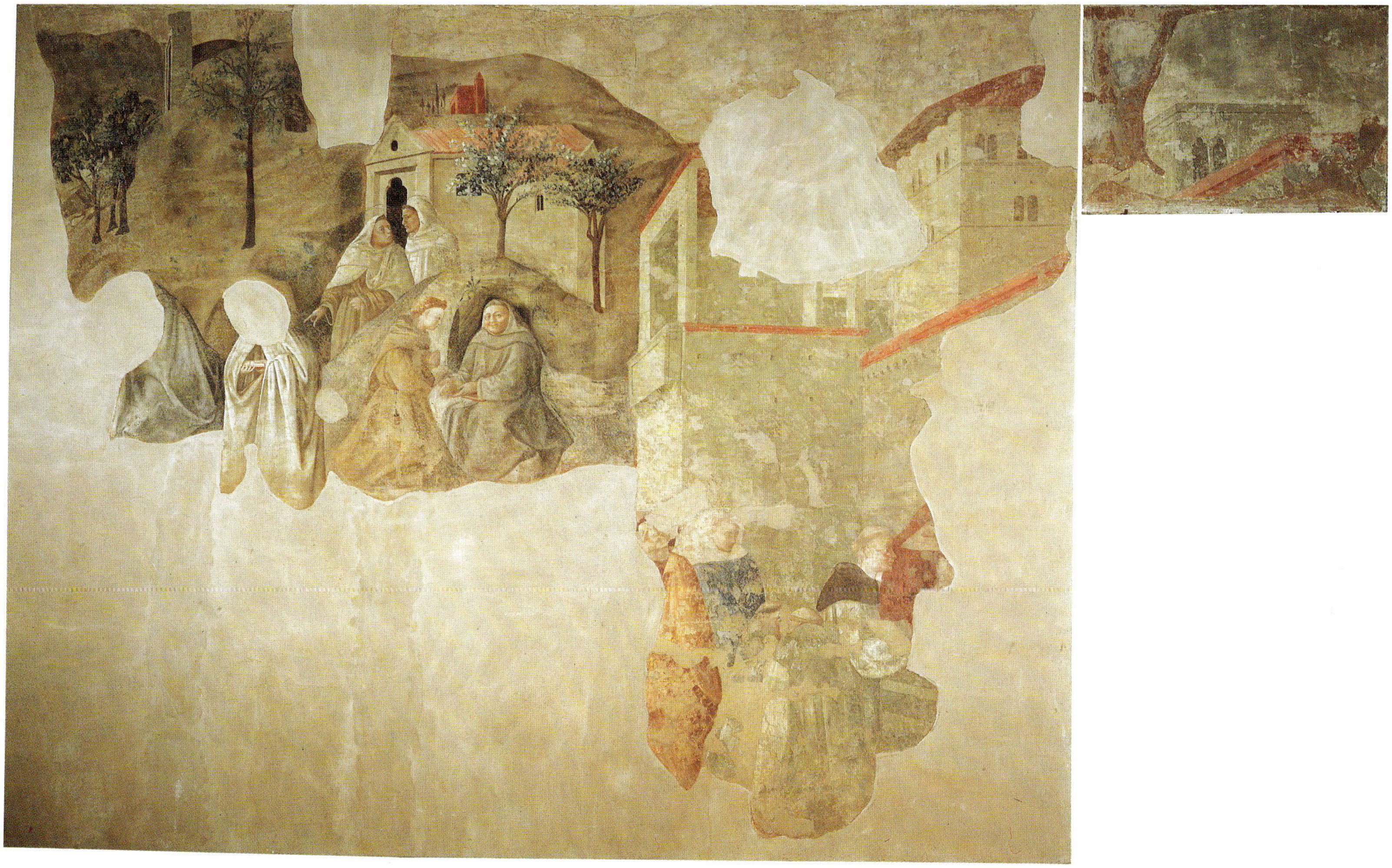

59 Filippo Lippi, *Confirmation of the Carmelite Rule*, c. 1430–34, detached fresco from the square cloister, Florence, Santa Maria del Carmine.

The fresco (fig. 59) is in fragmentary condition, with probably less than half of the original composition visible.[40] Vasari identifies the subject as the Confirmation of the Carmelite Rule, and there does indeed seem to be some sort of Carmelite embassy making its way toward an urban center where other ecclesiastics and monks congregate in the lower-right corner of the image. The art historian Giovanni Poggi, in an effort to date the fresco, suggested that it commemorates not the original confirmation of the Rule, but the mitigation approved by Pope Eugenius IV with a papal bull of 1432.[41] Miklòs Boskovits convincingly refuted Poggi's theory and argued that it represents an episode from the earlier history of the Order, either the confirmation of the Rule, as Vasari claimed, the approval of the white Carmelite mantle in 1287, or the first mitigation of the Rule in 1247 when the Order moved west.[42]

Whatever the subject of this scene, it is important to note that it occupies only the right third of the fresco composition, and that at least as much space is devoted to the antics of numerous hermits dispersed across a landscape. This has inspired some to suggest a "Tebaide" subject akin to that in the Uffizi attributed to Gherardo Starnina or the young Fra Angelico.[43] Boskovits, however, has offered an interpretation with a more overt Carmelite theme. He identifies the figures in the landscape as the Carmelite hermits who lived in the Holy Land in ancient times, during "a primordial phase in the history of the Order, prior to its transfer from Palestine to Europe."[44] He seems to be on the right track, and it is tempting to push his thesis further, even though the fragmentary state of the fresco discourages definitive conclusions. There are two areas that I think can be elaborated. One concerns the relationship between the two extant parts of the fresco necessary to understand how the subject as a whole should be construed. The second regards the scene at the lower right. If it is indeed the Confirmation of the Carmelite Rule, as Vasari claimed (and this seems the most plausible identification), what was at stake in representing this subject during the early *quattrocento*? Why would it have been chosen for the cloister wall in the Carmine?

I want to begin by looking very carefully at the fresco. The composition seems to have been conceived along lines similar to those of Masaccio's *Tribute Money* (fig. 60) in the Brancacci chapel. As in the latter, a rectangular format is utilized with a country and city dichotomy set up between the left and right

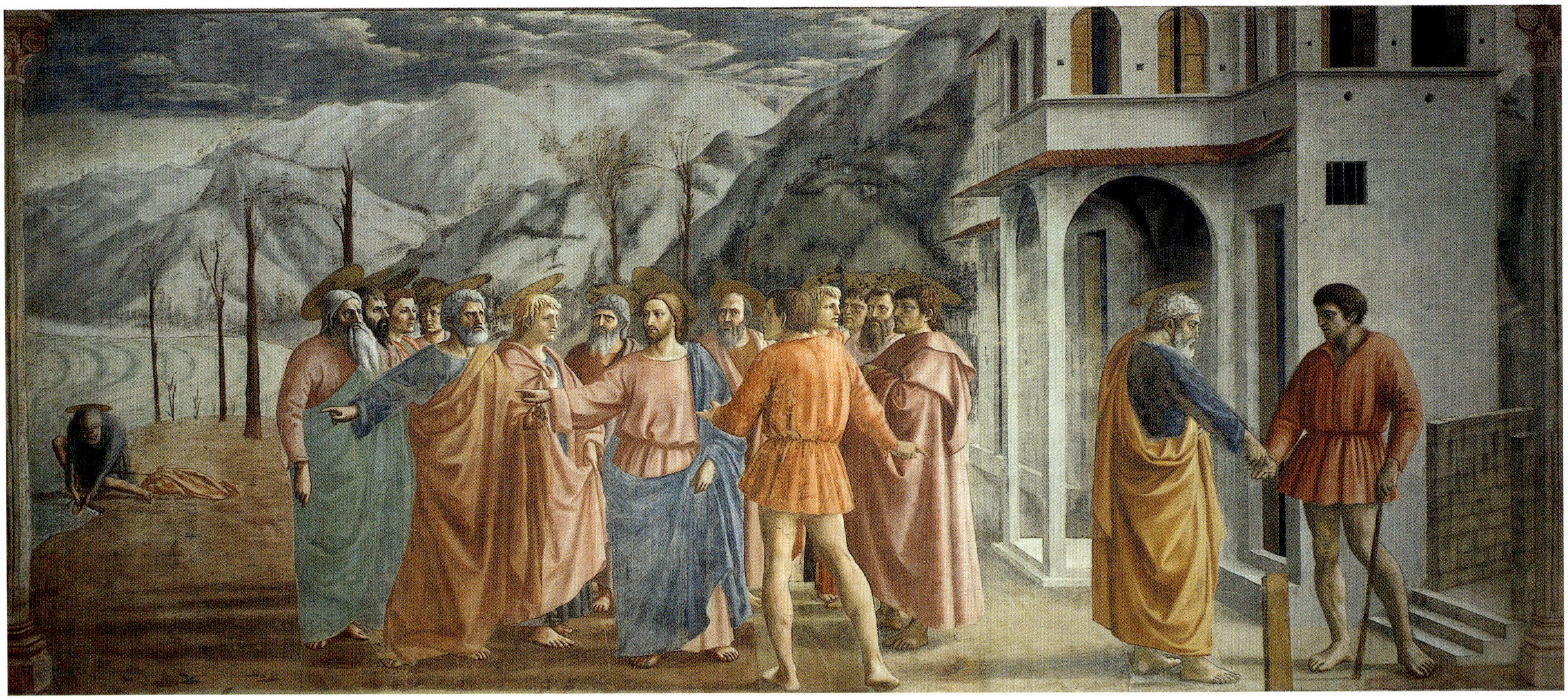

60 Masaccio, *Tribute Money*, c. 1425–27, Florence, Santa Maria del Carmine, Brancacci chapel.

sides of the fresco. (The width of the cloister fresco has been reduced by a quarter, with only the upper corner of the original right-hand part remaining.) The artist also follows Masaccio's scheme of multiple narratives within the same frame. In the background at the left (fig. 62), monks or hermits interact in the barren hills, while at the right (fig. 61) in an urban setting a group of clergymen concentrate their attention on someone or something up a flight of stairs. There must have been a dramatic focus in the central foreground of the fresco that no longer exists. This is evident from the standing figure with the red cloak looking off to the left, just at the edge of the damaged area of the fresco. This figure would have closed off the central scene from the narrative action at the right – very much like the apostle in the *Tribute Money* who seals the circle of apostles, separating the scene in which Christ instructs Peter to take the money from the belly of the fish from that in which Peter pays the tax collector.

There is a major difference between Masaccio's composition and that of the cloister fresco that helps to reveal a different narrative strategy employed by the painter of the latter. While Masaccio set his three narratives within a tripartite pictorial space, the three events in the cloister fresco are disposed within a composition divided in two. The urban setting takes up a good half of the composition. In addition, the country scene with the hermits does not really sit comfortably in the background, as

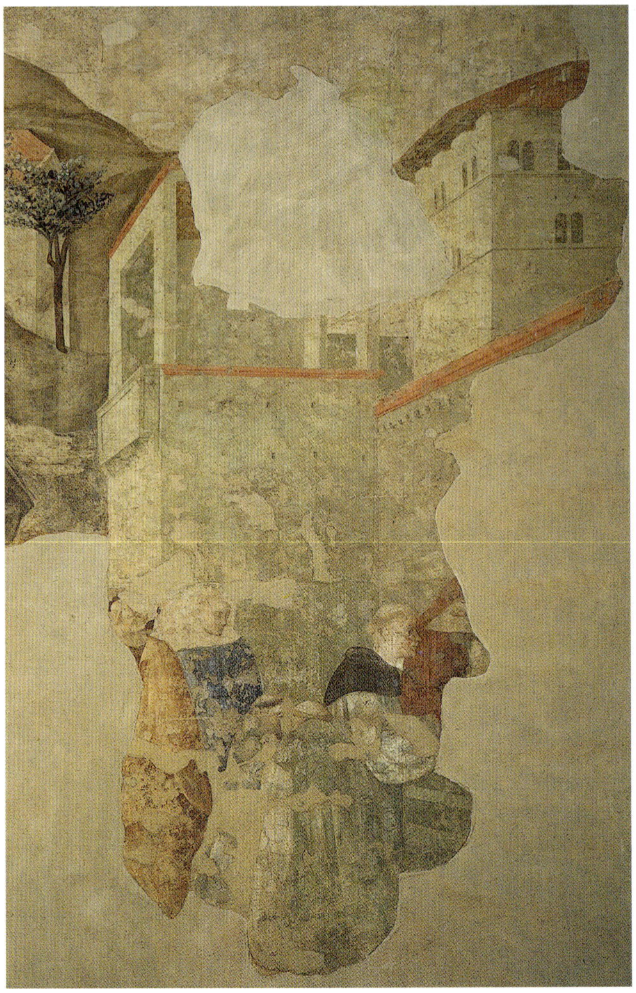

61 Filippo Lippi, *Confirmation of the Carmelite Rule*, detail of fig. 59.

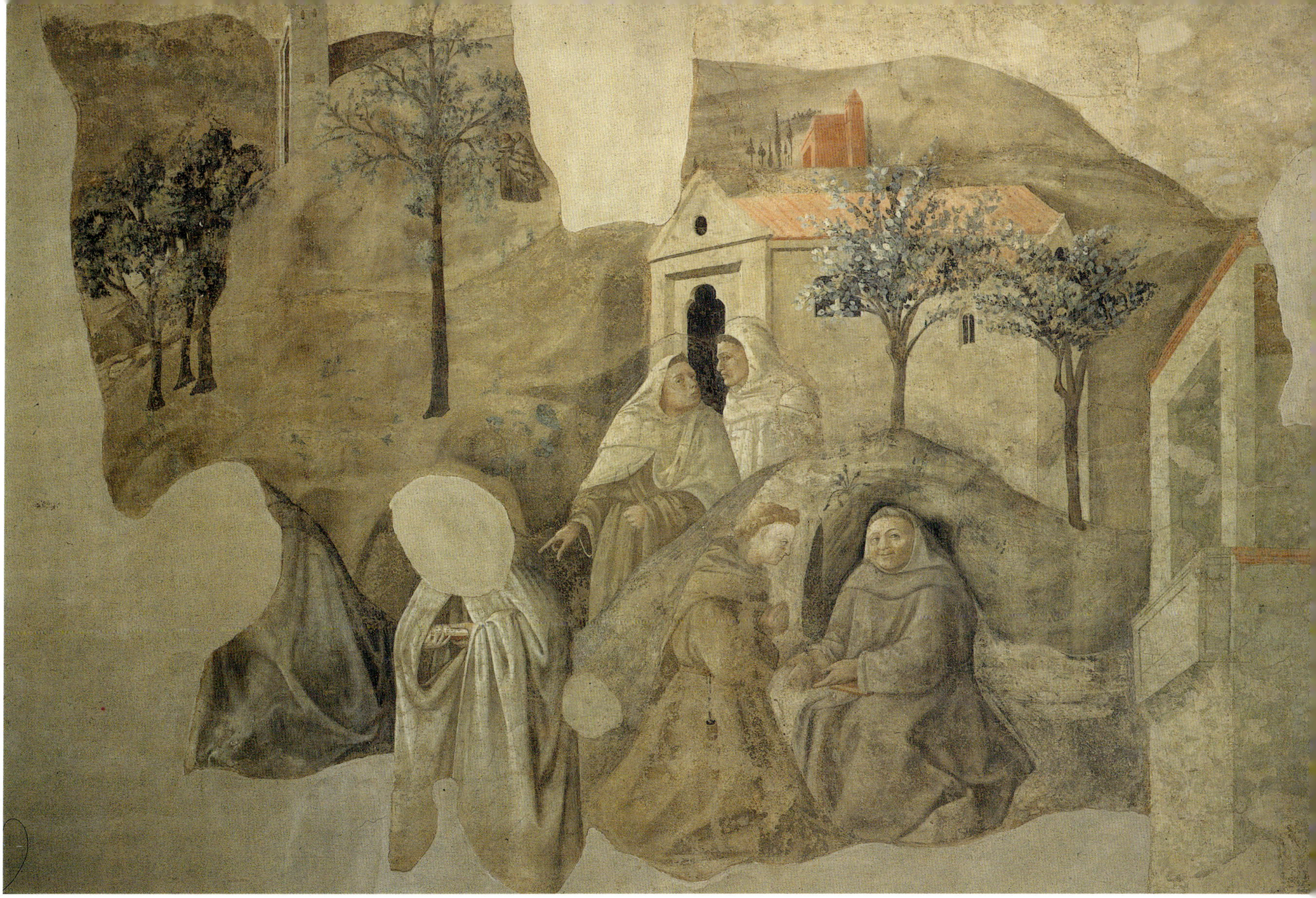

62 Filippo Lippi, *Confirmation of the Carmelite Rule*, detail of fig. 59.

does Masaccio's rendering of Peter with the fish (fig. 63) in the Brancacci chapel fresco. The painter has not employed diminishing proportions, so his hermits are on scale with the foreground figures, consequently lending equal weight to the landscape half of the fresco. The country and city dichotomy thus becomes less a backdrop for the narrative action and more the subject of the narrative itself. And this subject – the movement between country and city across a narrative scape – was of particular significance to the Carmelites. It served as an underlying theme in many of the events in the history of the Order, from the descent of Elijah from Mount Carmel to neighboring settlements, to the Carmelite's migration from the desert hermitages of the Holy Land to the urban centers of the West.

There are two Carmelite texts that may be of some help here in trying to determine more specifically what this fresco is about, one written just before the fresco was probably painted, and the other a few decades afterward. The first is the *Viridarium de ortu religionis et fratribus eiusdem*, composed between 1411 and 1435 by Fra Giovanni Grossi, who was the general prior of the Carmelite

63 Masaccio, *Tribute Money*, detail of fig. 60, with St. Peter removing the coin from the mouth of the fish.

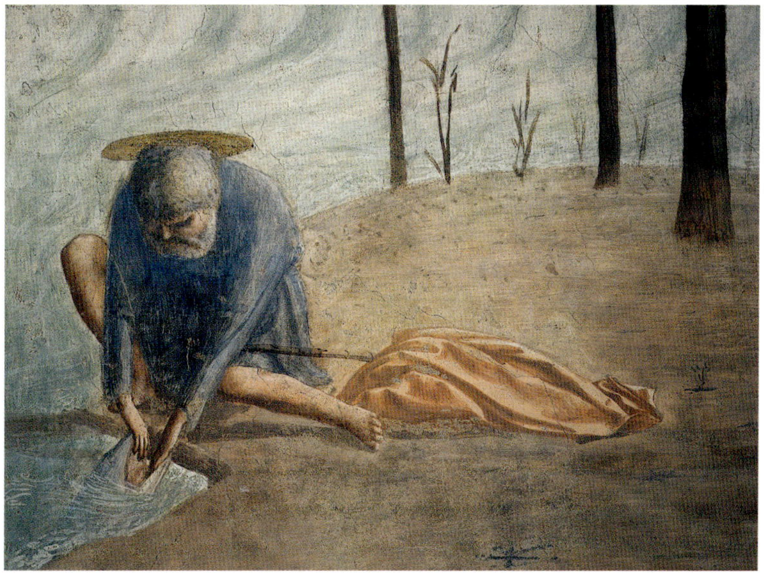

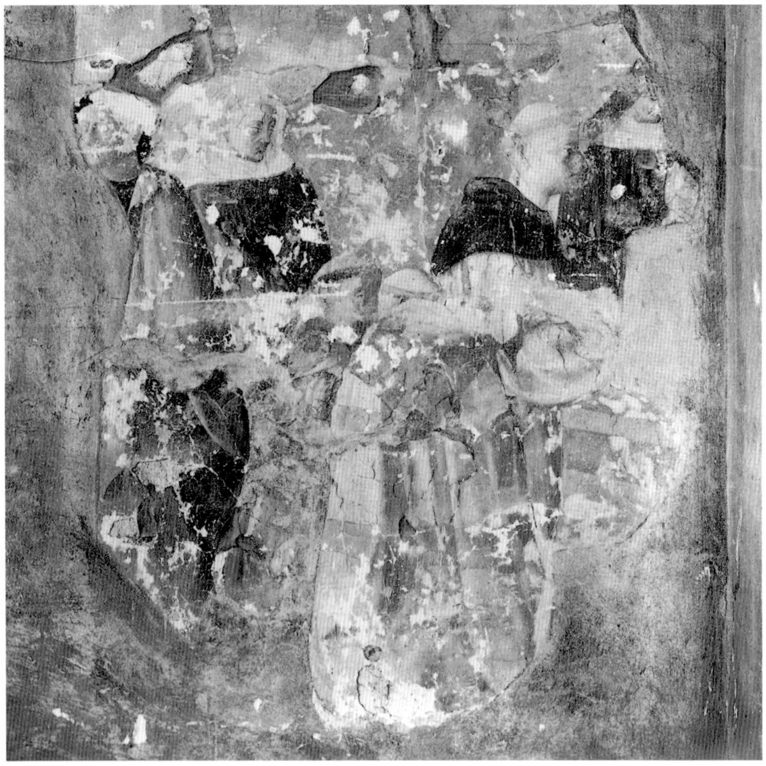

64 Filippo Lippi, *Confirmation of the Carmelite Rule*, detail of fig. 59 (before restoration).

Order.[45] This work represents the first Carmelite attempt to set, in a comprehensive fashion, modern events and personages into the Carmelite doctrinal and historical framework that had been worked out during the *trecento*. The second text is the *Vita fratrum del sancto Monte Carmelo*, written in 1461, in Tuscan *vulgare*, by Fra Nicola Calciuri from Messina, a Carmelite friar who resided in the Florentine Carmine and at Le Selve.[46] It is a much richer accumulation of material than Grossi's *Viridarium*, substantially longer, and composed of various genres of religious and spiritual discourse. Probably it was intended as a spiritual guide.[47] It is not that Lippi necessarily would have been personally familiar with the *Viridarium*, but rather that the material covered in the work – dealing with the history and notable figures within the Order – would have been common currency within Carmelite convents during the period. I shall look at the formal organization of these two literary works and their treatment of the two subjects discernible in the Carmine fresco – the primitive Carmelite hermits in the Holy Land and the confirmation of the Carmelite Rule.

Like the fresco in the cloister of the Carmine, Fra Giovanni Grossi's *Viridarium* is divided into two parts. The first, "On the Origins and Early Times of the Order" ("de Ordinis origine temporeque primo"), dates the origin of the Carmelite Order to the tenth century BC during the time of Prophet Elijah, and then follows the history of Elijah's followers through to the period in which Christ was born. The second, "On the Plants and Shoots that Spring from Below" ("de plantulis et germine quod surgit ab imo"), takes the Order from Christ's birth to the present (the early fifteenth century), ending with the general priorates of Grossi's successors.

In the first half of the *Viridarium*, emphasis is given to the establishment of customs and institutions that eventually became formalized in Carmelite doctrine and practices – the founding of the Order by Elijah, Elisha becoming the first disciple, Elisha receiving Elijah's scorched cloak, and the dedication of the Order to the Virgin. Grossi was also intent upon demonstrating the early hermits' status as witnesses to the coming of Christ and their apostolic undertakings following the death of Christ. Only very brief mention is given to the life of the early desert hermits:

> There on that mountain, Elijah himself performed many marvels . . . Then, taking as companions Elisha, Abdiah, Jonah and many other prophets, he instructed them to live in virginity in honor of . . . the Virgin. . . .
>
> Then Elisha himself, after the passing of Elijah, with the children of the prophets, led many to the dwelling and to devotion on that very Mount Carmel, in order to lead a distinguished life.[48]

Fra Nicola Calciuri's *Vita fratrum del sancto Monte Carmelo* is tripartite in structure, divided into three books, "Gloria," "Paradiso," and "Vita eterna." "Gloria" essentially corresponds to Grossi's "On the Origins and Early Times of the Order," elaborating on material from the Old Testament Book of Kings about the prophets Elijah and Elisha. The material is presented in such a way that the image of Mount Carmel begins to accrue resonant symbolic and analogic significance.[49] By the time Calciuri passes on to the second book, "Paradiso," the Carmelite convent on Mount Carmel is firmly in place as the archetypal monastery, and it becomes the centerpiece in his discussion of "Paradise in this World" ("paridiso in questo mondo").[50] The chapters discuss "Where the Holy Mount Carmel is," "How the Convent is Built and in what Form," "On the Manner and Form of the Divine Office," "On the Manner and Form of their Diet," "On Manual Labor."[51]

It is this sort of ideal and yet concretely detailed hermitage on Mount Carmel that is, I believe, represented in the fresco in the cloister of the Carmine. The way in which the hermits are disposed about the mountainscape, involved in various forms of religious devotion, reflects Calciuri's lines: "This most holy place was of such great sanctity, that with a license from the prior, the friars engaged in every kind of penitential act which they . . . desired."[52] A young novice dressed in a brown habit and scapular with his hood drawn back kneels before an older seated hermit who – so characteristic of Lippi works – looks out at the spectator with a slight smile, just as Calciuri tells us, "you see them all to be happy and content, living in holy penance."[53] The two hermits outside the small chapel on the hill ("leaving the church two by two") wear their white mantles with the hoods drawn over their heads – "in the church and in the cities, they always wore the mantle."[54] Even the straightforward and accessible narrative mode of the fresco reflects Calciuri's choice of the Tuscan vernacular for his text. Both chronologically and conceptually, the frescoed image of Mount Carmel falls somewhere between Grossi's historical gloss and Calciuri's spiritual exercise in imagining the actual site complete with measurements and the daily paces of the early Carmelite hermits.

One of the difficulties in placing the scene depicting the desert hermits in the fresco within some kind of historical and temporal frame lies in the type of mantles the hermits wear. They are dressed in brown and gray habits and scapulars with white cloaks. This combination was approved as the official Carmelite costume only in the thirteenth century. Until that time, the Carmelites had worn the *mantello barrato*, the brown and white horizontally striped cape supposedly modeled on Elijah's scorched white mantle. This mantle apparently became a source of embarrassment for the friars in the West and they were given permission by Pope Honorius IV to exchange it for a white one in 1287.[55]

While the *trecento* and *quattrocento* texts that allude to the early desert hermits never fail to describe their *mantelli barrati*, the pictorial representations of Elisha and the early desert hermits and Middle Eastern friars are not consistent with respect to their habits. Lorenzetti's predella scenes for the Sienese Carmine high altar (see figs. 22a–e) show the early hermits beside the fountain of Elijah on Mount Carmel in their striped robes and commemorate the papal permission to change the habit. In non-narrative *trecento* images, however – including that in one of the lateral panels of the Lorenzetti polyptych (see fig. 28) – Elisha always wears the white mantle.[56] The dress of the Carmelites in the Brancacci chapel frescos may help to explain the anachronism in the Carmine cloister fresco.

In Masolino's fresco of *St. Peter Preaching* (fig. 65) and in Masaccio's of *St. Peter in Cathedra in Antioch* (fig. 66), Carmelite friars wearing the white mantle are incorporated into the scenes representing events from the first century AD.[57] In these two frescos, the anachronism is rendered appropriate by the symbolic overlay: the figures are both historical witnesses and contemporary Carmelites from Santa Maria del Carmine in Florence. One of the ideological functions of the frescos was to demonstrate that among those who listened to Peter's sermons and who attended the apostle at Antioch were Carmelite friars, who, according to Carmelite history, were present in the Holy Land during the first millennium AD and had a convent in Antioch. Their presence in the company of St. Peter also alludes to a self-serving position put forth by the Carmelites in the late medieval period in an effort to gain legitimacy in the West. They insisted that the early Carmelites in the East were not exclusively hermetic but, like Western mendicant friars, had also followed the apostolic calling: "Together with the Apostles, in whatever region, they preached to the faithful of Christ."[58]

At least two of Masaccio's Carmelites (and possibly those of Masolino) are portraits (figs. 67, 68), probably of contemporary *frati* in Santa Maria del Carmine in Florence – the kneeling *frate* (fig. 69) with his distinctive beak-like nose and the elder *frate* behind him, clasping his wrist, with his large nose, baggy eyes, pursed mouth, and weak chin. One of the figures is probably R. M. Matteo d'Antonio, the *provinciale* of the Tuscan convents and regent of the Carmine *studium* during the 1420s, the dominant official personality in the Florentine convent during the period. Masaccio's easy integration of these contemporary figures into an early Christian narrative without recourse to "marking" devices like size differentiation, spatial separation, intercessory gestures, or labels – where likeness itself and portrait conventions become the marking device – was a revolutionary feature in Florentine painting in the mid-1420s. This practice developed out of the *Sagra* which had commemorated a contemporary

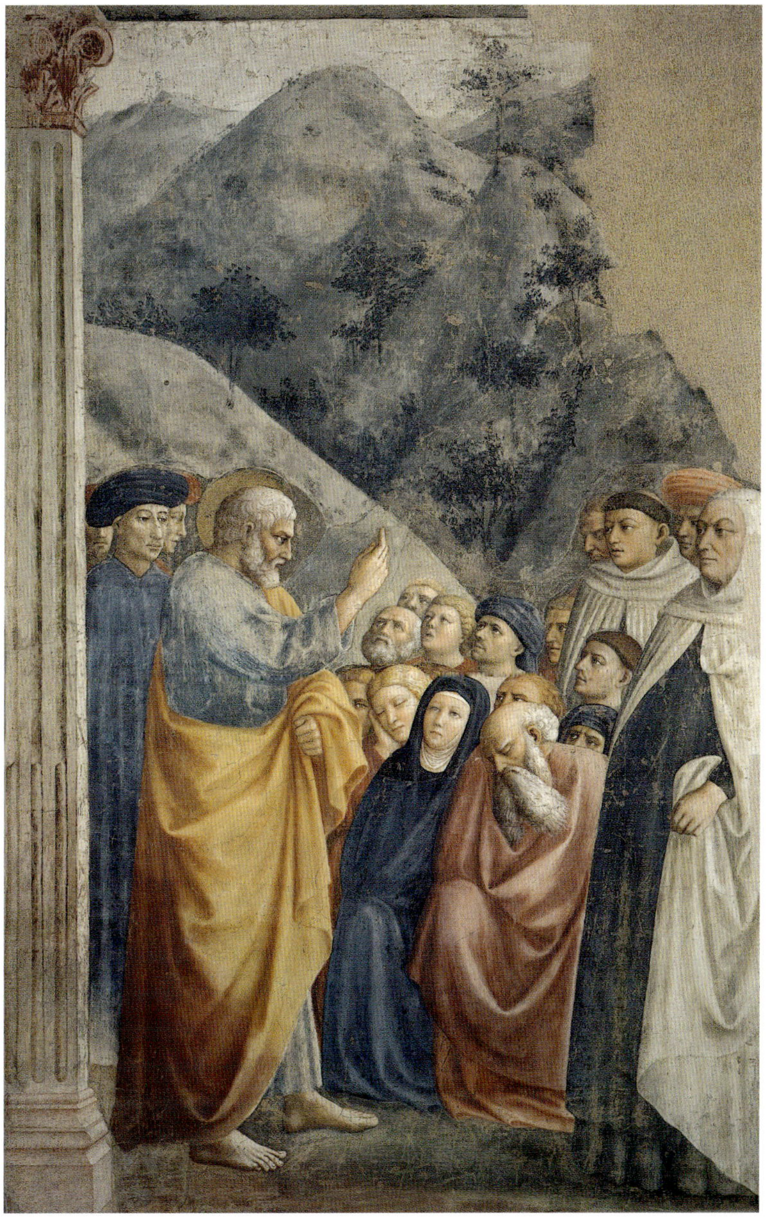

65 Masolino, *St. Peter Preaching*, c. 1425, Florence, Santa Maria del Carmine, Brancacci chapel.

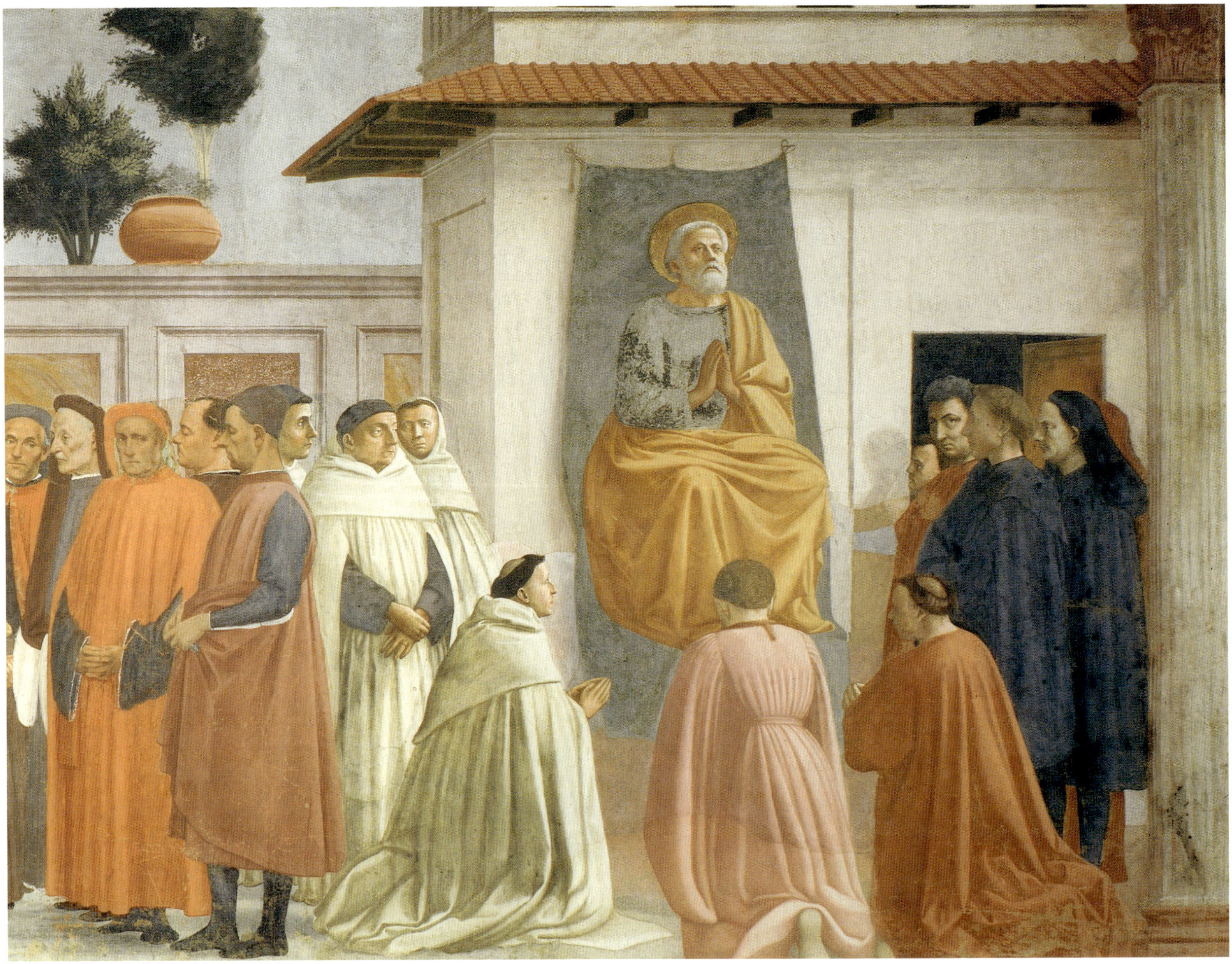

66 Masaccio, *St. Peter in Cathedra in Antioch*, c. 1425–27, Florence, Santa Maria del Carmine, Brancacci chapel.

historical happening at Santa Maria del Carmine, and it neatly represents the particular way in which the Carmelite Order was weaving its own version of its origins and development into the historical tapestry. Carmelites – fantastic conjurings of historical personages who were little more than self-images – were inserted into the Old Testament and early Christian past and invoked as *exempla* for contemporary monastic practices.

It is my contention that something similar is happening in the Carmine cloister fresco of the hermits on Mount Carmel. The early desert hermits are shown in the habit approved in 1287, because they are to be understood in terms of an idealized Carmelite religiosity realized through contemporary practices like those at the Observant Carmelite convent Le Selve.[59]

I shall turn now to the second subject depicted in the Carmine cloister fresco, the confirmation of the Carmelite Rule. The second half of Grossi's *Viridarium* concentrates on the legitimacy of the Order: the first Rule of St. Basil, the Rule of Patriarch Albert, the confirmation of Albert's Rule, the first mitigation of the Rule in 1247, the substitution of the white cloak for the original striated one in 1287, ending with a list of the prior generals of the Order. The treatment of the Confirmation of the Carmelite Rule in the *Viridarium* provides some insight into the significance accorded the event in the Carmine cloister fresco.

Grossi claimed that the initial Carmelite Rule was written in AD 340 by St. Basil.[60] This Rule was then presented to the papal

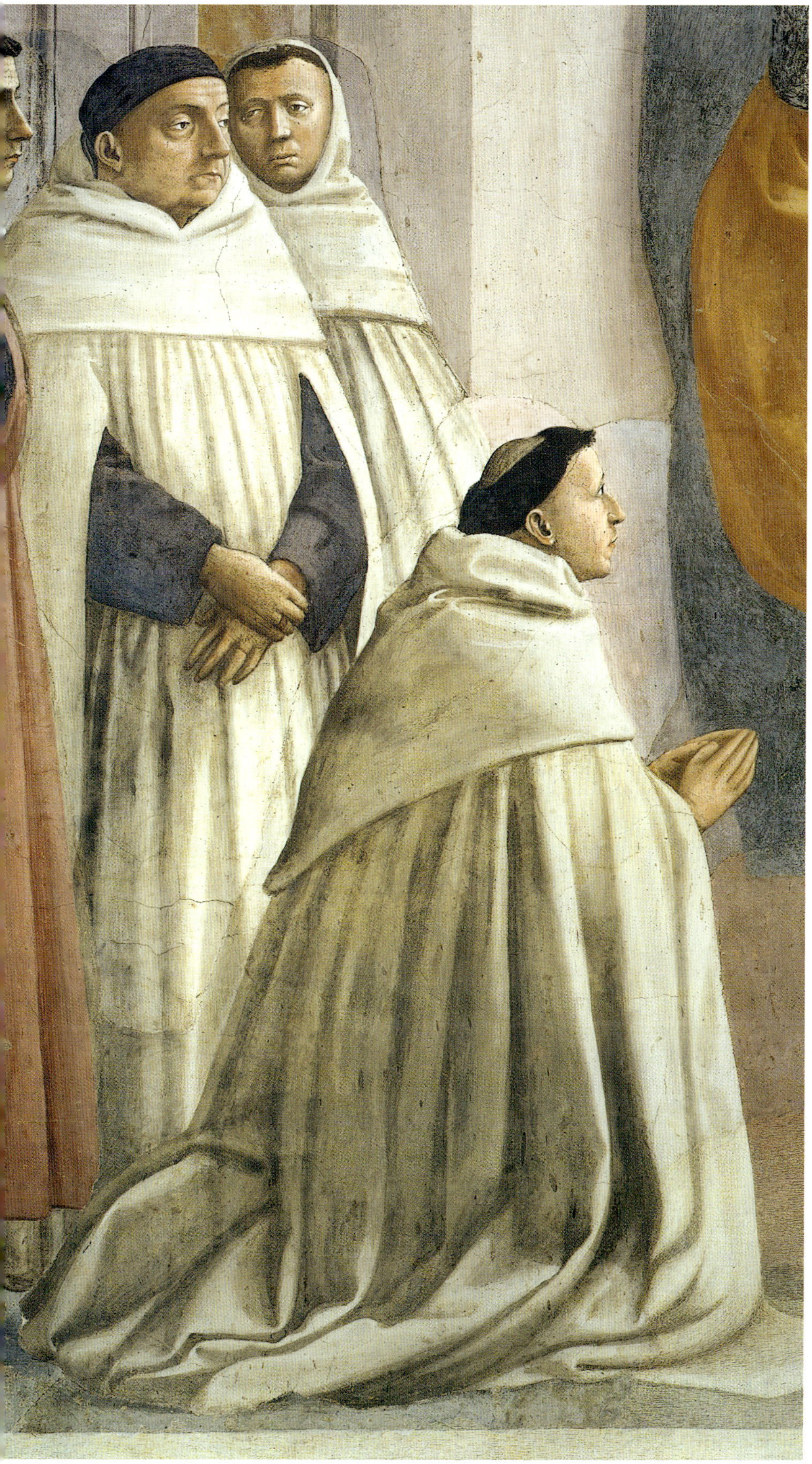

67 Masaccio, *St. Peter in Cathedra in Antioch*, detail of fig. 66.

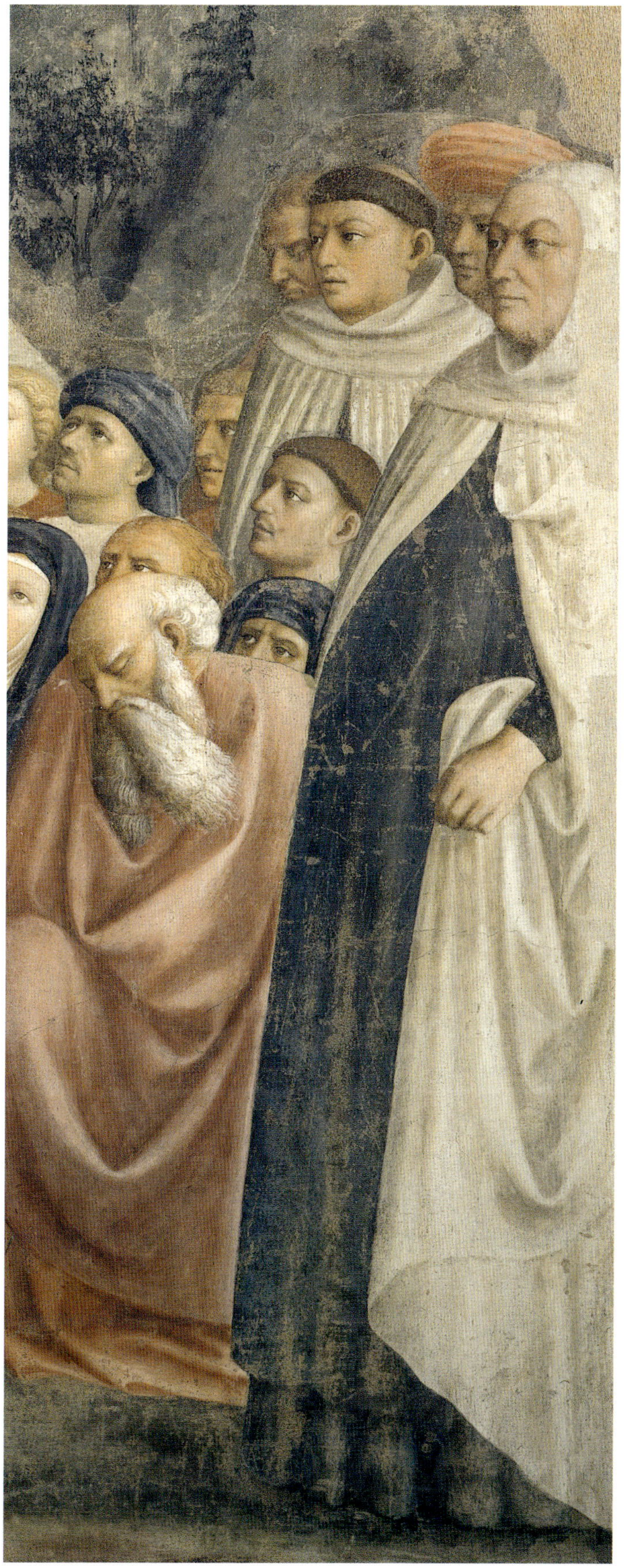

68 Masolino, *St. Peter Preaching*, detail of fig. 65.

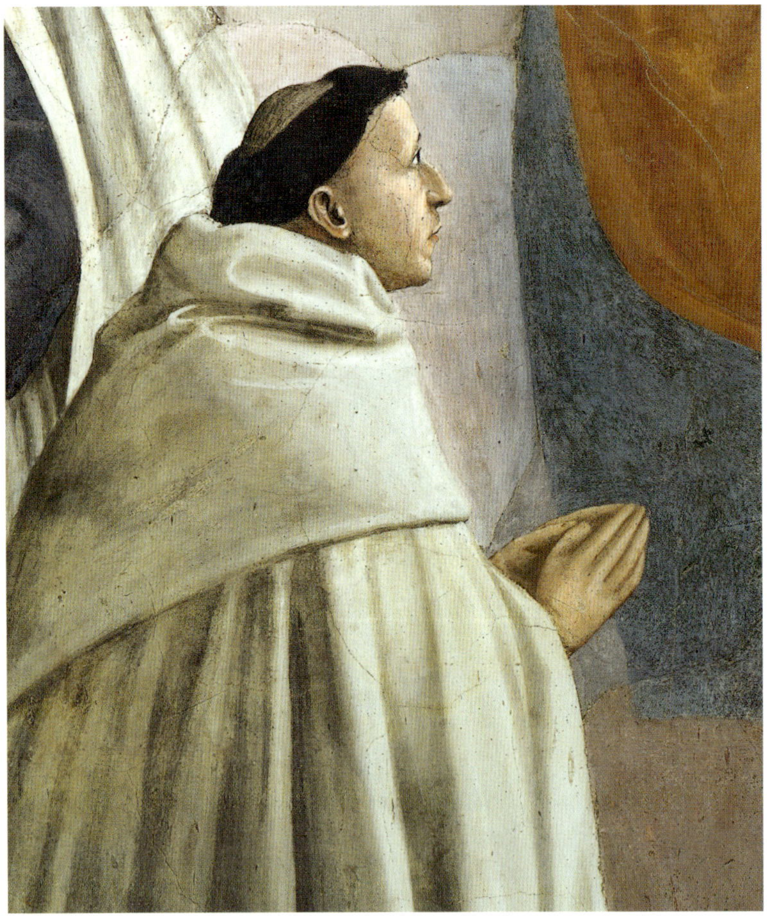

69 Masaccio, *St. Peter in Cathedra in Antioch*, detail of fig. 66.

legate Patriarch Albert in the late twelfth century by the third prior of Mount Carmel, Broccardus, to be "corrected."[61] In this way Grossi establishes the extreme antiquity of the primitive Carmelite Rule, and treats Albert's intervention as an official review of the Rule by a papal representative – rather than as the origin of the Rule, as most late medieval (and modern) accounts maintained. Grossi dates the first confirmation of the Rule to 1199: "At this time, Pope Innocent III confirmed the Carmelite Rule, during the first year of his pontificate."[62] He also asserts that the Rule was then confirmed a second time in 1216 with a papal bull of Honorius III and once again by Gregory IX in 1227.

The confirmation bull was, in fact, issued by Pope Honorius III in 1226.[63] The real date had become something of a problem for the Carmelites by the end of the thirteenth century.[64] In 1275, Pope Gregory X had declared at the Council of Lyon that no mendicant orders founded after 1215 would be recognized, and that the expansion of other mendicant orders, with the exception of the Franciscans and Dominicans, would be severely restricted. The situation was redressed somewhat in 1298, when the Carmelites were awarded the same exemptions as the Franciscans and Dominicans, but the issue remained a sensitive one. Pope John XXII reconfirmed the Carmelite exemptions in 1317 and 1326. However, this did not prevent the Carmelites from revising the historical record in their favor. In the Carmelite Constitutions written by John Ballistarius in 1369, the confirmation of the Rule was set securely within the papacy of Innocent III (1198–1216). Grossi essentially reproduced this account. His date for the second confirmation in 1216 is significant because, while falling in the first year of the pontificate of Honorius III, it is nearly contemporary with the Fourth Lateran Council of 1215 and is the same year in which the Dominican Rule was approved. Perhaps conscious of the shaky grounds upon which he had constructed the confirmation of the Rule, Grossi offers himself as a witness to the truth: "Bullam vidi ego Johannes in Tholosa." He himself had seen a copy of the bull of 1216 in Toulouse.[65]

The confirmation of the Carmelite Rule was discussed by Calciuri in a section devoted to the history of the Rule in the second book of his work, "Paradiso." Calciuri also provided a deceptive account of the confirmation, citing several authoritative texts as the proof of authenticity. He set the confirmation within a narrative. When the Carmelite St. Angelo of Licata journeyed to Rome, he met Sts. Dominic and Francis who had come to the city to petition the pope to confirm the rules governing their respective mendicant brotherhoods.[66] Angelo returned to Sicily where he was martyred in 1225, but his companions went back to Mount Carmel and reported on the historic encounter in Rome. The hermits convened a meeting of all the Eastern Carmelite provinces, and decided that they too must send a delegation to Rome and have the Carmelite Rule officially approved by the pope, "along with the other orders." Calciuri is somewhat ambiguous about precisely when the confirmation took place. Citing Vincent of Beauvais's *Speculum Historiale*, he writes that these events took place during the time of Emperor Frederick whose reign commenced in 1211. Dominic and Francis sought papal approval beginning "in the time of Innocent III; and when Innocent was dead, Pope Honorius succeeded him. And this Honorius . . . approved the Rule of the friars living on the Holy Mount Carmel."[67]

Thus, even in the *quattrocento* the confirmation of the Carmelite Rule was an important moment of legitimation in the history of the Order, which continued to require certain adjustments to the factual account. It is a pity that we do not have any more information about how this controversial subject was presented in the Carmine cloister fresco. Lorenzetti had dealt with the problem in the predella of the altarpiece for the Sienese Carmine (see fig. 25) by depicting the confirmation of the original "primitive" Rule by a pope (presumably Honorius III), with allusions to three other confirmations represented in the three popes with bulls in hand, hovering above.[68] The problematic question of exactly when during the papacy of Honorius III the bull was confirmed is masked by representing the act of legitimation validated three times over.

Lorenzetti depicted a group of eight Carmelites within the audience chamber where the pope, his two clerical ministers, and a congress of cardinals preside. The Carmelites alone are being received by the pope. In the Carmine fresco, the setting appears to have been somewhat different. The fragment representing the Confirmation (fig. 70) shows two kneeling Carmelites (fig. 64) – here, interestingly enough, shown wearing the *mantello barrato*, the stripes now barely discernible – in the company of other monastic delegates. There is a friar with a white hood and black mantle (possibly a Dominican) and another with a brown hood and white mantle. These figures are gathered in the right foreground, while up a flight of stairs on a higher plane – presumably, the dais where the pope is holding audiences – a cardinal is visible. The moment being represented is probably that when the Carmelites (and here I overlay my account with the words of Calciuri), "along with the other orders," stimulated by the example of Francis and Dominic, presented themselves before the pope, seeking the approbation of their Rule. The time, or date, would be that continuum "in the time of Innocent III; and when Innocent was dead, Pope Honorius succeeded him."

In this way, the Carmelites, along with the Franciscans, Dominicans, and the Umiliati, would fall within the pool of mendicants who were accorded legitimacy as independent orders through the proclamations of the Fourth Lateran Council of 1215.[69] The Carmelite case would thus parallel that of the Dominicans who sought confirmation from Innocent III, and following his death, were recognized during the first year of the papacy of Honorius III in 1216, just a year after the close of the Fourth Lateran Council. The artist's vivid evocation of this crucial moment in the Carmelite past using the representational idiom of Masaccio would have functioned something like Grossi's words bearing witness ("vidi ego Johannes"). It would have offered *quattrocento* Carmelites (among others) the possibility of participating as witnesses to the legitimation of the Carmelite Order (albeit to a falsified version).

I should like now to consider briefly what might have been the subject depicted in the left foreground of the fresco, which has all but vanished. Earlier, I suggested that the fresco sets up a division between the countryscape and the urban setting. These generic terms now can be replaced with more precise coordinates. The countryside represents the slopes of Mount Carmel (from the ninth century BC to the mid-thirteenth century) and the city, Rome (some time between the end of the papacy of Innocent III and that of Honorius III, c. 1215–26). In late medieval Carmelite doctrine, the relationship between the country and the city was a dialectical one, with the early desert hermitage on Mount Carmel serving as a constant point of renewal and spiritual purification. It is likely that the missing left-foreground scene in the fresco represented, in one way or another, the movement down from the mountain, away from the East, toward Western civilization and cenobitical monasticism. It could have shown the procession made by the embassy of Carmelites, at some point between their departure from Mount Carmel and their arrival in Rome. It is even possible that the

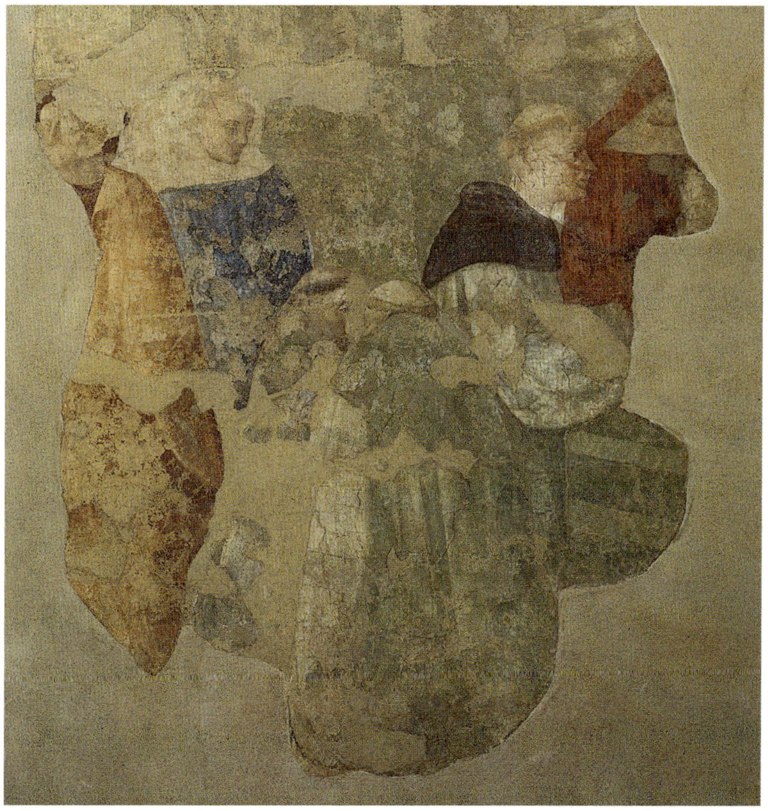

70 Filippo Lippi, *Confirmation of the Carmelite Rule*, detail of fig. 59.

artist depicted the apocryphal meeting in Rome between St. Angelo of Licata and Sts. Francis and Dominic. While this would have neatly set up a relationship of parity between the Carmelites and the two major mendicant orders, it is doubtful that such a bold claim (and intriguing sub-narrative) could have escaped comment by Vasari. My conclusion, then, is that the subject of the fresco as a whole is the historic passage of the Carmelites from eremitical monasticism on Mount Carmel and in the Eastern *provincie* to cenobitical monasticism in the West, legitimized through the confirmation of their monastic Rule by the head of Western Christendom, the pope.

It may well be that I am seeking too much closure in a discussion of a fresco that is a mere fragment. The handwriting on the wall, on the other hand, is less fugitive than the message conveyed, and I shall conclude by touching upon the question of authorship. Certain characteristics of the fresco that might at first sight be labeled inept or puerile become acceptable within the context of the particular project. The simple, direct representation of the hermits in the hills parallels Calciuri's use of the vernacular in his spiritual guide. The didactic quality of the presentation is understandable in a work intended, like a *speculum*, to reflect and instruct. The apparent naivety of the hermits is consistent with contemporary Carmelite representations of the "Children of the Prophets." The absence of diminishing proportions to depict the hermits in the mountainous background seems to be a refusal to consign them to a secondary role within

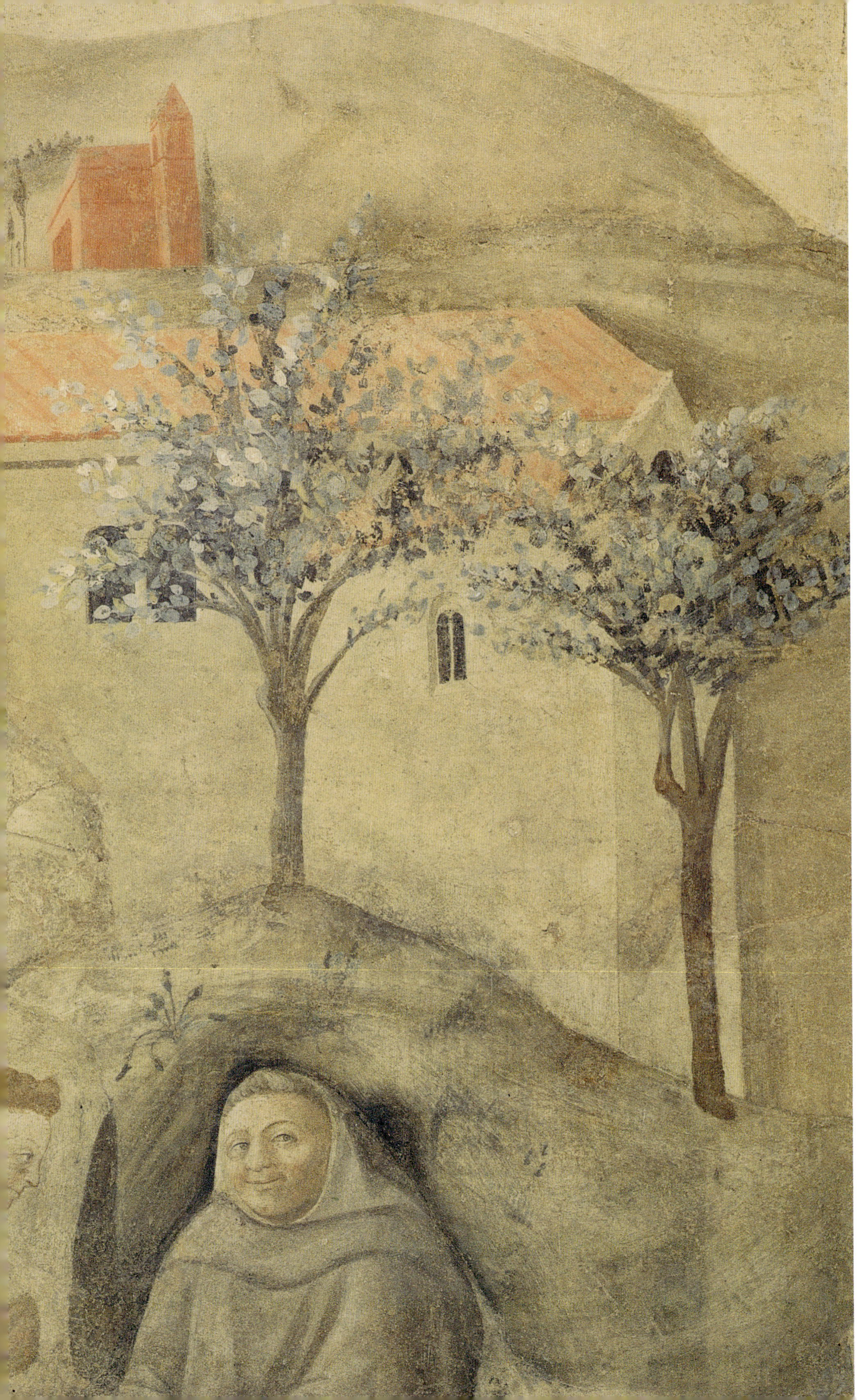

Carmelite doctrine, even as they receded into the narrative's past tense. The fresco seems to me to combine a deliberate archaism with a studied perception of Masaccio's work in the Brancacci chapel, treated by one thoroughly immersed in the Carmelite concerns represented, with a strong affective relationship to the subject depicted. And that fits the profile of the young Carmelite painter Fra Filippo Lippi.

As for the date, it has once again become anyone's guess, now that art historians have justly refuted the association of the fresco with the mitigation of the Carmelite Rule by Pope Eugenius IV in 1435, back-dated to 1432.[70] There are no neat concurrences of Carmelite events that help to explain the timing of the commission (as with Masaccio's *Sagra*). The fresco reflects a Tuscan Carmelite interpretation of subjects addressed in Grossi's *Viridarium*, anticipating Calciuri's *Vita fratrum del sancto Monte Carmelo* of 1461. The fresco should be associated with Masaccio's *Sagra* (painted some time after 1422), as a further embellishment of the cloister with representations of Carmelite themes, primarily for the benefit of the members of the convent who used the cloister daily as both a passageway and a quiet environment for religious reflection.[71] The Empoli *Madonna and Child with Saints and Angels*, the Trivulzio *Madonna of Humility*, and the Carmine fresco thus have been shown to be consistent with my notion of the early artistic production of "frate Filippo di Tommaso dipintore" (c. 1430–34). It follows logically that a monastic painter who learned his craft in the walls of his convent would begin with commissions generated in the immediate environment, reflecting the patronage network and iconographical concerns of the convent. In time, these patronage relationships and the growing reputation of the "frate dipintore" led to a broader socio-economic field of artistic production, new iconographic preoccupations, and a wider exposure to developments in the visual arts. And in this way, the artist would have progressed from these early works to the highly accomplished, radical paintings of the late 1430s – those that we attribute with confidence to Fra Filippo Lippi.

71 Filippo Lippi, *Confirmation of the Carmelite Rule*, detail of fig. 59.

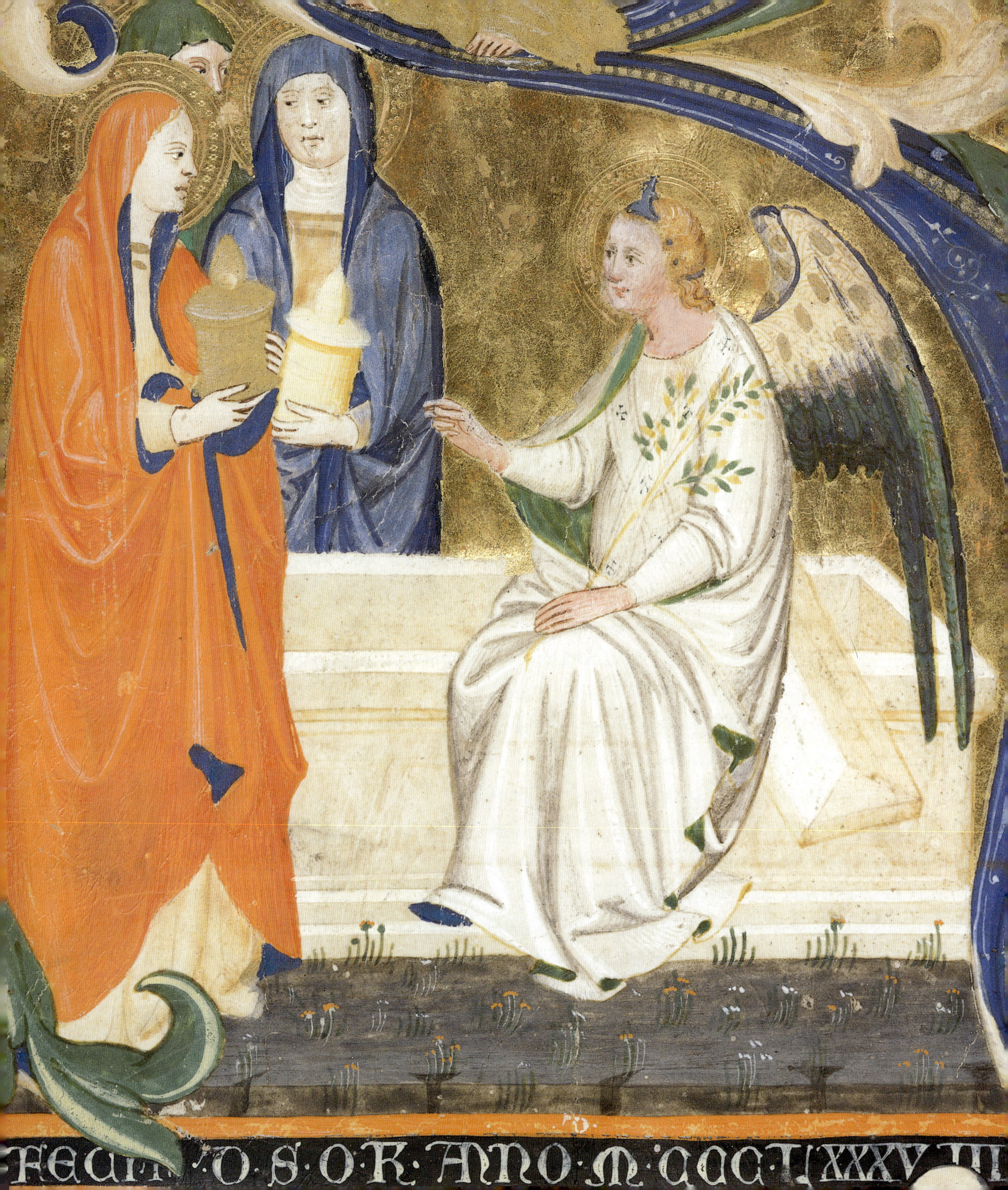
FECIT .O.S.O.R. ANNO.M.CCCLXXXV III

CHAPTER FOUR

THE *FRATE DIPINTORE*: MONASTIC ARTISTIC PRODUCTION IN QUATTROCENTO TUSCANY

"FRATE FILIPPO DI TOMMASO DIPINTORE." So reads an entry in the vestment list compiled in early January, 1431, in Santa Maria del Carmine (figs. 73 and 74).[1] Filippo di Tommaso was around twenty-five years old, and it is the first time that we find the two terms *frate* (friar) and *dipintore* (painter) converging upon his given name.

Frate and *dipintore* comprised two particular social identity markers in *quattrocento* Florence, which in turn referred to distinct, but interconnected, fields of social practice. Lippi was not the only monastic painter working in Florence at the time. "Guido di Piero dipintore del populo di Santo Michele Bisdomini" had some kind of artistic training and experience of the world before he was named anew at his profession "frate Giovanni;" and as "frate Giovanni dipintore" he lived a complicated life at the juncture of overlapping monastic, papal, and artistic concerns – a life that has been virtually effaced by a cultural memory constructed around his posthumous sobriquet of Fra Angelico.[2] There were others, too: Don Lorenzo "Monaco," Fra Diamante, Fra Domenico, Fra Bartolomeo, in addition to a host of illuminators. Apparently, an overlap was permitted between the religious activities of a member of a monastic order and the artistic (and economic) activities of a producer of painted representations. The question that I shall address in this chapter is just what this conjuncture of *frate* and *dipintore* may have involved in *quattrocento* Florence: under what conditions was it possible, how was it regulated, and what kinds of pictorial solutions did it generate?

THE PAINTER, THE FRIAR, AND THE FRIAR PAINTER

Upon matriculation into the Florentine Arte dei Medici e Speziali, the painter was required to take the following oath:

> I, who come to this Guild and Confraternity, swear before the Saints of God's Gospels, to practice my craft well and loyally and uprightly, and to obey the present and future consuls and their lawful and honest commandments, so long as they are not contrary to the Commune and People of Florence, and to the public good, and to observe all of the statutes and ordinances of the said Guild, and to do every other thing that the artisans of the Guild are required to do relative to the affairs of the said Guild.[3]

This oath was incorporated into the Arte statutes in the mid-*trecento* when the guild organized painters' economic, fiscal, political, and juridical activities. While the role of the guild had become less central within early *quattrocento* Florentine society, and patronage ties had become significantly more influential, nearly all of the practicing painters in the city continued to matriculate into the guild and pronounce the words of this oath.[4]

A mendicant friar, upon his profession, took another sort of oath or vow. With his hand placed in that of the prior of the convent, the Carmelite novice professed: "I ask for the mercy of God and of the Virgin Mary, and for the habit of the Carmelite religion, and that I might be worthy to be admitted to profess."[5] This would be followed by a pledge, here described by the Florentine notary Ser Filippo di Cristoforo in his record of the profession of Fra Filippo Lippi on June 18, 1421:

> He professed etc. before the said prior, the present stipulator and recipient, to the said Rule and Order and to the Reverend Father friar Johannes Grossus, General of the said Order etc. and he promised chastity, poverty and obedience, along with the customs of the said Rule, and he dedicated himself and his goods, present and future, to the said Order and chapter and convent etc.[6]

72 Don Simone Camaldolese, *Initial "R" with the Resurrection and the Three Marys at the Tomb*, detail of fig 77, with the Three Marys at the Tomb (larger than actual size).

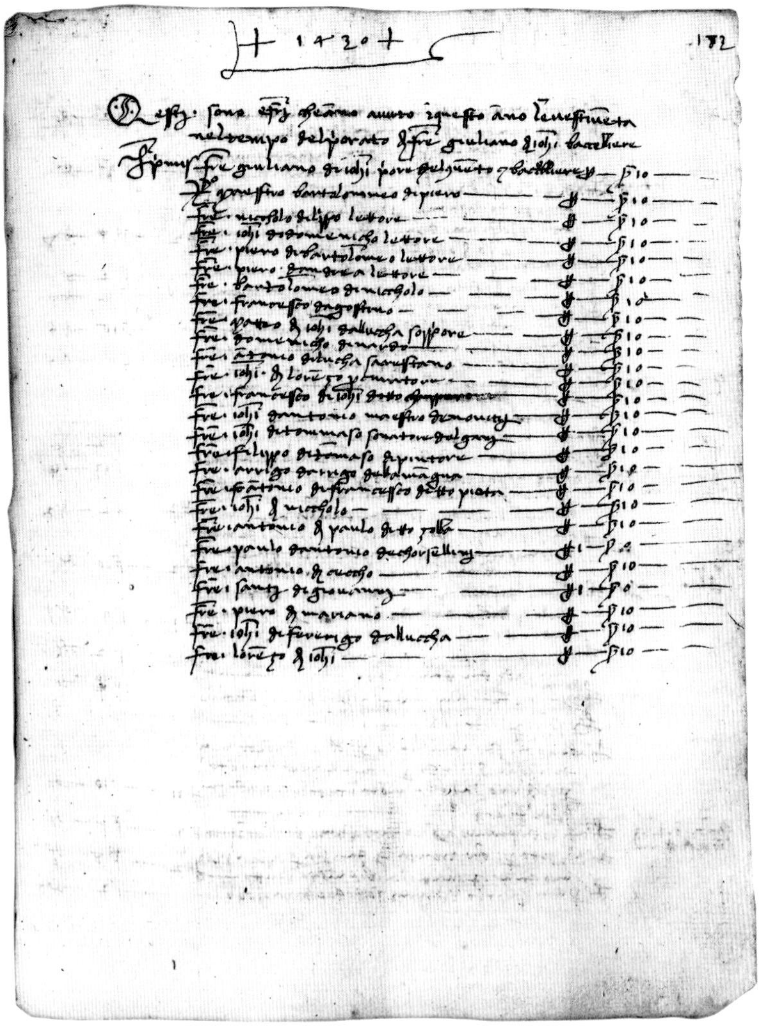

73 List of the friars in Santa Maria del Carmine recorded in early January 1431 (modern dating) in the convent *Libro di entrata e uscita*, Florence, Archivio di Stato (Con.Sopp. 113, n. 85, c. 183r).

74 "Frate Filippo di Tommaso dipintore" listed among the friars of Santa Maria del Carmine in early January 1431 (modern dating), detail of fig. 73.

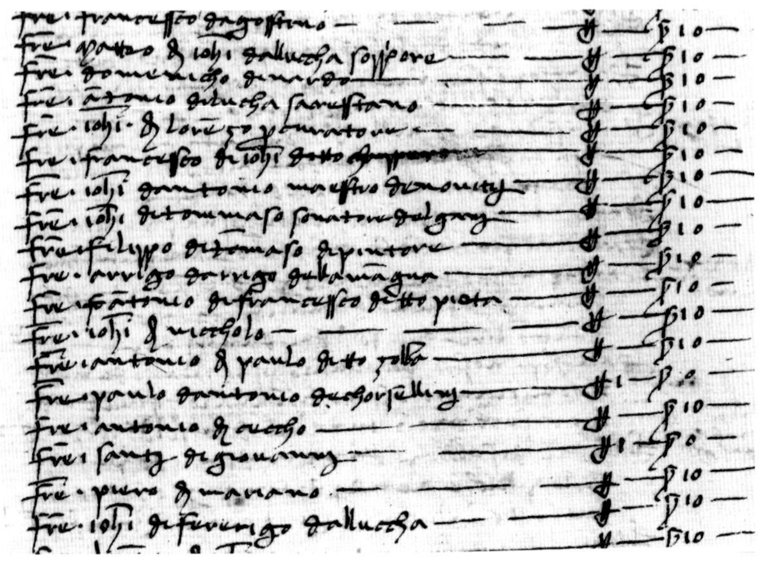

The formula for the Carmelite profession dated back to the early fourteenth century, after the Carmelites were recognized as a mendicant religious order; while strict adherence to the Rule and to poverty, chastity, and obedience were rare by the *quattrocento*, Carmelite novices continued to intone these words upon their profession.[7]

The different hierarchy of allegiance and emphasis that one finds expressed in the painter's oath of matriculation and the friar's profession is telling. The initiate painter states his ambition to "practice my craft," while the friar wishes to receive "the mercy of God and of the Virgin Mary" and to wear the Carmelite habit – here metonymous for living the Carmelite religious devotional life. Each then swears a fealty of sorts to a series of written tenets, corporations, individuals, and ideals.

At the beginning of the oath, the painter's focus is myopic, fixed at the level of his practice and certain regulating conditions. Then it broadens, culminating with the abstract ideal of public utility upon which the *comune* itself was founded and to which the painter, as a good and loyal worker and citizen, contributed. The friar's profession was organized somewhat differently. There are two series of relationships set forth, each preceded by "the Rule," with "the Order" as the key middle term: rule–order–general prior and rule–order–chapter and convent. In the first series, the corporate body of Carmelites (the order) is bracketed by the written, transcendent law (the rule) on one side and the highest temporal authority after the pope to whom the professed Carmelite would be responsible (the general prior) on the other. In the second series, the corporate body of all Carmelites is bolstered by the written law on one side and the smaller sub-divisions of chapter and convent, which would become the immediate environment in which the professed friar would live according to that rule, on the other.

The differences in the structuring of relationships and the hierarchy of obedience found in the painter's and the Carmelite's initiation oaths hint at some of the different ways that their lives were to be structured following their entry into their respective vocations. In the early *quattrocento*, a painter practicing in Florence was required to matriculate in the guild of the Medici e Speziali, pledging to abide by the guild's statutes governing membership, apprenticeship, contracts with patrons, a master's trade secrets, materials, and the quality of production.[8] In addition to his guild affiliation, the painter was also subject to the fiscal and legal sanctions levied by the *comune* and church. His liquid wealth, assets, and property were taxed directly by the *comune*, and his economic activity was taxed directly by the guild, and indirectly through *gabelle* payments on materials and trade.[9] If he happened to own any land in the *contado* – as did a number of the more financially successful painters of the time – he was also required to pay the *decima* (an annual tax in grain and wine, ostensibly equal to one-tenth of the value of the land) to the parish in which the land was located.

The painter's social activity and economic production fell within the jurisdiction of a number of legal bodies. The tribunal of the Arte dei Medici e Speziali, overseen by the guild consuls, adjudicated cases directly pertaining to his painting activity, while the Mercanzia tribunal, composed of members of each of the greater guilds, handled more serious disagreements and some civil cases. The Archiepiscopal Curia arbitrated issues involving canon law violations, and the Podestà, the Capitano del Popolo, and the Esecutore di Giustizia heard civil cases.[10] A painter's social identity was structured around his household and relatives, his guild affiliation, his local parish and *gonfalone* membership, his patronage ties, and his professional relationships within the workshop and in collaborations with other artisans. He participated in any number of lay confraternities (including the painters' Compagnia di San Luca). He was a member of a local parish within the Florentine archdiocese, and was expected to attend church at least on feast days and to take communion and confess, at minimum, once a year.

These conditions that governed the *quattrocento* Florentine painter gave rise to certain kinds of pictorial production. There were local masters who referred to a Florentine canon of painted precedents. There were dynastic workshops and joint practices. Painters exhibited a general skill in the application of a painted design to a range of surfaces – wall, panel, leather, parchment, cloth, gesso, terracotta, and marble. They had personal exchanges with patrons or their agents, resulting in commissioned work that followed conventional formats, with the iconography tailored to the patrons' needs. Production was decentralized, with the various manufactured components of the finished work often executed by different masters. While this may have been the norm, there were plenty of exceptions. The artistic sector of the late medieval and early Renaissance Florentine economy was based on a diversified production and extra-urban commerce, so that from the time that the statutes of the various guilds were written, their rubrics were applied flexibly, permitting local artists to work in multiple media and foreign artists to practice with relative freedom in the city. An artist like Apollonio di Giovanni was highly specialized within a single pictorial format (the *cassone*), while Uccello, Antonio Pollaiuolo, and Verrocchio worked across guild perimeters.

Non-Florentine artists, such as Gentile da Fabriano, Domenico Veneziano, and Pietro Perugino, also practiced in the city, introducing new influential artistic technologies. During the *quattrocento*, as the city's institutions and corporate bodies became increasingly dominated by a more exclusive group of Florentine patricians, and private initiatives increased, patronage relations and "clientelism" became more significant in determining an artist's practice than guild legislation and communal statutes.

The fifteenth-century mendicant friar, like the painter, was enmeshed in a network of loosely applied constraints and codes. His activities were regulated by the rule and constitutions of his order and by convent practices. He was immediately responsible to his convent superiors and to the ministers of the province and general order. The friar was not a member of civil society, and hence outside of the authority of the Florentine *comune*. While the friar was permitted limited movements and actions in the *seculum* (with the permission of his superiors), he was not subject to any of the guild or communal taxes, statutes, or penalties. His immediate superiors were responsible for his activities and transgressions in the *seculum*. At the same time, however, with a license from his superiors, the friar could himself appeal to secular law when his secular activities were compromised by lay influences.[11] He could also participate in lay confraternities, and not only those that were associated with his own convent church.[12]

Some friars were also benefice holders, acting as chaplains and rectors in parish churches, oratories, chapels, and in female monastic houses. They came under the jurisdiction of the archiepiscopacy and were subject to canon law, accountable to the regional archbishop and his vicars, and were responsible for the spiritual well-being of the souls under their care. Monastic priests with country benefices had to collect the annual *decima* on the lands within their parishes. But the archiepiscopacy was never very successful in making demands on the beneficed monastic clergy.[13]

Like the guild statutes, the monastic rules were loosely and pragmatically applied in most Florentine religious houses during the *quattrocento*, with the exception of the Observant convents. Most urban mendicant houses in the *quattrocento* followed mitigated versions of their original rules, where the more constricting dictates (pertaining to diet, isolation, and movement) were modified. Other rubrics, particularly those regarding private property, were notoriously bent.[14]

The *quattrocento* Florentine professional painter and mendicant friar thus occupied two distinctly demarcated yet overlapping social fields. The secular painter's social, religious, and economic activities were regulated by a greater number of institutional bodies, while the friar needed only to acknowledge the authorities within his order, the pope, and on occasion the archiepiscopacy. The friar was principally defined as a religious actor with restricted movements, while the painter was implicitly involved in a much wider range of social, cultural, political, religious, and economic practices and exchanges. What happened, then, when a friar was also a painter, or a painter a friar?

Monastic attitudes toward work had been significantly influenced by the Benedictine Rule and subsequent Benedictine practices. The Benedictine Rule stated:

> Craftsmen present in the monastery should practice their crafts with humility, as permitted by the abbot. But if anyone becomes proud of his skill and the profit he brings the community, he should be taken from his craft and work at ordinary labor [elsewhere defined as work "in the fields" or "manual labor"]. This will continue until he humbles himself and the abbot is satisfied. If any of the works of these craftsmen are sold, the salesman shall take care to practice no fraud.[15]

Work was also advocated in the Benedictine Rule as a means of alleviating idleness: "If anyone is so slothful that he will not or cannot read or study, he will be assigned work so as not to be idle," just as "sick and frail brothers should be given work that will keep them from idleness."[16] While the early monastic communities that followed Benedict's Rule tended to minimize the material support structure of the monastic life, this changed in the tenth and eleventh centuries, and monastic craftsmen played an important role in building and maintenance, and in providing the accessories used in the increasingly elaborate religious rituals of the monasteries.

The mendicant orders, proliferating in the early thirteenth century, rejected the Benedictine "possessionate" monastic model. Mendicant attitudes toward both religious art and monastic artistic production were heavily determined by the mendicant vow to poverty and by the itinerant existence of the early friars. The Dominican Order set the standards, enacting legislation against lavish artistic decoration within churches, which were then emulated by the Franciscans.[17] Mendicant artistic production was permissible nonetheless as a form of work, which the various mendicant rules and constitutions accepted both as a means of combating idleness and warding off abject poverty and indebtedness.[18]

Thus, strictly speaking, according to the rule, the *quattrocento frate dipintore*'s activity was contained within the parameters ascribed to the friar. He was a friar who had managed to fulfill his monastic vows to the satisfaction of his superiors and consequently was permitted to engage in the practice of painting, which was permissible under the various mendicant rules. And again, strictly speaking, according to the rule, the friar could live and paint in the convent and, under exceptional circumstances with the permission of his superiors, he could live and work outside the convent walls. Strictures regarding private property and wealth varied from order to order, with the stricter communities requiring that the friar turn over to the convent the profits he derived from his art. He worked around his primary religious devotions and curative duties – the daily routine of the Divine Offices and masses, and the religious calendar of feast days.[19] As a *frate dipintore*, he was not bound to observe the regulations laid out in the Arte dei Medici e Speziali, as he was not punishable in the guild or merchants' court. Hence, there was no recourse for an aggrieved patron regarding contract violations over time limit, materials, and quality of work, no regulations controlling his engagement of apprentices or his collaborations. Cases were indeed taken to the courts and judgments passed, but the court had no real power to enforce rulings reprimanding friars and had to hand the cases over to the monastic authorities or the ecclesiastical courts (if the friar was a priest).

This profile of the *frate dipintore* suggests real possibilities for a painting practice quite different from that of the lay professional painter, granted reasonably obliging monastic superiors. In the *quattrocento*, however, many of the distinctions between the professional and the monastic painter based upon thirteenth and fourteenth-century monastic and guild legislation disappeared in practice. Both secular and monastic artists worked in a relatively unregulated economic environment in which the demand for well-executed painted works was high.[20] Under auspicious patronage circumstances, both could count on support and leeway from their immediate authorities, whether secular or monastic. That said, the *quattrocento* Florentine cultural and religious economy was not a free-market free-for-all arbitrated by powerful financial bosses. One must not lose sight of the subtle dynamics that shaped patronage relationships and the intricate way in which men like Cosimo de' Medici, Palla Strozzi, and Giovanni Rucellai worked through existing social structures and traditional practices. Nor should the high incidence of monastic painters working in the city during the period be explained away simply by reference to the decadent conditions of Renaissance monasticism. It was not merely on account of lax regulations and high market demand that, for a brief moment, two painters considered among the most outstanding of their generation – Fra Angelico and Fra Filippo Lippi – were both mendicant friars. Therefore, I want to hold onto the distinction between the monastic and the secular painter.

Attempts have been made to locate "the world of the Renaissance secular painter"[21] but, until recently, little thought had been given to the terrain of the Renaissance monastic painter.[22] In order to retrieve some of the contours, surfaces, and spaces of this often mystified domain, one must consider how the *frate dipintore* went about his work: how he obtained commissions, was remunerated, developed patronage networks, balanced "prayer and labor," and managed to secure that all-important permission from his monastic superiors to paint, both within and without the convent. I shall examine diverse forms of monastic artistic activity, with the majority of examples taken from documented cases of book production. Manuscript illumination was the predominant artistic activity undertaken by friars and monks during the early Renaissance, and therefore there are more contemporary records regarding this practice. While I do not want to suggest that the conclusions drawn in the following sections about manuscript illumination were applicable necessarily to panel painting and fresco projects, nonetheless they reveal much about *quattrocento* attitudes toward monastic labor, monastic incursions into the *seculum*, and the conditions under which a professed monk or friar dedicated to the service of God was permitted to turn his attentions toward convent and private demands for the pictorial representation of the sacred.

The conditions of monastic artistic production during the *quattrocento* varied significantly from one order to another, between the Benedictines, Vallombrosans, Camaldolesi, Gesuati, Umiliati, and Olivetans, and the mendicant Carmelites, Dominicans, Servites, Franciscans, and Augustinian regulars, to name the most prominent. Some of the differences stemmed from the contrasting organizational and theological tenets of each order, set forth in their rules and constitutions, and from their different historical evolutions. But there was even significant variation in the character of monastic artistic production between the individual provinces and within the convents of a single province of a given order. Each monastery had its own particular character, established through a history of negotiations between the monastic community and the local lay community, with its own cultural, political, and religious traditions and practices, both official and popular. In evaluating the experiences and production of a *frate dipintore*, it is helpful to conceive of the monastery as a semi-dependent socio-economic system in which the production of painted images had a certain perceived value. This value was multi-valent, determined by the function of images within religious rituals, and by the complicated social role of the Renaissance monastery within contemporary cultural politics. This value was linked to socio-religious practices that were devotional, curative, and economic, which evolved out of the "political economy of the sign."[23]

ARTISTIC PRODUCTION IN THE CONVENT

Was there such a thing as a convent painter or a convent workshop? These terms have been applied loosely to explain a practice like Fra Angelico's, located within a specific convent (San Domenico first and afterwards San Marco), displaying a distinctly "Dominican" iconography, or an enterprise like the book production at Santa Maria degli Angeli during the fourteenth and fifteenth centuries, involving a number of Camaldolesi illuminators who collaborated with convent scribes, rubricators, authors, and binders.[24]

In the account books of Florentine monasteries dating from the *quattrocento*, certain laborers are referred to in the possessive: "our miller," "our gardener," "our servant." These were either salaried workers who lived in the convent proper, or laborers outside the convent who took care of all convent needs in a certain line of work. Laymen who performed artistic services for the convent on a regular, salaried basis were described in similar terms ("our illuminator").[25] Monastic artists and artisans were usually referred to in the convent registers by name alone. On the rare occasions that they were identified as practitioners, the possessive pronoun "our" was reserved for the religious affiliation: the painter Lorenzo Monaco was "Don Lorenzo painter from Siena of our Order."[26] The Olivetan illuminator Fra Bartolomeo da Ferrara illuminated manuscripts for Monte Oliveto in 1472 and was described as "our illuminator" in the convent books. However, when he was reassigned to a Venetian Olivetan convent the following year, he became "their illuminator."[27]

Thus, when the monastic records document "our illuminator" or "our painter," this artist, like "our barber" and "our cook," was a layman or a friar or monk working either exclusively for the monastery or responsible for all illuminated or painted commissions generated by the convent. This label would therefore not apply to a *frate dipintore* who was contracted out to another monastery, who was painting predominantly for lay patrons or who had a diversified production. The "convent artist," in so far as this existed as a concept or a position, would thus have been a very conditional title, no longer applicable once the lay or religious artist had terminated a project, or if the monk or friar were assigned to another religious house.

In describing the small artistic Renaissance that flourished in the Camaldolese monastery of Santa Maria degli Angeli around the time of Lorenzo Monaco, Vasari referred to a number of monastic illuminators who "flowered there for a long period of many years."[28] His characterization of the monastic artistic activity that he envisioned at Santa Maria degli Angeli in the early *quattrocento* is tinged by a retrospective nostalgia for those "former times [when] the monks ever applied themselves to painting and to design."[29] The picture he gave of Santa Maria degli Angeli falls somewhere between the classic convent *scriptorium* with monastic illuminators and scribes laboring away, and the *quattrocento* Florentine *bottega*, that privileged site of Renaissance artistic innovation.[30] This contrasts markedly with the convent environment that Vasari sketched in his *Vita* of Lippi where he transformed the Brancacci chapel into a proto-Accademia, offering the young Lippi something closer to the apprenticeship experience an aspiring painter would have encountered in the *seculum* in the *bottega*.

Speculation about the physical environment and working conditions of fifteenth-century monastic painters within the convent has swung between these two conceptions – the *scriptorium* (convent center of manuscript production) and the *bottega* (painter's workshop) – and traversed a third term, the *officina* (workshop), in the process.[31] A close review of documentary and artistic evidence suggests that *scriptorium*, *officina*, or *bottega* do not adequately describe the flexible, ever-changing scene of painting production within the monastery.

For the most part, the *quattrocento* convent supported only a small, fragmented field of production organized less around institutional regulations than the will of individual monastic authorities. The physical site, the work force, and working conditions changed continually with the particular requisites of each commission assigned by the convent or undertaken by the convent *frati*. A number of manuscripts can be demonstrated to have been executed by the Camaldolesi monks of Santa Maria degli Angeli during the late fourteenth and early fifteenth centuries (fig. 77), but we hardly find the monks assembled row by row, pen and brush in hand, one writing, one illuminating the text that the former had written. Instead, we see that the monks often left their own monastery and worked on the premises of the convent that had commissioned the illuminated book.[32] There were indeed situations in which one convent monk copied out a text and another monk illuminated the initials, but these projects must be seen less as part of an assembly line, on-site production, and more as arrangements utilized for single, specific projects. The same illuminator could be relocated to another convent the

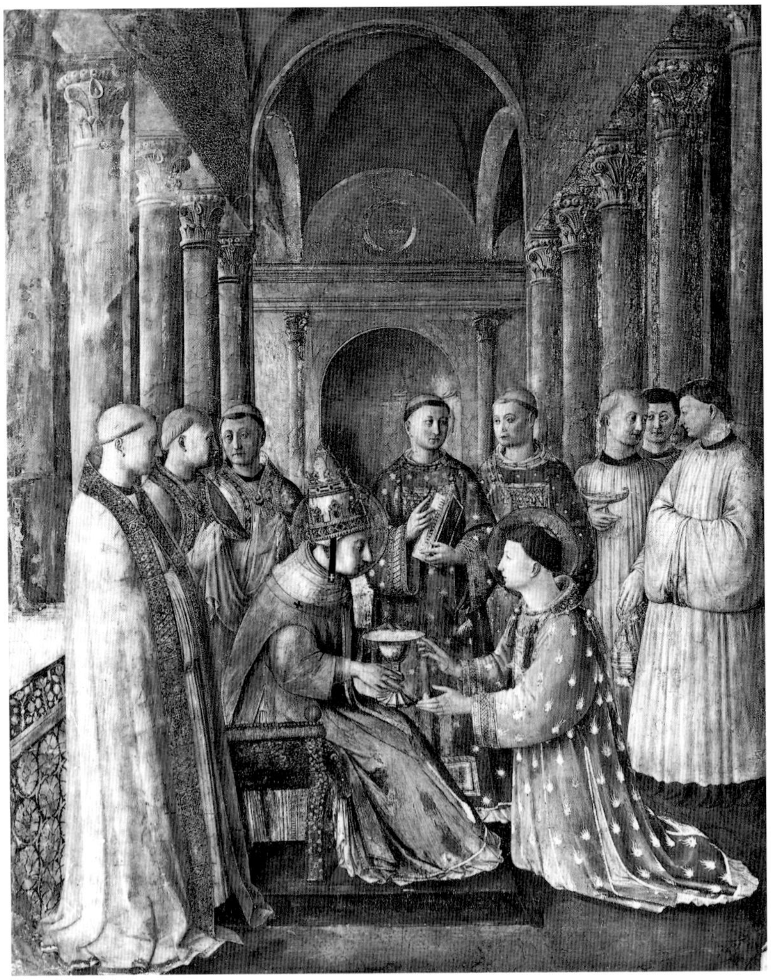

75 Fra Angelico, *Ordination of St. Lawrence*, 1448–50, Chapel of Nicholas V, Vatican.

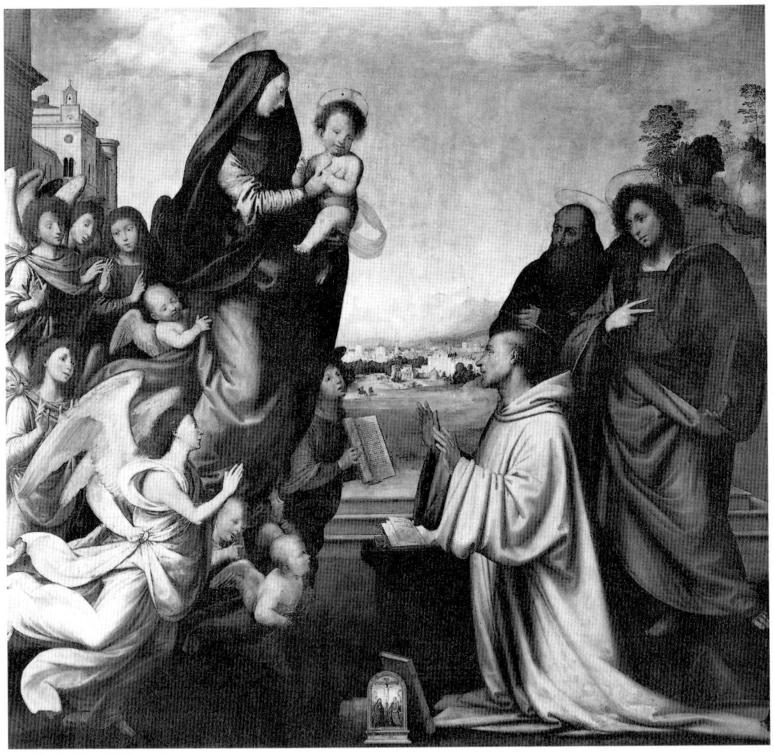

76 Fra Bartolomeo, *Vision of St. Bernard*, 1504–07, Florence, Uffizi.

following year, or could be contracted to work for another order or for lay patrons.[33]

Monastic artists sometimes worked collaboratively with other artists, monastic and lay. Many are documented working with *garzoni*.[34] The lay production team that Fra Angelico mobilized and took on the road with him to Rome and Orvieto from about 1445 to 1449 (fig. 75) consisted of a *consocio* or fellow master, Benozzo Gozzoli, and a contingent of *garzoni* (apprentices).[35] The Observant Dominican Fra Bartolomeo (fig. 76) entered into a partnership for three years (1509–12) with the lay painter Mariotto Albertinelli.[36] Miklòs Boskovits and George Bent both conclude that the manuscript production at the monastery of Santa Maria degli Angeli during the late *trecento* and early *quattrocento* was also a lay–monastic joint venture. Boskovits cites a group of miniaturists, some Camaldolesi – Don Silvestro dei Gherarducci, Don Simone (fig. 77), Don Lorenzo Monaco – and other laymen – Ser Miniato, Matteo Torelli, Bartolomeo di Fruosino, Paolo Soldini, and the Master of the Ashmolean Museum predella. He claims "it is justifiable to speak of a Camaldolese 'illumination center,' more than a *bottega*. The collaborators worked completely independently and probably not outside of their habitual environments; the convent was limited to organizational functions and did not serve as the site of a common *bottega*."[37]

Besides Santa Maria degli Angeli, there were two other monastic centers of manuscript production in Florence, the Badia (1435–50) and San Marco (1445–1505). Both relied predominantly on lay illuminators.[38] It is interesting to note that certain lay painters who are documented as having worked for, or are associated on the basis of stylistic evidence with these monastic illumination centers, apparently never matriculated into the Florentine Arte dei Medici e Speziali. Battista di Biagio Sanguigni and the young Guido di Piero (Fra Angelico), who are often thought to have trained under Lorenzo Monaco of Santa Maria degli Angeli, seem never to have matriculated, and nor did Zanobi Strozzi and Domenico di Michelino who are documented within the Fra Angelico orbit at San Marco.[39] It is possible that monastic artistic centers offered lay artists an alternative working environment to the guild system. Legally these artists would have been immune from guild repercussions as long as they did not work in the *bottega* of a guild-affiliated artist.[40]

Monastic plans and descriptions of the physical layout of monasteries have yielded little precise information about work sites. The Gesuati of San Giusto in Florence, who prepared pigments and manufactured stained glass, maintained "buildings used as workshops to make colors." Vasari wrote of *officine* at San Giusto in the second cloister and a large room for making stained-glass windows on the third floor.[41] Manuscript illumination probably took place in a *scriptorium*, or if such a facility was

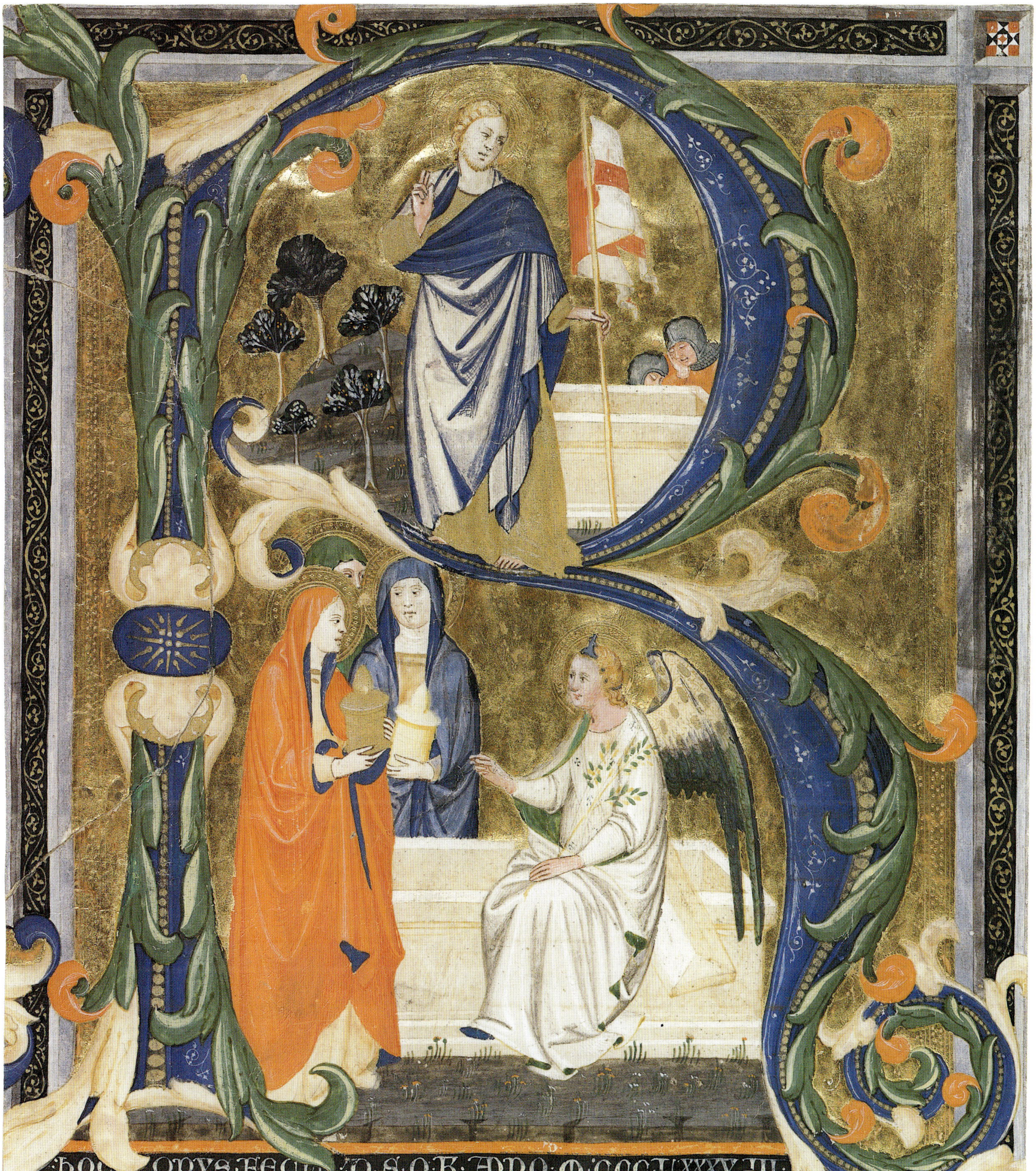

77 Don Simone Camaldolese, *Initial "R" with the Resurrection and the Three Marys at the Tomb*, 1388, New York, The Bernard H. Breslauer Collection.

lacking, in the vicinity of the convent library. Most monasteries had *officine* where maintenance work was done. We must assume that Don Lorenzo Monaco, Fra Angelico, Fra Bartolomeo, and Fra Filippo Lippi were given some space within their respective convent grounds where they could work on their panel paintings.

There is no information about the training of those monastic artists who did not acquire their skills in the *seculum* before taking their vows. Florentine secular artists were subjected to a lengthy apprenticeship lasting no less than three years, beginning when they were at least fourteen years old, according to guild statutes. They lived in their master's house and learned the rudiments of the art by performing the secondary, ancillary production tasks – grinding pigments, priming panels, cleaning the shop. The master paid the apprentice an annual wage (around ten florins), provided room, board, and certain articles of clothing in exchange for the apprentice's services.[42] The apprentice was obliged to endure the term of his indenture and could not work for another master until it was completed, subject to a fine if he violated the agreement.[43] In a guild system which encouraged the sons of masters to follow their father's trade by eliminating their guild matriculation fee, there was also a strong incentive to avoid the cost of indenturing apprentices by using family labor. Thus, the informal, unregulated apprenticeship of a master's sons and daughters could begin from the time the children were capable of holding a broom and last as long as they were unable financially to establish themselves independently, or in the case of the daughters, marry.

It is difficult to conceive how a monastic artist could have acquired a comparable immersion in the technical and practical foundations of craft production. There are no records of monks or friars serving as apprentices to secular artists. Monks and friars seem to have developed into artists almost exclusively when there was already a master or an artistic enterprise in place in the convent.[44] When Lorenzo Monaco became a Camaldolese in 1391, there was at least one Camaldolese miniaturist affiliated with his convent, Santa Maria degli Angeli, from whom he could have learned to paint.[45] We know that these monastic masters worked with *garzoni*, and it is feasible that on occasion these helpers were fellow *frati* engaged in a loose sort of apprenticeship. The Carmelite Fra Diamante trained under Fra Filippo Lippi – in this case outside the monastery, but with a fellow Carmelite. Vasari tells us that one of Fra Bartolomeo's disciples was the Dominican Fra Paolino Pistoiese.[46]

The very conditions of monastic production were such that a sustained high level of work over successive generations was a rarity. Monks and friars were frequently reassigned to new convents, in some orders every two or three years. Thus, a long period of close collaboration between two monastic artists would have been nearly impossible unless an exception were made. In addition, the Renaissance city represented a much larger potential talent pool than a monastic chapter or province. The child apprentices were often the sons of painters or artisans, as we have seen, and had already been socialized into the petty-bourgeois system which valued a production ethic and high standards of work.

This was probably not the case for the adolescents who entered the city's monasteries during the *quattrocento* – on account of personal choice dictated by religious devotion, a promise made by parents in thanks for an act of divine intervention, primogeniture, careerism orchestrated by the family, poverty, or the lack of an immediate family. The monastery did on occasion provide an alternative site for craft production, but this was not something given extraordinary emphasis in the rule or incanted daily in the Divine Offices. In one case involving Olivetans who practiced *intarsia* and wood carving in the late fifteenth and early sixteenth centuries, it took one established master, who had trained and worked in the *seculum* before joining the Order as a *converso*, or lay brother, and an inspired disciple, who himself may have been apprenticed to a craft before professing, to launch a monastic practice in which only a single generation of cloistered friars was able to learn the rudiments of the craft and carry on independently at something less than the level of their teachers.[47] Manuscript production at Santa Maria degli Angeli flourished for only fifty years. Most of the accomplished monastic artists during the early Renaissance received their training from lay professionals or were *conversi*.

I now want to take a closer look at the conditions under which monastic artists and craftworkers labored in their own convents. In-house production is defined as a situation in which a convent monk or friar produced work commissioned either by or for the convent, or by a patron or confraternity associated with the convent.

From 1379 through 1393, the name of the Olivetan friar Agostino Chiari of Florence appeared frequently in the account books of San Miniato al Monte. Over the fourteen-year period recorded, Fra Agostino Chiari seems to have been a "convent" illuminator and scribe (according to my definition of the term), working for his own monastery. He was engaged in the production of a manuscript from the purchase of the parchment through to the binding. He was supplied with (or reimbursed for) the necessary materials by the convent – pen, pigment, parchment, gold leaf, and leather for the book cover. He was never paid for his labor.[48] This accounting procedure is consistent for in-house monastic artists' production from the late *trecento* through the mid-*quattrocento*, persisting into the late *quattrocento* in the more observant houses like Monte Oliveto[49] and San Marco (Vasari tells us that Fra Bartolomeo kept only enough money "to pay for colours and other materials necessary for his painting"[50]).

By the mid-fifteenth century, the language used in the account books began to change. Instead of meticulously recording each individual payment for materials, the bookkeepers started to generalize: "for illuminating," "for making miniatures." There are two interesting Carmelite examples of this change. In 1436, a member of the Santa Maria del Carmine

78 Fra Giovanni da Verona, *Liturgical Objects*, 1503–05, intarsia from the choir stalls of Monte Oliveto Maggiore (Province of Siena).

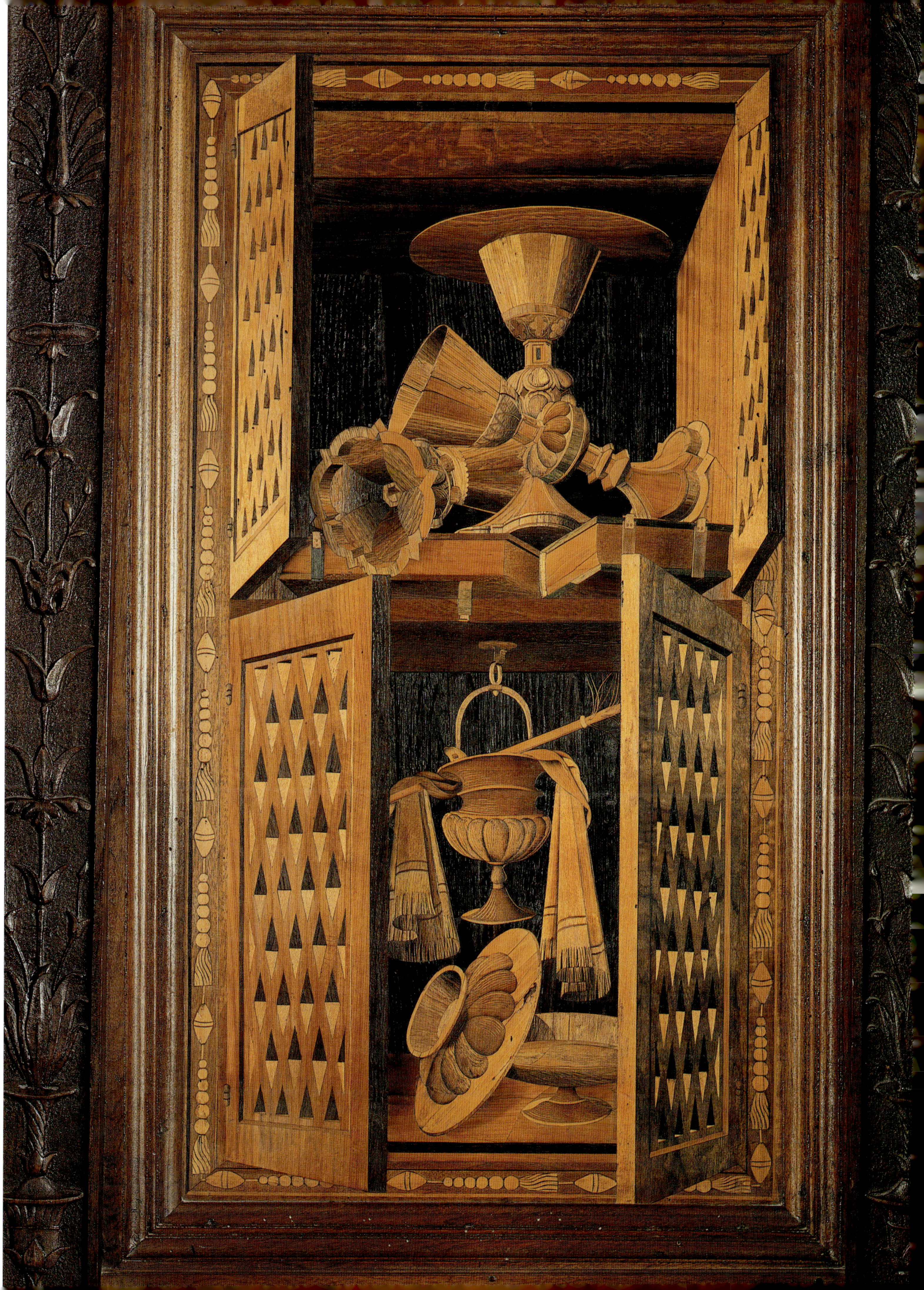

chapter, Fra Arrigo d'Arrigo, "remade" a painted crucifix and, in 1441, Fra Filippo Lippi painted a ceremonial casket for the body of the *trecento* Carmelite Beato Andrea Corsini. The Carmelite account book indicates that Fra Arrigo was reimbursed for his materials (wood and cloth) and for "the painting of the wood,"[51] while Fra Filippo was to be reimbursed "for a quantity of wood, for making the glue, for painting the casket of Beato Andrea."[52] The monastery was no longer merely providing the illuminator or painter with materials, but it was now supporting his artistic practice.

This development came about as the perceived value of painting was changing within society. A painter's ability to commemorate, honor, imitate, ornament, and beautify was increasingly regarded and sought after and, in turn, commanded higher prices. These transformations taking place in painting practice and theory outside the convent walls may well have encouraged the monastic support of those monastic artists who wielded the brush. The support extended to the relaxing of monastic regulations within the convent (even the Observant Dominican Fra Bartolomeo, Vasari informs us, "had a dispensation from attending any of the offices in the choir with the other friars," and was actively encouraged by his prior to paint).[53] It also led to the granting of permission for monastic painters to work outside the monastery walls.

MONASTIC ARTISTS WORKING OUTSIDE THE CONVENT

When the Olivetan illuminator Fra Bartolomeo moved from one Olivetan convent to another – from Monte Oliveto to Sant'Elena in Venice – from the perspective of the Monte Oliveto bookkeeper, "our illuminator" became "their illuminator."[54] When the Observant Dominican calligrapher Fra Benedetto di Piero of San Domenico in Fiesole (Fra Angelico's brother) copied out choral books for the Florentine Observant Dominican convent San Marco, his own convent was remunerated for his expenses and labor.[55] This in-house and out-of-house dichotomy became more pronounced when a friar worked for religious and lay patrons outside his own order. His painting practice at once began to resemble that of a professional secular painter.

A friar or monk needed permission from his superiors to leave the convent in order to undertake an artistic commission. While this was probably more often than not an informal procedure, under certain circumstances it required official sanction from the highest ranking administrator in the order or from the pope himself. The Dominican glazier Fra Giovanni de Lavezolis of Ferrara was requisitioned by Pope Nicholas V to glaze windows in the Vatican palace. The general master of the Dominican Order established the conditions under which he could accept this papal commission:

> On the day July 3 [1451], it was conceded to friar Johannes de Lavezolis of Ferrara that he be allowed to remain outside a convent of the Order in honest society while he executes the glass windows for the Supreme Pontiff, and that he be allowed to accept a benefice – curatorial or non-curatorial – with the authorizing intervention of the Apostolic See. He is also authorized to choose a suitable confessor of the Order who would absolve him four times a year of those [sins] that a master of the Order is able. He may also receive alms and distribute them within the Order.[56]

Fra Giovanni need not live in a Dominican convent, but he had to confess to a Dominican master four times a year, and while he was permitted to hold a benefice, any alms that he received had to be turned over to the Order. An anecdote describing the conditions under which Fra Angelico lived during his own stay in the Vatican working for the same pope was recorded by the chronicler P. Girolamo Borselli at the end of the *quattrocento*:

> This beatific man was so religious and observant that even while staying in the palace of Pope Nicholas V, he observed all of the rules of his . . . religious order. And Nicholas V, because of the veneration he held for him on account of his sanctity and virtue, going sometimes to visit him while he was painting the chapel that is in the papal palace, one day said to him: "Fra Giovanni, I desire that today, in acknowledgment of your work, you eat meat." To which he responded, "Most beatific Father, I haven't requested a license from my prior." And the Pope: "I give you permission."[57]

We have already seen that monastic illuminators could leave their own monasteries to reside in the monastery, often of another order, that was commissioning the manuscript. Other monastic artists took up lodgings in the *seculum*. Fra Angelico – considered to have been the most observant of monastic painters – nonetheless stayed in an inn in Orvieto with his *garzoni* and assistant before moving into a house owned by his patron, the Opera del Duomo, rather than retreating to the Dominican convent located across town.[58] Lippi is not the only monastic painter who lived in the *seculum* for an extended period. Lorenzo Monaco, who had professed in 1391, was living beyond the walls of Santa Maria degli Angeli by at least 1402, when he was residing in the parish of San Bartolomeo del Corso in Florence. He was frequently referred to as "Don Lorenzo fu degli Angnoli" from this point onward. In 1411, he bought a house from the monks of Santa Maria degli Angeli adjacent to the convent which he must have used as a habitation and a workspace. He had at least two lay assistants in his employ in 1421–22.[59]

From the *trecento* through the *quattrocento*, the friars and monks were paid rates competitive with professional lay painters, following standard contract conventions. Illuminators were paid by the painted letter or by the day. A Dominican glazier was paid per square *braccia* of glass.[60] The burning question is whether they were allowed to keep the money that they earned when painting, illuminating, glazing, and sculpting. While the various rules of the monastic orders declared that no property could be held individually by a member of the monastic community, by the *trecento* and *quattrocento*, both constitutional amendments and permissive priors and abbots of the monasteries had relaxed this rubric, even in mendicant houses. Certain religious curative duties were remunerated and ordained monks had a ready source of income from performing the sacraments. Singing a mass could bring in l.4, and a baptism l.1 s.16. Preaching was even more lucrative. The Dominican Fra Bartolomeo Rimbertini, Bishop of Cortona, netted f.28 l.2 in alms for preaching during Lent and Easter at Santa Maria Novella in 1441.[61] The understanding was that alms earned in this manner would go back into the service of God – pay for a monk's or friar's upkeep while traveling from one convent to another. However, monasteries had begun to make considerable concessions for the benefit of members from the patrician class. Monks and friars were no longer always required to turn over their personal patrimony to the convent upon their profession, and were often allowed to bequeath their property to whomever they chose. They held shares in the *comune*'s funded debt (the Monte) in their own names and collected the annual interest for their personal use.[62] Stefano Orlandi has demonstrated that during the *trecento* many of the Dominicans of Santa Maria Novella maintained personal financial accounts banked with the prior.[63]

Antonio Manetti insisted that Fra Angelico "never painted for a fee and if he received one for something, all was for the convent."[64] Fra Angelico's tomb epitaph poetically conveys something of the same: "Let me not be praised because I seemed another Apelles, but because I gave all my riches, O Christ, to Thine."[65] And in fact, Fra Angelico's payment records reveal deviations from standard practices. It is clearly the friars of San Marco and not the artist who were being paid for the panel mentioned in the following convent account book entry: "he leaves seven ducats for us as part of the payment of a painting that Giovanni [Fra Angelico] must paint."[66] When working in Orvieto, Fra Angelico negotiated a contract with the Opera of the Duomo where even his *garzoni* received a monthly salary from the patrons rather than being paid out of the master's earnings, as was the common *bottega* custom.[67] Lippi and his assistant Fra Diamante appear to have had a similar arrangement in Prato.[68] When Fra Bartolomeo's partnership with Albertinelli was dissolved in 1513, his half of the assets were clearly stated as belonging to the friars of San Marco.[69]

It appears that practices varied considerably and that the situation at San Marco was more the exception than the rule. The Dominican Fra Giovanni di Campi of Santa Maria Novella evidently kept the money given to him by the Florentine *comune* for his part in designing the Ponte alla Carraia in the early *trecento*.[70] Monks and friars who lived outside the convent like Lorenzo Monaco, Lippi, and Fra Diamante were apparently allowed to keep their earnings in order to support themselves. Lippi's finances were clearly independent from the Carmine and whatever he earned, received, or, like a good mendicant, begged for, was his own to spend as he wished.[71]

Within the Benedictine Order, the situation had apparently reached such a state that in 1461 the abbot general Niccolò da Reggio proclaimed a constitution to redress the problem of profit derived from monastic artistic activity. He decreed that those monks who were also artisans "may not practice a craft just for profit."[72] In contrast, at the end of the century, one Benedictine was granted permission, through a papal *breve*, to leave his monastery and work as a miniaturist in the *seculum* in order to pay off debts he had accrued as abbot.[73]

The fact that monastic artists worked outside the guild system and within the monastic chain of command could cause patrons problems. The Benedictines of the Badia in Florence noted in their account book that the Camaldolese miniaturist Don Niccolò Rossello, whom they had engaged to illuminate a psalter, "left on the day of September 2, 1443, because he was sent by his general to Venice with the intention of returning on the sixth of the said month in the morning to begin working."[74] They could only hope that he would be back at work when he said. In 1415, the Dominican glazier of Santa Maria Novella, Fra Bernardino di Stefano, took a 50 florin advance on two *oculi* windows for the Florentine Duomo and ran. The Opera del Duomo tried in vain for sixteen years to get its money back from the friar, who had moved to Arezzo and later Volterra.[75] Lippi's patrons, perhaps well aware that his monastic superiors gave him as much latitude as he desired in his secular pursuits, appealed not only to the ecclesiastical courts but also to his other patrons in order to insure that the *frate dipintore* would see through to completion their commissions.[76]

NUNS AND ARTISTIC PRODUCTION

There are few known examples of nuns engaged in artistic activities in Florence during the *quattrocento*. This reflects the state of archival research more than actual incidence. As more scholars take an interest in female enclosure, our knowledge of this field of activity will undoubtedly increase.

The nuns practiced crafts that were typical of the female labor force – embroidery, spinning, and weaving. They were also involved in book production. At Le Murate in Florence they sold cloth and manuscripts, and also painted gesso casts and produced essences. A surviving example of their needlework is the embroidered altarcloth decorated with golden doves made in 1449 for the high altar of the Collegiate church of San Gimignano (fig. 79).[77] Milanesi discovered that Paolo Uccello's daughter Antonia (1452–91), who was described as a "pittoressa" in the Florentine death registers, was a Carmelite nun.[78]

Nunneries had fewer opportunities to generate income than male monastic institutions and if a nunnery were not well endowed, art and craft production could play an important role

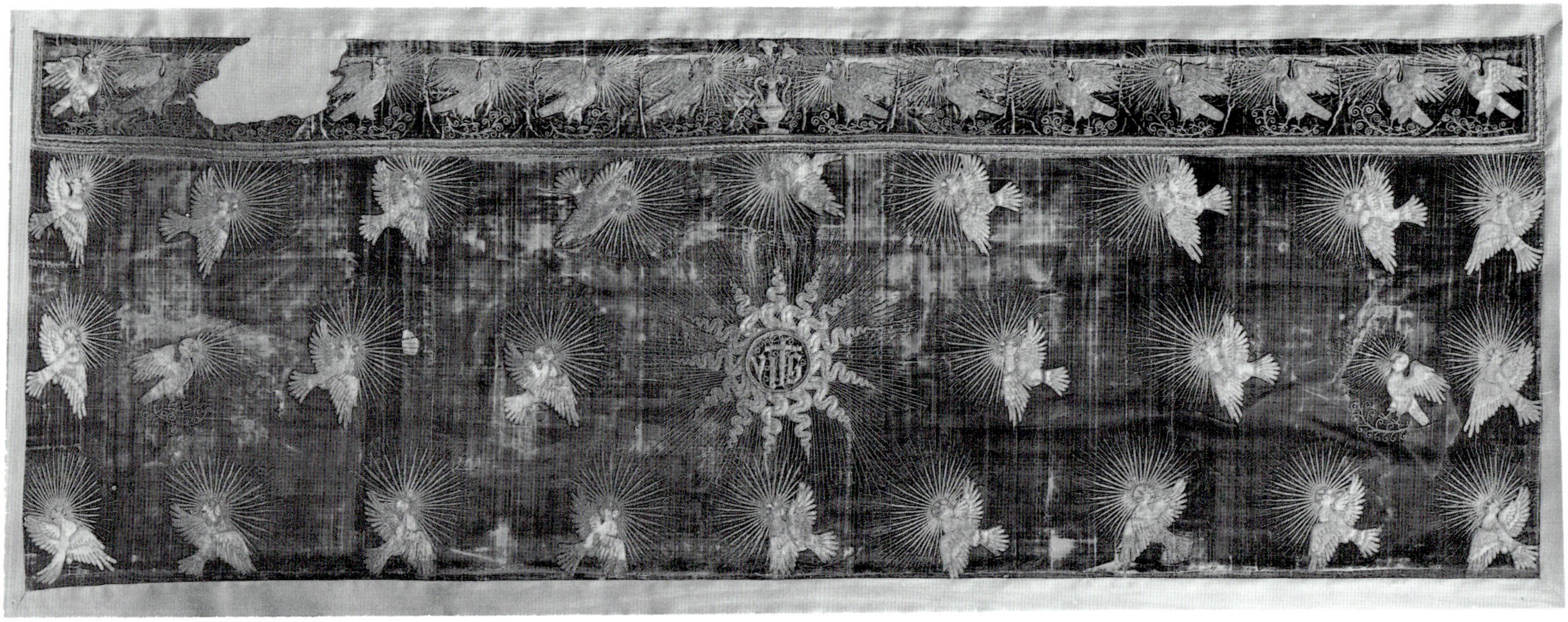

79 The nuns of Le Murate, embroidered altarcloth ("Paliotto delle Colombe d'Oro"), 1449, San Gimignano, Museo dell'Arte Sacra.

in supporting the nuns. It is not surprising to find the most "professional" production circumstances in Siena, where the historian Samuel Cohn has noted that nunneries were infrequent beneficiaries of lay pious donations during the *quattrocento*.[79] The nuns of Santa Maria Maddelena in Siena were actively engaged in book production, providing liturgical manuscripts for the Hospital of Santa Maria della Scala and the Opera del Duomo. In one case, they were paid by the illuminated initial like their male professional and monastic colleagues.[80]

One important difference between the artistic endeavors of the nuns and those of monks and friars was that the enclosure vow was much more strictly enforced for the women. The nuns' artistic activity necessarily took place within the convent. Joint projects with lay practitioners – such as the Roman missal copied at Le Murate in 1509 by the Benedictine Suora Battista Carducci and illuminated by a lay artist identified as Attavante Attavanti – were probably impersonal collaborations organized through male intermediaries.[81] Art historians, overly preoccupied with a quality criterion, note that the consequences of this enclosure – lack of adequate training, isolation, and lack of competition – limited the nun's achievements as illuminators.[82] What they fail to emphasize is that contemporaries were probably just as interested in a devotional criterion as in a quality criterion when evaluating the work of the nuns. In a field where manuscript production was increasingly dominated by lay professionals, the manuscripts produced in the nunneries were probably most valued as public manifestations of the devotion and industry of the enclosed nuns, which were of greater interest to the Florentines than the nuns' skill as painters.

* * *

80 Detail of fig. 79.

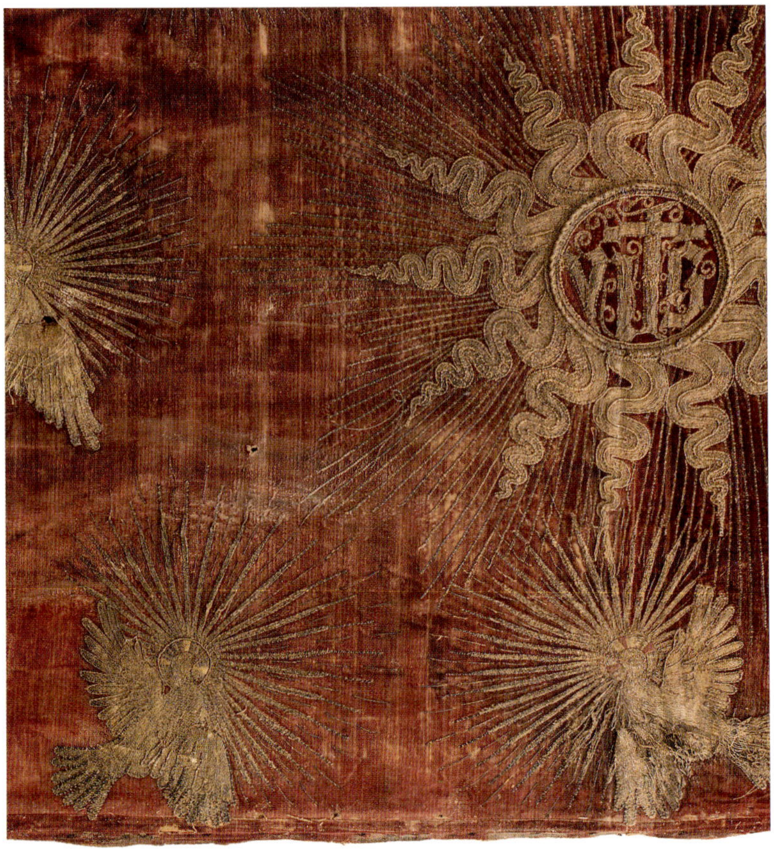

CONCLUSIONS

The Benedictine Order appears to have given its artisan members the greatest degree of freedom, which comes as no surprise considering the emphasis given to artisanal labor in the Benedictine Rule. There are a number of cases where artists left mendicant orders for the Benedictines or one of their derivative orders: Lippi's key assistant during the Prato and Spoleto projects, Fra Diamante, had switched from the Carmelite to the Vallombrosan Order by 1461.[83] The Observant Dominicans appear to have been among the most strict, insisting that their monastic artists follow the Rule and constitutions close to the letter. A large percentage of the monastic artists in all orders were *conversi*. These members of the monastic community had fewer religious obligations and hence more concentrated time to work as artists and artisans. They also had more contact with lay society and hence greater freedom to purchase their own materials, shop-talk with fellow practitioners, and procure commissions.[84]

Most of the Italian *quattrocento* religious painters, glaziers, miniaturists, sculptors, and intarsiasts learned their art before professing, so the secular sphere of patronage, collaboration, and profit was a familiar one to them. Even when the friar practitioners – like Fra Filippo Lippi – had not painted professionally before joining their religious orders, secular painting production inevitably influenced their artistic activity. The *quattrocento frati dipintori* purchased their materials from laymen and were often contracted by lay patrons. They collaborated with lay artists and had the technical value of their paintings translated into monetary value by lay artists assigned to *stimare* their work. Their painting was appraised for aesthetic, performative merit in the discourses of the lay literary class. There was considerable interaction and exchange between the social field of the *frate dipintore* tied to the monastery and the social field of painting production in the *seculum* (understood in its broadest terms).

While there is stylistic consistency within the works of a single monastic artist, one cannot point to a *quattrocento* "monastic pictorial style." The training of the artists was too diverse and, as Boskovits has pointed out, the fact that they moved from one convent to another exposed the monastic painters to a wide range of artistic influences.[85] In the early *quattrocento*, monastic painters produced almost exclusively religious subjects, but this changed toward the end of the century when monastic miniaturists began to illuminate a greater number of classical and secular texts.[86]

THE *FRATE DIPINTORE*

I want to close this discussion by returning to the specific case of the *frate dipintore*. It is important to emphasize that *frati dipintori* were not common among the monastic artists and artisans in Tuscany, who tended to be more involved in manuscript illumination, window glazing, and woodwork during the *trecento* and *quattrocento*.[87] Thus, the large number of monastic painters working in Renaissance Florence – Don Lorenzo Monaco, Fra Domenico, Fra Angelico, Fra Filippo Lippi, Fra Diamante, and Fra Bartolomeo – requires an explanation.[88] A second point regards the role that painting production played in the Florentine Renaissance monastic economy. Certainly, enterprises like the manuscript production at Santa Maria degli Angeli, the Badia, and San Marco (like the wool production of the Umiliati of Ognissanti and the pigment and stained-glass manufacture of the Gesuati of San Giusto) were money-making ventures important to the financial well-being of these monasteries. This was not the case for monastic painters. By the *quattrocento* in Florence, the monastic economy – including that of the major mendicant foundations of Santa Croce, Santa Maria Novella, Santa Maria del Carmine, and Santo Spirito – was generated principally by property revenues and pious bequests.[89] There must then have been other reasons that were not directly economic or tied to the relief of boredom that prompted monastic superiors to permit painter members to practice their craft. I shall begin with the obvious.

Considering the sectarian character of monasticism, evident in the insistence of each order upon certain tenets and scriptural interpretations, monastic religious art offered the possibility of clearly displaying the orthodoxy of an individual order. Paintings by monastic artists – particularly works commissioned for their own convents – display an iconography grounded in the religious beliefs and devotional traditions of their respective orders. Many of Fra Angelico and Fra Bartolomeo's frescos and panels display a distinctly Observant Dominican iconography, Lippi's early work conveys Carmelite themes (and some of his later painting too, as shall be demonstrated), and Lorenzo Monaco's altarpieces (fig. 81) represent Camaldolesi concerns.[90] This was particularly important to their respective orders in a period when monasteries were sacrificing control over the religious decorative programs within their churches and convents in exchange for generous and self-proclaiming patronage by wealthy patricians. Monastic artists, working for the convent, or for confraternities or private patrons within the monastery, offered the monks or friars one means of wresting back some part in the structuring of religious vision – in determining the disposition of the Divine and the character of the sacred.

Painting had also begun to play a more important role in lay religious devotion. A growing middle class had begun to invest in what amounted to a sort of religious insurance. Altars in monastic churches proliferated and were patronized by families and confraternities.[91] Monks, friars, and secular clergy were enlisted as chaplains to service these altars and recite masses before them. Religious images were installed in the chapels, both as devotional aids and visual testimony to the patrons' piety, evident in the apparent expense and aesthetic value of the work. Religious paintings were also placed above private altars, and on the walls and in niches in the home, and monastic painters were also commissioned to execute these private devotional works.

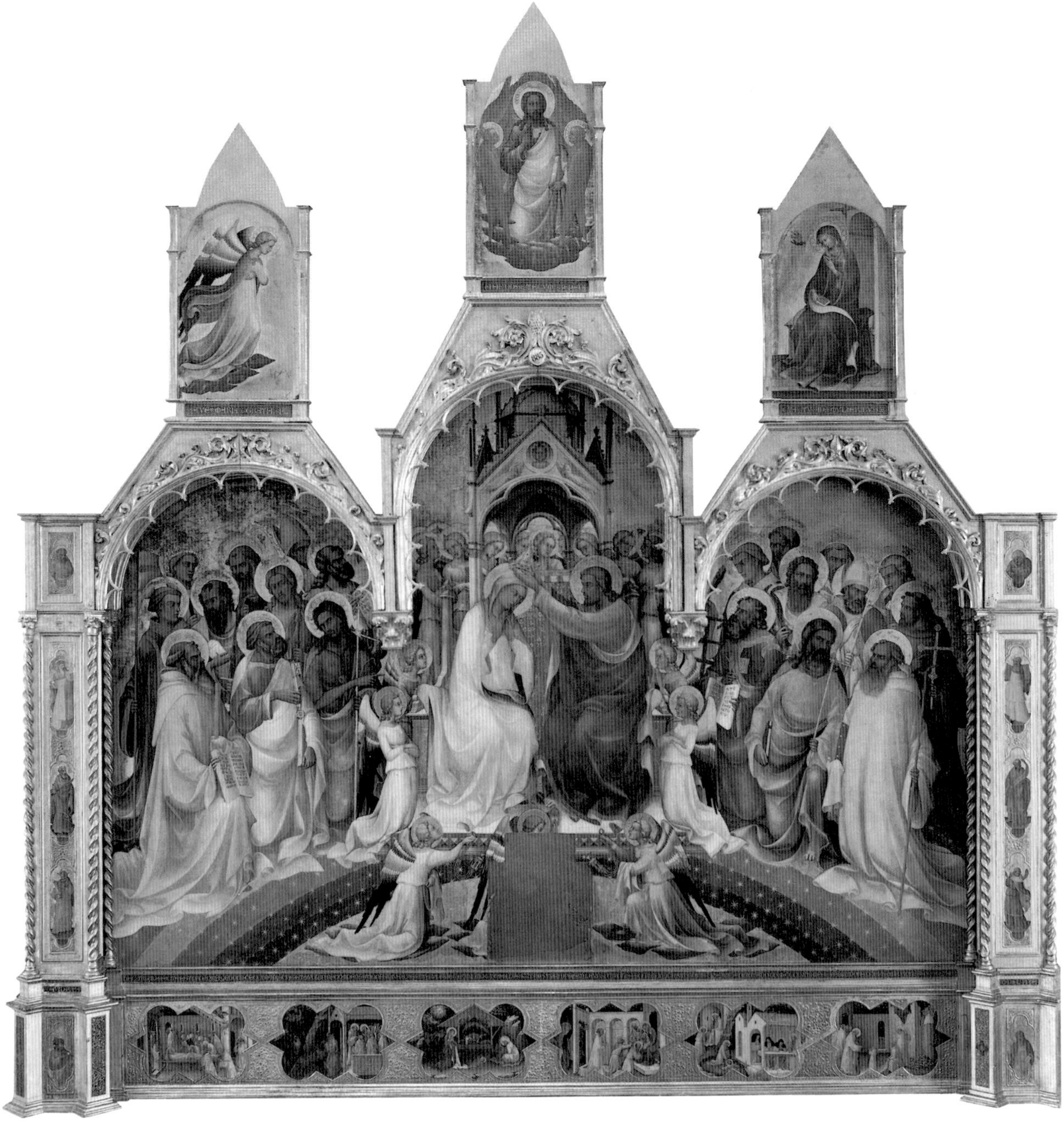

81 Lorenzo Monaco, *Coronation of the Virgin*, 1414, Florence, Uffizi.

It is possible, following the medieval discursive tradition, that people may have considered a religious representation produced by a monastic artist to be more devout, to have a more immediate, privileged claim on the sacred personage or scene depicted.[92] Cristoforo Landino described Fra Angelico's painting as "*devoto*," which Michael Baxandall translates according to contemporary usage as "easily understood and good for edifying and instructing people."[93] A fellow Dominican, Fra Domenico da Corella, wrote in 1469 of Fra Angelico that "above other painters, to him deservedly was given one grace, of rendering the Virgin."[94] Vasari noted that a St. Bernard by Fra Bartolomeo (see fig. 76) had "a certain celestial quality, I know not what, which seems to him who studies it with attention, to shine out over that work, into which Baccio put much diligence and love."[95] Could the laity of Santa Maria del Carmine have commissioned an image of St. Alberto from the Carmelite Fra Filippo Lippi because they thought it had a greater purchase on the sacred and would be more efficacious? There is no evidence to support this, but it is a provocative thought.

These explanations and suggestions do not, however, bring us any closer to understanding why there were so many monastic painters in Florence during the *quattrocento*. Is it possible to identify something particular to the Florentine experience – something related to the status accorded the art of painting in the city, the characteristics of that painting, and the nature of contemporary religious practices, even more specifically, of contemporary Florentine mendicant religious practices – that would explain the phenomenon? Of the six monastic artists mentioned, five were mendicants – two Observant Dominicans (Fra Angelico and Fra Bartolomeo), two Carmelites (Fra Filippo and Fra Diamante), and one probably Dominican (Fra Domenico). What was it about Florentine mendicant religious practices that encouraged the artistic enterprise and the patronage of these *frati dipintori*? This complex question is, in some sense, at the core of this study of Lippi's life and art. Here, I shall hazard some generalizations.

After the plague, in the late *trecento* and early *quattrocento*, the mendicant monasteries found themselves the benefactors of land and monied gifts, with their own ranks reduced by a half and, in some places, two thirds.[96] It was necessary to recruit new members, and at the same time to adjust to a new role as the bankers of the city's "religious patrimony." This new wealth gave the mendicant clergy a power base – of which rival interests like the *comune*, the local secular clergy, the papal curia, down to the neighboring land-owner, were very much aware. Savage attacks against the mendicants that caricatured their lax moral standards, lack of education, sexual license, greed, worldly pursuits, and spiritual depravity were not merely disinterested comments by objective observers noting what the documentary record confirms were frequent and flagrant transgressions.[97] They were criticisms by rival interests charged against a population that had been granted immunity from local laws and was flaunting wealth and power in contradiction of its traditional principles. This was not true of all mendicant foundations, particularly the smaller houses, and should not be exaggerated, as the mendicants were poor in comparison to the "possessionate" orders like the Benedictines. But nonetheless, the friars with their private incomes and convent endowments were visibly living a more luxurious life than their founders had.

Mendicant establishments were not impervious to the criticisms – they could not afford to be. Their well-being depended on their maintaining good relations with their ecclesiastical superiors, courting the laity that traditionally formed their patronage base, and keeping the secular clergy and *comune* off their backs. In addition, new trends in pious donations meant that lay people left their property more frequently in the hands of lay charitable institutions like the Hospital of Santa Maria Nuova, the Bigallo, and the Capitani di Orsanmichele, with instructions for annual payments to be made to the various mendicant houses among other religious foundations, often with provisions that the allocations be terminated if the friars failed in their obligations to the deceased. Thus, the mendicants received fewer direct property gifts and were more accountable to their lay patrons.

The mendicant clergy adopted several strategies to strengthen their position and to defend themselves against public criticism. One was to encourage the recruitment of patrician members, consolidating their ranks from within. The reform movements represent another response to public criticism. Yet another front was a sort of "media spectacle" generated by each order, promoting a positive image of monasticism. This involved the mobilization of a symbolic language emphasizing the monastic tradition, tenets, notable history, saints, and inspiring members of the order. This symbolic language permeated the sermons, texts, and visual images produced by the orders. It is here that the monastic artists played a role. Fra Angelico painted multiple images of the Madonna and Child flanked by the Dominican saints Dominic, Peter Martyr, and Thomas Aquinas – founder, defender, and codifier of Dominican orthodoxy (fig. 82). Fra Filippo Lippi represented the only two Carmelite *beati*, Fra Angelo of Licata and Fra Alberto of Trapani, and was directly involved in the celebration of a potential new local Florentine *beato*, Fra Andrea Corsini.

Monastic artists could also function as representatives or servants of their orders. Painting was a skill of increasing value in *quattrocento* Florentine society and monastic artists who offered their talents to notable patricians were themselves involved in power broking. Cosimo de' Medici's recourse to Fra Angelico's talent cannot be separated from Cosimo's relationship to the Observant Dominicans of San Marco. Perhaps the most blatant example of monastic artistic diplomacy occurred in 1509, when the prior of San Marco presented two small devotional images painted by Fra Bartolomeo to the Gonfaloniere of the Florentine Republic, Piero Soderini, in thanks for the return of the convent bell that had been confiscated in the aftermath of the Savonarolan episode. This exchange marked a thaw in relations between the new city government and the Observant convent.[98]

In so far as the mendicants were perceived as the most flagrant violators of their monastic rules and vows, and their behavior offered the greatest contradiction with that of the primitive monastic communities, efforts by the mendicants to clean up their public image were the most energetic. Their encouragement of the monastic painters within their ranks as ideologues and representatives outside the convent can be seen as part of this endeavor to generate a positive image of mendicant monasticism among the urban laity. (In Lippi's case, it would have been his art, as opposed to his comportment, that would have promoted such an image.)

There may be another explanation for the emergence of mendicant painters in *quattrocento* Florence, which is related to the role of mendicant monasticism in lay religious practices and to the changing character of religious representation.

During the *quattrocento*, the mendicants continued to serve as important orchestrators of lay religious activity. They were the clerical administrators of the private chapels and altars within their churches and were hosts of some of the city's most active confraternities.[99] John Henderson explains the appeal that the mendicant association had for the urban laity: "the smaller devotional companies of laud-singers or flagellants . . . provided the

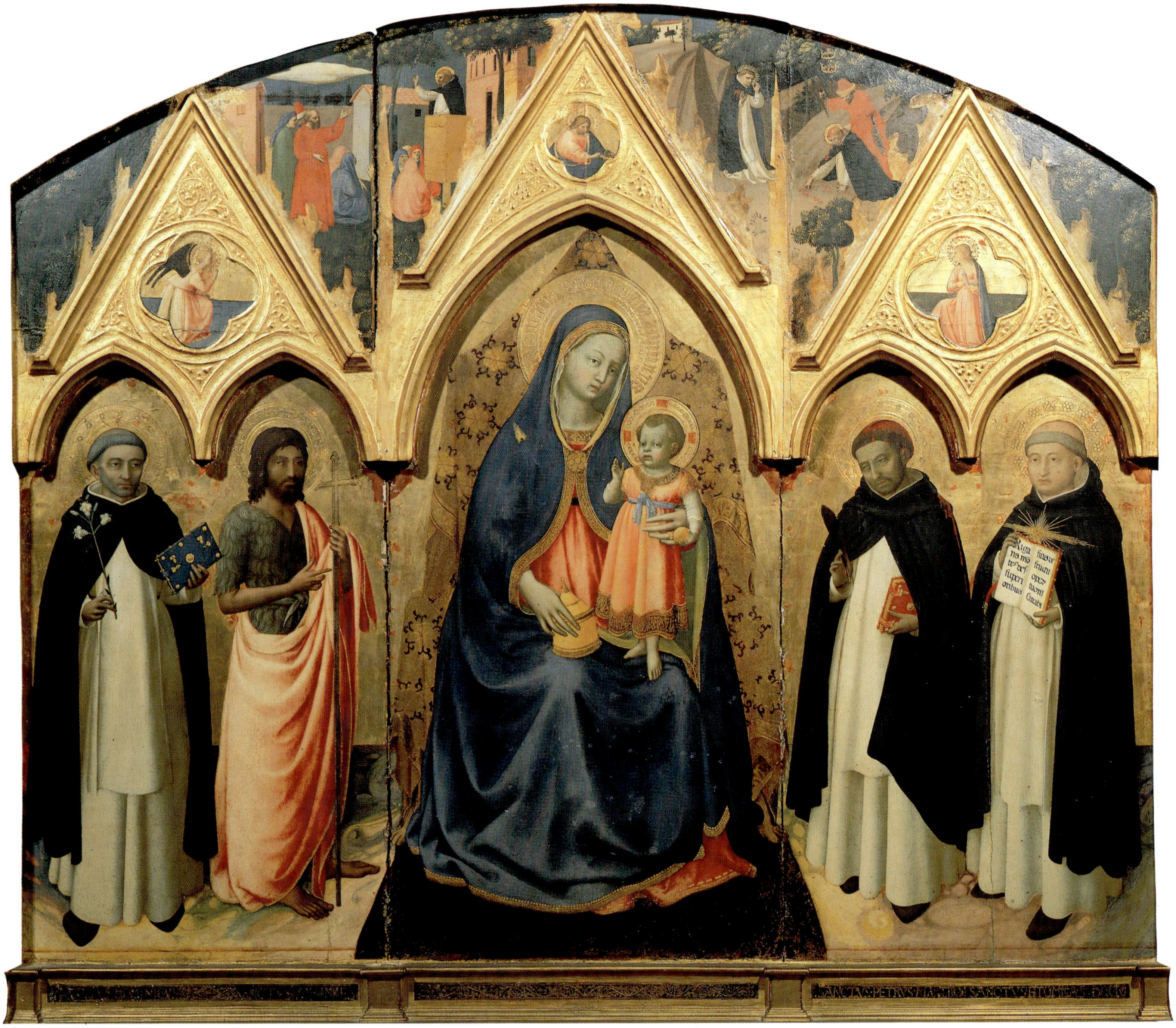

82 Fra Angelico, San Pier Martire altarpiece, 1428–29, Florence, Museo di San Marco.

layman with the opportunity to deepen his spiritual experience by taking part in para-liturgical services based on the monastic model."[100] In addition to offering the laity a model of religious devotion, the mendicants were, in a sense, co-producers of the *sacre rappresentazioni*, the festive processions, and the religious representations that were staged on their premises. The Observant Dominicans of San Marco hosted the Compagnia dei Magi and their church was the final destination of the Compagnia's annual Epiphany procession. An Annunciation play may have been performed annually in the Servite church of SS. Annunziata, while the Laudesi Compagnia di Sant'Agnese organized the Ascension Day play in Santa Maria del Carmine. The Dominicans of Santa Maria Novella promoted the Corpus Christi cult.

Meanwhile, during the *quattrocento*, religious representations – whether dramatic, processional, liturgical, painted, or sculpted – increasingly played on illusionism, as opposed to the *imitatione* of the previous century. Gone were the days when the Bianchi coursed through the city streets encouraging people to participate in the penitential acts to which they subjected themselves. Gone too were the times when flagellant brotherhoods seriously used their whips in *imitatio Christi*.[101] *Trecento* pictorial imagery encouraged the devotee to use the symbolic elements as points of departure for mental re-enactment of (or "shaping oneself to") the biblical dramas and saints' stories.[102] Instead, during the *quattrocento*, religious rituals were simulations carried off through acting, machinery, costume, and art. The century saw the elaboration, fine-tuning, and recording of the *sacra rappresentazione*. The Compagnia dei Magi dressed up in the guise of kings and retainers and processed through the streets. The altarpiece became a window into a discrete "other" place. These were all expressions of a gradual movement away from religious spectacles whose authority to represent the sacred was secured by occasional miraculous manifestations, toward spectacles whose authority to represent the sacred was purely representational. Instead of the guarantee of Real Presence – potent images and relics, holy men and women, the sacred directly manifest through miracles – this new religious art and spectacle offered a mediated presence, "likeness." In the process, the devotee was transformed into a spectator, observing the enactment with some detachment rather than actively participating or "witnessing" it.[103]

My argument is that for a brief period during the *quattrocento* in Florence, when the experience of religious viewing was becoming less empathetic and more intellectual than it had ever been, and the look of the sacred problematically close to mundane appearances, mendicants acted as the guarantors of the sacred relationship between the simulacrum and the referent in religious representations. The mendicant painters were, in a sense, called upon to produce a certain kind of religious pageant for a privileged sector of the Florentine laity – a performative religion. The so-called *sacre conversazioni* of Fra Filippo and Fra Angelico are altarpiece performances. The Albertian *istorie* in their frescos, narrative altarpieces, and predella panels display vivid enactments of Christian mysteries and episodes from saints' lives. The fact that Cosimo de' Medici's palace chapel altarpiece, the *Adoration of the Christ Child*, was painted by Fra Filippo Lippi Carmelitano, and the *Adoration of the Magi* in his private cell at San Marco was frescoed under the direction of Fra Giovanni (Angelico) Domenicano, were important confirmations of the sacred character of the religious ritual in which the Medici family head cast his "devotional gaze" upon these images.[104] In the palace chapel, Fra Angelico's lay artistic progeny, Benozzo Gozzoli, had been hired to represent the fanfare and pageantry of the Magi's procession along the walls (see figs. 175 and 176). But it was the Carmelite Fra Filippo Lippi who provided the scenography for the culmination of the journey – for the witnessing of the mystery of the advent of Christ (see fig. 178).

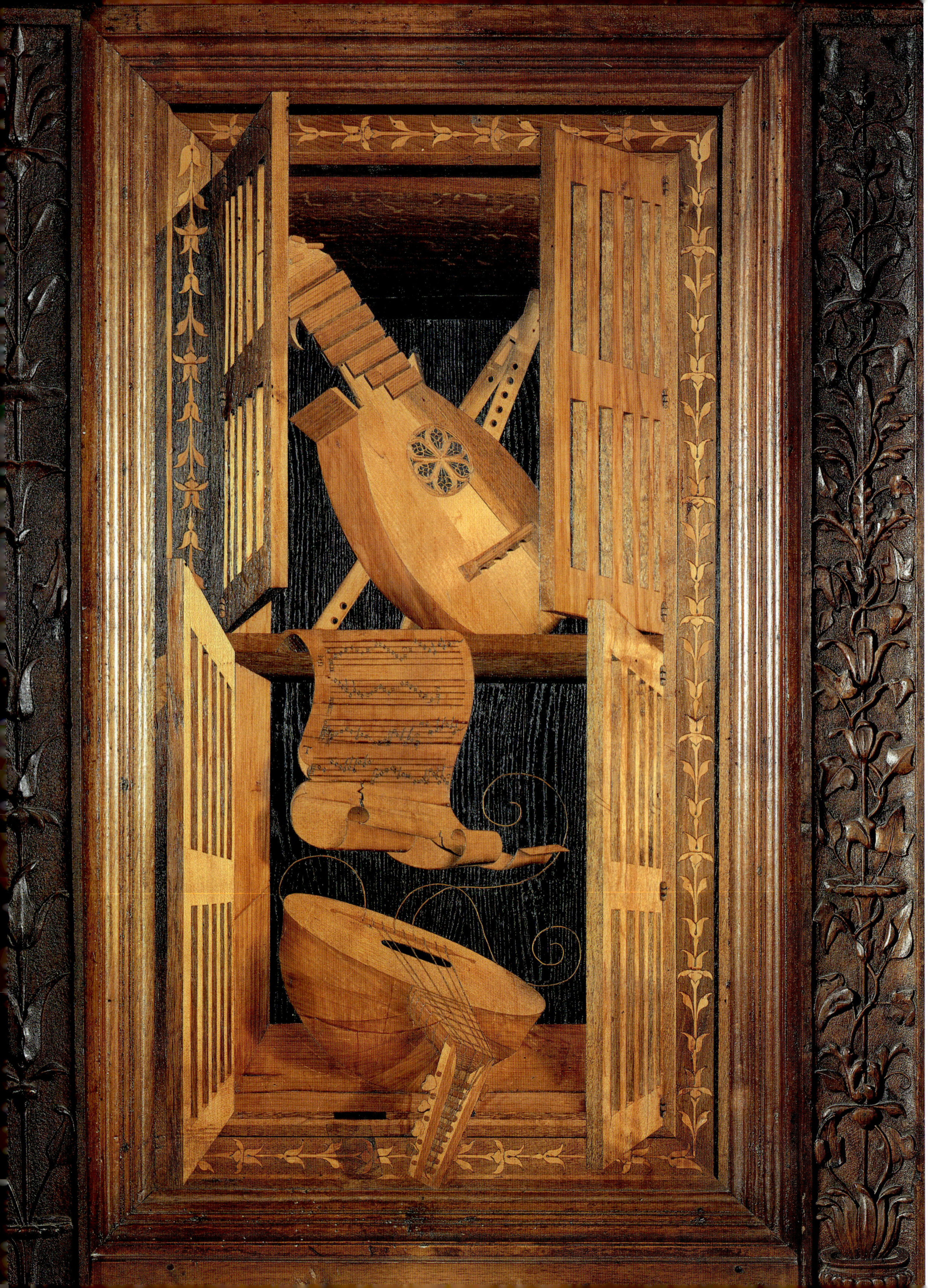

PART II

THE *SECULUM*

83 Fra Giovanni da Verona, *Musical Instruments*, 1503–05,
intarsia from the choir stalls of Monte Oliveto Maggiore (Province of Siena).

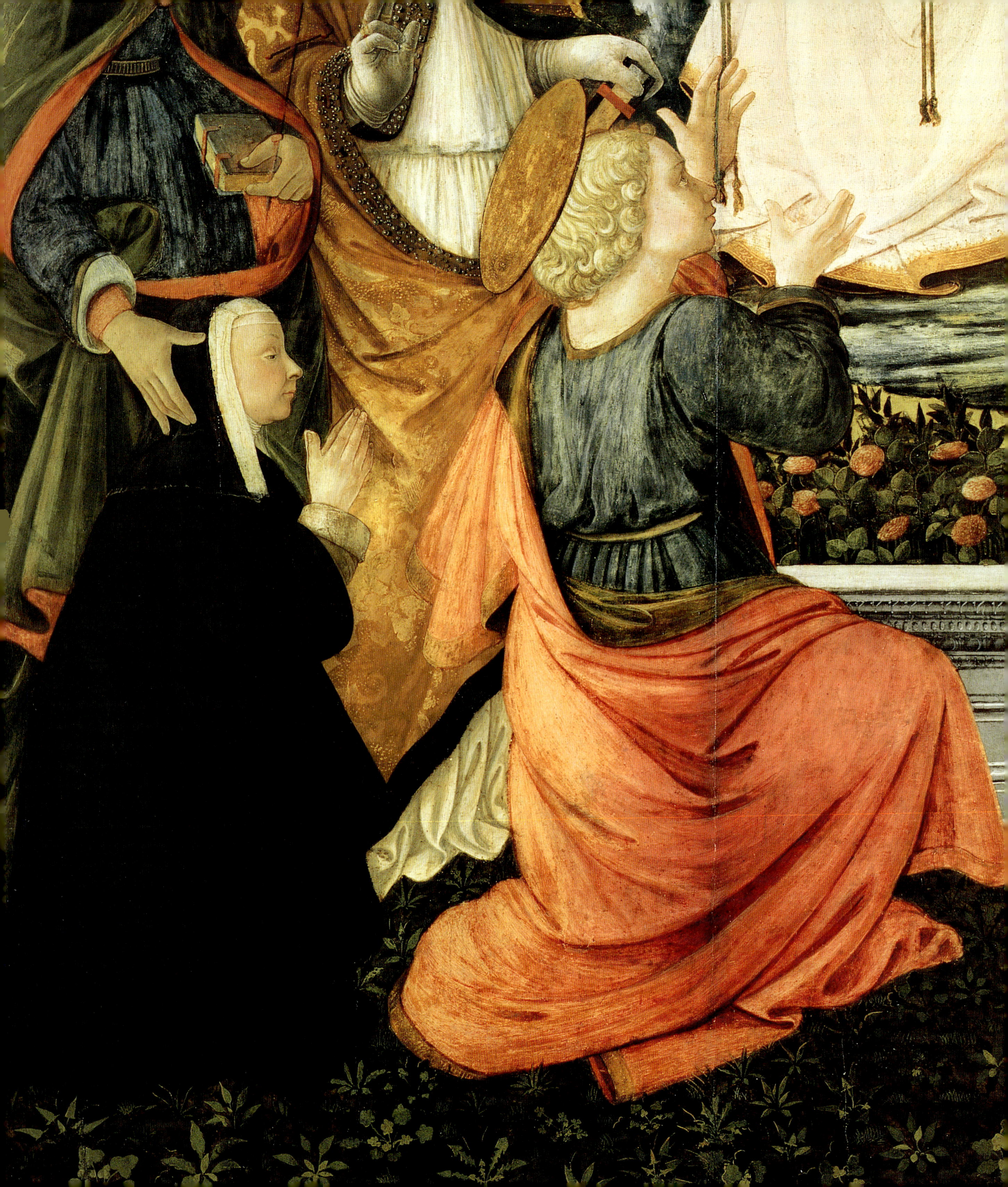

CHAPTER FIVE

FRA FILIPPO LIPPI IN THE *SECULUM*: FRIAR, RECTOR, CHAPLAIN, AND ROGUE

As Lippi passed from the *claustrum* to the *seculum* some time after 1432, his position within Florentine society became considerably less clear.[1] The Carmelite corporate condition had provided him with an identity, a code of behavior, fixed positions on controversial questions, and ready relationships with a particular group of the laity, the patrons of Santa Maria del Carmine. Outside the cloister, these positions were no longer as relevant, and they had to be redefined in relation to a new and pressing concern – the economic survival of the professional painter. Fra Filippo's social identity and status as a "religious" subject in contemporary Florentine society, however, remained. He was still a vested friar of the Carmelite Order with close ties to the Florentine Carmine. He became the rector of the parish church of San Quirico at Legnaia in 1442 and chaplain of the nunnery San Niccolò de' Frieri in 1450, and of the nunnery Santa Margherita in Prato in 1456. With these new positions, he entered the milieu of the beneficed friar, another ambiguous area, falling between the jurisdiction of the general prior of his order and the Florentine Archiepiscopacy. My argument here is that it was the indeterminacy of Lippi's social place and his exploitation of this condition that afforded him the degree of elasticity (and audacity) with which he handled his personal, professional, and religious affairs in the *seculum*. From this indeterminant position, he worked the edges and pushed the limits of the various social and representational fields in which he acted. During the *quattrocento*, the parameters of the permissible, while defined institutionally, and maintained through socio-economic relations, were ever changing according to the discretionary power of the prior of the convent, a well-placed patron, or the pope himself. They also could be manipulated by an artist's display of *ingegno*.

One of the central premises of this study is the primacy – or the over-arching determination – of the religious sphere in relation to Lippi's life and art. I shall devote this chapter to tracking and contextualizing his religious affiliations and activities during the years, the mature phase of his career, when he lived and worked in the *seculum*.

LIPPI AND THE FLORENTINE CARMELITES

Fra Filippo maintained his relationship with the friars of Santa Maria del Carmine in Florence after he moved his artistic enterprise to the *seculum*. Whether he actually remained a member of the Florentine chapter of Carmelites is difficult to determine. While he is always called "frate" in the documents, his Carmelite affiliation is recorded in a number of different ways. He is referred to as "Friar Filippo di Tommaso," "who was once a friar of the Carmine," "of the Carmelite Order," "of the friars of Santa Maria del Carmine," and "of the Carmelites of Florence." This variation was probably caused by the actual ambiguity of his position. He had been a member of the Florentine chapter of Carmelites and had been given permission by his monastic superiors to live and paint outside the convent, while retaining his status as a Carmelite. He was technically accountable to his Carmelite superiors for his actions in the *seculum*.

Lippi's name is absent from Carmelite records between January 1432 and January 1439. During this time, he is recorded working as a painter in Padua in 1434, and he must have been back in Florence by at least 1437. He appears to have resumed close contact with the friars of Santa Maria del Carmine between 1439 and 1441 – years that proved to be of particular significance for the Carmelites. This period overlapped with the year served by his brother, Fra Giovanni di Tommaso, as sub-prior of the Florentine Carmine. This familial relationship seems to have been important for Fra Filippo.[2] The onset of this renewed involvement with the Carmelites also coincided with the rather pathetic letter that he wrote to his patron Piero de' Medici in August 1439. Perhaps the precariousness and fragility of his situation expressed so melodramatically should be taken

84 Filippo Lippi and Fra Diamante, *The Madonna Giving her Girdle to St. Thomas, with Sts. Margaret, Gregory, Augustine, Raphael, and Tobias*, detail of fig. 86.

seriously: "it's clear that being one of the poorest friars that there is in Florence, I am."[3] While Fra Filippo was experiencing a very productive moment in his burgeoning artistic practice, his material base was neither extensive nor guaranteed.[4] His very identity as a *frate dipintore* situated in secular society had yet to be stabilized. It was not until he was granted the benefice of San Quirico at Legnaia in 1442, with the title of rector and commendatory abbot and the substantial sixty-florin annual yield, that his situation in the *seculum* became more precisely defined and financially secure.

On January 19, 1439, Fra Filippo's name appears again in the Carmelite ledgers, when he is recorded as one of five priests from outside the Carmine who joined twenty Carmelites in conducting commemorative masses in the chapel of Forte di Piero da Vico in Santa Maria del Carmine.[5] The following year, along with sixteen other Carmelite *frati*, he donated money to the Compagnia di Sant'Agnese toward the Ascension Day *sacra rappresentazione*.[6] But the play in 1440 was to be far overshadowed by an extraordinary event that occurred in Santa Maria del Carmine about a month before the planned performance – an event that had a resounding impact on the Florentine Carmelites and, ultimately, on the Carmelite Order as a whole. The celebrations and validations surrounding this event drew many people into the Carmelite orbit, and an active participant in the proceedings was Fra Filippo Lippi.

In 1440, the Florentine *comune* was involved in a territorial struggle with the Milanese, then under the rule of the Duke of Milan, Filippo Maria Visconti. By mid-April, the Milanese had hired the *condottiere* Niccolò Piccinino and had moved into the northern Tuscan *contado* with a force of 6,000 men.[7] As Piccinino's men made forays into the area along the Arno east of Florence, coming within three miles of the city, peasants and inhabitants of the towns in the countryside fled to Florence and took refuge within the city walls.

It was during this tense stand-off, a time characterized by crowding, confusion, fear, and rampant rumor, that reports of the miraculous deeds of the Carmelite Fra Andrea Corsini began to circulate in Florence. Fra Andrea had been a distinguished member of the Carmine during the previous century, attaining distinction as Bishop of Fiesole. According to the report of a young Florentine named Giovanni Dazzi, he descended from his stone sepulchre in the nave of Santa Maria del Carmine in order to make a prophetic pronouncement regarding the fate of the city then under seige (illustrated in an early sixteenth-century predella [fig. 85]).[8] He spoke to Dazzi on several occasions, culminating in his prediction that there would be an important Florentine victory on the evening of June 29 at Anghiari, and that word would reach Florence on the following day.[9] This information was conveyed to the Florentine authorities.

Indeed, on June 29, hoping to catch the Florentines off guard, Piccinino waged a surprise attack on the Florentine camp at Anghiari. In an unorthodox move, he made a frontal assault during the height of the early afternoon summer sun. The situation initially looked bleak for the Florentines, but after a four-hour battle, Piccinino's men were beaten into a retreat, leaving many dead and wounded on the battle field.[10]

On the Sunday following the victory, in acknowledgment of the miraculous foresight of Andrea Corsini, the magistrates, clergy, and city *popolo* made a procession from the Duomo to Santa Maria del Carmine to hear mass and to behold the body of Andrea Corsini. The corpse was found to be "fresh and palpable," as if Corsini had only recently died. Roused by devotional fervor, the people cried out "Sancte Andrea, ora pro nobis; Sancte Andrea intercede pro nobis." Pope Eugenius IV granted permission for an annual procession to be held in honor of the Carmelite on the second Sunday each June.[11] A cult began to take root as people came to pray before the body of Beato Andrea, and miraculous interventions were reported.[12]

On July 31, Fra Filippo Lippi heard the testimony of Domina Betta from Prato, claiming that she had been cured of partial deafness and an impaired left arm through the intercession of Beato Andrea.[13] She had come to Florence in procession with others from Prato in order to leave a wax head beside the tomb of the Carmelite in thanks for his miraculous cure. The woman's story was recorded before Fra Filippo and three lay witnesses by the notary Ser Paolo di Lorenzo Dieciaiuti in the cloister of the Carmine. Ser Paolo di Lorenzo presented Fra Filippo according to standard notorial protocol, in a manner so as to lend maximum solemnity to the forum – selecting adjectives which we rarely find associated with the friar: "an honest, religious and upright man, friar Filippo di Tommaso."[14]

In January, 1441, following the Anghiari miracle, Lippi was involved in the construction and decoration of "la chassa del Beato Andrea."[15] This painted wooden casket has not survived.

85 Florentine, *St. Andrea Corsini's Miraculous Prophecy of 1440*, early sixteenth century, painted narrative scenes on a predella, Florence, Santa Maria del Carmine.

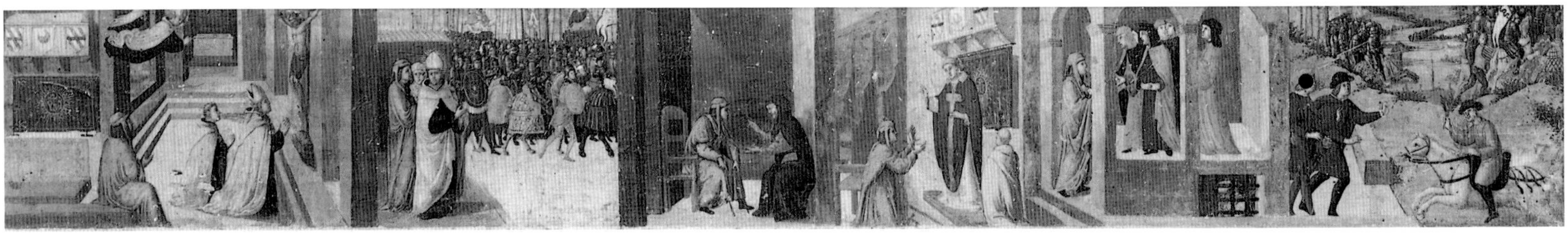

Paolo Caioli has suggested that it was a ceremonial presentation casket raised on scaffolding in which Andrea's body was placed when on view before the crowds.[16] It would have been conveniently portable, rendering Beato Andrea's body more accessible to the crowds than it would have been in the old elevated stone sarcophagus. We cannot tell how elaborate Lippi's painted casket was, since not enough of these wooden structures survive to give us a sense of the norm. Those that still exist run the gamut from the large, ornate (and obviously costly), painted and gilded *cassa* of the ninth-century Beato Andrea in San Martino, Ponte a Mensola, dating from the late *trecento* – which served as a permanent receptacle for the corpse – to the tiny wooden casket of the fifteenth-century Carmelite Beato Angelo Mazzinghi, adorned with a simple inscription, in the sacristy of the Carmine.

Lippi's renewed close association with Santa Maria del Carmine continued to the end of 1441. In the wake of the miracles of Andrea Corsini, this was a very festive year at the Carmine. New patrons came forth, subsidizing feast day meals in the convent.[17] On April 19, the anniversary of the *Sagra* (the consecration of the church) was elaborately celebrated, while regular feast days passed with additional pomp and display. Fra Filippo was once again active with the Compagnia di Sant'Agnese in May, paying them s.5 d.4 "per chalcina" (gesso – for a fresco project?) and singing a mass.[18] On July 3, he was paid for the "chest that he left in the room when he was staying in the infirmary," indicating that he had spent some time in the convent, perhaps during an illness. On October 8, he was reimbursed 4 *grossi* which he had lent to the prior for the subsidy of a convent meal.[19]

Early in the following year, Lippi's circumstances changed fundamentally when he was elected rector and commendatory abbot of the parish church of San Quirico at Legnaia. However, his continued interaction with the Carmelites can be documented on numerous occasions. In 1447, on July 10, the *frati* of Santa Maria del Carmine journeyed to San Quirico for the celebration of the Sunday mass (the Carmelite account book refers to San Quirico as "the church of friar Giovanni di Tommaso and friar Filippo" – Fra Filippo and his brother).[20] During the two-and-a-half years that he served as chaplain of the Gerusalemite nunnery of San Niccolò de' Frieri (1450–52), Fra Filippo relied on the friars of the Carmine to stand in for him when he was unavailable to conduct the services.[21] He was also one of the officers of the Ascension Day festival committee of the Compagnia di Sant'Agnese during 1451.[22]

The court records of a property dispute that Lippi brought before the Florentine Tribunale della Mercanzia in 1457 are revealing regarding both his relationship with the Florentine Carmelites at this advanced date, when he was working predominantly in Prato, and the manner in which his status as a friar was publicly perceived. In making his case before the court, Lippi invoked a privilege that the Carmelites traditionally had with the Tribunale, entitling him to an exemption from the mandatory fees.[23] His adversary in the case, Mona Lucia, insisted that as a friar Fra Filippo was not allowed to utilize the court system without a license, nor was he permitted to own property. Lippi responded that he had a special license from the provincial prior of his order. He seems to have evaded the second issue by declaring that the half-house in question was the property of the friars of Santa Maria del Carmine. He showed up in court on one occasion during the proceedings accompanied by the eminent Carmelite Fra Bartolomeo di Maso Soderini – presumably to add weight and authority to his argument.

The Carmelites were also present many years later at the funeral of Fra Filippo Lippi in Spoleto in 1469. Payments were made by the Opera of the Duomo "to the priests and friars and neighbors for the funeral of Fra Filippo" and "to friar Giovanni when he came to Spoleto the last time."[24] Could this friar Giovanni have been Lippi's brother?[25]

Fra Filippo's continued relations with Santa Maria del Carmine, punctuated by at least one period of actual residence, suggests that the boundaries between the *seculum* and the *claustrum* – and here *claustrum* is to be understood as a cultural site and not just the physical space of the monastic cloister – were considerably permeable during the Renaissance. Fra Filippo remained a member of the Carmelite Order under the authority of his Carmelite superiors, while the Carmelites gave him considerable leeway in his application of the Carmelite Rule and Constitutions when living in the *seculum*. Within the complex socio-political network of patronage and power relations in *quattrocento* Florence, the Carmelites ultimately valued the high regard in which he was held as a painter and the patronage he received from powerful members of the Florentine patriciate and the ecclesiastical hierarchy. His status as a Carmelite *frate dipintore* evidently outweighed the embarrassment or inconvenience he may have caused the Order through his transgressive behavior.[26] As shall be demonstrated, when Fra Filippo was called to account for questionable commercial and religious acts, it was the archiepiscopal authorities and not the Carmelites who raised the challenge.[27]

RECTOR AND COMMENDATORY ABBOT OF SAN QUIRICO AT LEGNAIA

On February 23, 1442, Fra Filippo Lippi was elected rector and "commendatory abbot for life" of the parish church of San Quirico at Legnaia, west of Florence along the Via Pisana. The appointment was proclaimed in a bull by Pope Eugenius IV. Four days later, Lippi was invested by the archiepiscopal vicar and Florentine canon, Ugolino Giugni. He was formally presented with the keys to the church and the bells were rung.[28]

San Quirico was an old ecclesiastical establishment, dating back at least to the eleventh century. It was dedicated to Sts. Quirico and Giulitta, the fourth-century child-martyr from

Antioch and his mother. The patronage of the church, including the right to elect the presiding clerics, was traditionally the prerogative of the local landed nobility, the dei Bostichi. By the fifteenth century, the Florentine archiepiscopacy seems to have assumed the right to assign the benefice, although, as will be seen, the dei Bostichi maintained a powerful voice in matters related to the church.[29]

As rector and commendatory abbot of San Quirico, Lippi was responsible for maintaining the parish property and seeing that the local parishioners received the necessary spiritual and sacramental ministrations.[30] The first responsibility entailed making sure that the church was serviceable, the altars functional, and the Host, Holy oil and chrism obtained and preserved with the respect they merited. All parish properties were to be inventoried, parish lands kept up, and parish prerogatives carefully guarded against encroachment. As an ordained priest, Lippi was qualified to minister the sacraments personally to his parishioners, or – although technically not permitted by the Episcopal Constitutions – he could delegate the responsibility to another. During the *quattrocento* the duties of the parish priest were not as rigorous as they became after the Counter Reformation. He was to celebrate the major feasts in the Roman calendar and the feast of the patron saint of the church; to celebrate the mass each Sunday and encourage his flock to attend; to provide the parishioners with the opportunity for confession (at least once a year) and assign the necessary penance. Marriage vows were to be announced publicly in the church and the sacrament of matrimony administered by the priest. The priest provided last rites for the dying and performed memorial masses for the dead. He also collected the annual land tax, the *decima*, from the parishioners, which he turned over to the Florentine archiepiscopacy.

A profile of Lippi's flock can be culled from Elio Conti's analysis of the 1427 *catasto*. San Quirico was the fifth wealthiest out of the fifteen parishes in the *pieviere* of San Giovanni (*quartiere* Santo Spirito), and the fourth most populous. There were 343 parishioners in sixty-three households. Forty percent of these had no taxable goods, falling into Conti's category of "the very poor" (*miserabili*), 26% were "poor" (*poveri*; 1 to 50 florins), 24% were reasonably well off (51–200 florins), while 10% topped the 200 florin mark.[31]

The San Quirico benefice provided the holder with an annual income of 60 florins.[32] In addition, the priest was paid for special services such as burials and memorial masses. According to the Florentine Episcopal Constitutions, one-third of this income was supposed to go back into the church, in the form of building improvements, decorative projects, feast day activities, and alms.

In the *quattrocento* ecclesiastical abuses were rampant. Benefices figured prominently in contemporary cries for reform. Treated primarily as sources of income and prestige, they were bought and sold, accumulated, and administered by unqualified proxies. Benefices tied to country parishes were among the least profitable (hence, among the least desirable) and, as a result, they tended to be occupied by clerics with minimal Latin and little potential to enlighten their parishioners in matters spiritual and practical.[33] Clerics holding parish benefices in the Florentine *contado* are singled out for criticism and ridicule in the popular *burle*, episcopal pastoral visits, sermons, papal bulls, legal cases, and literary tracts.[34] Monks and friars who occupied these posts were particularly difficult to call to task because they were not directly accountable to the local archbishop and bishops, whose responsibility it was to oversee the parish benefices.

Fra Filippo Lippi appears to have been just the sort of parish rector to inspire this criticism. While we can document that he was in residence at least on one particular Sunday in 1447 when the Carmelites of Santa Maria del Carmine journeyed to San Quirico to celebrate mass, absenteeism was apparently the norm.[35] Lippi appears to have established his principal residence in Florence before moving to Prato around 1453, and maintained his benefice through an occasional visit and by proxy. By 1447, his brother Fra Giovanni di Tommaso was serving as his chaplain, and on October 14, 1451, in a notarized document, Fra Filippo officially designated him as his stand-in to administer the parish affairs during his absence.[36]

On May 19, 1455, Fra Filippo was stripped formally of his benefice at San Quirico as the result of a court case brought before the Archiepiscopal Curia. Lippi was accused of having forged a payment receipt in 1451, to the painter Giovanni di Francesco de Cervelliera da Rovezzano.[37] Lippi audaciously responded to his dismissal, which had been engineered by the court of the Florentine Archbishop Antonino. He went over Antonino's rather lofty head, presenting his case to the Ecclesiastical Appeals Court. He engaged the sympathies of the Bishop of Fiesole, Leonardo Salutati, and pleaded directly to Pope Callistus III. Antonino informed the pope that Fra Filippo had falsely represented the situation, and the pope gave way. On July 15, a papal *breve* was issued confirming the sentence of the Florentine Archiepiscopal Curia against Lippi. Lippi was referred to as one "who perpetrated many and wicked crimes" ("qui plurima et nefanda scelera perpetravit") and was dismissed as rector of San Quirico. The benefice was turned over to a canon of San Lorenzo, ser Domenico, who had been nominated by the patron of San Quirico, Leonardo dei Bostichi.[38] In a desperate effort to hold onto the benefice, Fra Filippo initiated a countercase in late August. He claimed that he had admitted to the forgery under torture, and that his confession was therefore invalid. He noted that Giovanni di Francesco had originally verified that the payment receipt was legitimate, and then later contradicted his own testimony. Fra Filippo challenged the legitimacy of Leonardo dei Bostichi as the rightful patron of San Quirico, and insisted that the newly appointed rector, ser Domenico, had been improperly invested as a priest and was therefore unqualified to serve as rector. It followed, therefore, that Fra Filippo was still the rightful rector of San Quirico. Fra Filippo's rather slanderous appeal was eventually dismissed, although he was still referred to as the rector of San Quirico when he appeared before the Tribunale della Mercanzia in 1457.[39]

CHAPLAIN OF SAN NICCOLÒ DE' FRIERI

In the meantime, Lippi had been given another religious appointment. From February 20, 1450, to July 2, 1452, he served as chaplain ("cappellanus") of the nunnery of San Niccolò de' Frieri, a small oratory and hospital with a college of Gerusalemite nuns in residence since 1392, just outside the gate of San Pier Gattolino in Florence.[40]

The appointment was not of the same magnitude as the San Quirico benefice. Nunneries were dependent upon the male clergy to perform the religious services and sacraments since no woman could enter the priesthood. The duties of a chaplain in a nunnery could range from officiating at the festive and weekly masses, to confessing the nuns, and seeing to their burial rites. Male clerics in nunneries also often represented the interests of the nunneries outside the convent walls, where the nuns were not free to roam and where the abbesses themselves often lacked connections and influence. The fourteenth-century Florentine Episcopal Constitutions had established that the *cappellano* of a nunnery be a priest or cleric over forty years of age, that his appointment be confirmed with a license from the bishop, and that he exhibit "honesty in social relations and in [his] way of life."[41] During the fifteenth century, the position came under increasing scrutiny as the number of nunneries rose steadily, and the necessity to preserve the purity of the girls and women became a communal and episcopal undertaking.[42] Archbishop Antonino increased the minimum age of the *cappellano* to forty-one.[43]

The previous chaplain of San Niccolò – the Augustinian friar Giovanni da Foligno – had died in mid-August 1449. A series of monks, friars, and lay clergy were hired "mass by mass" until Fra Filippo became the official replacement early in 1450.[44] From January 6 to 15, Fra Filippo was called in on a provisional basis by the nunnery, and paid by the mass. His appointment as the official chaplain must have occurred in the middle of the month and, on February 20, a contract of sorts was drawn up in the nunnery's *Libro dei debitori e creditori*:

> Frate Filippo di Tommaso of the friars of the Carmine must have, because he is with, that is, with us as our chaplain, on the day the 20th of February, 1449 [1450], and he must say the mass every Sunday and then two times a week and do the other things that our other chaplains have done . . . And we must give him for his salary, in the form of alms, nine florins . . . a year.[45]

Fra Filippo said mass at San Niccolò on average three to four times a week. When he was unable to be present himself, he sent one of the Carmelites of Santa Maria del Carmine to stand in for him.[46] He was paid 5 soldi for each mass. He also attended to other needs of the convent, including the Lent services. His income for two and a half years was 91 lire and 4 soldi.[47] In early January, 1450, when Fra Filippo said mass at San Niccolò on a temporary basis, he is described in the nunnery account book as residing on Via Chiara, a street close to Santa Maria del Carmine and near the San Pier Gattolino gate where the nunnery was situated. It is not known whether he continued to stay there during his chaplaincy.

There is an interesting incident connected with Lippi's chaplaincy at San Niccolò. In the summer of 1450, he engaged the services of Michelozzo and his associate, the goldsmith Bartolomeo di Frusino, to cast a new bell for the nunnery church.[48] The old bell was broken and was sold to Michelozzo and Bartolomeo, to be replaced by a heavier bell made of a superior grade of metal. The transaction did not go entirely smoothly. To quote the account book from San Niccolò,

> They cast it two times and the first time it came out incomplete because of an error by Michelozzo who is such a good master in the making of bells; the second time, also on account of him, because the crown was not dry, the metal, when it encountered the humidity, spurted out of the mold.[49]

The defective crown was removed because Michelozzo was no longer on hand to supervise the project and was eventually repaired by a local smith. Funds covering the cost of the new bell were provided as alms donated by the convent's patrons. Lippi played the role of the intermediary ("mezzano") between Michelozzo and Bartolomeo, on one side, and the nunnery, on the other.[50]

Fra Filippo's last recorded salary payment at San Niccolò is dated July 2, 1452. By this time he had already been engaged to work on the frescos in the Pieve Santo Stefano in Prato, a project that demanded his residence there. It is probable that his chaplaincy was terminated on this account.[51]

CHAPLAIN OF SANTA MARGHERITA IN PRATO

The next ecclesiastical appointment for Lippi – that of chaplain of a small Augustinian nunnery in Prato, Santa Margherita – was a posting over which he has attained some notoriety.

If Fra Filippo was awarded the Santa Margherita chaplaincy in 1456 – as Milanesi says, after he was stripped of his San Quirico rectorship – then one can only conclude that he must have been receiving very strong backing from a quarter that Archbishop Antonino dare not challenge, even though it was an appointment that did not fall so clearly within Antonino's jurisdiction (a prebend tied to an Augustinian nunnery as opposed to a parish church).[52] Perhaps Lippi's guardian angel was Callistus III or the combined Medici *consorterie*. Prato fell under the immediate jurisdiction of the bishop of Pistoia, who happened to be Donato de' Medici at the time, and it is possible that he had a hand in Lippi's receiving the benefice. Nonetheless, the nuns of Santa Margherita should have been forewarned: Lippi did not distinguish himself as an exemplary *cappellano* in their nunnery any more than he had in the country parish of San Quirico at Legnaia.

So embroidered with roses and scandal have Lippi's activities as *cappellano* been that it is a task indeed to unravel this tangle in search of the historical record. Santa Margherita was a very small Augustinian convent, supporting around six nuns. The abbess at the time of Lippi's appointment was Bartolomea de' Bovacchiesi.

Vasari would have us believe that the *frate cappellano* of Santa Margherita was also its painter, executing the altarpiece for the main altar for the convent church.[53] It was during the painting of this altarpiece that Lippi's ardor was supposedly aroused for the young Lucrezia Buti, who Vasari claims – with the abbess's permission – posed for his painting of the Virgin Mary. This painting has been associated with an altarpiece now in the Galleria Comunale in Prato (figs. 84, 86, 87, 88), depicting the Madonna giving her girdle to St. Thomas, with Sts. Margaret, Gregory, Augustine, Raphael, and Tobias. There is a donor portrait of a kneeling nun, possibly the abbess of Santa Margherita. Technical and stylistic evidence suggests that the picture was executed in two campaigns – designed and begun by Lippi and finished later by Fra Diamante.[54]

Regarding Lippi's relationship with the nuns of Santa Margherita, we know more about what went on outside the convent than within – thanks to Milanesi's effort to provide a corrective to Vasari's account of the Lucrezia Buti affair (as described in Chapter 1). Shortly after Lippi became *cappellano* of the convent in 1456, one of the nuns, Lucrezia Buti, left the convent and went to live in Lippi's Prato residence. She was followed soon afterwards by her sister Spinetta.[55] Three other nuns – Piera d'Antonio Sensi of Prato, Simona di Michele Lottieri, and Brigida d'Antonio Peruzzi of Florence – who were alleged to have had illicit relations with men licensed to enter the convent, also left Santa Margherita at this time. For two years, these five nuns (representing the bulk of the population of the convent) lived outside the walls. Then, on December 23, 1459, in a solemn ceremony, they renewed their vows before the high altar of Santa Margherita in the presence of Ottaviano Guasconi, abbot of Santa Maria di Grignano and vicar of Prato, Donato de' Medici, Bishop of Pistoia, and Jacopa de' Bovacchiesi, the new abbess of the nunnery (replacing her sister, who had died).[56]

A year later, in late January 1461, we find Fra Filippo involved in a complicated property transaction, purchasing a house in the country outside Prato in the name of his nephew, which he then sold to the convent of Santa Margherita with the condition that following the abbess's death, the house be given to "one of her disciples" to use during the latter's lifetime.[57] In May of that same year, in a *tamburazione* (anonymous complaint), Fra Filippo and ser Piero d'Antonio di ser Vannozzo, the procurator of the convent, were denounced to the Ufficiali di Notte e Monasteri on account of their comportment with the nuns of Santa Margherita.[58] According to the denunciation, two months earlier, a child fathered by ser Piero had been born in the nunnery and had been smuggled out one night through "a certain hole" and baptized in Prato the following morning. Fra Filippo also had a son ("he is big, and has the name Filippino") by one of the nuns "named Spinetta [sic]."[59] The informant tells the officials that "ser Piero has frequented and frequents the convent of Santa Margherita in Prato," and "when you want to find him, every day you will find him there and another who is called friar Filippo: and one [i.e. Fra Filippo] with the excuse of being the chaplain, and the other, of being the procurator."[60]

There is no record indicating whether Lippi was apprehended for his comportment with the nuns of Santa Margherita.[61] That news of the affair was circulating publicly we know from the anonymous *tamburazione* and perhaps also from the Medici correspondence. In a letter written by Giovanni de' Medici to one of his agents in 1458, he refers to having laughed at "the error of Fra Filippo."[62] It is probable that Lippi was eventually removed from his post of *cappellano*, although there is no documentary evidence to support this. We know from his son Filippino's will that Lippi must have continued his liaison with Lucrezia Buti, because four years after the *tamburazione* a second child was born to Filippo and Lucrezia, named Alessandra.[63]

When Fra Filippo was called to the Umbrian town of Spoleto early in 1466 to undertake the painting of the apse of the Duomo, perhaps his patrons, associates, and adversaries in Florence and Prato all breathed a sigh of relief. Certainly he was not awarded any additional ecclesiastical benefices, and with all his problems and distractions left behind in Prato, the two and a half years he spent in Spoleto were productive (despite recurring illness): he managed to cover the apse and two out of three of the narrative scenes below with frescos before he died in 1469.

LITIGATION AS A THEME

While Lippi's liaison with Lucrezia Buti has received much attention from historians, art historians, and the Romantics of the nineteenth century, Rudolf and Margot Wittkower are the only authors who have treated the broader implications of Lippi's transgressive behavior. In *Born Under Saturn* (1963), they approached the affair from the standpoint of religion and morality. They challenged what they took to be an anachronistic worry latent within the critical literature on Lippi: "How was it possible that a man of his moral fiber could produce pious works and spend a lifetime painting them?" They conclude that "except for Savonarola's brief interlude, few people in the fifteenth and early sixteenth centuries saw a contradiction between the licentious behavior and the religious works of an artist." They offer the following explanation:

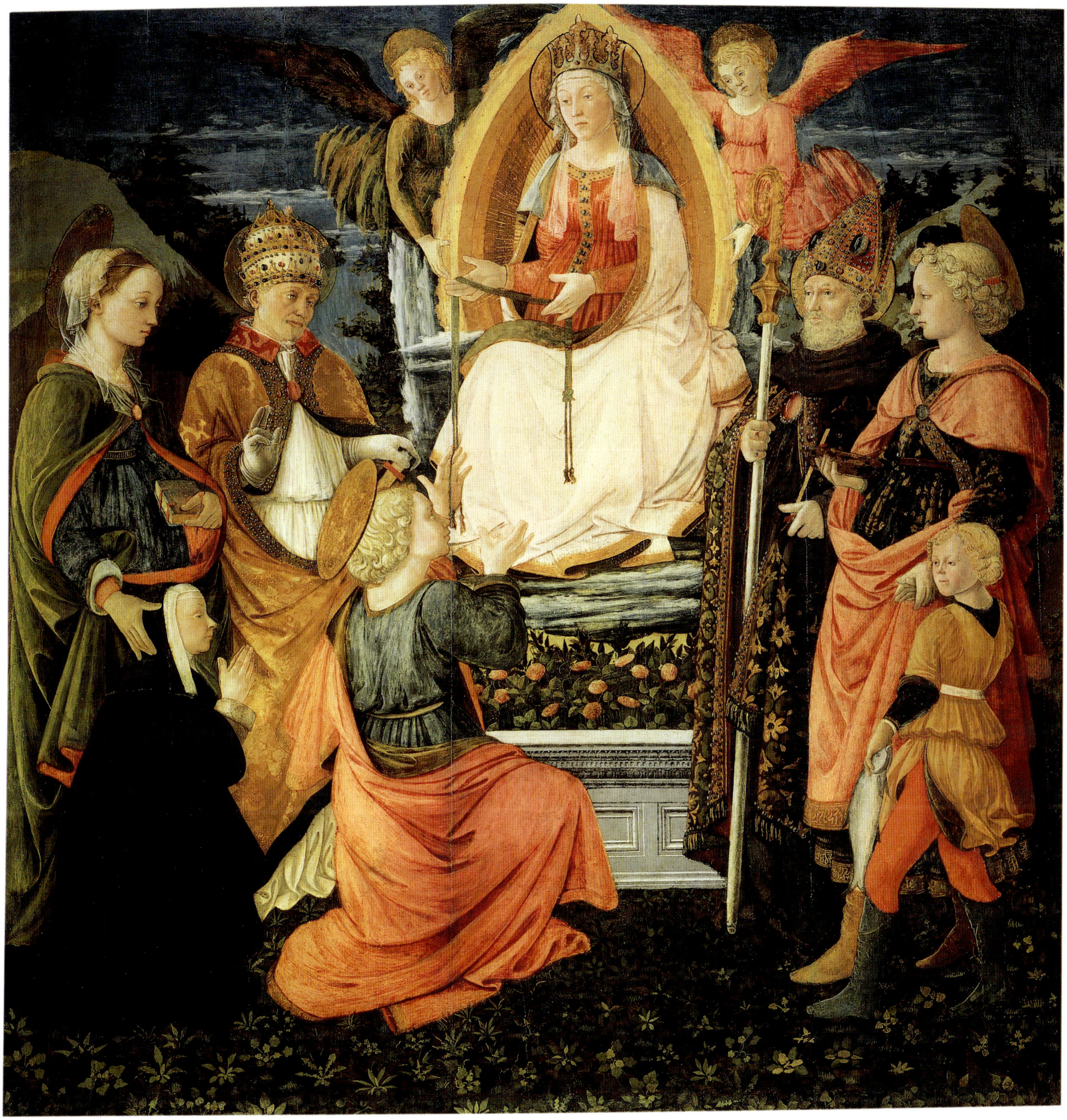

86 Filippo Lippi and Fra Diamante, *The Madonna Giving her Girdle to St. Thomas, with Sts. Margaret, Gregory, Augustine, Raphael, and Tobias*, c. 1455–65, Prato, Galleria Comunale di Palazzo Pretorio.

Like so many other orphans, Filippo and Lucrezia, who had both lost their parents in early youth, had been destined by their relatives for a monastic life at an age when they themselves had no choice in the matter. The practice of handing over to monasteries children who would later find they had no vocation whatever for a religious life inevitably produced a great many cynical monks and nuns.

The Wittkowers realized, however, that this is not the whole picture: "But this can only partly explain the extraordinary moral laxity among members of the clergy, which is confirmed by many documents of the time and which, in later years, was one of the chief complaints of all church reformers."[64] And they leave the matter at that. Elsewhere in the book, in a chapter entitled "Artists and the Law," they observe that fifteenth-century Italian society was a particularly litigious one, and while many artists had run-ins with the law, artists do not appear in the court records disproportionately to other professionals and social groups.[65] Thus, Lippi's transgressive behavior comes off as fairly conventional for the times, and not unusual in an artist or a beneficed friar.

I want to push this point a little further. It should be apparent by now that Lippi's conflicts with secular and clerical authorities did not arise solely as a result of his comportment with the Augustinian nun Lucrezia Buti. Between 1450 and 1463, his name appears in documentary records related to contested legal issues no less than twelve times. I believe there are two forces at work here. On the one hand, the frequency with which Lippi began to tussle with the law – both as plaintiff and defendant – intensified after 1450, as the painter was gaining increasing confidence in his negotiations in secular society. And, at the same time, transgression emerges as one of the means by which he explored the parameters of his world during his mature years – both its sacred and secular terrain.

It is worth reviewing the chronology of Lippi's numerous litigations:

1451 January 27: involved in litigation with ser Bastiano di ser Giovanni Boccianti da Pisa in the Archiepiscopal Curia. Subject unknown.[66]

1451 September: took the Perugian Antonio del Branca before the Tribunale della Mercanzia because Antonio had refused to pay him for a painting which Antonio insisted wasn't executed by the master's hand. It appears that Lippi won the case.[67]

1451 November 15: came to terms with the brothers Leonardo and Bastiano di Domenico di Giovanni from Septimo over an unknown conflict, before the notary ser Donato di Bartolo di Donato.[68]

1453 April 16: failed to finish a painting for Lionardo Bartolini by the contracted deadline and was forced to pay a fl. 22 fine, with his Prato patrons acting as the guarantors.[69]

1453 July 13: with Lorenzo Manetti went into arbitration over the price of a painting which he had executed for Manetti, with the archiepiscopal vicar Ugolino Giungi acting as arbiter.[70]

1455: Giovanni di Francesco de Cervelliera accused him of having forged a payment receipt of 1451. The case was adjudicated before the Archiepiscopal Curia and finally settled in 1455, after he confessed to the crime under torture. As a result, on May 19, he was stripped of his benefice as rector of San Quirico at Legnaia.[71]

1455 April 26: with the painter Barnaba di Giovanni went into arbitration before the Archiepiscopal Curia for unknown reasons.[72]

1455 September 6: launched a counter-case against the patron of the San Quirico benefice, Leonardo dei Bostichi, and the man chosen to replace him as rector, ser Domenico. He also claimed that he had been deprived of his benefice under false pretenses and that he was therefore still the rightful rector.[73]

1457 October 13: took Mona Lucia before the Tribunale della Mercanzia over her failure to pay him money she had received for renting part of a house on Borgo San Frediano which he claimed was his rightful property. The court ruled in his favor.[74]

1461 May 8: a *tamburazione* was filed against him and Piero d'Antonio di ser Vannozzo over their free comportment with the nuns of Santa Margherita in Prato.[75]

1462 August 11: a dispute with the painter Giannino working for the *comune* was heard before the *comune* in Prato, with the ruling apparently in Lippi's favor.[76]

1463 October 26: the *consiglio generale* of Prato, frustrated with the slow and costly progress of the frescos in the Pieve, decided to suspend Lippi's fresco activity and audit his account. It was determined that he had kept within his budgetary limitations. However, the matter still went into arbitration early the next year, with Carlo de' Medici resolving the dispute.[77]

Insight into the situation is gained by paying attention to the kinds of legal disputes and where and how they were adjudicated. While the nature of one case (1451, November 15) cannot be determined, two were commercial cases, initiated by Lippi before the Tribunale della Mercanzia, in which he sought to recover money that was owed to him by a patron and a tenant. Another was a contract breach in which a second patron acted as guarantor and made certain that Lippi paid the agreed fine for failing to finish a painting on time. Two of the cases were communal affairs – one involving a painter working for the *comune* in Prato and the other the violation of the nuns of Santa Margherita, an area in which the *comune* of Florence had concerned itself since 1421. The other six disputes were brought

87 Filippo Lippi and Fra Diamante, *The Madonna giving her Girdle to St. Thomas, with Sts. Margaret, Gregory, Augustine, Raphael and Tobias*, detail of fig. 86.

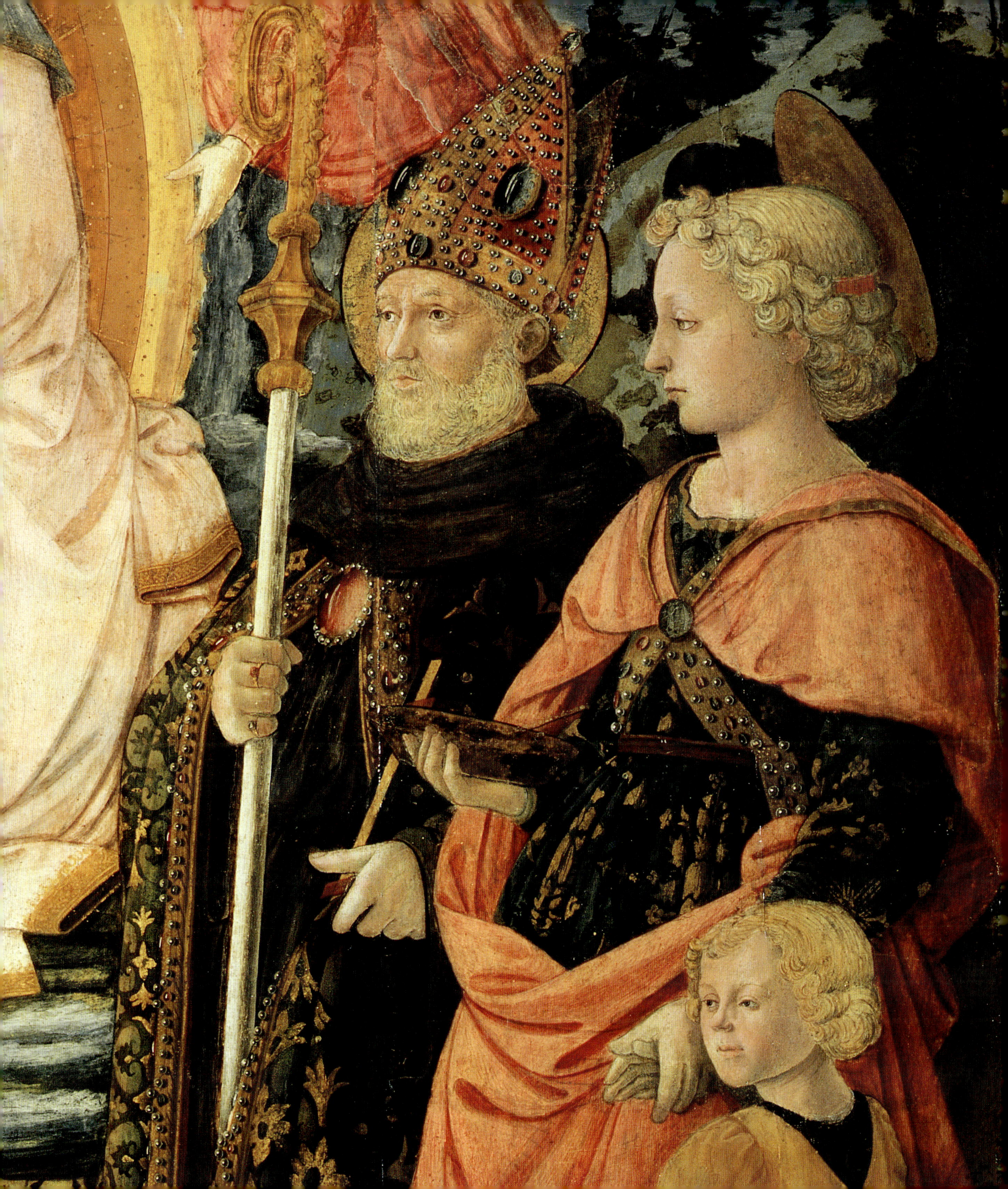

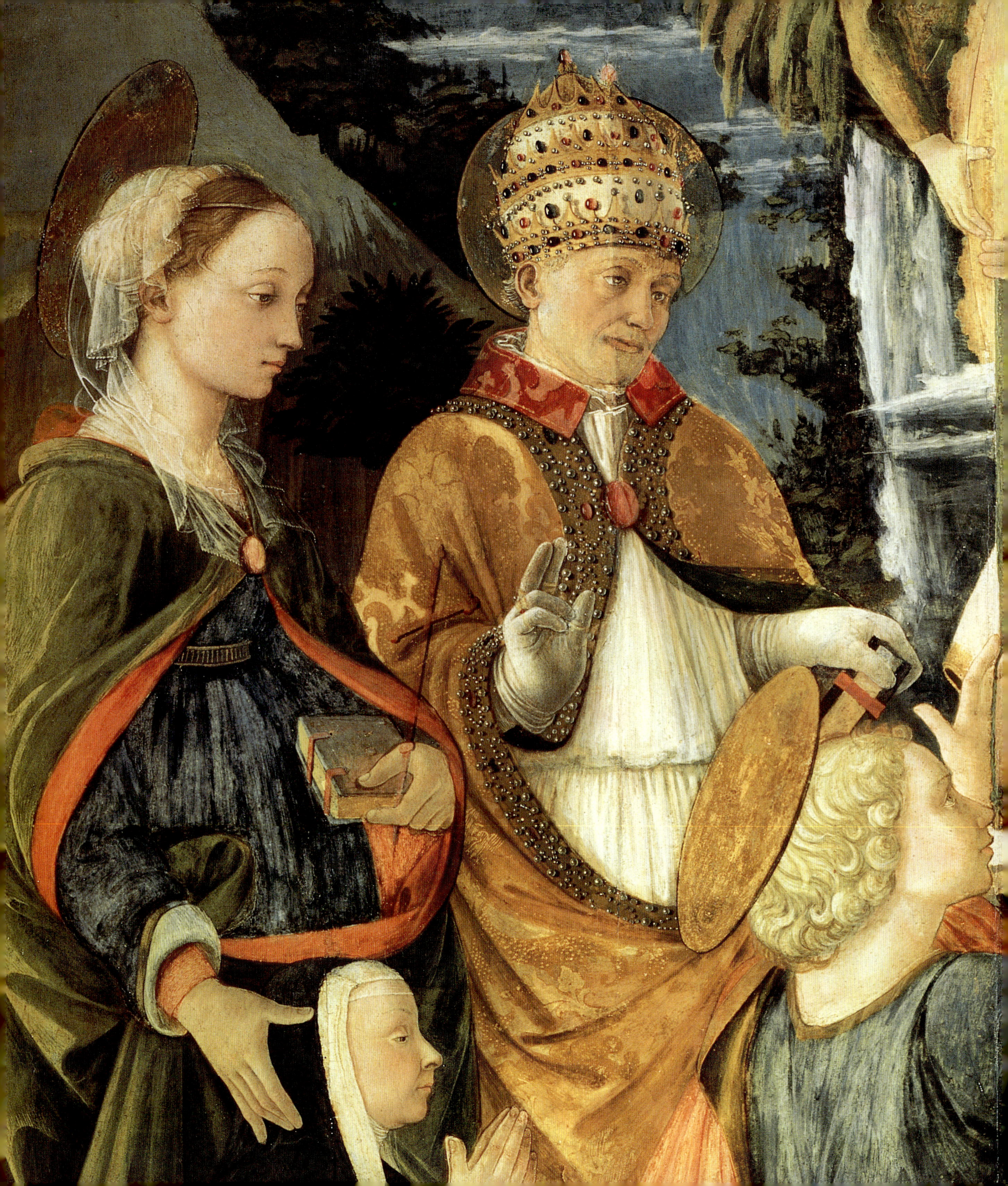

before ecclesiastical authorities – three before the Archiepiscopal Curia, two before episcopal notaries acting as arbiters, and one before the cleric Carlo de' Medici acting as arbiter. With the exception of the San Quirico benefice case, the issues in these six cases were all commercial, rather than ecclesiastical, and for the most part, the charges were initiated by the other party.

What emerges is this: as Lippi's investments in secular matters increased over the years, in the form of personal property and business interests, he learned how to work the civil legal system in order to protect these investments. In contrast, when others wished to prosecute him over commercial disputes, his ambiguous status as a *frate dipintore* forced them to have recourse to his patrons or to ecclesiastical officials who had some authority over him. In one instance, the archiepiscopal vicar and arbiter declared that if Lippi refused to abide by his determinations, the friar should be publicly excommunicated. The Archiepiscopal Curia also had the power to remove Lippi from his position as rector of San Quirico. This ultimately came to pass, as the result of a legal dispute which was, in part, a commercial affair.

To attempt to explain Lippi's multiple litigations, all concentrated within thirteen years before the artist left for Spoleto, one has also to look at the manner in which he transacted his personal and professional affairs. "See toward what danger the man is headed!" the Medici agent Francesco Cantansanti had expostulated when Lippi's workshop materials were pawned in order to pay his rent. This precariousness extended to all aspects of his life. In his professional work, to be discussed in the next chapter, he failed to meet his contract deadlines, allocated the work to his assistant if a commission did not interest him, and repeatedly exasperated his patrons. His perpetual cash-flow problems affected his relationships with his professional colleagues, when he was unable to pay his debts on materials he had purchased or pay his collaborators for their work. Nor was the execution of his paintings a smooth process. He seems to have been prone to distraction, to have reworked compositions continually, and to have had trouble bringing projects to completion.

In the religious sphere, the Carmelite friar often had little to do with his Order; the rector of San Quirico was more absent than present; and the chaplain of Santa Margherita was all too present in the convent and familiar with the nuns under his care. Even his few surviving literary endeavors reveal a transgressive, haphazard style.[78] One of Lippi's patrons whom the artist prosecuted for refusing to pay for a painting, complained to the Tribunale della Mercanzia that Lippi's petition before the court had been "obscure, inept and badly drawn-up, and it doesn't proceed or conclude and lacks the customary requirements, and the matters contained and named in it were and are not true."[79]

Lippi's transgressive behavior emerged out of his continual movement between diverse social spheres, each of which had its own rules, mores, and traditions. Within Santa Maria del Carmine, he had been brought up on the Carmelite Rule and Constitutions. These regulations were applied relatively flexibly during the *quattrocento*, and even more so in Fra Filippo's case, once he became a painter. Outside the monastery walls, the conditions were considerably different. It was inevitable that Lippi would run up against the limits defining each social sphere – his very profession as a beneficed *frate dipintore* mandated it. Transgression proved, perhaps subconsciously, to be a means of testing what was ultimately permissible, in situations where the norms were not always applicable. Fra Filippo approached problems pragmatically and flexibly. When tortured, he confessed; when pushed up against a wall, he defended himself with whatever means available, be it the court, a powerful patron, a stretched truth, and perhaps lies and deliberate falsification.

88 Filippo Lippi and Fra Diamante, *The Madonna giving her Girdle to St. Thomas, with Sts. Margaret, Gregory, Augustine, Raphael and Tobias*, detail of fig. 86.

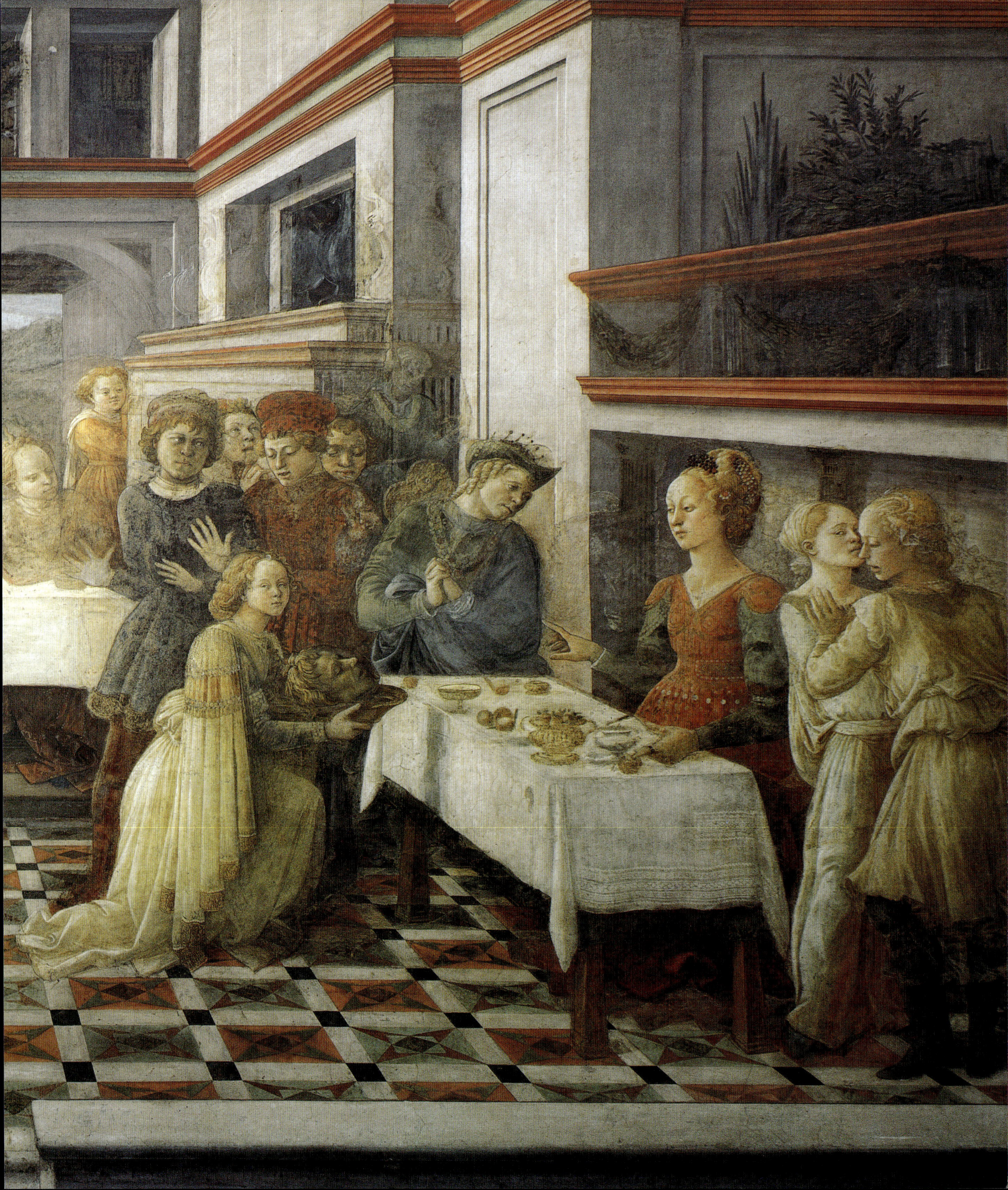

CHAPTER SIX

PAINTING PRACTICE

IN THIS CHAPTER I SHALL DISCUSS Lippi's mature artistic practice, focusing on the distinctive characteristics of his painting, his workshop organization, and patronage network. My interest will be in situating his artistic production in relation to that of his contemporaries, and within the broader context of *quattrocento* Florentine pictorial practices. While I shall point to specific examples of Carmelite influence in his mature work in Chapter 7, I do not want to lose sight of "Frate Filippo di Tommaso dipintore" in this more general discussion of his practice. A sub-text running through this chapter will be that his unique position as a Carmelite friar painter who moved between the *claustrum* and the *seculum* influenced the manner in which he organized his practice and explored critical artistic issues, particularly in religious representation. I begin by reviewing the major works, describing the character and valence of his painting over the course of his mature years as a painter.[1]

THE PAINTINGS: THE CURRENCY OF STYLE AND INNOVATION

The first documentation of Lippi's activity as a painter is the reference to "frate Filippo di Tommaso dipintore" in an account book from Santa Maria del Carmine in January, 1431 (see figs. 73 and 74).[2] In Chapter 3, I discussed the early works attributed to the friar painter when he was still a resident member of the Florentine Carmelite chapter. The next record of his artistic activity comes in 1434, when he is documented in Padua, painting a reliquary tabernacle for the Santo and evaluating the work of two little-known painters along with Francesco Squarcione. Nothing is known about his accommodations in Padua or his contact with the Carmelites in the city. No paintings from this Paduan stay survive, although there are several works by Paduan artists that appear to be based on lost compositions by Fra Filippo.[3]

He was back in Florence by 1437 but did not, however, return to Santa Maria del Carmine, taking up residence instead beyond the convent walls.[4] In 1437 he painted the dated Tarquinia *Madonna and Child* (see fig. 90), apparently for the Florentine archbishop Giovanni Vitelleschi. That same year, he began the Barbadori altarpiece (see fig. 103) for the sacristy chapel in Santo Spirito, commissioned by the heirs of Gherardo Barbadori, in accordance with his testamentary bequest. Dated to this period (c. 1439–40) on the basis of pictorial style are the San Lorenzo *Annunciation* (see fig. 104) and the Metropolitan *Madonna and Child*. By 1439, Fra Filippo was working for the Medici. He referred to an unidentified painting he was executing for them in a letter written to Piero de' Medici in August of that year (see below p. 154). This was also the year that he received the commission for the *Coronation of the Virgin* (see fig. 91) for the high altar of Sant'Ambrogio from the chaplain Francesco Maringhi. He worked on this painting through the first half of the next decade.

During this first period of his professional painting practice in the 1430s and early 1440s, Lippi demonstrated a robust and lively pictorial style that had its roots in the art of Masaccio and Donatello.[5] As I discussed in Chapters 1–3, the work of Masaccio was pivotal in the formation of Lippi's painting. Masaccio worked on site in the Brancacci chapel and the cloister of Santa Maria del Carmine in the mid-1420s, as well as painting a polyptych for the Carmelite church in Pisa. In these paintings, Carmelite interests were represented in both the subject matter and in the formal style that Masaccio employed.

Like Masaccio, Fra Filippo was interested in modeling his compositions with *rilievo* (relief). In fashioning forms, he used a system of highlights, reflections, middle tones, shadows, and cast shadows to approximate the effects of light falling upon physical bodies and materials in a defined spatial setting (as in the Tarquinia *Madonna and Child*, the San Lorenzo *Annunciation*, and the Barbadori altarpiece). His hardy three-dimensional figures and objects were set in a pictorial space created through perspective. In his painted interiors he fashioned the floor designs and the horizontal lines of his *all'antica* architecture into receding orthogonals leading toward a central vanishing point along the horizon

89 Filippo Lippi, *Banquet of Herod*, detail of fig. 98.

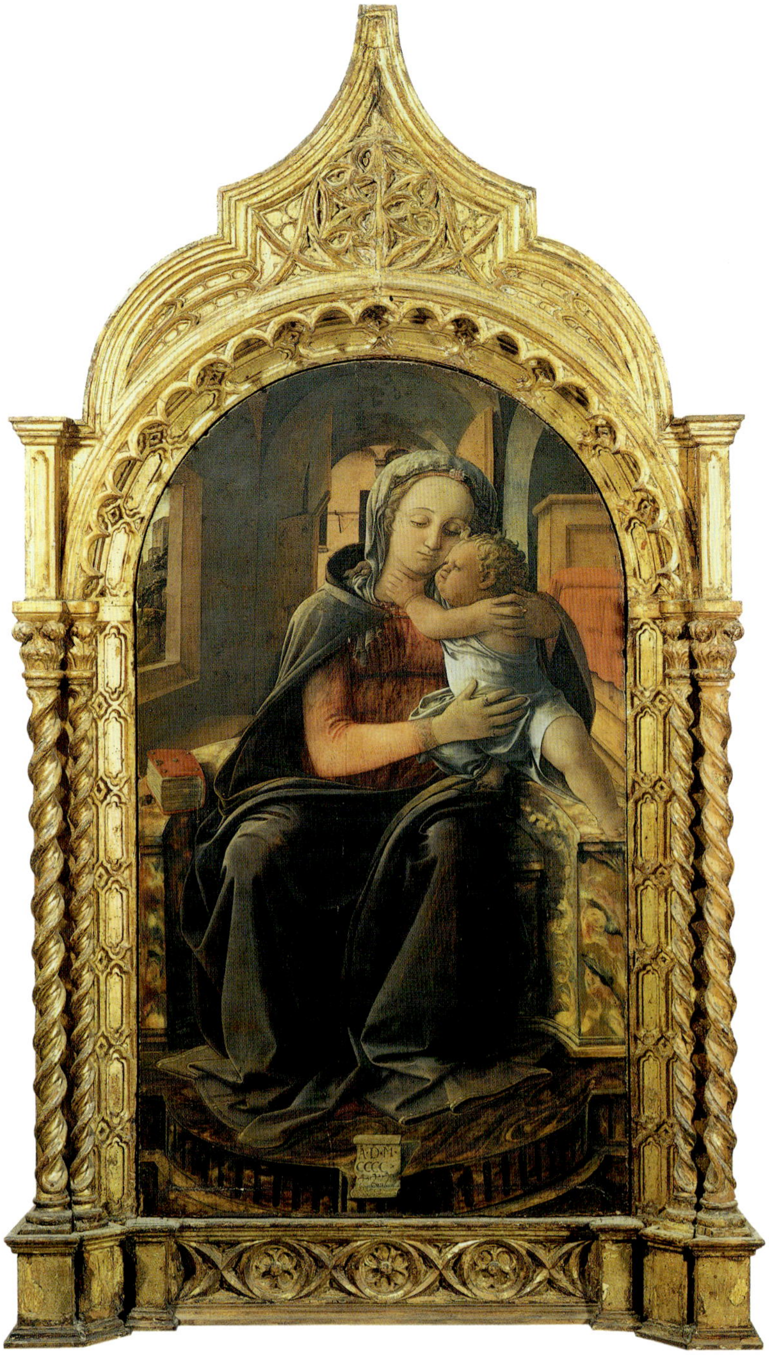

90 Filippo Lippi, Tarquinia *Madonna and Child*, 1437, Rome, Galleria Nazionale d'Arte Antica (Palazzo Barberini).

line, as in, for example, the Barbadori altarpiece, the Sant'Ambrogio *Coronation of the Virgin*, and the Santa Croce novitiate chapel *Madonna and Child with Saints* (see fig. 92). In Chapter 3, I argued that this kind of tangible, concrete, and corporeal representation of the sacred was consistent with the Carmelite tendency to dramatize and reenact mysteries and events associated with the early Carmelite history in the Holy Land.

At the same time, and perhaps also motivated by his sensibilities as a friar painter, Lippi never allowed his three-dimensional modeling or perspectival space to dominate the pictorial composition. His mathematical perspective does not exhibit the consistency and rigor found in that of Masaccio and, in a manner similar to Donatello's, functioned more as a design element or a conceptual framework that could be readily undermined for practical purposes or dramatic effect, as in the San Lorenzo

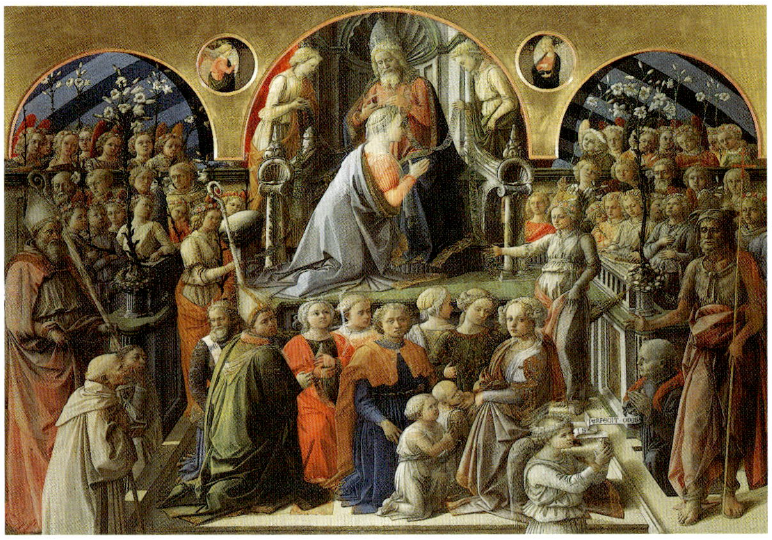

91 Filippo Lippi, *Coronation of the Virgin* from Sant'Ambrogio, 1439–46, Florence, Uffizi.

92 Filippo Lippi, *Madonna and Child with Sts. Francis, Damian, Cosmas, and Anthony of Padua* for the novitiate chapel of Santa Croce, c. 1440–45, Florence, Uffizi.

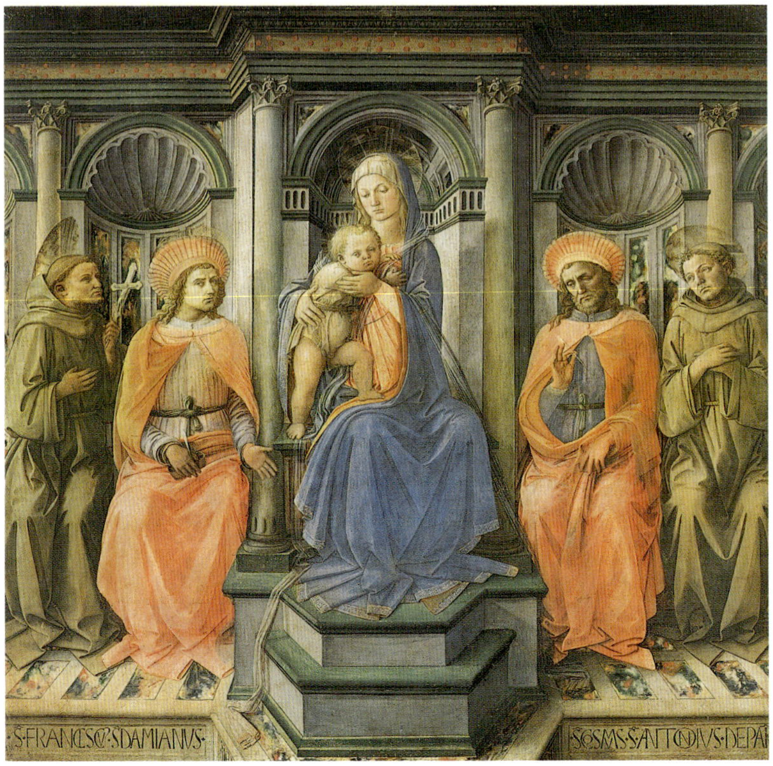

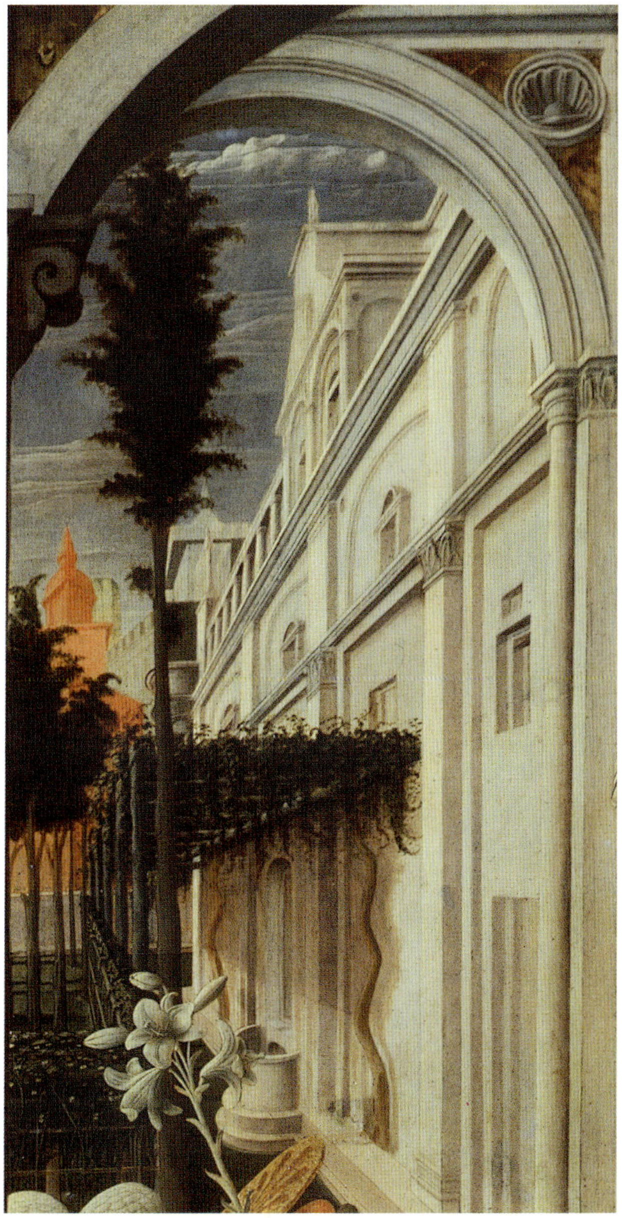

93 Filippo Lippi, *Annunciation*, detail of fig. 104.

Annunciation. For this reason, perspective was merely one of many technical means he used in his highly structured, vital compositions. Of equal importance was the interrelationship of color values within individual forms, distributed across the picture surface and within the pictorial space. Another key element to his compositional structure was the dramatic unfolding of his *istorie* (narratives) through expressive, varied figure dispositions and the interrelationship between figures (again, as in the San Lorenzo *Annunciation*).[6] His animated figuration (*figure*) demonstrates an acute awareness of Donatello's narrative reliefs (fig. 94).

Fra Filippo provided an active spectator position and guaranteed a certain variety of viewing pleasure.[7] In this way his art was similar to that of Masaccio and Donatello, and quite distinct from that of his contemporary Fra Angelico, where the relationship between the viewer and the sacred representation was a more mediated one. In Lippi's paintings, the beholder's viewpoint is loosely positioned very close to the picture by the perspectival scheme of the paintings. The principal subjects are very often pushed up against the picture plane, and figures frequently meet the eye of the beholder in a direct address. The picture plane, reminiscent of Alberti's window metaphor in *De pictura*, is articulated as a transparent barrier between the viewer and the represented space. Fra Filippo set into play a game of temptation and frustration along this liminal zone. The viewer is often tempted to "enter" the pictorial space through a break fashioned along the lower picture edge – in the San Lorenzo *Annunciation*, the Barbadori altarpiece, and the Sant'Ambrogio *Coronation*. Frustration of course ensues, enhanced by the obscuring of the vanishing point or some other obstruction to the spectator's attempt to "see into" the pictorial space.

All of these elements combine to give Lippi's paintings the effect of being staged with immediacy before the beholder, as if the sacred and secular subjects represented were in fact tangibly present. As I have indicated, this variety of dramatic enactment of the sacred was consistent with Carmelite representational practices in the early fifteenth century. It is also possible that Fra Filippo's interest in exploring this kind of provocative

94 Donatello, *Assumption of St. John the Evangelist*, c. 1435, Florence, San Lorenzo, Old Sacristy.

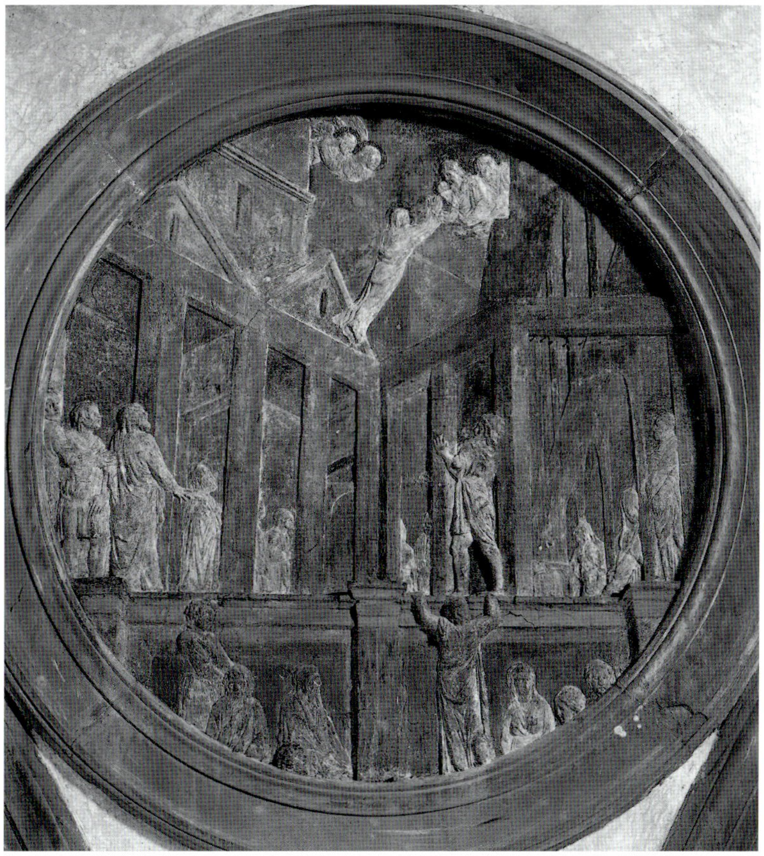

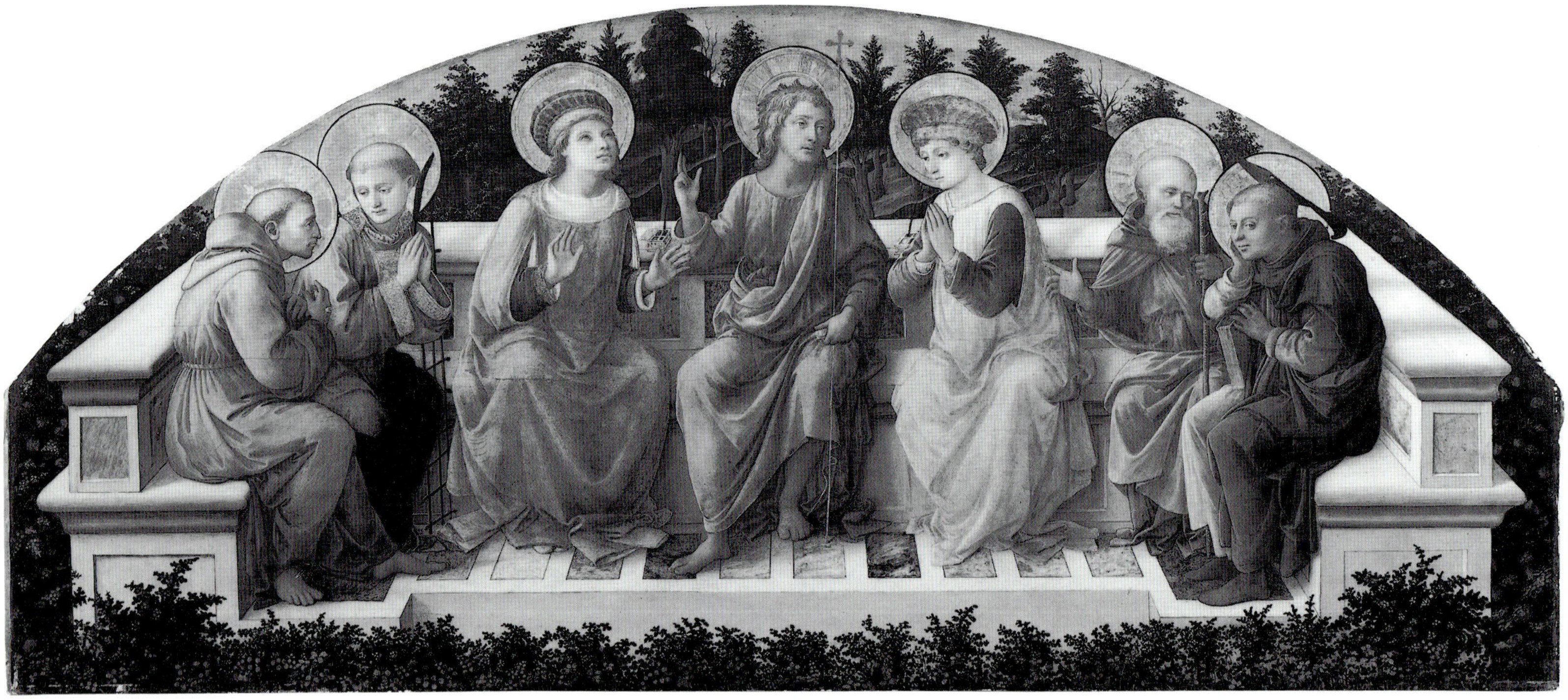

95 Filippo Lippi, *Seven Saints*, c. 1450, London, National Gallery.

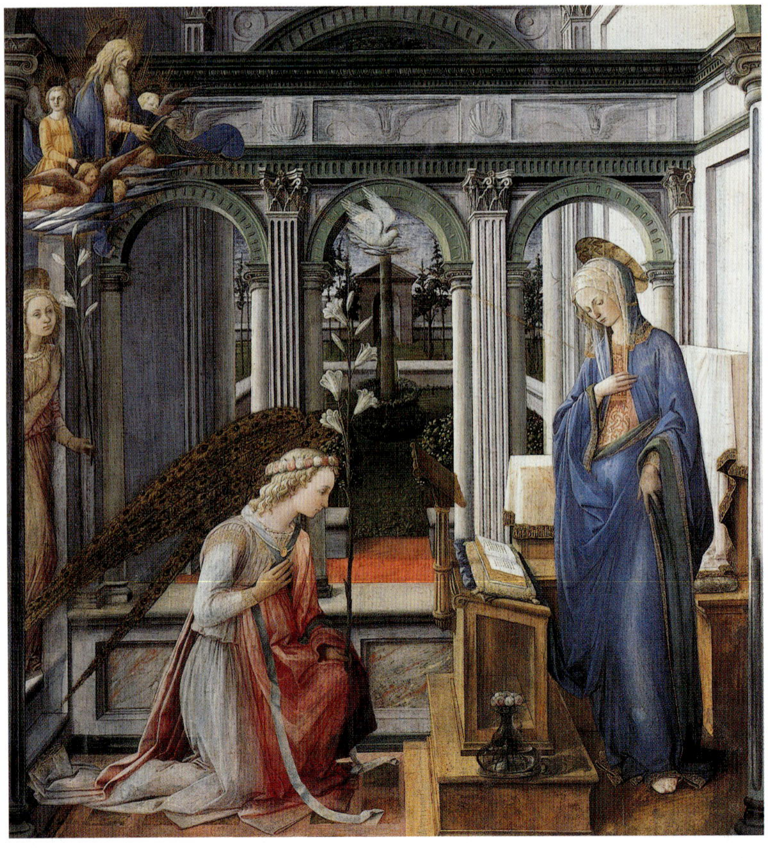

96 Filippo Lippi, *Annunciation* from Le Murate, c. 1443, Munich, Alte Pinakothek.

confrontation between the sacred and secular (or "profane") grew out of his own experiences in negotiating the social spaces of the *claustrum* and the *seculum*.[8]

In the late 1440s and early 50s, during the second decade of his professional work in the *seculum*, Fra Filippo veered away from this pictorial style. Dating from the early 1440s are the *Annunciation* (see fig. 96) for the high altar of Le Murate, commissioned by Giovanni Benci, and a number of undocumented paintings including the *Annunciation* (see fig. 121) in the Palazzo Barberini in Rome, the *Madonna and Child with Saints* for the novitiate chapel of Santa Croce for the Medici, and the two portrait panels (see figs. 113 and 114). He also executed an altarpiece for Sant'Egidio, the church attached to the hospital of Santa Maria Nuova, at this time.[9] To the mid-1440s to the early 50s, art historians have assigned the following undocumented works: the *Coronation of the Virgin* executed for Carlo Marsuppini for the church of San Bernardo in Arezzo, the *St. Lawrence Enthroned with Saints and Donors* painted for Alessandro Alessandri (fig. 97), the Doria Pamphili *Annunciation*, the Washington tondo (see fig. 128), and the *Annunciation* and the *Seven Saints* (see figs. 223 and 95) painted for the Medici. Two documented works from this period are a *Vision of St. Bernard* which he painted for the chancellery of the Palazzo della Signoria in 1447, considered to be the panel in the National Gallery in London (see fig. 150), and an altarpiece, now lost, painted in 1451, for the Perugian Antonio del Branca for the church of San Domenico in Perugia (over which the patron took Fra Filippo to court).

Toward the end of this period, Lippi left experimentation with perspective, volume, and animated figuration to the lay painters

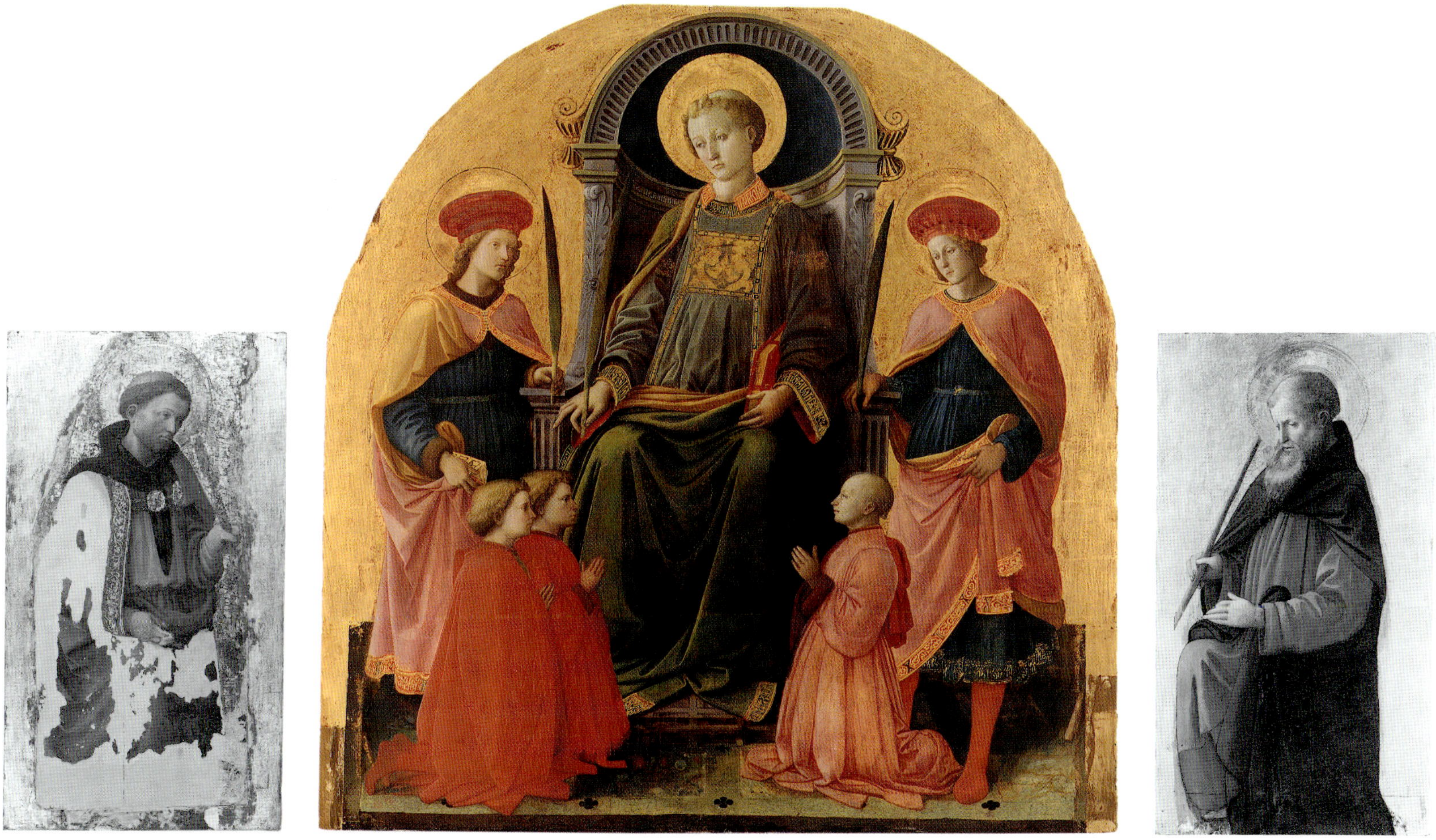

97a–c Filippo Lippi, *St. Lawrence Enthroned with Saints and Donors*, early 1450s, New York, Metropolitan Museum of Art, Rogers Fund, 1935 (35.31.1a,b,c).

Paolo Uccello, Domenico Veneziano, and Andrea del Castagno and moved closer to the pictorial mode of Fra Angelico. His paintings were more static, with softer modeling. Dramatic action and narrative were played down. The terms *devoto* and *vezzoso* that Cristoforo Landino later used to describe the painting of Fra Angelico (which Michael Baxandall loosely translates as "devout" and "blithe")[10] apply to a number of Fra Filippo's works from this period – the *St. Lawrence Enthroned with Saints and Donors*, the Marsuppini *Coronation of the Virgin*, the *Vision of St. Bernard*, and the *Annunciation* and the *Seven Saints* for the Medici.[11] This shift may have been inspired by the recently completed and quite remarkable fresco decoration of San Marco by Fra Angelico and his assistants (1439–45).[12] At the same time, influenced by the work of the sculptor Lorenzo Ghiberti, Fra Filippo began to elaborate a new formula for physical beauty in these staid sacred figures, which communicated *grazia* (grace), *bellezza*, and *pulchritudo* (beauty), and became an important feature in his later painting.

In 1452, Lippi was called to the neighboring town of Prato to work on the frescos in the main chapel of the Duomo, then the Pieve Santo Stefano (see figs. 98, 145, 148, 149, 160, and 179). This project was completed fourteen years later, in 1466. During this period he divided his time between Prato and Florence, maintaining a workshop and residence in Florence, and executing panel paintings for patrons in both cities.[13] Works carried out for Florentine patrons include a tondo of the *Madonna and Child* (see fig. 130) painted for Lionardo Bartolini in 1453, considered to be the picture in the Palazzo Pitti, a *St. Jerome* for Lorenzo Manetti in 1453 (now lost, which resulted in another of Fra Filippo's many litigations), and the Adoration of the Christ Child paintings. These include the triptych commissioned by the Medici as a gift for Alfonso of Naples (1456–58; see figs. 172–73), the altarpiece for the Medici Chapel (see fig. 178), painted circa 1459, and the altarpiece thought to have been commissioned for the cell founded by Piero de' Medici and Lucrezia Tornabuoni at the Camaldoli hermitage during the mid-1460s (see fig. 171). In Prato Fra Filippo painted the *Madonna del Ceppo* (see fig. 99) for the Ceppo Nuovo in 1453, the *Death of St. Jerome* (see fig. 180) and lost frescos for the provost of the Pieve, Gemignano Inghirami, and the *Circumcision* for the Servites of Spirito Santo, which was completed after he left for Spoleto. He executed works in the Palazzo del Podestà in Prato which have not survived. From this period also

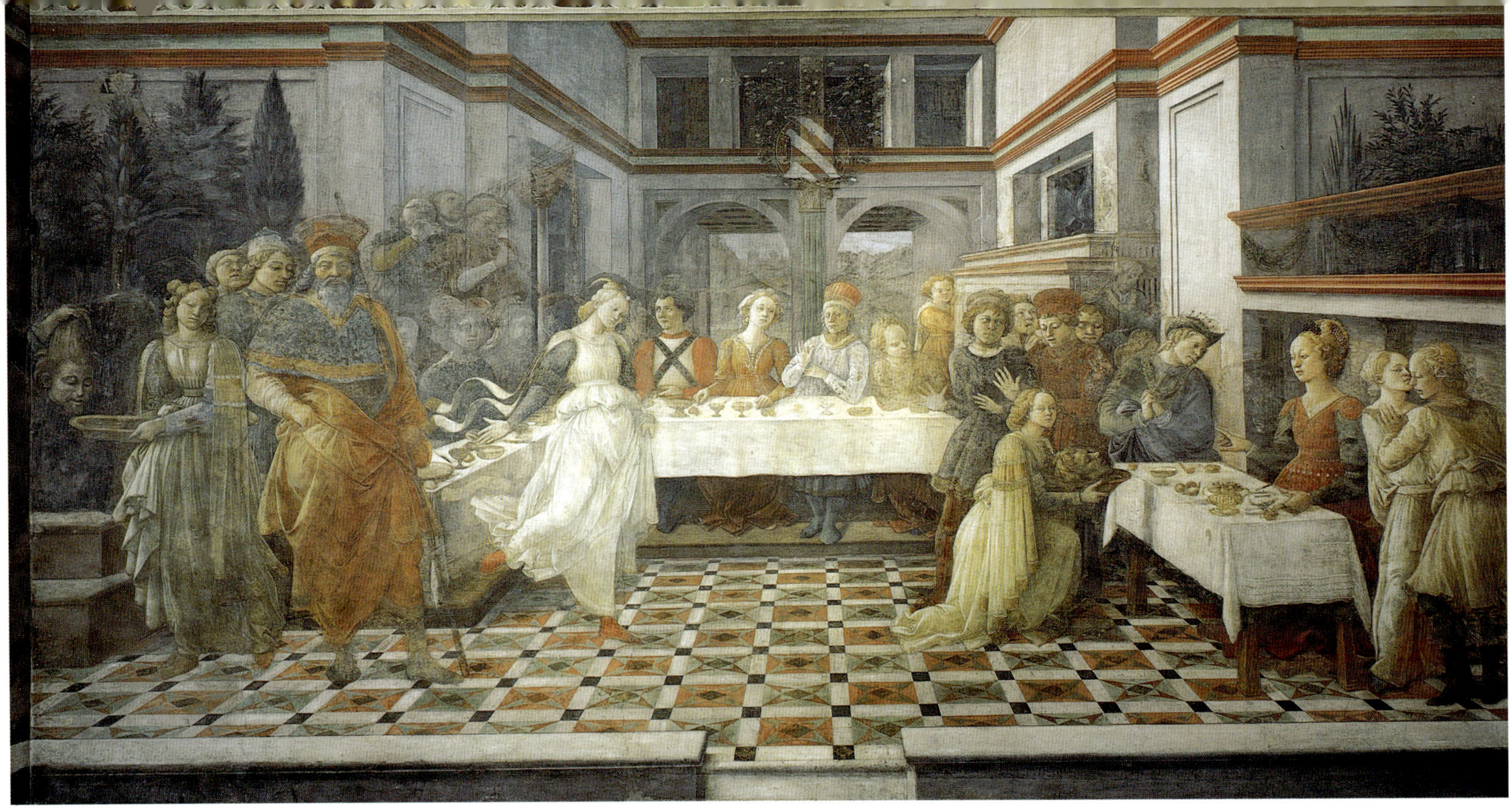

98 Filippo Lippi, *Banquet of Herod*, early 1460s, Prato, Cathedral of Santo Stefano, main chapel.

are the *Trinity* for the Confraternity of the Holy Trinity in Pistoia, begun by Pesellino, which Fra Filippo completed between 1458 and 1460, the *Annunciation* (see fig. 122) for the provost of the same Confraternity, Jacopo Bellucci, and the undocumented Uffizi and Munich *Madonna and Child* panels (see figs. 138 and 139). In 1466, Fra Filippo left Tuscany, moving to Spoleto where he worked on the frescos in the apse of the Duomo (see figs. 164 and 165) until his death in 1469.

The paintings from these final decades of Fra Filippo's life exhibit dramatic vitality tempered by elegant and graceful figurations. Both his *arte* (technical skill) and *ingegno* (innate talent) are self-consciously performed in work from this period, which includes some of his most innovative and interesting compositions (the Bartolini tondo, the Adoration of the Christ Child paintings, and the *Banquet of Herod* and the *Funeral of St. Stephen* in Prato). The fresco cycle in the *cappella maggiore* of Santo Stefano in Prato afforded the artist the opportunity to respond to the recent developments in Florentine monumental wall painting introduced by Fra Angelico at San Marco (1439–45), Uccello in the Chiostro Verde at Santa Maria Novella (1445–47) and in the cloister at San Miniato al Monte (late 1440s), and Domenico Veneziano and Andrea del Castagno at Sant'Egidio (1439–44; 1451–53; no longer extant).[14] Lippi became masterful at devising complex *istorie* on a grand scale, with multiple *effetti* (episodes) distributed across the pictorial field and set deep within the pictorial space. For this, and for the increasing clarity of his narrative composition, he was particularly indebted to Ghiberti's "Gates of Paradise" (see fig. 166), which had been installed on the Florence Baptistery in 1452. He introduced sophisticated linkages between the different scenes of the Prato cycle, even incorporating the actual corners of the chapel within the pictorial space of the martyrdom scenes (see figs. 148 and 149).[15]

Material richness and *varietà* (variety) are increasingly evident in works of this period. In the frescos at Prato and Spoleto, he selectively applied gold leaf, both on flat surfaces and in relief, to heighten the luminosity and to decorate the elaborate costumes, accessories, and architecture (fig. 102). It was the artist's skill in rendering ornament in particular that was singled out by Landino in his description of Lippi's painting (1481)[16] and by Fra Filippo himself in his letter to his patron Giovanni de' Medici, regarding progress on his triptych for Alfonso of Naples in 1457. In this letter, he justified the high price he was asking for the painting "because of the beauty of ornament" ("perchè bella d'ornamenti"; see fig. 101). In later works, Fra Filippo's representation of the landscape backgrounds to his narratives became both more intricately detailed and more capable of characterizing a broader range of natural settings.

Lippi's mature work demonstrates a fascination with contemporary Netherlandish painting.[17] I suggested in Chapter 1 that the presence of the German Fra Arrigo d'Arrigo – who may have been a painter – in Santa Maria del Carmine during Lippi's youth, could have stimulated this interest. The Tarquinia *Madonna and Child* (1437; see fig. 90) exhibits several features that recall northern painting – the Madonna and Child set in a domestic interior, the precise description of the open shutters at the back of the room and the pellucid light illuminating what appears to be a courtyard beyond, and the tantalizing glimpse of a landscape

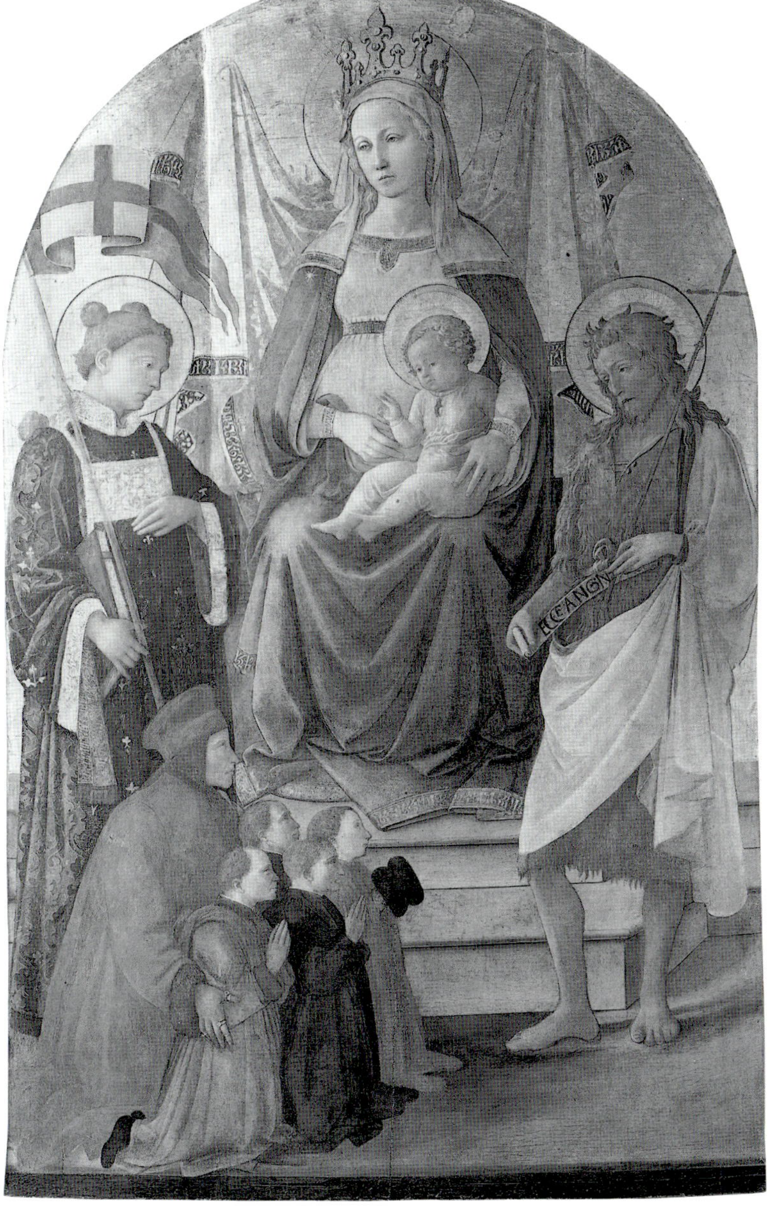

99 Filippo Lippi, *Madonna del Ceppo*, 1453, Prato, Galleria Comunale di Palazzo Pretorio.

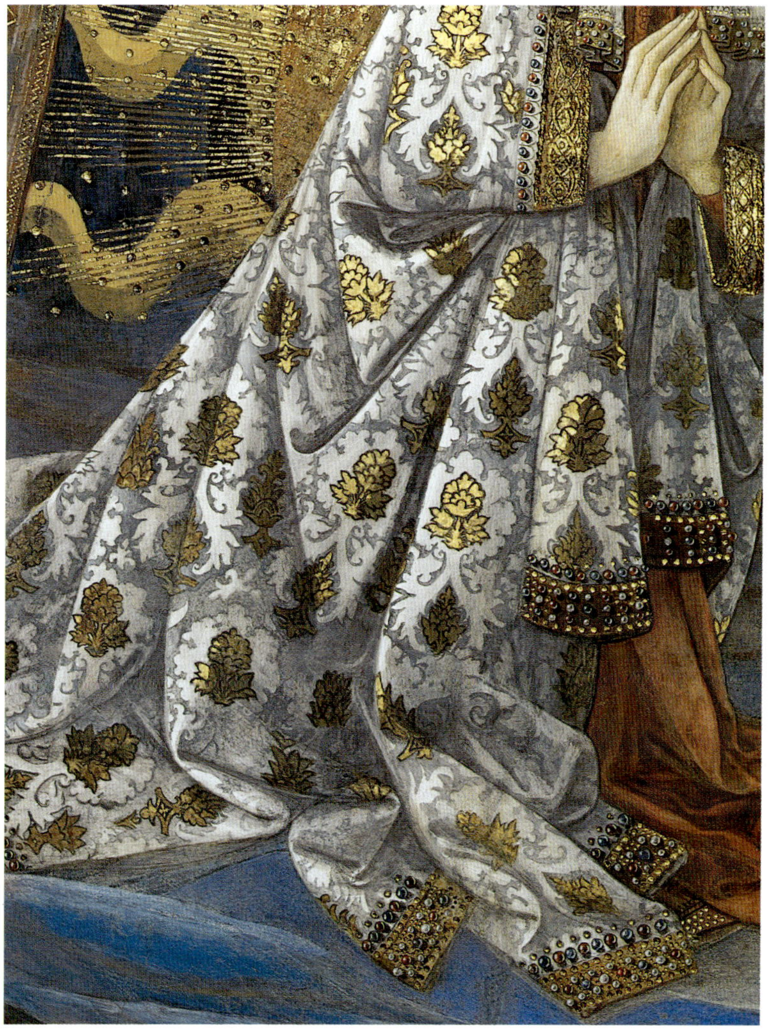

100 Filippo Lippi, *Coronation of the Virgin*, detail of fig. 165.

101 Filippo Lippi, *St. Michael*, detail of fig. 173b.

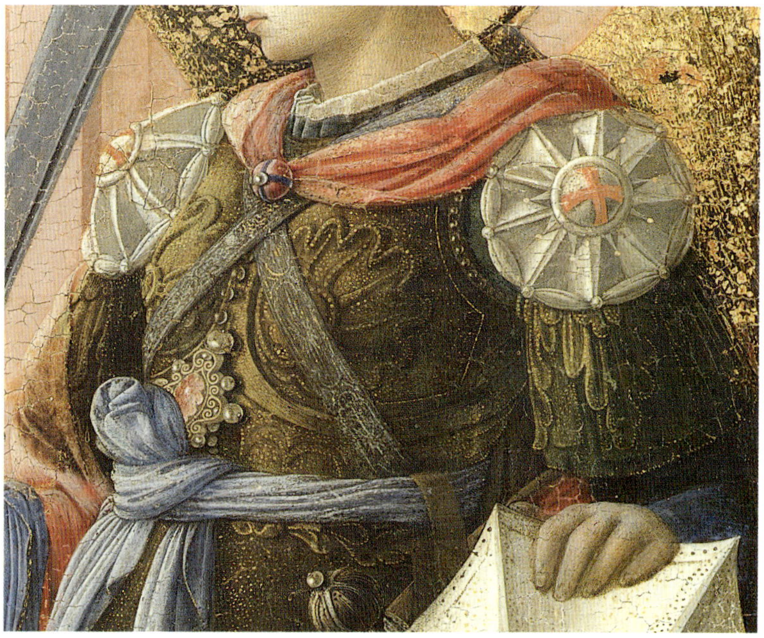

visible through the window at the left. The confident handling of reflected light and transparency in the glass vases that appear in the San Lorenzo and Munich *Annunciation*s (see figs. 104 and 96) do indeed suggest a careful study of Netherlandish painting. Lippi's interest in portraiture and the use of a window setting in his two surviving individual portrait panels may derive from exposure to Flemish portraits like those by the Master of Flémalle, Jan van Eyck (see fig. 111), and Rogier van der Weyden. The elaboration of landscape, which became more pronounced in his later panel painting and monumental fresco cycles, may have been influenced by the highly detailed, atmospheric renderings of nature in northern painting. His experimentation with these features of Netherlandish painting complimented his

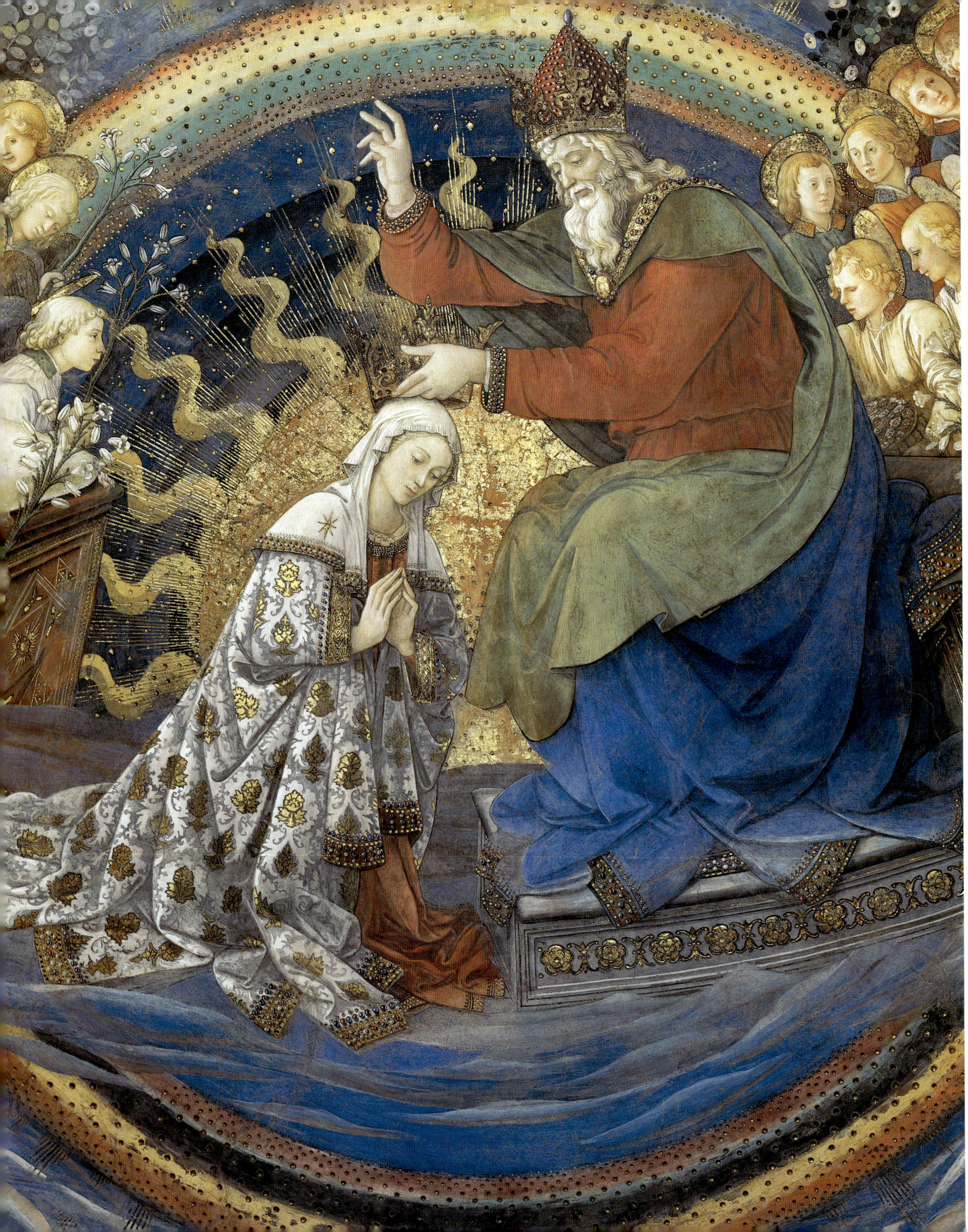

Florentine preoccupations with perspective, three-dimensional modeling, ornament, and composition, and represent yet another element of the appeal that his vital pictorial style had for his patrons, particularly as the Florentine consumption of northern European art increased in the 1450s and 1460s.[18]

I shall turn now to the specific areas of *quattrocento* Florentine painting where Lippi most distinguished himself. In each case, Fra Filippo proved to be working at the cutting edge of artistic practice, participating in the gradual redefinition of art and the role of the artist that we have come to associate with the "Renaissance."

The Tavola quadrata

Fra Filippo Lippi was one of the preeminent producers of altarpiece paintings in Florence from the late 1430s to the mid-1460s, when he left Prato for the Umbrian town of Spoleto. His success in this category of religious image was tied to the evolution of a new rectangular altarpiece format in Florence, which art historians term the *tavola quadrata* or the "Renaissance *pala*."[19]

The adoption of the *tavola quadrata* for altarpieces was influenced by Alberti's *De pictura* written in 1434, and by Brunelleschi's design for the interior of San Lorenzo (c. 1433). Alberti conceived of the painting as a rectilinear *quadro* and made the analogy between a painting and a window looking onto a tangible space. He also likened a painting to a cross section through the base of the "visual pyramid" formed by the visual rays traveling between the eye (at the apex of the pyramid) and the objects of vision (framed at the base). A painting could thus display a proportioned view of objective reality equivalent to the image transmitted by the visual rays to the eye.[20] This manner of conceptualizing a painting depended upon a mechanical system for producing a transcription of three-dimensional space upon the two-dimensional panel, and Alberti provided practical instructions for the painter. Mathematical perspective, as first experimented with by Filippo Brunelleschi, and then by Alberti, posited a monocular viewer, standing in a fixed position at a measured distance from the painting, who was willing to participate in the fiction that the painter's markings upon the two-dimensional picture surface offered a representation of pictorial space as continuous with the physical space in which the viewer was situated. The painted figures and forms within the pictorial space were modeled on appearances found in the natural world and to be understood as having a tangible physical presence.[21]

This new way of conceptualizing a painting formed the theoretical basis for the *tavola quadrata* altarpiece. It differed substantially from the conceptual underpinnings of the traditional gold-ground, gabled polyptych, grounded in medieval theological expositions on the symbolic status of the *imago* and in popular piety that empowered the image with an affective response to devotional address.[22] The religious imagery of a gold-ground polyptych was not charged with the task of capturing the "likeness" of unfathomable divinity and the sacred cosmos. Religious images were grounded in what Georges Didi-Huberman calls a "pictorial practice of *nonverisimilitude*, in opposition to every poetics or rhetoric of verisimilitude, . . . a pictorial practice of *dissemblance*."[23] They were considered to be material aids for the contemplation of the sacred – conceived of by theologians as figurations, simulacra. And, unlike Albertian or Brunelleschian perspectival pictorial space, the compartmentalized panels of the polyptych, while constituting a formal entity, were not proposed as parts of a continuous, unified composition. Representational subjects were segregated according to a hierarchy of sacrality and positioned in a formal structure that privileged the central vertical and horizontal axes.

Normative devotional practices were predicated upon the expectation of what Mircea Eliade terms "hierophany" – the manifestation of the sacred through a break in the customary experience of space, so that the absolute reality of the sacred cosmos could be revealed, momentarily, within a mundane setting.[24] The pivotal instance of "hierophany" occurred during the mass, when the eucharistic wafer became the body of Christ. In image devotion, manifest signs of sacred presence occurred when a devotee's prayer addressed to an image was followed by some kind of palpable demonstration of sacred intervention (a miraculous cure, conception, a change in the weather) or, on rare occasions, when a painting "came alive" (by speaking, moving, bleeding, sweating). Hence, it was not continuity but *discontinuity* which was of importance. Michael Camille has described the efficacious religious image as one which had broken out of "the ornamental and ritual encasement that kept it separate from the onlooker."[25] The gold-ground polyptych was thus implicated in a kind of religious devotion that emphasized hierarchy, division, separation, dissimulation, and hierophany, rather than unity, verisimilitude, and continuity.

Fra Filippo Lippi's Barbadori altarpiece (1437–39; fig. 103) offers a lively critique of the transition toward the *tavola quadrata*.[26] This altarpiece for the Barbadori chapel in the sacristy of Santo Spirito presents the Madonna and Child with Sts. Frediano and Augustine and a host of angels.[27] Scenes from the lives of these two saints and the Virgin adorned the predella. Fra Filippo devised a unified pictorial space for these sacred figures which nonetheless keeps the conception of the traditional triptych fully in play through both the framing element and certain architectural features in the representation. The original frame does not survive, but the replacement reproduces Fra Filippo's scheme of a wide central arch flanked by two smaller arches springing from pendant bosses. Painted columns in the pictorial space flank the bosses of the frames, suggesting the dividing framing columns of a Gothic polyptych.

The altarpiece, however, playfully proclaims that it is not a triptych. These painted marble columns do not quite line up with the bosses and do not segregate the two attendant saints into separate compartments – to the contrary, Frediano and Augustine are placed directly in front of the columns.[28] What is more, the three arches of the frame seem arbitrarily

102 Filippo Lippi, *Coronation of the Virgin*, detail of fig. 165.

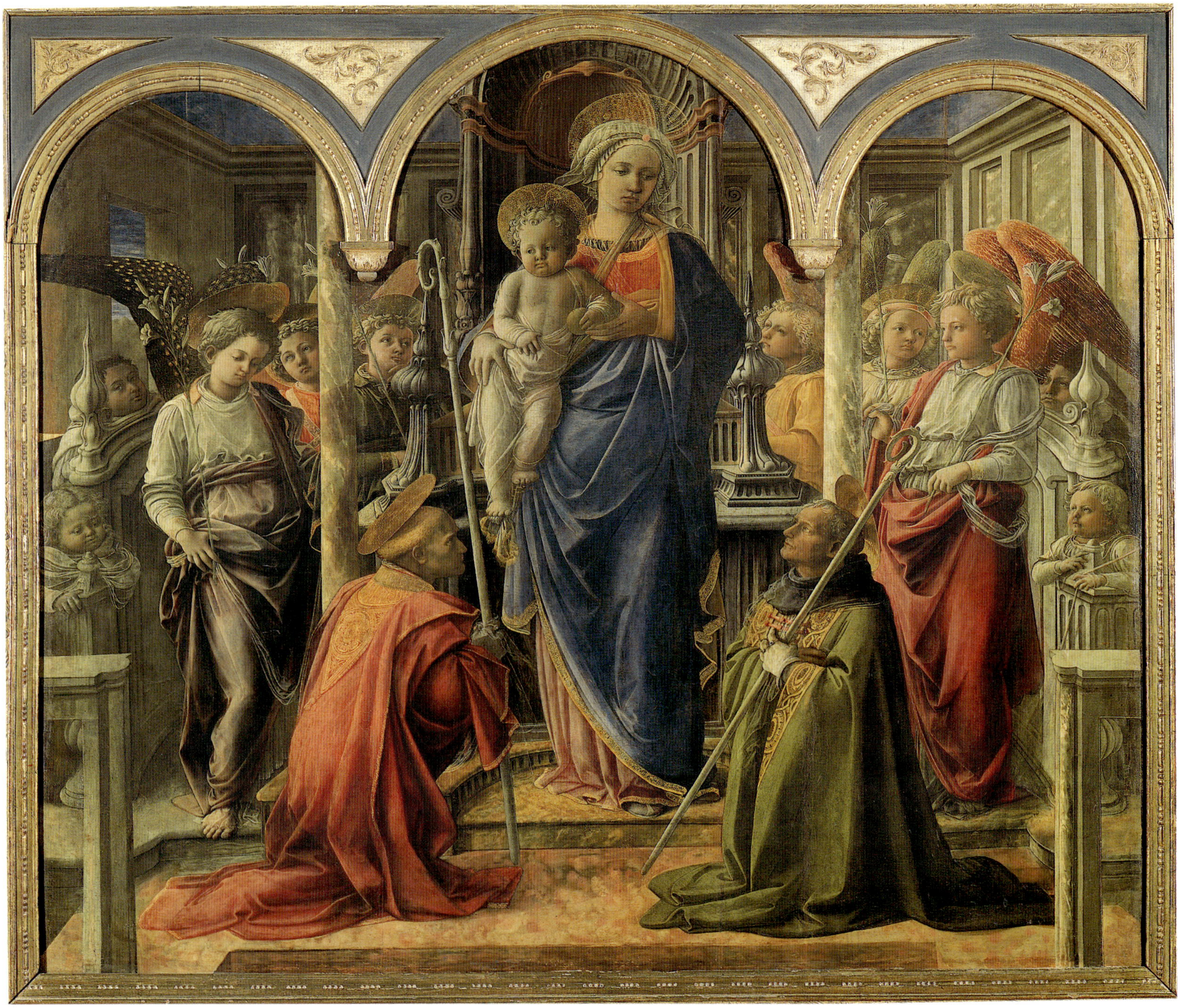

103 Filippo Lippi, Barbadori altarpiece, central panel, 1437–39, Paris, Louvre.

superimposed over the pictorial space, which appears continuous behind them. The picture plane and lower edge of the composition are very consciously articulated to imply a continuous space between the viewer and the represented figures. A stone balustrade opens up at the center foreground and a recessed, negative space is cut into the marbled dais, suggesting both continuity and access. John Shearman suggests that this apparent accessibility to the principal sacred figures is offset by a "compensating distancing" created through the unusual standing position of the Virgin, elevating her above the devotee and intercessing saints.[29]

The adoption of the *tavola quadrata* within the altarpiece appears to have been influenced by Brunelleschi's design for the interior of San Lorenzo. A document of 1434 confirms that he introduced a uniform program for the chapels in the church that provided for rectangular altarpieces ("cum tabula quadrata et sine civoriis, picta honorabiliter").[30] Lippi's San Lorenzo *Annunciation* altarpiece (fig. 104) in the Martelli chapel in the left transept

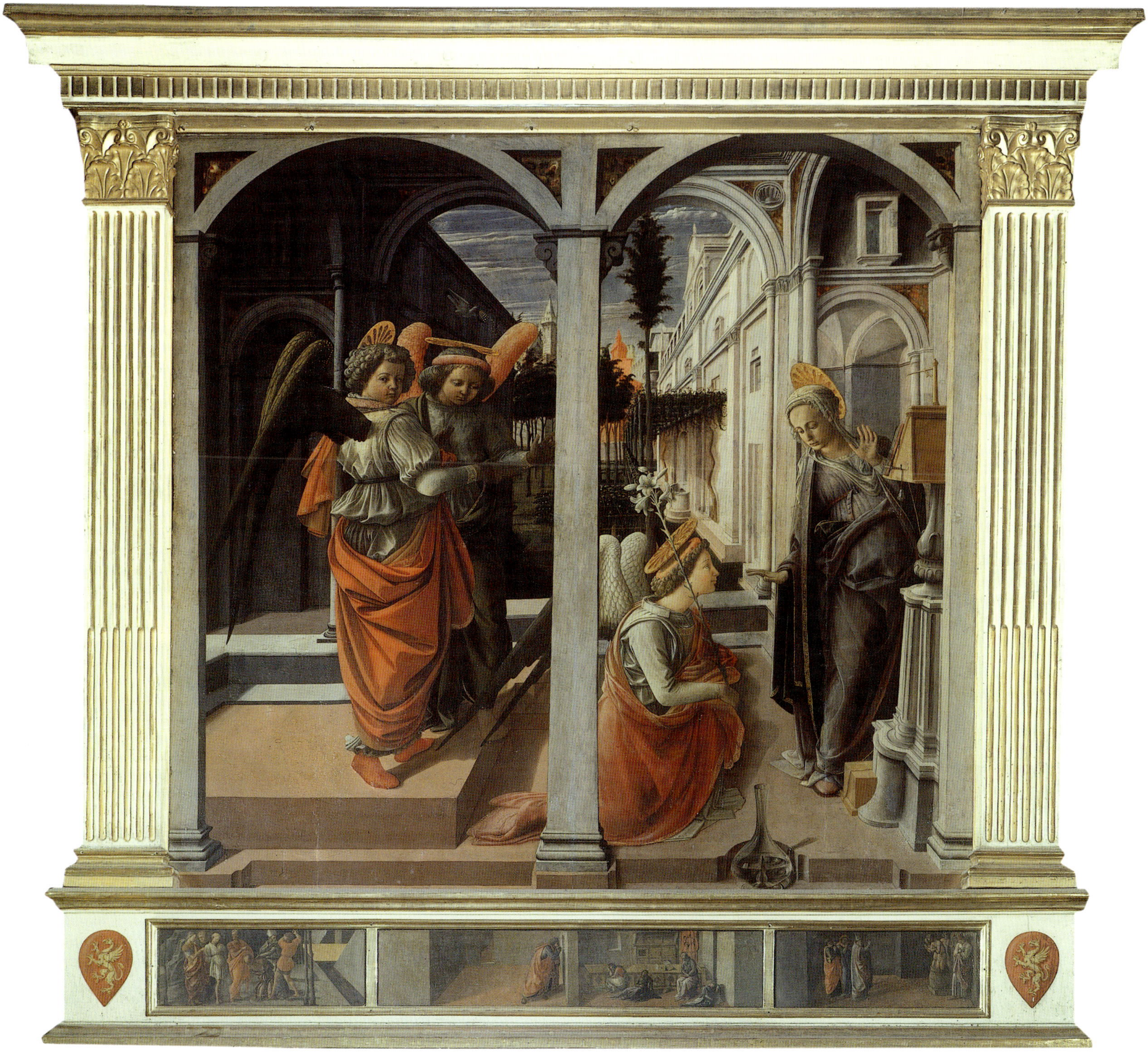

104 Filippo Lippi, *Annunciation*, c. 1439, Florence, San Lorenzo, Martelli chapel.

was one of these new *tavole quadrate* installed in the church (fig. 106).

The *Annunciation* is nearly square. The simple, *all'antica* frame is a later addition, but it seems likely that the original frame was Classical in style.[31] Lippi employed an ingenious, illusionistic painted frame that calls attention to the picture plane, highlighting that all-important juncture where the actual chapel space above the altar merges with the pictorial space construed as "beyond" the altar wall. This fictive frame consists of two arches supported by tall, square pillars, rendered in a gray tone to simulate *pietra serena* – the stone used for the *all'antica* architectural members within the church of San Lorenzo. To further the illusion of a continuous space between the chapel and the pictorial space, the moldings of the bases of these pillars are very similar to those in San Lorenzo.[32] The viewer is tempted to "enter" the pictorial space along the lower step, which seems flush with the framing pillars, and to "touch" – or in some way sensually apprehend – the vase of water (fig. 105) that is set so realistically within a recess in this step. Behind the frame, Fra Filippo situated the Annunciation drama in the shallow foreground space. The principal figures – Gabriel and the Virgin – are confined to the right-hand arch of the illusionistic frame, although the trailing folds of Gabriel's cloak and the points of his wings demonstrate that the space behind the two arches of the frame is a continuous one. At left, two angels attend. Behind this shallow space representing the Virgin's chamber, Fra Filippo depicted a deep *hortus conclusus* (enclosed garden) that extends back along the steeply receding orthogonals of the neo-classical buildings on either side. Urban edifices are visible in the distant background, accentuated by their clear silhouettes against the blue sky and their vermilion color.

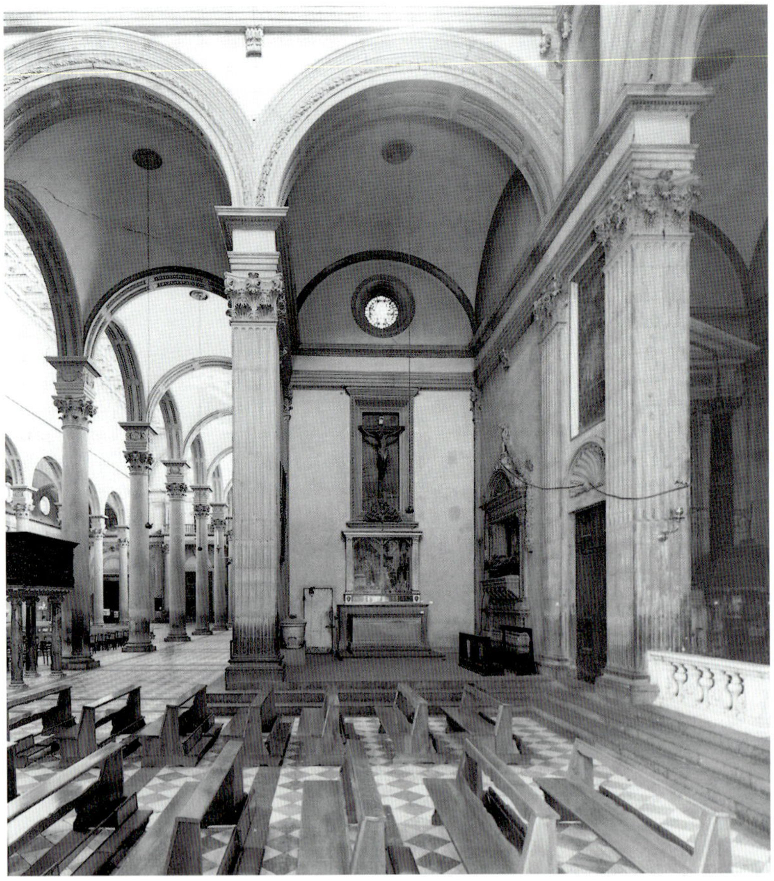

106 Interior of San Lorenzo, looking into the Martelli chapel, Florence.

105 Filippo Lippi, *Annunciation*, detail of fig. 104.

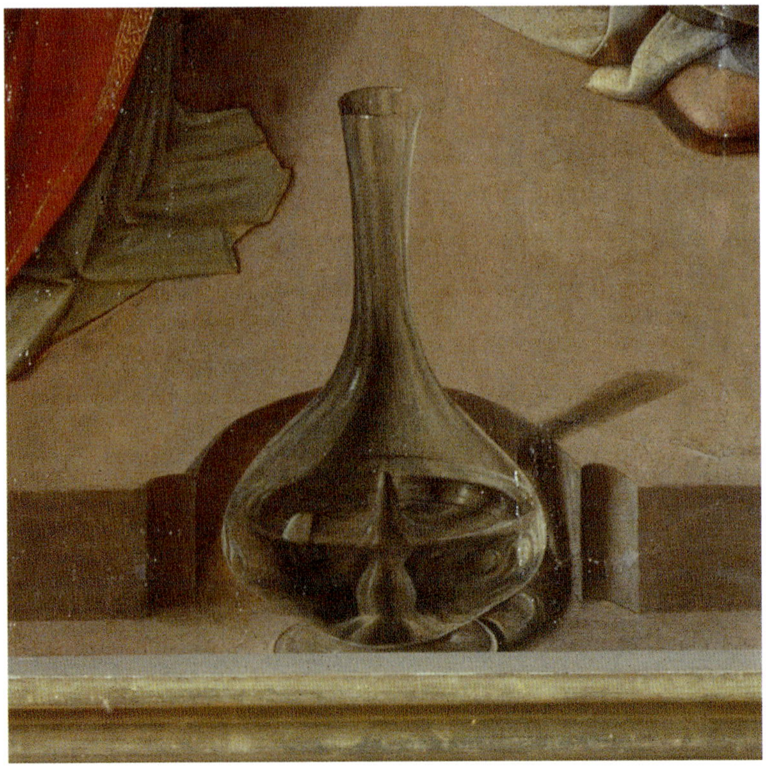

But Fra Filippo didn't render up this unified pictorial space and robust naturalism without making the very precepts upon which it is based problematic. His clever illusionistic frame, which calls attention to the picture plane, also serves to undermine one of the most important features of this new *costruzione legittima* – the vanishing point. The vanishing point is situated just to the right of the central pillar of the frame (at the level of the angels' gesticulating hands) and, as John White has observed, "the eye is called back to the surface at the very point of greatest penetration."[33]

The *Annunciation* is not dated and is usually accepted as around 1439–40 on the basis of style.[34] To make matters more complicated, on close examination, the altarpiece proves to be composed of two painted panels that do not quite line up, united at the center of the composition with a series of butterfly joins.[35] The predella, displaying scenes from the life of the name-saint of the chapel patron, Niccolò Martelli, is painted in a divergent style from that of the central panel, suggesting either that it was executed at a later date or by another artist.[36] These factors have led some scholars to maintain that the *Annunciation* was originally designed around 1440 as a set of movable shutters for an organ or reliquary cabinet and then reconfigured in the mid-1440s or later as a square *pala d'altare* for the Martelli chapel.[37] The ambiguity over the dating and the original function and location has prompted some to point instead to Fra Angelico's San Marco altarpiece (fig. 110) – also without a precise date (c. 1440–43) – as the first indisputable *tavola quadrata*. More recently, William Hood has argued that Fra Angelico's earlier Annalena altarpiece (dated to around 1434–35 on the basis of style) (fig. 107) was originally painted for the Medici chapel in the left transept of San Lorenzo, and fashioned as a *tavola quadrata* according to the Brunelleschian chapel prescriptions. For this reason, he claims, it should legitimately be considered the first Renaissance *pala*.[38]

The Annalena altarpiece, composed on a rectangular panel, displays the Virgin and Child enthroned within a very shallow pictorial space, set before an architectural backdrop and flanked by six saints who are splayed outward to either side of the throne.[39] The predella displays narrative scenes from the lives of Sts. Cosmas and Damian. Hood observes that the composition "suggests that Fra Angelico approached this entirely new type with some trepidation."[40] The figures are set against a tooled gold cloth that is reminiscent of the gold ground of the traditional polyptych. A hierarchy of sacrality is imposed through the subtle differentiation of three levels upon which the figures are situated. The outermost saints (Peter Martyr and Francis) stand upon a grassy carpet in the foreground, while the privileged Medici saints (Cosmas, Damian, John the Evangelist, and Lawrence) are raised slightly upon a white stone platform, with the Virgin and Child enthroned upon an elevated, decorated marble throne in the center of the composition.

Much more sophisticated in conception is Fra Angelico's altarpiece for the high altar of the Observant Dominican monastery church of San Marco.[41] The range of pictorial considerations that engaged Lippi in the Barbadori altarpiece and the San Lorenzo *Annunciation* are clearly evident in the San Marco work. The altarpiece displays a congregation of Dominican and Medici saints with angels in a unified pictorial space, gathered around the Madonna and Child who are seated upon a splendid *all'antica* throne. The panel is rectangular in shape and was probably originally set in an *all'antica* frame.[42] While Lippi evokes the traditional triptych in the Barbadori altarpiece through the play on the tripartite frame and columns, Fra Angelico ingeniously alludes to the variant religious representational mode through the inclusion of the illusionistic little gold-ground Crucifixion panel (*tavoluzza*) (fig. 108) rendered as though flush with the picture plane at the lower edge of the composition. The Lippi altarpiece tantalizingly suggests access and continuity between the viewer's space and the pictorial space, while Fra Angelico gives greater emphasis to a dramatic spatial rupture. The gold-ground Crucifixion, in addition to its iconographic purpose prefiguring the sacrifice of Christ, serves to communicate to the beholder that entry into this Albertian pictorial space is nonetheless effected through mental prayer rather than physical access.

The illusionistic curtains gathered at either side of the picture serve a similar function. They suggest the actual curtains which traditionally covered sacred images when they were not being invoked in ritual devotion. The curtains in the altarpiece signify a highly mediated access to the sacred subject depicted. And while Fra Angelico has employed the mechanics of mathematical perspective, with the receding orthogonals of the kelim rug and a vanishing point in the center of the Virgin's womb, he has undermined the rules of proportional diminution by enlarging the figures of the Virgin and Child relative to their position in the middle ground. They are on scale with the two Medici saints Cosmas and Damian in the foreground. Nor does the carefully defined pictorial space offer a readily recognizable frame of reference. The setting is that of a temporary ceremonial ground erected out of doors, with a patterned cloth *spalliera* separating the sacred figures from a grove of trees and distant hills beyond.

The designation of the first *tavola quadrata* altarpiece must necessarily remain a matter of conjecture, given the fragmentary state of the documentary record, although the balance of evidence points toward Fra Angelico's Annalena altarpiece. What perhaps is more interesting and of greater significance is the role played by the two *frati dipintori* in the second half of the 1430s and early 1440s, in working through the representational problems implicit in the adoption of this new pictorial form.[43] Both painters explored the paradox underlying the conceptualization of religious representations as coextensive with actual profane settings, and in the adoption of a greater degree of naturalism for the rendition of Christian mysteries and sacred figures. Both Fra Angelico and Fra Filippo also found ingenious means of potentially intensifying the religious experience of the devotee before the altarpiece in their applications of the new artistic technology.

Fra Filippo used the *tavola quadrata* to effect a new kind of dramatic "hierophany." He brought a heightened attention to the encounter between the sacred protagonists and the spectator, and structured this dynamic confrontation around the liminal zone of the altarpiece frame and picture plane. The viewer's act of looking into the altarpiece thus ruptures the customary modalities of time and space. During a brief moment, at the onset of the more extended temporal span of beholding the painting, the sacred personages represented in the shallow foreground of the perspectival pictorial space were offered up to the viewer as if palpably present within their figurations. Divinity, sanctity, and Christian mysteries – invisible, unknowable, distant, and historical – presided for a fleeting moment within his radically embodied figural receptacles. This encounter with "Real Presence" did not last long; the matrix of Fra Filippo's illusionism was not designed to sustain it. The hierophany ceased when the inconsistencies in the perspectival construction and the ambiguities in the pictorial space began to undermine the

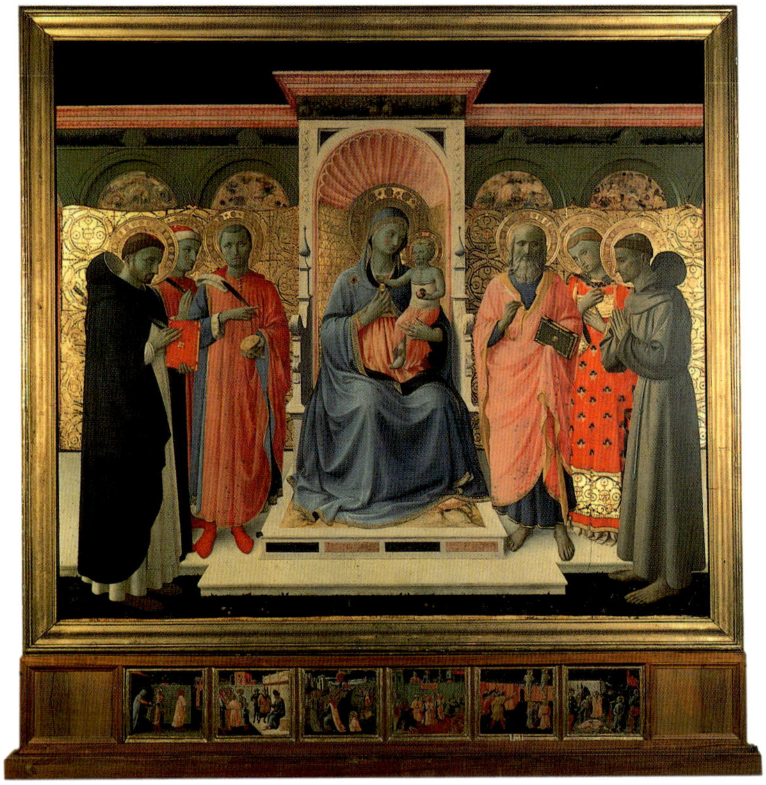

107 Fra Angelico, Annalena altarpiece, c. 1434–35, Florence, Museo di San Marco.

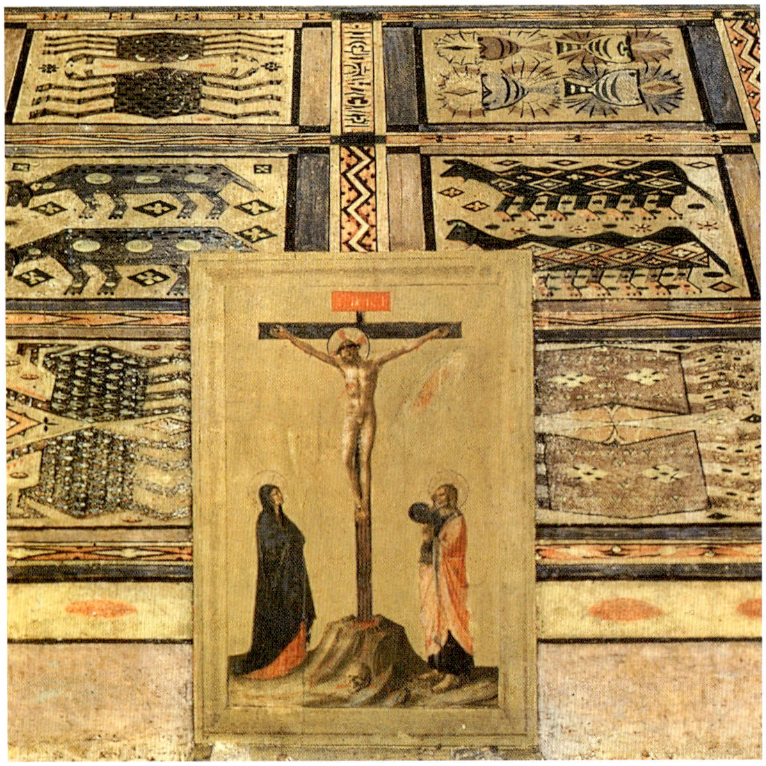

108 Fra Angelico, San Marco altarpiece, detail of fig. 110.

apparent concreteness of the vision. At this point, Fra Filippo's recourse to a more traditional mode of religious representation took over, as the primary subjects in the altarpiece were eloquently glossed in the proliferation of vividly rendered visual metaphors.

The *tavola quadrata* quickly became a popular feature of Florentine painting. Domenico Veneziano's *St. Lucy* altarpiece (c. 1445; fig. 109), commissioned for the high altar of Santa Lucia de Magnoli, offers a striking variation with its rigorously plotted spatial configuration and architectural setting, complex lighting arrangement, and pleasing chromatic harmony. Neri di Bicci's *Ricordanze* testify to how the *tavola quadrata* had become the standard altarpiece format within a very active and successful painting practice during the third quarter of the *quattrocento*.[44]

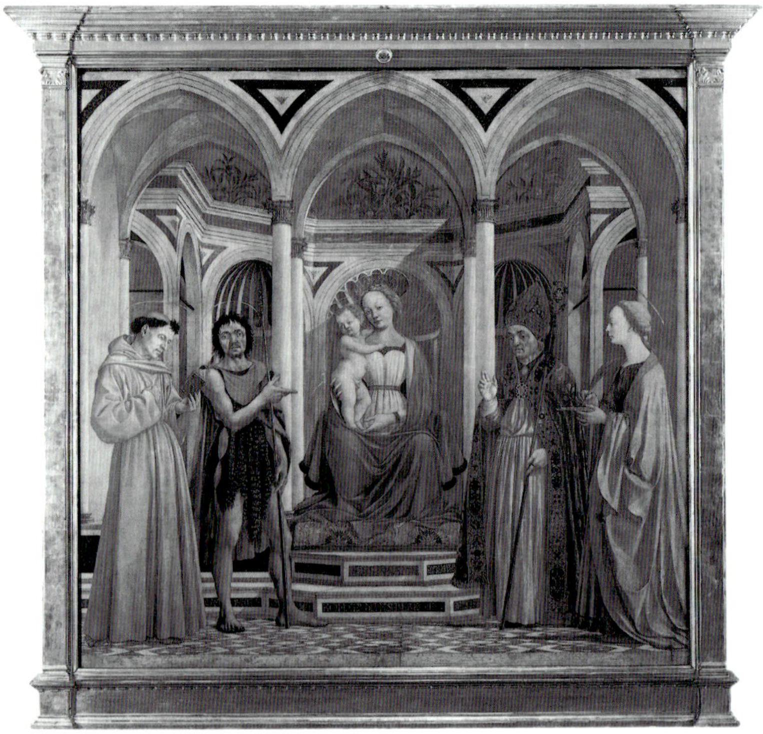

109 Domenico Veneziano, *St. Lucy* altarpiece, c. 1445, Florence, Uffizi.

However, the gold-ground polyptych persisted as a powerful alternative, even in the work of the two artists responsible for introducing and popularizing the new format.[45] Fra Angelico painted a stunningly beautiful gold-ground polyptych for the church of San Domenico in Perugia (see fig. 204). Fra Filippo executed a gold-ground altarpiece, *St. Lawrence Enthroned with Saints* (see figs. 97a–c), for Alessandro Alessandri.[46] In this work, Fra Filippo also resorted to another characteristic feature of the *trecento* polyptych, utilizing a scale variation to differentiate the principal sacred figures from the diminutive donor and his two sons kneeling in the foreground below. Thus, while the *tavola quadrata* involved an important paradigm shift in visual representational practices, and this new form became the prevailing

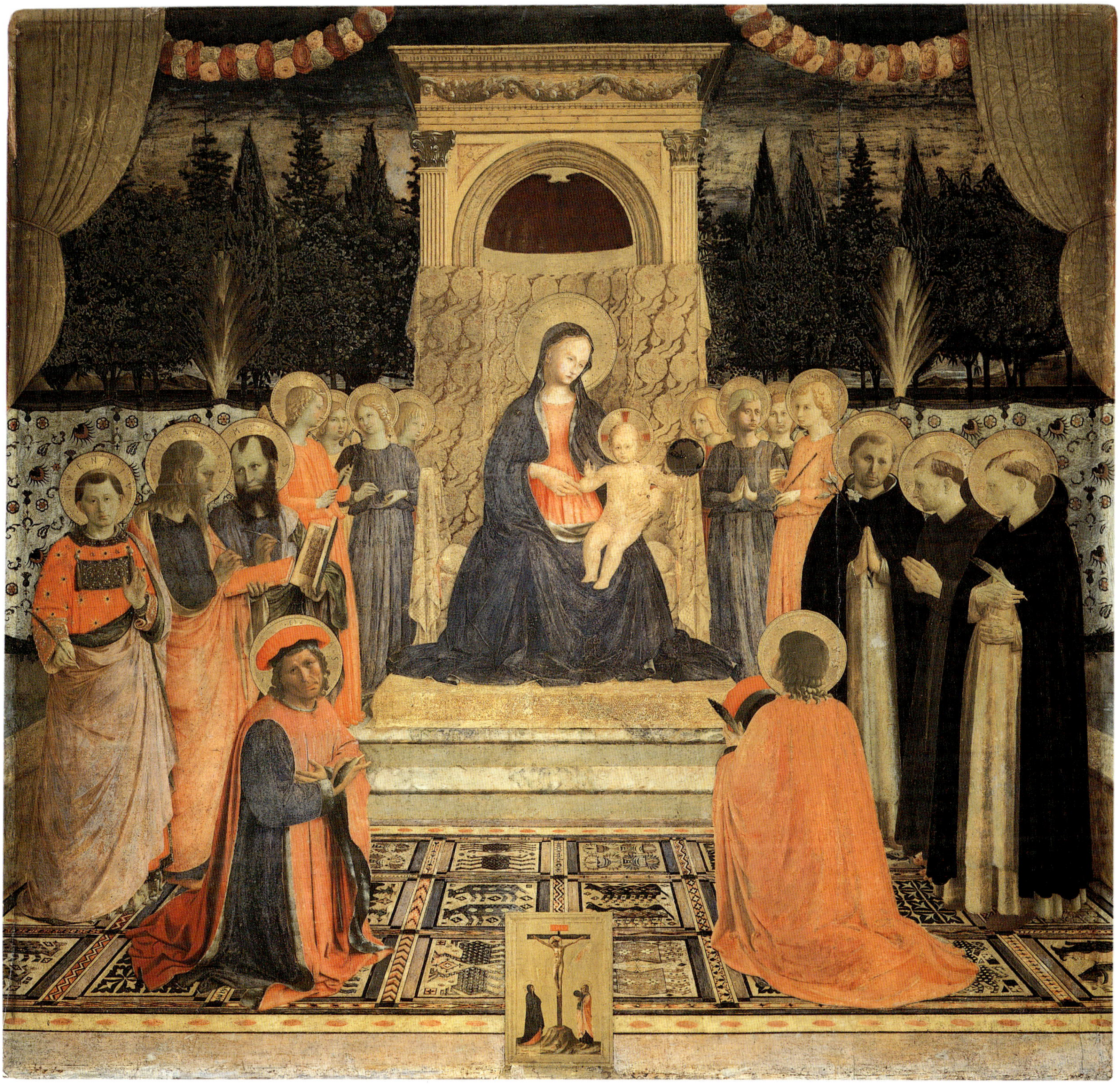

110 Fra Angelico, San Marco altarpiece, c. 1440–43, Florence, Museo di San Marco.

model in more progressive artistic production, it was nonetheless one among a number of altarpiece configurations produced during the Italian Renaissance and must be studied in relation to these other competing variants.[47]

Portraiture

Fra Filippo Lippi's activity as a painter of portraits involved three principal categories: 1) the rectangular panel painting that isolates a half-length figure shown in profile, 2) full and half-length donor figures integrated into religious paintings, and 3) the likeness of contemporary individuals incorporated as witnesses or among the crowd in religious narrative frescos.[48]

An attempt to analyse Lippi's portraits in the light of general developments in Italian, and more specifically, Florentine portraiture runs up against innumerable problems. While portraits are documented in Europe during the fourteenth century and the incidence of portraiture increased significantly during the fifteenth century, the rate of survival of portrait panels is very low.[49] Furthermore, many of the extant works lack documentation so that the subjects cannot be identified, nor can dating be established with much certainty. Because portraits were so directly tied to the specific interests of individual families and lineages, their perceived value and very survival was dependent upon the fortunes of the families and the persistence of family memories. This began to change by the end of the fifteenth century, as collecting patterns altered and portraits became of interest as aesthetic objects associated with celebrated artists. There is also the problematic question of the influence of Netherlandish portraiture (fig. 111), which was more technically and conceptually advanced, upon Italian practices during the first half of the *quattrocento*.

111 Jan van Eyck, *Cardinal Niccolò Albergati*, c. 1432, Vienna, Kunsthistorisches Museum.

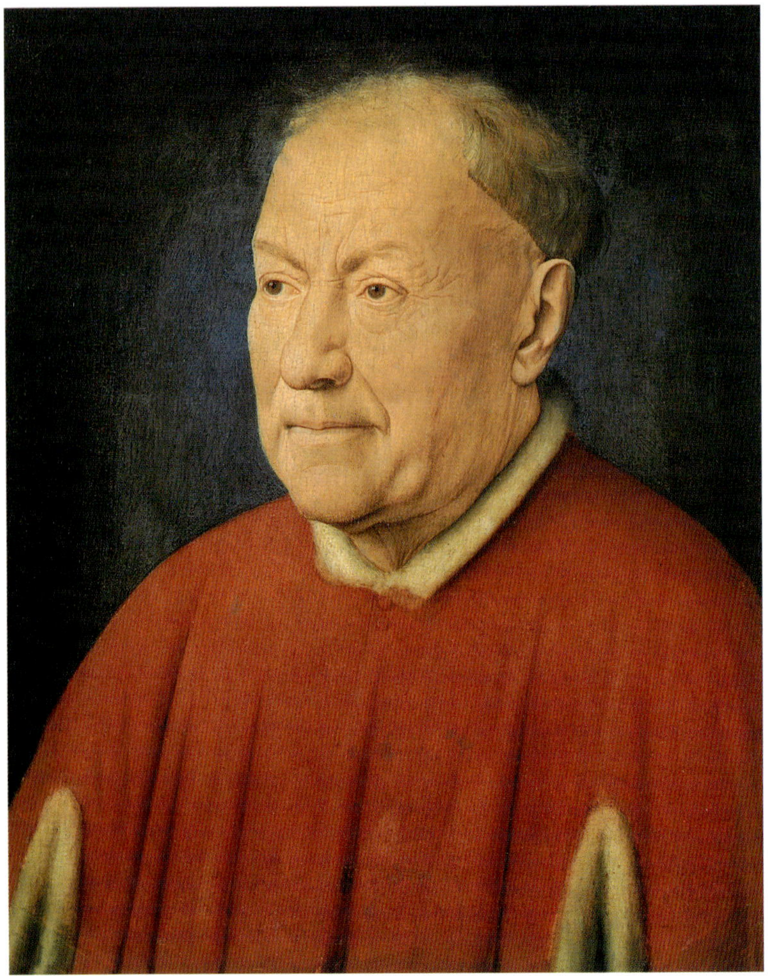

The emergence of the independent portrait panel in early Renaissance Italy reflects changing attitudes toward the family, social identity, personal subjectivity, and commemoration. Portraiture isolated the individual human subject and defined that subject both as a distinct being and as a member of any number of social aggregates (family, lineage, class, corporate body, institution, geographic locale, and political entity). This identity was established through the depiction of distinguishing physiognomic features, personal and corporate devices and attributes, and character traits elaborated through visual metaphors. The development of portraiture was also predicated upon changes in the visual and material culture, whereby images of recognizable contemporary and historical subjects were displayed and viewed within secular and ecclesiastical settings.

By the 1430s, portraiture, which had initially functioned as a means of commemorating royal lineages within European courts, had been appropriated by the merchant class in the Netherlands and, probably around a decade later, by the same class in the Italian republics and signorial states.[50] During the fifteenth century, the practice of portrait painting was bolstered by an increasingly more sophisticated theoretical apparatus derived from Classical example and humanist elaboration, the courtly love and chivalry traditions, and the celebration of illustrious statesmen, poets, artists, and men of arms from the more recent past.

The two extant portrait panels by Lippi in New York and Berlin are among the earliest surviving independent portraits in Florentine art.[51] They appear to have been painted shortly after a group of portraits displaying young men in profile wearing elaborate *cappucci*, although none of these early Florentine portraits is documented and the dates ascribed to them by art historians range from the 1430s to the 1450s.[52] In the male portrait panels, the pictorial language of commemoration is very spare.[53] The sitters' features are generalized, with the line of the profile the principal characterizing device, and the gaze out of the picture the most evocative sign of memorial presence. Somber but expensive fur-lined clothing and elaborate knotting on the hats are the only signs of patrician status and wealth, while the static pose may signify formal decorum.[54] The nuances of individual character and subjectivity are clearly not of interest in these portraits, which promoted familial remembrance by "making the absent present" in very essential terms.[55] Most revealing about the function of these early male portraits are the two works attributed to Domenico Veneziano (c. 1440). If the inscriptions on these panels added in the sixteenth-century are to be trusted, they represent Matteo Olivieri and his son Michele (fig. 112). The commission appears to have been a commemorative gesture by another member of the Olivieri lineage, since both subjects are shown with idealized youthful visages, and were painted at a time when the older Olivieri had been dead for decades and the younger probably recently expired.[56]

Both Fra Filippo's portraits feature women as their principal subjects. The New York panel (fig. 113) is an unusual double portrait showing a woman in profile in the center foreground, with a male figure only partially visible at the left, leaning through a window embrasure and situated in a deeper spatial plane.[57] The Berlin portrait (fig. 114) displays a single female subject in profile against an open window.[58] We know from Petrarch's sonnets that Simone Martini painted a portrait of Petrarch's beloved Laura, but Lippi's portraits are among the earliest Italian individual female portrait panels to have survived.[59] While there is no documentary verification, Fra Filippo's portraits and other *quattrocento* Florentine representations of youthful, elegantly attired women have been associated with the commemoration that accompanied the union of two patrician lineages through marriage.[60]

In the *Double Portrait*, the subjects' specific identity is established through the coat of arms hanging over the window sill associated with the man (that of the Scolari family) and through what must have been a personal motto embroidered onto the sleeve of the woman ("lealtà").[61] The *Portrait of a Woman* lacks any such referents, and in neither portrait is there an attempt to distinguish particularizing physiognomic features or personalized attributes. In both, the facial features are very generalized and the profile lines are not strongly accentuated or exaggerated.[62] Evidently, characterizing "likeness" is not what is at issue in these portraits. Instead, they present a visual discourse on female virtues valued by Florentine patrician society – beauty, piety, chastity, fidelity, fertility, and lofty social status.[63] The portraits elaborate upon the "dowry of virtue" that was an important component of the perceived identity of a patrician young woman, along with her lineage, that of her husband, and her wealth. These virtues are physically embodied by the sitters, displayed by the clothing and jewelry that ornament their bodies, and elaborated through the elements within the setting.

Attention is brought foremost to the visages of the women. In each case, the face is the feature of the painting that is rendered with the brightest illumination. The profile of each woman stands out against the more muted tones of the background. The modeling of the faces is exquisitely subtle, with gradual, almost indiscernible tonal transitions, giving the effect of a hard, smooth, fair surface – evoking the metaphors of ivory and marble used in the Petrarchan poetic tradition when describing the skin of a beautiful woman. Both female subjects have plucked eyebrows and foreheads and exhibit the blond hair that accorded

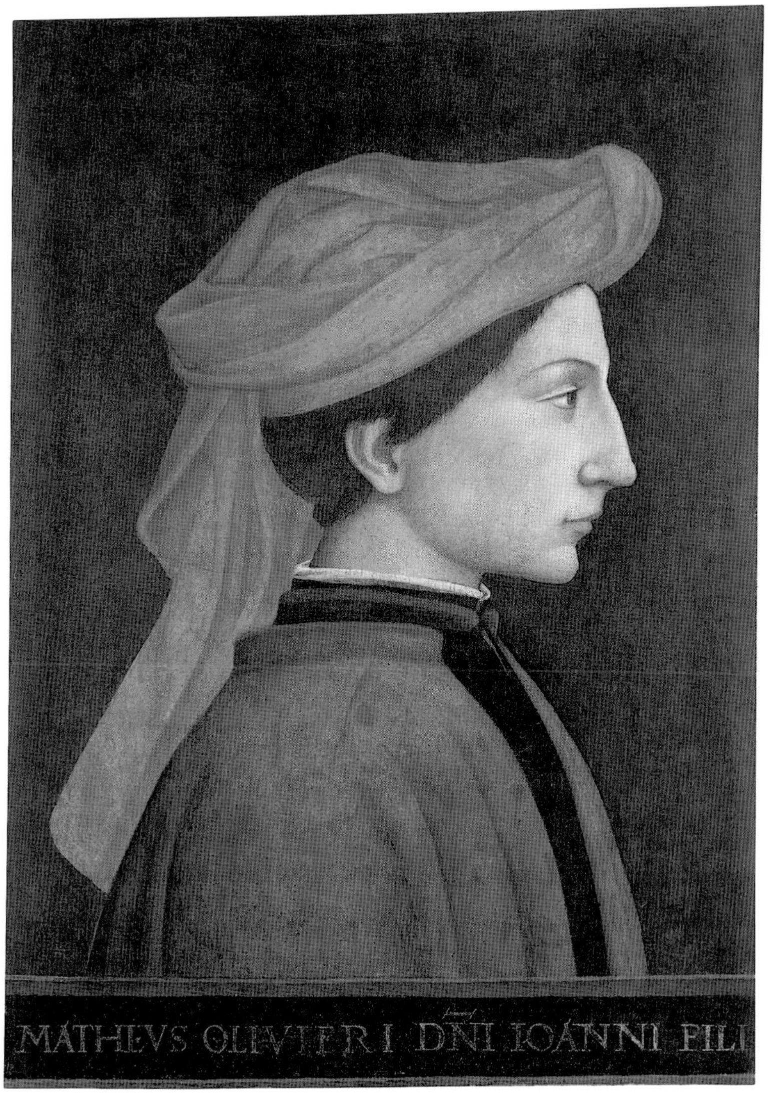

112 Domenico Veneziano, attr., *Portrait of Matteo Olivieri*, c. 1440, Washington, National Gallery of Art, Andrew W. Mellon Collection.

with the prevailing canon of female beauty. In the *Double Portrait*, Fra Filippo set the woman's generalized visage against the atomized detailing of the landscape visible through the window (fig. 115). The petrified, beautiful face resists penetration and demands to be apprehended as a surface, while the deep space of the landscape encourages a visual mode of "seeing into," setting up a dialectic between the physical beauty of the woman and her "inner" character elaborated through framing elements and ornament. Piety and chastity are suggested by the monastery visible through the window, which calls attention to itself as the most legible feature within the landscape. The lush vegetation in the landscape may suggest fertility.

Fidelity is implied by the conjunction of male and female subjects in the presence of the man's coat of arms, and affirmed in the motto "lealtà" on the woman's sleeve. The lofty social status of these individuals is displayed through the Scolari arms, and in the extraordinarily rich costume and jewelry worn by the

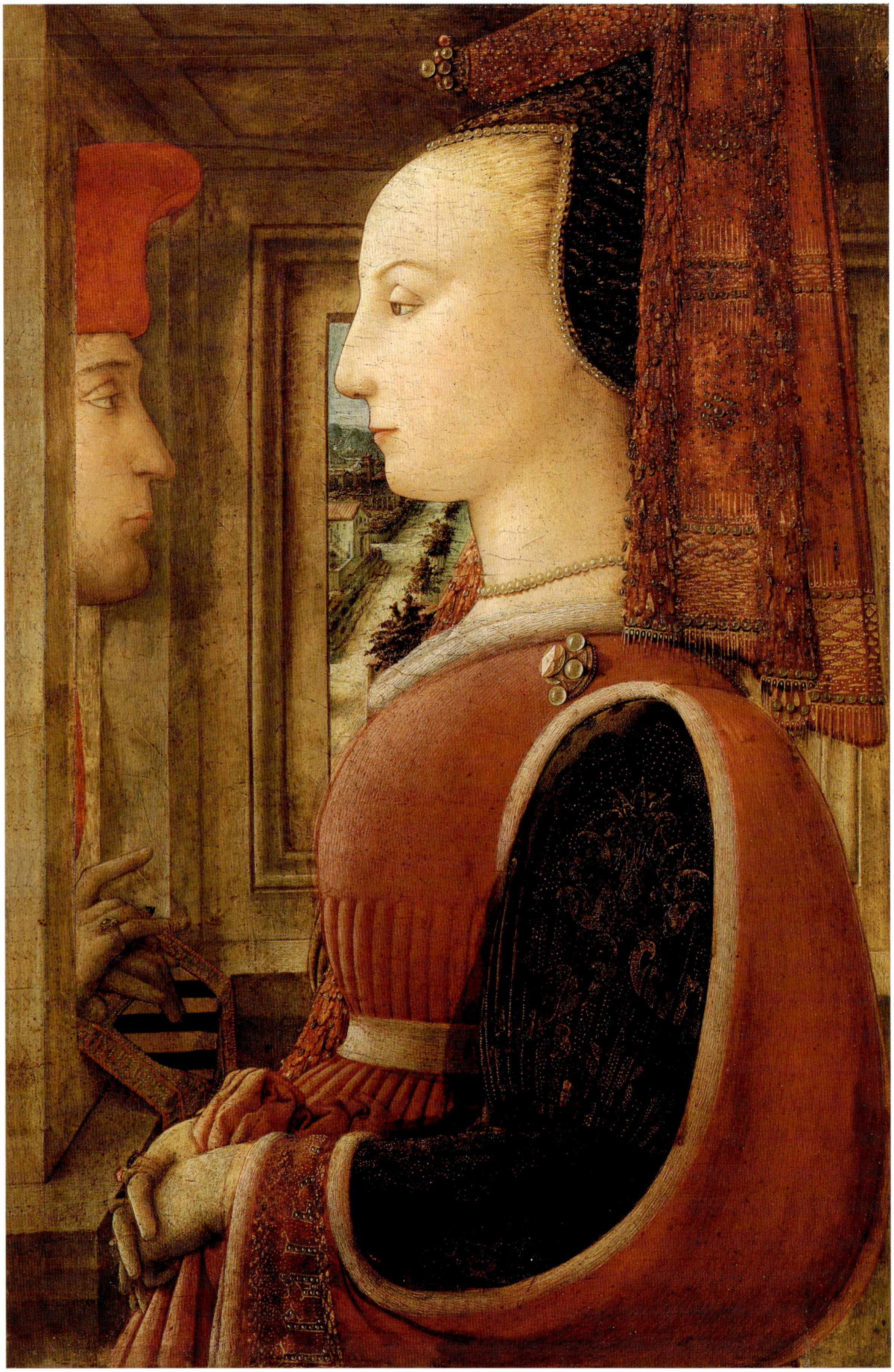

113 Filippo Lippi, *Double Portrait*, early 1440s, New York, Metropolitan Museum of Art, Gift of Henry G. Marquand, 1889. Marquand Collection (89.15.19).

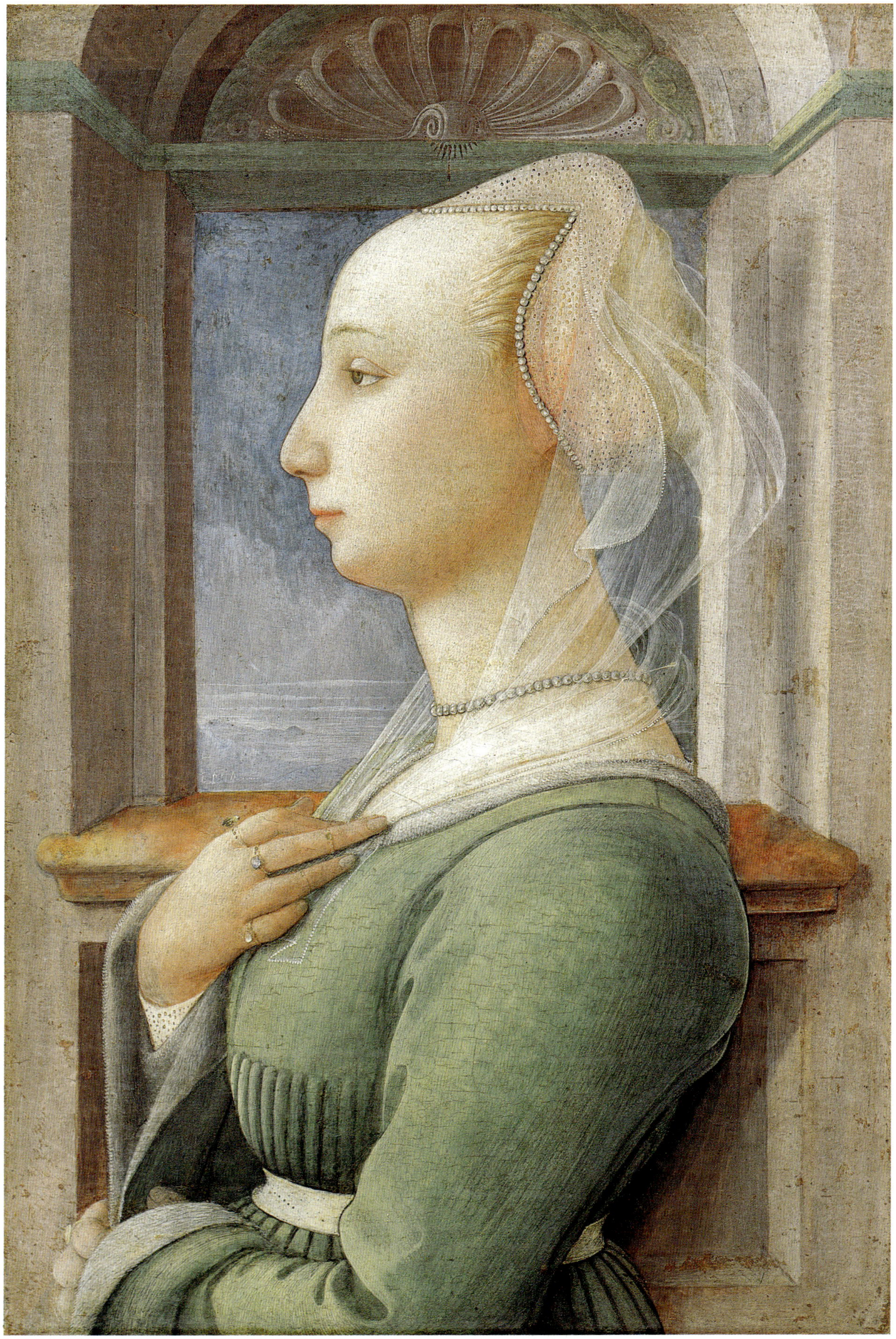

114 Filippo Lippi, *Portrait of a Woman*, early 1440s, Berlin, Staatliche Museen Preussischer Kulturbesitz, Gemäldegalerie.

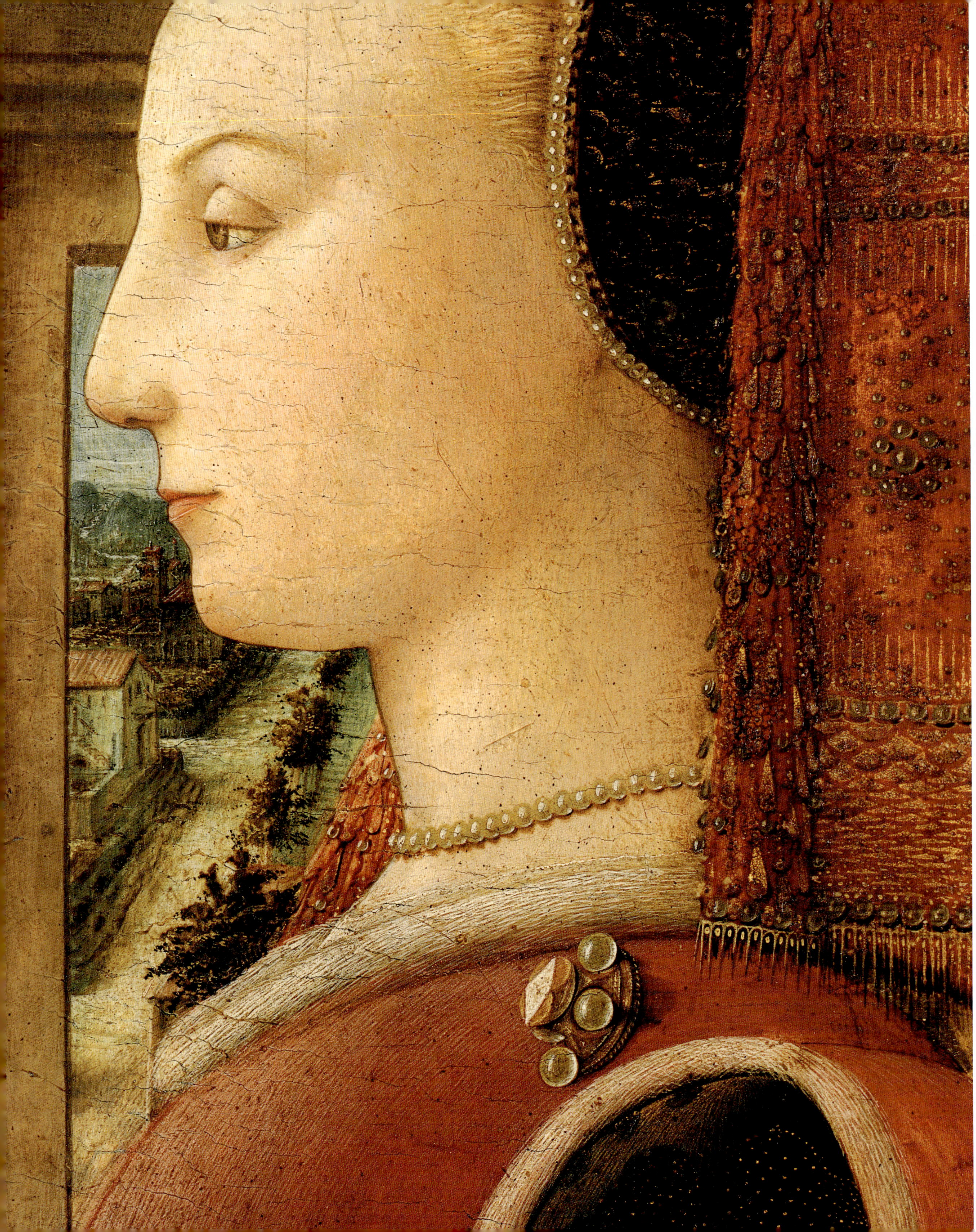

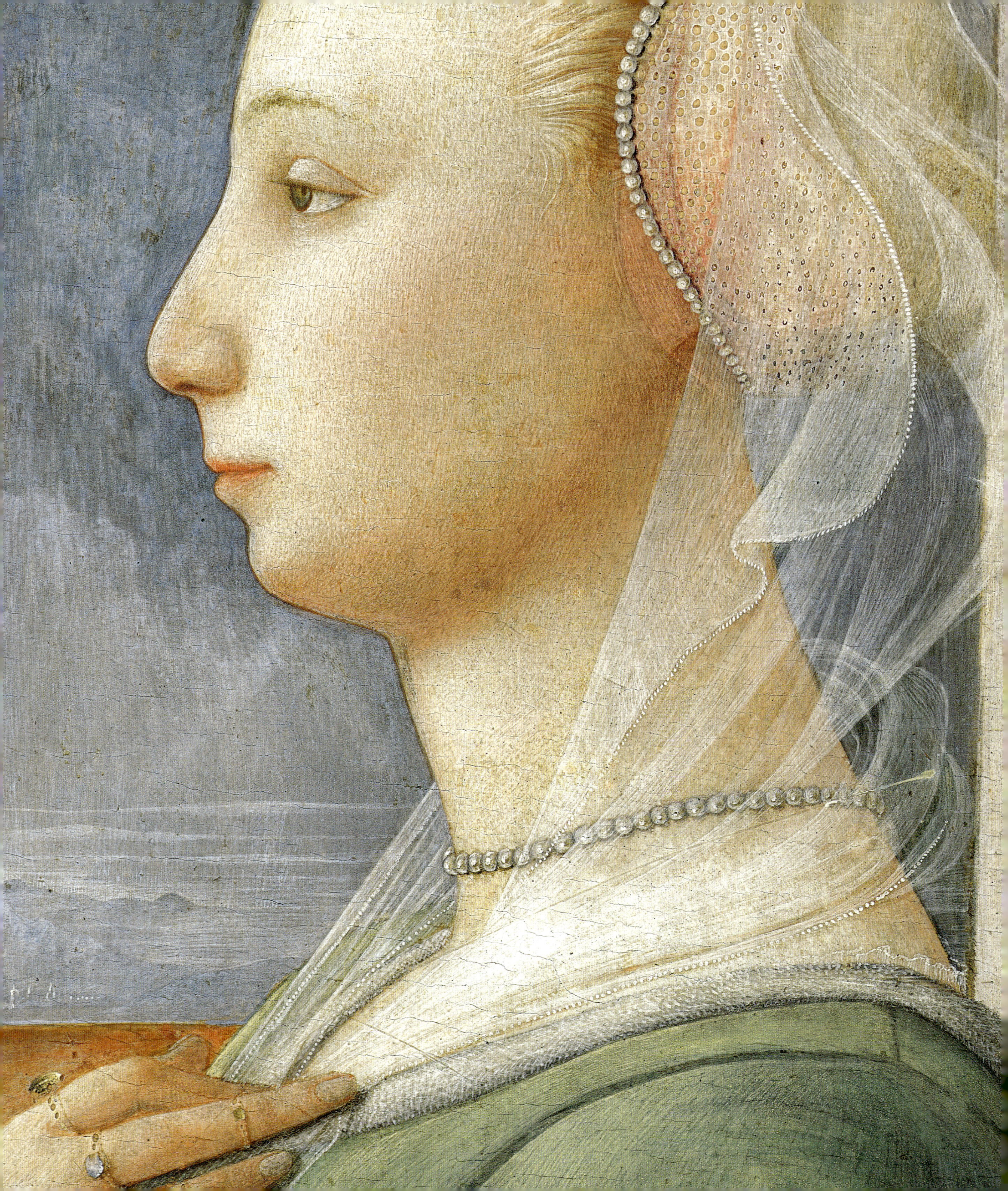

woman. Her outer dress (*giornea*) is lined with fur, the sleeves of her inner dress (*cioppa*) appear to be of gold-embroidered velvet, while her *alla parigina* headdress is encrusted with pearls.[64] She wears a necklace of pearls, rings upon her fingers, and a shoulder broach featuring a faceted stone set within pearls. In both the New York and the Berlin portraits, the pearls which adorn the women's necks and headdresses were conventional symbols of purity, as well as being a typical wedding gift. This treatment of the woman's attire differs significantly from the somber dress found in the five male portraits discussed above and points to a different economy of display in female portraiture, which featured physical beauty and rich ornament. The clothing and jewelry worn by the female subject in the *Double Portrait* suggest that the commemorative effigy served to memorialize a festive (as opposed to a quotidian) presence in which costly dress and ornament functioned as signs of family patrimony.[65]

Central to Lippi's portraiture is a process of objectification. Both of his female portrait subjects are pushed up against the picture plane and tightly framed by the architecture, offering clearly defined, accessible, and intimate objects for beholding. They are both animated by the modeling of their flesh and features, but are also firmly anchored, fixed, with a lack of engagement, and thus easily objectified by the viewer's gaze.[66]

The New York portrait is the earliest double portrait found in Italian art. Pictorial precedents for this composition may be seen in Flemish paired portraits and in manuscript illumination.[67] Attempts have been made to situate Fra Filippo's panel within the discourse about beauty, love, and art in which female portraiture was increasingly bound up during the *quattrocento*. It has been argued that in the *Double Portrait*, the encounter between the male and female subjects through an open window is derived from the Song of Songs, and reflects the poetic love tradition in both its religious and secular variations.[68] The shadow cast by the male figure has been related to Pliny's remark in his *Natural History* that painting originated with the circumscription of the lover's shadow falling upon a wall.[69]

What must be taken into account, however, is the fact that the female figure occupies the central and primary position in the composition and that there is a lack of interaction between the man and woman.[70] Technical examination of the panel has revealed that the male figure was added after the primary composition had been blocked out and the female figure painted in.[71] The male subject is also situated in a deeper spatial plane and at a slightly lower level than the female subject, and hence their gazes do not actually meet. The most banal conclusion to be drawn is that this member of the Scolari family should be understood as a secondary figure within the composition, as an element of the broader frame of references within which the primary female figure is explicated. It is also possible that the double-portrait conception evolved over the course of the execution of the panel, and that Fra Filippo gradually elaborated a thematics of love and marriage (and perhaps even death) that incorporated the male figure, as he went along. Another possibility is that, on one level, the portrait formalizes an aspect of the courtly love tradition, whereby desire is generated out of the perpetual deferral of gratification through a continual displacement of the object of desire.[72] In this case, the very failure of

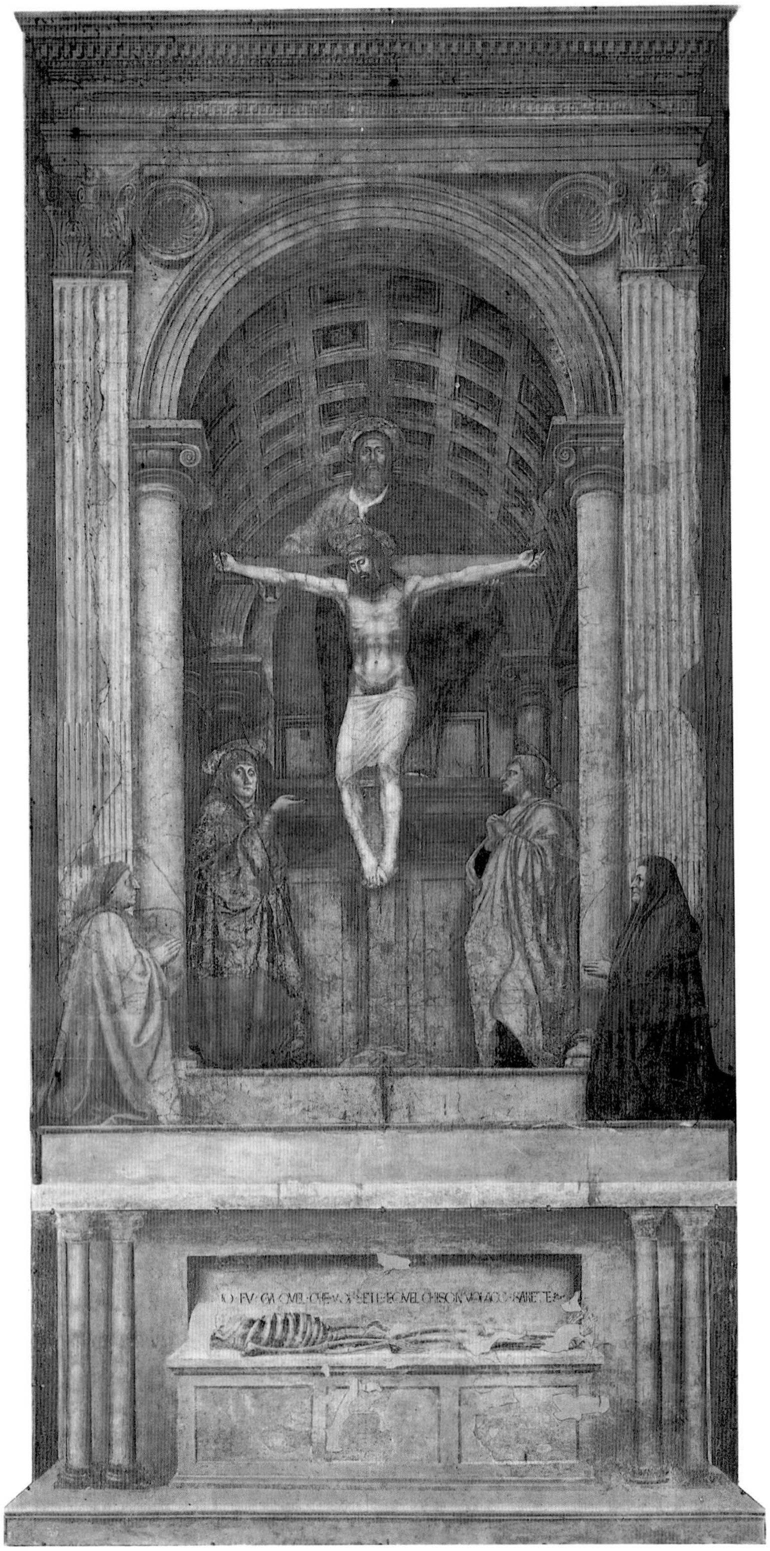

117 Masaccio, *Trinity*, c. 1427, Florence, Santa Maria Novella.

115 (*page 132*) Filippo Lippi, *Double Portrait*, detail of fig. 113.

116 (*previous page*) Filippo Lippi, *Portrait of a Woman*, detail of fig. 114.

the two figures to engage directly would echo the inability of the (male) beholder to possess the beautiful young woman in the painting, proffered so tantalizingly before his eyes.

The New York and Berlin portraits demonstrate Fra Filippo Lippi to have been among the earliest Italian artists to offer the individual portrait panel to a patrician clientele. His pictorial style leant itself particularly well to female portraiture, where he combined his skills in rendering figures with convincing physical presence and immediacy, with an idealized, generalized beauty and grace.

The portraits of donors in religious representations by Lippi are heavily indebted to the innovative work of Masaccio, best exemplified in the *Trinity* (fig. 117).[73] Masaccio departed from the *trecento* practice of working with a hierarchy of scale where the sacred figures were represented in one size and the donor figures in smaller dimension, often segregated in a separate pictorial register in the immediate foreground and isolated like cut-out stencils against a flat ground. In the *Trinity*, Masaccio integrated the Lenzi patron and his wife within a unified pictorial space. They are depicted on scale with the sacred figures according to the logic of proportional diminution that underlay his perspectival scheme. While they occupy a different zone of the pictorial space from that of the sacred figures, it is a continuous space and one that is defined and measurable. They kneel upon what appears to be a projecting stair in the interior of the church, effectively within the same space as the beholder.

Donor portraits appear in ten of Lippi's religious representations, from his earliest works like the devotional panel in the Cini Collection (see fig. 47) and the small Fitzwilliam triptych (see fig. 46), to his later altarpieces like the Corsham Court *Annunciation* (see fig. 122) and the *Death of St. Jerome* (see fig. 180).[74] This is a higher percentage of donor portraits in religious images than is found in the work of any of his contemporaries. I take issue with John Pope-Hennessy's dismissive assessment of Lippi's donor images, which he considers regressive in the aftermath of Masaccio's accomplishment.[75] Instead, I contend that Lippi demonstrated a similar interest and creative imagination in portraying donors and integrating their portraits into his religious compositions.

Furthermore, it is compelling in the case of this *frate dipintore* to conceive of the painting of donor portraits as a kind of religious ministration. As an ordained member of the monastic clergy, the chaplain of two nunneries, and a parish priest, even if notoriously lax in his responsibilities, Fra Filippo was trained to offer a variety of religious services to the individuals and communities under his care. The painting of a donor portrait is not so far removed from the curative and sacramental duties that a member of the monastic clergy was called upon to perform, like confession or the recitation of memorial masses.[76] Fra Filippo, the *frate dipintore*, was, in effect, laboring on behalf of the patron to bring about an act of saintly intercession by positioning the donor-as-supplicant in a reverential attitude in proximity to a designated saint or a sacred mystery, within the imaginary space of visualized prayer. If the theoretical model offered by Alberti for portraiture as "presence" is considered in relation to donor portraits, than Fra Filippo was well positioned to provide a representational embodiment that asserted the continual presence of the supplicant – effectively a non-stop prayer for heavenly intercession.

The artistic means that Fra Filippo developed to represent his patrons included a technique for making his donor portraits stand out from the altarpieces, tabernacles, and devotional panels into which they were incorporated. He used a strong black line (figs. 119 and 120) to define the profile of the donor and to set the face off against its surroundings. As an accomplished portraitist, Fra Filippo also used this heavy profile line to delineate the characterizing contours of the donor's forehead, nose, mouth, and chin. He depicted individuating features like skin tone and texture, facial hair, hair style and color, and dress. These details indicated age and social position – two important components in the construction of identity (particularly male identity) in *quattrocento* Florence. The donor's body position, gesture, and attitude before the sacred figures within the composition characterized and elaborated upon the patron's piety.

With two exceptions, Fra Filippo's donor effigies are on scale with the sacred figures within his complexly structured compositions.[77] While he set the donors and sacred subjects within a common pictorial space, he nonetheless maintained a careful distinction between the different spatial zones of the constructed space, following a strict decorum in separating the sacred from the secular. In the Sant'Ambrogio *Coronation of the Virgin* (see fig. 212), the deceased patron Francesco Maringhi is placed within a tomb-like recess at the right of the composition, and is further designated as the patron by the inscribed banderole ("Is perfecit opus") held by an angel before him. The unidentified donors in the *Annunciation* in the Palazzo Barberini (fig. 121) kneel behind a wooden balustrade that extends from the Virgin's tarsiated *prie dieu* in the extreme right foreground, in a scenography that anticipates Bernini's Cornaro Chapel.[78] The patron in the Corsham Court *Annunciation* (fig. 122), Jacopo Bellucci, kneels behind a low parapet, set apart from the foreground space where the Annunciation takes place – with the bold implication that he is situated even more deeply within the Virgin's private quarters than the sacred protagonists.[79]

An unusual degree of narrative interaction was introduced by Fra Filippo between a donor and the figures in the religious *istoria*. In the *Death of St. Jerome* (figs. 118 and 180), the donor, Gemignano Inghirami, is shown in profile in the foreground before the bier upon which the dead saint lies. He kneels in supplication alongside a crippled youth who has come seeking a cure from the saint's body. The Gerolomite brother at the left motions toward both the cripple and Inghirami in a gesture that recalls traditional saintly intercession directed toward a donor. This gesture, however, effectively situates both of these potentially peripheral figures immediately within the historical narrative of mourning over the body of St. Jerome.

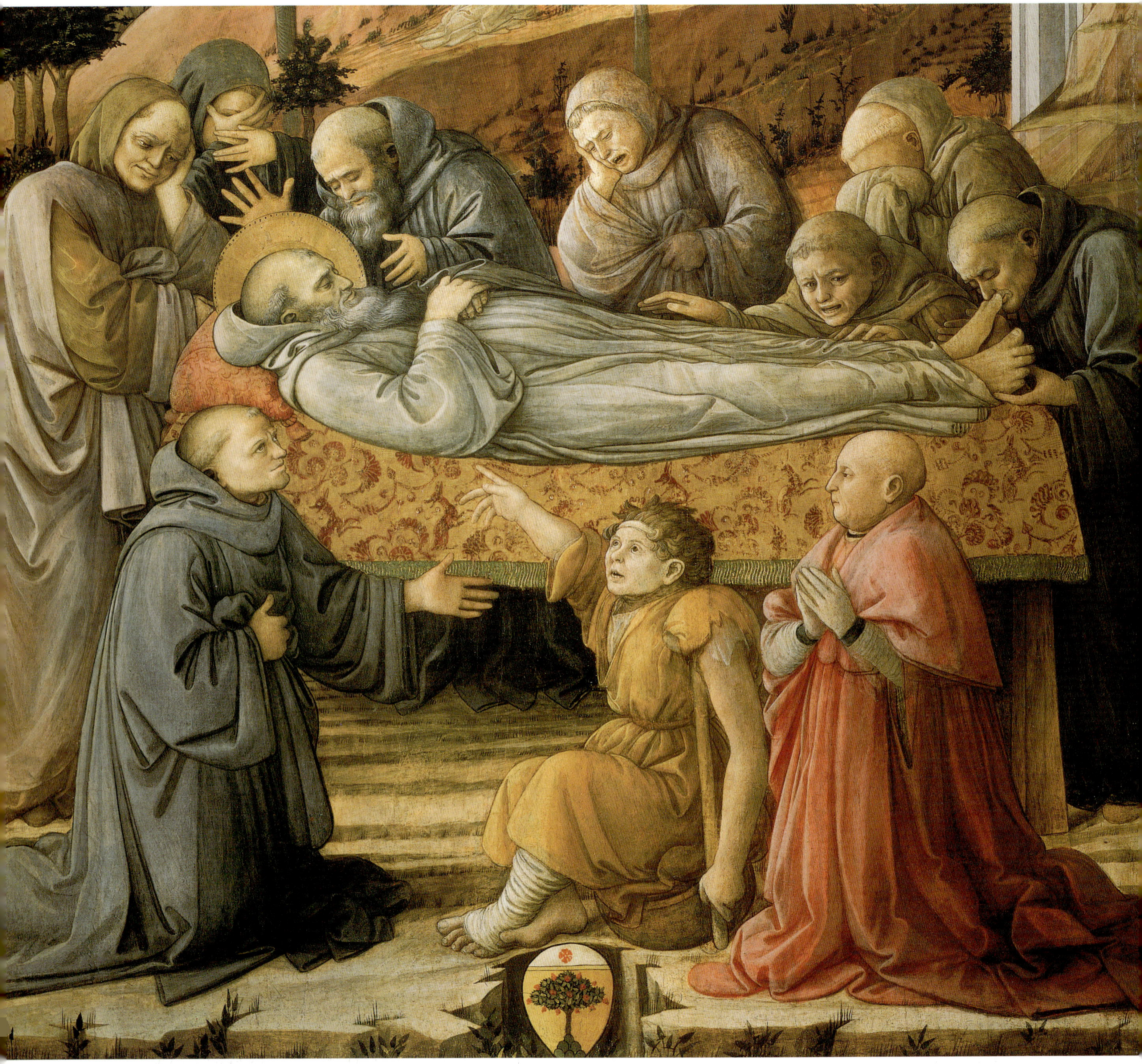

118 Filippo Lippi, *Death of St. Jerome*, detail of fig. 180.

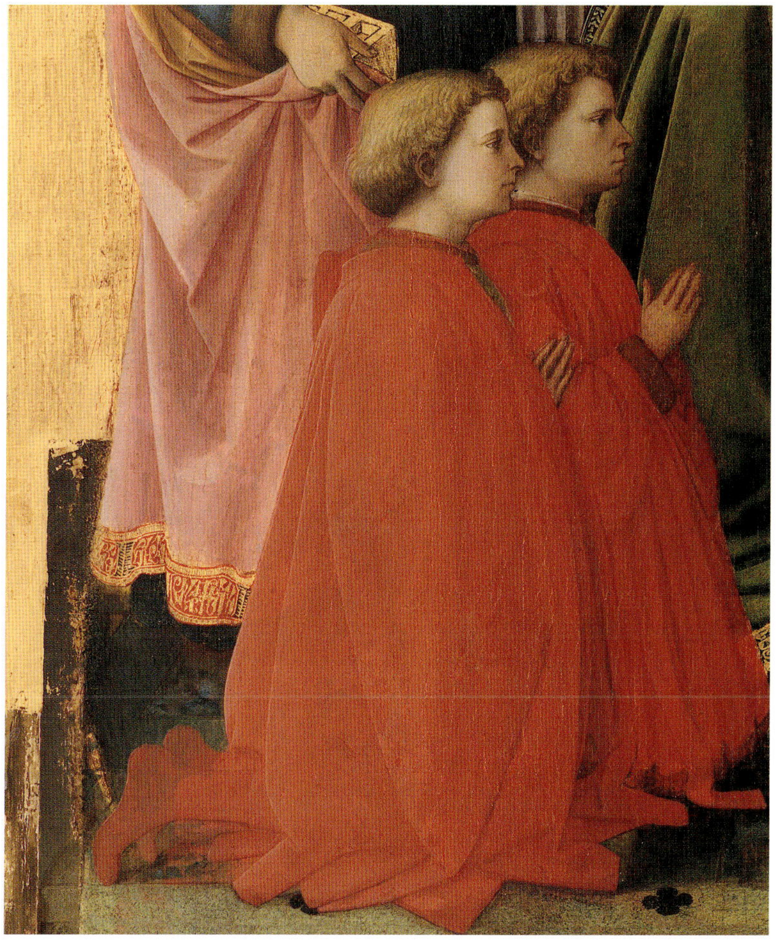

119 Filippo Lippi, *St. Lawrence Enthroned with Saints and Donors*, detail of fig. 97, with the sons of Alessandro Alessandri.

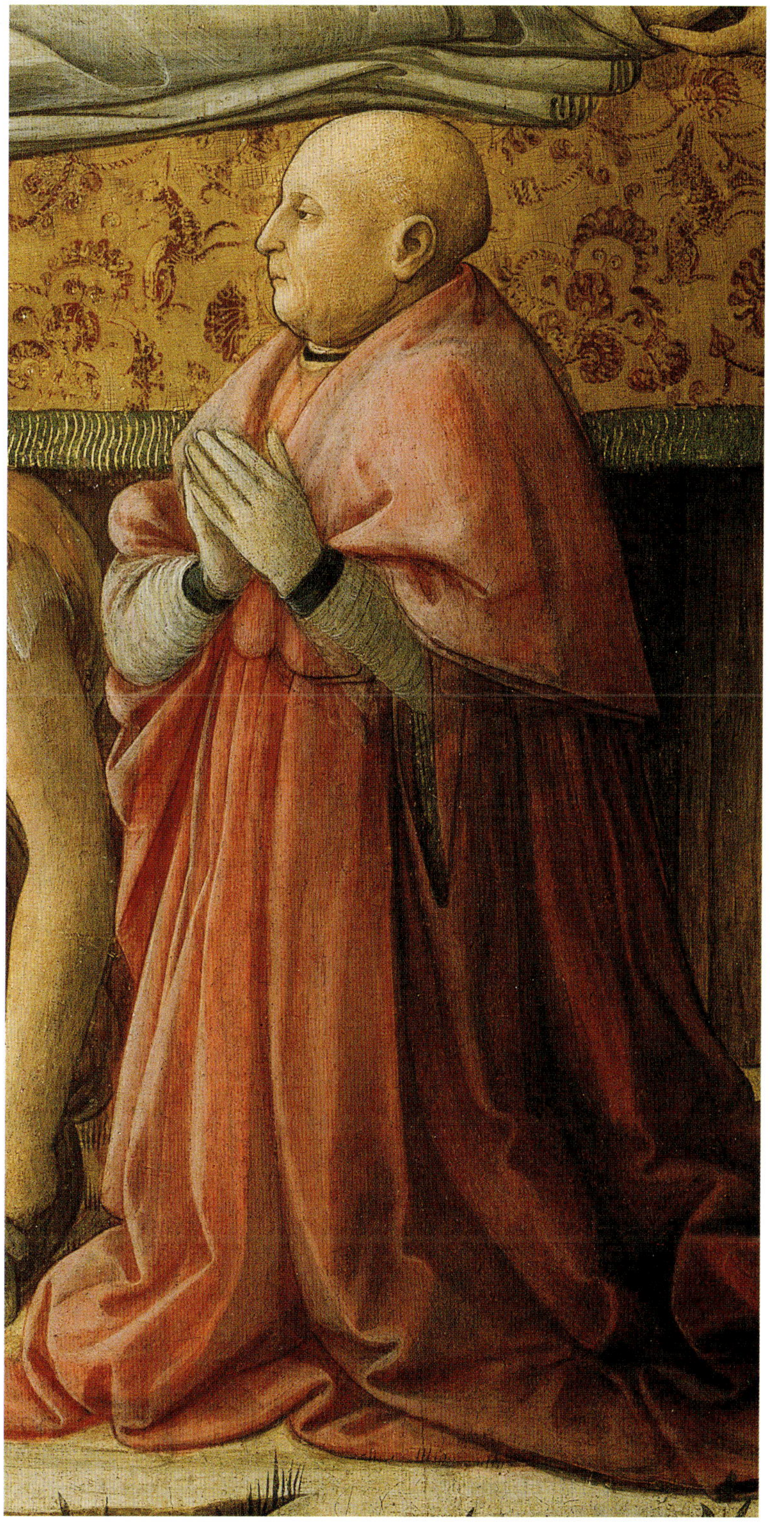

120 Filippo Lippi, *Death of St. Jerome*, detail of fig. 180, with the donor portrait of Gemignano Inghirami.

Lippi also departs in a more radical manner than did Masaccio from the strict profile presentation of the donor. In the Palazzo Barberini *Annunciation* (fig. 121), one of the two donors is shown in three-quarter view. Even when the faces of the donors are shown in profile, their bodies are often turned toward the viewer in three-quarter view, investing their figures with greater volume and a sense of movement, and rendering them more "present" within the sacred scene depicted.

While Fra Filippo Lippi's two earliest works with donor portraits – the Cini *Madonna and Child with Saints* and the Fitzwilliam triptych (see figs. 47 and 46) – appear to have been small, personal devotional images, seven out of the ten paintings with donors are large altarpieces that were displayed in ecclesiastical settings.[80] Lippi offered his patrons the possibility of a new degree of public engagement in working out the patrons' identity.[81] He encouraged a sort of game of recognition on the part of the spectator, which in turn guaranteed the direct acknowledgment of the donor's religious patronage by the church-going public – the parishioners, neighbors, kin, friends, clergy, and other patrons of the institution. The donor effigy also affirmed the personal link between the religious institution and this personage of high status, rank, power, and wealth. The donor figures in Lippi's altarpieces demonstrated a manifest, privileged, personal purchase on the sacred, through the mediation of a friar painter, in a specific act of religious patronage.

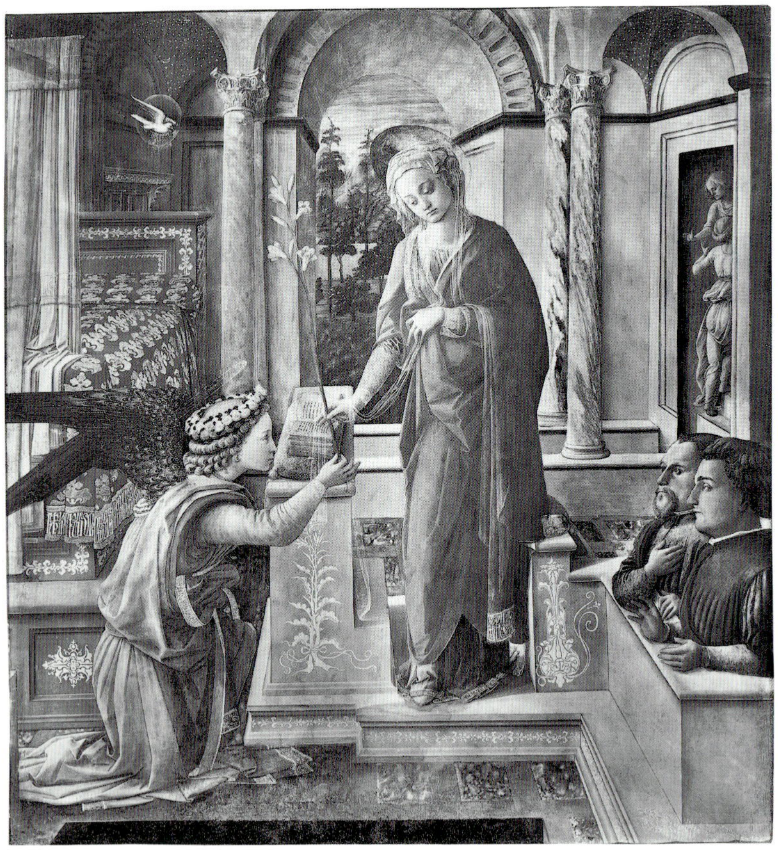

121 Filippo Lippi, *Annunciation*, early 1440s, Rome, Galleria Nazionale d'Arte Antica (Palazzo Barberini).

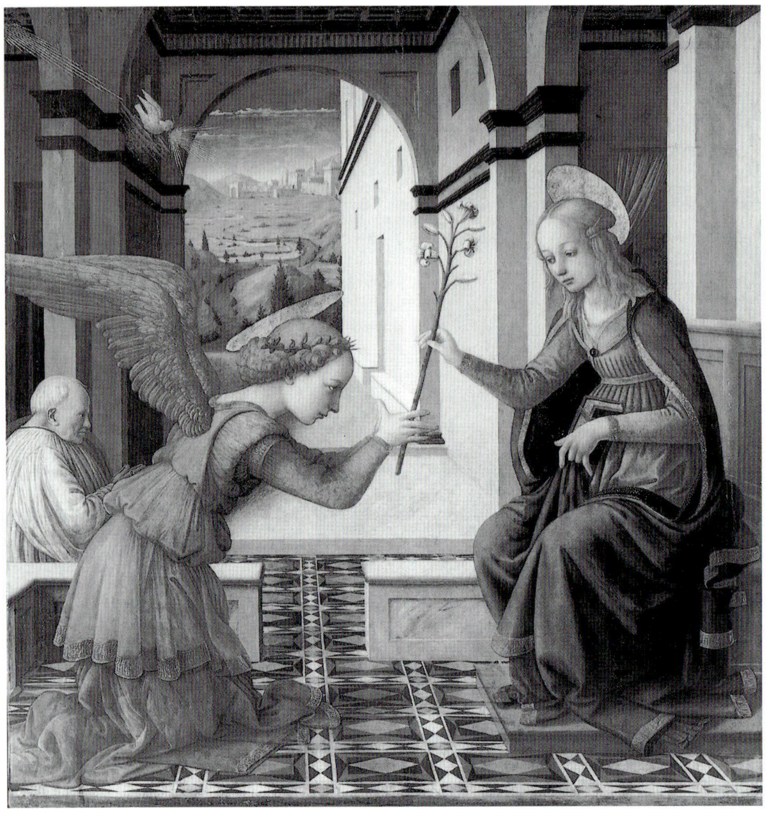

122 Filippo Lippi, *Annunciation*, 1466, Corsham Court (Wiltshire), Methuen Collection.

Contemporary Florentines also appear in Fra Filippo's narrative fresco painting. Here he was following the example of Masaccio in the Brancacci chapel (see fig. 66),[82] of Benozzo Gozzoli in the more recent *Procession of the Magi* (1459; fig. 123) in the chapel of the Medici Palace, and very probably of Domenico Veneziano at Sant'Egidio.[83] Like Masaccio, he concentrated the portraits within the lowest tier of his fresco cycle in the *cappella maggiore* of the Pieve Santo Stefano in Prato, where they would be most visible by his patrons and the public. The portraits appear on the left wall in the *Funeral of St. Stephen* (fig. 124). This narrative – which Eve Borsook has convincingly

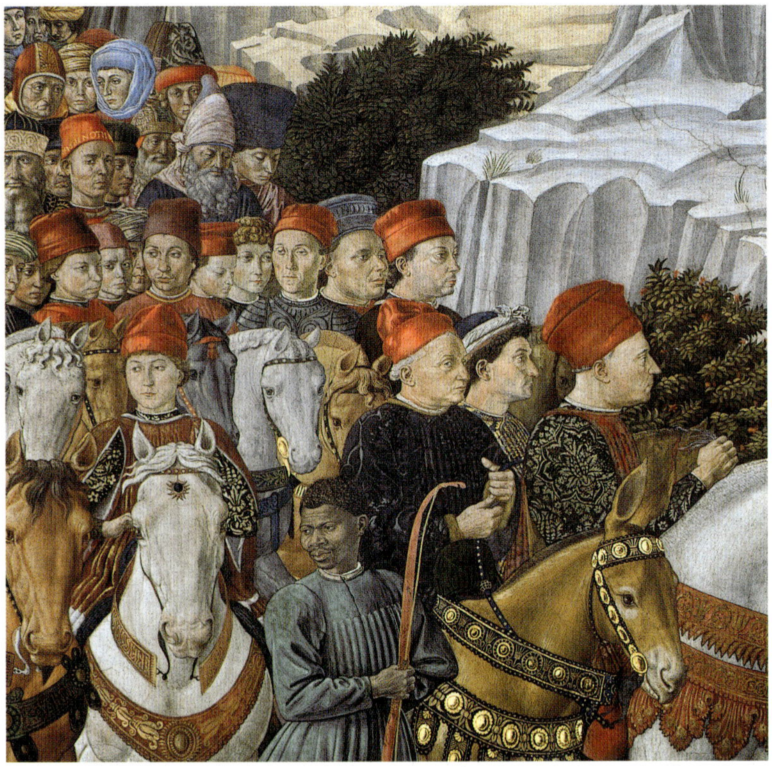

123 Benozzo Gozzoli, *Procession of the Magi*, detail of fig. 176, 1459, Florence, Palazzo Medici-Riccardi, chapel.

demonstrated represents the "Celebration of the Relics of St. Stephen" – lends itself more readily to portraiture than the dynamic *istoria* representing the *Banquet of Herod* (fig. 98) on the bottom register of the opposite wall of the chapel.[84] Borsook also suggests that the fresco had a commemorative function that helps to explain the presence of the contemporary portraits, including that of Cardinal Carlo de' Medici, son of Cosimo Il Vecchio. She connects the date, 1460, inscribed in the fresco, not with the completion of the work, but with the ceremony when the new Provost of Santo Stefano, Carlo de' Medici, was received in the church on the feast day of the relics of St. Stephen, August 3 of that year.

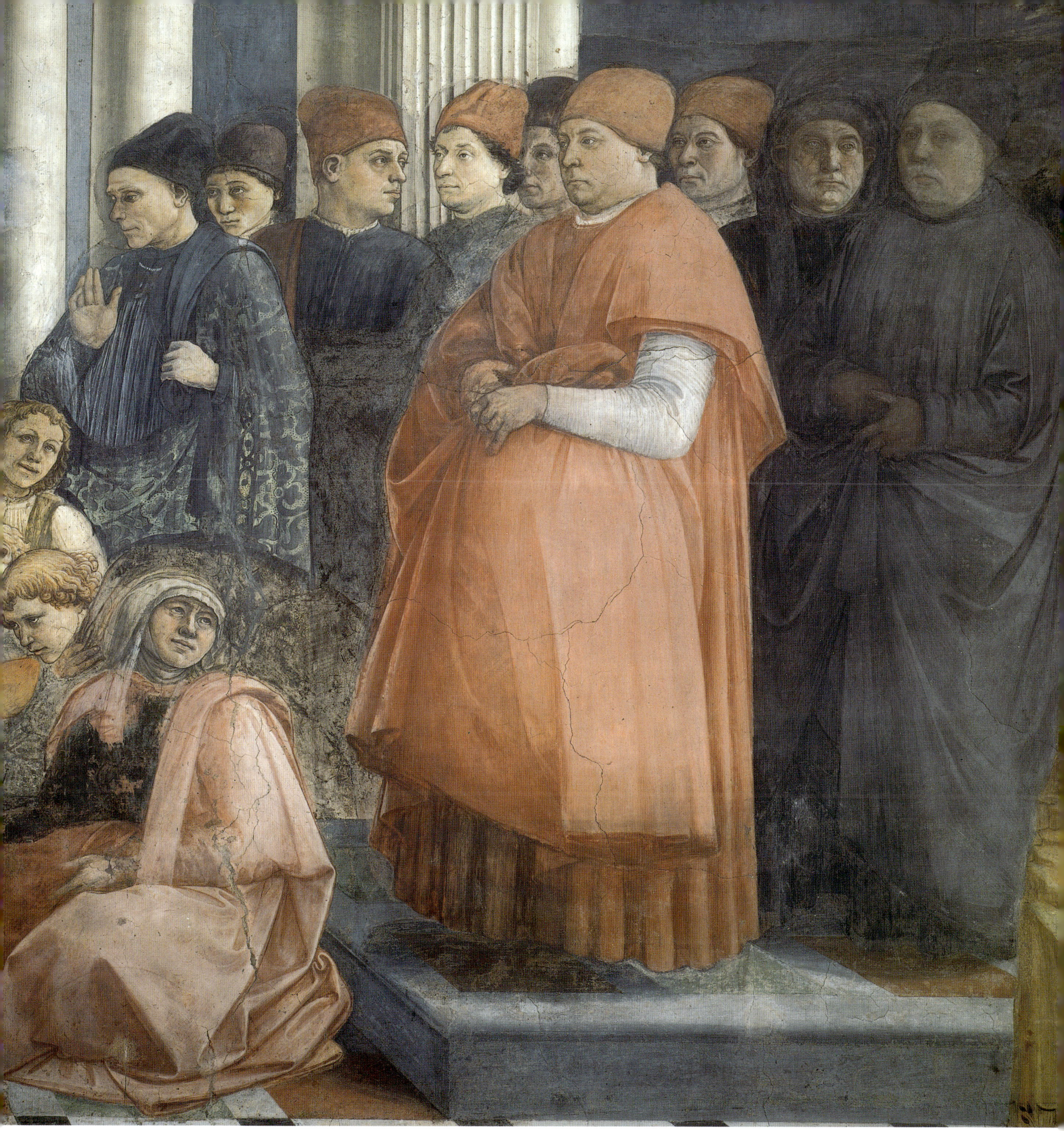

124 Filippo Lippi, *Funeral of St. Stephen*, detail of fig. 145.

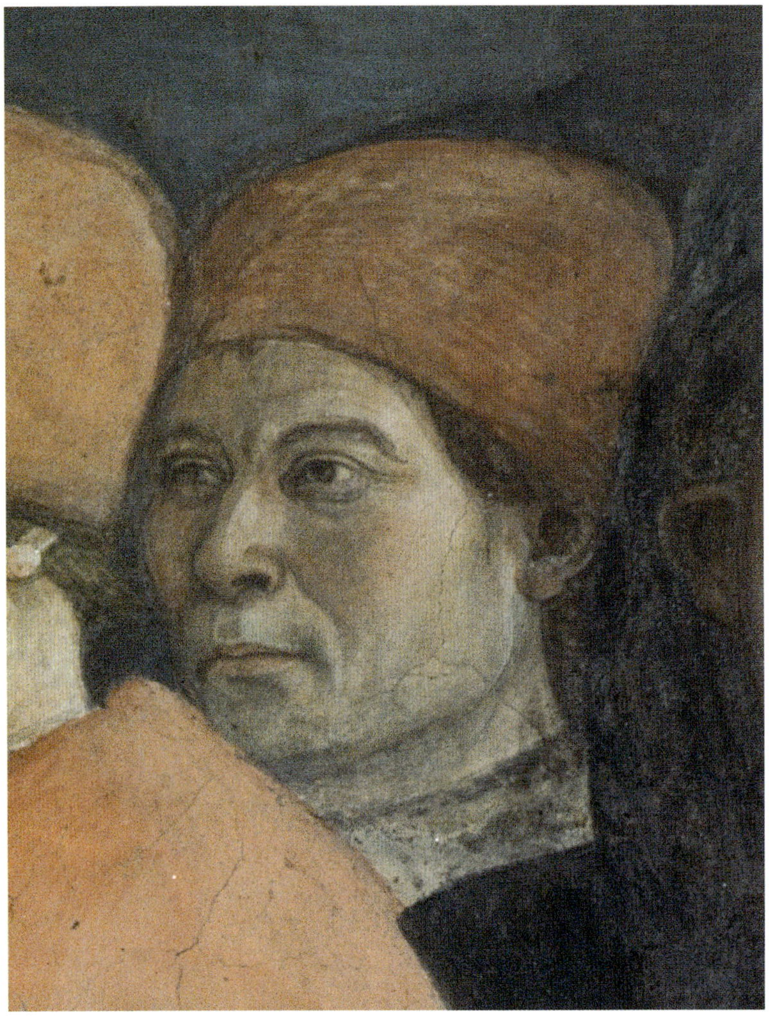

125 Filippo Lippi, *Funeral of St. Stephen*, detail of fig. 145, with Carlo de' Medici.

Portraits are distinguishable among the relatively static, composed group of mourners who gather around the body of St. Stephen, by the differentiation of facial features, age, and stature, and the use of contemporary dress to clothe the figures. It was Vasari who first recorded that Cardinal Carlo de' Medici is represented in this scene.[85] The Cardinal has been identified as the figure at the right (fig. 125) standing behind the portly cleric in red and just to the left of the two figures in black. This portrait head bears marked similarities to the portrait panel of Carlo de' Medici painted by Andrea Mantegna (fig. 126).[86] Eve Borsook has identified the portly cleric in the red robe at the right as Pope Pius II.[87] Vasari also stated that Lippi painted his own portrait and that of his principal assistant, Fra Diamante, in this scene (see fig. 142). Scholars have attempted to give other figures in the crowd specific identifications.[88] However, while a number of lay and clerical officials can be demonstrated to have been directly involved with the fresco commission, there is not enough visual evidence available to confirm these identifications.

This practice of incorporating contemporary portraits into narrative painting became a standard feature in Florentine monumental wall painting during the last quarter of the fifteenth century. It is found in the frescos of Benozzo Gozzoli, Botticelli, Ghirlandaio, Cosimo Rosselli (see fig. 232), and Filippino Lippi. The mixing of sacred and profane, of biblical and prosaic, within religious narratives in an ecclesiastical setting generated criticism from Savonarola later in the century. The Dominican reformer insisted that it violated the decorum of religious representation, showing dishonor to the sacred subjects.[89] The practice, however, persisted and must have been a valued characteristic of Florentine painting by the end of the century.[90]

There is one other category of portraiture that Fra Filippo appears to have practiced – self-portraiture. I shall deal with this subject at the end of the chapter when discussing the painter's negotiation of artistic identity.

* * *

126 Andrea Mantegna, *Carlo de' Medici*, c. 1460–66, Florence, Uffizi.

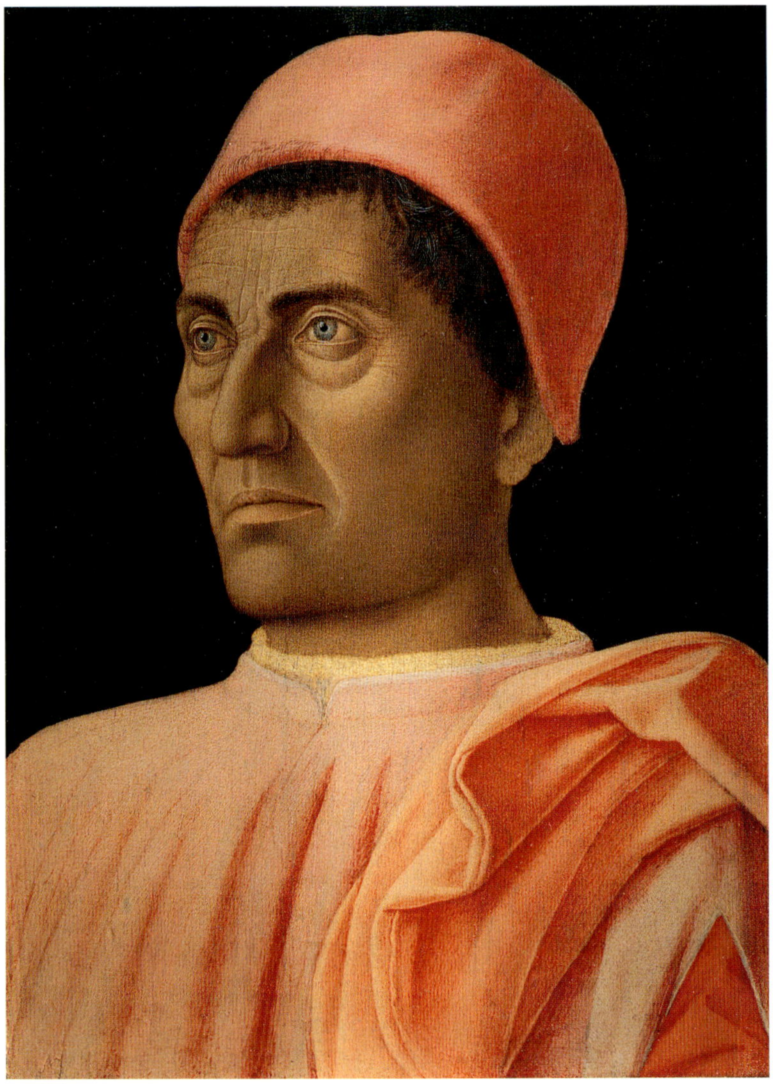

Demand for decorated furnishings and display objects for the palazzo interior rose significantly in the *quattrocento*.[91] This was, in part, a consequence of the redefinition of domestic space. The palazzo interior was increasingly used for a variety of social, economic, and cultural activities – social gatherings, business transactions, religious devotion, and marriage rituals. At the same time, patrician women circulated less frequently in the city at large, and the palazzo became their principal reserve. The palazzo interior thus became an important site for the demonstration through artistic display of status, wealth, lineage, and acculturation, as well as civic and domestic virtues. Rooms were decorated less often now with frescos and more frequently with a variety of cloth and painted wall-hangings (*spalliere*), tarsiated paneling, and carved and painted furniture, painted portraits and sculpted portrait busts, Marian devotional images, bronze figurines, and more elaborate birth trays (*deschi da parto*). Evidence for the physical disposition of these objects within the palazzo interior comes from inventories and from visual representations of interior scenes, usually dating from the late fifteenth century.

Some painters specialized in specific categories of images, like Apollonio di Giovanni and his production of painted marriage chests (*cassoni*). More often, however, as in the case of Fra Filippo Lippi, painters added small devotional images and portraits to their workshop repertoire.

I have discussed Lippi's contribution to one category of painting for the domestic interior, the portrait panel. A second category – the half-length Madonna and Child devotional image – will be treated below as a new variation of a traditional kind of religious image. There was a third type of domestic painting, the tondo, that first made its appearance in the work of Fra Filippo and Domenico Veneziano.

Tondi were independent devotional panels of a circular shape that became very popular in Florentine palazzi interiors during the late *quattrocento*.[92] Visual evidence found in the woodcut illustrations to Savonarola's *Predica dell'arte del bene morire* (1496; fig. 127) and archival inventories suggest that tondi were hung in the townhouse bedroom (*camera*) or antechamber (*antecamera*) and were used for domestic devotional purposes.[93] The circular form developed out of the use of figurated tondi in architectural embellishment and sculptural decoration – particularly Madonna and Child images on tombs, goldsmiths' designs, and in altarpiece frames.[94] The tondo was also a standard feature of both Brunelleschian and Michelozzian architecture and this may have encouraged a more versatile and creative attitude toward it as a design element in the *quattrocento*. Designs for the eight historiated circular stained-glass windows for the drum of the cupola of the Florentine Duomo were executed by Donatello, Lorenzo Ghiberti, Paolo Uccello (see fig. 170), and Andrea del Castagno between 1434 and 1445, which must have stimulated interest in the tondo form among contemporary artists. It is also

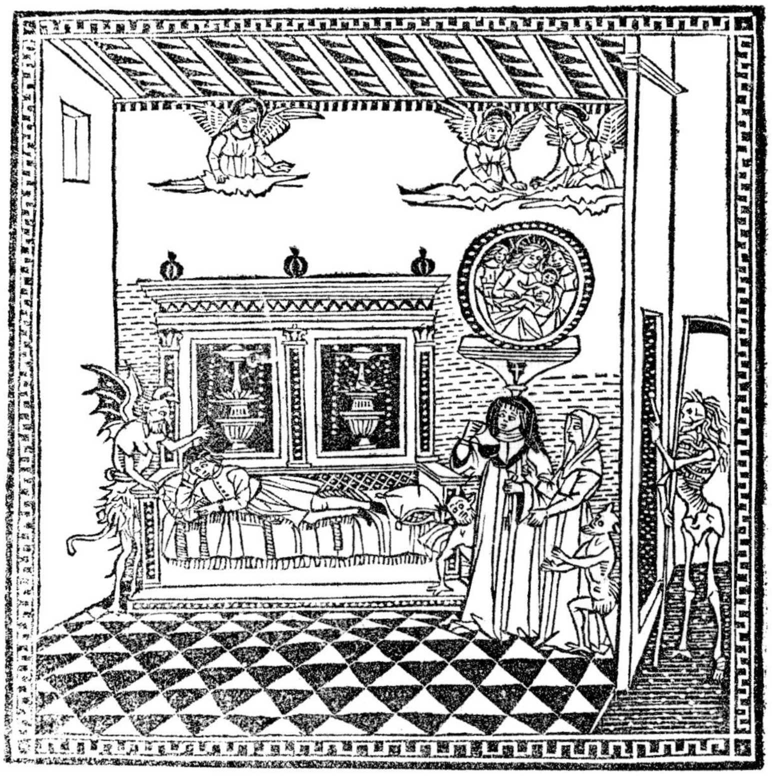

127 Woodcut from Savonarola's *Predica dell'arte del bene morire*, (1496, Florence).

very possible that this new image type associated with the domestic interior was influenced by another category of circular paintings made for domestic use and display during the *quattrocento*, the birth tray.[95]

The attraction that the tondo offered the *quattrocento* painter lay in the challenge that it posed to pictorial composition. It encouraged a centralized composition in which foreground and background relationships had to be worked out with precision. The tondo also encouraged a degree of playful illusionism in the seemingly arbitrary truncation of the painted scene by the circular frame.

There are two surviving tondi painted by Lippi – the *Adoration of the Magi* (fig. 128) in the National Gallery in Washington and the Bartolini tondo *Madonna and Child* (fig. 130) in the Pitti Palace in Florence, dating from 1452–53. These works, along with the *Adoration of the Magi* attributed to Domenico Veneziano in Berlin (fig. 129), dated to c. 1440, constitute the earliest surviving examples of the independent painted tondo. The Washington tondo is not documented and poses extremely difficult problems of authorship and dating, which have been extensively treated by Jeffrey Ruda and need not be rehearsed here.[96] His conclusion that the painting was executed over a period of twenty years (c. 1435–1455), with the assistance of an artist working in a manner very close to that of Fra Angelico (perhaps Benozzo Gozzoli), however, makes it difficult to discuss the painting in terms of Lippi's artistic intentions and formal

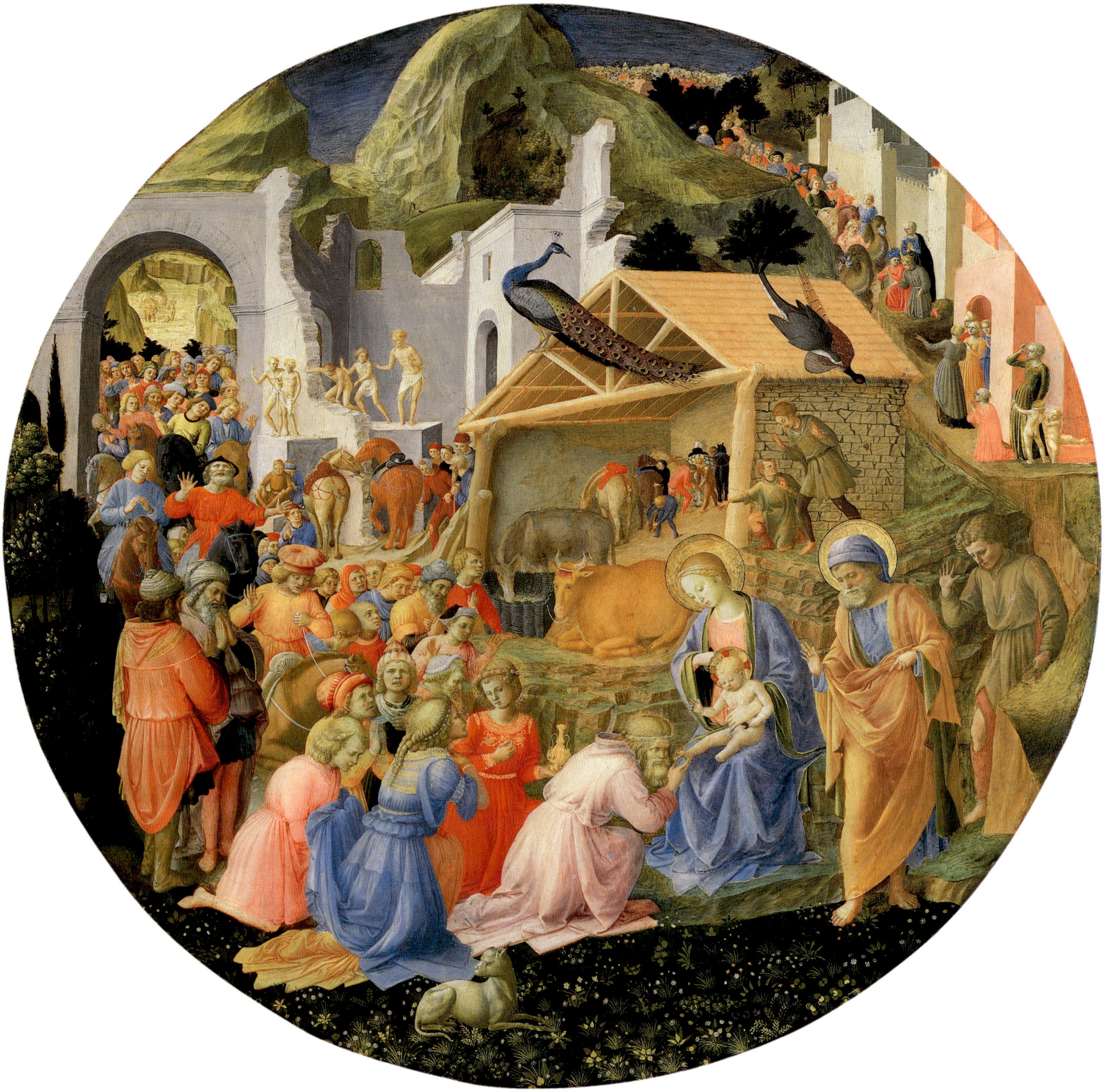

128 Filippo Lippi, *Adoration of the Magi* (the Washington tondo), c. 1435–55?, Washington, National Gallery of Art, Samuel H. Kress Collection.

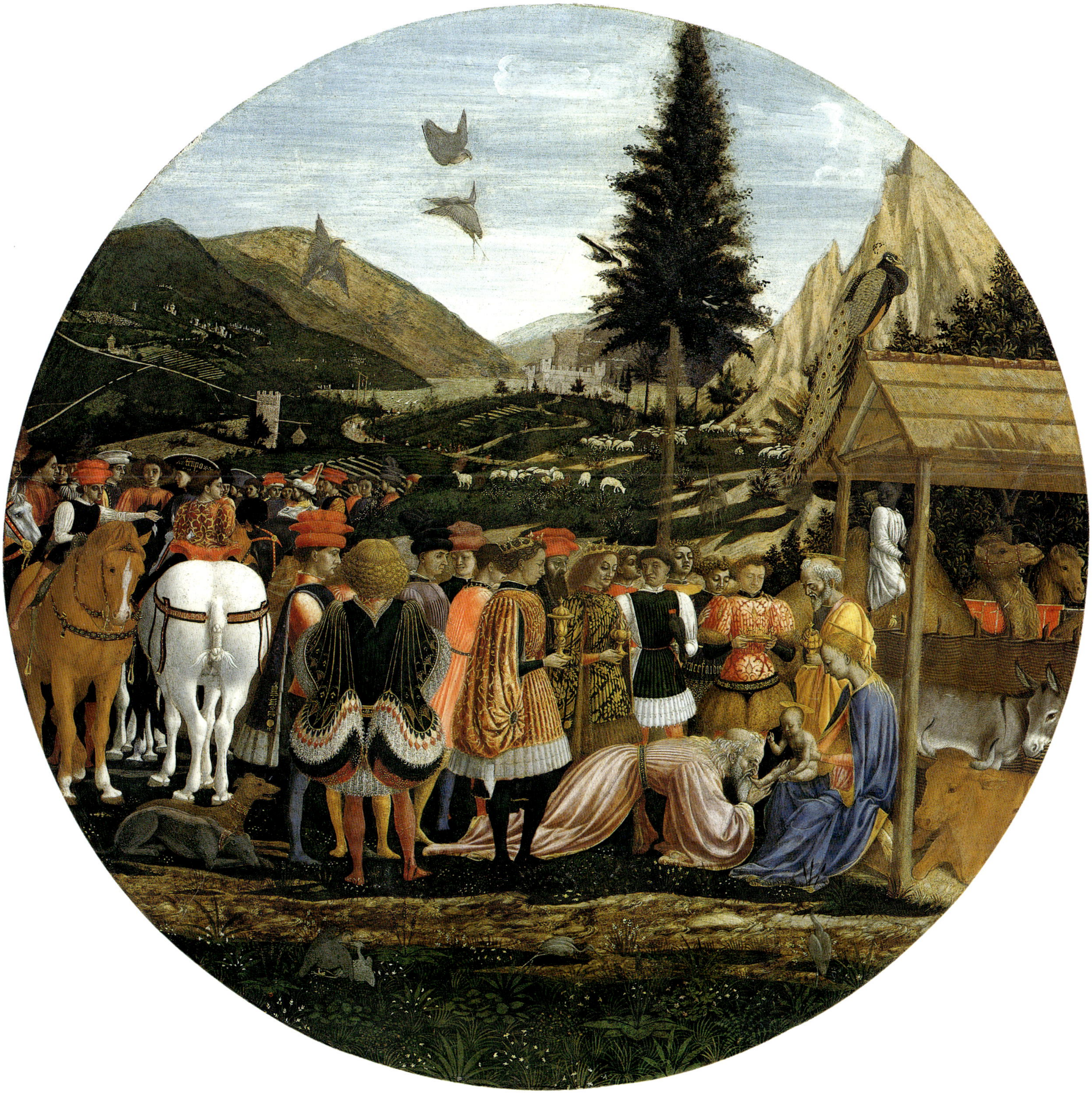

129 Domenico Veneziano, *Adoration of the Magi*, c. 1440, Berlin, Staatliche Museen Preussischer Kulturbesitz, Gemäldegalerie.

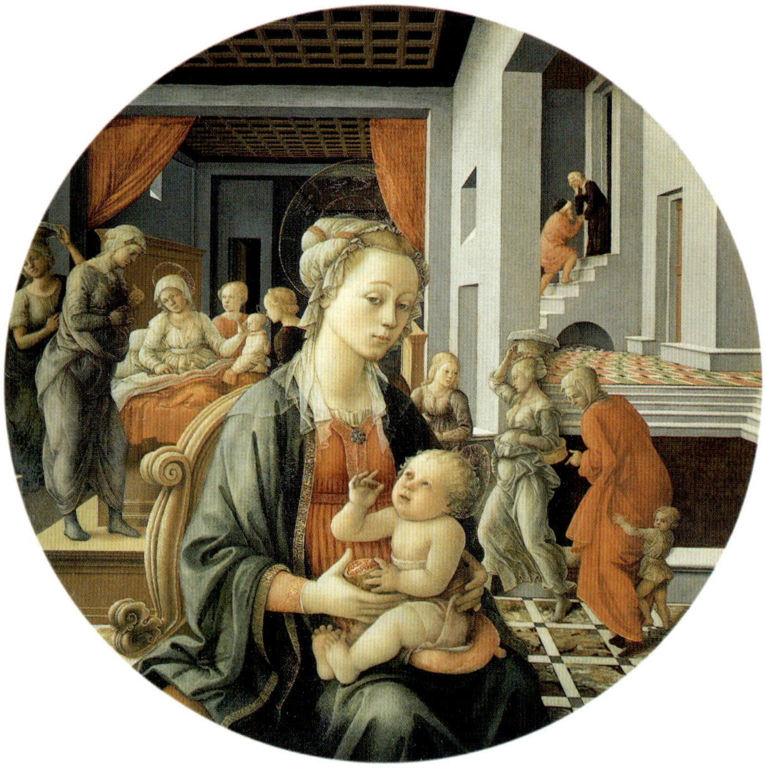

130 Filippo Lippi, *Madonna and Child with the Birth of the Virgin* (the Bartolini tondo), 1452–53, Florence, Galleria Palatina (Palazzo Pitti).

invention. The Bartolini tondo was painted for the Florentine banker and statesman Lionardo Bartolini. It is referred to in a contemporary document as "a certain tondo of wood" with "a certain narrative of the Virgin Mary."[97] I shall discuss this painting in detail in the following chapter, identifying possible Carmelite influence on Lippi's highly innovative composition and iconography. Here I shall merely provide a very brief discussion of how the tondo form was utilized by Fra Filippo in these two paintings, and how the intended location within the domestic interior may have influenced the choice and presentation of the subject matter.

Both tondi are very large paintings of similar dimensions: the Washington tondo measures 137 centimeters in diameter and the Bartolini tondo 135 centimeters.[98] This suggests that Lippi conceived of their form in a uniform manner, endowing them with a monumentality and material substance appropriate to their probable intended display on the walls of the bedroom or antechamber of Florentine townhouses. The paintings no longer have their original frames.

The tondi represent religious subjects associated with birth. That in Washington depicts the Adoration of the Magi and the Bartolini, a Madonna and Child with the Birth of the Virgin represented in the background. In the Bartolini tondo, the themes of birth and fecundity and the possible intention of having a family coat of arms painted on the reverse of the panel,[99] suggest that the painting was intended to commemorate the birth of one of the Bartolini children.[100]

The circular format of the Washington tondo is not utilized very effectively. The all-important center of the circular panel does not hold. The artist clearly had difficulty in juggling narrative and spatial elements within the composition. The principal action takes place in the shallow foreground space in the lower third of the painting. Kneeling upon a crescent moon of floral carpeting, the Magi bow down before the Christ Child. The Virgin and Child are raised on a short grassy ledge. A little dog – probably an addition by the later, Fra Angelicesque hand – awkwardly fills what may have been an unaccustomed and uncomfortably open area in the circular composition. The Magi's attendants crowd the left section of the composition in near illegible confusion. The procession appears again at the upper right, during an earlier moment in the narrative, outside the walls of Bethlehem, in a more satisfying arrangement which follows the curve of the tondo. The central zone of the picture is given over to the manger, at some distance behind the Virgin and Child and the Magi. While the blank gray stable wall at the absolute center of the tondo does provide some clarity amid the confusion of figures, incidents, and problems in scale and recession, this is not enough to satisfy the compositional demands of this vital area of the painting.

The tondo represented in the woodcut in Savonarola's *Predica dell'arte del bene morire* is placed relatively high on the wall of the palazzo bedroom. The Washington tondo, however, seems to demand a lower viewpoint so that the beholder could examine the detailed composition from close up and at some length.[101] The painting, notable more for its rich concentration of detail, panoply of color, and variety of incident than for its compositional clarity, has the quality of a highly elaborated, precious, material object. This may mark a taste in domestic consumption characterized by the accumulation and display of such expensive goods as illuminated manuscripts, tapestries, ivory boxes, and *cassoni*, which functioned as material signs of patrician magnificence.[102]

If Ruda's proposed chronology for the painting of the Washington tondo (c. 1435–55) is accepted, then this work would have been begun before, and completed long after, Domenico Veneziano painted his *Adoration of the Magi* tondo around 1440.[103] Following the art historians' tendency to value historic "first" endeavors, perhaps the laurels awarded for the first tondo deserve to be shared by both Fra Filippo Lippi and Domenico Veneziano. Domenico's painting, however, is much more successful in accommodating the Adoration narrative within the circular frame. The artist lined up the principal figures in frieze fashion across the picture space, with their heads marking the horizontal diameter of the circle.[104] The center of the tondo features the heads of the two standing Magi, with the elder king kissing the foot of the Christ Child at the right. The Magi's entourage turns the corner at the left of the composition (accented by a lovely display of front and rear views of horses) and then cuts back into the middle ground. There is a gradual transition from the foreground narrative to the background landscape. Domenico's tondo is on a smaller scale (84 centimetres in diameter) than Fra Filippo's Washington tondo, but it exhibits a similar quality of visual splendor achieved through an abundance of small scale, highly refined detail, and ornament.

With the Bartolini tondo, Lippi introduced new features that became standard to the tondo during the second half of the *quattrocento*. Fra Filippo had become highly skilled at composing in the circular format, introducing provocative spatial relationships and figural juxtapositions that nonetheless work together symphonically. The Virgin and Child are placed in the foreground of the painting, with the Virgin's head situated just above, yet dominating, the center of the composition. The lower edge of the tondo cuts off the Virgin at the knees, and has the effect both of constituting an arbitrary truncation of the pictorial space and a curve that elegantly follows the lines of the Virgin's lower body in this three-quarter view. In the background scene depicting the Birth of the Virgin, there is a continual play between the rectilinear lines of the bedroom interior rendered in perspective and the graceful curves of the figures, which repeat the arc of the tondo edge.

By virtue of a strong, centralized composition, the monumentality of the Virgin and Child, and the riveting gaze of the Virgin down upon the spectator, the Bartolini tondo would have effectively commanded the attention of the viewer in its domestic setting. This is a painting that could have dominated a room, like the tondo of the *Madonna and Child* illustrated high on the wall in *Predica dell'arte del bene morire* (see fig. 127). The successful accommodation of the round format anticipates the centralized tondi from the last quarter of the fifteenth century painted by Botticelli, Lorenzo di Credi, and Luca Signorelli – artists who must have been considered specialists in the form.

The Half-Length Madonna and Child

Single-panel half-length devotional images of the Madonna and Child were produced in Tuscany in increasingly greater numbers during the *quattrocento*.[105] The popularity of this category of image was tied to the relatively small scale of the panels and their comparably low cost, their versatility and portability, and the intimacy and visual accessibility of the sacred figures represented – appropriate for private devotion. There were also many venerated half-length Marian icons of both local and Byzantine manufacture (see fig. 17) displayed in Tuscan churches, which must have had some bearing upon the appeal of this Madonna and Child configuration. Half-length Madonna and Child images were utilized in a variety of devotional contexts, displayed in churches, oratories, roadside tabernacles, public buildings, work spaces, and domestic interiors.[106] A great area of growth in the market for these images seems to have been the domestic interior where Marian images were replacing the small Crucifixion tabernacles which had been popular during the previous century. Like the tondi, half-length Madonna and Child paintings were displayed on the walls of the *antecamera* and *camera*.[107]

Interesting new configurations of the painted half-length Madonna and Child emerged only after sculptors like Donatello and Ghiberti had popularized marble, terracotta, and cast gesso variations in the round and in relief, during the second quarter of the century. Donatello's sophisticated experiments in *rilievo schiacciato*, in particular, were key to the development of painted versions. It was the illusionism of *rilievo schiacciato* (low relief) in a work like the Pazzi *Madonna* (c. 1422; fig. 131), which presupposed a pictorial space receding and extending beyond the framing elements, that precipitated the development of the painted variation. Compared to their *trecento* predecessors, *quattrocento* Tuscan paintings of the half-length Madonna and Child were larger, framed in *all'antica* tabernacles, with architectural settings, richly brocaded cloth, or landscapes replacing the traditional gold-leaf ground. The shorthand terminology used in Neri di Bicci's *Ricordanze* for these small-scale images in their elaborate frames was *tabernacolo* or *cholmo*. Commissions for both half-length Madonna and Child cast-gesso reliefs and paintings abound in the *Ricordanze* (described as "una meza Vergine Maria di gesso di pocho rilievo" and "una meza Nostra Donna di piano dipinta") and are frequently ordered in bulk by individuals who

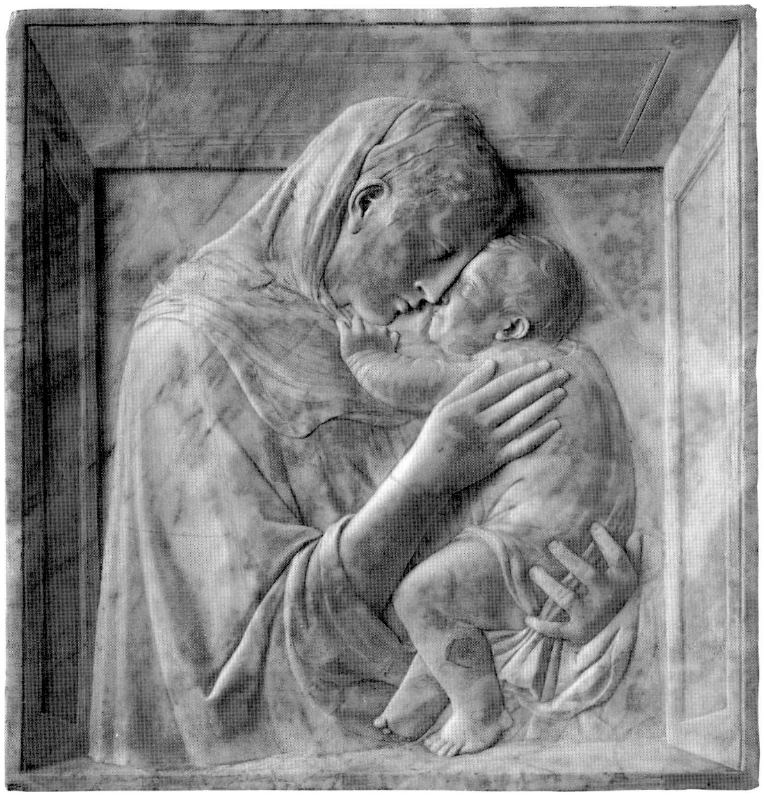

131 Donatello, Pazzi *Madonna and Child*, c. 1422, Berlin, Staatliche Museen Preussischer Kulturbesitz, Skulpturensammlung.

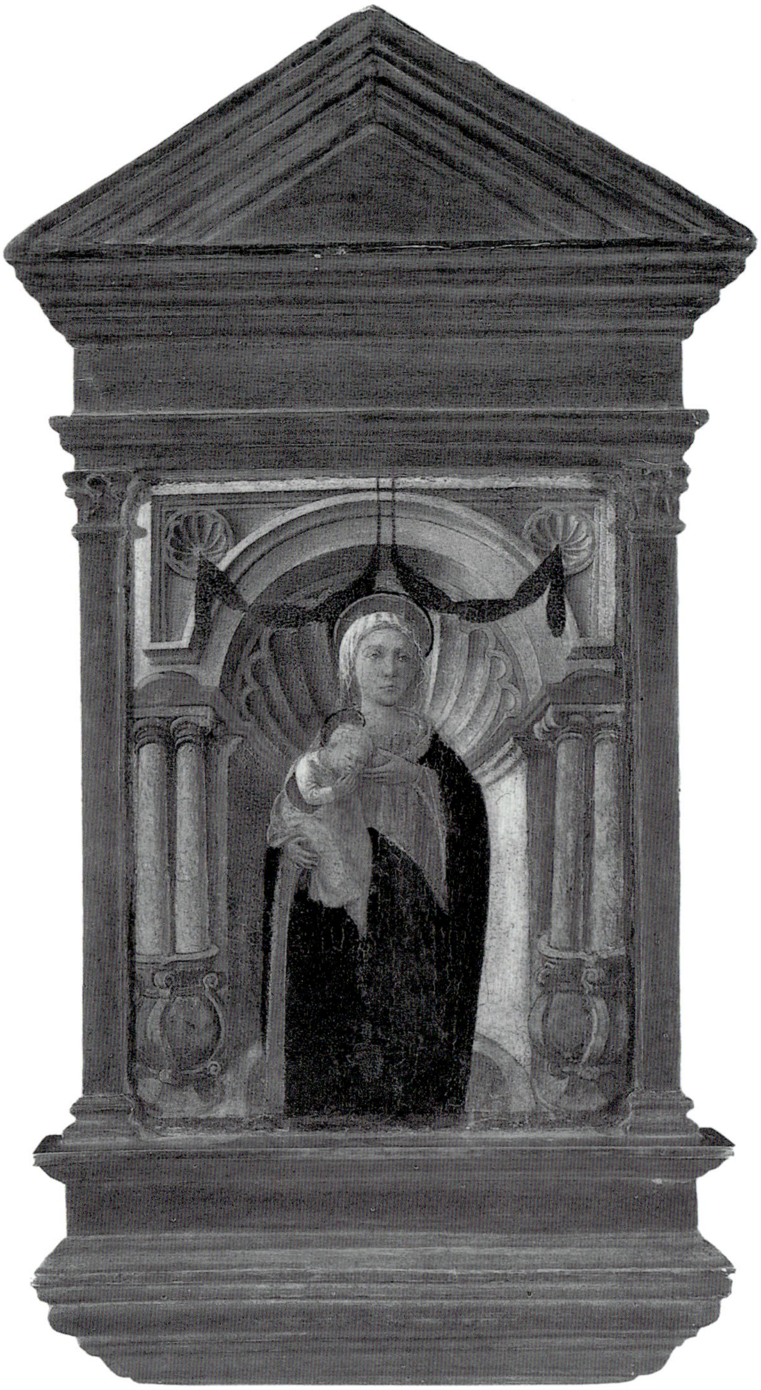

132 Filippo Lippi, *Madonna and Child*, early 1430s, Pavia, Turini Collection.

must have been dealers.[108] Lippi was the painter who perhaps most influenced the evolution of this image type, which had become so popular by the second half of the century.

None of Lippi's nine surviving Madonna and Child panels is documented or dated, and I shall therefore restrict myself to commenting on the evolution of the pictorial composition.[109] The paintings range in size from the very small early work in the Turini collection (29 × 22.5 cm), to the monumental panel in the Palazzo Medici in Florence (115 × 71 cm) among the late works of the painter, with the average dimensions around 75 × 55 cm (roughly 1¼ × 1 braccia).

The Turini *Madonna and Child* (fig. 132) is among the earliest works attributed to the young friar.[110] This small three-quarter-length Madonna and Child, set within an architectural niche and *all'antica* frame, is dated to the early 1430s. Giuseppe Marchini has convincingly argued that the figure-in-the-niche configuration recalls Donatello's *St. Louis* of 1423, while the painted architectural features were inspired by Masaccio's *Trinity* of c. 1427 (see fig. 117).[111] However, Fra Filippo's integration of the figures within the architectural setting is not successful and it was not until he had a more sophisticated understanding of Donatello's *rilievo schiacciato* that he was able to provide a more satisfactory composition.

133 Filippo Lippi, *Madonna and Child*, early 1440s, Washington, National Gallery of Art, Samuel H. Kress Collection.

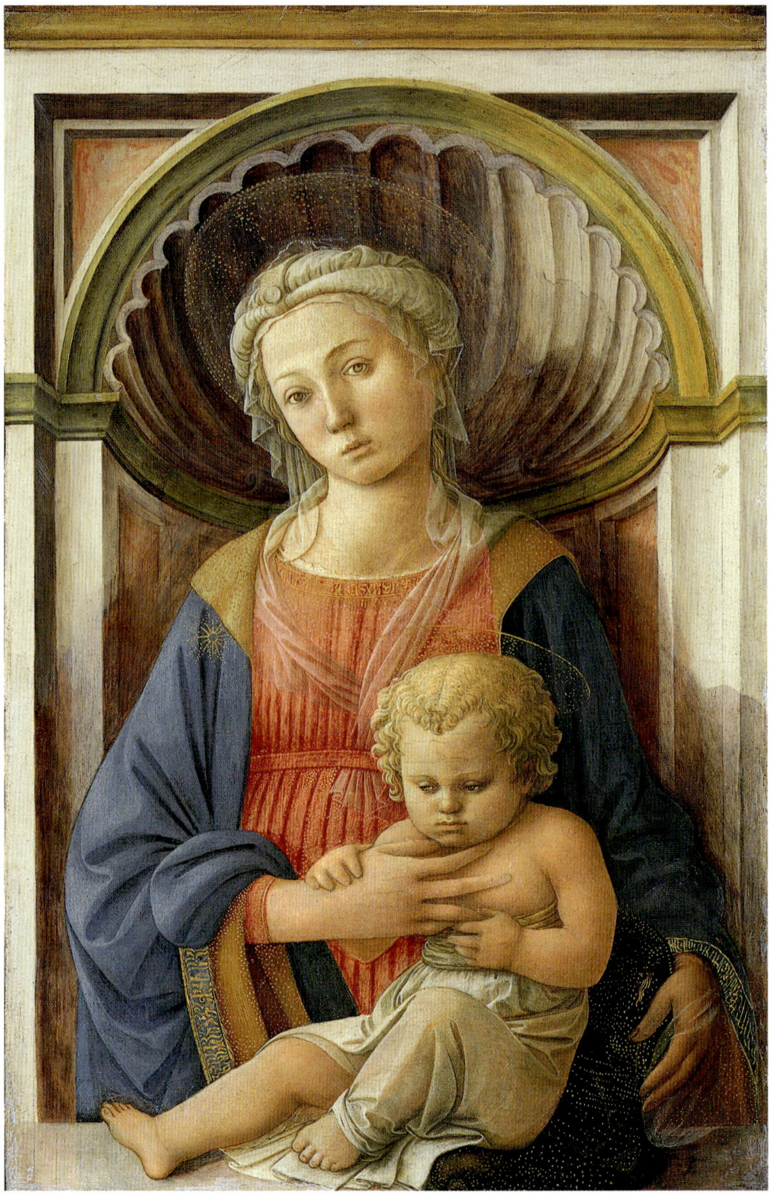

The *Madonna and Child* in the National Gallery of Art in Washington (fig. 133) dates to the early 1440s.[112] Its numerous *pentimenti* bear witness to the painter's struggle with the composition. There are traces of two incised halos visible in the upper third of the panel (fig. 134), which indicate that the Virgin and Child were originally positioned higher up, perhaps with the Christ Child standing. The ledge along the lower edge of the picture appears to have been added at a later stage in the design, as the Virgin's ultramarine robe and the incisions marking the lower left lateral dimensions of the niche are visible through the now transparent paint film of this structure.

The painter's final solution evinces the characteristic features that were to make his half-length images so appealing. Foremost among these is the intimate confrontation effected between the viewer and the sacred subjects depicted. The pictorial space is very shallow and the Madonna and Child, painted on a large scale, are pushed up against the picture plane. The presence of the Virgin is made more tangible and imposing by her cast shadow falling in soft hues against the back of the stone niche, giving physical dimensions also to the compressed space. The Virgin meets the eye of the beholder, who must have been positioned close to the panel in the more intimate viewing circumstances of these *tabernacolo* images. The Child sits upon a cushion propped up against the Virgin's hand, on the ledge at the base of the picture, with his foreshortened knee suggestively projecting out into the viewer's space. It is not until the Madonna and Child paintings of Raphael that we encounter such an intimate relationship established between the viewer and the sacred figures through the manipulation of pictorial space and figure disposition.

134 Diagram of the incisions visible in Filippo Lippi's *Madonna and Child* in the National Gallery of Art, Washington.

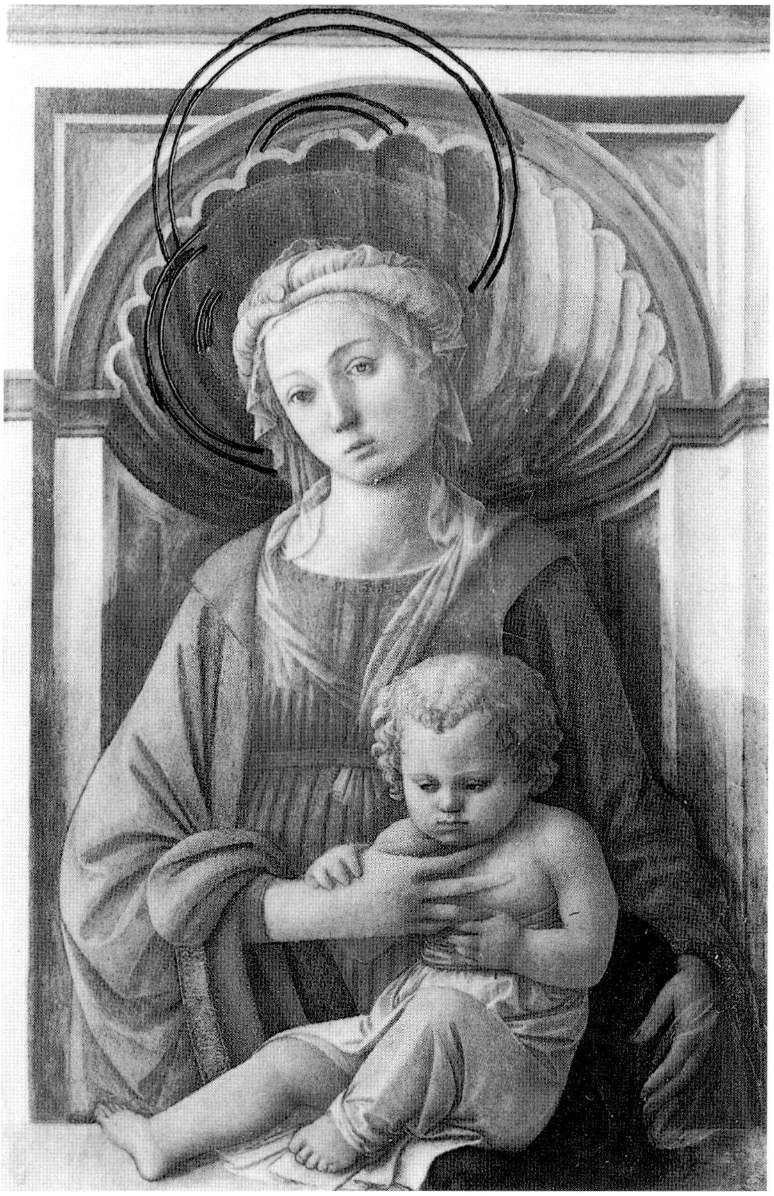

Fra Filippo refined the half-length Madonna and Child composition over the next two decades, working out variations and enriching the setting with brocaded cloth backdrops and more elaborate architecture like that found in the painting now in the Medici Palace in Florence (fig. 135).[113] This large picture dating from the mid-1460s has an interesting tabernacle sketch on the verso (figs. 136 and 137) that may be a design for an *all'antica* frame for the painting.

The most significant modifications to the format, however, came in the 1460s, when Fra Filippo introduced a narrative element and opened up the background to landscape. In the *Madonna and Child with Angels* in the Uffizi (fig. 138), the Virgin is shown in three-quarter view, sitting at a thirty-degree angle to the picture plane, in an extraordinarily shallow, compressed space, in front of a window or doorway opening onto a landscape.[114] Her substantial body casts a shadow against the moldings of the window or door frame. She is shown absorbed in prayer, with her eyes unfocused, and her hands together before the Christ Child who looks upon her face and reaches out to touch her. The devotional gravity of the image, however, is undermined in characteristic Lippi fashion through a playful appeal directly to the spectator by the youthful angel holding aloft the Christ Child. This angel is situated indeterminately, standing between the Virgin's legs, in front of the fictive frame, with his left wing projecting out toward the viewer. The second angel supporting the Child is even more ambiguously placed within the shallow space in front of the opening. He is almost entirely obscured behind the other figures, visible only through glimpses of dismembered body parts – fingers on the knee and wrapping round the back of the Christ Child, and a face cut off at the eyes by the arms of the Child.

The sacred figures are separated from the viewer by the most richly tactile features in the painting – the ornamented armrest of the low-backed wooden chair upon which the Virgin is seated, and the gold-embroidered cushion nestled between the volutes of the armrest. Adorning the cushion are pearls, deftly painted with translucent luster, tantalizingly close to the viewer's

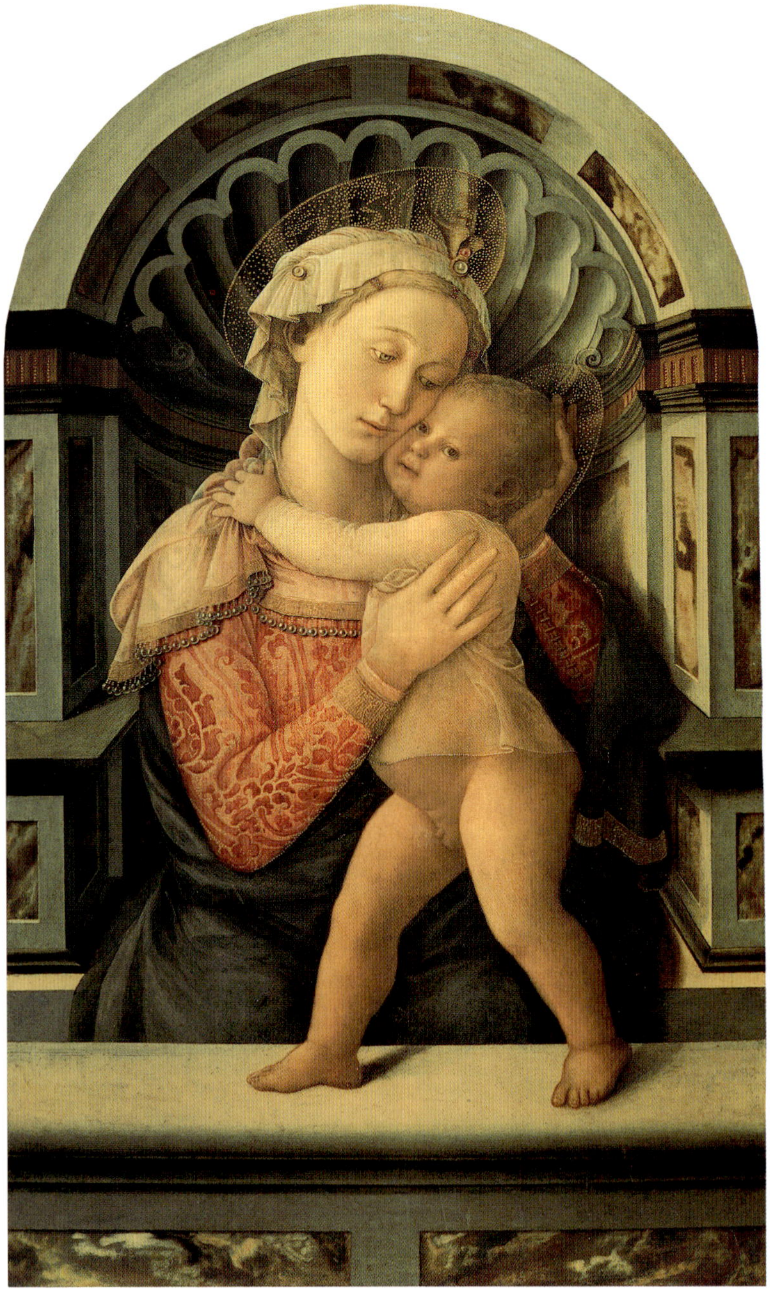

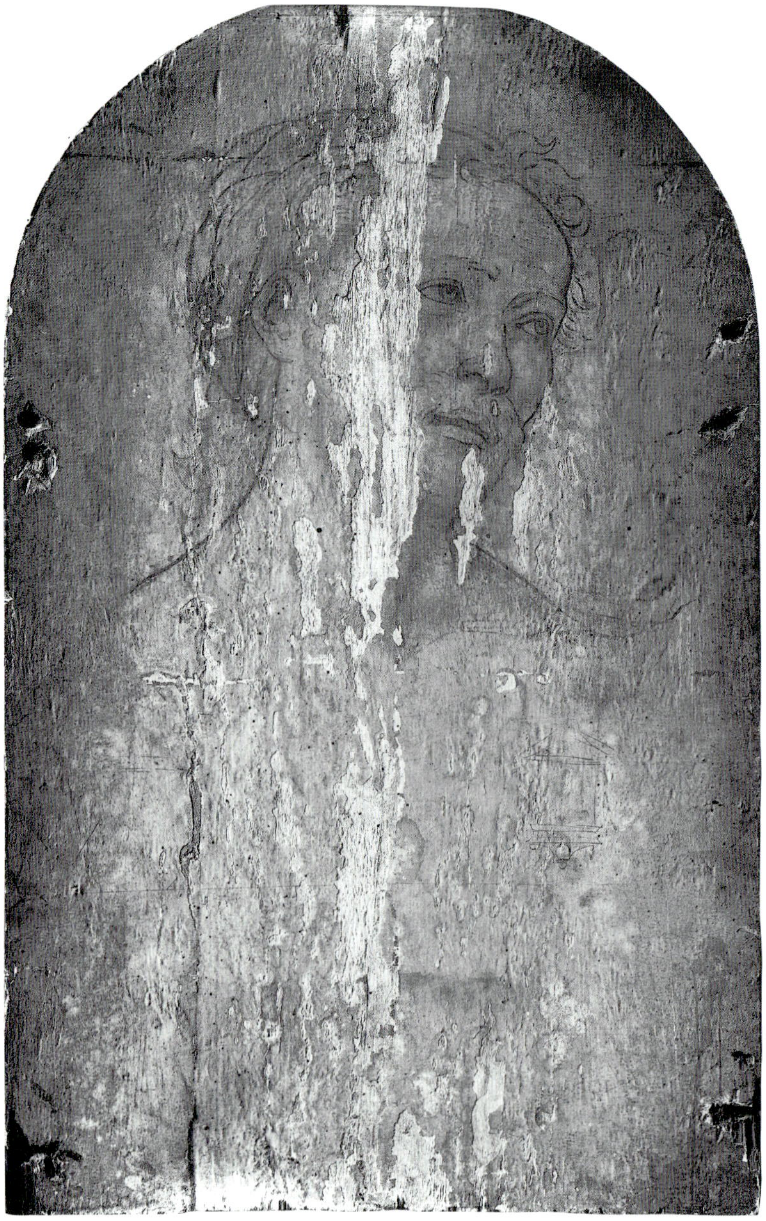

135 (*above left*) Filippo Lippi, *Madonna and Child*, c. 1465, Florence, Palazzo Medici-Riccardi.

136 (*above right*) Filippo Lippi, drawing on the verso of the *Madonna and Child*, c. 1465, Florence, Palazzo Medici-Riccardi.

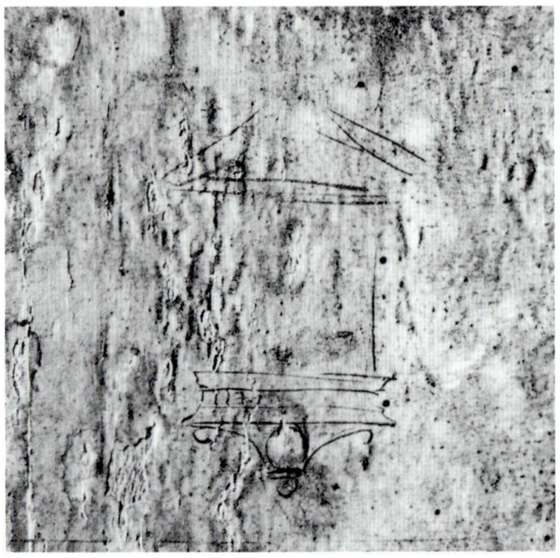

137 (*right*) Filippo Lippi, detail of the tabernacle sketch on the verso of the *Madonna and Child* (fig. 136).

138 (*facing page*) Filippo Lippi, *Madonna and Child with Angels*, c. 1460–65, Florence, Uffizi.

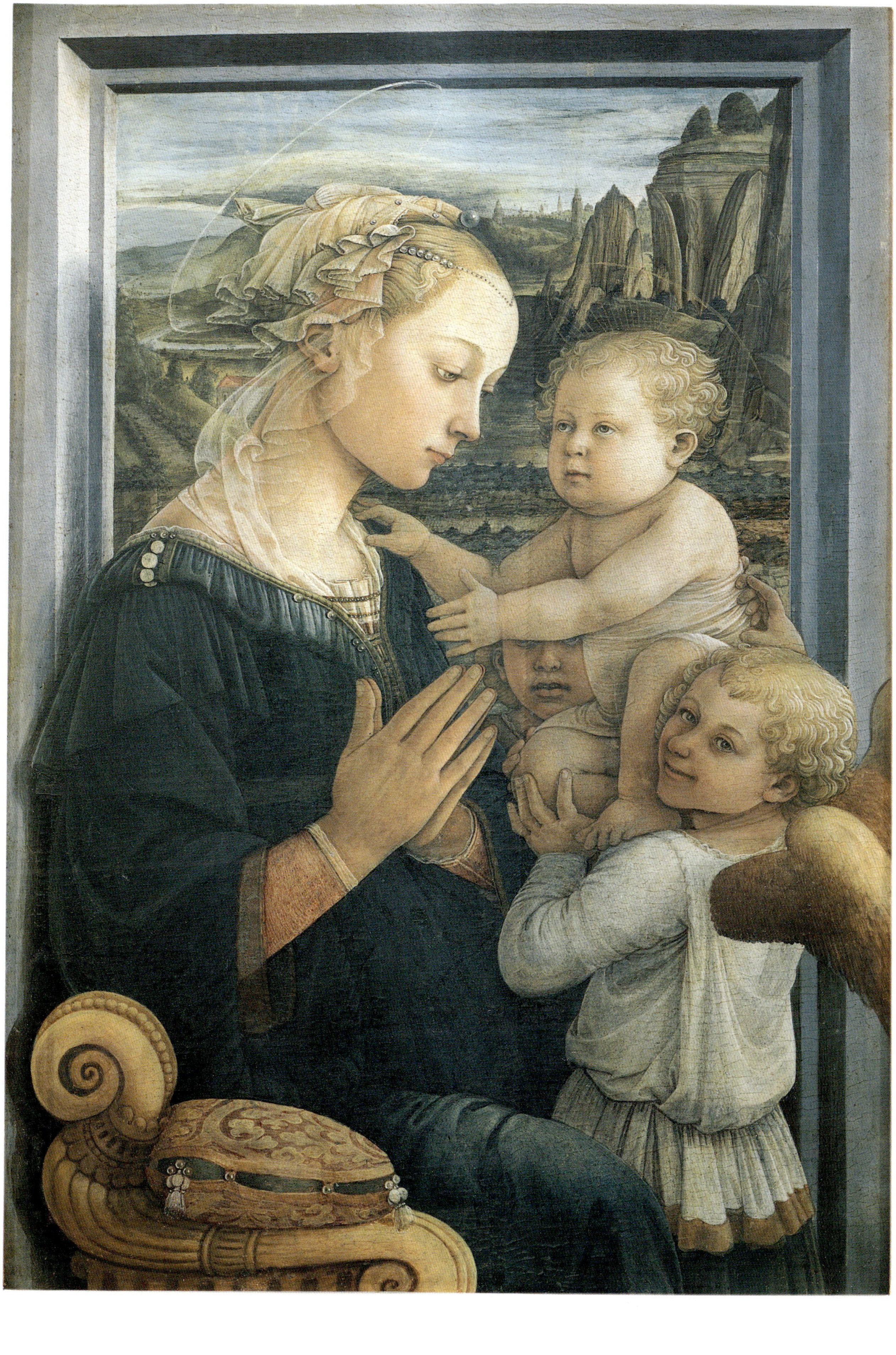

space. These elements assert a provocative and alluring materiality. There is the suggestion here that entry into this sacred domain comes about through an appeal to, if not the seduction of, the senses.

The landscape seen through the *pietra serena* frame contains cultivated fields and a building in the foreground, a craggy mountain in the upper right middle ground, and an expanse of sea and a distant city set against the high horizon line. As proposed in the following chapter, these landscape features that demonstrate a contrast between nature tamed by people and the uninhabited wilderness had particular significance within the Carmelite symbolic order. Mountains, deserts, forests, and the sea all had associations with the Middle Eastern geography where the Carmelites had first settled before moving to the West and becoming established as mendicants in European urban centers. Similar landscape elements are evident in Fra Filippo's Munich *Madonna and Child* (fig. 139) of roughly the same date.

139 Filippo Lippi, *Madonna and Child*, c. 1465, Munich, Alte Pinakothek.

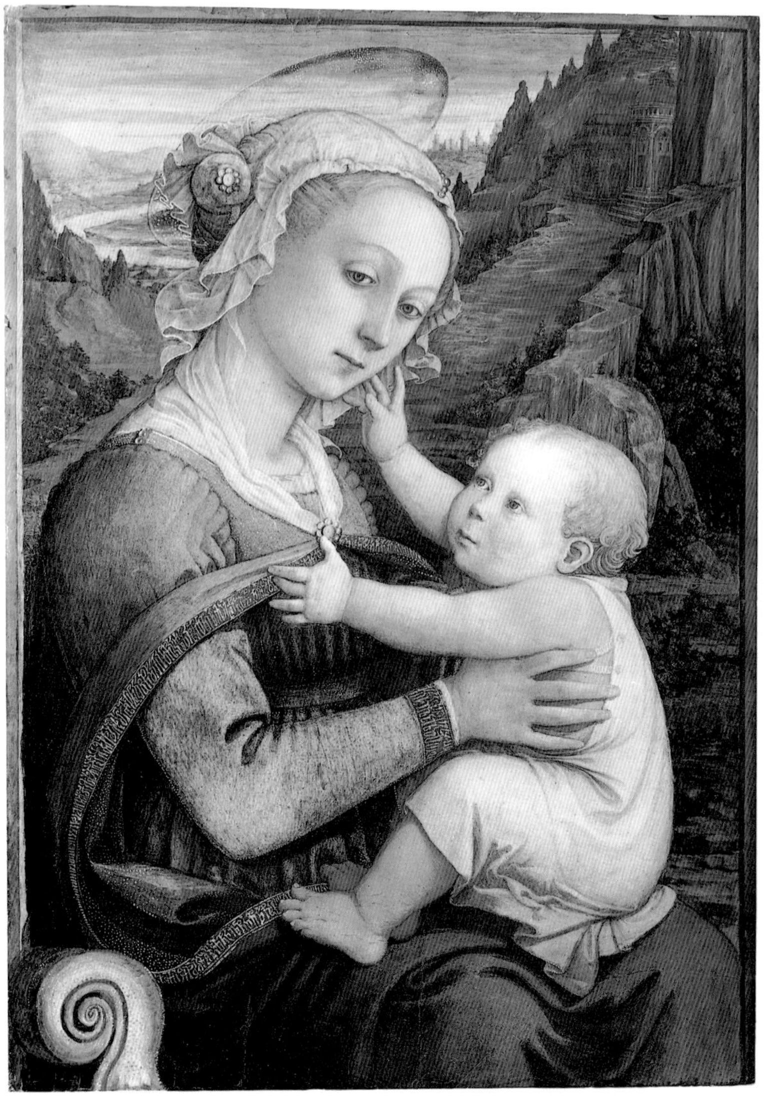

The close encounter orchestrated by Fra Filippo between the Virgin and Christ Child and the viewer in these *tabernacolo* panels may have owed something to the painter's particular perception of the Virgin as a Florentine Carmelite friar. The Carmelites claimed the special favor of the Virgin. She was the patron of the Carmelite Order, the titular saint of Santa Maria del Carmine, and the privileged focus of Carmelite doctrine and devotion.[115] The intimacy of address which is bound up in the formal construction of these half-length Madonna and Child panels is of a similar order to the direct and personal mode used by the Carmelites in their special prayers to "La Vergine Maria Carmelita": "Flower of Carmel, and flowering vine, Splendor of the Heavens, and singular Virgin mother . . . Give privileges to your Carmelites, Star of the Sea."[116] The striking visual idiom that Fra Filippo used in rendering the Virgin and Child in such images seems to bring together the medieval Christian allegorizing tradition where secular metaphors were invoked to describe the sacred, and more recent vernacular poetics. Considerable attention is given to defining the physical beauty and grace of the Virgin, seen in her refined features, elegant carriage, and ornamented hair and clothing. The Christ Child is robust and active, and physically demonstrates his attachment to his mother. The boldness implicit in representing the Virgin and Child in this manner is masked by the artist's ease and fluency. It is the confident manner with which Fra Filippo negotiates this merging of the sacred and secular, and different literary genres, that suggests his saturation in the religious representational conventions of the monastic *claustrum* and his exposure to the diverse representational practices in the *seculum*. Nor should Fra Filippo's personal experiences with women and children be discounted – experiences that bridged the *claustrum–seculum* divide, particularly when the Carmelite friar became the father of an illigitimate child born of a nun who had been under his care as a chaplain.

Fra Filippo Lippi's Madonna and Child images greatly influenced contemporaries such as Domenico Veneziano and Pesellino, as well as two minor painters, often directly associated with Fra Filippo's workshop and who generated derivative works, known as the Master of the Castello Nativity and the Pseudo-Pier Francesco Fiorentino.[117] Artists of the next generation – Baldovinetti, Verrocchio, Botticelli, Lorenzo di Credi, Ghirlandaio – were particularly inspired by Fra Filippo's later half-length Madonna and Child compositions, as landscape and narrative incident became standard features in their Marian devotional panels.

The *tavola quadrata*, portraiture, the tondo, and the half-length Marian devotional image represent four important categories of *quattrocento* painting which Lippi worked to define with his innovative pictorial formulations. To these can be added his dynamic *istorie* (narrative compositions) – particularly those in his fresco cycle in Santo Stefano in Prato, which I have discussed in passing in this chapter and which arguably deserve a separate section to themselves.

After Fra Filippo left the Carmelite milieu and established himself as a painter in Florence in the late 1430s and early 1440s, he lacked the necessary resources to support a large workshop. In this regard, his practice was markedly different from that of his contemporary Fra Angelico, who had an impressive production base complete with professional assistants and apprentices by virtue of his monastery, San Marco. Not unlike many lay painters during the period, Fra Filippo seems to have taken on only one principal apprentice at a time, and handled an increasing volume of work by entering into contractual relationships with established shops and independent masters.

The first of Lippi's apprentices of whom we hear is Giovanni di Francesco de Cervelliera. On June 1, 1440, a contract was drawn up between Fra Filippo and Giovanni di Francesco.[118] In his characteristically loose and imprecise manner, Fra Filippo recorded:

> [In the name of] Jesus, on the day the first of June, 1440
>
> Let it be noted to each and every person how, on this day, the first of June of the year above, Giovanni di Franciescho with this [agreement] comes to stay with me – that is, friar Philippo di Tommaso, painter, according to these terms and agreements – that is, that the said Giovanni must be and do all those things that by the above-mentioned Fra FFilippo [sic] would be commanded of him in the manner of a good disciple. And I owe him and am obliged [to teach him] that which I know regarding the art of painting, obliged to teach him and show him that which I know about the art of painting. And furthermore, I, the above-mentioned, oblige myself to give him for his labor and salary, [providing] he does that which is said above in the manner of a good disciple, forty florins.[119]

Giovanni di Francesco was probably fairly advanced in his artistic training by 1440. The forty florins that Fra Filippo agreed to pay him was high for an apprentice salary, and just two years later he matriculated into the Arte dei Medici e Speziali as an independent master.[120] In 1442 Fra Filippo and Giovanni di Francesco entered into a brief partnership – *compagnia* – which lasted only a month (from some time in September to November 16, 1442). Upon dissolving the partnership, they negotiated a further agreement regarding unfinished business – the restoration of a painting by Giotto:

> I, friar Philippo, painter, rector of San Chiricho a Llegniaria, make today, this day the 16th of November, 1442, in agreement together with Giovanni di Franciescho, painter, that each and every agreement we have made together or spoken of or written in the name of the company, on this above-mentioned day, must be considered and we want to be annulled; and this we will do, one with the other and the other with one, with these accords, that is: that the said Giovanni has received to repair a large panel by Giotto which he must complete in all respects with a gilded frame and a blue background and decorations in the drapery and helmets and other armor, according to the custom of good, finished work. And his payment shall be six florins immediately, [adjusted according to] that which will then come to him, then that must be and is intended to be his payment. And if that mentioned here and [in relation to] the said painting not be received, then a complaint will be made and his intentions heard in the presence of one who is able to bring us to an agreement, [and] for as much as it can be sold, let it be sold; and if this one should get more, it should be given to that one here, that is, to me, friar Filippo. And moreover, I am content that in the said [circumstances] Giovanni would have seven lire and fifteen soldi and in this way it finishes: he with me and I with him of each and every thing which, from the day in September in 1442 in the past, until now, the day the 16th, mentioned above and the century. And for clarification I say I, friar Philippo, the above-named, for clarification, I say that I have made this statement with my own hand and the said Giovanni will sign below with his own hand, to be content with that which is contained above.[121]

The painting by Giotto described in the contract does not correspond with any extant work by the artist. It appears to have belonged to Lippi and was being touched up and reframed to be sold. This is an early instance of a *trecento* painting being restored for its antiquarian value rather than for its importance as an efficacious sacred image. The restoration was apparently satisfactorily accomplished by Giovanni di Francesco. There is a note at the bottom of his version of the contract which reads "I, Giovanni di Francesco, declare myself to be content and completely paid on this day, the 16th of February, 1451".[122] He was later to insist that he had never been paid money that he was owed by Fra Filippo, and that the signature on the contract had been forged.[123] I have discussed the ensuing litigation between the two painters over the payment in Chapter 5, when considering Lippi's loss of his benefice at San Quirico at Legnaia and his numerous court battles.

The documents pertaining to the production of the *Coronation of the Virgin* (see fig. 91) for the high altar of Sant'Ambrogio, which occupied Fra Filippo Lippi during the first half of the 1440s, provide interesting insight into his workshop organization and collaborative practices. Among the six painters with whom Lippi worked on the altarpiece, only Fra Carnevale and Fra Diamante (employed at different times) belonged to his immediate shop. The others – Piero di Lorenzo, Frossino di Serro, Bernardo di Giovanni, and Stefano di Francesco – were independent masters who assisted Lippi predominantly when the altarpiece was near completion, with gilding and accessories such as the curtain to cover the painting.[124]

The relationship that Lippi established with Fra Diamante was long-lasting and became a crucial factor in his workshop production. Fra Diamante is first mentioned as an apprentice of Fra Filippo's ("discepolo di fra filipo") on July 17, 1447, when he was a seventeen-year-old Carmelite friar,[125] and he remained Lippi's principal assistant for over twenty years. He is documented in Prato with Fra Filippo working on the frescos for the *cappella maggiore* of Santo Stefano from 1454 to 1466, receiving a salary which was paid to him by the commissioning body out of Fra Filippo's earnings. During this period in Prato, Lippi produced a substantial volume of work in addition to the Santo Stefano frescos, relying on Fra Diamante's assistance.[126] Fra Diamante followed Fra Filippo to Spoleto where he contributed to the fresco decoration in the apse of the Duomo, staying on to finish the project after Lippi's death in 1469. The money he received for his part of the Spoleto frescos came to one fifth of the total payment. As a member of a religious order – first the Carmelites, and later, by 1460, the Vallombrosans – he never obtained the official status of an independent master by matriculating into the painters' guild. Perhaps for this reason, after Fra Filippo's death in Spoleto, when Fra Diamante went to collect the balance of payment for the fresco cycle in 1470, the forty-year-old painter is referred to in the documents as Fra Filippo's "apprentice" (*garzone*).[127]

Two other known painters are documented as having been apprenticed under Lippi for brief periods. Fra Carnevale – then known as Bartolomeo di Giovanni Corradini da Urbino, before he became a Dominican – was a "dipintore e disciepolo di Frate Philippo" when Fra Filippo was working on the Sant'Ambrogio altarpiece. He moved from Urbino to Florence in May 1445 and remained with Lippi at least through January of the following year.[128] The Umbrian painter Piermatteo d'Amelia (who later worked on the vault of the Sistine Chapel) was a "garzone di Frate Filippo" in Spoleto in 1468.[129] During the final years in Spoleto, Fra Filippo's young son Filippino assisted his father, coming under the guardianship of Fra Diamante following Lippi's death. While there is no extant documentation, it seems highly probable that the young Botticelli passed through Lippi's workshop during the final years of the Carmelite painter's life.[130] Other minor members of the workshop appear in the documents, mentioned sometimes by name ("Lo Spanguolo",[131] "Jacopo,"[132] and "Domenico"[133]), or generically as "his apprentices" ("garzoni suoi"[134]). These *garzoni* and *discepoli* rounded out a relatively small artistic practice dominated by Fra Filippo and his trusty collaborator Fra Diamante.[135]

There is very little information regarding the physical location and organization of Fra Filippo's work space. When the Sant'Ambrogio altarpiece was completed in early 1446, it was delivered from Fra Filippo's house ("cha[sa] sua") to the convent of Sant'Apollonia where it was kept until its installation at Sant'Ambrogio a year later.[136] This may indicate that he worked out of his house at this time, rather than maintaining a separate *bottega*. On the other hand, when Fra Filippo returned to Florence from Prato during 1457–58, to work on the Medici altarpiece for Alfonso of Naples, he maintained a shop separate from his living quarters. This is clear from the wording of Francesco Cantansanti's letter to Giovanni de' Medici describing Fra Filippo's erratic work on the altarpiece, where he writes that soon after he left Fra Filippo working on the painting, the artist "went home from there."[137] In Prato and Spoleto much of his work involved on-site fresco painting, although he did execute a number of panel paintings while in Prato, and probably had a workshop either in his residence or elsewhere.

Fra Filippo's painting practice was small and relatively diverse. He specialized in high-quality, expensive altarpieces. He made the occasional tabernacle image, portrait, and devotional panel, restored paintings on at least three occasions,[138] and made designs for niello.[139] He had engaged in minimal fresco work before accepting the commission to fresco the *cappella maggiore* of the Pieve in Prato. With the exception of his portraits, his paintings were all of religious subjects, intended for both ecclesiastical and secular settings. In this regard, his practice was closer to that of Fra Angelico, and distinct from his lay contemporaries Paolo Uccello, Domenico Veneziano, and Andrea del Castagno, who painted both religious and secular subjects.

In the execution of his paintings, Fra Filippo followed many of the standard *bottega* practices. For the large altarpieces and frescos, he seems to have been responsible for the overall design and the key figures, allocating preparatory work, secondary figures, and some background detail to his assistants (fig. 140).[140] It appears that he also left certain projects in the hands of his

140 Filippo Lippi, *Death of St. Jerome*, detail of fig. 180, with the Nativity in the background.

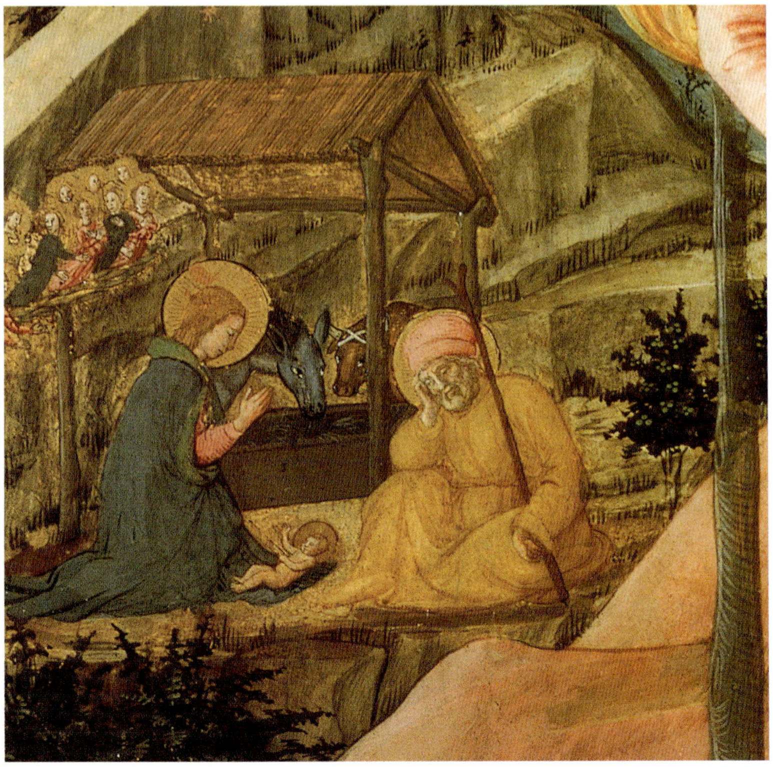

assistant, particularly those where the prestige was low.[141] With important projects, however, such as in paintings commissioned by the Medici, the work was carried out with maximum care and artistry. He took an unusually long time to finish his paintings, causing many of his patrons great consternation. In one case, he was levied a fine of 22 florins for his tardiness,[142] while Giovanni de' Medici advised that a Neapolitan nobleman who had shown an interest in obtaining a painting by Fra Filippo could do so "if he's not in a hurry."[143]

The prices that Lippi commanded were relatively high. He received just under 400 florins for the densely figurated Sant'Ambrogio *Coronation of the Virgin* (1439–46; see fig. 91). The patron of the *Annunciation* (see fig. 96) for Le Murate paid 200 florins for the painting and the altar fittings. In 1451, the Perugian Antonio del Branca agreed to give Lippi 70 florins for an altarpiece of the Madonna and Child with saints for San Domenico in Perugia, a sum which the dissatisfied patron later refused to pay.[144] Lippi received 85 florins for the *Madonna del Ceppo* (see fig. 99) in Prato.[145] In 1457, in a letter to Giovanni de' Medici, Lippi insisted that 100 florins would be a fair price for his labor on the triptych for Alfonso of Naples.[146] In 1458, the *Trinity* was evaluated at 200 florins *di sugello*, with 85 allocated to the heirs of Pesellino and 115 to Fra Filippo.[147] Lippi was paid just under 2,000 florins for labor and materials for the frescos in Prato and a little over 1,000 florins for the frescos in Spoleto (1466–69).[148] It is difficult to put these figures in perspective, as there is no satisfying study of the cost of *quattrocento* Florentine paintings.[149]

While Lippi followed many traditional production methods, his painting technique was fluid and pragmatic, like that of the more innovative painters in Florence, Domenico Veneziano, Paolo Uccello, and Andrea del Castagno. The most striking characteristic of his practice was the way that he developed a composition. The conception was never securely fixed in a preparatory study, in the under-drawing, or even in the blocking out and modeling of the figures and setting on the panel or fresco itself. He continued to work and rework elements, never securing the design solution until the final stages of painting. We see this clearly in the many *pentimenti* that are visible in his paintings (fig. 141), and in his fresco work where he eschewed cartoons and would leave large passages undefined, working up the details *a secco*.[150] Fra Filippo Lippi would also appear to have been among the early *quattrocento* Italian painters to experiment with oil glazes.

We have a brief glimpse of the artist at work in the letter written by the Medici agent Francesco Cantansanti to Giovanni de' Medici in 1457, reporting on Lippi's progress on the triptych for Alfonso of Naples.

> Fra Filippo has to gild those pinnacles of the panel [and?] he was in debt to the Buondelmonti, and I urged him on every day until Saturday evening I stayed with him for an hour to make him work. He stayed there doing it for a day. As I left him that business got [to] him, he went home from there and yesterday evening he took off. Those things are staying as security for the rent. I'm leaving this weft for [Bartolomeo] Seragli to untangle, if not, when I get back I'll handle it myself. But see toward what danger the man is headed![151]

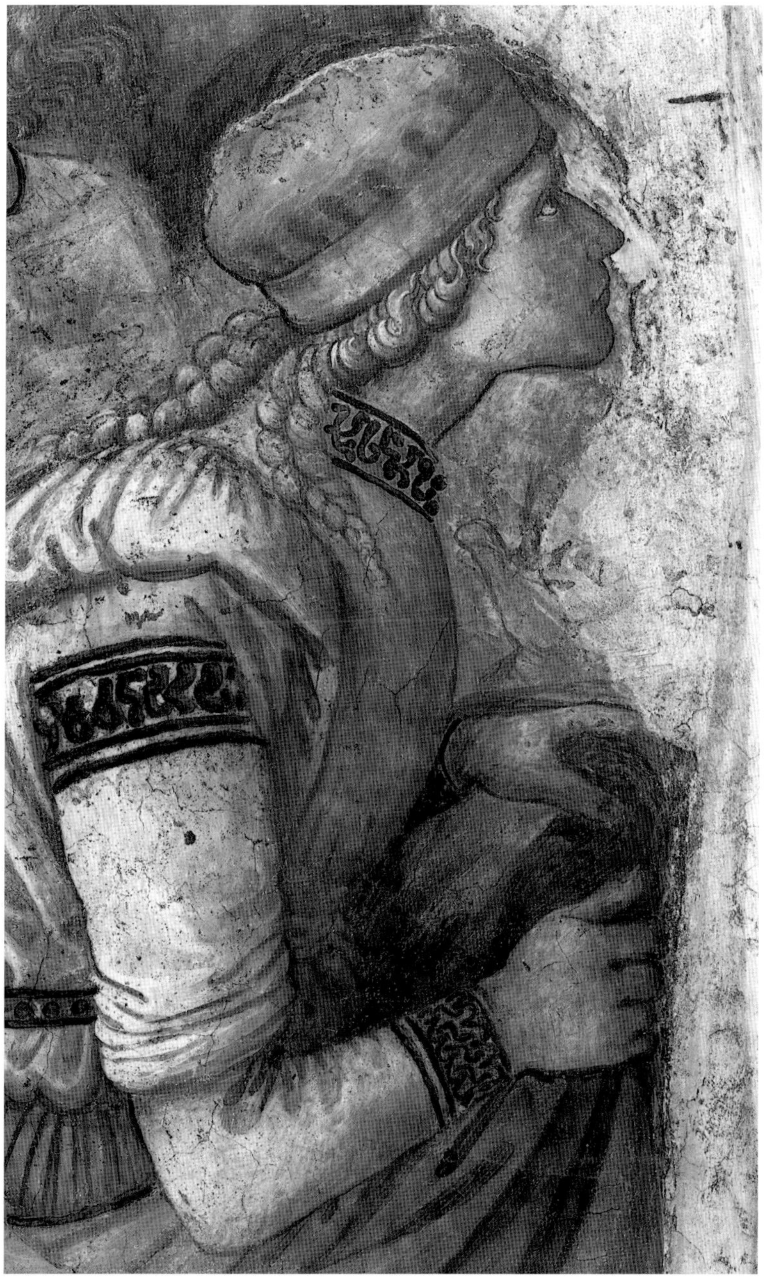

141 Filippo Lippi, *St. John in the Wilderness*, detail of fig. 160, showing one of the figures at the left with *pentimenti* visible in the left hand and profile.

Fra Filippo's own letter to Giovanni de' Medici regarding the same painting confirms Cantansanti's account of the painter's insolvency and anxious state: "I'm stuck because I have no more gold, nor money to have it put on. I beg you not to leave me like this, it's three days that I've done nothing waiting for you here."[152] He seems to have been a temperamental character who lived precariously. The restlessness and over-extension that characterized the manner in which the painter conducted his personal and professional affairs are manifest, too, in Fra Filippo's painting technique and pictorial style.

PATRONAGE

As a Carmelite friar painter working in the *seculum*, falling outside conventional monastic and secular institutional formations and jurisdictions, Fra Filippo Lippi was dependent upon patronage in a different way from other Florentine artists of the period. While other painters built up a patronage network through family, neighborhood, confraternal, and professional ties, Fra Filippo came to rely upon the strong backing of the Medici family and others within the family's orbit. This is not to say that he did not maintain fluid relations with the Carmelites, members of his family, the Compagnia di Sant'Agnese, powerful ecclesiastics, influential patricians, and his professional colleagues. However, the very manner in which he dealt with these various bodies – occasionally, inconsistently, opportunistically, and transgressively – is indicative of his strong reliance upon the support of the most powerful faction in the city, the Medici.[153]

When Fra Filippo returned to Florence around 1436, after his brief stay in Padua, we find him immediately plugged into a network of Medici family members, allies, agents, and friends. How he came into contact with this dominant faction is difficult to establish from the paucity of documentation for the painter during the 1430s. The Medici had little involvement with Santa Maria del Carmine, its principal patrons, and confraternities during this time.[154] It is possible that Fra Filippo had developed a reputation outside the Carmine by the middle of the decade, and came to the attention of the Medici in this manner. Or perhaps an introduction was made through an ecclesiastical patron of Fra Filippo's, such as the Florentine Archbishop Giovanni Vitelleschi who commissioned the Tarquinia *Madonna and Child* (1437; fig. 6) and was a friend of Cosimo de' Medici.

The first record of Fra Filippo's contact with the Medici is his remarkable letter to Piero de' Medici of August 13, 1439, which deserves to be quoted in full.

> [In the name of] Jesus, 13 Aug. 1439
>
> In reply to one [i.e. a letter] I sent you, I've received yours which took thirteen days to get here which has done me real harm. You answer me in closing that you can't make any other choice about the panel – that I should keep it for you which by God is bad for me if I leave, and more you can't give me a penny. This has hurt me really badly in a lot of ways and this is one of them, and it's clear that being one of the poorest friars that there is in Florence, I am, and God has left me with six sick and useless nieces to get married off and however little and much good to them, I am. If you could have them give me a little grain and wine at your house that you'd sell me, it would be a joy to me, putting it on my account. I burden you with this with tears in my eyes so that if I go away I can leave it for these poor children. I want you to know that I've been with Ser Antonio about the Marchese and wanted to know from him what he wanted me to do, he says going to serve the Marchese he'll lend us five florins each and leaving home I see I couldn't make myself a pair of stockings. I beg you, it won't be much trouble, two lines to him, to Ser Antonio, to recommend me to him, and may your answer be quick, I'm leaving the next day, I'm sure if I stay here eight days I'm dead such is [my] fear. For God's sake answer to your house where I'll leave this so it doesn't get held up like the other.
>
> Fra Filippo painter in Florence
> To Piero di Chosimo at Trebbio in Mugello[155]

The letter provides insight into the dynamic that attended the exchange of services between the artist and his Medici patrons. Fra Filippo was financially dependent upon the Medici while in their employ, maintaining an account with them to cover his work and living expenses, but he seems to be manipulating sentiment in order to obtain a hand-out (for those "sick and useless nieces"). He does not acquiesce with grace to the opinion of his social superior, voicing his unhappiness with Piero's refusal to pay any more money for the painting or concede to any "other choice[s] about the panel." As a client of the Medici, he readily turns to Piero in order to secure his influence with another princely patron (the Marchese of Mantua or Ferrara) whom he is interested in serving.[156] Fra Filippo's tone in the letter is in turn familiar, disgruntled, audacious, demanding, and pathetic. It is a far cry from the careful, deferential, and yet intimate attitude assumed by Domenico Veneziano when writing to Piero de' Medici.[157] Clearly Fra Filippo did not "know his place," or if he knew it, he certainly didn't keep to it – and yet the Medici seem to have tolerated this.

The letters exchanged on the occasion of the triptych commissioned by the Medici from Fra Filippo as a gift for King Alfonso of Naples further demonstrate that the painter was no easy client.[158] They also suggest why the Medici may have been willing to put up with Fra Filippo Lippi's antics. In the first of these missives, dating from July 20, 1457 to Giovanni de' Medici, Fra Filippo indicated that there had been some disagreement between them over the painting. He informs him that the Medici agent Bartolomeo Martelli, who was acting as a go-between, "said . . . that I should do absolutely everything that you wanted and he went over it with me repeatedly showing that it was I who had done wrong to you."[159] As a result, Fra Filippo assures Giovanni, "I did what you ordered me about the panel and held myself to the line on everything." Further down, he reiterates this with hyperbole, declaring "Now Giovanni, I am here absolutely to be your slave and I will produce."[160] He then proceeds, however, to put pressure on his patron to pay him more for the painting, raising the price in dizzying and roundabout argumentation from the fourteen florins that he had already received, to thirty florins, sixty florins, and finally, "for love of you I don't want to get from you more than a hundred florins."[161] He concludes, rhetorically, "if I've been presumptuous in writing to you forgive me and I will always do whatever more and whatever less will please your reverence."[162] A month later, the Medici agent Cantansanti was sent to monitor Fra Filippo's progress on the painting. He even had to stay with Fra Filippo in order to get him to work. His exasperation with the artist is clear in the letter that he wrote to Giovanni de' Medici (quoted above), concluding "see to what danger this man is heading!"

In spite of these difficulties, the painting was finished and delivered in the spring of 1458 to Alfonso of Naples, to the great satisfaction of both patron and recipient. Giovanni de' Medici wrote to his agent in Naples, Bartolomeo Serragli, "I understand that you have presented the panel to His Majesty the King, and that he was highly pleased with it." In another letter he wrote, "I see you write how much His Majesty has valued the panel, which is good news." Apparently it was so well received that one of the Neapolitan courtiers wanted a copy made by Fra Filippo.[163] This "minor ploy in Medici diplomacy" – as Michael Baxandall has called it – was one of the maneuvers the Medici made in an effort to secure a stronger Florentine alliance with the Neapolitan kingdom.[164] It demonstrates the value of an artist like Lippi to his Medici patrons and the importance of artistic production within the political economy of conspicuous display and gift-giving that prevailed in the Italian courts and republics during the period.

Over the course of his career, Lippi produced at least nine paintings for members of the Medici family. These include "la tavola" mentioned in Lippi's letter to Piero de' Medici (1439);[165] the *Madonna and Child with Saints* painted for the novitiate chapel of Santa Croce which Cosimo de' Medici had endowed, dating from the mid-1440s;[166] the *Adoration of the Christ Child* painted for the chapel in the Palazzo Medici around 1459;[167] a *St. Jerome in the Wilderness*;[168] "alcune storiette" which Vasari says Cosimo de' Medici commissioned from Lippi for Pope Eugenius IV; the *Annunciation* lunette with Medici insignia and the companion piece, the *Seven Saints* lunette with Medici saints Cosmas, Damian, John the Baptist, Francis, Peter Martyr, Anthony Abbott, and Lawrence of around the 1450s;[169] the triptych commissioned by the Medici for Alfonso of Naples in 1456, completed in 1458, representing the *Adoration of the Christ Child with Saints*;[170] and the *Adoration of the Christ Child* for the cell founded by Piero de' Medici and Lucrezia Tornabuoni at the Camaldoli hermitage, of around 1465.[171] The surviving works demonstrate a uniformly high quality of execution and extremely innovative and creative pictorial features. I shall look more carefully at the relationship between the artist and his Medici patrons in Chapter 8, where I focus on the altarpiece that he painted for the novitiate chapel at Santa Croce.

A significant number of Fra Filippo's patrons were Medici associates. Among the first works Fra Filippo painted upon returning from Padua is the dated Tarquinia *Madonna and Child* (1437), which was probably commissioned by the Florentine Archbishop Giovanni Vitelleschi, a friend of Cosimo de' Medici, who took over the diocese on Cosimo's return from exile. In the early 1440s, Fra Filippo painted two altarpieces for Giovanni d'Amerigo Benci, one of the most important members of the Medici bank, for the nunnery church of Le Murate, which I shall discuss in Chapter 9. Among his other patrons was the banker and statesman Alessandro Alessandri, who acted on behalf of the Medici in their maneuvers for position and influence.[172] Lionardo Bartolini, who commissioned a tondo from him, was a Medici agent.[173] The Provost of the Pieve of Santo Stefano at Prato, Gemignano Inghirami, was a Pratese with Medici connections. He was directly involved in Lippi's fresco project for the *cappella maggiore* of the Pieve, in addition to engaging the artist on two projects for his private chapels in Prato. Following Inghirami's death in 1460, he was succeeded as Provost by Carlo de' Medici, an illegitimate son of Cosimo.

Strong backing in ecclesiastical circles was important to the *frate dipintore* Filippo Lippi, and it must have been through his Medici connections that certain powerful ecclesiastical patrons came to stand behind the friar. Pope Eugenius IV conferred the San Quirico benefice upon Lippi in 1442 and Vasari says that Lippi also painted certain "storiette" for him.[174] Eugenius had strong Medici–Florentine leanings. The Dominican Prior of San Marco, Fra Giuliano di Filippo Lapaccini, who acted as the mediator between Lippi and his Perugian patron Antonio del Branca, worked closely with Cosimo de' Medici on the reconstruction of San Marco."[175] Pope Callistus III initially listened sympathetically to Lippi's pleas for justice after the Florentine Archbishop Antonino had deprived him of his benefice in 1455. Lippi probably also had strong support from Donato de' Medici, who as Bishop of Pistoia was responsible for the ecclesiastical affairs in the city of Prato.

These Medici dependents and allies, who either commissioned works from Fra Filippo or lent their support to him, were enacting important procedures of *quattrocento* Florentine patronage. A Medici supporter like Bartolini emulated his patron by commissioning a tondo from Fra Filippo Lippi – who may well have been perceived as a "Medici artist." Alessandri had Lippi include images of the Medici saints Cosmas and Damian in the altarpiece that he had painted, making a public demonstration of his association with the Medici but also appropriating these potent saintly intercessors for his own devotional needs.[176] Medici allies who lent their support to the friar, like Pope Eugenius IV, were negotiating their own relationships with the Medici in extending their patronage to a Medici retainer.

* * *

Fra Filippo Lippi worked in a discursive space that was opening up in *quattrocento* Italy, where both the status and practice of the artist were being redefined.[177] Fra Filippo's representational strategies and pictorial solutions evident in his paintings demonstrate a set of interests and values that were integral to the conceptions about art being worked out in theoretical terms by humanists and in practical terms by contemporary artists.[178]

While Fra Filippo did not leave a record of his perspective on art as clearly articulate as Ghiberti's *Commentarii*, there are a number of ways in which he expressed his views within the context of his painting. One of these is through his attempts at self-portraiture, with its implicit self-reflection and negotiation of artistic identity. In the *Vita* of Lippi, Vasari noted that in the *Funeral of St. Stephen* fresco in Santo Stefano in Prato, "he painted himself with a mirror, dressed in black in the robes of a prelate, and his disciple Fra Diamante."[179] Following Vasari's lead, the two figures to the far right of the scene (fig. 142), both looking out at the viewer, have been identified as the artist and his assistant.[180] The artist and his young son Filippino are recognized in the *Dormition of the Virgin* in the apse of the Duomo in Spoleto as the two figures standing at the foot of the Virgin's bier, with Fra Filippo this time in a Carmelite habit (fig. 143).[181] These frescos were executed shortly after the first securely documented case of an artist's portrait included among the figures in the crowd – Benozzo Gozzoli's signed self-image among the attendants in the Medici Chapel *Procession of the Magi* fresco of 1459 (fig. 144). In *De pictura* Alberti had provided theoretical grounds for the practice of commemorating artists through portraiture in narrative frescos by encouraging painters "to paint my portrait in their *historie*, and thereby proclaim to posterity that I was a student of this art and that they are mindful of and grateful for this favour."[182]

142 Filippo Lippi, *Funeral of St. Stephen*, detail of fig. 145, with the artist's self-portrait (right) and Fra Diamante (centre), early 1460s, Prato, Cathedral of Santo Stefano, main chapel.

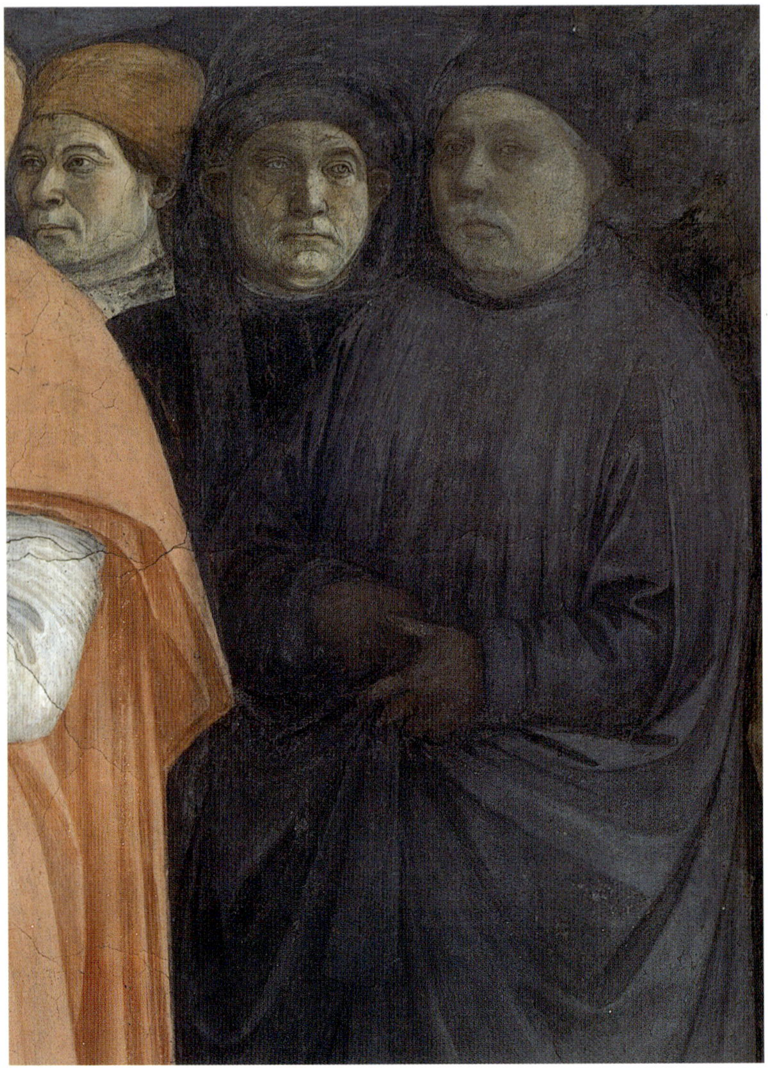

143 Filippo Lippi, *Dormition of the Virgin*, detail of fig. 159, with the artist's self-portrait.

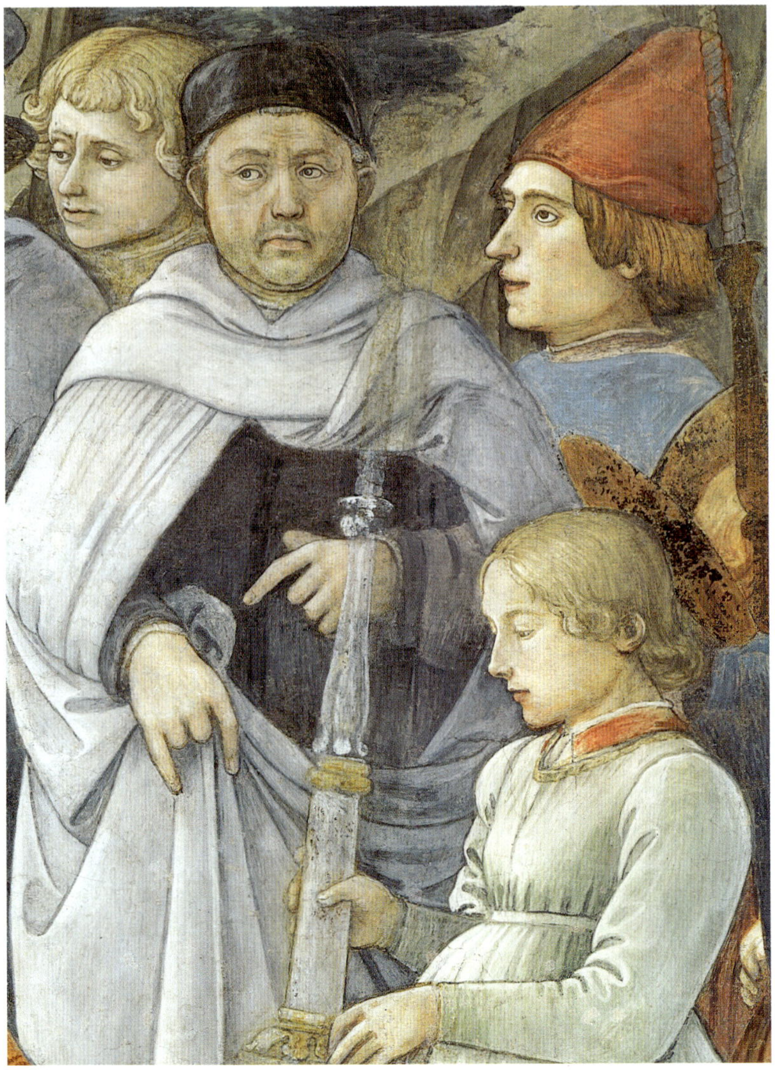

In the *Funeral of St. Stephen* (fig. 145), the artist portrayed himself in full figure, standing to the right of the imposing cleric in red, emulating his pose, shadow-like in darker robes.[183] The self-portrait is positioned at the juncture of a curious rupture in the visual logic of the narrative setting. The painter's shoulder abuts the rocky terrain encasing the scene of St. Stephen's martyrdom to the right. This rocky ground cuts diagonally across the front of a pillar and invades the church interior where the saint's body is displayed in the *Funeral of St. Stephen*. Fra Filippo here eschews the illusionistic architectural framing to separate sequential narrative scenes that he uses elsewhere in the fresco cycle, proposing instead a sort of pictorial elision that functions something like the representation of "temporal flow." The artist stands by to orchestrate this demonstration of artistic *ingegno*, literally embodying artistic license. The inspiration for this odd scenography may have come from the fresco of the *Burial of St. Cecilia* (fig. 146) attributed to Lippo d'Andrea in the sacristy of Santa Maria del Carmine in Florence.

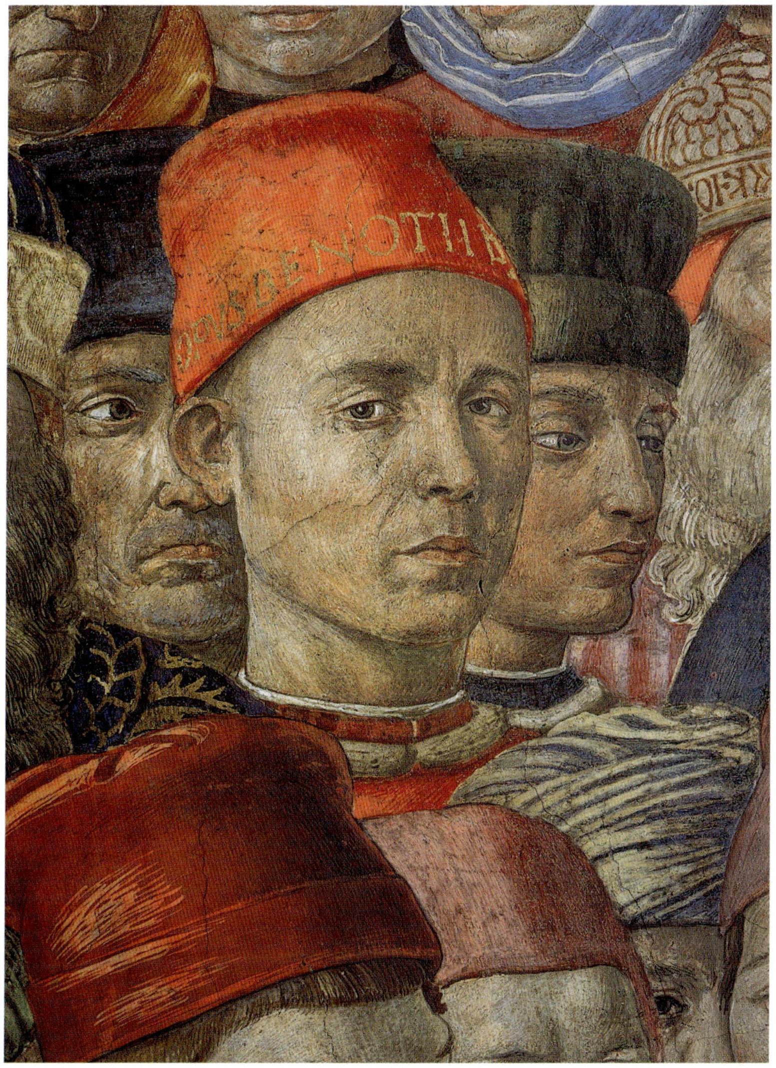

144 Benozzo Gozzoli, *Procession of the Magi*, detail of fig. 176, with the artist's self-portrait, 1459, Florence, Palazzo Medici-Riccardi, chapel.

In the *Dormition of the Virgin* in Spoleto, the painter inserted his self-portrait conspicuously, dressed in his Carmelite habit, at the very foot of the Virgin's bier. Here, Fra Filippo's proximity to the Virgin may serve as a demonstration of the Carmelite's special devotion to the "Madonna of Monte Carmelo," particularly at a time when, aged and increasingly infirm, he may have been meditating upon his own mortality. As a Carmelite, Fra Filippo was entitled to the Sabbatine Privilege whereby the Virgin would accompany him to the "mountain of everlasting life" on the Saturday following his own death.[184] The figure in the fresco also seems to be making a very self-conscious reference to his status as the author of the fresco cycle. Shown in full figure and facing outward, the Carmelite artist points toward his right hand, reifying the contractual signature "mia propria mano" and the literary trope of the *manus pictoris*.[185] Poliziano later versified this hand in the epitaph on Fra Filippo's tomb in the Duomo of Spoleto (fig. 147) as the very "grace of hand" with its "craftsman's fingers" that "gave colour life and fooled the living with its long-awaited voice."[186]

Another example of a highly self-conscious signature in Fra Filippo's painting can be seen in the way that the painter signed his name in the altarpiece in the chapel in the Medici Palace (see fig. 177). "Frate philippus p" ("p" standing for "pictor") is inscribed along the foreshortened handle of an axe in the lower left corner of the painting.[187] Within the sylvan setting of the *Adoration of the Christ Child*, the axe is the implement that has felled the trees that lie strewn about the forest floor around the Virgin and Child. This dead wood is a metaphor for the obstructions that must be cleared away in forging a path toward a fruitful Christian practice (Luke 3:9). The signature axe may stand for the painter's brush, as Fra Filippo demonstrates that he has fashioned a fertile ground for spiritual reflection within the pictorial imagery of the painting with his artistry. The important relationship with Fra Filippo's most prestigious patrons, the Medici, and the prominent display site of the painting in their palace chapel, seem to have provoked this reflection upon the painter's activity and identity.

Lippi's involvement in the restoration of a painting by Giotto in 1442, mentioned above, can also be seen within the context of changing attitudes toward the value of painting and the status of the artist. The fact that Giotto is named as the painter of the panel ("uno quadro grande di Giotto") in the contract drawn up between Fra Filippo and Giovanni di Francesco de Cervelliera suggests that Fra Filippo was aware of the high estimation in which Giotto was held during the *quattrocento* and the significance accorded the new style of painting that he had introduced, as described, for example, in Ghiberti's *Commentarii* (c. 1450). This point, however, should not be pushed too far, as the restoration was clearly a commercial affair calculated to enhance the resale value of the painting. It is striking that Fra Filippo did not undertake the work himself, assigning the repair

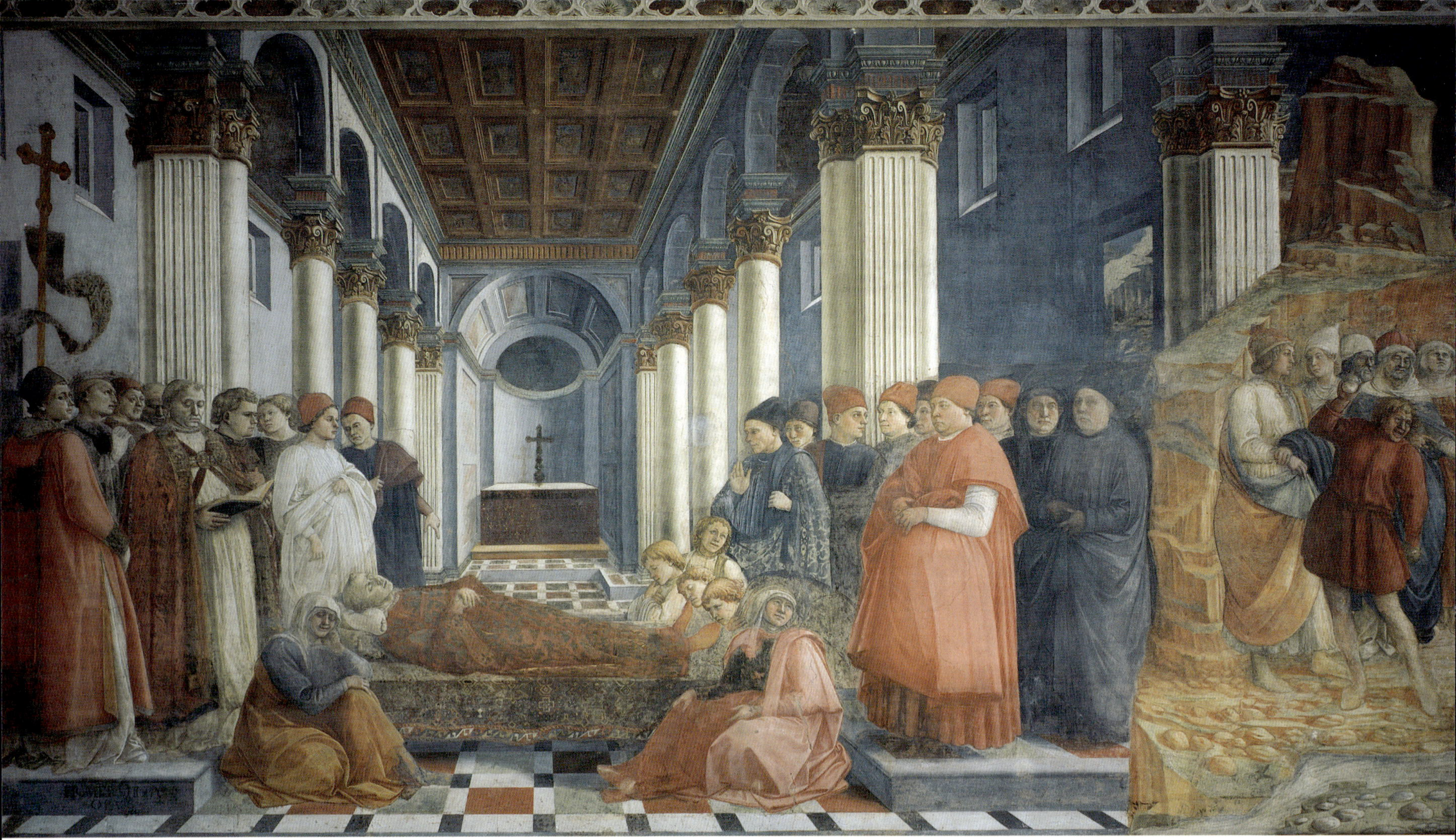

145 Filippo Lippi, *Funeral of St. Stephen*, early 1460s, Prato, Cathedral of Santo Stefano, main chapel.

instead to his ex-apprentice in an accord drawn up specifically for this one project.

Along with the work of artists like Donatello, Luca della Robbia, Domenico Veneziano, Andrea del Castagno, and Fra Angelico, Lippi's painting embodied artistic values that had currency within progressive cultural circles, influenced by humanists' redefinition of the arts and fostered by a patrician elite with a vested interest in fashioning a new image of themselves and their city through artistic patronage.[188] Fra Filippo evolved a highly individual painting style where he self-consciously performed his artistic *ingegno* for the viewer's delectation, in the form of clever compositional innovations, imaginative pictorial *invenzioni*, and manifestations of *fantasia*. Let us look at examples of each of these three critical terms in Lippi's painting.

In the fresco cycle in the *cappella maggiore* of Santo Stefano in Prato, the Martyrdom of St. Stephen (fig. 148) is represented in the lower left corner. Roguish young men in short tunics hurl stones at the kneeling saint who raises his eyes toward the heavens. A more mature and sympathetic crowd gathers behind, while Christ hovers above, atop a cloud, surrounded by a ring of cherubs and seraphs, directing an angel who offers a martyr's

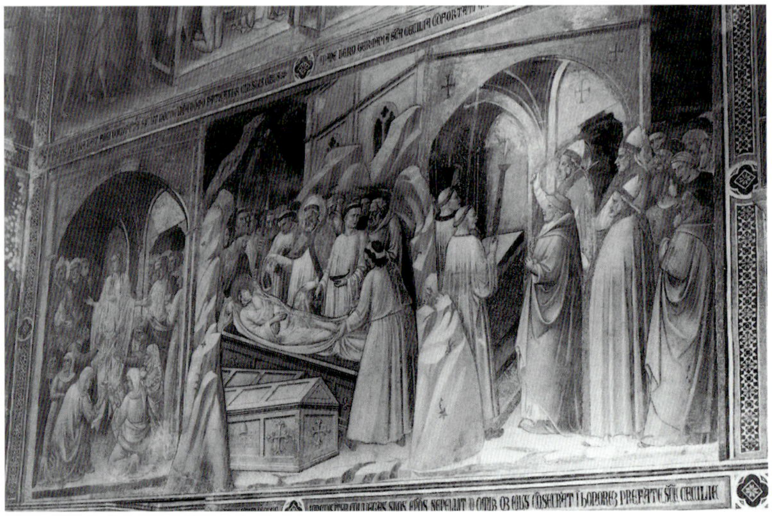

146 Lippo d'Andrea (attr.), *Burial of St. Cecilia*, c. 1395–1400, Florence, Santa Maria del Carmine, sacristy.

147 Tomb of Filippo Lippi, c. 1490, designed by Filippino Lippi, Spoleto, Cathedral of Santa Maria Assunta.

crown to the dying saint. What is most remarkable about this dramatic martyrdom scene is that it takes place across the corner of the chapel. The pictorial space wraps around the right-angled corner, incorporating into the narrative the physical space of the chapel itself, as a figure on the left chapel wall prepares to hurl a stone diagonally across the corner at the saint depicted on the end wall. The rugged outcrop of rock behind the figures and a small stream at their feet both turn the corner in the chapel, providing a continuous setting along the left lateral and end walls. On the other side of the chapel, the Beheading of the Baptist (fig. 149) takes place. The executioner reaches out across the corner of the chapel to hand the decapitated Baptist's head to Salome, with the bend in his elbow following the angle where the two walls meet. Unlike in the *Martyrdom of St. Stephen*, the settings along the end wall and the right lateral wall are not continuous. The two different backgrounds merge abruptly in the corner angle, possibly thematizing the violent severing of the saint's head from his body in the *istoria*.

Lippi's highly imaginative use of the corner spaces within the chapel would have been understood by his more educated audience (and perhaps by other artists) as evidence of the *ingenium* or *ingegno* (innate talent) that he brought to his pictorial composition.[189] This is the kind of inspired solution that was to earn him Cristoforo Landino's praise for his pictorial composition ("valse molto nelle compositioni") – composition being the *quattrocento* category used by Alberti to describe the formal organization of an *istoria*.[190] Similar imaginative experimentation with formal composition – guided by technical skill and knowledge (*ars*, or *disciplina*, and *dottrina*) – also characterized Fra Filippo's efforts in developing the *tavola quadrata* altarpiece and modifying the half-length Madonna and Child image, described above.[191] *Ingenium* was a creative quality increasingly valued by commentators on the arts during the *quattrocento*.[192] In the Preface to Alberti's *Della pitture*, *ingegno* is the term he invokes when praising the accomplishments of the Florentines Brunelleschi, Donatello, Ghiberti, Luca della Robbia, and

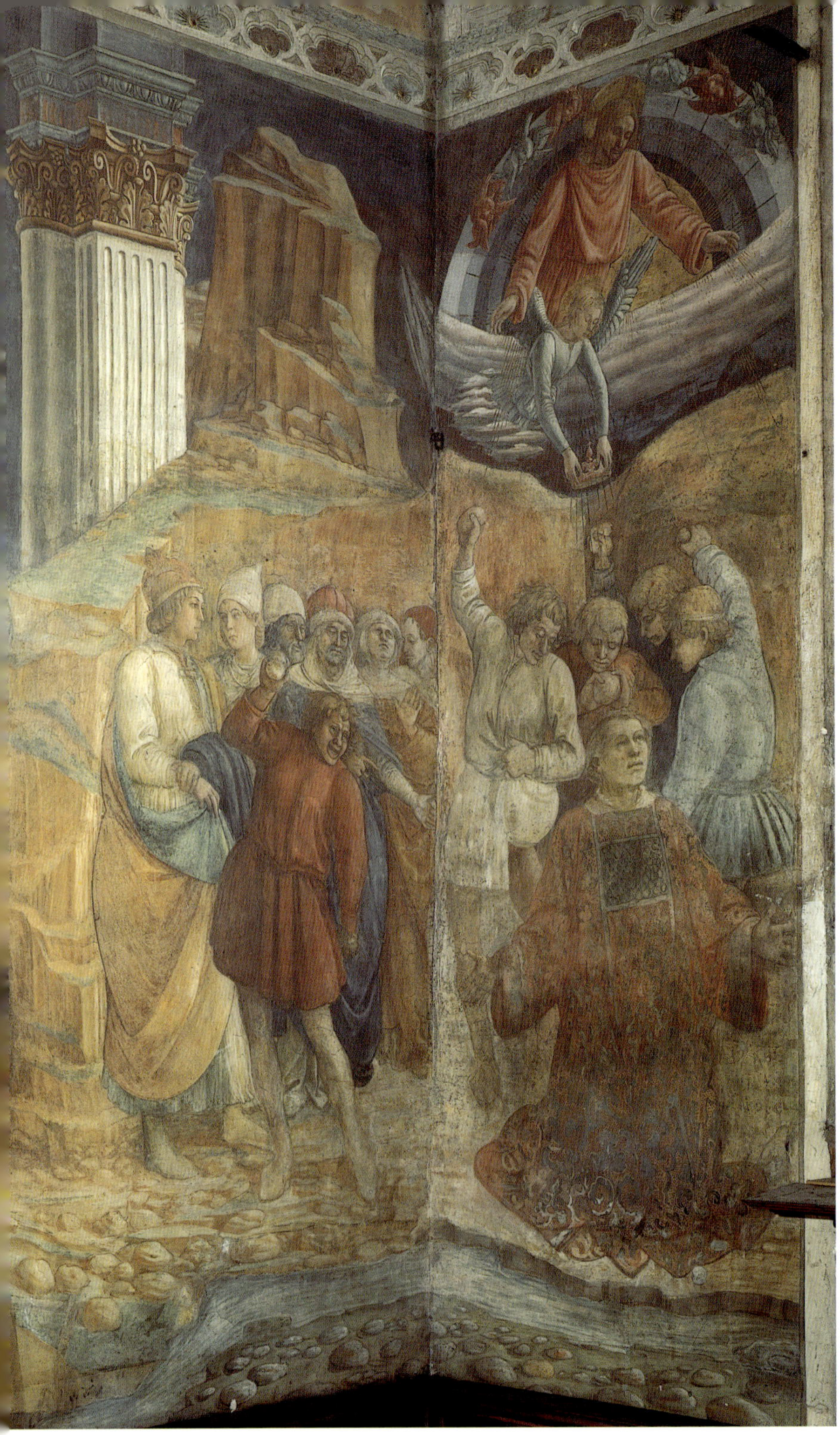

148 Filippo Lippi, *Martyrdom of St. Stephen*, early 1460s, Prato, Cathedral of Santo Stefano, main chapel.

Masaccio over those of the ancients.[193] As Stephen Campbell observes, "The conception of the painter as an authorial figure possessing *ingenium*, and the pictorial composition as analogous to literary invention, is central to the most powerful fifteenth-century claim for painting's dignity and status as a liberal art."[194]

Imaginative *invenzioni* were also exhibited in Lippi's paintings. Following the poetic tradition, when applied to painting, *invenzione* referred to a pleasing elaboration of the pictorial content.[195] The Bartolini tondo (see fig. 130), with its novel juxtaposition of the Madonna and Child against a narrative backdrop within a new circular framing would have struck contemporaries as a radical *invenzione*. Fra Filippo's Adoration of the Christ Child altarpieces (see figs. 169, 171, 178), which depart from the conventional Nativity iconography, and his images of the Madonna and Child with and without accompanying saints, animated by

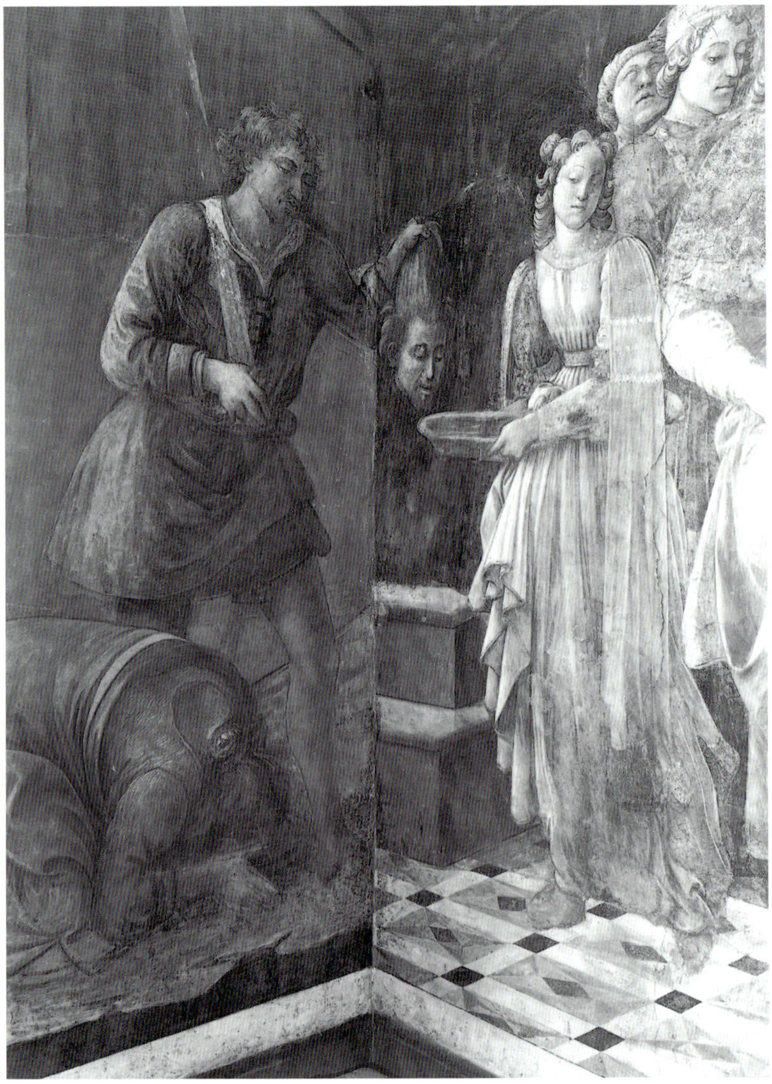

149 Filippo Lippi, *Beheading of the Baptist*, early 1460s, Prato, Cathedral of Santo Stefano, main chapel.

narrative incident and anecdotal details, would also fall into this category of striking *invenzioni*.[196] In the *Annunciation* lunette he painted for the Medici (see figs. 223 and 224), he provided a visual interpretation of the penetration of the Virgin's body without precedent, showing the dove of the Holy Spirit descending in serial images toward a hole in the Virgin's gown from which gilded rays emerge. In the companion image, the *Seven Saints* (see fig. 95), Fra Filippo introduced an element of narrative into the representation of an assemblage of saints. He endowed the saints with distinct actions and interactions, while preserving an atmosphere of quiet contemplation by placing the figures in a forested grove reminiscent of his Adoration of the Christ Child paintings.

Martin Kemp has traced a trajectory within fifteenth-century art theory whereby the manifestation of an artist's imagination and *fantasia* was given an increasingly more positive valuation and greater emphasis as the century progressed.[197] *Fantasia*, as it came to be used in artistic theory, referred to an artist's imaginative faculty and was manifest in his inspired insight and formal invention.[198] An interesting and provocative demonstration of artistic *fantasia* can be seen in Fra Filippo's *Vision of St. Bernard* (fig. 150), associated with a documented commission of 1447 for the chancellery in the Palazzo della Signoria.[199] Rather than represent the demon which tempted the saint in a precisely defined form – like the devils hiding among the rocks in the *Harrowing of Hell* fresco painted under the direction of Fra Angelico in one of the *conversi* cells at San Marco – Fra Filippo depicted the creature partially truncated by the lower left picture edge, in loosely applied, translucent black pigment, lurking in the shadows within the recesses of the rock behind the saint (fig. 151). This not fully realized, fragmentary fantasm seems to literalize and deconstruct Cennino Cennini's definition of an artist's *fantasia* as the ability "to discover unseen things, hiding under the shadow of nature, and to fix them with the hand, demonstrating what actually does not exist."[200] This monstrous creature of Fra Filippo's *fantasia* hovers between form and non-form, between representational fixity and the fluid fantasmagorical transmutations of the fertile imagination.

Fra Filippo Lippi produced distinctive, innovative, highly accomplished panel paintings and frescos for his patrons. These works were characterized by visual splendor, animated figurations, and intricately structured compositions. His playful and imaginative solutions to pictorial problems had both an intellectual and a sensual appeal, and actively engaged the spectator. Particularly among the Medici and members of their faction, his paintings were sought-after commodities within fifteenth-century Florentine economic and cultural exchange.

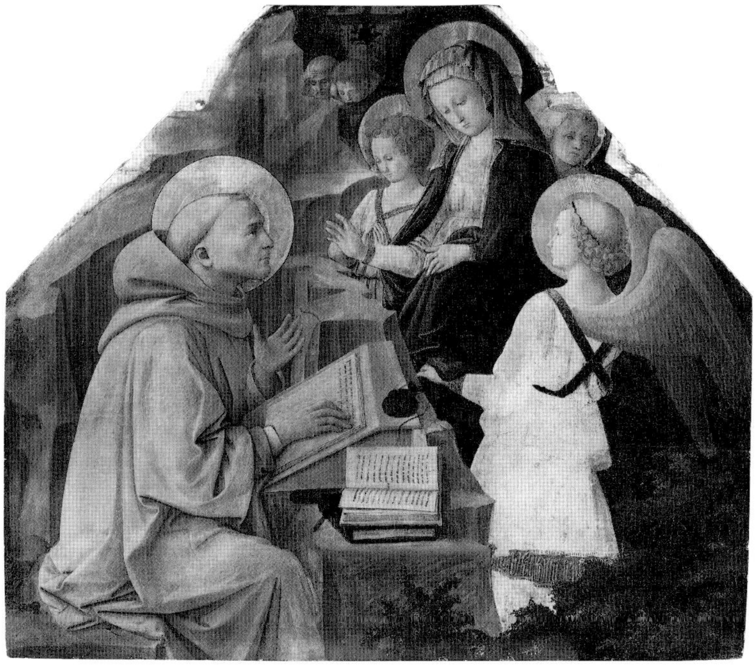

150 Filippo Lippi, *Vision of St. Bernard*, c. 1447, London, National Gallery.

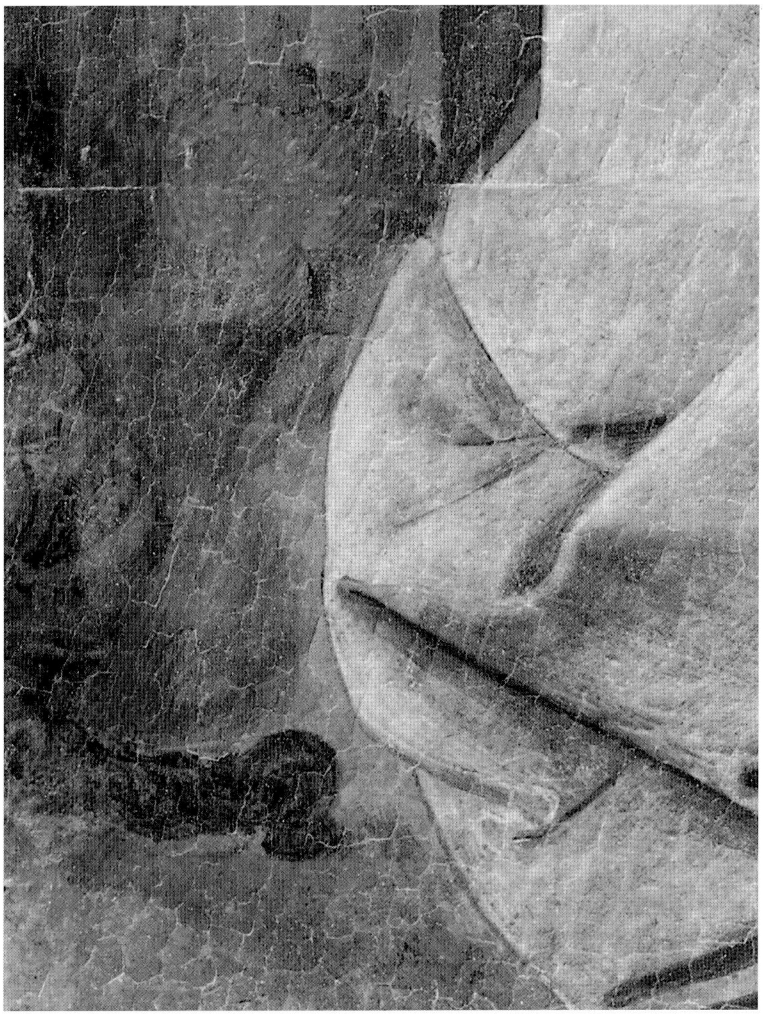

151 Filippo Lippi, *Vision of St. Bernard*, detail of fig. 150, with the demon in the lower left corner.

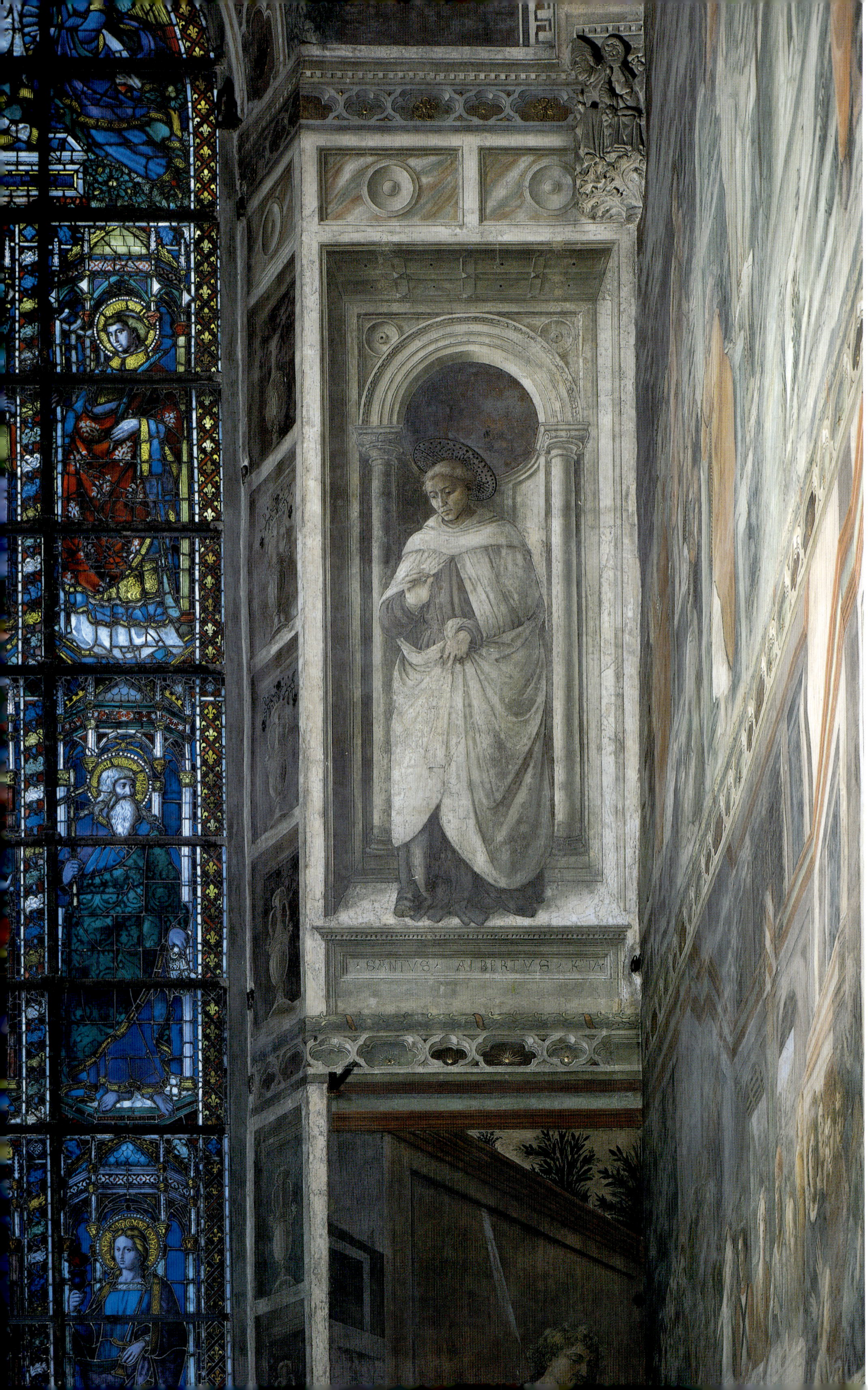
SANTVS ALBERTVS KTA

CHAPTER SEVEN

CARMELITE IN NAME ALONE? CARMELITE INFLUENCE IN FRA FILIPPO'S MATURE WORK

Fra Filippo Lippi's documented paintings were produced from his mid-thirties to his death at roughly age sixty-three in 1469. During this period, the painter lived in secular society and his relationship with his own Carmelite Order was somewhat attenuated, as described in Chapter 5. But Lippi had passed sixteen-odd years in the Carmelite cloister. He had been exposed to a Carmelite indoctrination and the devotional practices of the convent of Santa Maria del Carmine. In addition, he maintained his status (and hence, at some level, his identity) as a Carmelite friar. To what extent can one consider the mature artist a Carmelite painter? How did his Carmelite past and continued status as a Carmelite friar influence the way that Fra Filippo Lippi, the professional painter, conceived of his religious subjects? These are some of the questions I shall address in this chapter.

The *cassa* of Beato Andrea Corsini discussed in Chapter 5 is the one securely documented work undertaken by Lippi for either the Carmelites or a Carmelite institution after he left Santa Maria del Carmine. At some point during his artistic career, he may also have painted the *Annunciation* that once adorned the wall above the main portal leading from the piazza into the Florentine Carmelite convent, just to the right of the church, visible in a seventeenth-century print (see fig. 153).[1] However, certain Carmelite themes and iconography, as well as a mode of visualizing the sacred involving enactment and manifestation, worked their way into the pictorial fabric of his mature work. There is the obvious example of his fresco of the Carmelite St. Alberto of Trapani (fig. 154) occupying a prominent place on the end wall of the *cappella maggiore* in Santo Stefano in Prato. Eve Borsook suggests that this may represent a gesture of appreciation made by the patrons to the Carmelite painter who had toiled long, laboriously, and very successfully on the chapel decoration.[2] Other Carmelite themes and iconography are not as overtly evident in Lippi's mature paintings, being subordinated by the primary iconographic program of individual works, and they require a bit of excavation in order to bring them to the surface. I shall touch briefly upon four such examples here. First I shall address the influence that the Carmine Ascension Day *sacra rappresentazione* had on Fra Filippo's pictorial imagery. I shall then discuss how one pictorial innovation of Fra Filippo's, and another new pictorial genre, both owe

153 Stefano della Bella, *Procession to the Tomb of St. Andrea Corsini*, etching from Benedetto Buonmattei, *Descrizione delle feste per la canonizzazione di S. Andrea Corsini* (Florence, 1632).

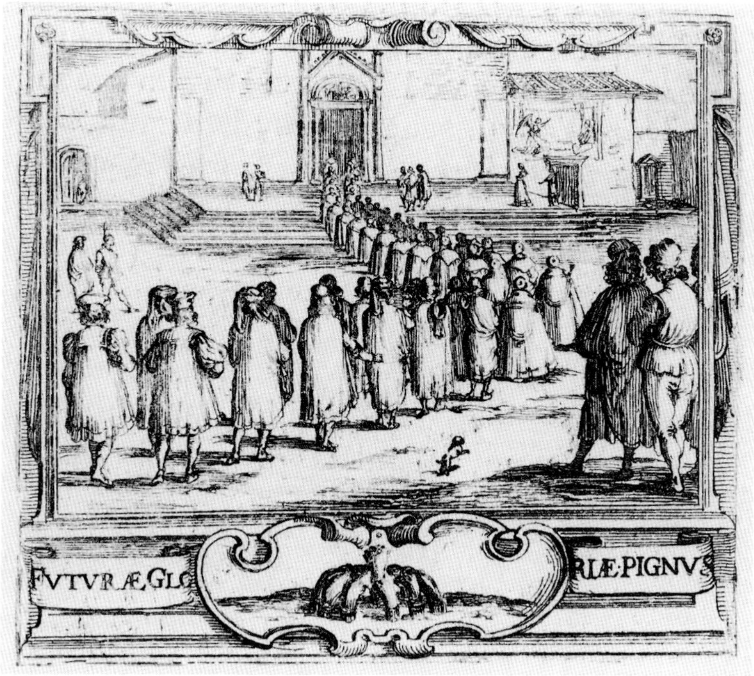

152 Filippo Lippi, *St. Alberto of Trapani*, late 1450s, Prato, Cathedral of Santo Stefano, main chapel.

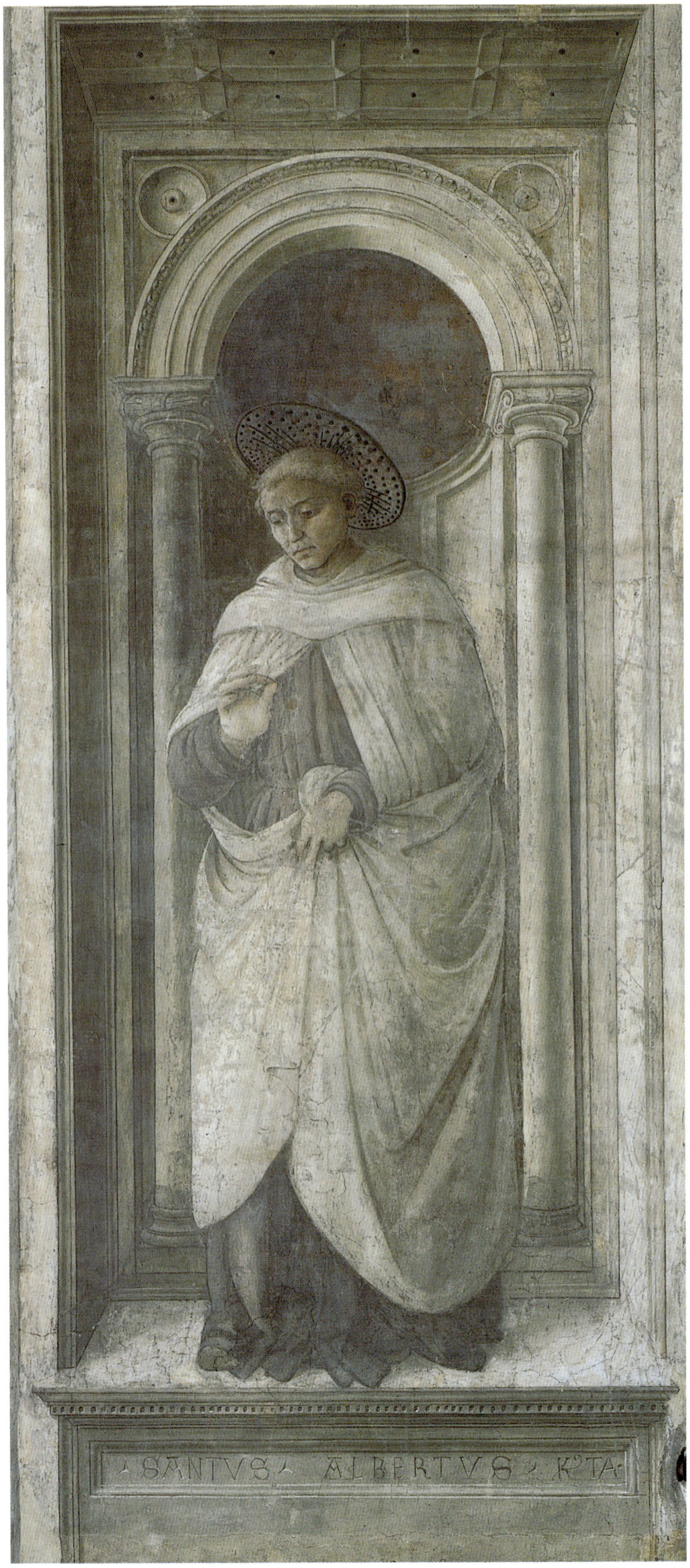

154 Filippo Lippi, *St. Alberto of Trapani*, late 1450s, Prato, Cathedral of Santo Stefano, main chapel.

something to his Carmelite perspective on representing the sacred. I shall conclude with a look at Carmelite mountain imagery in his landscapes.

THEATRICALITY AND THE ASCENSION DAY *SACRA RAPPRESENTAZIONE*

The Ascension Day *sacra rappresentazione* staged each year in Santa Maria del Carmine by the Compagnia di Sant'Agnese had a significant impact on the way that Lippi visualized – or rendered visible – sacred subjects in his paintings.[3] One has only to read through Bishop Abraham of Suzdal's long description of the 1439 play (provided in full in Chapter 2) to recognize the many features in Fra Filippo's art that derive from the dramatic enactment. Lippi's angels – in particular, those in the Barbadori, Sant'Ambrogio, and San Lorenzo altarpieces (see figs. 103, 91, and 104) – resonate with Bishop Abraham's evocation of the "four young children, resembling angels in their head-dress and clothes, each with a flowering branch in his hand" and the "two children dressed as angels, with golden wings." The account books of the Compagnia di Sant'Agnese inform us that the young actors representing angels in the play had wings made of ostrich and peacock feathers – as does the angel Gabriel in Lippi's Barberini and Munich *Annunciations* (see figs. 121 and 220).[4] The choir of music-making angels in the Vatican *Coronation of the Virgin* is akin to the "throng of little children who represent angels with pipes and lutes and lots of tiny bells" that encircles God the Father in the heavens in Bishop Abraham's description.

Lippi's conventional means of portraying a divine intervention by God or Christ in the earthly realm was indebted to Brunelleschi's wizardry in engineering the complicated hoisting mechanisms and lighting devices used in the Ascension Day drama. Lippi's half-length, fully modeled God and Christ figures, surrounded by angels and cherubs, emanating rays of light, hovering above a cloud, have something in common with Bishop Abraham's descriptions of God the Father revealed in the heavens, and Christ's ascension from the Mount of Olives: "Heaven open[s] and God the Father [is seen] floating above, suspended in the air in wondrous fashion, in a great light, which comes from innumerable lamps; little boys, who represent the heavenly Powers, move around him." Christ is drawn aloft toward a suspended cloud and upon reaching it, he disappears and then is dramatically revealed as "two Angels bow before him on the left and the right, and in the same instant the *nuvola* is lit up by a multitude of lights which send their splendour everywhere." See, for example, the God and Christ figures in Lippi's Medici chapel *Adoration of the Christ Child* (see fig. 178), the Munich *Annunciation* (see fig. 220), the *Martyrdom of St. Stephen* in the Prato Duomo (see fig. 148), the *Death of St. Jerome* (see fig. 180), and the *Annunciation* in the Spoleto Duomo.

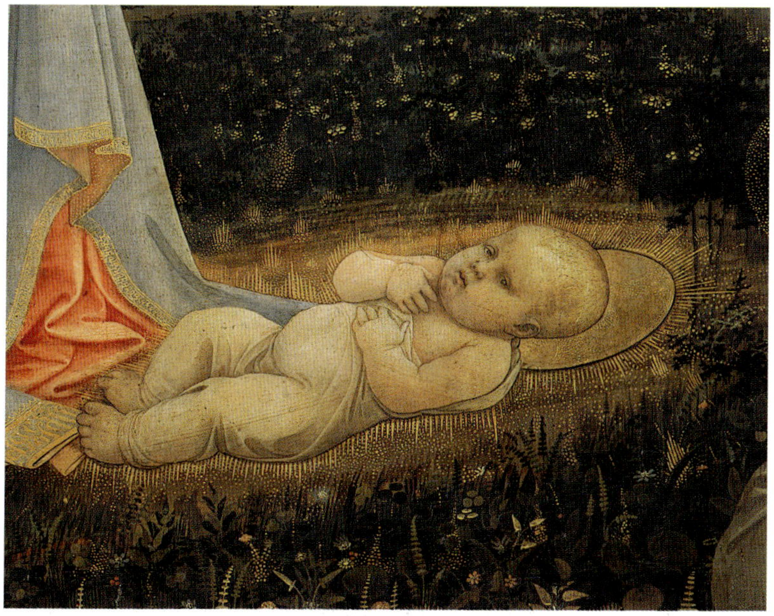

155 Filippo Lippi, *Adoration of the Christ Child*, detail of fig. 171.

The artist's conception of divine illumination and his technical means of representing it may well be related to the effects produced by the five hundred clay lamps, the glass containers full of colored water through which light was passed, the dyed parchment lanterns, and the lighted aureole surrounding God the Father used in the *sacra rappresentazione*.[5] Take, for example, Lippi's *Adoration of the Christ Child* scenes (see figs. 169, 171, and 178) where an intense glow reflects off the smooth pale skin of the Madonna and Child and golden ogee flames descend from the Holy Spirit and dance around the numinous Christ Child (fig. 155). There is also his unique depiction of light on reflective surfaces through a dense sprinkling of little gilded buttons (fig. 156).

156 Filippo Lippi, *Madonna and Child with the Birth of the Virgin*, detail of fig. 168, with St. Anne in bed.

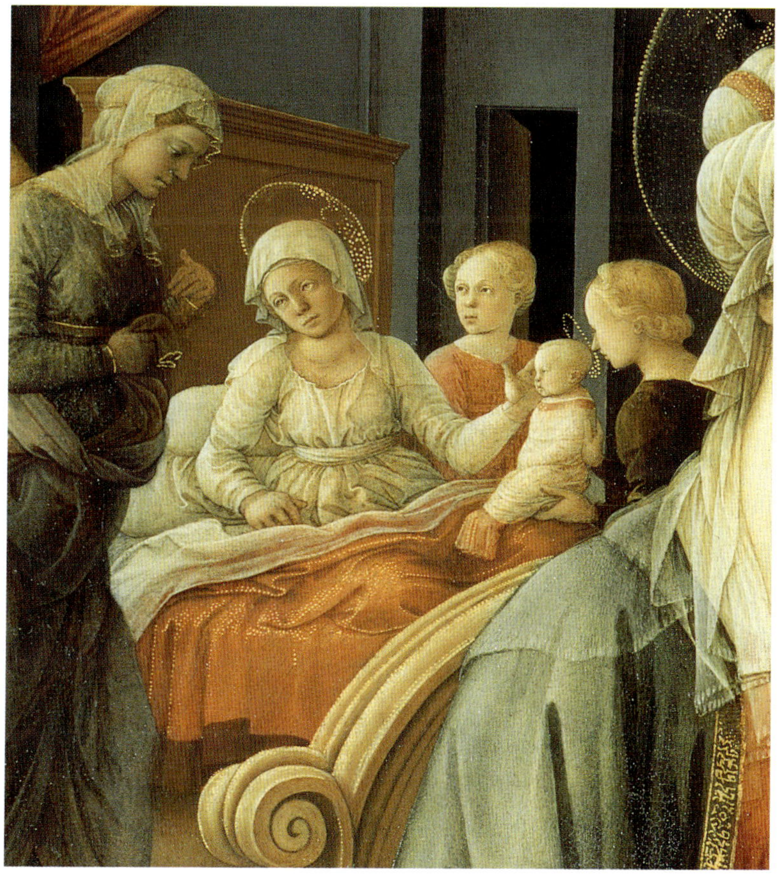

Detailed descriptions of the illumination devices used in the play, found by Cyrilla Barr, were provided by one of the officers of the Compagnia di Sant'Agnese in 1467, Neri di Bicci. The iron frame that supported both Christ and the two angels during the ascension was called the *seste*, and the wooden mandorla that enframed Christ was the *sole*, lit with a lantern "of parchment, dyed red, with a small lamp behind."[6] Neri also listed the *stella nuova*, which was "a large wooden star standing above the cloud in an edifice made of cloth and decorated with painted angels, in which structure is hidden the said star of wood which has many rays and at each ray is a square copper lantern with much fireworks which is lit when Christ enters the cloud and not before."[7] These mechanisms seem to be illustrated in the *Zibaldone* (c. 1470; figs. 157 and 158) of Buonaccorso Ghiberti. The *stella nuova* and lighting scheme bring to mind Lippi's Coronation scene in the epicenter of the apse of the Duomo in Spoleto (see fig. 165). God the Father sits enthroned within a golden orb emanating shimmering rays of light. The Virgin's face is bathed in the light, and is almost as bright as the reflecting gold leaf of the orb behind her. The *seste* and *sole* devices seem to have been borrowed more explicitly in the narrative fresco of the *Dormition of the Virgin* below (figs. 159 and 161), where the Virgin rises

157 and 158 Buonaccorso Ghiberti, drawings of (*left*) an illumination device and (*right*) the stage machinery used in the Ascension Day *sacra rappresentazione* in Santa Maria del Carmine, from his *zibaldone* c. 1470, Florence, Biblioteca Nazionale, MS. Banco Rari 228, c. 115r and v.

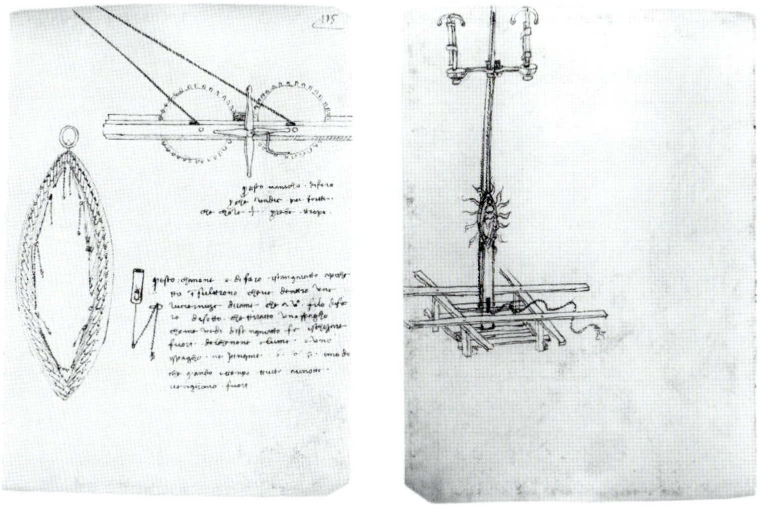

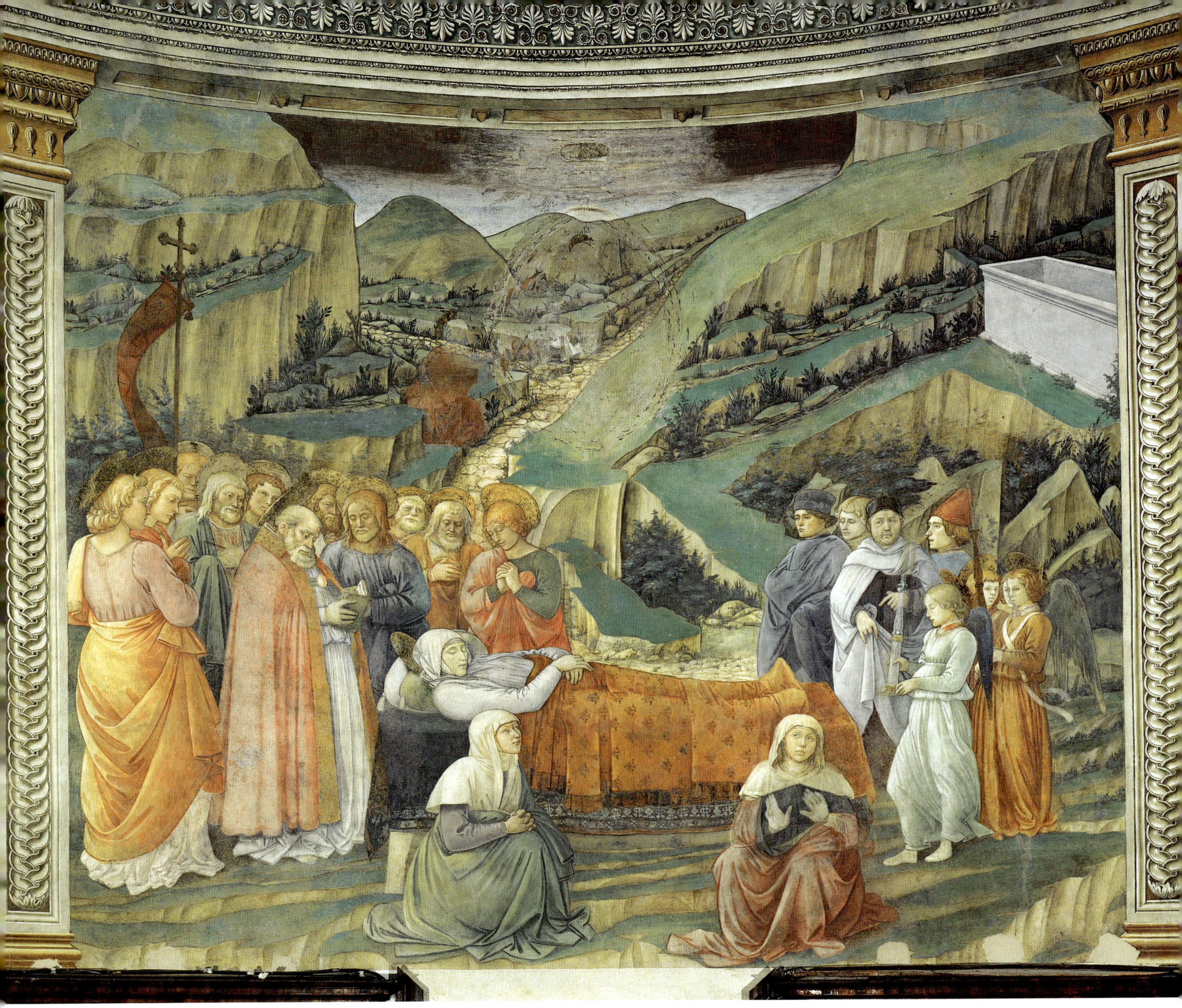

159 Filippo Lippi, *Dormition of the Virgin*, 1466–69, Spoleto, Cathedral of Santa Maria Assunta.

to the heavens in a mandorla (painted *a secco* and hence now barely discernible).

Even the fact that this mandorla was painted *a secco* is telling. It is as though Lippi, the artist, conceived of his pictorial narratives in a dramatic way, with events unfolding in time and space. First the Virgin died and then – *miracolo!* – through a divine intervention painted *a secco*, she was transported to heaven. The angel who comes to speak with the young Baptist in the wilderness in the Prato fresco (figs. 160 and 162) entered (and vanished from) the narrative composition in a similarly theatrical manner. Lippi devised the stage – a rocky desertscape with the young Baptist kneeling down in prayer – and then, as the true fresco set into the drying plaster on the chapel wall – *miracolo!* – the angel appeared from the celestial realm and delivered his message (that is, was realized *a secco* in pigments superimposed on the frescoed scene).

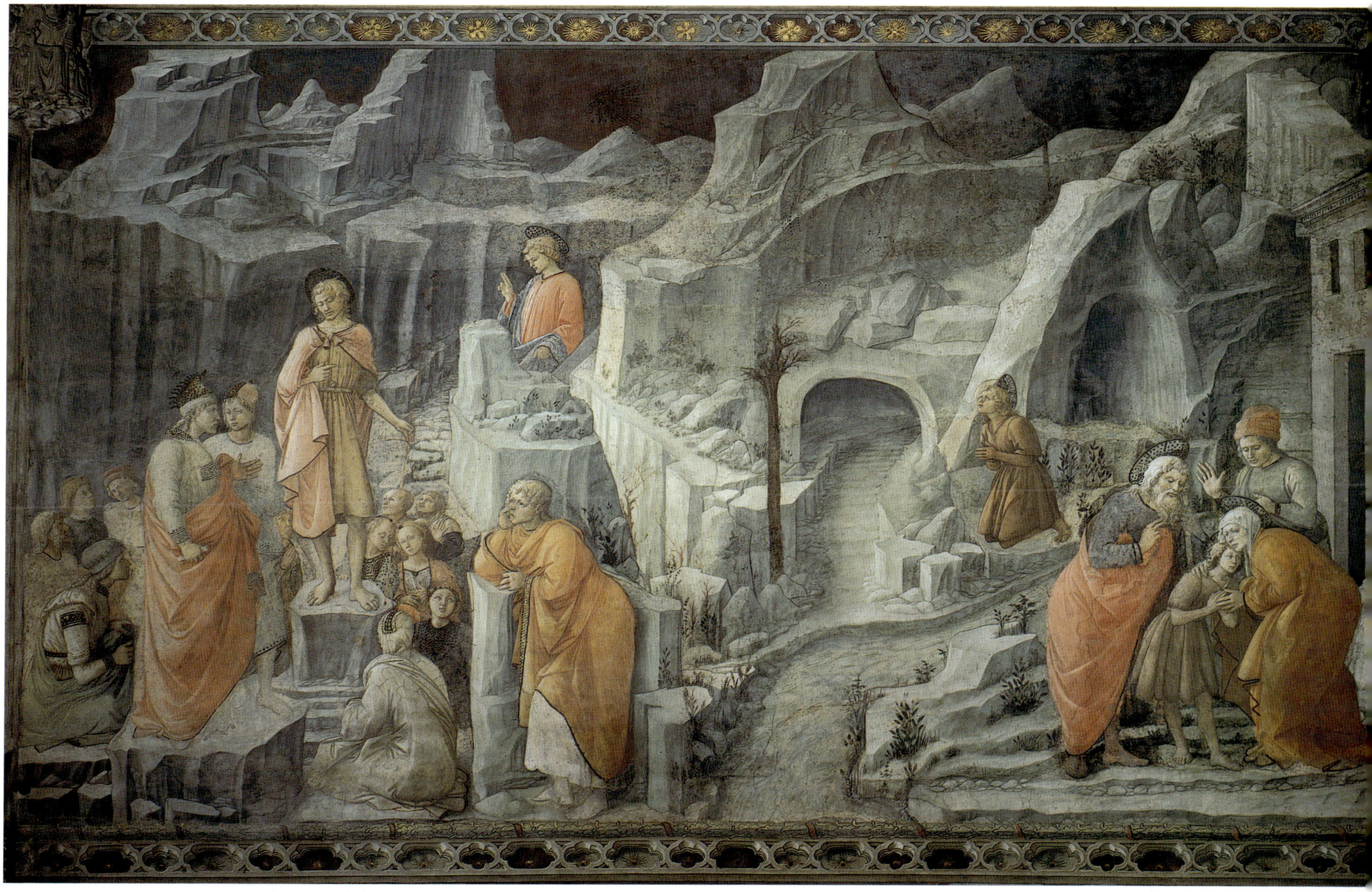

160 Filippo Lippi, *St. John in the Wilderness*, late 1450s, Prato, Cathedral of Santo Stefano, main chapel.

There are other ways that the Ascension Day *sacra rappresentazione* left its imprint on Lippi's pictorial idiom. His paintings leave one with the powerful impression of being staged. The figures are fully realized in three dimensions and are endowed with the effects of self-consciousness and an awareness of the presence of a viewing audience on the other side of the picture plane. This is particularly true of the attendant figures – who, not immediately engaged in the principal dramatic action of the narrative, as though lacking in concentration, seem to slip out of their assigned roles. Baxandall has made the connection between a figure type found frequently in *quattrocento* painting that directly engages with the beholder and the *festaiuolo* in contemporary *sacre rappresentazioni*. The *festaiuolo* mediated between the audience and the religious drama being staged.[8] These mediating figures abound in Lippi's paintings – such as the attendant angels in the San Lorenzo *Annunciation* (fig. 163) and the young Baptist in the *Adoration of the Christ Child* for the Medici chapel (see fig. 178). *Festaiuoli* were also abundantly present in the Carmine Ascension play. By 1488, each of the different sets on which the various scenes of the play were enacted had its own *festaiuolo*.[9] There was one for the city of Jerusalem represented as a castle at the left of the *ponte*, another for the Mount of Olives rising to the right, another for heaven, some fifty-six feet up and set back above the *cappella maggiore* on a wooden *tribuna*, and a fourth for *paradiso* – distinct from heaven, apparently constructed somewhere above it.

Lippi's very tendency to organize the pictorial space of his compositions into an amalgam of separate spatial cells is reflective of these numerous stage-settings of the Ascension play.[10] In just this way the narrative unfolds across the expanse of the wall space in Lippi's two major fresco cycles in Prato and Spoleto. This is apparent particularly in Spoleto where the scenes from the life of the Virgin are set within an illusionistic architectural frame that runs along a semi-circular strip of wall space in the

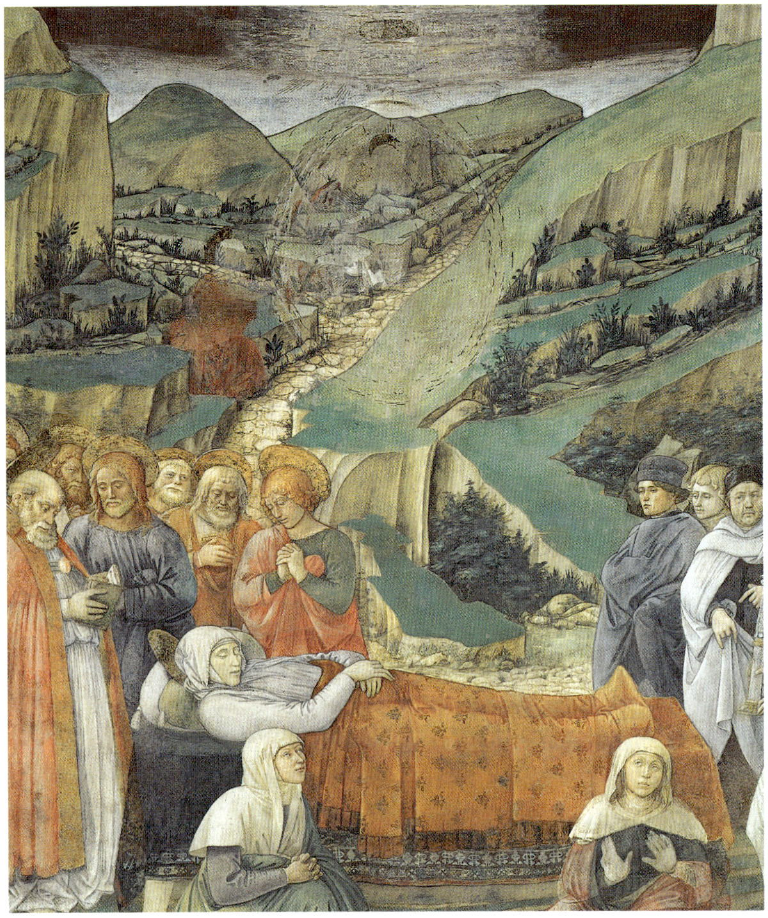

161 Filippo Lippi, *Dormition of the Virgin*, detail of fig. 159, with the fugitive *a secco* painting.

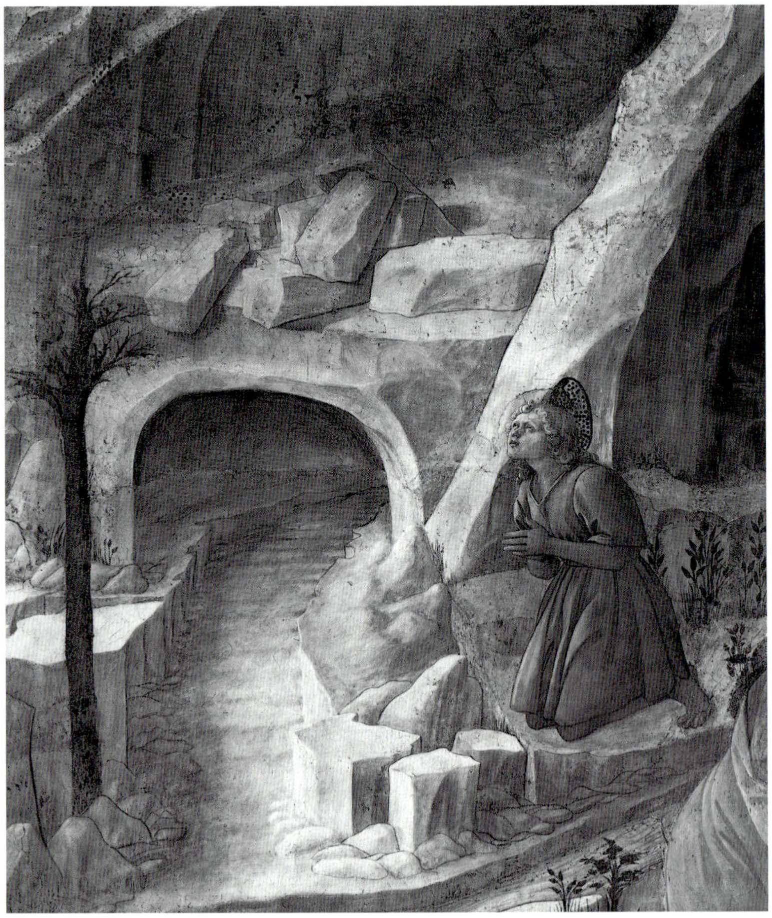

162 Filippo Lippi, *St. John in the Wilderness*, detail of fig. 160.

apse of the Duomo (fig. 164). The drama reaches a climax in the bowl of the apse above (see fig. 165) and is played out by monumental figures. (Is it mere coincidence that the crumbling manger wall in the Nativity is considered to be modeled after the old Roman theater in Spoleto?[11])

The Carmine Ascension Day drama was not the only one staged in Florence, nor the only *sacra rappresentazione* that made use of Brunelleschi's complex lighting and hoisting devices.[12] Bishop Abraham of Suzdal reported seeing a spectacular performance of the Annunciation mystery.[13] He noted how the Angel Gabriel descended from the heavens (located in a chamber set up against the inner wall above the entrance) down the nave of the church along a lengthy cable. Gabriel reached the Virgin's bedroom atop the stone choir screen and then, after delivering his message, returned to the heavens in a shower of fireworks, with his wings beating to and fro like those of a bird. Vasari, too, described an Annunciation play at the monastery church of San Felice in Piazza.[14] According to Vasari, Brunelleschi designed the heavenly sphere which hung from the rafters, complete with a rotating choir of angels suspended below and an illuminated mandorla device which transported Gabriel down to a platform where the Virgin's bedchamber was set up. It is very likely that Fra Filippo frequented these other dramatic productions in Florence, and that they too had an impact on his religious representation. It was the Carmine Ascension Day drama, however, staged in Fra Filippo's own monastery, which appears to have had the most profound impact upon the painter's work. The descriptions of these plays, inventories of the equipment used to stage them, and the few scripts that survive from later productions[15] indicate that it was in the Carmine *sacra rappresentazione* that the full vertical dimensions of the church were utilized in setting up multiple stages for the various scenes of the drama. And in the Carmine Ascension, the visual element, rather than the words of the dialogue, appears to have been the primary dramatic means of presenting the religious mystery.

NEW PICTORIAL CONVENTIONS: THE BARTOLINI TONDO

In Chapter 6, I demonstrated how Fra Filippo Lippi was among the most innovative painters of his generation, unhinging traditional iconographic conventions, blurring the distinctions between pictorial genres, and forcing provocative questions

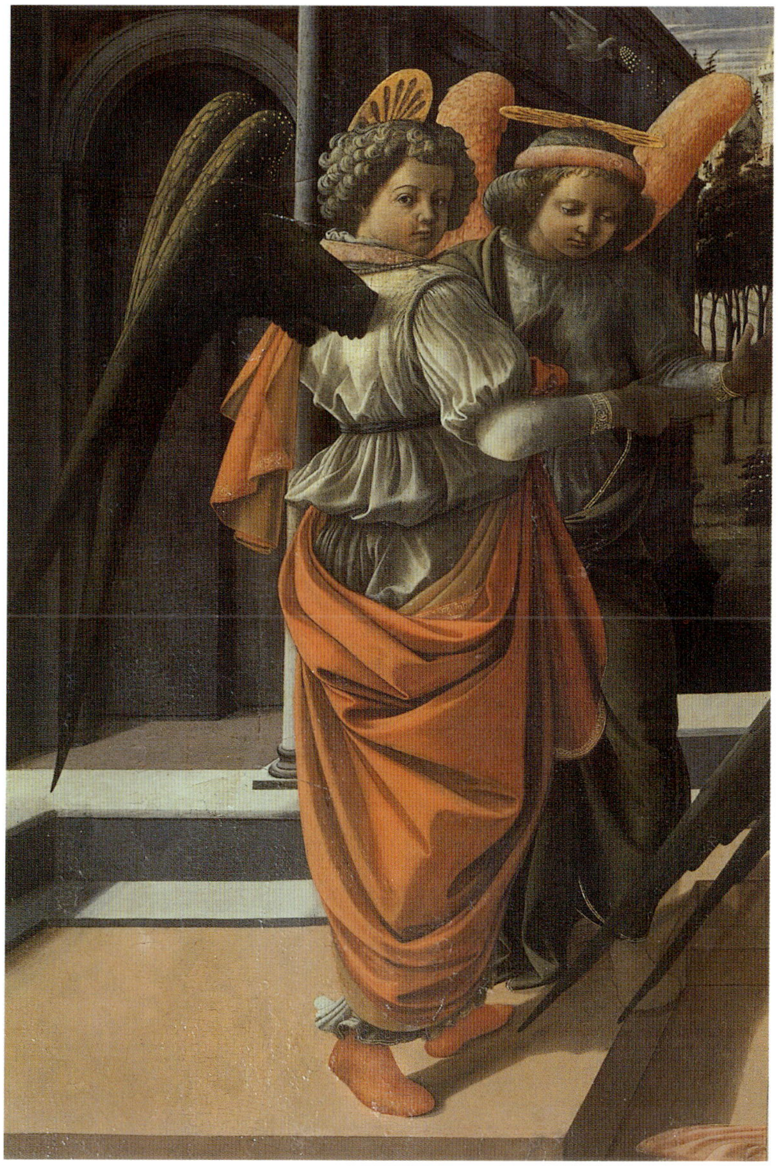

163 Filippo Lippi, *Annunciation*, detail of fig. 104.

regarding religious painting's claims to represent. It would be a gross exaggeration to insist that Lippi's Carmelite orientation to religious subjects was the significant factor in this process, but that it contributed may indeed have been the case. Take, for example, Lippi's fascination with framing and with the relationship between the pictorial space and the beholder's space in his religious paintings. This interest, found also in the relief work of Donatello, could have been enhanced by Lippi's experiences as a *frate dipintore* that gave him insight into both secular and sacred perspectives, and the necessary mediations required when maneuvering between the two positions. There are two instances, however, where I believe that the painter's Carmelite perspective directly influenced the novel way he approached his subject matter. One is the Bartolini tondo, while the other centers on the Adoration of the Christ Child paintings that Lippi produced in the last two decades of his life.

The Bartolini tondo *Madonna and Child* (see fig. 168), now in the Pitti Palace, was painted in 1452–53 for the Florentine banker and statesman Lionardo Bartolini.[16] It may seem odd to suggest Carmelite precedents for a picture that owes its most radical characteristic to secular painting conventions. The tondo form, the themes of birth and fecundity, and the possible intention of having the family coat of arms painted on the reverse of the panel all suggest that the tondo was intended to commemorate the birth of one of the Bartolini children and derives from the *desco da parto* tradition. But there is also a deliberate doubling up as a Madonna and Child image. Here, however, narrative – usually relegated to the predella zone of a devotional image – is presented as the backdrop. The Virgin's low-backed throne affords a view into the distance, where one beholds narrative action transpiring within a series of linked settings reminiscent of the *Jacob and Esau* relief on Ghiberti's newly installed "Gates of Paradise" (fig. 166).[17] In a scene of the Nativity of the Virgin, we see St. Anne's bedroom with the curtains drawn back from the bed and the swaddled new-born being given to her mother. Other women enter from the right, bearing gifts of food and livestock.[18] In the upper-right background, Joachim and Anne meet during an earlier moment in the story – a scene known as the "Meeting at the Golden Gate" (fig. 167). This pictorial treatment represents a collapsing of what art historians sometimes refer to as the "iconic" and "narrative" modes (or *imago* and *istoria*). The Virgin and Child are no longer isolated against a gold ground or framed within an architectural niche, but appear with narrative references integrated into the constructed space around them. Fra Filippo had experimented earlier with this approach in the Tarquinia *Madonna and Child* (see fig. 6), where the Annunciation scenery is represented in the background. It may be no mere coincidence that both these pictures involve Marian mysteries that were of particular significance to the Carmelite Order.

The Carmelites had two convents in the city of Jerusalem. By the fifteenth century, one of these, dedicated to St. Anne, had acquired a formidable heritage:

> The Convent of St. Anne in Jerusalem, facing the Temple of Solomon, [is located] at the bottom of the street that leads to the Gate of St. Stephen, on the left-hand side. And this is that place where the Virgin was born, that place that was given to our hermit friars thirty years after the death of St. James.[19]

The Carmelites claimed to have settled in the very house where the Virgin had been born, late in the first century AD (the Apostle St. James had died in the year 44). They had a second convent in Jerusalem located at the Golden Gate, that sacred city gate where Anne and Joachim had been united after the double annunciation of the Virgin's birth. This meeting at the Golden Gate was considered to be the moment of the Virgin's Immaculate Conception: "In Jerusalem at the Golden Gate, where Anne and Joachim, the parents of the Virgin Mary, met each other,

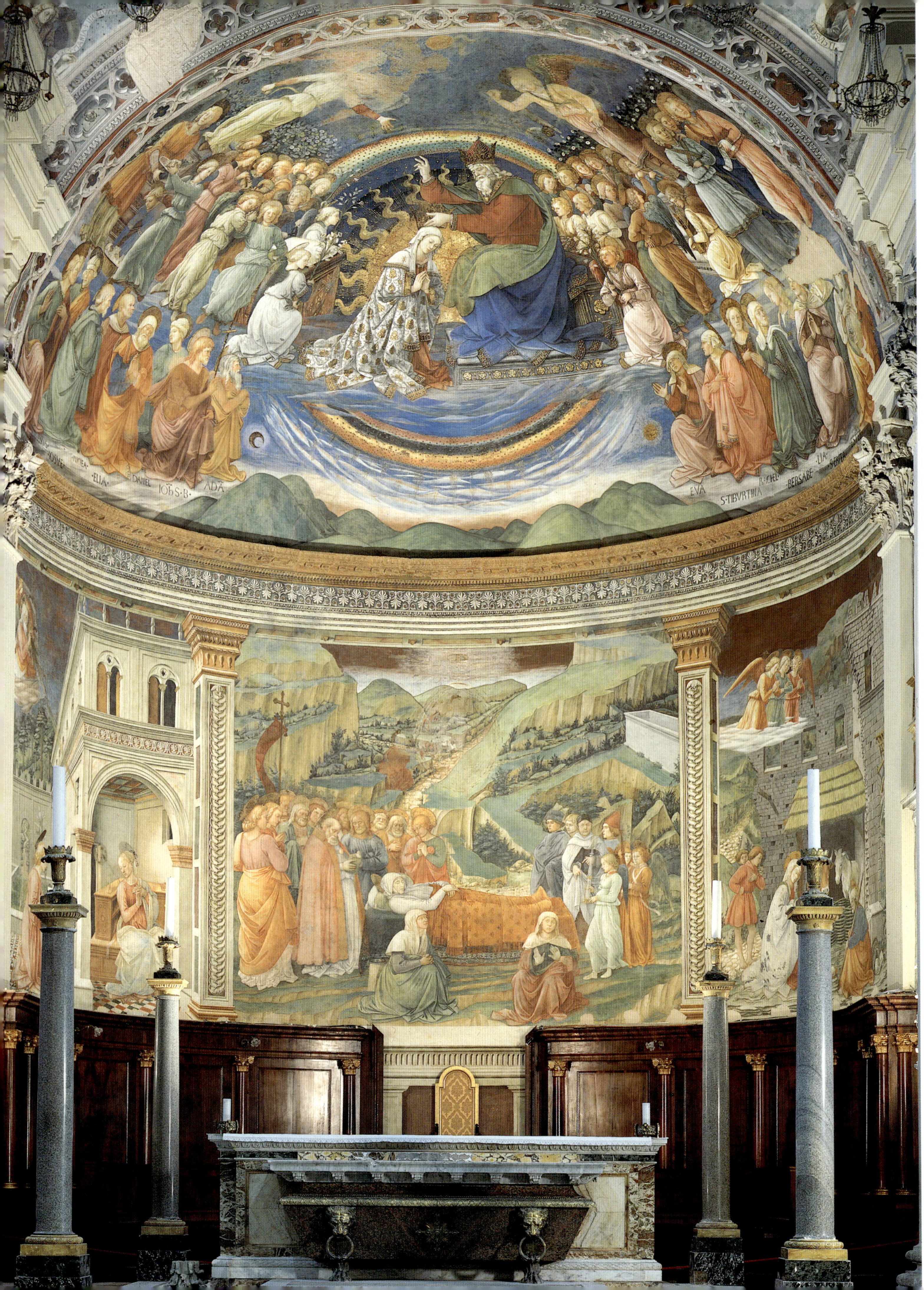
IOSVE
ELIA
DANIEL
IOБS·B
ADĀ
EVA
S·TIBVRTINA
RACHEL
BERSABE
LIA

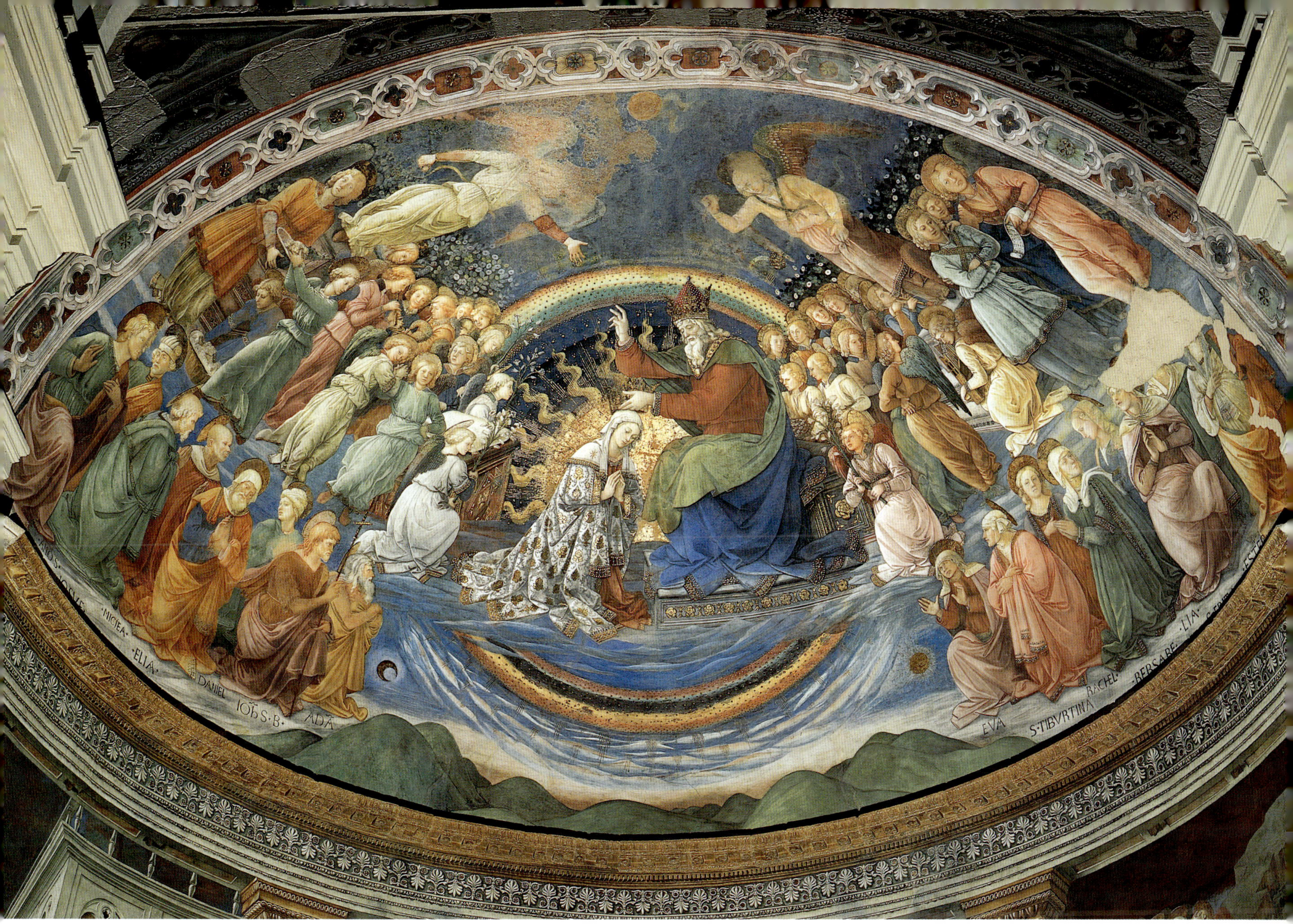

165 Filippo Lippi, *Coronation of the Virgin*, 1466–69, Spoleto, Cathedral of Santa Maria Assunta.

they piously conceded and built a church there, in honor of the Virgin, where she was conceived."[20]

In this way, these most sacred places associated with the Virgin's conception and birth were physically appropriated by the Carmelites and ideologically imprinted by the Carmelite "Doctrine of Origin," which had the friars present in the Holy Land at the time of the advent of Christ, as discussed in Chapter 2. Moreover, the Order was dedicated to the Virgin. The friars claimed that St. Anne had carried the Virgin to Mount Carmel while she was still a baby and that she had later returned to visit the friars at their hermitage there. They dedicated their oratory to the Virgin and lived in celibacy in her honor. She was the Carmelite "Patrona" and "Matrona." Ludovico Saggi suggests that the Carmelite appropriation of the Virgin's home turf helped to advance their claim that they had been "tied to Mary ever since that very first moment of their [and her!] terrestrial existence."[21] This Carmelite privileged access to the Virgin, to her relics and sacred *loci*, was the subject of numerous Carmelite representations, and conditioned the descriptive language in which the Virgin was invoked.[22]

The imagery in the Bartolini tondo is organized in such a way that the Virgin and Child trigger an immediate association with the events that transpired at the sites of both Jerusalem Carmelite convents. The Virgin and Child are represented lifesize and are pushed up against the picture plane. The Virgin meets the eye of the beholder squarely and is intimately accessible to the viewer's gaze. Thus the beholder enters the spaces of the background narratives by grace of the Virgin's invitation, through the Virgin's eye. The tondo becomes a round window, a gratifyingly large peep-hole into St. Anne's bedroom and surroundings. The birthing chamber is represented as a private female space, which only nurses, servants, and female

164 View of the apse of the Cathedral of Santa Maria Assunta, Spoleto, 1466–69.

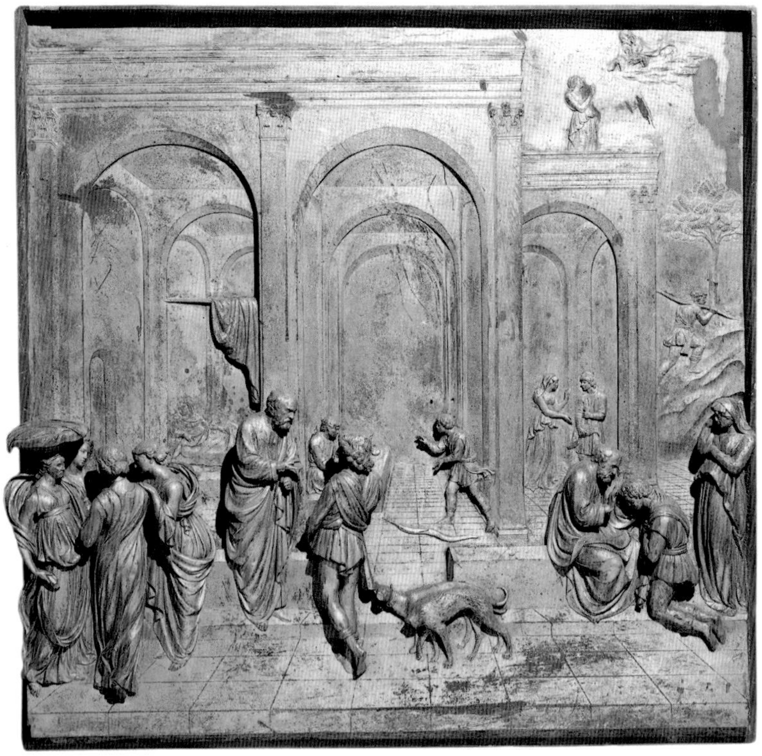

166 Lorenzo Ghiberti, *Jacob and Esau*, c. 1429–37, installed in 1452, from the "East Doors" of the Florentine Baptistery, now in Florence, Museo dell'Opera del Duomo.

companions may frequent. This is a private viewing of the Virgin's house.[23] Even more exclusive is the view onto the meeting at the Golden Gate. Joachim and Anne are all alone as they embrace at the Golden Gate (which is more like a doorway off the courtyard of a private residence). The viewer becomes the sole witness to the Immaculate Conception.[24]

The Carmelite influence, I believe, lies in the nature of the relationships set up between the foreground and background subjects. The visual linkage established between the Virgin and Child group and the narrative scenes of the Birth of the Virgin and the Meeting of Joachim and Anne at the Golden Gate, depended upon a Carmelite chain of associations and a privileged Carmelite intimacy with these historic places in the city of Jerusalem. Similar Carmelite associative links function in other works by Fra Filippo. In the Trivulzio *Madonna of Humility* (see fig. 53), the Virgin and Child are represented in the company of an aged St. Anne. In the *Death of St. Jerome* (see fig. 180), a scene of the Nativity of Christ is painted in the background, alluding to St. Jerome's burial which was considered to have been close to the site where Christ was born, in the Church of the Nativity in Bethlehem – where the Carmelites also had a convent. In the Tarquinia *Madonna and Child* (see fig. 6), an Annunciation setting is visible in the background behind the Virgin and Christ Child. The viewer is thus transported into the Madonna's private bedchamber in her home in the city of Nazareth, where, once again, the Carmelites had a convent.

NEW PICTORIAL GENRES: THE ADORATION OF THE CHRIST CHILD

From the mid-1450s through the mid-1460s, Filippo Lippi evolved a new presentation of the Virgin and Child that became popular in the second half of the *quattrocento* in Florence. He created the theme of the Adoration of the Christ Child, or "Nostra Donna che adora il Figliuolo," to use the fifteenth-century Florentine nomenclature.[25] The composition and iconography were grounded in two traditions: St. Bridget of Sweden's account of her vision of the Virgin adoring the Christ Child lying upon the ground, and early Renaissance Tuscan depictions of the Nativity. Fra Filippo transformed the subject into a distinct devotional image set within an elaborate forested landscape with a rich imagery of sylvan flora, geological features, and atmosphere, which functioned as visual metaphors for the Incarnation, penitence, and eremitical religious devotion.[26] In

167 Filippo Lippi, "Meeting at the Golden Gate," detail from the *Madonna and Child with the Birth of the Virgin* (fig. 168).

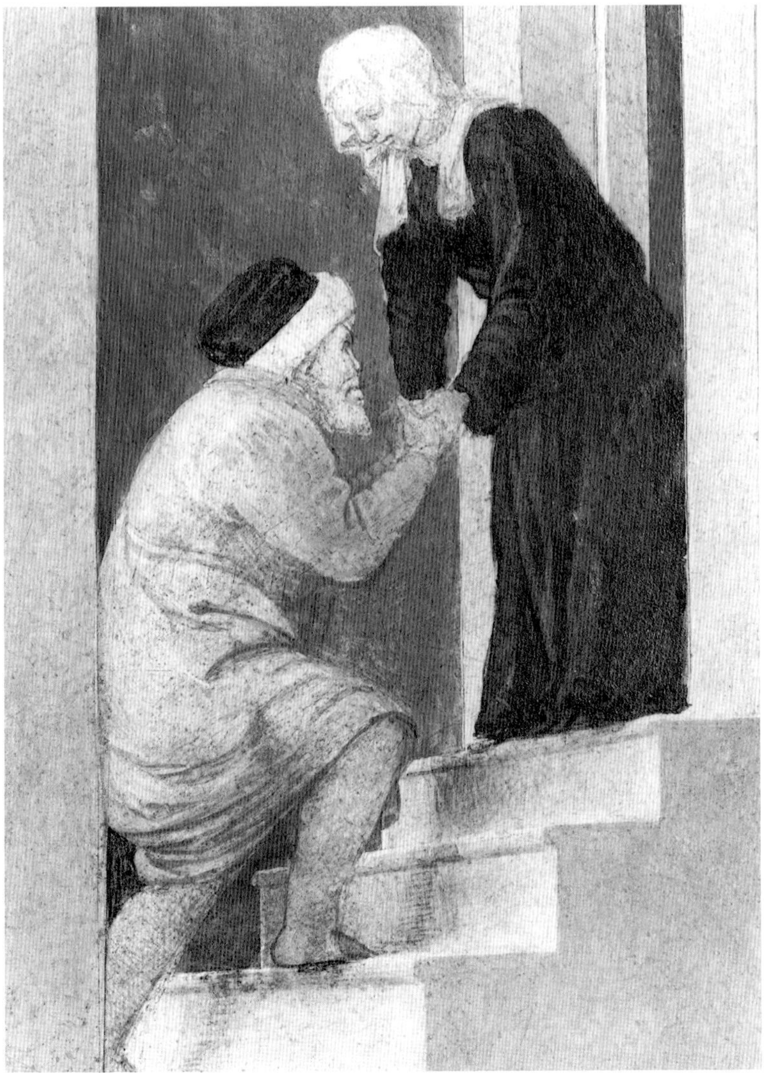

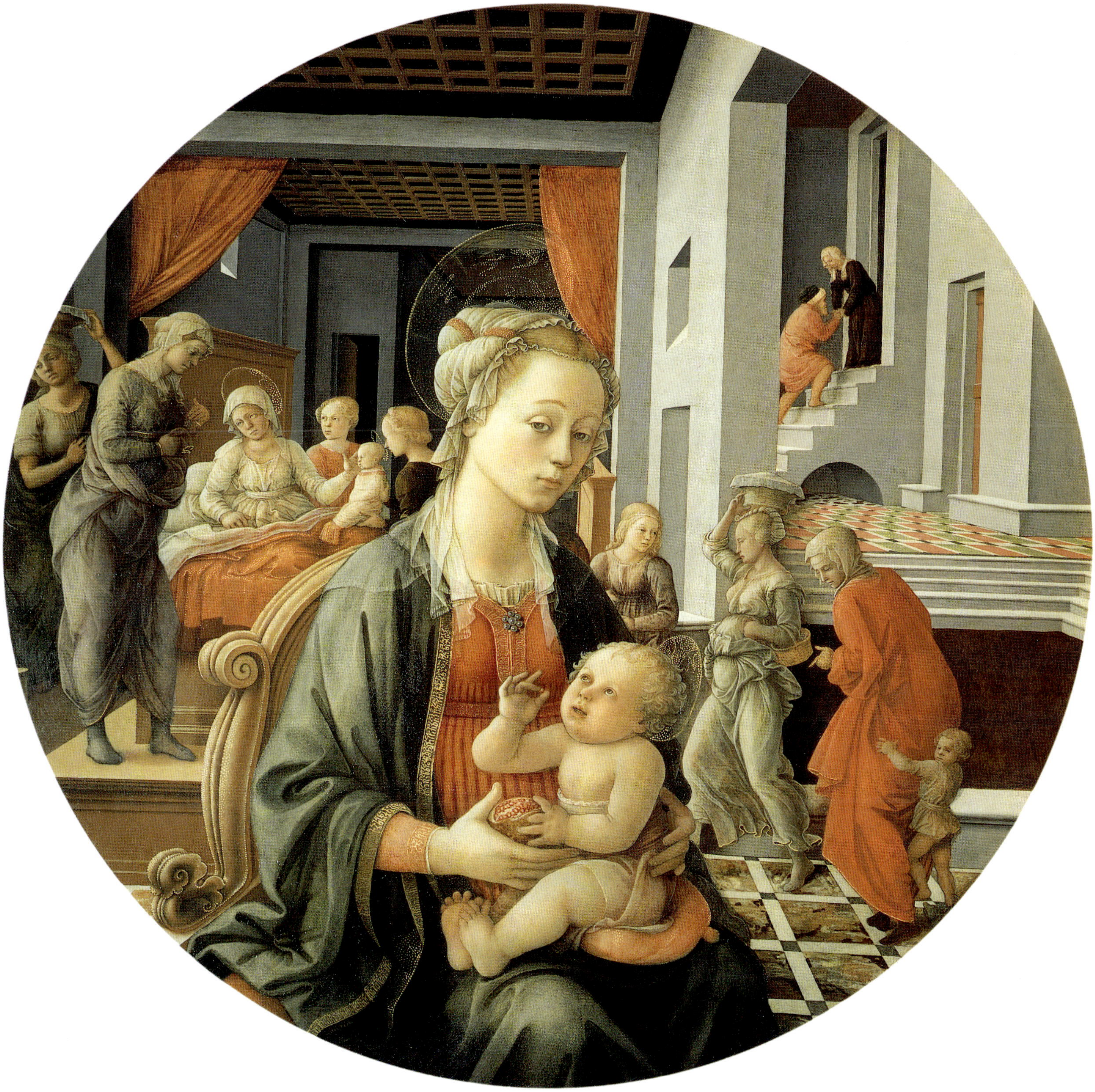

168 Filippo Lippi, *Madonna and Child with the Birth of the Virgin* (the Bartolini tondo), 1452–53, Florence, Galleria Palatina (Palazzo Pitti).

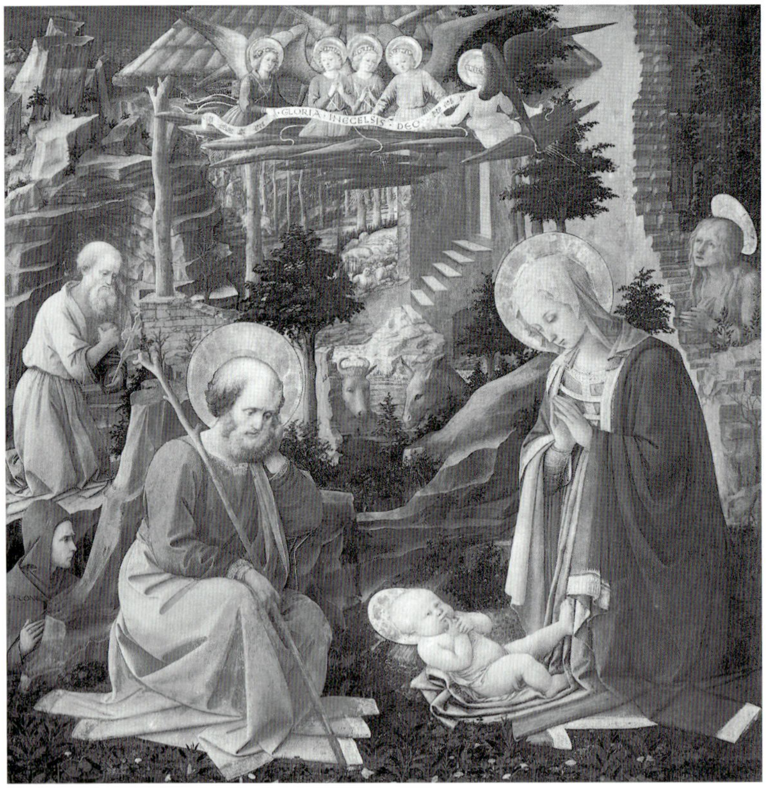

169 Filippo Lippi, Annalena *Adoration of the Christ Child*, c. 1455, Florence, Uffizi.

addition to this interesting development in contemporary religious devotional imagery, the Adoration of the Christ Child paintings offered a new means of visualizing the wilderness, of rendering the landscape within a painted composition, and, more generally, of representing nature.

Fra Filippo's first version of this new type, probably made for the Benedictine Annalena nunnery around 1455, was ostensibly a Nativity (fig. 169). In a composition highly derivative of Uccello's 1443 design for the stained-glass window in the Florentine Duomo (fig. 170), St. Joseph is present beside the Virgin and Child, the ass and ox lie placidly in the manger, and shepherds look on, while angels bearing the inscription "Gloria in excelsis Deo" hover above. Lippi's subsequent elaborations of this type, however, omit these narrative markers – the triptych for Alfonso of Naples commissioned by Giovanni de' Medici, whose lost central panel is known only through a rapid sketch by Fra Filippo (fig. 172) and the surviving wings (fig. 173), the altarpiece for the chapel in the Palazzo Medici (fig. 178), and a painting said to have come from a cell in the Camaldoli hermitage (fig. 171), dedicated to the Baptist and patronized by Piero di Cosimo de' Medici and his wife Lucrezia Tornabuoni, built in 1463.[27]

These images are set in a dark wooded landscape where the Madonna kneels, her hands clasped together in devotion, before the Christ Child lying virtually nude upon the verdant forest

170 Paolo Uccello, *Nativity*, 1443, oculus window from the drum of the cupola of the Florentine Cathedral of Santa Maria del Fiore.

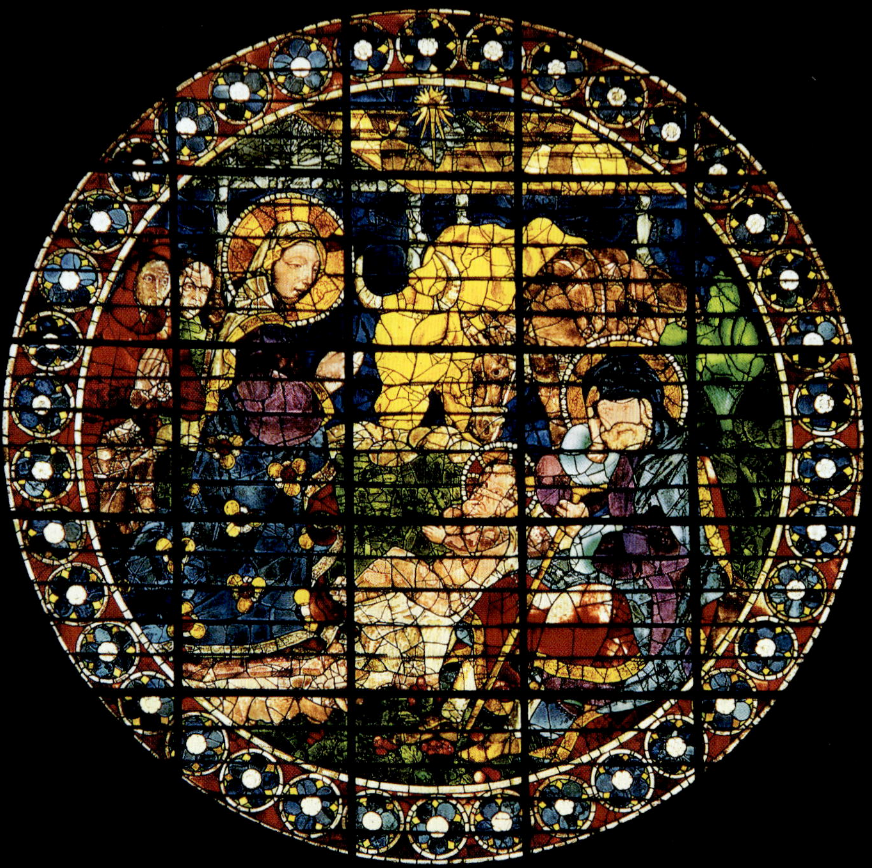

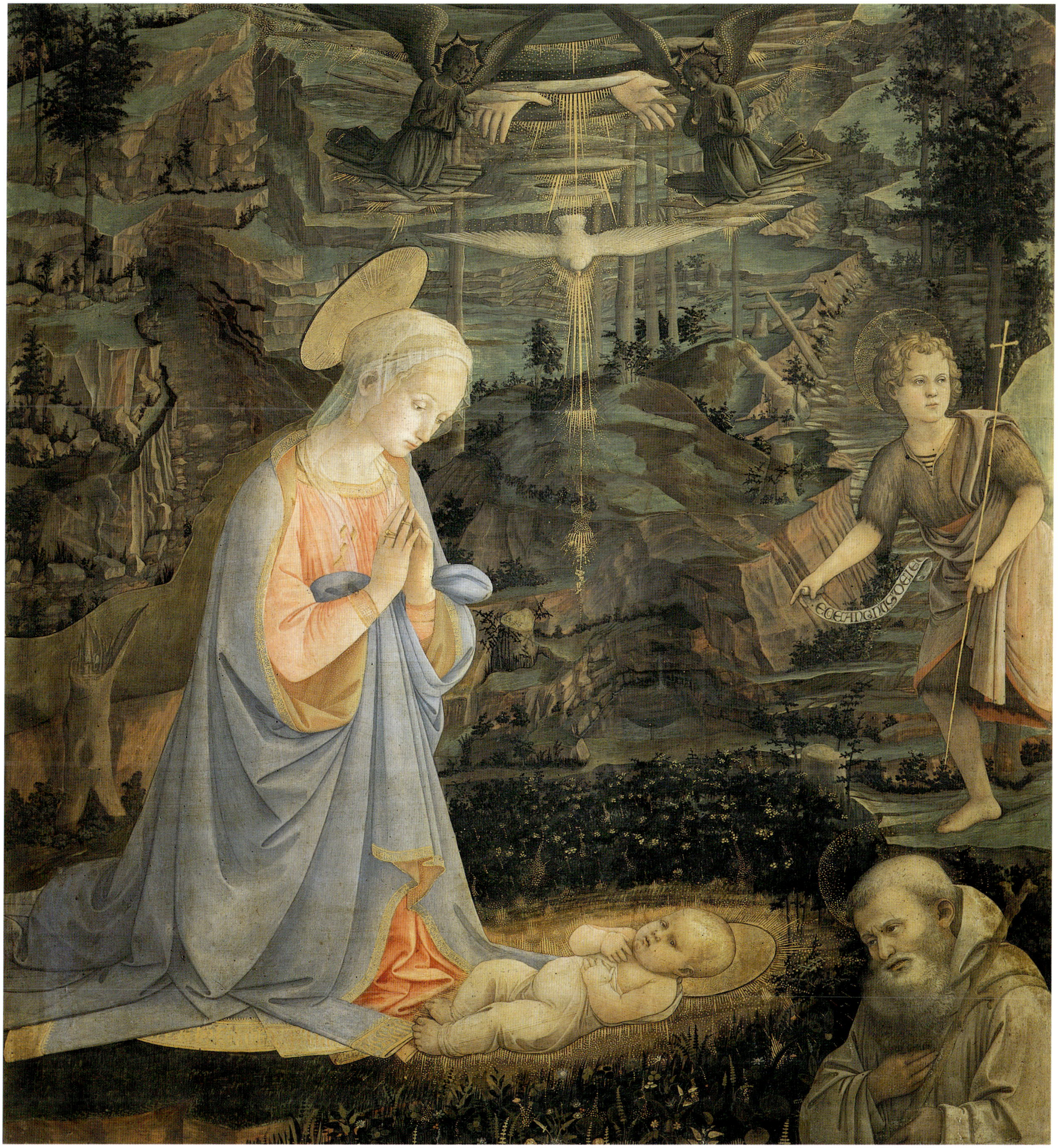

171 Filippo Lippi, *Adoration of the Christ Child*, c. 1463, from the hermitage at Camaldoli, now in Florence, Uffizi.

ground. God the Father (or simply his hands in the Camaldoli picture) appears above and the Holy Spirit descends toward the Child, proceeded by tongues of fire. The Child is surrounded by an aura of dancing gilded flames and the Virgin and Child truly glow with divine light. Hermit saints assemble along the periphery, absorbed in their contemplative or penitential acts. An interior or spiritual awareness of the Madonna and Child is suggested on the part of these saints. Only the young Baptist in the Medici chapel altarpiece recognizes the Christ Child, carrying his proclamation "Ecce Agnus Dei" on a banderole. But even his active presence does not shatter the atmosphere of concentrated contemplation and religious devotion that permeates the scene.

As Jeffrey Ruda has observed, "With regard to their original ownerships, it is extraordinary how much the establishment in these paintings of a new iconography overrode the differences of situation among an urban convent, a palace chapel, and an exceedingly austere hermitage in a real wilderness."[28] Art historians have looked for sources for this new iconography in the Old Testament Book of Isaiah, the writings of St. Bernard, in the "naturalism" of Franciscan devotional sites and religious metaphors, and in the penitential brotherhoods and Observant movements of the fourteenth and fifteenth centuries.[29] The *Adoration of the Christ Child* from the Medici Palace chapel, in particular, has been given a more precise interpretation with Cristina Acidini Luchinat's recent recovery of Gentile Becchi's Latin verses about the chapel imagery.[30] It is not my purpose here to offer a critique of the various interpretations or to propose a variant reading of these fascinating paintings. I simply wish to suggest that there is a *quattrocento* Tuscan Carmelite theme that may also help to explain the hermetic atmosphere in which the Adoration takes place. In addition, I shall try to establish why this kind of imagery would necessarily have appealed to the patrons of the paintings, despite the variant locations in which the works were displayed. For it is not merely fortuitous that three of the four images painted by Fra Filippo were Medici commissions. If I am going to argue for a Carmelite devotional strategy underlying the imagery, then this must be shown to have been compatible with Medici family interests and religious practices. I shall take my cue from the Medici chapel and the narrative and thematic context in which the *Adoration of the Christ Child* altarpiece by Lippi was originally set.

The frescoed walls of the tiny chapel were transformed into an illusionistic processional scene by Benozzo Gozzoli in 1459 (fig. 174). Richly attired courtiers accompany the three Magi on a serpentine road that takes them, moving from left to right, across three walls of the chapel, through a lush landscape filled with game and cultivated fields. This countryside recalls the Medici landed holdings north of Florence in the hilly verdant Mugello. At the rear of the cortege, at the far left of the right wall of the chapel, are portraits of the Medici family and associates among the attendants of the Magi (fig. 176).[31] Attention has been brought to the fact that these are no mere symbolic

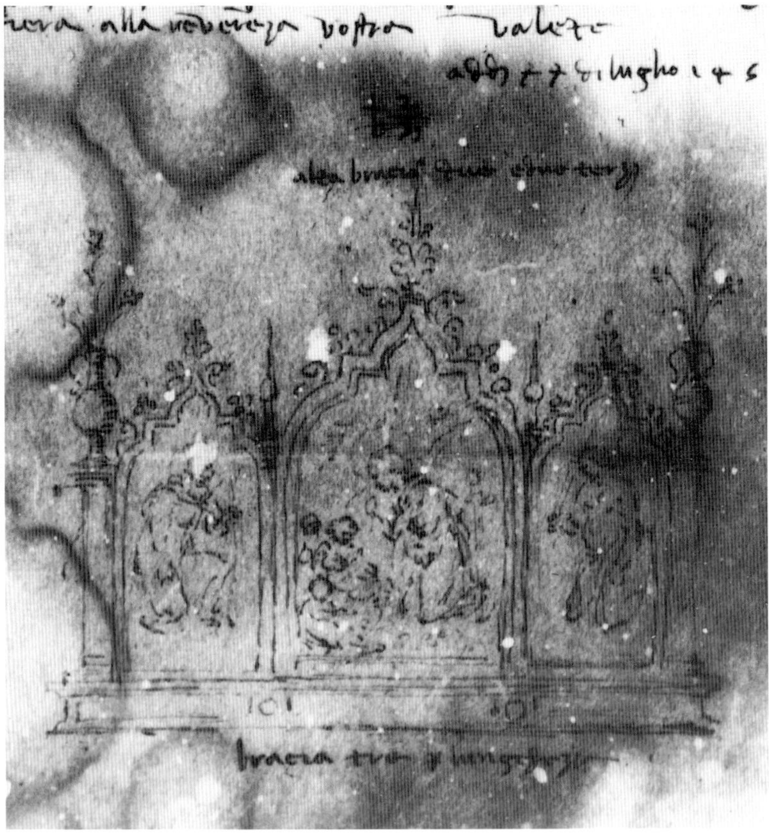

172 Filippo Lippi, drawing of the triptych for Alfonso of Naples on the letter written to Giovanni de' Medici, 1457, Florence, Archivio di Stato, MAP, f.VI, c. 255.

allusions. On the Feast of the Epiphany, members of the Compagnia de' Magi rode in procession from the Piazza della Signoria, up Via Larga, to the Piazza San Marco where, within a makeshift manger, actors represented the Virgin and the Christ Child.[32] Cosimo de' Medici and his son Giovanni were prominent members and patrons of the Compagnia. One year, Cosimo took part in the procession as one of the Magi, dressed in a fur cloak and wearing a gold crown upon his head.[33] This "performative" character of the religious experience is important, too, for understanding the significance of the Lippi *Adoration of the Christ Child* in the chapel.

Benozzo Gozzoli's Magi end their procession at the extreme right of the fresco along the left wall. They halt before the raised chancel where the altar and altarpiece were originally located. The chancel walls are adorned with frescos of singing angels who have the words of the hymn "Gloria" running through their halos (fig. 175). These angels denote that the altar space is of a very different order from the festive setting in which the procession takes place. It is a sacred space. And this progression toward the sacred is confirmed by Gentile Becchi's verses on the chapel:

> In Cosimo's chapel, where was painted in the first part the Magi, in the second the singing angels, and in the third Mary

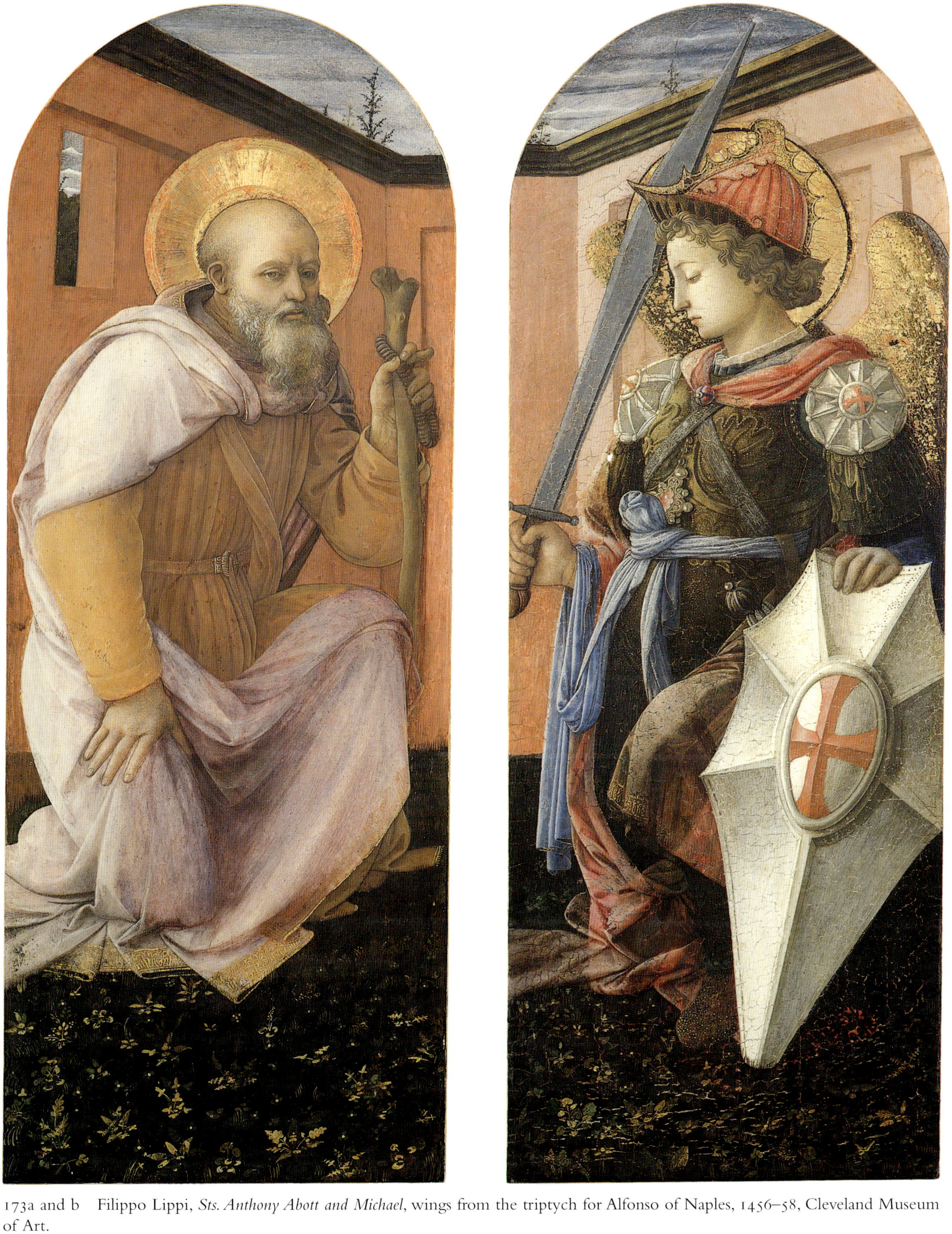

173a and b Filippo Lippi, *Sts. Anthony Abott and Michael*, wings from the triptych for Alfonso of Naples, 1456–58, Cleveland Museum of Art.

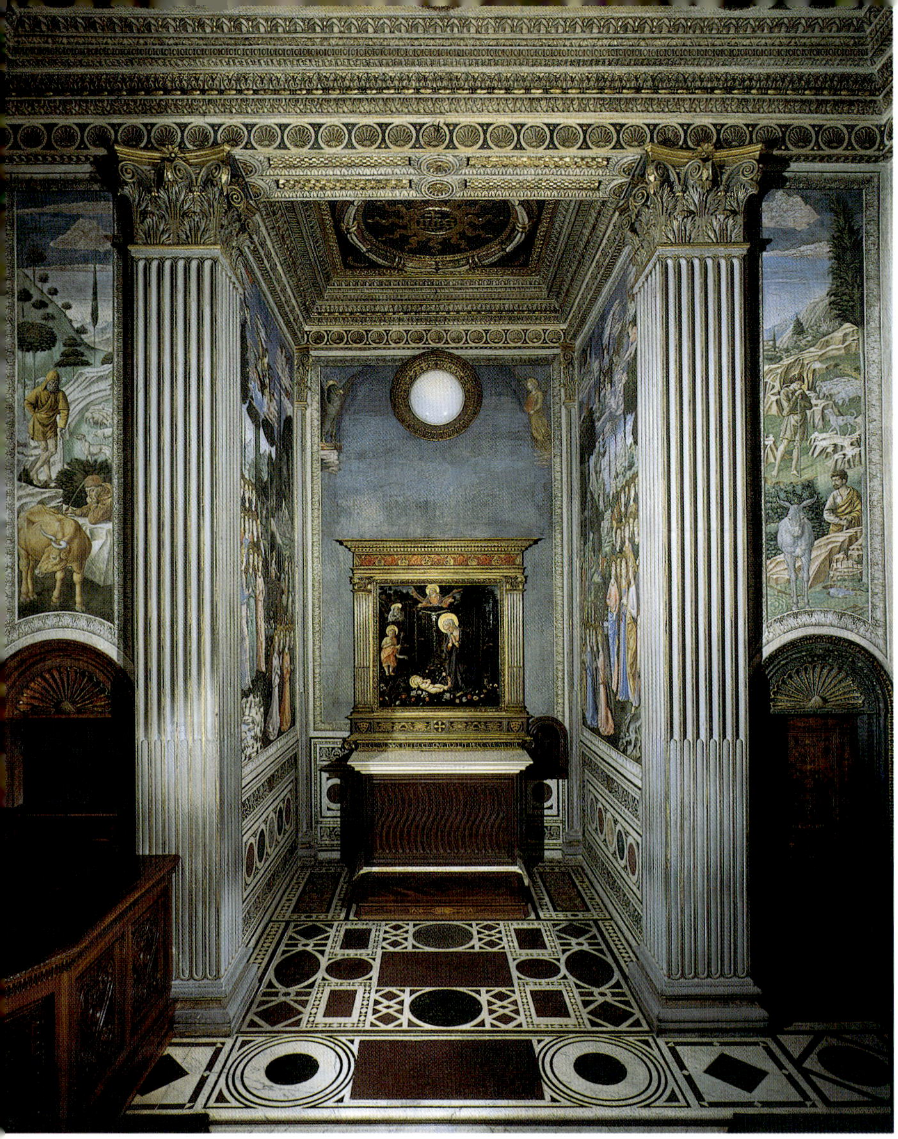

174 Chapel in the Medici palace, with a copy (c. 1470) of Filippo Lippi's Berlin *Adoration of the Christ Child* above the altar, Florence, Palazzo Medici-Riccardi.

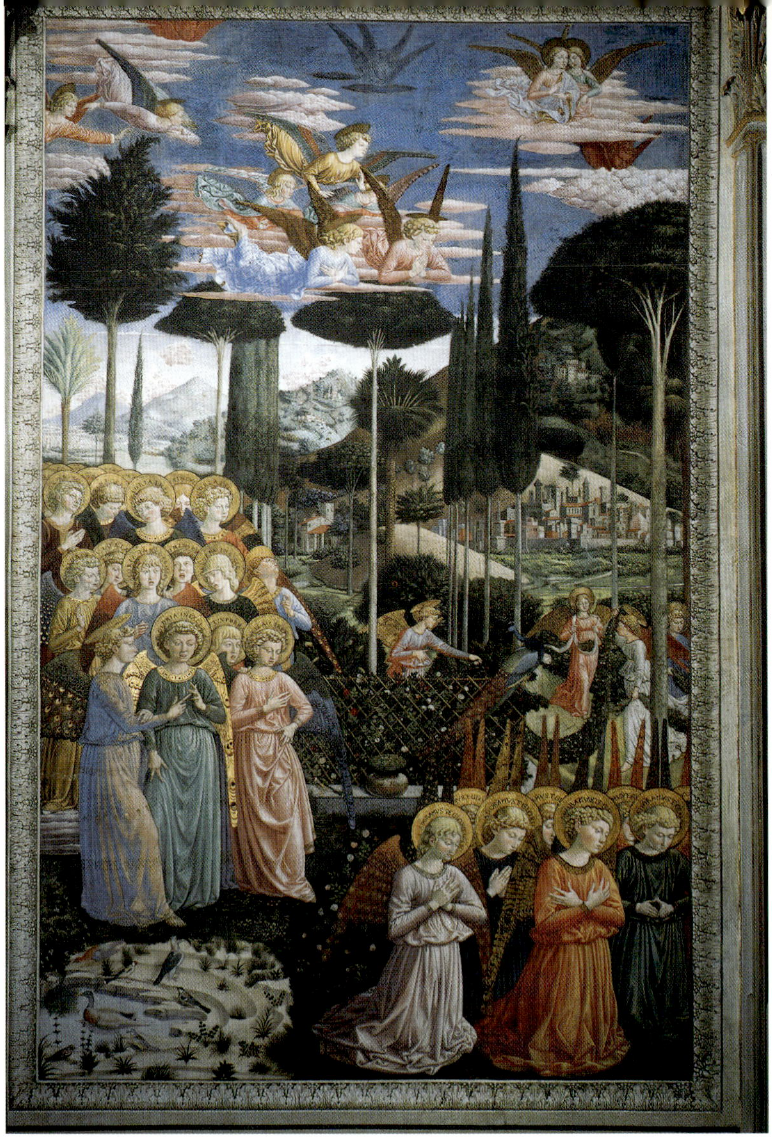

175 Benozzo Gozzoli, *Singing Angels*, 1459, Florence, Palazzo Medici-Riccardi, chapel.

who adores her Child, so that the visitors sacrifice with their hearts, words and deeds.

The gifts of the Kings, the prayers of the celestial spirits, and the soul of the Virgin are the sacred elements in the little temple. Keep thy foot distant, O profane crowd.[34]

We must imagine Lippi's Berlin *Adoration* back in place above the altar in the Medici chapel.[35] The *quattrocento* viewer would have encountered Lippi's painting as the culmination of a visual progression beginning elsewhere – perhaps in the Florentine streets or in another part of the palace – and then moving into the palace courtyard, up the stairway, into the chapel, and continuing across the frescoed chapel walls. The setting of Fra Filippo's *Adoration* was quite different from what the viewer would have encountered in the mock-manger set up in Piazza San Marco at Epiphany.[36] Here there was no manger, no pageantry, indeed, no references to the Epiphany narrative at all. The Virgin and Christ Child appear in a flowery grove in the heart of a forest, with the young Baptist and St. Bernard unobtrusively present. The beholder would have been encouraged to sidle up, unnoticed, like St. Bernard, and assume a devotional attitude just beyond the edge of the pictured space, below the steps to the *scarsella*, in the main body of the chapel. At the end of the long procession, characterized by garrulous detail, self-conscious display, and anecdote, the narrative collapsed on its objective, and the beholder passed into a state of religious contemplation.

This progression is present in the altarpiece itself, through the imagery of the axe, the felled trees, and the path cleared through the forest leading to a spiritual epiphany. Texts associated with both the Baptist and St. Bernard made use of a similar imagery. The Baptist, when preaching in the desert, had described how "the axe . . . laid unto the root of the trees" so that "every tree . . . that bringeth not forth good fruit is hewn down" (Luke 3 : 9).[37] St. Bernard, who peers down upon the Virgin and Christ Child from behind a truncated branch in the painting, invoked the metaphor of cutting into the rocks and earth to describe the contemplative state in his *Super cantica canticorum* and referred to

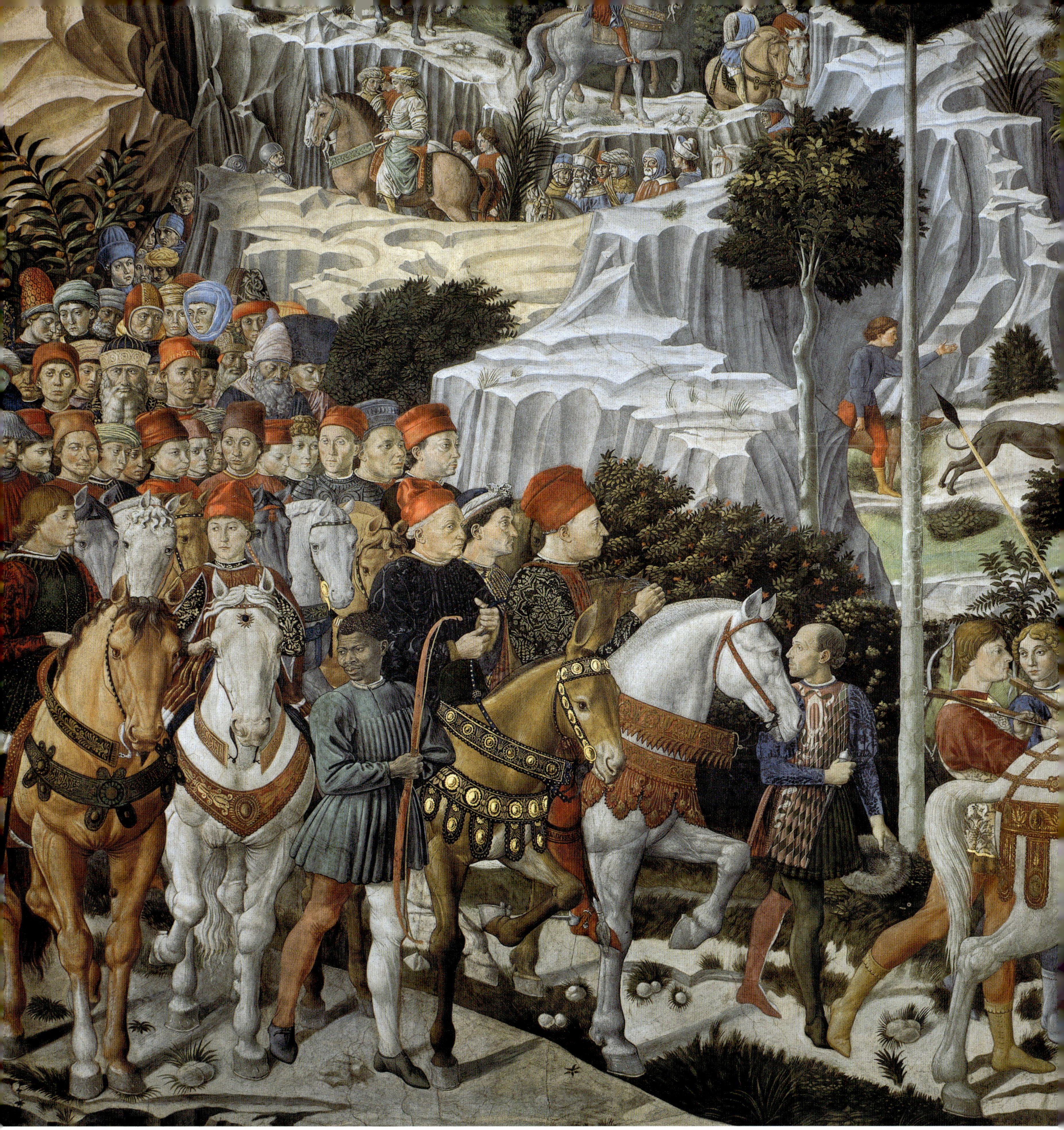

176 Benozzo Gozzoli, *Procession of the Magi*, 1459, Florence, Palazzo Medici-Riccardi, chapel.

the axe and cut branches frequently in his letters.[38] Fra Filippo Lippi signed his name along the forshortened handle of the axe (fig. 177). In this way, the painter, in a self-conscious display of his artistry, indicated that he had cleared the way for this spiritual progress with his brush.

A pilgrimage of sorts could thus have been effected as a contemplative journey by meditating upon an image of the Adoration of the Christ Child.[39] In the case of the Annalena and the Medici chapel *Adoration of the Christ Child* paintings, a devotional posture before the image could effectively transport the beholder from the city where he or she engaged in devotional exercises to a forested "other" place. And in this way, these Adoration scenes functioned rather differently from the perspectival paintings by Fra Filippo that proposed a continuity between the physical space inhabited by the beholder and the pictorial space.[40] Here, instead, a radical rupture was set into play, one that even stripped the altarpiece in the Medici chapel of its narrative ties to the procession of the Magi frescoed on the walls of the chapel.

The concept of a hermetic retreat, far from the city, where a purer, more direct, and fervent religiosity could be practiced, was no mere fantasy of an earthly paradise lost for the Tuscan Carmelites during the early *quattrocento*. The sacred preserve and the hermitage in the wilderness were potent images for members of a religious order that had started as an eremitical community of ascetics in Syria along the slopes of Mount Carmel. Inspired by thirteenth and fourteenth-century descriptions of the lives of the Eastern Carmelite hermits, the Tuscan Carmelite *provincia* approved the foundation of a reformed convent in the woods above Lastra a Signa, known as Le Selve. I have written in some detail about Le Selve in Chapter 2, demonstrating the important role it played in off-setting the urban integration of Santa Maria del Carmine in Florence, the central convent of the Tuscan *provincia*. I have also discussed in Chapter 3 how the early history of the Order was represented by the young Fra Filippo in the fresco in the cloister of Santa Maria del Carmine (see fig. 59).

Eremitical monasticism remained an ideal within the Carmelite Order and was a model for the Carmelite Observance at Le Selve. As the locus of eremitical monasticism was transposed in the Carmelite visual imagination from a schematic conception of the distant wooded slopes of Mount Carmel and the desert friaries in the Holy Land, to the local Tuscan forested hills, the wilderness imagery took on a more concrete visual aspect. This terrain could now be more precisely mapped. Fra Filippo's Adoration of the Christ Child paintings – with their variety of flowers, trees, mountain streams, and dry river beds, rocky outcrops, shaded glades, shadows, and distant vistas where the visible bleeds into dense forestation and obscurity – reflect such a Carmelite sensibility in defining a sylvan hermetic retreat where a more direct contemplation of the sacred could transpire.

Furthermore, the symbol of the axe and the metaphor of tree-felling represented in the Medici chapel *Adoration* had an important Carmelite frame of reference tied to the foundation of the

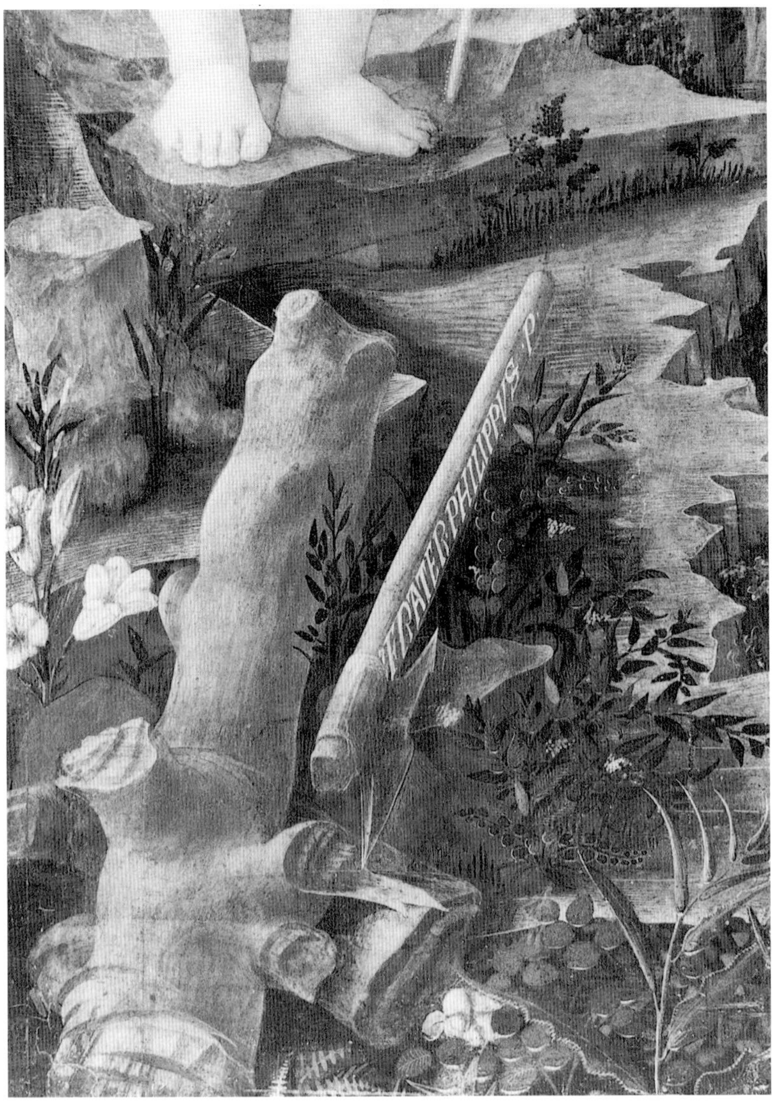

177 Filippo Lippi, *Adoration of the Christ Child*, detail of fig. 178, with the axe handle.

early Carmelite hermitages in the Holy Land. In the second Book of Kings, in a passage that was incorporated into Carmelite *Vitae* of the Prophet Elisha and accounts of the early hermits, the followers of Elisha began to construct a new settlement along the banks of the River Jordan:

> Now the sons of the prophets said to Elisha, "See, the place where we dwell under your charge is too small for us. Let us go to the Jordan and each of us get there a log, and let us make a place for us to dwell there." . . . And when they came to the Jordan, they cut down trees. But as one was felling a log, his axe head fell into the water; and he cried out, "Alas, my master! It was borrowed." Then the man of God said, "Where did it fall?" When he showed him the place, he cut off a stick, and threw it in there, and made the iron float. And he said, "Take it up." So he reached out his hand and took it. (2 Kings 6 : 1–7)

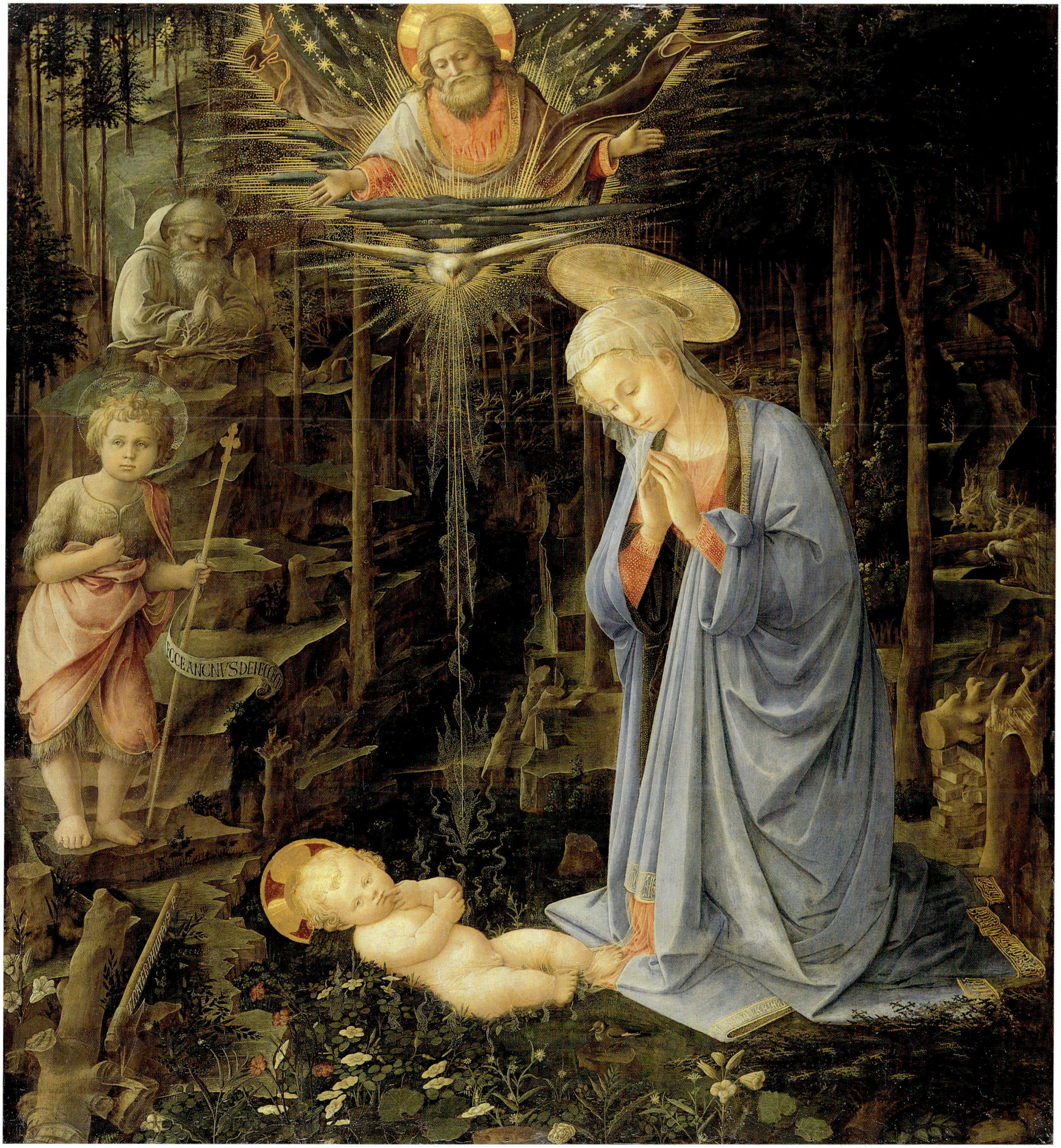

178 Filippo Lippi, *Adoration of the Christ Child*, c. 1459, from the chapel in the Medici Palace, now in Berlin, Staatliche Museen Preussischer Kulturbesitz, Gemäldegalerie.

In this context the axe is the tool miraculously recovered by Elisha, used to construct what the Carmelites considered to be among their earliest hermitages along the banks of the Jordan river. The felled trees here have positive connotations, being the building material used for the habitations of the "Children of the Prophets."[41] The fact that Fra Filippo chose to sign his name on the axe handle certainly calls attention to it and may denote multiple and possibly contradictory meanings. More conventional meanings, like those associated with the Baptist and St. Bernard, may have coexisted with a discrete Carmelite symbolism which thematized the process of fashioning the hermetic retreat as a representational act, a devotional exercise, a physical withdrawal to the Tuscan countryside, and an "historical" memory recorded in the Bible.

The variety of religious experience afforded by meditating upon the Virgin and Child within the context of a hermetic wilderness retreat obviously fulfilled different needs for the Medici from those for the Carmelites. The Medici required another sort of reversal, a different kind of undoing and offsetting. While the Carmelites' motivation in invoking the hermetic ideal lay in the incongruity between their historic past as desert hermits and their contemporary status as urban mendicants, the Medici family need arose from the contradictions underlying their condition as Christian bankers and Florentine oligarchs. The wooded retreat in Lippi's Adoration of the Christ Child paintings[42] provided a contemplative space for a direct, fervent religiosity that offered Medici family members, their associates, and political allies the experience of religious asceticism.[43] The beholder could thus enact a contemplative pilgrimage to the site of Christ's Nativity, or a meditation upon the Incarnation, and, in a self-effacing gesture, significantly place him or herself in the humble devotee's position just outside the sacred pictorial space. For the Florentine public attentive to Medici symbolic displays and maneuvers, this would have been an important sign of religious asceticism, offsetting other public displays of Medici power and position in the city. At the same time, this space for religious contemplation was a private Medici space, reminiscent of the family property in the Mugello (before the deforestation of the seventeenth and eighteenth centuries), where Medici roots ran deep. This final personalized touch in this new iconography, specifically tailored to meet the Medici devotional requirements, brought the Medici back to their own epiphany. The Carmelite Fra Filippo Lippi was particularly predisposed to visualize this idea.[44]

MONTE CARMELO

In the Carmelite cosmography, Mount Carmel, located in Syria some three miles from the city of Nazareth, beside the sea, was considered to be one of the holiest places on earth. It was what the scholar of comparative religion Mircea Eliade calls a "cosmic mountain," one of many images found in different religious systems that serve as an *axis mundi*, constituting "a break in the homogeneity of space . . . symbolized by an opening by which passage from one cosmic region to another is made possible (from heaven to earth and vice versa; from earth to the underworld)."[45] Mount Carmel was the site where the Carmelite Order had originated in the Holy Land, and continued to serve as a point of return and spiritual renewal, through prayer and pilgrimage. It was visited numerous times by God, frequented by the Prophet Elijah, and settled by his followers. The Virgin herself was said to have visited the Carmelite hermits in their sanctuary on Mount Carmel. It was also a point of passage from this world to celestial paradise. The Carmelites held that it was on Mount Carmel that the Prophet Elijah received word of his impending death. Many hundreds of years later, in 1291, Carmelite friars were martyred by the Saracens in the convent on Mount Carmel, as they sang the hymn *Salva Regina*. Mount Carmel was also an analogue for earthly paradise. It was "the Holy Mountain Carmel," which "because of the singular graces and privileges that God has conceded . . . is a mountain of sweetness and honey, a mountain of gentleness, a mountain of corporeal and spiritual fruit."[46] The mountain figured prominently in Carmelite liturgy, in the *laudi* the friars sang, and the images they evoked in their literary endeavors.

A striking mountain imagery permeates Fra Filippo Lippi's compositions. There is the rugged, desert mountainscape with faceted rock faces rendered in pastel monotone so notable in the Prato frescos. There is another more verdant, wooded, mountain setting found in his Adoration of the Christ Child paintings. The most impressive mountain evocations are those permitted by the monumental scale of his fresco projects in Prato and Spoleto. In the Duomo at Prato, along the wall decorated with scenes from the life of St. Stephen in the *cappella maggiore* (fig. 179), a rugged red mountain breaks through the frame of the middle and upper registers, forcefully becoming the armature upon which the narrative episodes rest and a compositional device to encourage the ascent of the eye to the uppermost scene. Lippi does a similar maneuver in Spoleto (see figs. 159, 164 and 165), uniting the ascending green slopes in the background of the *Dormition of the Virgin* in the lower register with the rolling summits that line the horizon at the base of the *Coronation* in the apse above.

Sometimes the mountains or mountainous scapes in his pictures are mere references, relegated to the background. In these cases, they function associatively. In the Palazzo Barberini and Spoleto *Annunciations*, the mountain in the background alludes to the fact that the Annunciation occurred in Nazareth near Mount Carmel. The mountains in the Uffizi *Madonna and Child with Angels* and the Munich *Madonna and Child* (see figs. 138 and 139) may even identify the Virgin as the "Madonna del Carmine" or "Madonna del Carmelo." In the latter, a path visible just behind the Virgin's head leads upward through rocky terrain to a church – a possible reference to the Carmelite oratory dedicated to the Virgin on Mount Carmel. In other paintings, the

179 Filippo Lippi, *Life of St. Stephen*, 1453–65, left wall of the main chapel in the Cathedral of Santo Stefano, Prato.

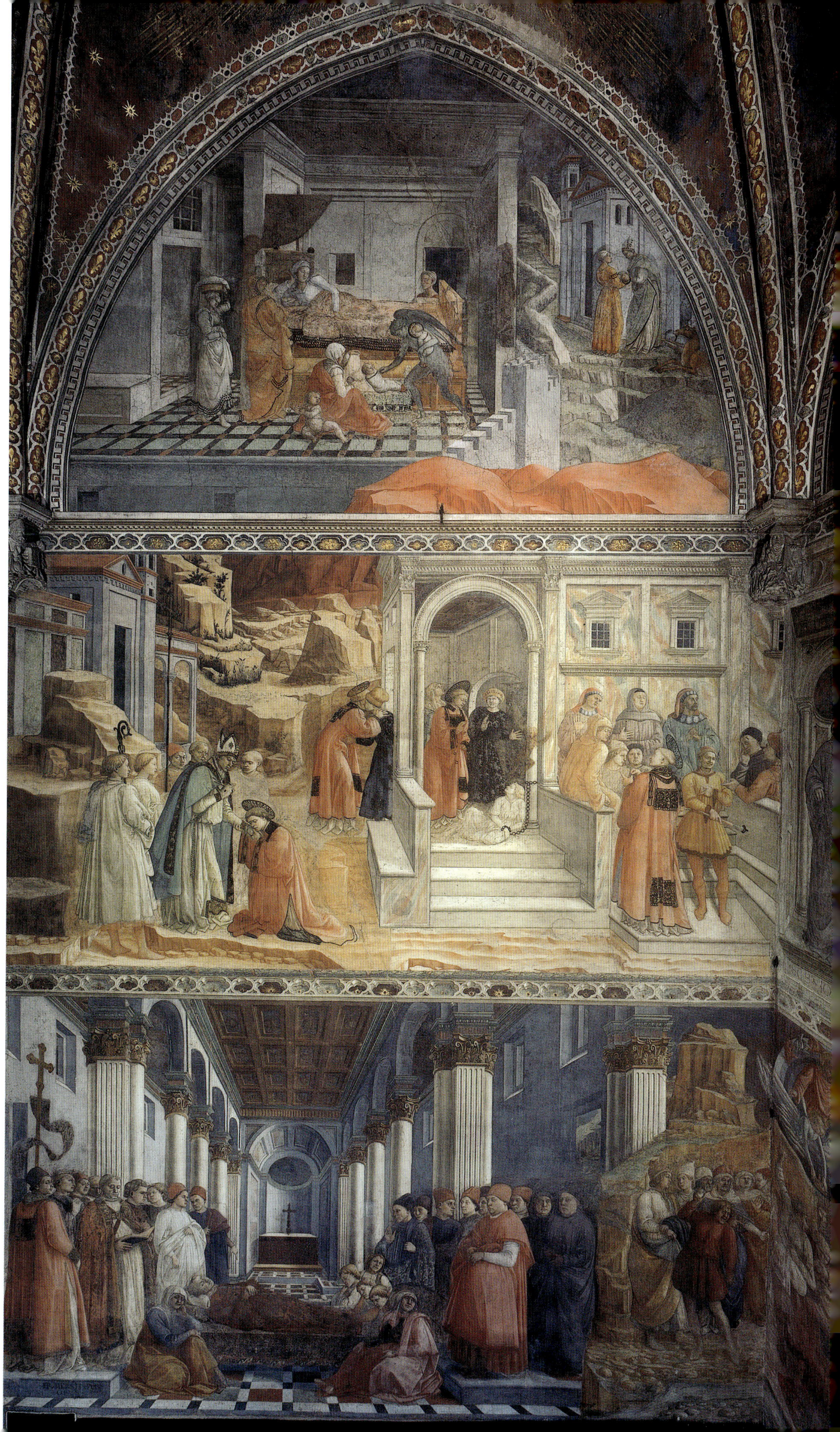

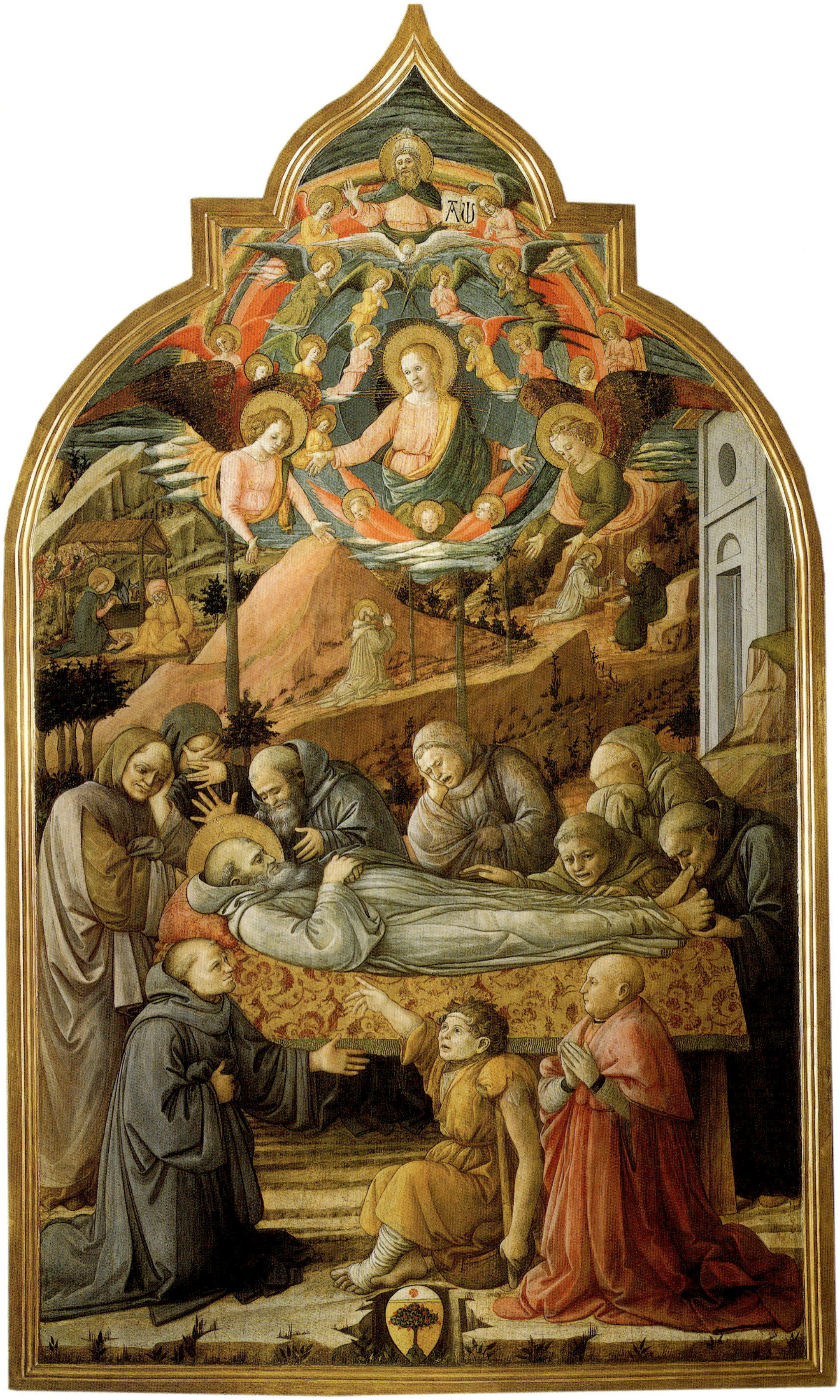

180 Filippo Lippi, *Death of St. Jerome*, mid-1450s, Prato, Museo dell'Opera del Duomo.

mountains are integrated into the narrative, referring metonymically and generically to the Holy Land where the various biblical events depicted took place – the Washington tondo, the *Nativity with Saints* and the *Death of St. Jerome*, which all occurred in Bethlehem; the *Entombment*, which took place on Mount Golgotha, outside Jerusalem; the *Baptist in the Wilderness*, which occurred along the banks of the River Jordan; and the *Martyrdom of St. Stephen*, which transpired in Jerusalem.

Mountains figure in all three of Fra Filippo Lippi's "obsequy" paintings. In the *Death of St. Jerome* (fig. 180), which Fra Filippo painted in the mid-1450s for the provost of the Pieve of Prato, Gemignano Inghirami, the dead saint is laid out on a bier in the foreground and narrative events are dispersed throughout the mountainous landscape background. In the *Funeral of St. Stephen* in the Duomo in Prato (see fig. 145), the body of the saint lies within a church setting, but at the right of the scene, through an open door, there is a glimpse out onto the sharp incline of a mountain scape – a curious detail in the somber scene. Even more bizarre is the rugged rock that actually intrudes into the church interior. Compositionally, this rock outcrop links the funeral scene with the adjoining martyrdom of the saint. In the *Dormition of the Virgin* (see fig. 159) in the Duomo in Spoleto, the dormition takes place out of doors, in a valley sloping up at either side of the scene, with a path leading into the distant mountains. As I mentioned before, the green pigment of the mountain slopes is picked up in the mountain tops in the *Coronation* scene directly above, giving the impression of a continuous mountain with God the Father enthroned above.

In each of the three scenes, an indication of the passage of the dead saint from this world to the next is provided. In the *Death of St. Jerome*, the Trinity is ready above to receive the soul of the saint into heaven, and the kneeling figure of St. Jerome in one of the background narratives doubles as a diminutive soul en route to the heavens. In the *Funeral of St. Stephen*, angels bearing a martyr's crown hover above the martyred saint in the adjoining scene. In the *Dormition of the Virgin*, one can barely make out the outlines of the mandorla painted *a secco* that once contained the figure of the Virgin rising toward her coronation as Queen of Heaven in the apse above.

These obsequy scenes set in mountainous landscapes paralleled one of the most potent Carmelite mountain images – the "Holy Mountain of Everlasting Life," to which the Virgin herself would personally convey each Carmelite friar after his death. This extraordinary guarantee of salvation, the Sabbatine Privilege, was inspired by a dream of Pope John XXII, one of the Carmelite's greatest advocates. The Madonna del Carmelo had appeared to him in his sleep and declared:

> Let the professed members of the said Order be freed from punishment and from guilt on what day they go from this world; so that with hastened step they may pass over Purgatory, I, the Mother of Grace, shall descend on the Saturday after their death and whoso I shall find in Purgatory, I shall free, so that I may lead them unto the holy mountain of life everlasting.[47]

The pope wrote the dream up into a papal bull, which he confirmed on March 3, 1322. This was much coveted by the Carmelites, and it was reconfirmed by Pope Alexander V in 1409.[48] The remarkable privilege, so recently reconfirmed, could be claimed by the vested Carmelite Fra Filippo Lippi. It is almost inconceivable that it would not have influenced the way he meditated upon death and the departure of the Christian soul from this earth. And it appears that the Sabbatine Privilege (shown here in a late sixteenth-century illustration [fig. 181]) also influenced the manner in which Fra Filippo represented this subject in his paintings.

* * *

181 *Sabbatine Privilege*, from the *Necrologium Carmelitanum* (1593), Florence, Biblioteca Nazionale, Conventi Soppressi, C.5.786, frontispiece.

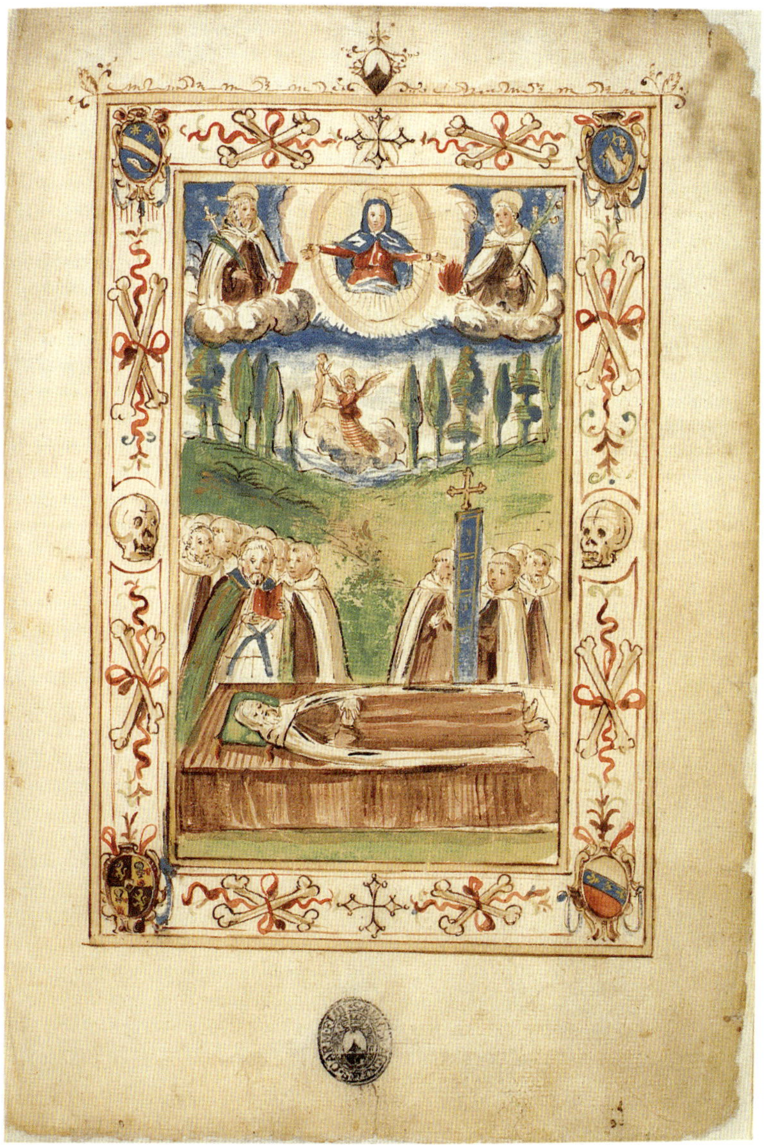

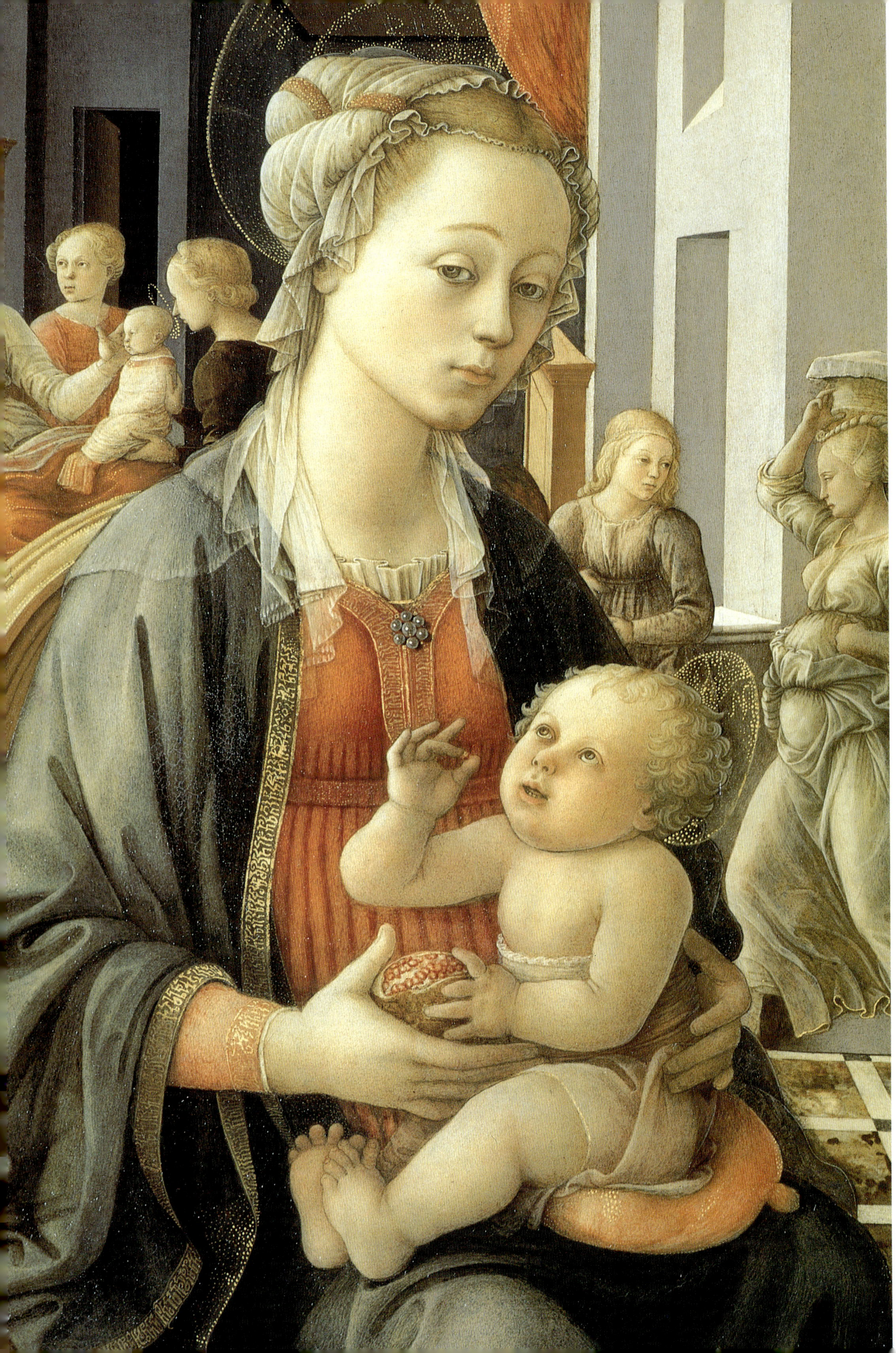

CONCLUSION

Was the mature Fra Filippo Lippi, then, a "Carmelite painter" in the same way that Fra Angelico can be described as an "Observant Dominican painter"? Yes, in that he was a Carmelite friar who painted. And no, given that he was not called upon to represent Carmelite subjects to the same extent that Fra Angelico worked with an overtly Dominican imagery. One could not write the kind of account about Fra Filippo that William Hood presented in his *Fra Angelico at San Marco* (1993). However, in concluding this chapter I should like to maintain that Fra Filippo's religious perspective was shaped in relation to the Carmelite interests and representational practices to which the friar was exposed when he lived within the cloistered environment of Santa Maria del Carmine, which I defined in the first section of this book. And, when based in the *seculum* during his mature years, his social identity continued to be that of a Carmelite *frate dipintore*. While Fra Filippo's patrons had commanding control over the choice of subject matter in his paintings, and Fra Filippo fashioned the pictorial imagery according to the particular requisites of each commission, the manner in which he gave visual form to the sacred was nonetheless influenced by Carmelite themes and the Carmelites' particular relationship to the sacred sites in the Holy Land and biblical personages.

182 Filippo Lippi, *Madonna and Child with the Birth of the Virgin*, detail of fig. 168.

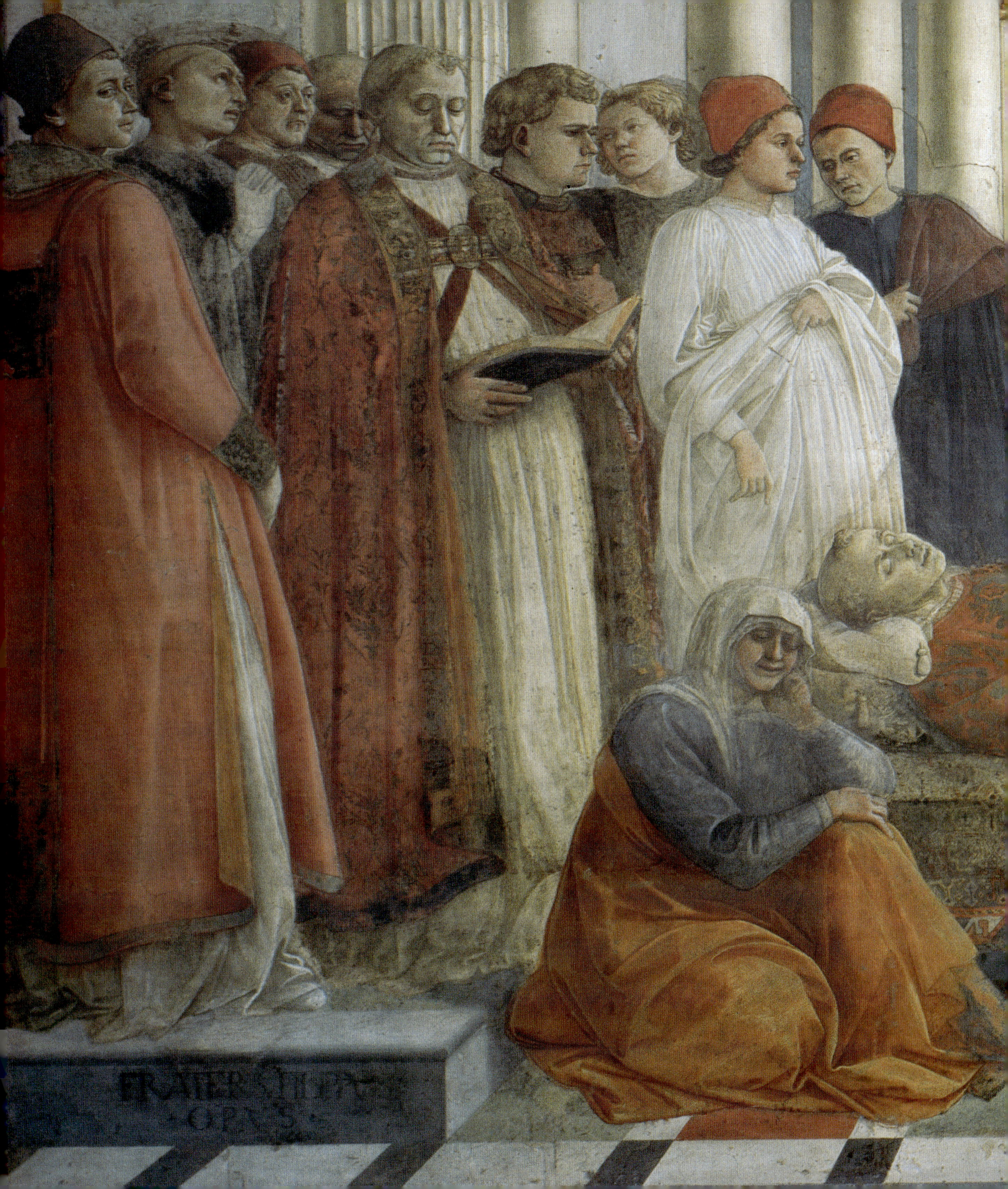
FRATER
OPVS

PART III

ART AND RELIGION IN FIFTEENTH-CENTURY FLORENCE

183 Filippo Lippi, *Funeral of St. Stephen* detail of fig. 145.

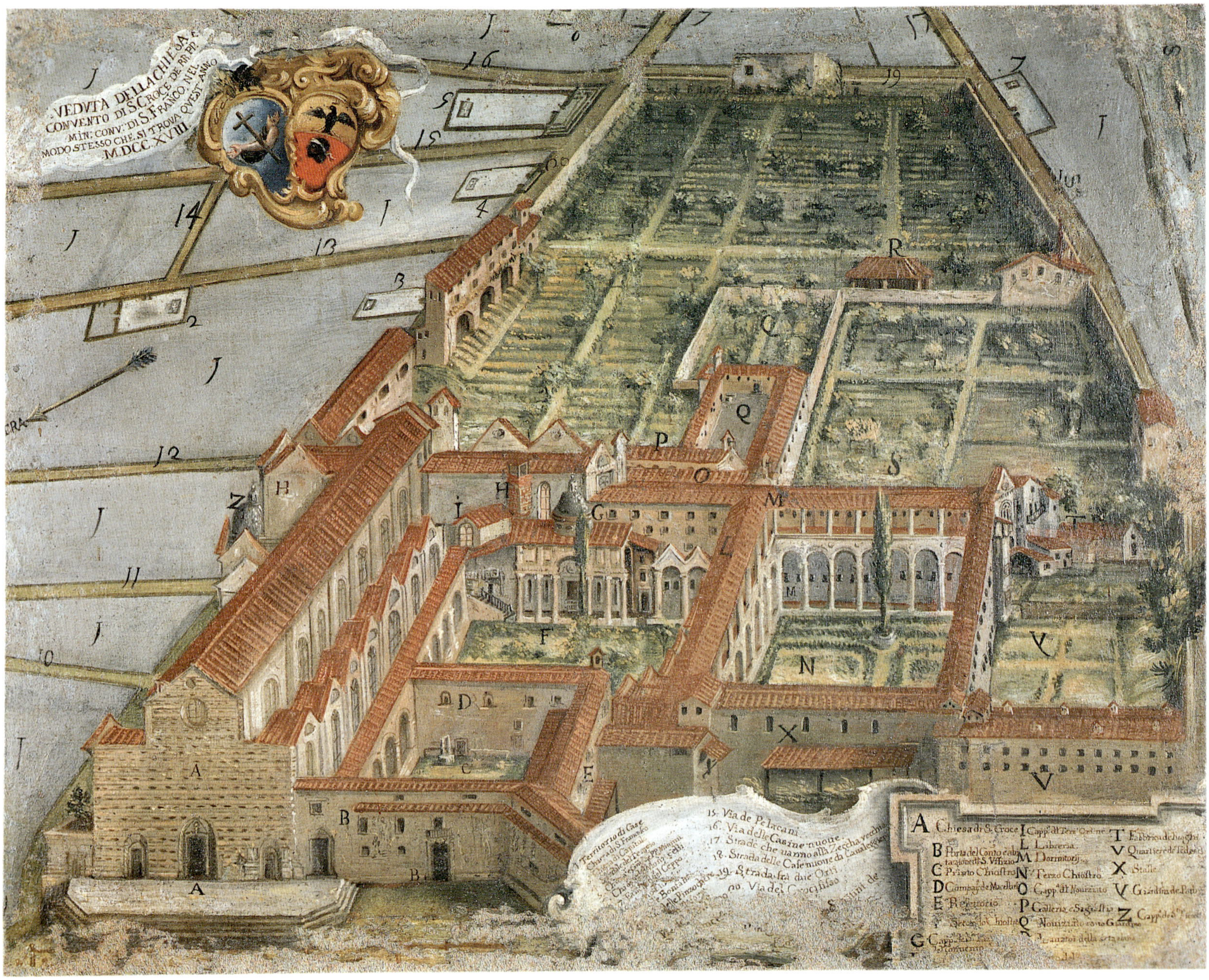

184 Anon., *View of the Church and Convent of Santa Croce*, 1718, Florence, Museo dell'Opera di Santa Croce.

CHAPTER EIGHT

THE NOVITIATE ALTARPIECE FOR SANTA CROCE

Cosimo de' Medici financed the construction of a new novitiate at Santa Croce in the late 1430s and early 1440s.[1] The buildings of the novitiate complex included the corridor leading from the church transept to a chapel, a stairway, and a dormitory above. The chapel (fig. 185) seems to have been finished by 1439, with the interior adornment and that of the adjoining sacristy continuing through the 1450s.[2] Vasari identified the architect who designed Cosimo's project as Michelozzo, and architectural historians have accepted this both on the basis of style (Michelozzo's) and habit (Cosimo's). The painter chosen to execute the altarpiece for the novitiate chapel was Fra Filippo Lippi.

Fra Filippo's Santa Croce altarpiece (fig. 186) is a standard variant on the *Madonna lactans*, or "Nursing Madonna" type.[3] Rather than actually nursing the Christ Child at her breast, the Virgin in Lippi's painting holds the standing child on her lap, while one of her breasts is exposed to the viewer. The *Madonna lactans*, or "Galactotrophousa," was a very old motif in Byzantine art and also had a pre-Christian precedent in the representation of the Egyptian Isis nursing Horus.[4] While the image was not widely used in Byzantium, it became very popular in Italy during the late Middle Ages, when the cult of the Virgin was at its height. Over the *trecento*, the *Madonna lactans* was often conflated with the "Madonna of Humility" where the Virgin is shown seated on the ground with the Christ Child in her lap (see fig. 201). The iconographic emphasis was on the "humanity" and "humility" of the Virgin as the Mother of Christ who nourished her son with her own milk. While this may have been the general religious doctrine underlying the *Madonna lactans*, the specific meanings were as diverse as the broad range of applications. In biblical commentaries, prayers, visions, and sermons, the *Madonna lactans* was invoked historically, metaphorically, categorically, and as *exemplum*. In visual representations, the image had a wide dissemination, appearing as the central panel of altarpieces, in frescoed street tabernacles, in small devotional panels, and as single-image altarpieces in private and corporate chapels, in monastic and parochial churches.

An effort to come to terms with the religious meaning of Fra Filippo Lippi's altarpiece for the novitiate chapel at Santa Croce is hampered by the wide relevance of the *Madonna lactans* theme within late medieval and early Renaissance piety. It is a tricky business searching for contingent meanings, because

185 The novitiate chapel, Florence, Santa Croce.

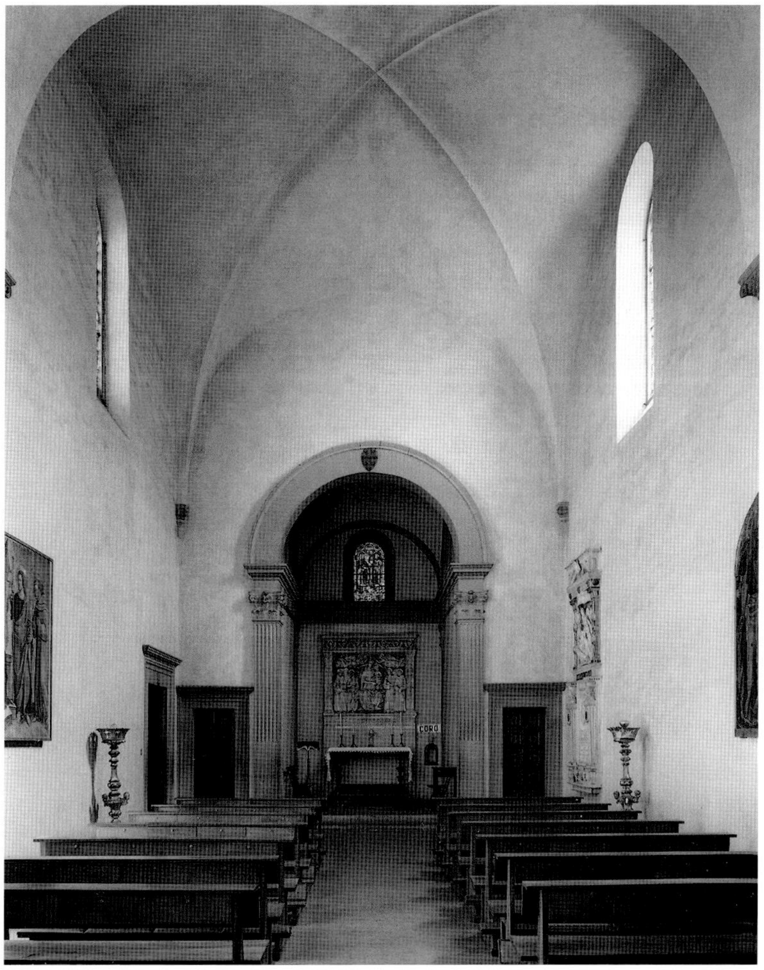

the *Madonna lactans* seems to offer itself up as a blank silhouette accommodating any number of historical attitudes toward women, mothers, virgins, superiors, inferiors, brothers, sisters, and institutions – lay, governmental, monastic (Cistercian, Franciscan, Vallombrosan, and so on).[5] The discrimination in determining contingency, then, must lie in the projection rather than in the accommodation, and I shall try to select possible meanings in accordance with the particular drama of the context. This drama of context can be defined as follows: behind the commission of the Santa Croce *pala*, there were four parties exerting an immediate influence upon its production and intended use – the patron Cosimo de' Medici and his family, the Franciscans from the convent of Santa Croce in Florence, the novices of Santa Croce, and the artist Fra Filippo Lippi. Each had some kind of claim to make on the world through the altarpiece. Each had a range of needs the painting was called upon to fulfill. Some of these needs overlapped, some were complementary, others were in conflict. The degree to which each of the four sets of claims was manifest in the pictorial imagery and subsequent use of the altarpiece depended upon the relative power relations between the parties and their respective relationship to the production and reception of the painting.

THE PATRON COSIMO DE' MEDICI

The fifteenth-century Florentine bookseller Vespasiano da Bisticci's explanation for Cosimo de' Medici's religious patronage is well known: "He had prickings of conscience that certain portions of his wealth . . . had not been righteously gained, and to remove this weight from his shoulders he held conference with Pope Eugenius [IV]," resulting in various pious donations which took the form of architectural endowments. Vespasiano listed each project and the number of florins spent on it: the church and convent of the Observant Dominican San Marco (fl. 40,000), the sacristy, nave, and priests' lodgings of Cosimo's local parish church San Lorenzo (fl. 60,000), the church and convent of the Benedictine Badia of Fiesole (fl. 7,000), Santo Spirito in Jerusalem, and two Franciscan houses – the convent and church of the Observants of Bosco ai Frati in the Mugello (fl. 15,000), and the novitiate and chapel of Santa Croce (fl. 8,000).[6] Ernst Gombrich ironically refers to these tallies as the Medici "Account with God."[7]

Beside this traditional explanation of Cosimo's donations as acts of contrition for usurious gains, we can posit another analysis that construes Medici religious patronage as an important element in the political and cultural hegemony that the family established in the Florentine republic during the *quattrocento*. As Richard Trexler has observed,

> Florence's classical system of ritual times, spaces, and objects resisted the building of individual reputation through pomps, and Cosimo learned he could only compete within that system, not overturn it. . . . Generally speaking, Cosimo avoided the formal personalization of the official [religious] calendar, and sought to create significant familial times through more subtle means. One such means was to build chapels in honor of Sts. Cosmas and Damian in several major churches in the city, ensure that divine services were said in them, especially on those saints' feast, yet resist the temptation to make the feast an official communal celebration.[8]

The chapel dedicated to Sts. Cosmas and Damian in the novitiate of Santa Croce can thus be seen as one of these incursions of Cosimo de' Medici's personal saints into an important city religious space. The strategic implications of this maneuver become apparent if we cast a look over the political geography of Florence around 1435–40.

The Santa Croce quarter of the city was the traditional habitation of a high concentration of patrician families with anti-Medici leanings. The Albizzi, Peruzzi, Castellani, Ricasoli, and Gianfigliazzi had opposed the Medici in the 1433–34 showdown, and were exiled or declared politically ineligible in the aftermath.[9] These families were also prominent patrons of the Franciscan church. Cosimo's religious patronage in Santa Croce may thus have been a subtle inroad into a hostile urban territory.[10] A Medici presence was physically established within the convent in the new novitiate complex – stamped through and through with the Medici arms.[11] In addition, the Franciscans and their novices were engaged to solicit sacred intervention on Cosimo's behalf, and the Medici saints entered into the Santa Croce saintly congregation, alongside Sts. Francis, Anthony of Padua, Louis of Toulouse, and the other saints and mysteries honored within the chapels of the convent.[12] Cosimo's political allies, too, directed their religious patronage toward the Franciscan convent and church. Andrea de'Pazzi built the new chapter house,[13] Giovanni d'Amerigo Benci, a manager of the Medici bank, endowed a chapel in the transept, while another Medici partisan, Niccolò Cavalcanti, is thought to have commissioned Donatello to sculpt the *Annunciation* (see fig. 10) for an altar in the church.[14]

Cosimo's patronage was somewhat different from traditional lay ventures within the convent. The very phenomenon of a novitiate chapel, altar, and altarpiece was not only new to Santa Croce in the 1430s, but also was unusual in monasteries at this time. The appearance of similar chapels in the following century reflects how the inchoate but fluid organization of the *quattrocento* monastery gradually gave way to a more ordered, hierarchic institution, in which the distinct parts were differentiated by separate spaces, rituals, and patronage spheres.[15] Cosimo de' Medici's role as patron of the Santa Croce novices indicates that a large convent like Santa Croce, supported by a resourceful patron, could sustain a separate internal structure for its novices. But more significantly, it pointed to the extent to which the Franciscans were willing to relinquish internal authority to a powerful layman. Cosimo was doing more than just subsidizing

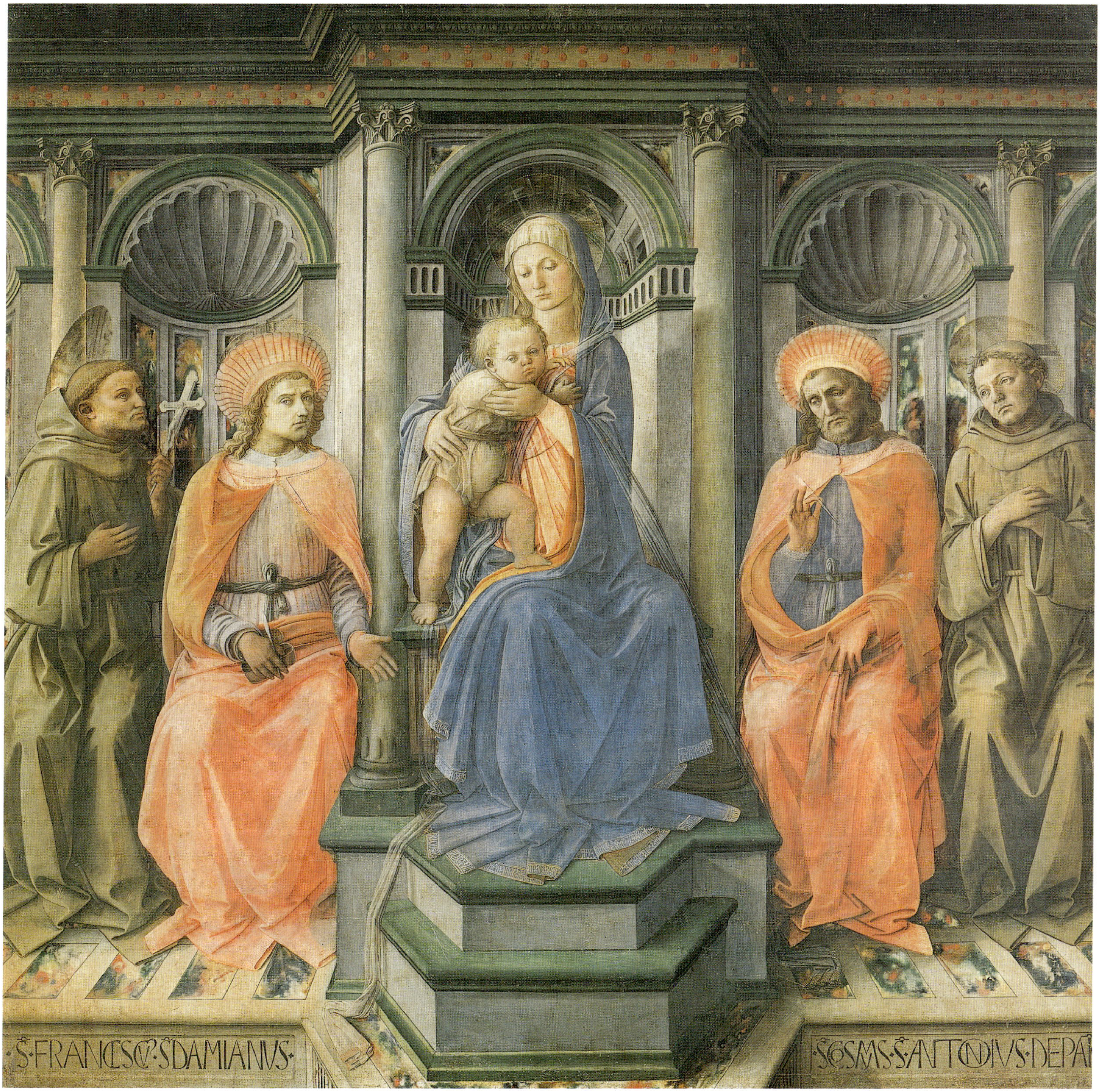

186 Filippo Lippi, *Madonna and Child with Sts. Francis, Damian, Cosmas, and Anthony of Padua* for the novitiate chapel of Santa Croce, c. 1440–45, Florence, Uffizi.

the construction of convent buildings and dictating the decoration of the chapel. He was offering himself as the patron of the novices. The scope and implications of this position can be inferred from evidence dating from later in the century. Lucrezia Tornabuoni, the wife of Cosimo's son and heir Piero, and later Lorenzo, her son, were involved in the selection of the master of the novices at Santa Croce. The novices of Santa Croce, on one occasion, appealed to Lorenzo as "our lord and patron," calling themselves the "sons of your Majesty" and the novitiate of Santa Croce, "your house."[16]

The terms of the agreement established between Cosimo and the Franciscans for the novitiate chapel were apparently spelled out in a papal bull that no longer survives.[17] A letter written by the Minister General of the Franciscan Order, Fra Giacomo da Mozzanica, in 1457, gives some indication of the accord:

> As I heard from worthy [people] on faith, how, a most agreeable place having been completed and brought to conclusion for the preservation and protection of the novices of our said Florentine convent, a pleasing accord was made between the friars and the most illustrious man Cosimo de' Medici, for some satisfaction, being his repayment for many benefits and for the construction of residences, so that every morning at dawn, a mass should be sung in the chapel of the holy martyrs, Cosmas and Damian, in reverence of the glorious Virgin Mary, Mother of Christ, by the same novices; and it should be established that during whatever preferred seven days, an ordained friar should sing the designated mass without error, and perform the commemoration of the above-mentioned Saints and Martyrs Cosmas and Damian.[18]

One sees in this agreement a give-and-take between the host institution and the lay patron. Cosimo had subsidized major building within the convent, and in return for this pious donation, religious services were rendered. The novices' chapel was dedicated to his personal saints who were to be honored with an unofficial octave annually. Daily masses dedicated to the Virgin were to be performed ("per l'anima di detto Cosimo," according to a late sixteenth-century convent ledger).[19]

Within the imagery of the Santa Croce *pala*, Medici claims were established in a number of ways. The signature mark of Fra Filippo Lippi (like that of the architect Michelozzo in the chapel design) functioned as a sign itself. The Medici were engaging one of the top painters working in the city of Florence at the time, and his pictorial style would have been associated with the innovative and acclaimed Barbadori altarpiece.[20] Fra Filippo was employed by the Medici by at least 1439, the date of the Carmelite painter's remarkable dispatch to Piero de' Medici (reproduced in Chapter 6) regarding a picture in progress for the Medici. The artist may thus have already been publicly perceived as a "Medici painter." Similarly, the fictive architecture in the picture – a Michelozzian, Brunelleschian pastiche with a Lippi inflection – was a signifier of the kind of modern architectural projects in the new classicizing style which the Medici had

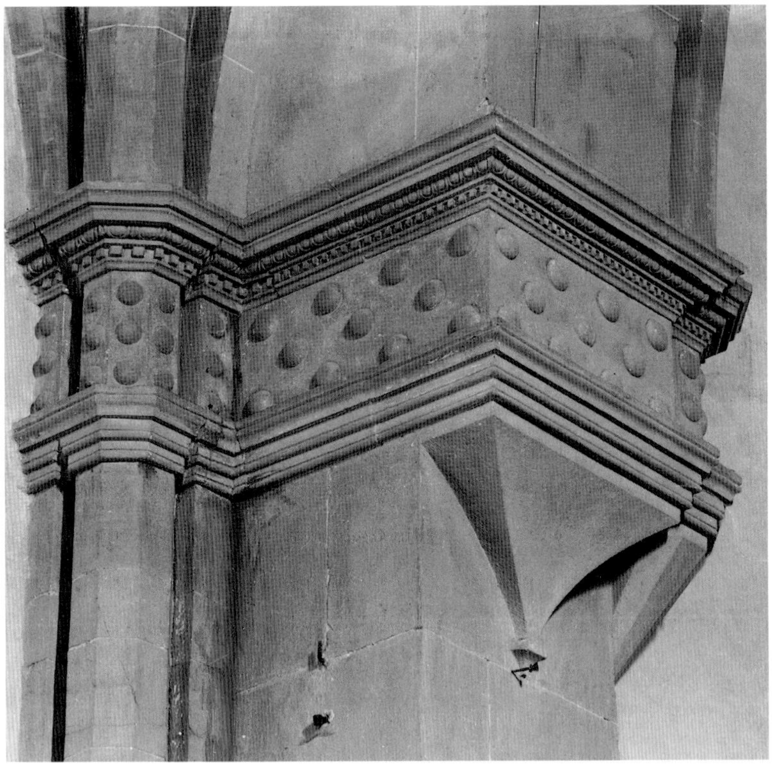

187 Architectural detail from the interior of the convent church at Bosco ai Frati (in the Mugello, Province of Florence), attributed to Michelozzo, mid-1430s.

undertaken at Bosco ai Frati, San Marco, San Lorenzo, and in the palace on the Via Larga.[21]

The Virgin and Child and the saints in the altarpiece all perch beneath a frieze displaying the Medici balls or *palle*. It had been Michelozzo's ingenuity in the monastic churches at Bosco ai Frati and San Marco to generate a decorative frieze motif out of the Medici *stemma* (fig. 187).[22] While this feature is absent in the actual architecture of the novitiate chapel at Santa Croce, it appears in the fictive architecture in Lippi's altarpiece. The Medici saints Cosmas and Damian, as the titular saints of the novitiate chapel, occupy the privileged positions to the immediate right and left of the Virgin, with the Franciscan saints Francis and Anthony of Padua in the outer positions. The Medici saints are directed outward, toward the viewer in the chapel space. Damian enacts a standard intercession gesture: he points to the Virgin and Child with one hand, and down with the other, toward a posited supplicant praying before the chapel altar – a position assumed by the beholder. He is interceding not just on behalf of the soul of the patron, Cosimo de' Medici. Along with St. Cosmas, he offers himself to the Franciscan novices as an extension of Cosimo de' Medici's patronage largess. Here Sts. Cosmas and Damian serve as saintly *palleschi*, or members of the Medici band.

By 1440, Cosimo had already been alluded to as *Pater Patria* – a title that was officially granted him by the Signoria following his death.[23] He was later to be called "father, patron, perpetual supporter and helper"[24] and, in specific relation to his religious patronage, a "magnanimous man."[25] As the patron of the novices of Santa Croce, Cosimo was embodying another perceived sentiment: "Above all, Cosimo loved the multitude of the lower populace."[26] Within the pecking order at Santa Croce, the novices were clearly the *basse genti* and in offering himself as the patron of this lowest body, Cosimo was also demonstrating the pious virtue of humility. It is Cosimo's "pudor" that Alberto Avogadro singled out when praising Cosimo's patronage of the novices' quarters in *De Religione, et Magnificentia Illustris Cosmi Medices Florentini*.[27] Sts. Cosmas and Damian can thus be seen as analogic representations of Cosimo de' Medici's role as the beneficent, charitable, and propitious religious patron.

We know, however, from literary sources, that this image of Cosimo was not a stable one. Just as the *encomia* to Cosimo the statesman were carefully conceived so as not to play into the fear that Cosimo was undermining republican processes, so the *encomia* to Cosimo the religious patron were counterpoised by criticisms that his munificence was self-serving and self-proclaiming. A *converso* of the Badia di Fiesole – another of Cosimo's religious endowments – is said to have asked Cosimo "Why do you have so many *palle* placed on all sides of the monastery?"[28] In Abbot Timoteo Maffei's defense of Cosimo, *In Magnificentiae Cosmi Medicei Florentini Detractores Libellus* (1460s), he has the detractor comment that "his arms can be seen painted and sculpted in various places in clerical and religious buildings – a deed which seems to manifest a lust for glory more than for divine veneration. Nor will I ever believe that he built so many and such great structures if not for obtaining a certain immortality of his name and empty glory."[29]

The frieze lined with the Medici *palle* in Fra Filippo's altarpiece could thus have been perceived as a clever artistic flourish – or, negatively, as the exaggeration of a patron's negotiated right to display his or her arms in an ecclesiastical space.[30] And this is not the only point of ambiguity in the painting. The pictorial space is compressed – almost to the point of being claustrophobic. Sts. Francis and Anthony (figs. 189 and 190) seem to be sliding off of the bench, moving out of their allotted niches and pushing in toward the center, invading the space of the Medici saints (as if to counter the Franciscan saints' displacement to the outside position in the painting). They are thus positioned in front of columns and may be interpreted metaphorically as foundation figures – literally pillars – of the Order. But it is a tense arrangement.[31] Tension is made manifest in a curious passage in the altarpiece where the Virgin's veil falls to the ground on either side of her throne (see fig. 195). On the left, it cascades loosely to the floor like a waterfall while, on the right, the veil is drawn taught between the crook of the Virgin's arm and the edge of the upper stair of the throne (almost as though it were pinned by St. Cosmas's leg). Is Lippi painting the tension implicit in a powerful patron's claim for a privileged position, for a personal iconography, in the space of religious representation in a Franciscan convent? St. Cosmas is shown in a contemplative attitude, holding his martyr's palm like a pen (fig. 188). It is almost as if he were writing, recording authorship – the signature of Cosimo de' Medici.

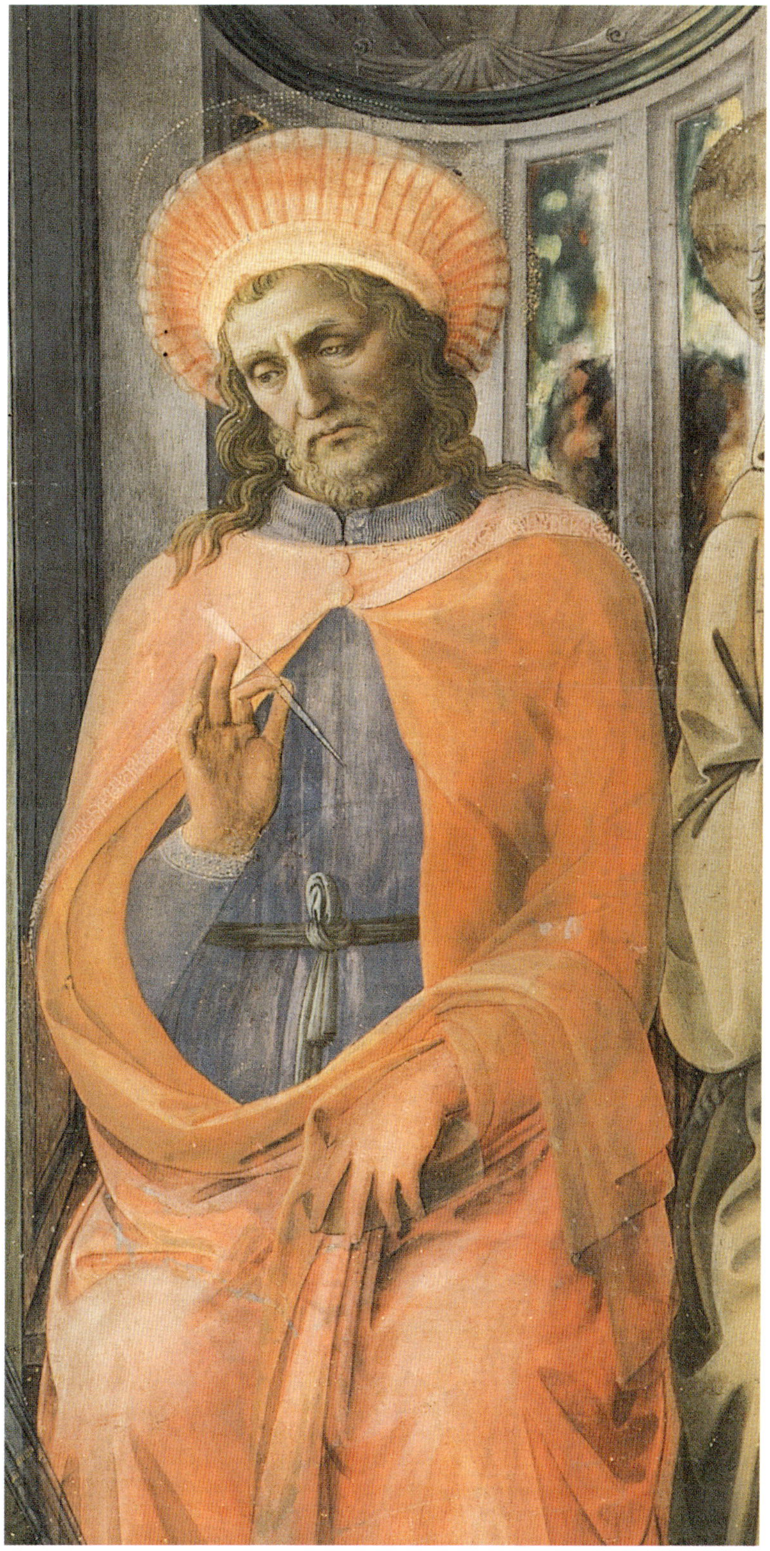

188 Filippo Lippi, *Madonna and Child with Sts. Francis, Damian, Cosmas, and Anthony of Padua*, detail of fig. 186, with St. Cosmas.

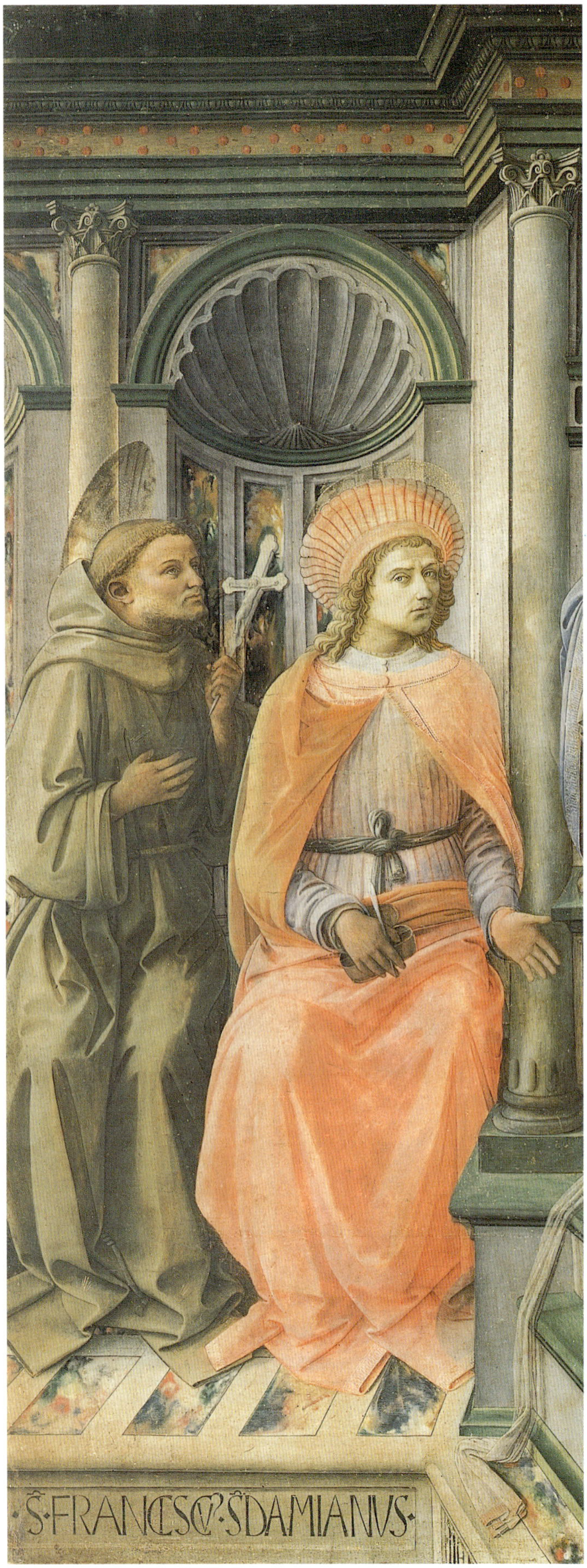

189 Filippo Lippi, *Madonna and Child with Sts. Francis, Damian, Cosmas, and Anthony of Padua*, detail of fig. 186, with Sts. Francis and Damian.

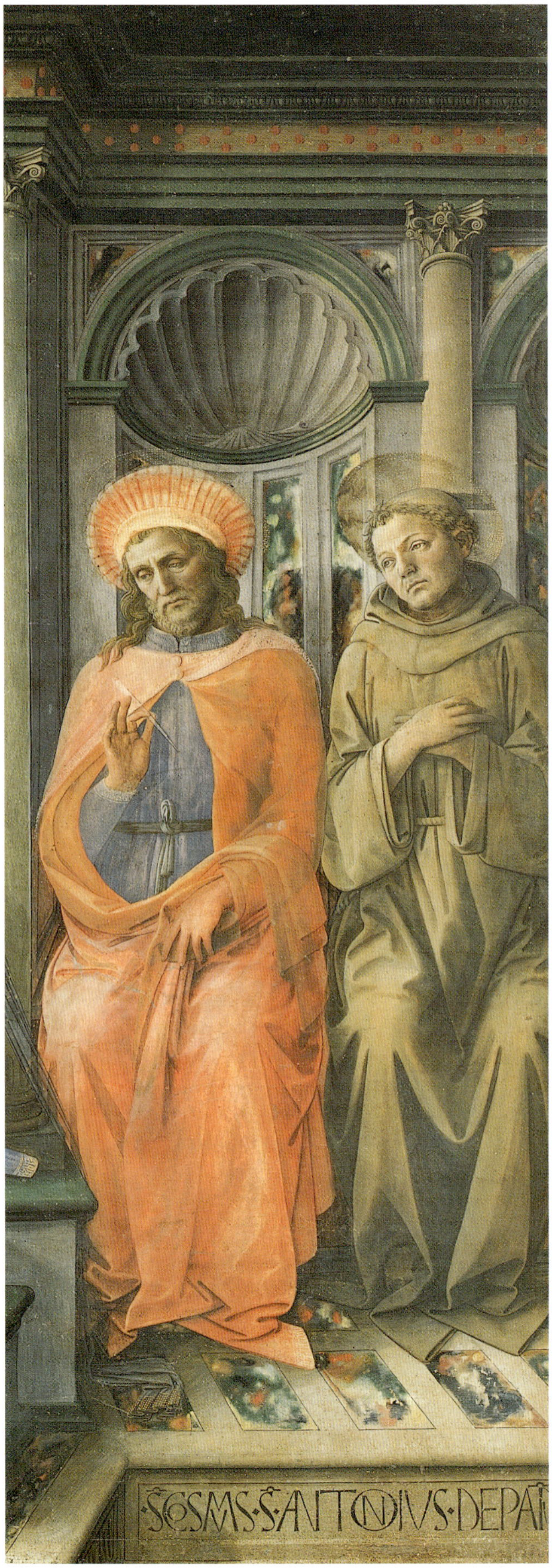

190 Filippo Lippi, *Madonna and Child with Sts. Francis, Damian, Cosmas, and Anthony of Padua*, detail of fig. 186, with Sts. Cosmas and Anthony of Padua.

Just as Vespasiano da Bisticci translated Medici acts of piety into their exact monetary values, so did the Franciscan chroniclers. A late sixteenth-century chronicle very baldly lists the expenditures made by the various patrons at Santa Croce during the first half of the *quattrocento*, including Cosimo's outlay of 6,000 florins.[32] This equation of piety with lavish expenditure on convent construction was historically problematic within the Franciscan context.

Building patronage in Franciscan churches and convents was a sensitive issue during the late medieval period and early Renaissance. As one of the fundamental (and expensive) material needs of the monastic community, building was implicated in the bitter controversy surrounding the interpretation – both in principle and in practice – of Franciscan Poverty. There was a fine line, never adequately defined by Francis of Assisi, between church building as a virtuous act of devotion to God, and church building as a sinful celebration of wealth and worldly pride. On the one hand, Francis had been commanded by the miraculous crucifix: "go and repair my house. You see it is falling down." And yet, Bonaventura relates, "On a number of occasions, he ordered the friars to leave a house, or even had it pulled down, if he thought that it offended against Gospel poverty, either because the friars claimed the building as their own or because it was too sumptuous."[33]

In the Constitutions of Narbonne drawn up in 1260, the Franciscans attempted to clarify and codify the appropriate building and decorative program for a Franciscan church. The dimensions of the church were to be kept to a minimum, with vaulting only over the choir. Only the window of the principal chapel should be historiated, limited to representations of the Crucifixion, the Virgin, the Baptist, and the *beati* Francis and Anthony of Padua.[34] Of course, the primary Franciscan seat at Assisi, which was being built at the very time of the Narbonne council, embodied the absolute contrary of the Narbonne dictates and one has only to survey the principal Franciscan churches in the various Italian provinces to discern that the Narbonne building dictates were never strictly upheld.

But the critical position against opulent building persisted and became a standard trope in Franciscan discourses. In fact, in one cautionary tale, the Florentine church of Santa Croce itself (fig. 191) features as an example of an excessively decorated edifice:

> Friar Jovenale de Aliss of Florence was one of the main friars who founded and built the convent of Santa Croce in Florence. According to Master Bartolomeo of Pisa, he has this punishment in Purgatory: until Judgment Day, there are two hammers above his head which continually beat against his skull. He himself revealed this, appearing to a friar, declaring it the punishment and the suffering he endured for his sin against Holy Poverty.[35]

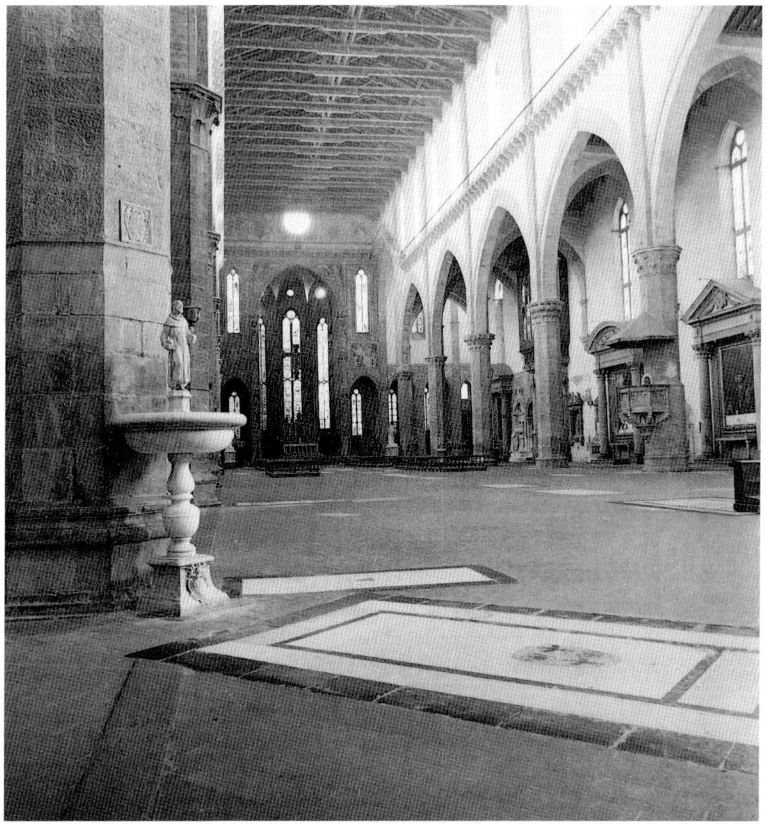

191 Interior of Santa Croce, looking toward the main chapel, Florence.

Franciscan Poverty was also the key term in the rift that had been steadily developing within the Order between the Observants, who interpreted the Rule of St. Francis narrowly, and the Conventuals, who were more accommodating. A split had begun to manifest itself while Francis himself was still living, and came to a head soon after his death. The Observant movement, however, is considered to have originated during the following century, when the friars of Brugliano in Umbria were given official permission in 1368 to follow the strict reforms they had adopted, which were at odds with the statutes of the general Order. Observant houses were quickly established throughout Western Europe with varying degrees of autonomy.[36]

Similar reform movements developed among the other prominent orders during the early decades of the *quattrocento*, reflecting the concurrent but often conflicting values that Renaissance religious culture placed, on the one hand, on resplendent pious donations and material display, and on the other, on religious asceticism. In Chapter 2, I demonstrated how the Carmelites adapted to the situation by ascribing complementary values to the different forms of religious life practised in their urban convents where the mitigated Rule was followed, and in the hermitages, where a stricter version of the Carmelite Rule was observed. The two Franciscan elements coexisted with relative equanimity through the beginning of the fifteenth century.

The year of 1430 was a watershed of sorts. The Franciscan Observant movement had been gaining momentum under the influence of three charismatic figures – Fra Bernadino of Siena, Fra Giovanni of Capistrano, and Fra Alberto of Sarteano. Until this point there had existed a genuine spirit of cooperation between the Minister General of the Order, William of Casale, and Fra Giovanni of Capistrano, representing the Observant interests. It quickly became clear, however, that the stringent reforms drafted by Fra Giovanni of Capistrano for the Order with the endorsement of Pope Martin V (known as the "Martinae") would not be enforced by the pope as promised.[37] This further polarized the groups, and Martin's successor, the strong advocate of monastic reform, Eugenius IV, formalized the division by establishing two vicars general, presided over by a minister general with significantly reduced powers. The Franciscans were officially split into two independent Orders by Pope Leo X in 1517.[38]

In 1429, Martin V had passed a bull declaring that no new Franciscan houses could be established within five leagues of an existing convent.[39] Despite this bull, Observant houses sprang up on the outskirts of Florence and in the *contado*. By the 1440s – the period that concerns us – the Observants were established in San Francesco in Fiesole (1390), San Salvatore beside San Miniato al Monte (1420s), the Ospizio dello Spedale del Ceppo under the care of San Francesco, Bosco ai Frati in the Mugello (1420s), and in three Florentine houses of Franciscan tertiaries – San Giorgio (1420s), San Nofri (1420s), and Santa Orsola (1430).[40] The Observants did not, however, have a monastic seat in the heart of the city of Florence. Within the city walls, the Conventual convent Santa Croce dominated the Franciscan scene (see fig. 184). Founded in 1228, it was one of the oldest mendicant establishments in the city, and was the administrative center of the "Custodia Fiorentina," which included the Franciscan convents of Prato, Castelfiorentino, Borgo S. Lorenzo, Figline, and Barberino.[41] Santa Croce was also intricately integrated into the urban surrounds, functioning as one of the four *quartiere* churches in the city and one of the principal Florentine burial grounds.

There is some reason to believe that the Conventual friars of Santa Croce felt threatened by the growing popularity of the Observant Franciscans. According to the *catasto* report of 1427, Santa Croce was among the poorest convents in the city of Florence.[42] Daniel Lesnick has characterized the Franciscans of Santa Croce during the previous century as coming predominantly from families of low economic resources, many of whom had very recently immigrated to Florence. The friars in turn – through their sermons and religious services – catered to a Florentine public composed of artisans, shopkeepers, and professionals from the *popolo minuto*.[43] Roberto Bizzocchi observes that while the Franciscans did not necessarily lose their popular support during the *quattrocento* in Florence, the Augustinians and the Dominicans were attracting a more powerful group of patrons – both as benefactors and as professed members and key office holders within the orders themselves and among the secular clerical ranks.[44]

This situation was particularly problematic for the Franciscans in the light of changing trends in early Renaissance Florentine religious life. There was a move away from mass participation in public displays of penitential piety (in which the Franciscans had played a central role) toward more formalized religious activities in which clerics and privileged patrons performed the rituals before an audience of devotees. Because a number of Santa Croce's traditional patrons were magnates and political exiles (the Bardi, Peruzzi, Alberti, Strozzi, Cerchi, and Ricasoli), they had little prestige and influence in the city.[45] In addition, the Benedictines, Augustinians, and particularly the Franciscan's chief rivals of the *trecento*, the Dominicans, populated the ranks of the secular clergy. The Dominicans also consolidated their civic importance in their traditional conventual seat at Santa Maria Novella by accommodating the papal entourages during Martin V's stay in Florence (1419–20) and Eugenius IV's lengthy sojourn (1434–43), and in hosting the papal court during the celebrated Council of Florence in 1439.

There was also significant popular and official support in Florence for the Observant reform movements, particularly that of the Franciscans.[46] Eugenius IV granted privileges and property to Observant convents within the various orders and encouraged the founding of new houses. Cosimo de' Medici had personally overseen the resettlement of the Observant Dominicans from San Domenico in Fiesole to the newly renovated monastic complex at San Marco, and had built the Observant Franciscans at Bosco ai Frati a new church and convent.[47] He is also said to have offered to finance the building of the Observant Franciscan convent at San Salvatore al Monte (beside San Miniato al Monte), but the Franciscans supposedly turned him down.[48] The Observant Franciscans were generously patronized by the Florentine *comune*[49] and by eminent individual patrons like Guido del Palagio, Niccolò da Uzzano, and Castello Quaratesi.[50]

The Franciscans of Santa Croce were also touched by topical political events. As mentioned above, the Santa Croce quarter of the city of Florence was the heart of the urban territory dominated by anti-Medicean forces. The Albizzi, Peruzzi, Castellani, Ricasoli, and Gianfigliazzi had been major patrons of Santa Croce in the *trecento*, along with the Bardi family which sustained four chapels in the church – even though their habitations were concentrated in the Santo Spirito quarter of the city. After Cosimo de' Medici returned to Florence, many members of these families were exiled or prohibited from holding public office, and in some cases, stripped of their property.[51]

Thus, by the third and fourth decade of the *quattrocento* the friars of Santa Croce were in need of a new generation of patrons with more financial and political power in the city to participate in religious rituals that were increasingly more oriented toward pageantry and spectacle. And indeed, there was a major turnover. The patrons who stepped forward following a fire in 1423 in the convent (Tommaso Spinelli, Michele di Guardino, Andrea de' Pazzi, and Cosimo de' Medici) were all new faces. In 1441, the Calimala guild was appointed by the city priors to oversee the condition of the church and convent. Castello Quaratesi was Gonfaloniere di Giustizia at the time, and there is a tradition that says that he himself offered to pay for the facing of the facade, but was refused by the Operai of Santa Croce because he insisted on having his coat of arms emblazoned across it.[52] The patronage rights to the facade were granted to the Parte Guelfa, which placed their arms over the three portals and set Donatello's statue of St. Louis into a niche above the central door at around this time.[53] It was the grand sepulchral monument erected for the Florentine chancellor Leonardo Bruni (d. 1444) that initiated the series of monumental wall tombs commemorating eminent Florentines in the nave, which centuries later gave rise to Santa Croce's reputation as the Florentine Pantheon. The church that the Franciscan Cardinal protector Bessarion consecrated in a ceremony attended by Eugenius IV in 1443 had a very different complexion from the *trecento* church.

Although it is difficult to gauge, it appears that similar transformations were taking place within the convent of Santa Croce.[54] Prior to the 1348–49 plague, the convent had been among the largest Franciscan houses in existence, with well over 100 friars.[55] The few surviving lists of friars from the *quattrocento* indicate that the numbers had stabilized at around fifty.[56] During the first half of the century, the social composition of the convent appears to have been similar to that in the *trecento*, consisting of Florentines from humble backgrounds. The ministers of the convent and masters of the *studium* – positions usually held by the more educated and well positioned friars – were, for the most part, occupied by non-Florentines.[57] This pattern changed by the end of the century, when many of the friars began to carry patronyms, interestingly enough, of the families that had been the traditional patrons of the church and quarter: Strozzi, Peruzzi, Castellani, and Machiavelli. There were also representatives of the new group of patrons: Quaratesi, Spinelli, and Medici.[58]

Thus, it is very likely that there were strong diplomatic motives behind the agreement made between the friars of Santa Croce and Cosimo de' Medici. At a time when the debate on Franciscan poverty raged within the Order and the Franciscans were particularly targeted in criticisms against monastic excesses,[59] the friars of Santa Croce permitted Cosimo de' Medici to bring in his personal architect, Michelozzo, and construct a novitiate complex in the new, classicizing architectural idiom.[60] While Santa Croce may have refused an offer for a facade that would have proclaimed the arms of Castello Quaratesi, the friars accepted a novitiate stamped through and through with the Medici *palle*. The Franciscan saints in Fra Filippo Lippi's altarpiece for the novitiate chapel (see figs. 189 and 190) perch beneath a frieze run through with these same Medici *palle*. They stake out the Franciscan context of this act of Medici piety, proclaiming the religious authority under which it occurred.

But the Franciscans of Santa Croce had another vested interest in the altarpiece imagery beyond that of competing for the seats of honor and religious jurisdiction with their powerful patron. The altarpiece was to stand above the altar in the chapel that their novices would use in their daily devotional exercises. The painting had to communicate basic Franciscan principles and *exempla* to the initiates during their year's novitiate.

THE NOVICES

Ostensibly, the novices within the convent of Santa Croce had little power to determine much of anything.[61] One of their objectives during their year's novitiate was to learn Obedience – to suppress their individual wills and obey their superiors within the Order and convent. Their power to influence the pictorial imagery of Lippi's altarpiece thus lay primarily in the institutional necessity within the Order for a novitiate, with its corresponding rules, rites, and, in this case, chapel and altarpiece.

St. Francis had decreed:

> If anyone is inspired by God to live our life and comes to our brothers, they should welcome him; and if they see that he is determined to profess our Rule, they should bring him to their minister. . . . The candidate should sell all his possessions and give the money to the poor. . . . The minister should clothe him as a novice for a year, giving him two tunics without a hood, a cord and trousers, and a caperon reaching to the cord. When the year fixed for the novitiate is over, he should be allowed to profess obedience; and once that has been done, he may not change to another Order, or wander about beyond the limits of obedience, as the pope has commanded.[62]

The vague intentions of St. Francis as stated in the Rule were elaborated in subsequent Constitutions and amendments – particularly the Constitutions of Narbonne in 1260 and the "Martinae" of 1430. By the 1440s, Franciscan novices were required to be over fourteen years of age; they had to be of sound body, unmarried, free individuals, and freely committed to the novitiate, without debts or under excommunication. Those who had petitioned to enter the Order were received by the provincial minister and assigned to the care of a regional or provincial master of the novices in one of the *guardie* in his province.[63] The novices were essentially a separate body only partially integrated into the regular activities and routines of the monastic community. They were distinguished from the friars by age and by dress, and they slept in a separate dormitory.

The specific program of the novices is not spelled out in the Franciscan Rule or in any of the Constitutions, but there are a number of thirteenth-century Franciscan texts dedicated to the novitiate that provide some idea of the novices' indoctrination. The most influential of these were Davide da Augusta's *De exterioris et interioris hominis compositione*, Bonaventura's *Regula novitiorum* and the *Speculum disciplinae* attributed to Bernardo da Bess.[64] These guides (Bonaventura's is addressed in second person to the novice) touch upon the daily routine of the novices and describe a series of attitudes and activities that the novices were expected to learn.

One sees the religious community at its most essential in these clearly laid out prescriptions: there is a Rule to be followed within a semi-sequestered environment; a series of ritual behaviors designed to maintain this Rule regulating bodily and spiritual activities (eating, sleeping, manual labor, and religious practices). There are appropriate ways to comport oneself both within and without the convent, toward one's superiors, *frati*, and fellow novices, toward laymen, and toward women. The convent ministers – particularly the *guardianus* and the *magister novitiorum* – monitored the gates between the convent and the world outside; they oversaw the novices' observance of the Rule, and they insured that the novices' bodies obeyed the more highly valued mandates of the soul. The program is distinctly not erudite. In fact, the novices were strictly forbidden, in accordance with the Constitutions of Narbonne, to enter the convent schools. They were expected to master the Rule, to learn the Divine Offices and the appropriate prayers. Aside from learning these basic texts, novices had to embrace humble Obedience and Poverty, participate in the sacraments of confession and communion, learn how to behave in the choir of the church and around the altar, and how to partake in austere meals, and acquire hands-off sleeping habits.

Novices were also encouraged to spend at least an hour a day engaged in mental prayer. This variety of prayer, given special emphasis by the Franciscans, played an important role in structuring the friars' vision of the sacred, and had implications for the way in which they viewed religious images. The *Speculum disciplinae* advised: "Let the novices learn to find the time and leisure – at least for one hour during the day or night – after retreating into themselves and entering into the chamber of their minds, to pray to their Father in secret; with contrite and humbled heart, let them remain intimately before the Lord of the universe."[65] Giovanni of Capistrano gave some indication of how this mental prayer could be shaped:

> Let the Master encourage and instruct his novices repeatedly to meditate on the Passion of Christ, [their] own misery, day of death, infernal punishment, sins committed, and the glory promised to them. . . . Each day they should make the crown of the Virgin Mary with seven meditations, just as seven are the parts of her crown. . . . The first meditation is when the Angel Gabriel greeted the Virgin Mary; the second, when Christ was born; the third, when the Virgin Mary presented him in the temple; the fourth, when Christ left his mother and went to celebrate the supper with his disciples; the fifth, when the Virgin Mary wept for her son before the cross; the sixth, when Christ was placed in his tomb; the seventh, when Christ rose from the dead and appeared to his mother.[66]

This essentially followed the Franciscan tradition of mental prayer best exemplified in the famous late thirteenth-century *Meditations on the Life of Christ* attributed to Giovanni de Caulibus. Using a configuration akin to the rosary, the novices were encouraged to envision in the mind's eye a biblical narrative cycle like the Passion of Christ or the Seven Joys or Seven Sorrows of the Virgin, assuming an attitude of empathetic identity with the exemplary protagonist.

There is a popular strain of Franciscan literature stemming from the anecdotal *Vitae* of St. Francis written by Bonaventura and Tommaso del Celano and found in Fra Salimbeni's *Chronicle*, that offers a more dynamic conception of how novices may in fact have engaged in mental prayer.[67] These stories provide not so much a fleshed-out portrait of life in the convent as an indication of how certain kinds of stories were held up as *exempla* and were told and retold to successive generations of friars. A number of these narrative tropes are devoted to novices. They are particularly interesting here because they attest to the importance of images – mental images, dreams, visions, and paintings – in the devotional practices of Franciscan novices. They give us an idea of the expectations and the economy of visual desire that the novices might have brought to an image like Fra Filippo Lippi's Santa Croce *pala*.

The typical novice tale involves a doubting oblate who is unable to endure the rigor of the novices' routine during his year of probation. It is all the better if the novice is of high birth, and the contrast between *il secolo* and *l'ordine* is all the more extreme and unbearable. Sometimes the novice confesses his desire to leave the convent to the master of the novices; in other cases, he simply plans to slip away during the night. He pauses for prayer before an altar to pay a parting homage to the Virgin, Christ, or St. Francis. Inevitably, the novice has a vision and receives some kind of manifest proof of the virtue of the Franciscan calling. Sometimes the miraculous vision itself is enough to convince the novice to remain in the convent. In other stories, it requires more to change his mind. In Fra Dionisio Pulinari's *Cronache dei Frati Minori della Provincia di Toscana* (1580), a doubting novice at Neve in the 1440s was personally challenged by the crucified Christ in his vision: "Why are you thinking of leaving me!" He was consequently filled with humility by the magnitude of Christ's suffering as compared with his own.[68] One troubled novice fell asleep before the altar and dreamed of paradise. His blissful vision offered a subtle promise for his own salvation, were he to remain in the Order: there, alongside St. Francis and St. Anthony of Padua, he beheld a recently deceased Franciscan friar ("et quillo ultimo cosi resplendente, . . . quillo si è uno frate novamente morto").[69]

In nearly all of the stories, some kind of tangible representation of divinity ignites the vision. A novice falls asleep while reading a psalter and dreams that Christ presents him with his cross to bear.[70] Another doubting novice is instructed by the master of the novices to pray before the altar of the Sacrament and "then he clearly saw Jesus Christ come out of that little cupboard where the sacrament is kept, and come toward him."[71]

There is a particularly compelling story about two newly professed friars rather than novices, which nonetheless follows the same pattern.

> There were two close young companions who left secular society and became Franciscan friars with extreme devotion. But one of them, tempted by the devil, said to the other: "You promised me that you would return to secular life if I wasn't content to remain a friar. I'm telling you now that I don't wish to be a friar any longer." His companion strongly urged him to try just a little longer, but the other, while agreeing to stay a few more days, remained fixed in his bad intentions. To which his companion said, "I beg you that before we leave the Order, we go into the church and make several prayers to the Virgin Mary, so that she may help us to make the best choice." The other consented and they went together before the image of the Madonna. And both of them said prayers, and the one who was reluctant to leave, with many tears, said fervent prayers for his companion. And with these tears so heartfelt, the one who wanted to leave the Order saw St. Francis come there, and collect the tears of his companion in a golden vessel and present them to the Virgin Mary, praying to her that in her kindness she would be pleased to give satisfaction to the tears of the charitable and devoted friar. Seeing this miraculous thing, the friar who had been tempted was completely stunned and retreated into himself. He felt completely freed of that diabolical temptation, and lived and died in a saintly way in the religion.[72]

Fra Filippo's *Madonna and Child with Saints* in the novitiate chapel too must have served as a visual stimulus for "gli occhi della mente" (the mind's eyes) of the novices of Santa Croce. The novices assembled before this image at least once a day when they sang a mass to the Virgin each morning at dawn, in accordance with the agreement between the patron Cosimo de' Medici and the Franciscans, quoted above.[73] We can expect to find an iconography in the altarpiece responsive to some of the doubts and needs that the initiates, learning how to cast aside their customary way of life in the *seculum* for a new communal existence in the convent, invariably would have brought to their mental prayer.[74]

First and foremost, the altarpiece offered the novices a visual program reinforcing certain basic Franciscan tenets. It complemented the primary, pared-down Franciscanism they were exposed to in the *Regula novitiorum*, the Rule and Constitutions, the writings of St. Francis, and the *Vitae* of Francis and other Franciscan saints and *beati*.

Saints Francis and Anthony of Padua are presented in the altarpiece as the two essential exemplars of Franciscanism (see figs. 189 and 190). As mentioned above, they are visually linked with the columns of the architectural backdrop, signifying literally as pillars of the Order. (This metaphor had been established in the Assisi narrative cycle where Francis is shown in Pope Innocent III's vision propping up the listing Lateran basilica like a strong pillar of the Church [fig. 192].)[75] They are the two Franciscans singled out in the Narbonne Constitutions (1260) who could be represented, in addition to the Virgin, the Baptist, and the Crucifixion, in the windows above the high altar of a Franciscan church.

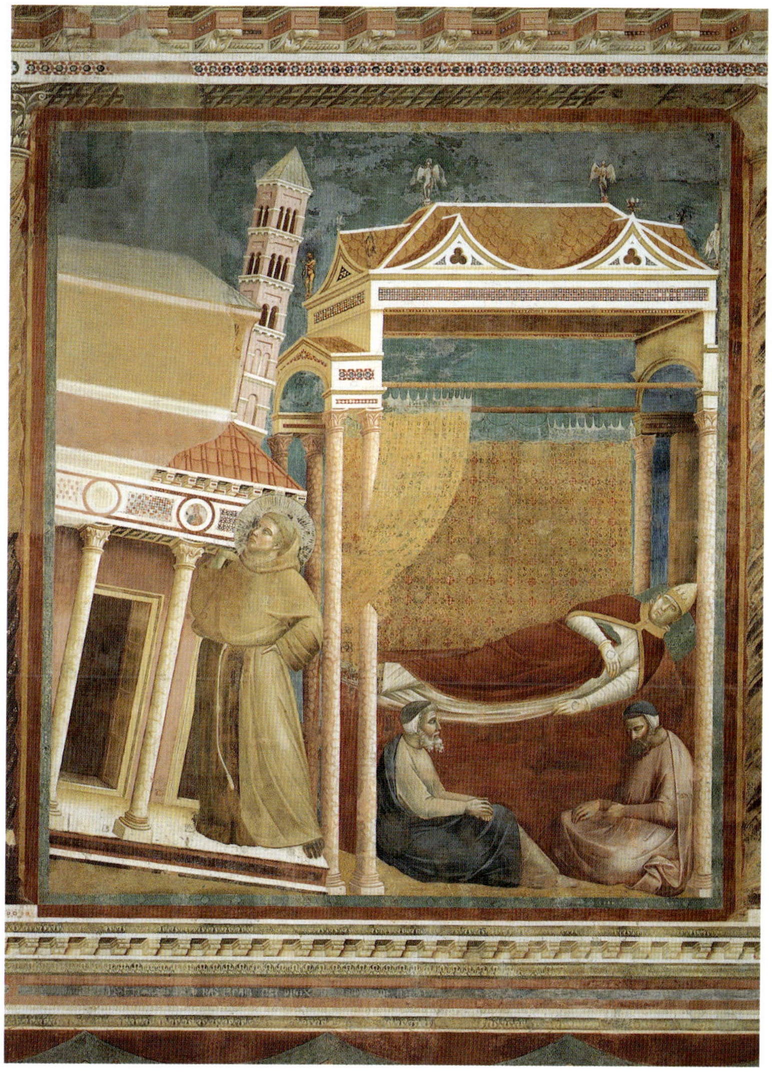

192 Master of the St. Francis Cycle, *Dream of Pope Innocent III*, 1290s, Assisi, San Francesco (upper church).

St. Francis was the founder of the Order, and Anthony one of his most accomplished followers. In an anonymous Franciscan panegyric, Anthony was called the "spiritual son of Beato Francis; good and excellent, because he imitated his father Beato Francis in everything."[76] This was a common characterization of the relationship between the two saints and would have been particularly relevant to the novices, who were emulating Anthony in following the example of Francis.[77] The two also exemplified different but complementary Franciscan religious ideals. In another panegyric, they are compared to the first two orders of angels (seraphim and cherubim): "Of these first was Beato Francis, truly speaking, because, among the other gifts of God, the passion of love shone in him. . . . Of the second order

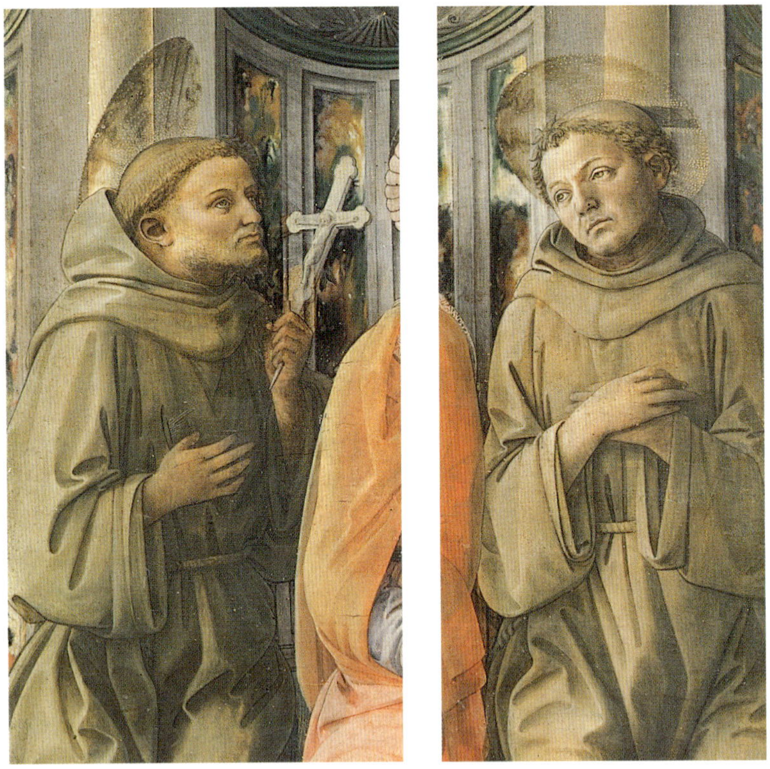

193 and 194 Filippo Lippi, *Madonna and Child with Sts. Francis, Damian, Cosmas, and Anthony of Padua*, detail of fig. 186, with (*left*) St. Francis and (*right*) St. Anthony of Padua.

came Beato Anthony, because, among the other gifts of God, brilliance in knowledge and in learning was preeminent in him."[78]

The comportment of Sts. Francis and Anthony in the altarpiece is suggestive of specific Franciscan doctrines and devotional attitudes.[79] St. Francis (fig. 193) holds a small cross, denoting the Franciscan devotion to the Crucifix and demonstrating the highest category of devotion, *latria*, which was accorded images of Christ. But both his body and his gaze are turned toward the Virgin, in a display of *hyperdulia*, the variety of devotion accorded the Virgin. His right hand rests on his breast – a devotional posture which conveniently reveals to the beholder the marks of his stigmata (emphasized by Lippi with golden rays emanating from the wounds) – which in turn articulates the doctrine of *imitatio Christi*. Anthony (fig. 194) crosses both hands over his breast in a classic devotional stance, and looks in the general direction of the Virgin. Their contemplative concentration contrasts with the more active engagement of the Medici saints.

The figure of the Virgin in the altarpiece too would have provided an effective focal point for some of the devotional exercises and concerns of the novices. While the altar in the chapel was dedicated to the Medici saints Cosmas and Damian, daily masses to the Virgin were recited at dawn in the chapel. The imagery in the altarpiece accommodates this liturgical routine of the novices in a number of ways. As mentioned above, the two Franciscan saints turn toward the Virgin and fix their eyes upon her, serving as devotional models for the novices during the mass. The unusual semi-seated position of all the lateral saints is actually quite similar to the posture that Franciscan friars assumed in the wooden stalls in the choir during the recitation of the night Office of the Virgin,[80] here described in a novices' guide:

> And always, during the entire Office, stay upright . . . except during the Night [Office], known as the Matins of the Virgin, when it is permitted for you to lean. . . . and for all the time of the Office, be worthy in such a way that you never look around or talk to anyone, but remain with your head bowed down slightly, your eyes lowered, your hands before you either crossed or held, one in the other, at your breast.[81]

The altarpiece could thus have offered a "How to comport yourself in the choir" visual *exemplum* to correspond to the directives in the novices' guides.

Julia Miller has suggested that the convex spatial construction in the altarpiece effectively thrusts the Virgin forward into closer proximity with the (novice) viewer, encouraging the direct, unmediated engagement and empathetic identification with the Virgin that the Franciscans emphasized.[82] This blurring of the boundaries between the novices' space and the sacred pictorial space is reinforced by the seemingly arbitrary truncation of the inscription along the bottom of the Virgin's throne by the lower edge of the painting and the indeterminant zone above the frieze in the upper regions of the altarpiece.

It is the *Madonna lactans* iconography in the altarpiece (fig. 195), however, which addressed most profoundly the condition in which the novices would have found themselves as new entrants into the Franciscan community. There was a long-established monastic context for *Madonna lactans* imagery, originating with St. Bernard and his Cistercian followers. The Virgin's breast-milk was made analogous to the spiritual and temporal guidance that an abbot offered to the monks under his care. St. Bernard had proclaimed, "We learn to feed the needy with the milk of doctrine." He discussed the lactating Virgin under the heading of "those who have undertaken the direction of souls."[83]

Not surprisingly, in contrast with the Cistercian tradition, Franciscans invoked the *Madonna lactans* theme less often as a metaphor for indoctrination than as a representation of spiritual and practical nurturing. In his *Office of the Passion*, following an antiphon to the Virgin, St. Francis had incorporated Psalm 21: "you have been my guide since I was first formed, my security at my mother's breast. To you I was committed at birth, from my mother's womb you are my God. Be not from me."[84] Bernardino of Siena elaborated on the theme in a sermon:

> Only the blessed Virgin Mary has done more for God, or just as much, as God has done for all humankind . . . God fashioned us from soil, but Mary formed him from her pure blood; God impressed on us his image, but Mary impressed hers on God . . . God taught us wisdom, but Mary taught

Christ to flee from the hurtful and follow her; God nourished us with the fruits of paradise, but she nourished him with her most holy milk.[85]

In accordance with the 1223 Rule of St. Francis, the friars themselves were to take on the roles of "mothers" and "sons" within the hermitage or convent:

> The friars who are mothers must be careful to stay away from outsiders and in obedience to their *custos* keep their sons away from them, so that no one can speak to them. The friars who are sons are not to speak to anyone except their mother or their *custos*, when he chooses to visit them, with God's blessing.[86]

Elsewhere in the Rule, St. Francis stipulated that the friars "are bound to love and care for one another as brothers, according to the means God gave them, just as a mother loves and cares for her son."

This metaphor of the guiding, nurturing parent was also applied to the novitiate. The novices, on their part, were required to "satisfy, immediately, with devotion, whatever the superior, prelate, or master should command, as an order almost divine, like sons true to the [vow of] obedience."[87] But in contrast to other orders like the Benedictine and Dominican, where hierarchy was firmly defined within the Rule and was maintained rigorously within the monastery, St. Francis had emphasized the fraternal relationship among his friars. "Ministers" were appointed to "administer" to the needs of the other friars, as opposed to act as their masters.[88] In fact, the "novice" offered an occasion for Francis to demonstrate the necessary subversion of power hierarchy in the name of extreme humility. In the *Vita di San Francesco*, Bonaventura has Francis explain, "I would obey a novice only one hour in the Order, if he were made my guardian, just as willingly as if he were the oldest and most experienced friar in the Order."[89] The *Speculum disciplinae* uses both "father" and "mother" images to describe different aspects of the master of the novices' ministrations to his wards: "Let him show himself toward them as a mother in the sweetness of his leniency, as a father in the strictness of his correction."[90]

There was thus a well-established precedent by which the novices of Santa Croce could recognize in the *Madonna lactans* represented in the altarpiece in their chapel a metaphor for the nurture and guidance that they could expect to receive during their year's novitiate from their Franciscan superiors and from their Medici patron. The nursing Madonna also contained other associations particularly relevant to Franciscan doctrine.

Leo Steinberg, Caroline Walker Bynum, and Margaret Miles have all discussed the *Madonna lactans* image in terms of the doctrinal significance of the Virgin's "nudity."[91] For Steinberg, the Virgin's exposed breast is an adjunct means to the primary explication of the Incarnation of Christ: "The image . . . assured the believer that the God rooting at Mary's breast had become man indeed; . . . the meaning of the subject was plain: Christ has to

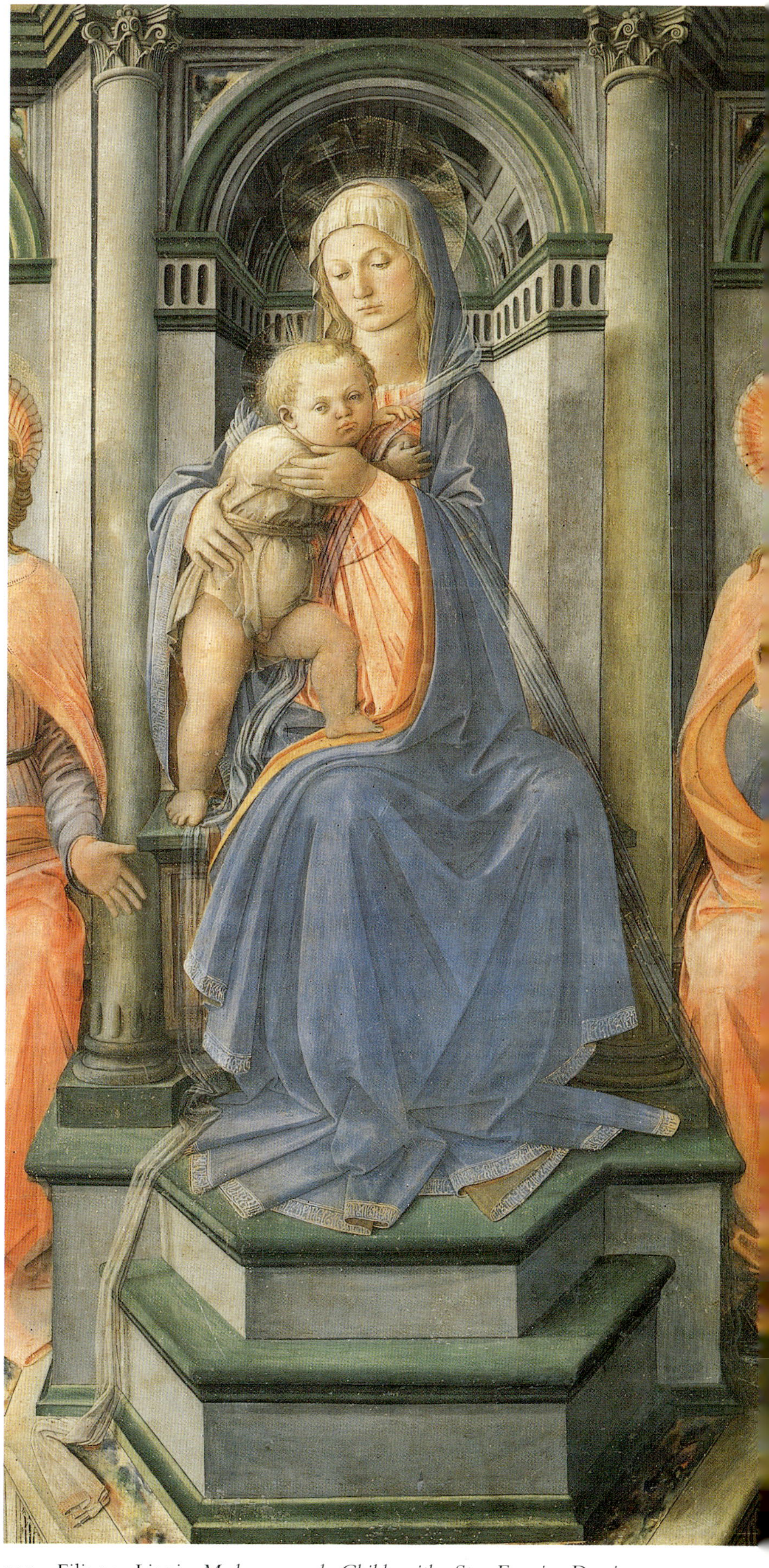

195 Filippo Lippi, *Madonna and Child with Sts. Francis, Damian, Cosmas, and Anthony of Padua*, detail of fig. 186.

eat. His taking food, initially as an infant . . . tendered the living proof that the substance assumed by the Trinity's Second Person . . . was human flesh subject to hunger." Lippi's Santa Croce altarpiece is in fact mentioned by Steinberg as an example of the most complete exposition of the Incarnation where both the Virgin's breast and the Christ Child's phallus are exposed to the viewer.[92] Bynum and Miles, responding to Steinberg, demonstrate that the Virgin's nudity also refers directly to her own humanity, which in turn, guarantees the full humanity of Christ. And in this role the Virgin was celebrated during the late Middle Ages as the principal intercessor and protector of humankind.[93]

The humanity of Christ and the Virgin were very important concepts within Franciscan theology. The Franciscans identified with this dimension of Christ and the Virgin, using their earthly deeds and sufferings as *exempla* to be emulated in their own religious observance. Christ, in becoming flesh, and the Virgin, by consenting to bear the God-child, exhibited both their supreme humility and their acceptance of an impoverished condition for the sake of the salvation of humankind. Francis proclaimed,

> Every day he humbles himself [during Mass] just as he did when he came from his "heavenly throne" into the Virgin's womb.
>
> Our Lord Jesus Christ is the glorious Word of the Father, so holy and exalted, whose coming the Father made known by St. Gabriel the Archangel to the glorious and blessed Virgin Mary, in whose womb he took on our weak human nature. He was rich beyond measure and yet he and his holy Mother chose poverty.[94]

Bonaventura declared in a sermon, "it is delightful . . . and sweet to see and to hear the Mother of kindness, she who is delightful to everyone, who offers milk and honey to her children [as if they were] her Child, with the result that the honey has the taste of the Divine and the milk, the taste of humanity."[95]

It is also possible that in a Franciscan *Madonna lactans*, the bare breast of the Virgin, as a sign of "nudity," signified "Poverty."[96] The two were established associative values in Franciscan descriptive language. In the early *Vitae*, Francis's repeated undressings and his gift of his clothes to the poor were presented as manifestations of his embracing of Poverty.[97] The link between physical nudity and Franciscan poverty was a standard trope in the writings of St. Bernadino and was invoked rather spectacularly by an Observant friar who preached nude before the public in Anagni in 1428.[98]

The *Madonna lactans* was thus a most appropriate vehicle for communicating the essential tenets of Franciscan Obedience, Humility, and Poverty, to the young Franciscan novices – a visual program to match the chapters in Bonaventura's *Regula novitiorum* devoted to "De humili obedientia" and "De paupertate."[99]

There are, however, some problems in presenting the Santa Croce *pala* as the quintessential Franciscan *Madonna lactans* image. The most obvious is that the painting, with its regally

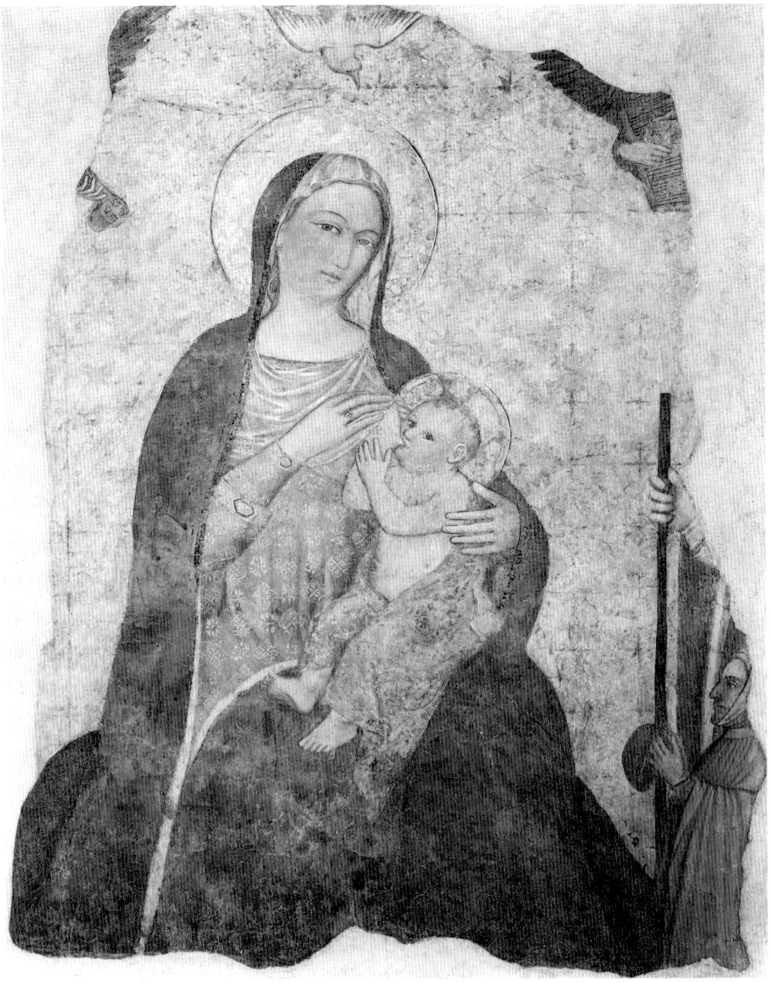

196 Florentine, *Madonna of Humility*, early fifteenth century, Florence, Museo dell'Opera di Santa Croce.

enthroned Virgin, prominent Medici doctor saints and rich fictive architecture, hardly embodies the principles of poverty or humility. While the image type may have had the potential to convey these religious themes, they are clearly not given emphasis in Lippi's painting. It is not a *Madonna lactans* of the "Humility" type where the Madonna sits directly on the ground, found in most of the few other *Madonna lactans* images that I have been able to trace to Franciscan sites,[100] like the early fifteenth-century fresco fragment from the nave of Santa Croce (fig. 196). Nor does Lippi's Santa Croce *pala* incorporate standard pictorial conventions for demonstrating "poverty" like the large bare feet of the Virgin in Domenico di Bartolo's *Madonna of Humility* (1433; see fig. 11).[101]

In Lippi's altarpiece (fig. 197), the Christ Child is clad in a white tunic tied with a cloth belt with gold-embroidered ends. The Virgin wears a white *camice* with a red *gamurra* over it, both gathered at the neck – very much in style in the 1440s – with a long blue mantle lined with orange fabric covering her body from head to foot, gathered on the ground in characteristic Lippi fan-folds. The border of the mantle and *gamurra* both have gold-

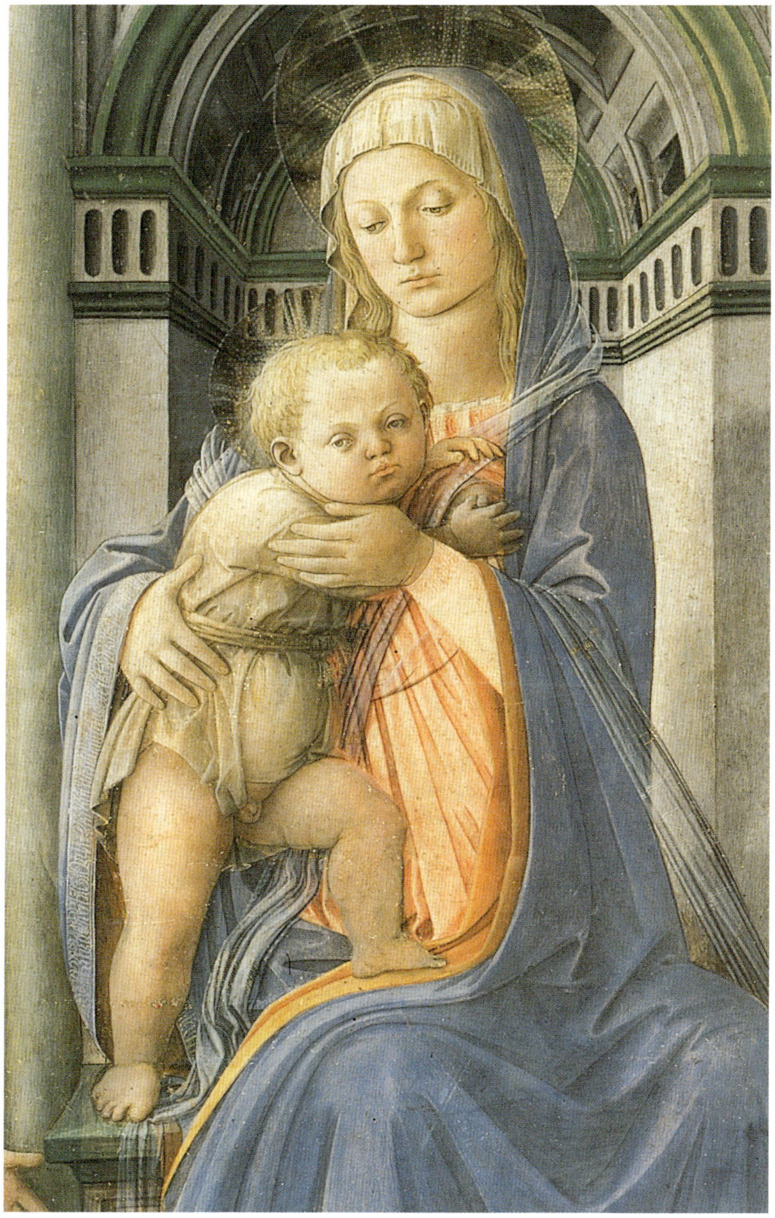

197 Filippo Lippi, *Madonna and Child with Sts. Francis, Damian, Cosmas, and Anthony of Padua*, detail of fig. 186.

embroidered simulated kufic script, another Lippi signature. This is standard early Lippi Christ Child and Virgin dress, nearly identical with that in the Barbadori altarpiece (see fig. 103). It is clearly a "Fra Filippo Lippi" Virgin and Child, with no alterations in form or decorative effect conceded to the iconographic dictates of Franciscan poverty.[102] The very characteristics of Lippi's painting style as noted by the Florentine Cristoforo Landino (1481) were not conducive to representing this Franciscan ideal: "*gratioso*," "*ornato*," "*artificioso*," "very good in composition and variety, in coloring, relief, in ornaments of every sort."[103] In introducing a Lippi altarpiece into the chapel of their novitiate, the friars of Santa Croce were also endorsing this painting style, so different from that of the Fra Angelico shop's pared-down formulaic imagery in the novices cells at San Marco (fig. 198),[104] or Sano di Pietro's explicit depictions of the Observant Franciscan Bernadino. In this choice (even if made indirectly through the Medici patrons), and in the imagery of the altarpiece painted by Lippi, one can sense resonances of the problem that the Conventual Franciscan friars of Santa Croce had in upholding the vow they had taken to "Lady Poverty."

It is also important to reiterate that in contrast to verbal and written descriptions, visual images of the *Madonna lactans* seem to have been relatively rare in a Franciscan context. I believe that there are complicated reasons underlying this notable absence, related to the highly visual element in Franciscan mental prayer.

The Virgin's exposed breast in Lippi's altarpiece may well have suggested at some level the humanity and poverty of Christ and

198 Fra Angelico and assistants, *St. Dominic before the Crucifix* from the novices' dormitory, c. 1439–45, Florence, San Marco.

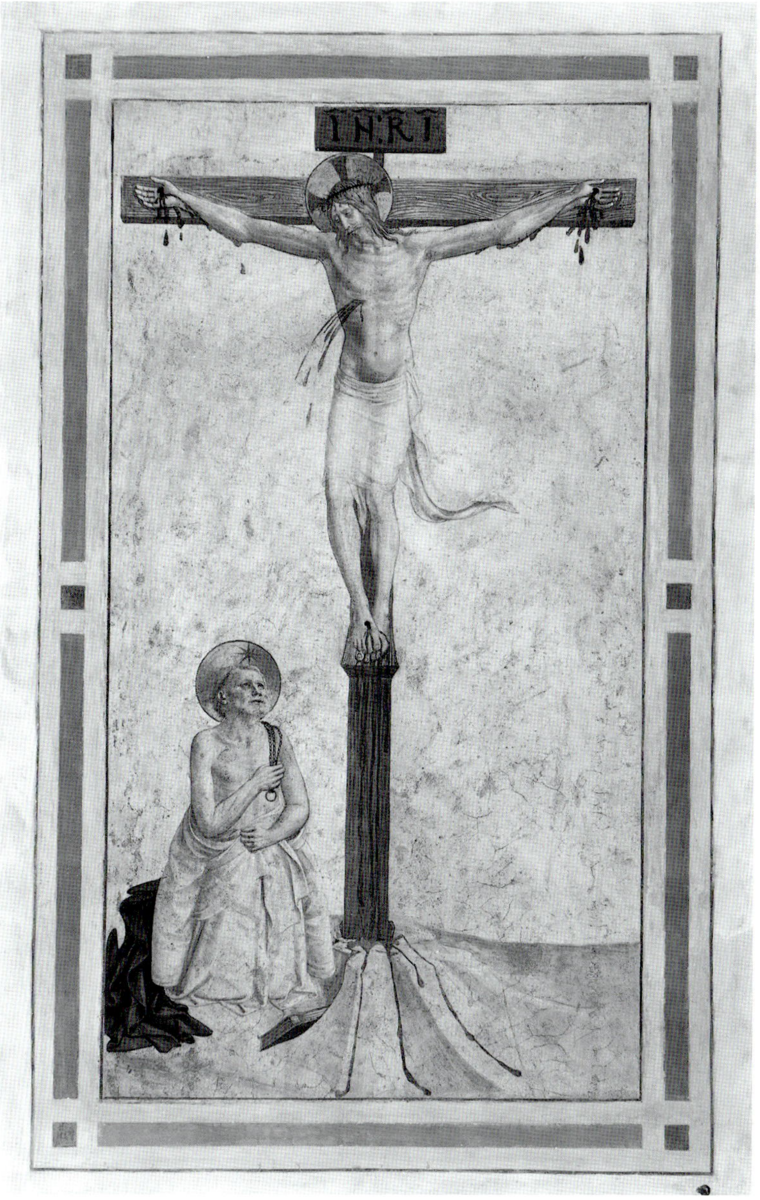

his Mother as Franciscan *exemplum*. But "nudity" was a dangerously unstable term in late medieval and early Renaissance religious representation. St. Francis may have taken off "his trousers in his fervor and enthusiasm and stood there naked before them all" when he renounced the world to follow "the Lord whom he loved, who hung naked on the cross."[105] But not all Franciscans could boast, as Bonaventura boasts for the founder of the Order, that he "had arrived at a point where his body was in perfect harmony with his spirit, and his spirit with God."[106] The author of the Novice guide *Speculum disciplinae* warns "It is base, in fact, to expose the nudity of the flesh of a religious person; whoever is honest, take care that his nude flesh is never visible except as much as shall be compelled by an obvious necessity."[107]

This double valence of Franciscan nudity – slipping readily between virtuous Poverty and sinful Temptation of the flesh – is evident in a story Pulinari tells about a novice in the convent of La Verna. The master of the novices instructed the novice "because you were a worldly and lascivious youth, these friars doubt your dedication; therefore, we want to see if you are in truth totally dead to the world; therefore, I want to lead you nude to the refectory and beat you before the friars."[108] The novice immediately began to undress, but the master stopped him. By demonstrating his very willingness, he had passed the test. To have carried out the undressing and to have made a visual spectacle of nude display would have pushed nudity as a sign of Obedience and Humility into the dangerous realm of nudity as temptation.

And nudity, when it came to women, was declared to be even more dangerous. Pages of instruction in the novices' guides were devoted to how the probate should comport himself toward women. Contact with women within the Convent of Santa Croce was controlled: we know from a 1386 notarial transaction that women were not permitted beyond the massive stone *tramezzo* dividing the nave of the church from the choir with its access to the convent.[109] But the Franciscans, like the other mendicant orders, interacted with lay urban society – performing masses in oratories and for confraternities, hearing the confession of private citizens – and the novices would have participated in some of these activities and encountered women in the process. Physical contact with women was to be eschewed, carried to the extreme in the *Speculum disciplinae*: novices "may not even easily kiss their own mothers."[110] And the all important Franciscan "occhi della mente" were not to be fixed on women. According to Bonaventura, Francis "was convinced that it was dangerous to allow any representations of them to enter one's mind because the flames of passion could easily be rekindled or the purity of a clean heart be stained."[111]

No women to enter the mind's eye, no kisses from the mother. And yet the Virgin Mary – unique among women as "celibate" daughter, handmaid, mother, and spouse all at once – was a central feature in Franciscan visions, in these imagined personal encounters with the sacred. What about the Virgin Mary as *Madonna lactans*? What about the Virgin as the mother of Christ who guaranteed His humanity with her own humanity, manifested in her nude breast. Was she permitted to enter into "gli occhi della mente" and become part of the pious visions of the novices? St. Bernard and Henry of Suso (d. 1363), both Cistercians, had visions where the Madonna offered them her breast to drink from. Both the Dominicans and Cistercians told the tale of the miraculous healing of the "Man with the Putrid Mouth" when he drank the palliative breast milk of the Virgin.

The Franciscans, however, had no such traditions. The Virgin offered up her Child to devout friars to hold – but not her breast.[112] Francis miraculously induced the flow of milk in the breast of an eighty-year-old woman whose daughter had died leaving an unweaned infant child.[113] In this instance, Francis effectively emulated the *Madonna lactans*, as he did in a vision of St. Claire's in which he offered her *his* breast to drink from.[114] But Francis himself is never reported as having been directly nourished by or within sight of the Virgin's breast in his mental prayer. The *Madonna lactans* did figure in the widely disseminated Franciscan text *Meditations on the Life of Christ*. In a brief passage corresponding with the period between the Nativity and the Purification of Christ, the "visitor" to the manger was encouraged not so much to envision the act of lactation as to empathize with the emotional state of the Virgin.[115] Perhaps it is on account of the strong visual element in Franciscan devotion that visions of nursing Madonnas are virtually absent among the myriad Franciscan miraculous sightings recorded during the late medieval and Renaissance periods, and absent, too, from the images of the Virgin and Child that were set up above altars in Franciscan churches and chapels.

Indeed, the Virgin's bare breast is considerably de-emphasized in Fra Filippo's *Madonna lactans* (fig. 199). The bare breast is exposed through a slit in the Madonna's gown, but is simultaneously concealed by her veil and by the Christ Child's hands. The slit in the Virgin's gown would have been sufficient to trigger the string of signifieds, from "*Madonna lactans*" to "nurture and guidance of the master of novices," to "St. Francis as a loving mother," and so on. Perhaps there was fear that a fuller, fleshier breast could have awakened visual desire in "gli occhi della mente" of the Franciscan novices, stimulating visions of real nursing mothers or beloved wet-nurses left behind in secular life, or, more dangerously, of seductive women.[116]

THE ARTIST

At the beginning of this chapter, Fra Filippo Lippi is designated as one of four parties with something at stake in what I termed the "drama of context" behind the production of the altarpiece. In social and economic terms, the contractual relationship with the Medici and the broader patronage implications were of key importance to the artist at this point in his career. He was obviously intent (and dependent) on pleasing his illustrious employ-

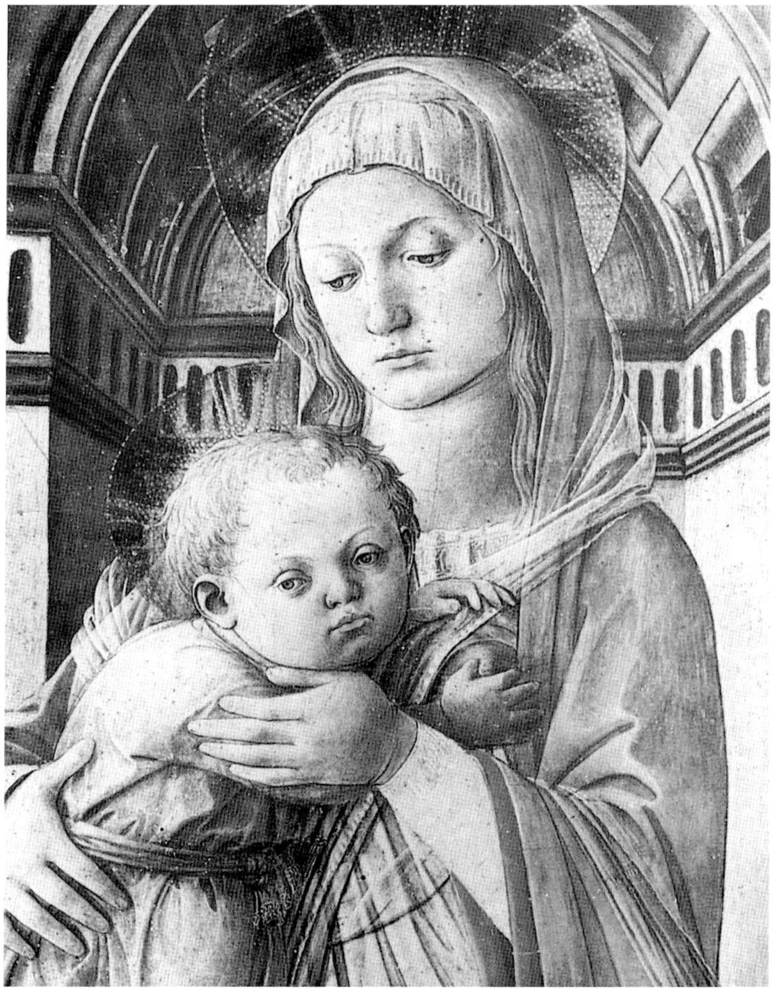

199 Filippo Lippi, *Madonna and Child with Sts. Francis, Damian, Cosmas, and Anthony of Padua*, detail of fig. 186, with the Virgin's breast.

ers by producing a painting to their liking that would generate further commissions from both the Medici and their allies. In artistic terms, the Santa Croce commission afforded him the opportunity of developing ideas about the altarpiece that he had begun to explore along with the other major innovative painters in Florence in the late 1430s and early 1440s. My conception of authorship or the role of the artist, however, extends far beyond the effort to realize these primary socio-economic and artistic ambitions. I see Fra Filippo as the articulator of the altarpiece – the one who made concrete in a material construction of wood, gesso, and paint a series of codified semiotic prescriptions mandated by the circumstances of the commission, which were not completely fixed, stable, or necessarily compatible.

Cosimo de' Medici or the Franciscans of Santa Croce evidently requested a *Madonna lactans* from Lippi. In a major altarpiece of this kind, it is not the sort of feature that an artist would have been at liberty to introduce on his own. And yet, one good look at the Santa Croce novitiate altarpiece is not, in itself, enough to assure the viewer that this is indeed the type of Madonna depicted. Because the crucial sign – the bare breast of the Virgin – is presented with a relative lack of clarity, the painting is easily readable as a straightforward Madonna and Child with attendant saints, in the modern, dynamic, and interactive Masaccio mode. And, as in Masaccio's Pisa polyptych (fig. 200), the iconography hits home only when the viewer strives to read the image in terms of a narrative of figure movement (*istoria*): what is that baby Christ up to? In Masaccio's work, he's munching on a bunch of eucharistic grapes, while in Lippi's Santa Croce altarpiece, he's tweaking the lactating Virgin's nipple. It is my contention that the *Madonna lactans* references in the Santa Croce *pala* are kept discreet for three reasons. The first, as I have suggested, is that the bare-breasted Madonna was not a stable symbol within the specific Franciscan devotional context for which the painting was intended. The second is that the experimentation in pictorial naturalism by Fra Filippo and his contemporaries around this time placed this particular Marian image under considerable pressure. And finally, the iconographical imperatives of the *Madonna lactans* seem to have taken a back seat to other concerns of the painter's that were more overtly artistic, centered upon the formal composition of the altarpiece. I shall discuss these latter two conditions in this section on Fra Filippo's stake in the Santa Croce *pala*.

The *Madonna lactans* had emerged as a popular devotional image within Sienese culture during the second quarter of the *trecento*.[117] The most widely disseminated version was produced by painters associated with Simone Martini who combined the *Madonna lactans* with the Madonna of Humility iconography (fig. 201). Characteristic of this rendition is an elegant Madonna clad in rich, tooled-gold brocade beneath her ultramarine robe, sitting upon a cushion on the ground and cradling the nursing Christ Child in her arms. The Child clutches the Virgin's breast, crosses his legs, and looks out at the viewer. The scene is set against a flat gold ground, and angels may hover round. The popularity of the image extended well beyond Siena, and it was taken up in Florence, particularly by Bernardo Daddi and his followers.[118] Variations on the composition included a version in which the Madonna and Child were lifted off the ground and enthroned. This type appeared frequently in the last quarter of the century, particularly in the paintings of Agnolo Gaddi.

Margaret Miles has argued that in early Renaissance *Madonna lactans* images, certain representational devices worked to guarantee religious as opposed to secular (and, more particularly erotic) readings of this bare-breasted, nursing female figure.[119] The Virgin's breast was partly covered by a veil and drapery. It was displaced to the level of the collarbone, and distorted in size and shape. These can be characterized as defensive strategies within the visual idiom designed to render the potential profane content neutral. Such strategies became too disruptive in the *quattrocento* when a premium was placed on naturalism in the visual arts as a representational means to more didactically efficacious images.[120] A new coherence was demanded among the separate parts that came together to constitute a picture. Anatomical correctness – or at least its approximation – was

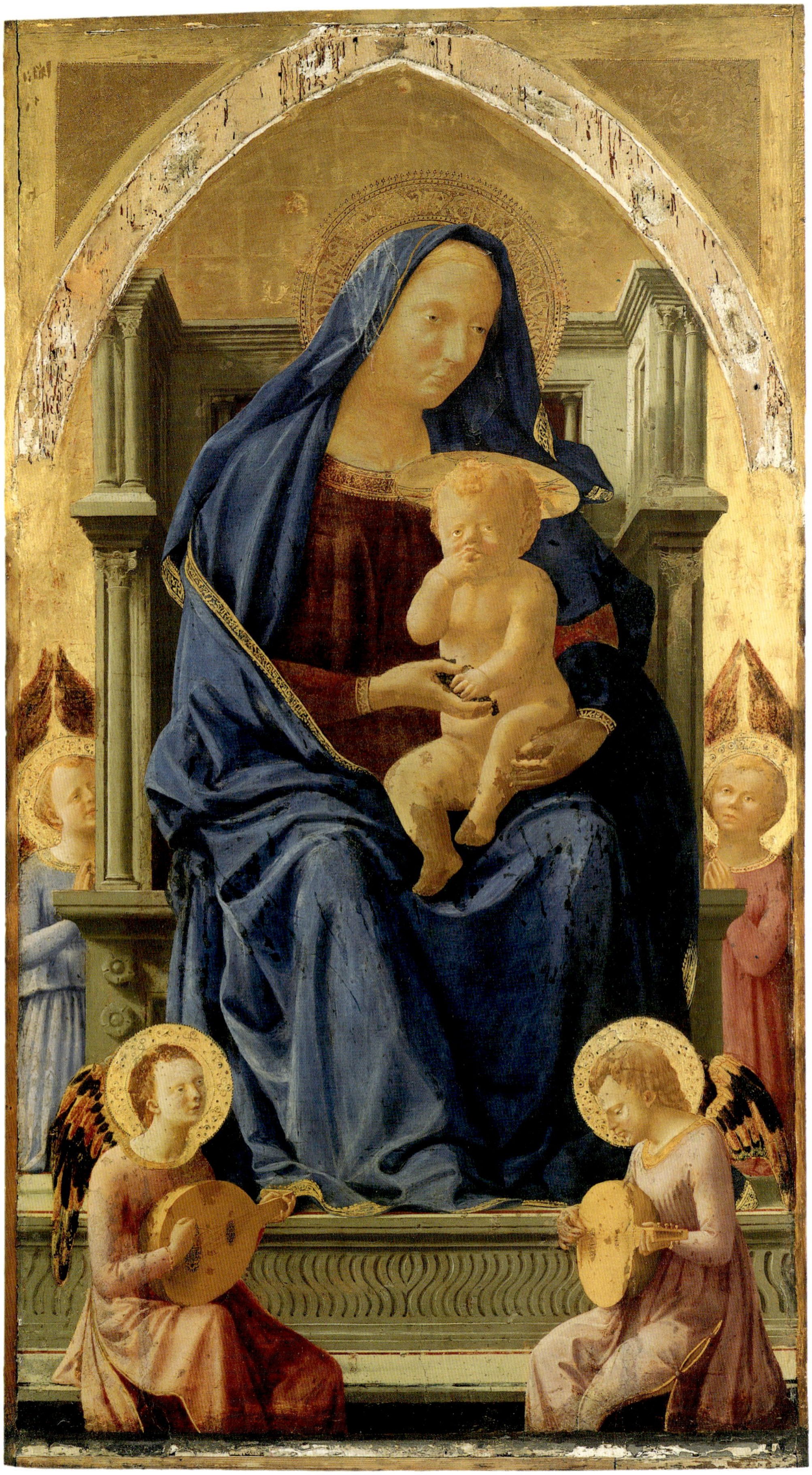

200 Masaccio, *Madonna and Child* from the Pisa polyptych, 1426, London, National Gallery.

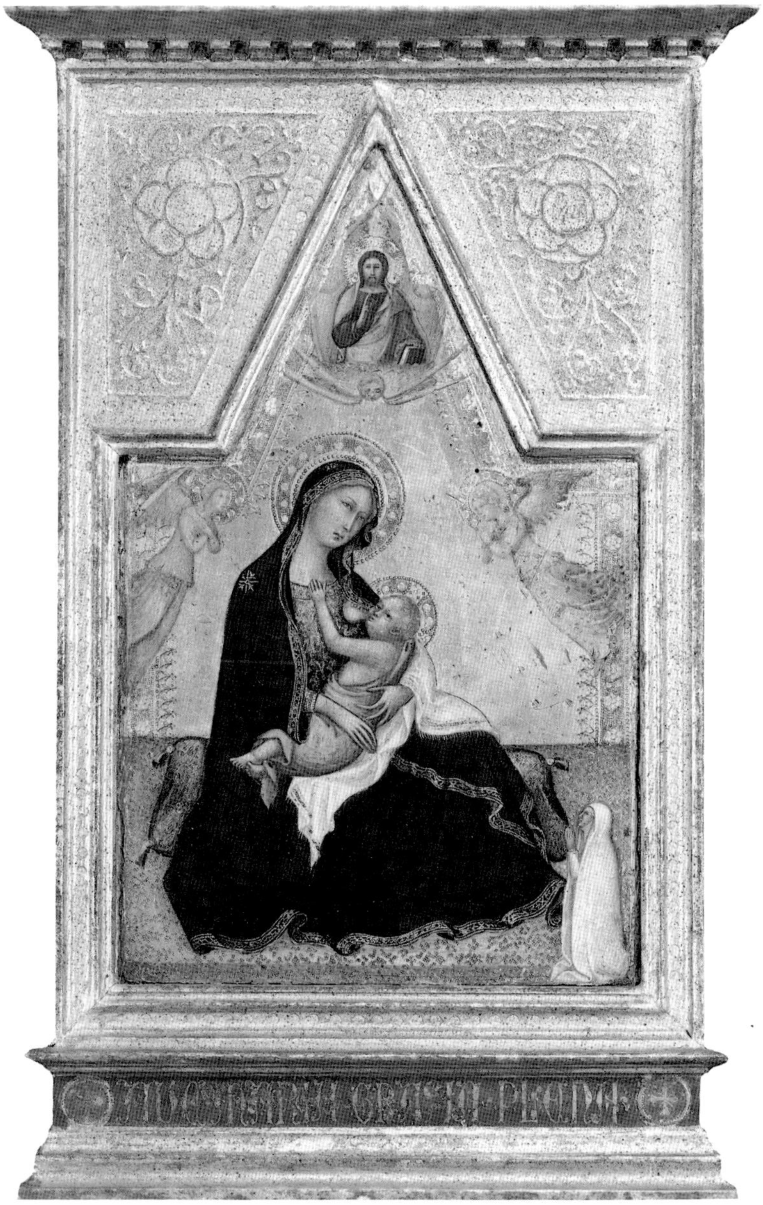

201 Andrea di Bartolo, *Madonna of Humility*, c. 1380s, Washington, National Gallery of Art, Samuel H. Kress Collection.

desirable in rendering the human figure, even when that human figure functioned as a sign for a sacred being like Christ or the Virgin. The Virgin and her bare breast could now be rendered with a much greater degree of physical volume and aspect, anatomical precision, surface detail, and spatial definition – according to a new technology of painting that the *quattrocento* viewer would have understood in terms of "l'imitazione della natura" or "l'imitazione del vero."

It is interesting, in this light, that the *Madonna lactans* seems to have gone out of vogue in Florence during the first half of the *quattrocento*. There are two gold-ground *Madonna lactans* panels by Lorenzo Monaco dating from the 1420s and versions attributed to retrospective artists like Niccolò di Pietro Gerini and Bicci di Lorenzo, which essentially reproduced *trecento* compositions.[121] There are two renditions painted by Masolino, including a very interesting panel in Munich (fig. 202), dated around 1425.[122] The artist adopted many elements of the traditional *trecento* composition described above. However, the Virgin's bare breast is considerably larger in relation to her body and adheres more closely to Renaissance principles of female anatomy. There is no attempt to conceal the juncture where the breast emerges from the opening in the red *gamurra* (gown). To the contrary, the slit in the *gamurra* is tailored along the edges with gold embroidery, evoking a more elaborate version of the contemporary wet-nurse's attire.[123] Masolino's nursing Virgin constitutes the most radical interpretation of this Marian image during the first half of the *quattrocento* in Florence.

In contrast, Fra Filippo avoided such a direct, full, and

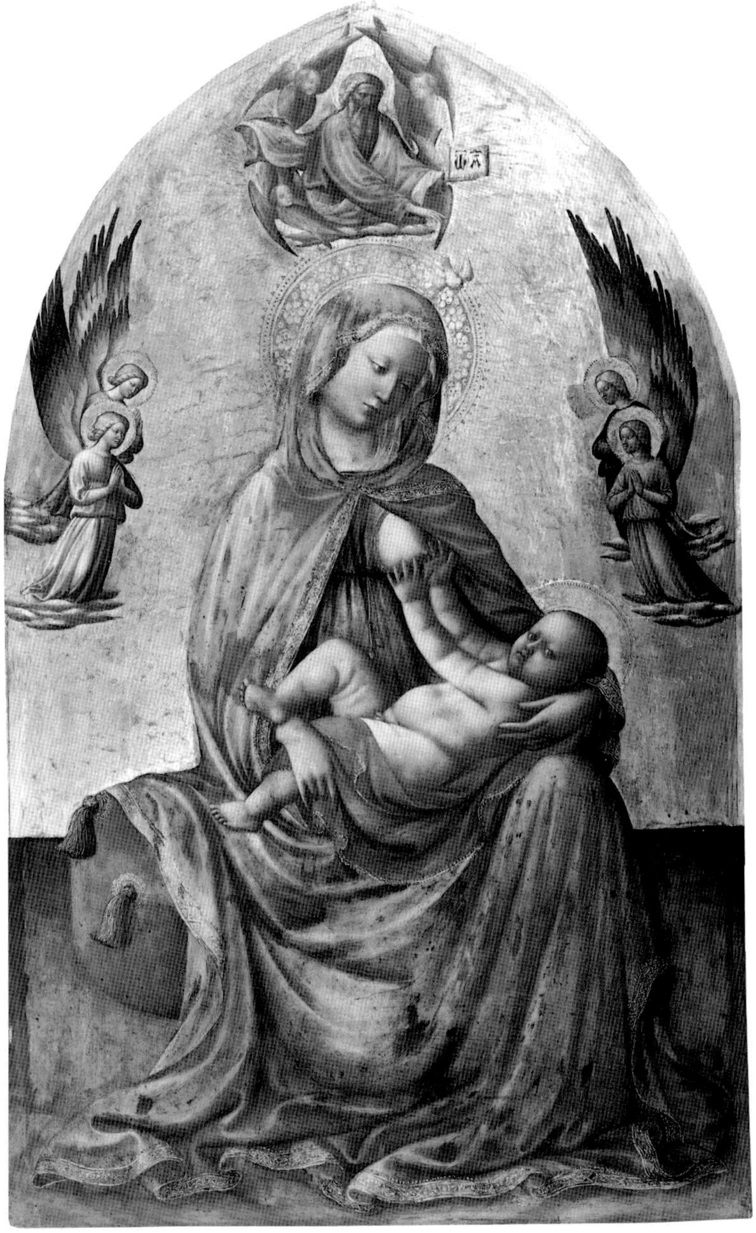

202 Masolino, *Madonna of Humility*, c. 1425, Munich, Alte Pinakothek.

veristic presentation of the *Madonna lactans* iconography in the altarpiece for the novitiate chapel at Santa Croce. He did so, however, without compromising either the naturalism used to render the sacred subjects or the religious decorum within this naturalistic representation. The Virgin and Child are elevated upon a throne and set within an architectural niche, establishing a hierarchy in which they are clearly differentiated as sacred figures.[124] The *lactans* signifiers are understated. The Christ Child does not nurse, and the disposition of the Virgin's veil and the positioning of the Child's hands deny the viewer unimpeded visual access to the Virgin's bare breast. There is, however, some indication that the artist had difficulty in stabilizing the design in the region of the Virgin's breast. There are *pentimenti* visible through the transparent paint film (see fig. 199) – traces of earlier, misplaced hands of the Christ Child, tentatively fingering the Madonna's flesh and cloak. The unsure character of the underdrawing in this overdetermined region of the female anatomy suggests that Lippi may not have been entirely at ease.[125]

The *Madonna lactans* is virtually absent from the work of the next generation of Florentine painters, Andrea del Castagno, Benozzo Gozzoli, and Neri di Bicci.[126] The image type reappeared during the last quarter of the century in the paintings of Cosimo Rosselli, Lorenzo di Credi, Botticelli, Filippino Lippi, and Ghirlandaio (fig. 203).[127] These later works are predominantly altarpieces and large, half-length devotional images. By this time the visual language of religious representation was moving toward a more comfortable accommodation within the fully fleshed metaphor of an idealized human body.[128] The *Madonna lactans*, however, seems to have been supplanted in popularity by two other devotional images – the half-length Madonna and Child and the Madonna adoring the Christ Child (with Lippi playing a key role in the evolution of each, as we have seen in Chapters 6 and 7).

From the art historian's perspective, the Santa Croce *pala* was executed at a critical moment in the history of Florentine art. If we think of the early 1440s (when the style of the painting suggests that it was executed), then the picture stands out as a radical innovation in the technology of contemporary altarpiece design. In Lippi's earlier Barbadori altarpiece (1437–9), Fra Angelico's Annalena (c. 1435) and San Marco (c. 1440–43) altarpieces (see figs. 103, 107, and 110), and Domenico Veneziano's *St. Lucy* altarpiece (c. 1445; see fig. 109), traditional compartmentalizing framing elements were eschewed and the saints were united together within the same pictorial space as the Madonna and Child. If these innovative works marked the explosion of the traditional *trecento* polyptych, then it could be argued that the Santa Croce *pala* represented an implosion. It should be seen as a parallel development worked out alongside this new type of altarpiece, offering a provocative re-dimensioning of the standard *trecento* polyptych in which a central figure, group, or scene is flanked by saints, all aligned and set within separate compartments without any fixed spatial or temporal coordinants.

In the Santa Croce *pala*, Fra Filippo brought the saints together into a unified pictorial space and framed them within a perfect square, but kept the conception and the operative principles of the traditional polyptych more or less intact by emphasizing the autonomy of each of the individual saints on either side of the Virgin and Child. The picture space is very shallow, and the lateral saints are lined up as in a frieze, so that they do not seem to mingle with one another or with the Virgin and Child. These saints have been released from a rigid confinement within polyptych compartments, but at the same time, the fictive architectural screen with shell niches and engaged columns that runs behind them recalls the separate spatial cells of the polyptych. The final Lippi twist is that Sts. Francis, Damian, Cosmas, and Anthony are not aligned with the tidy architectural divisions of the screen, and the net effect is similar to that in the Barbadori altarpiece, where the painted columns in the pictorial space lie slightly off-axis from the hanging bosses of the frame, and both propose and contradict the conception of a polyptych.

It was not only in Fra Filippo's oeuvre that these two altarpiece types co-existed. Fra Angelico also painted the so-called *sacra conversazione* type where all of the saints were grouped together within a unified pictorial space (see fig. 110) and, at the same time, executed other works like the Perugia polyptych (fig. 204) where the lateral saints are isolated in their own spatial cells with the absence of framing elements to perform this task.[129] Later in the century, too, while painters were working to elaborate the relationship between saints within the altarpiece, the compartmentalized, gold-ground polyptych continued to be produced in Florence.[130] There was also a more innovative altarpiece line which developed out of paintings like Lippi's Santa Croce *pala*. Botticelli, Lorenzo di Credi, and Cosimo Rosselli fashioned altarpieces where the accompanying saints are situated in a common pictorial space with the Virgin and Child, but are lined up at either side and are perceived by the viewer individually, rather than as part of an interactive ensemble.[131]

Martin Kemp, in his introductory essay to a volume reevaluating the Renaissance altarpiece, describes the development of the rectangular altarpiece with a unified pictorial space as a product of artistic, as opposed to religious concerns:

> The experiments with spatial unification, which reached a peak around 1440 with Filippo Lippi's Barbadori altarpiece . . . and [San Lorenzo] *Annunciation* . . . and Fra Angelico's San Marco altarpiece, do not seem to have been driven by theological or liturgical considerations but rather by an ambition to revivify the formal and emotional possibilities of a stock type in the light of new potentialities which were being developed across a range of genres by the pioneers of Renaissance art and architecture.[132]

There were, however, rumblings of reform within contemporary discussions of the liturgy, which have all the Renaissance signifiers and can be shown to have something in common with these transformations in the Florentine altarpiece.

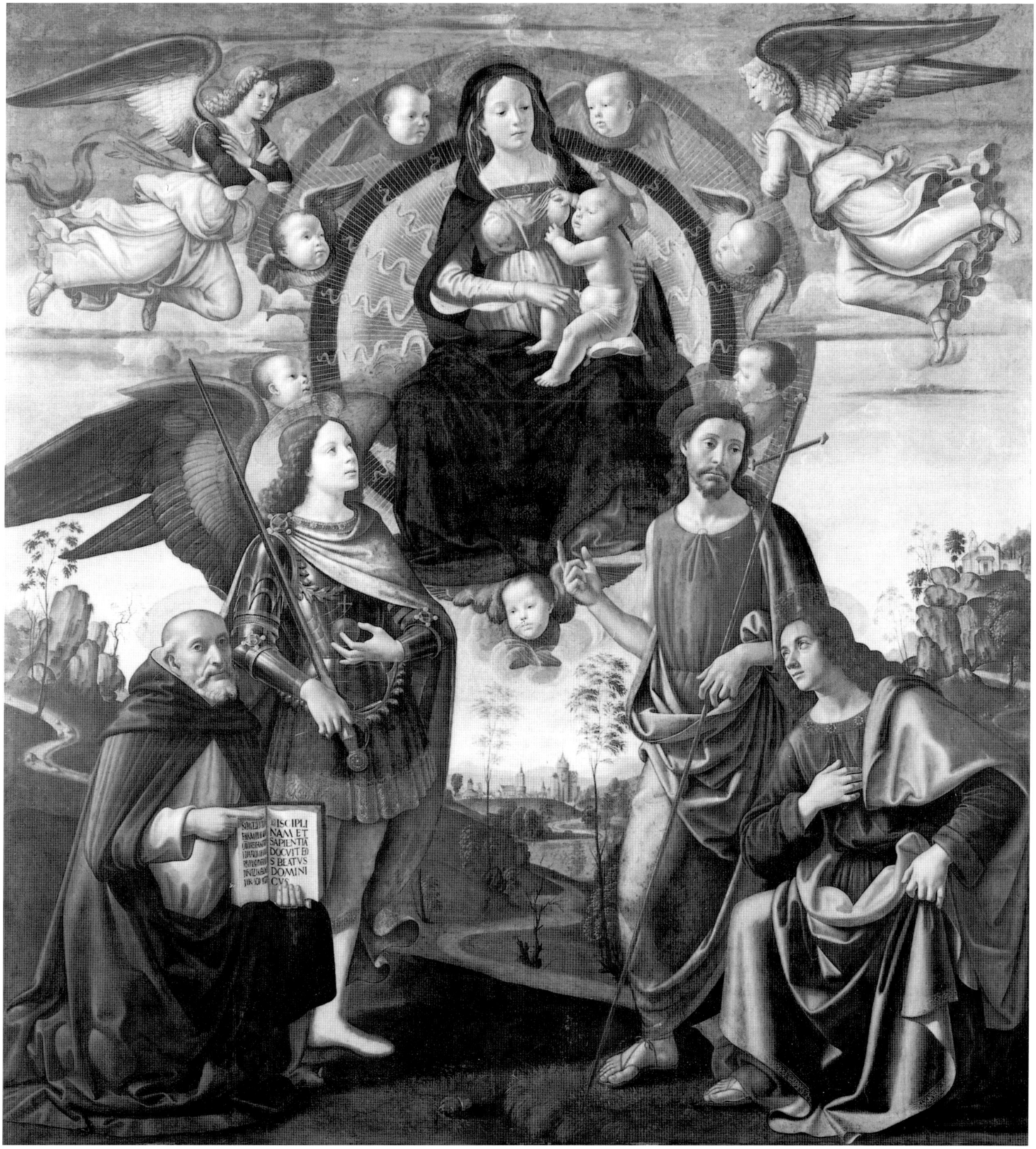

203 Domenico Ghirlandaio, *Madonna and Child with Saints*, c. 1490, the front of the high altarpiece of Santa Maria Novella, now in Munich, Alte Pinakothek.

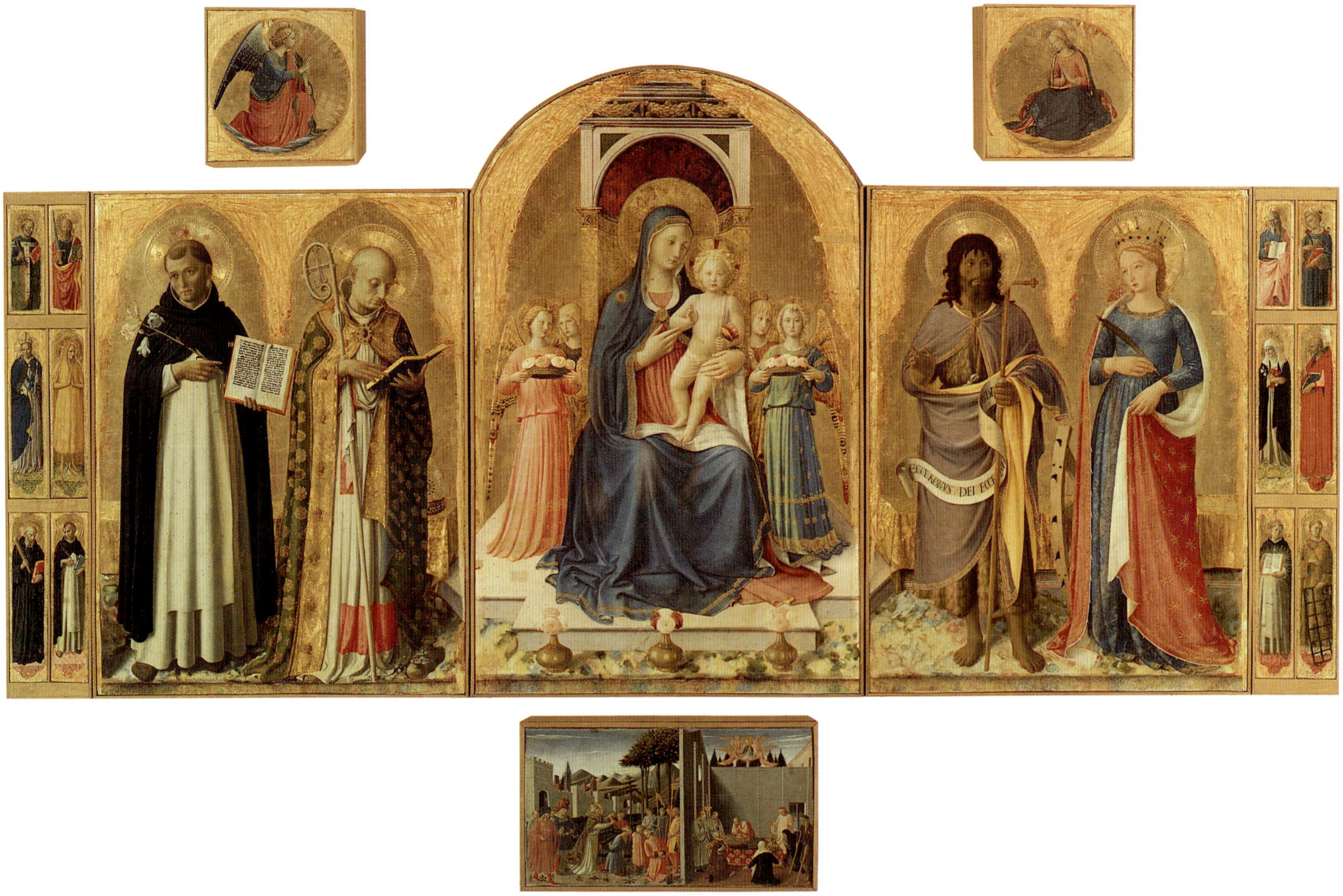

204 Fra Angelico, Perugia polyptych (without the complete predella), c. 1440s, Perugia, Galleria Nazionale.

In the late *trecento*, Rudolph de Tongres (d. 1403), a Dutch canon who had spent some time in Rome, launched an attack on the standard breviary then in common use.[133] This was a Franciscan breviary that had been officially accepted by Pope Nicholas III (1277–86), where the weekday Offices were lavishly embellished. Minor saints were accorded octaves and translations, and the liturgy was elaborated with apocryphal events from the saints' lives, the repetition of psalms, and supplementary prayers. Rudolph advocated a return to the antique Roman liturgy that was still observed by the canons of St. John Lateran and other churches in Rome, based upon biblical texts and concentrating on the essential canonical Offices.

To some extent, the altarpiece configuration where all the saints gather around the Virgin and Child within a unified pictorial space and the compartmentalized pseudo-polyptych resonate with these two liturgical currents. In the Barbadori and San Marco altarpieces, the various saints and angels are perceived in relation and in proportion to the central, privileged figures of the Virgin and Child. This parallels a liturgy in which the daily Offices and masses concentrate on the figures of the Trinity and the Virgin.[134] But the Florentine Renaissance religious cosmos was, and continued to be, composed of spheres of influence presided over by myriad saintly mediators. The city was under the patronage of the Virgin and the Baptist. Every individual had his or her personal name saint, as did larger corporate bodies like *consorterie*, guilds, and confraternities. Sts. Sebastian and Roch protected people against the plague. The Madonna del Parto and Madonna del Popolo were appealed to by pregnant women. There were separate prayers and festive rites addressed to these different saints and aspects of the Virgin, designed to insure that each would continue to remain efficacious in his or her respective area of sacred influence. The persistence of an altarpiece type with each saint either apportioned in a separate compartment or presented separately, in isolation, reflects social practices and a liturgy with distinct offices, special prayers, and elaborate *vitae* ascribed to each saint. Perhaps it is not surprising that Fra Filippo Lippi followed this particular altarpiece model when devising an image for a Franciscan convent, given the fact that the Franciscan breviary had codified this type of worship of the saints.

CONCLUSION

The altarpiece for the novitiate chapel at Santa Croce registered the interests of the diverse individuals and corporate bodies that had an investment in its production and use. The patron, Cosimo de' Medici, posited within the imagery an array of Medicean references and mobilized a visual style associated with his characteristic *magnificentia*. He also elaborated upon the public image of himself as a generous, pius patron of Florentine religious institutions. The Franciscan context of the commission predicated the inclusion of the two primary Franciscan saints alongside the Medicean saints, and a pictorial idiom that could articulate a set of Franciscan religious values. The altarpiece also had to be accessible to the principal audience within the novitiate chapel, the Franciscan novices. It had to serve as a focal point in the mass that they celebrated daily in the chapel and as a vivid stimulus for their mental prayer. It also had to present very basic Franciscan religious tenets to the postulants. Fra Filippo Lippi had to negotiate these competing concerns and devise a satisfactory, appropriate accommodation for them within the altarpiece imagery. He was working in an artistic culture that placed an increasingly higher value on the painter's *ingegno* and *invenzione* in introducing interesting solutions to problems in pictorial representation. However, as successful and imaginative as his solutions may have been, certain tensions are evident in the altarpiece. There is an uneasy spatial relationship between the Franciscan saints and the Medici patron saints at either side of the Virgin and Child that underscores the thorny problem of conspicuous lay patronage of a Franciscan convent. The paradoxical implications of Franciscan "unmediated" vision when applied to the image type of the *Madonna lactans* are also revealed. Certain Franciscan associations – nudity and poverty; desire and desire for God; mother and the Virgin Mother; a nursing woman and the Virgin in her humanity and humility – prove to be unstable when linked to a visual image of the *Madonna lactans* painted in a naturalistic mode.

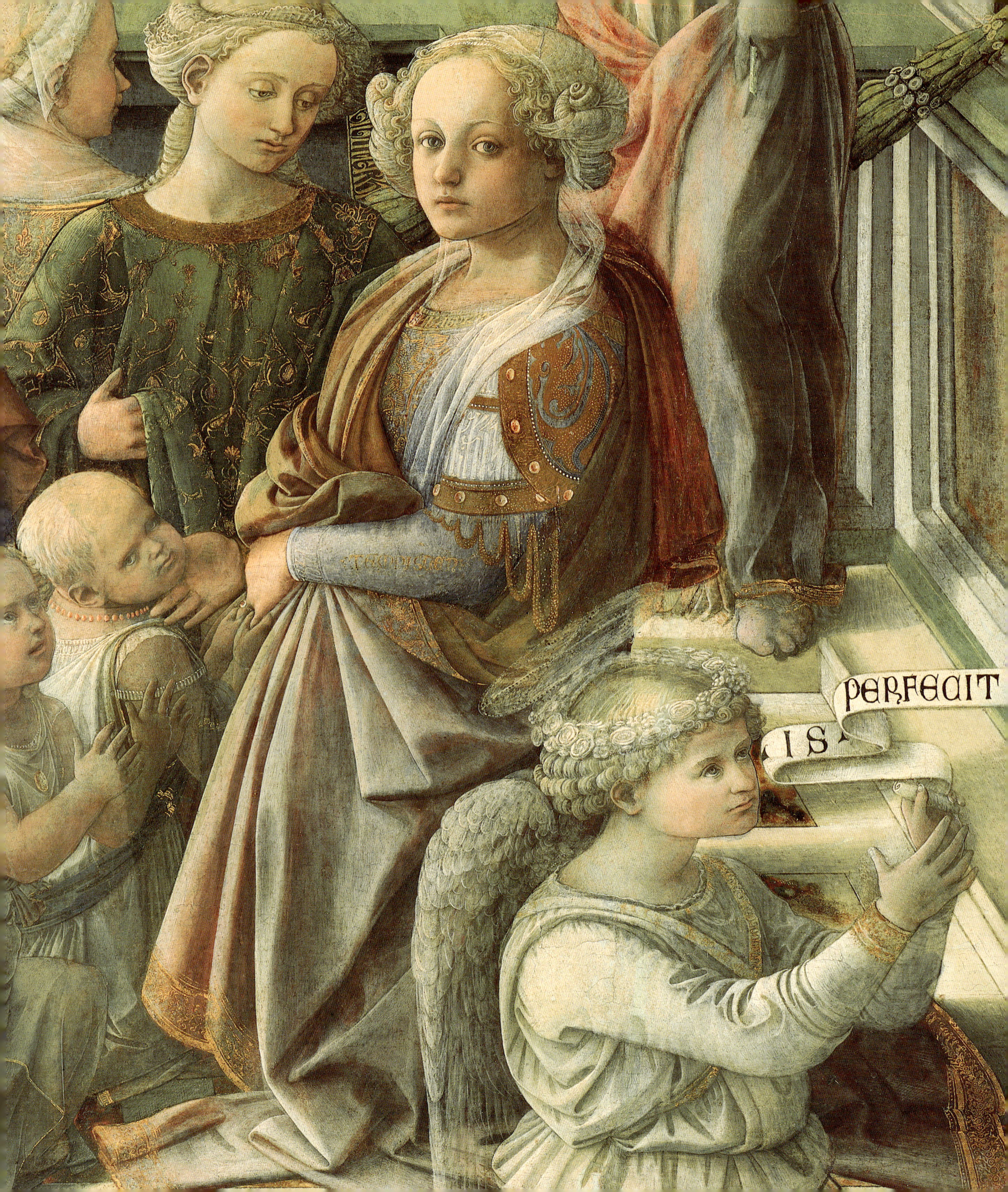
PERFECIT
IS

CHAPTER NINE

REPRESENTING *LE SUORE*: ALTARPIECES FOR TWO FLORENTINE BENEDICTINE NUNNERY CHURCHES

On December 2, 1424, an agreement was drawn up between the Benedictine nuns of Sant'Ambrogio in the city of Florence and a group of thirteen Benedictine nuns known as "Le Romite della Annuntiata." "Le Romite" were moving from their cramped quarters on the Ponte Rubiconte to a new residence on Via Ghibellina, just inside the city walls in the parish of Sant'Ambrogio (figs. 206 and 207). The Portuguese Abbot Gomez of the Badia was orchestrating the transfer and helping to set up the necessary conditions. In accordance with concessions granted by Florentine bishops during the *trecento*, any new religious foundation in the parish of Sant'Ambrogio had to have the approval of the small congregation of Benedictine nuns established at Sant'Ambrogio.[1] "Le Romite" were requesting permission to construct a small church and convent with the agreement that they observe certain traditional prerogatives of the nuns of Sant'Ambrogio. Only "Le Romite" and their chaplains could be buried within their new *sepultura* – implying, no local parishioners. Sant'Ambrogio chaplains would preside over their feast day worship and celebrations. Their church would have one, or at most, two altars, and the bell that would call them to mass and sound the canonical hours would be less powerful than the bells of Sant'Ambrogio. The five nuns of Sant'Ambrogio accepted the terms of the agreement a month later.[2] On December 14, "Le Romite," accompanied by the prior and priests of Sant'Ambrogio and a crowd of Florentine laymen, made a grand procession from the Ponte Rubiconte to the new monastery of Santa Maria Annunziata, which became known as Le Murate.[3]

But the agreement proved unsatisfactory for "Le Romite," who were becoming known now as the "Walled Sisters," or Le Suore Murate. In spite of the terms of the agreement and the requisite licenses obtained by Abbess Agata from the Florentine episcopacy, the parish priest of Sant'Ambrogio hassled the nuns continually. Efforts on the part of the abbess to build a small church and oratory at Le Murate were impeded, and the nuns were obstructed in celebrating the two most important feasts in their religious calendar, those of the Annunciation and of St. Benedict.[4]

The nuns turned to their intermediaries among the male clerical ranks – Abbot Gomez and their confessor Giovanni di Lorenzo da Fighino – and with their help approached Pope Eugenius IV who was residing in Florence at the time. On August 23, 1434, the pope issued a bull that granted Le Murate independence from Sant'Ambrogio and gave the abbess considerable autonomy.[5] Abbot Gomez was appointed protector of the nuns and any attempt to interfere with their activities would meet with papal censure leading to excommunication.

The new independent circumstances and the growing number of nuns at Le Murate gave rise to the need for a larger consecrated space within the confines of the monastery. According to a chronicle written in 1598 by one of the nuns of Le Murate, Giustina Niccolini, they had had a little church on the Ponte Rubiconte with an "alterino" adorned with an image of the Annunciation. During the first ten years in the new convent, they had managed with "a bit of a little church" with an oratory above and a bell "of the smallest weight."[6] The 1424 pact had limited the number of altars in the church to one, with a second altar negotiable if the nuns so desired. Shortly after the separation bull of Eugenius IV, plans were made to rebuild the church and construction was already under way when the Florentine banker Giovanni d'Amerigo Benci stepped forth and undertook the financing. The church was planned with three altars – a high altar dedicated to the Annunciation and two lateral altars dedicated to St. Bernard and to the Crucifixion. The construction of the church and adornment of the altars took place in a very short time, between 1439 and 1443.[7] The artist chosen to paint

205 Filippo Lippi, *Coronation of the Virgin* detail of fig. 214, with St. Theopista.

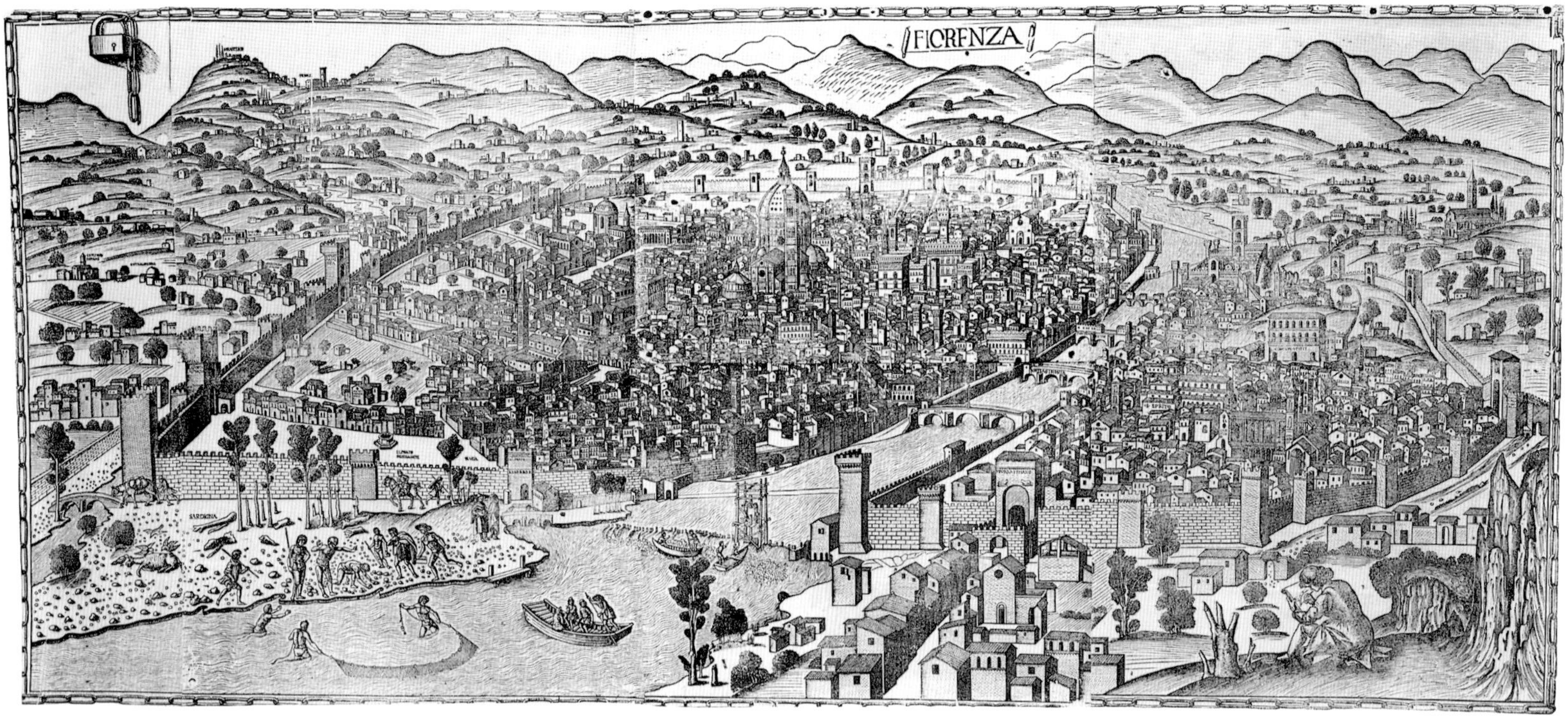

206 "Catena View of Florence," woodcut, c. 1470, Berlin, Staatliche Museen Preussischer Kulturbesitz, Kupferstichkabinett.

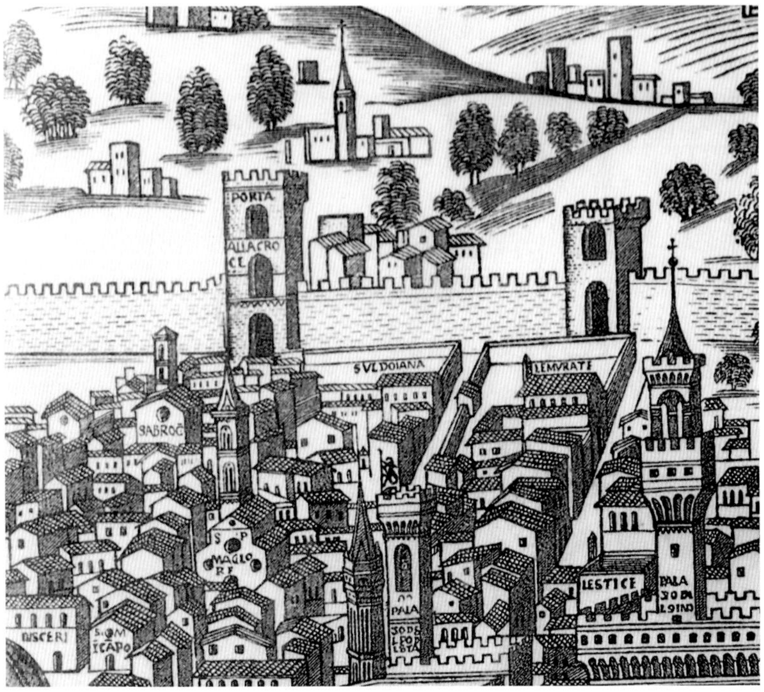

207 "Catena View of Florence," detail of fig. 206, showing the parish of Sant'Ambrogio.

the altarpieces for the main altar and that of St. Bernard was Fra Filippo Lippi.[8]

A twist to the story will provide the occasion for this chapter. During the very years that Fra Filippo was painting the *Annunciation* and *St. Bernard* for Le Murate, he was also working on the main altarpiece for the church of Sant'Ambrogio. How is this coincidence to be understood? Was it a case of continued rivalry between the two religious institutions, played out through their competing claims on the time and skill of one of the most highly regarded Florentine painters of the day? Or is this evidence of a new relationship between Sant'Ambrogio and Le Murate, involving cooperation, common ground, and commerce? The situation is complicated by the fact that the patrons of the altarpieces, Giovanni Benci and Francesco Maringhi, while sensitive to the interests of the nunneries, had personal investments in their religious patronage that conditioned the production and use of each painting. In addition, Sant'Ambrogio was both a Benedictine nunnery and the local parish seat, and thus there were parish as well as convent considerations involved in the high altarpiece commission. I should like, nonetheless, to take as my primary focus the two Benedictine nunneries, their colleges of nuns, and their high altar images. I shall argue that the nuns themselves had a share in the two altarpiece commissions, and shall try to identify where their interests are made manifest in the pictorial imagery.[9] I shall raise the question of whether the circumstances underlying the conflict that raged between the two nunneries from 1424 to 1434, in some way or another, may have left their mark on the two paintings that Lippi executed in the early 1440s.

* * *

Sant'Ambrogio (figs. 208 and 209) was one of the oldest nunneries in Florence. The parish church first appears in a documentary citation in the year 1001, and the convent a century later, in 1141, when it came under the protection of the Holy See.[10] Sant'Ambrogio was initially located just outside the Florentine walls, to the east of the city. It fell within the jurisdiction of the Florentine Badia. Typical of Benedictine foundations, it did not have complete autonomy from the local bishopric. During the early years of its existence, the convent probably drew its members from the families of the Florentine landed nobility.[11] When the Florentine walls were enlarged in the late thirteenth century, the convent of Sant'Ambrogio was incorporated into the city proper, in one of the largest but poorer parishes.[12] It appears that Sant'Ambrogio underwent a slow transformation from one of the more exclusive convents located just outside the city, to an urban institution with a strong local, neighborhood base. By the mid-*trecento* the convent was experiencing financial problems.[13] While the number of convent nuns had been formally fixed at twelve in 1305, by the early *quattrocento*, the numbers had settled well below this ceiling.[14] Through the 1430s, there were only five to six nuns attached to the convent, for the most part from local parish families of middling wealth.[15]

At the time that "Le Romite" from the Ponte Rubiconte moved into Le Murate in 1424, Sant'Ambrogio was thus a small Benedictine convent in a poor section of the city whose financial security was threatened by the arrival of the new congregation of Benedictine nuns in the same neighborhood. The terms of the 1424 agreement between the two nunneries were designed to keep local parochial involvement at Le Murate to a minimum, protecting the nuns of Sant'Ambrogio against the loss of their traditional patronage base.[16] But the conditions of female enclosure in the city at large were changing, and this inevitably had some effect on the relationship between the two nunneries.

In what has become a classic study on Florentine nunneries during the Renaissance, Richard Trexler tracked a phenomenal rise in the number of female monastic establishments from the *trecento* through the mid-*cinquecento*.[17] He observed that between 1378 and 1552, the number of nunneries in the city of Florence rose from eighteen to forty-seven.[18] The increase during the first half of the *quattrocento* was gradual but steady. Over the same period, the average number of nuns within each establishment grew from around fourteen to seventy-three.[19] From the 1427–28 *catasto*, it is evident that roughly 2.25% of the women in the city were cloistered as nuns, increasing to a remarkable 11.5% by 1552.[20] In 1427–28, the majority of the women enclosed in the nunneries – between 65 and 75% – were from patrician families.[21]

With the steady rise in demand for places, Sant'Ambrogio was guaranteed a ready supply of endowered applicants. The convent began to broaden its patronage base and accept women from all parts of the city – no doubt necessitated in part by the local competition posed by Le Murate where the number of nuns was climbing steadily. Throughout this period, Sant'Ambrogio was unusual in resisting the pressure to expand its facilities and open its doors to a greater number of nuns. The numbers went up, but never much beyond the capacity established in the previous century.[22]

From the survival of the convent's *Ricordo di Monache e doti* that covers the years just following the installation of Fra Filippo's altarpiece, we can get some idea of the Florentine public to which the nunnery of Sant'Ambrogio now appealed.[23]

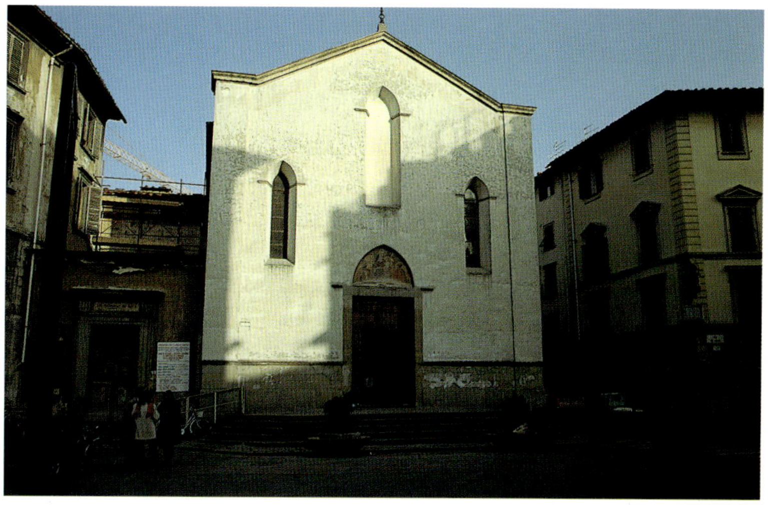

208 The Church of Sant'Ambrogio, Florence.

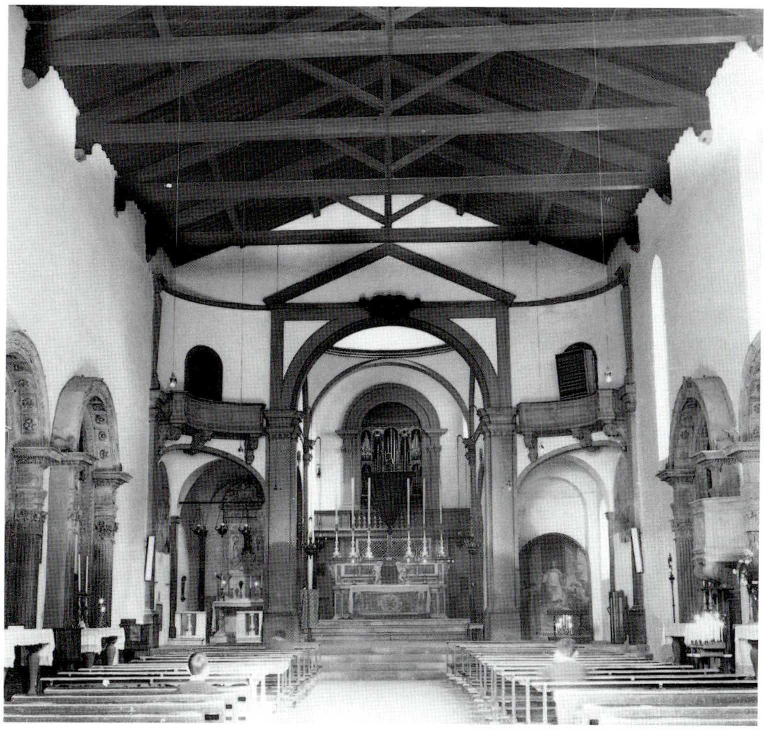

209 Interior of the Church of Sant'Ambrogio, looking toward the main chapel, Florence.

Twenty-three nuns and boarders, recorded from 1440 to 1470, were for the most part from the less established families of the Florentine patriciate – many of them *novi cives*, or "new citizens."[24] These included the Bagnesi, Barbadori, Barducci, Bartolini, Brancacci, Buonaccorsi, del Caccia, del Cassa, Formiconi, Lorini, Pecierotti, Peruzzi, Piccardi, and Strozzi. The Strozzi and Peruzzi nuns were from minor branches of these more illustrious families (until 1468, when three *fanciulle* from the Palla Strozzi branch of the family entered the convent).[25] The families came from all four quarters of the city, relatively evenly distributed, representing ten different *gonfaloni*. The dowries paid by the nuns' families ranged from 70 to 100 gold florins – middling for convent dowries.[26] Three of the family heads placed two of their daughters within Sant'Ambrogio.[27] While the convent opened its doors to very young boarders, it does not appear as though Sant'Ambrogio made a practice of accepting oblates not yet in their teens.[28]

The abbesses of Sant'Ambrogio during this period were both from families with strong patronage ties to the parish church of Sant'Ambrogio. Abbess Niccolaia Buonaccorsi[29] was the daughter of Stefano di Giovanni Buonaccorsi, a prominent doctor of law and politician in the city.[30] During the early years of her long tenure as abbess, her father occasionally acted on the convent's behalf.[31] After her father's death in 1432, there seems to have been a shift in the convent patronage away from the Buonaccorsi toward the Maringhi and Barducci families. Niccolaia's successor as abbess was Antonia di Stagio Barducci.[32] The Barducci were *novi cives*, slowly gaining influence in the parish of Sant'Ambrogio.[33] Antonia's father, Stagio, had founded a chapel dedicated to St. Eustace in Sant'Ambrogio, located to the right of the *cappella maggiore*. Her brother Giovanni, who was a banker, assisted the convent in various financial negotiations, including the payments made to Lippi for his work on the painting for the high altar.[34]

The nunnery of Le Murate (fig. 210) had a very different history and public image from Sant'Ambrogio. The founder had been a poor woman named Apollonia from the Sienese countryside who had moved into a small house on one of the piles of the Ponte Rubiconte (where the current Ponte alle Grazie is located) in 1390.[35] Apollonia was joined by another woman, Agata di Domenico Lucente, in 1396, and four years later, the two walled themselves into the house, pledging to live like desert hermits. Agata went out on occasion to gather alms and a local parish priest came to confess the women and to say mass in a small church that was erected beside the house. Gradually they were joined by other women. Their numbers had climbed to seven by 1413, when they were persuaded to join the Benedictine Order.[36] By the time the nuns moved to their new convent on Via Ghibellina in 1424, they numbered thirteen.

The nuns gained a reputation for their extreme religious practices. Their hermetic existence in the little house on the Ponte Rubiconte under Agata earned them the title "le Romite di suora Agata."[37] When they joined the Benedictine Order in 1413,

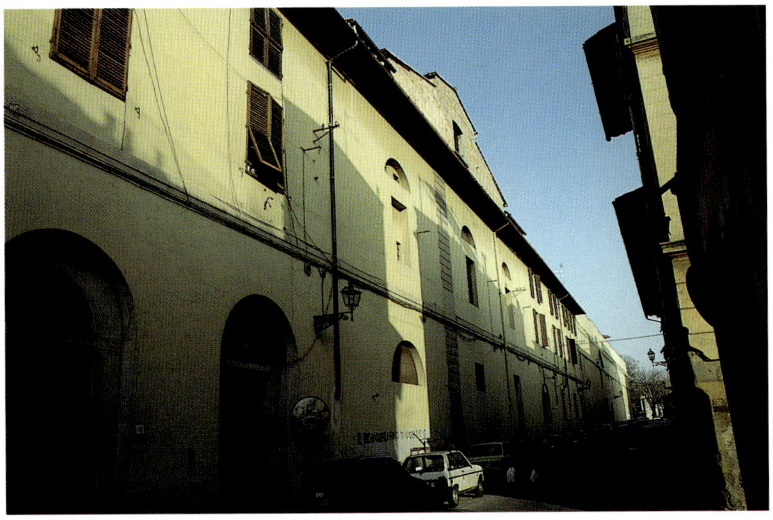

210 The ex-nunnery Le Murate, Florence.

211 Stefano Buonsignori, *View of Florence*, 1584, detail showing Le Murate (from the 1660 De Rossi edition).

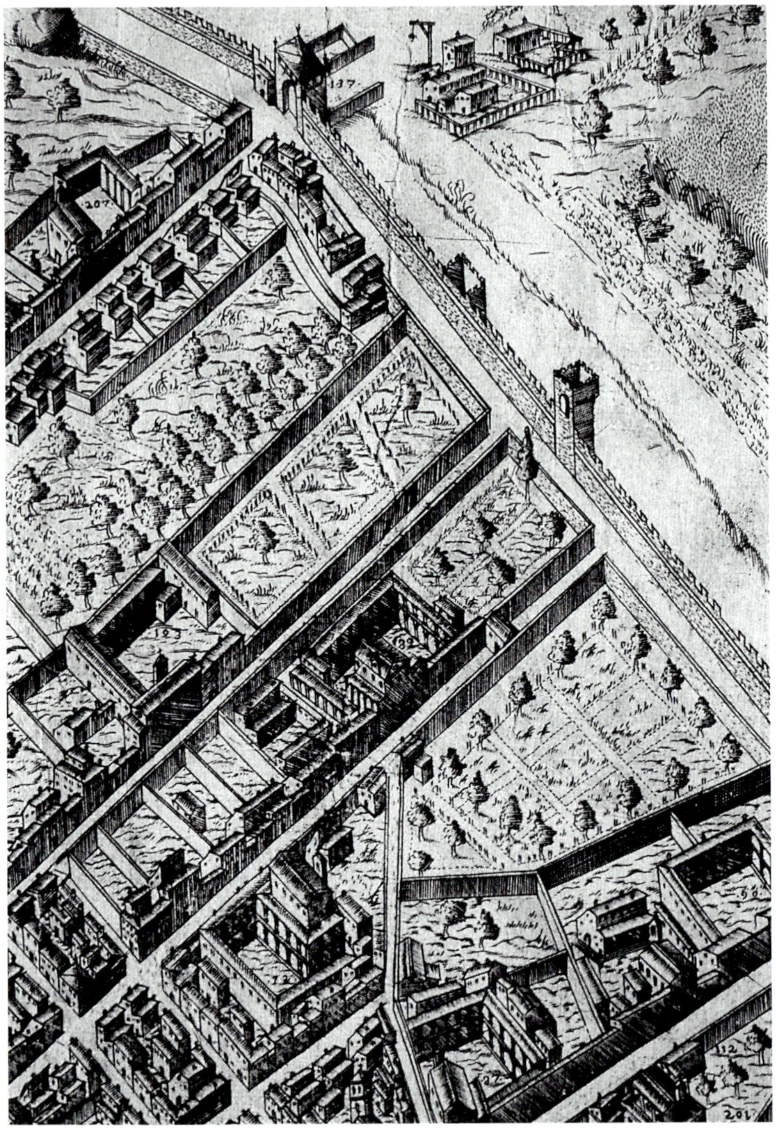

they followed the Rule with strict observance. They donned a blue and white habit, said to emulate the dress of the Virgin, and wore sandals without stockings. Once in their new monastery on the Via Ghibellina, they instituted a symbolic reenactment of Apollonia's historic "walling off" on the Ponte Rubiconte. One of the doors to the convent was sealed shut, to be reopened each time a nun professed and then walled in once again.[38] It is interesting that the nuns became known as "Le Murate" only during this later phase of their monastic existence, when the symbol of the wall was self-consciously and ceremoniously mobilized.[39]

A small church and oratory were constructed, in addition to convent facilities, for the ever-increasing numbers. The nuns began to put aside time from their devotional exercises in order to support their growing material needs through various sorts of manual labor.[40] A "Sala della Telaia" was built where the nuns wove cloth and did embroidery work (see figs. 79 and 80) for sale. They also became involved in manuscript production, casting and painting gesso reliefs, and manufacturing essences.[41] In 1433, the nuns changed their habit, replacing their blue and white robes with the more conventional Benedictine black habit and veil, and professed anew.[42]

On close examination, it would appear that the social status of the women had begun to change as soon as the group renounced its marginal status as an independent house of non-aligned religious extremists and came under the Benedictine Rule. This affiliation gave them legitimacy in the eyes of the Florentine patriciate, and neutralized the fears that independent congregations of religious women inevitably aroused within the male clerical ranks and among the governing class.[43] In the *Cronache del Monastero* (1598), Giustina Niccolini notes that the early nuns "were not of noble blood."[44] The founder Apollonia, she claims, was "born of a poor man."[45] It was Agata, a woman of substance ("una Donna da Bene"), and not Apollonia, who became the first abbess in 1413. The subsequent two abbesses were new arrivals to the nunnery, and seem to have been elected for reasons of social position, maturity, and administrative power. Abbess Simona, elected in 1433, was the daughter of the Florentine patrician Giovanni da Panzano. She had been a nun in the Marches before entering Le Murate two years before her appointment as abbess at the age of forty-two. The next abbess, Scolastica Rondinelli, who assumed the title in 1439 at age forty-five, was renowned for having passed from widow to oblate to prelate, all within the course of seven months.[46] She was the daughter of Ugolino Rondinelli and the widow of Piero dell'Antella – both members of patrician families proscribed in the 1434 confrontation with the Medici faction.[47]

It was following the years that Lippi painted the high altarpiece, 1439–43, just after Scolastica became abbess, that Le Murate underwent the most dramatic transformation. There were thirty-six nuns in 1439 and when Scolastica died in 1475 at the venerable age of eighty-one, the number of nuns at Le Murate was just under two hundred. The convent's *Libro di vita et morte* disappeared long ago, and we have only fragmentary information on the women who joined the convent as boarders, *converse*, and oblates. We do know that Scolastica put two of her own daughters in the convent, and that three members of the Strozzi family entered between 1445 and 1453.[48] The man who paid for the construction of the convent church, Giovanni Benci, placed his daughter Caterina in the convent in the mid-1440s as a boarder.[49] During the second half of the century, women from the Albizzi, Bardi, Benci, Capponi, Medici, and Strozzi families joined the convent.[50]

As a complement to the Benedictine Rule, Abbess Scolastica drafted a set of Constitutions detailing the strict devotional practices of the nuns of Le Murate.[51] The nuns were to hasten to the choir whenever summoned and were to be present at all of the Divine Offices. In the refectory they were to be silent as the lesson was read, with their eyes downcast. They were to recite penitential psalms as they worked. The kitchen was debarred without a license from the abbess. In the *parlatorio* where relatives came to visit, the nuns were never to be alone, and could only exchange gifts or letters with a license from the abbess. They were constrained to maintain complete silence on Wednesdays and Fridays. The penalties for disobedience are spelled out: penitential psalms recited in the chapter house with hands tied behind the back, a meager meal of bread and wine eaten on the refectory floor, apologies offered by bowing to the foot of the offended party.

According to Le Murate's Chronicle, however, in practice these strict regulations and punishments were not always upheld. The Chronicle informs us that "the standards began to decline, and [only] with difficulty, [the nuns] were able to live, as time went on, with such rigor and strictness with which they had started out."[52] Certain contradictions were in evidence: the nuns slept in a common dormitory, as the Benedictine Rule prescribed, but separate servants quarters were built to house the lay women who attended them.[53] While the nuns had initially produced their embroidery work, manuscripts, gesso reliefs, and essences to meet their material needs, the financial base of the convent was now secured through pious donations from the laity. Therefore, the nuns' work figured primarily in the cycle of devotion and manual labor outlined in the Benedictine Rule. (The nuns were in fact gaining a reputation for their handiwork, but the convent Chronicle insists that most of the 500 florins that the nuns earned annually from the sales were given away as alms to the poor.)[54]

In spite of these discrepancies between the letter of the Rule and the tenor of life inside Le Murate, the public reputation of the nuns remained crystallized in the image of extreme piety and unremitting devotion associated with the convent founders. In 1443, the lawyer Tommaso Salvetti wrote of Le Murate, that "the venerable nuns, who are present in great numbers, engage in extreme acts of submission without ever expecting that with their own merit they could ever satisfy [God]."[55] Archbishop Antonino, writing some ten years later, used a more elaborate rhetoric to praise the nuns:

> They who now number over one hundred, [maintain] extreme observance, fasting, silence and discipline, through the simplicity of their manner and attire. All unite for the Divine Offices, while outside the canonical hours, continuously, day and night, two of them read the psalter in the choir of the church, taking turns, one after the other. . . . While property is at the disposal of some, generally the nuns are allowed neither possessions nor income. They procure their meager livelihood through manual labor and alms generously given to them. Exhibiting the greatest charity, [they are] of one heart and one spirit with God.[56]

This is indeed lavish praise from the Florentine archbishop who condemned the general state of the city's nunneries as a "public scandal."[57]

Later in the century, another religious reformer of a more radical bent saw the situation quite differently. In 1495, Fra Savonarola told a lay Florentine audience of a visit he had made to Le Murate:

> I went to Le Murate last Friday. . . . I preached to them . . . that they must leave their trinkets, headdresses, hair-nets and the olive [branches] that they make of gold and silver and their little books. Secondly, if they are the "Walled Sisters," they must be as they are named. And I say that it is a terrible thing to open [the convent] to gentlemen who go there; I know too, I do, who are the courtiers who are lightweight like a boat, and I said to them that that dramatized song was invented by Satan, and that they must throw away these books of songs and organ [music]. And if the head who has the governorship is not able to cope, she should renounce her office.[58]

Savonarola's criticisms speak toward the gap that existed between the encomiastic rhetoric on Le Murate and the loose application of the Benedictine Rule within the walls by the late fifteenth century. But Florentines were not yet ready to relinquish their polished image of the convent. They had heard of Savonarola's stern admonitions to the nuns of Le Murate uttered two days earlier, and were apparently not pleased. Savonarola was on the defensive before the crowd: "But why, oh Friar, have you said this? Not because I say that they are bad, because I say they are good; but it is necessary that they return to this simplicity."[59] Even in the 1490s, the nunnery continued to hold its reputation as one of the city's most exemplary convents and Savonarola had to clarify the nature of his criticisms. His uncompromisingly austere standards and his particular conception of female monasticism were in contradiction with the character of the religious life that the patrician women of Le Murate had established over the century.[60]

I should now like to pull some comparative features out of these profiles of the two Benedictine nunneries. Sant'Ambrogio was distinguished as one of the oldest convents in the city, while Le Murate was one of the newest. By the fifteenth century, Sant'Ambrogio was not attracting the daughters of the high Florentine patriciate, and the dowry prices were correspondingly in the middle range. We can assume that this represented something of a fall in the fortune and prestige of the convent. Le Murate, on the other hand, was in the process of radical transformation. Over a period of thirty years, it had changed from a marginal, unaffiliated group of extreme anchorites to one of the most reputable congregations of nuns in the city in which the Florentine patriciate enthusiastically sought to place their women. And while the size of Sant'Ambrogio had been fixed at twelve during the early *trecento*, the numbers soared at Le Murate, and the convent was continually enlarged to accommodate the additional women. At Sant'Ambrogio, the nuns' application of the Benedictine Rule was probably relatively loose, while the nuns of Le Murate pledged a strict observance modeled after Benedict's followers at Monte Cassino. While the extreme character of the observance at Le Murate slackened after mid-century and probably came somewhat closer to that practiced in other Benedictine houses in the city like Sant'Ambrogio, the rhetoric about the convent continued to stress the nuns' devout piety and strict following of the Benedictine Rule.

Sant'Ambrogio had the advantages and disadvantages of being both a convent and the parish seat. The nuns shared the same church, clerics, altars, and relics as the parishioners. They may have benefited from the presence of a large male clerical staff, the ready-made patronage base in the parish, and a wide range of public religious ceremonies – particularly those associated with the Corpus Christi relic kept in the church – but this exposure to the parish meant that the nuns experienced regularly and directly those flexible boundaries that separated the nunnery from the *seculum*. Le Murate, on the other hand, was independent from the parish, and consequently had a very different relationship to the Florentine laity. The "Suore Murate" were symbolically "walled into" their convent, with access to the inner sanctum strictly limited. They probably lived their enclosure more intensely than did the nuns of Sant'Ambrogio. They selectively courted particular patrons, including the wealthy general manager of the Medici bank, Giovanni Benci, and later in the century, Lorenzo de' Medici.

Earlier on, the two convents had been in direct competition for members and patronage from the same city neighborhood. By the late 1440s, the sheer demand for places within the city nunneries had increased to such an extent that Le Murate no longer posed a significant threat to the livelihood of the nuns of Sant'Ambrogio. In addition, each cultivated a different public image. The Benedictine convent at Sant'Ambrogio was able to offer patrician women (and their concerned relatives) its reputation as the oldest nunnery in the city, and small and stable numbers. Le Murate, on the other hand, was known for the austerity and devoutness of the religious life practiced by the Benedictine nuns and the security offered by the high walls.

The question of precedence between Fra Filippo Lippi's altarpieces commissioned for the high altars of Sant'Ambrogio and Le Murate cannot be determined from the documentation as it now stands – although the balance of evidence points toward the Sant'Ambrogio *Coronation of the Virgin*. While there is a rich collection of documents permitting one to follow the progress of Lippi's work on the *Coronation* from start to finish in great detail,[61] the material on his commission for the *Annunciation* for Le Murate is scanty – a single contemporary reference in an account book, followed by brief descriptions in several late fifteenth and sixteenth-century sources.[62]

Lippi's involvement in the decoration of the high altar of Sant'Ambrogio commenced in 1439 – just as the construction of the convent church at Le Murate was beginning. At the time, he was completing the Barbadori altarpiece for the sacristy of the Augustinian church of Santo Spirito – a high-profile project if we are to judge from Domenico Veneziano's letter – and he was also engaged on an unknown Medici project.[63] At some point during this year, Fra Filippo made a contract with Francesco Maringhi, the chaplain of Sant'Ambrogio and patron of the high altar. Lippi began work on the *Coronation of the Virgin* by April of the following year. The monumental painting took him five-and-a-half years to complete, and was finally installed above the high altar in January, 1447.[64] The sum paid for his labor and materials was just under 400 florins.[65]

The *Cronache del Monastero* of Le Murate state that soon after Scolastica Rondinelli became abbess in 1439, Giovanni Benci contributed funds toward the rebuilding of the new convent church. According to the *Cronache*, by 1443, the construction of the church and the decoration of the altars were completed.[66] In fact, it is an account book from Sant'Ambrogio which provides the only contemporary reference to Lippi's work for Le Murate: in 1445, a payment was made by Lippi regarding the "agreement made for the panel of Giovanni Benci," which indicates that Lippi's account for one of the altarpieces for Le Murate was still not completely settled by this date.[67] The chronicle – citing as a source the convent's early records – claims that Giovanni Benci spent 200 florins on the high altar and all of its trappings.[68] This contrasts with the 400 florins spent on the high altarpiece alone at Sant'Ambrogio, just as the dimensions of the *Annunciation* for Le Murate (203 × 186 cm) are smaller by a third than those of the Sant'Ambrogio *Coronation* (200 × 287 cm). One must, of course, remember that Fra Filippo was also painting a second image for the church of Le Murate, thus giving the interior of the new building a distinctly modern and uniform pictorial style.[69]

The patron of the Sant'Ambrogio *Coronation of the Virgin* was Francesco Maringhi (fig. 212). He was a canon of San Lorenzo and had served as chaplain, rector, governor, and procurator of Sant'Ambrogio for many years, dating back to the period of open hostility between Sant'Ambrogio and Le Murate.[70] By 1439, he had acquired patronage rights to the high altar of Sant'Ambrogio, and arranged the rededication of the *cappella maggiore* to St. John the Baptist "Decollato." He was acting both as a private individual and as a member of the male clerical community of Sant'Ambrogio, appropriating a privileged space within the church that had traditionally belonged to one of the prominent families in the Sant'Ambrogio parish, the Baldesi.[71] He was decorating the high altar of a church that served both the parish of Sant'Ambrogio and the small Benedictine convent. This was to be his burial place and the site of memorial masses for himself and his relatives. In addition, he was also associating his name and memory, and that of his family, with a celebrated relic of the Eucharist, which was stored in the *cappella maggiore*.[72] Until the relic was moved to another location within the church in 1471, Francesco Maringhi's *cappella maggiore* served as the framing (both architectural and ritual) around the tabernacle that housed the relic.

Francesco died during the early stages of the embellishment of the *cappella maggiore* and his nephew, Domenico Maringhi, saw the project to completion. It is not known which Maringhi chose the subject of the altarpiece – although the coincidence of Francesco's death with the Feast of the Assumption of the Virgin (August 15), suggests that Domenico selected the Coronation of the Virgin to commemorate his uncle's passing.[73]

The patron of Lippi's *Annunciation* for Le Murate had a very different profile from that of Francesco Maringhi.[74] Giovanni

212 Filippo Lippi, *Coronation of the Virgin*, detail of fig. 214, with Francesco Maringhi.

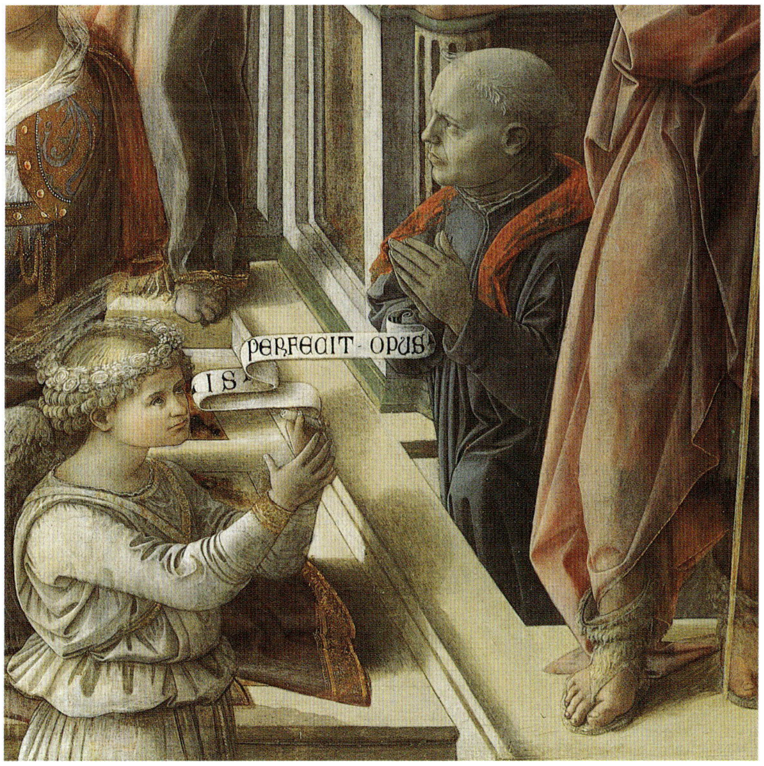

Benci was just coming into his own as one of the principal figures in the operation of the Medici bank. Born in 1394, he had been employed at the bank since age fourteen, and had spent most of his adult life outside Florence, working first in the Rome branch of the bank and then successfully managing the Geneva and Basel branches. He had come back to his native city in 1434, following the return of Cosimo de' Medici from exile, and was appointed joint general manager of the bank. Thereafter, his family, fortune, and standing in the city grew. The years during which he assumed the patronage of the church of Le Murate (1439–43) correspond with the period in which he held important government offices, being appointed prior in 1439 and Gonfaloniere di Giustizia in 1443.[75]

His association with Le Murate was a timely pious investment. It occurred simultaneously with the consolidation of his financial and social situation, and was part of an overall restructuring of his position within the city. Distancing himself from his petty bourgeois roots, he was building himself a new image and a fresh patronage base. The area of Le Murate was across the river from the traditional Benci territory in the parish of Santa Lucia de Magnoli. It was, however, a stone's throw away from the neighborhood of his wife's kin, the famous *trecento* banking family, the Peruzzi. Giovanni eventually chose to settle in this part of the city, by 1454 moving to the parish of San Jacopo tra'Fossi where the Peruzzi presided.[76]

In his religious patronage, Giovanni Benci modeled himself after his own benefactor, Cosimo de' Medici. Like Cosimo who championed the Observant Dominicans of San Marco and the Observant Franciscans at Bosco ai Frati, Giovanni Benci also patronized a religious foundation known for austere practices and strict observance. But Giovanni Benci, only recently returned to the city, selected a relatively new religious house to support. He thus entered the scene at Le Murate as the principal patron of a new convent, without having to contend with traditional patronage prerogatives or maneuver for position from within the institution, as did the cleric Francesco Maringhi. The new Abbess, Scolastica Rondinelli, was a friend and, as a result of the 1434 accord established by her predecessor with the parish of Sant'Ambrogio, she had control over the building projects and burial privileges within her convent.[77] This worked to the advantage of the wealthy and ambitious Giovanni Benci. He became the patron of the convent church and at least two of its altars, and established a burial site beneath the main altar (although he was ultimately buried in the *sepoltura* of the chapel he had endowed at Santa Croce).[78]

The church of Le Murate was a primary feature in the image that the convent offered the city. While most of the convent grounds were forbidden to the laity, the church was open to the public. A portal leading into the church from the Via Ghibellina was incorporated into the prominent walls that encircled the convent. Florentines could enter at will to attend Mass or to listen to the Divine Offices recited (and later sung) by the nuns in their oratory above.[79] The church was thus one of the few convent sites where a patron's pious investment was visible to the public at large. The interior adornment of the church, including Lippi's painting above the main altar, functioned as a direct reflection of Giovanni Benci's beneficence. His recourse to Fra Filippo may also have been in emulation of Cosimo de' Medici, as the painter had been working for the Medici since at least 1439. On the other hand, Giovanni Benci had contact with the Barducci family who were prominent patrons of Sant'Ambrogio, and may have selected Fra Filippo through this channel.[80]

Some years later, probably in the late 1440s or early 1450s, Giovanni Benci contributed again to the building projects at Le Murate, financing the construction of a new refectory and the enlargement of the monastery walls (fig. 210). He purchased several properties along the border of the nunnery with the intention of building a grand new church, but he died before this project came to fruition.[81] By 1448, he was reputed to have spent over 10,000 florins at Le Murate.[82] Archbishop Antonino wrote rather sweepingly in his *Chronica* (c. 1460) that "the monastery was built from the start by Giovanni Benci, and through to the finish, it was perfected by him."[83]

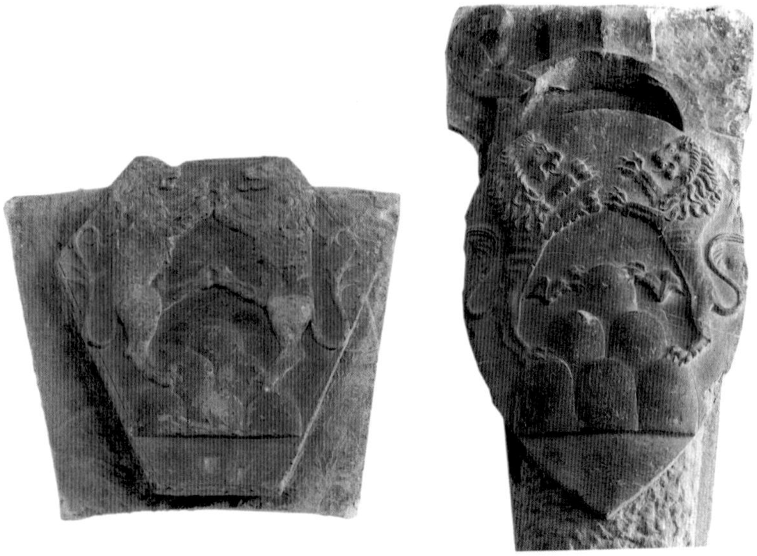

213a and b Benci coat of arms from Le Murate, now detached, (original location in the convent unknown), Florence, Le Murate.

The most probable scenario is that Francesco Maringhi was the first to engage the services of Lippi and then Giovanni Benci, whether motivated by Cosimo de' Medici's example or through his Sant'Ambrogio connection, followed suit. There would have been a period during the first half of the 1440s when the artist was working on the two altarpieces simultaneously. According to this scenario, there would have been no overt competition between the two active patrons vis-à-vis the altarpieces. Domenico Maringhi – the nephew of the deceased Francesco –

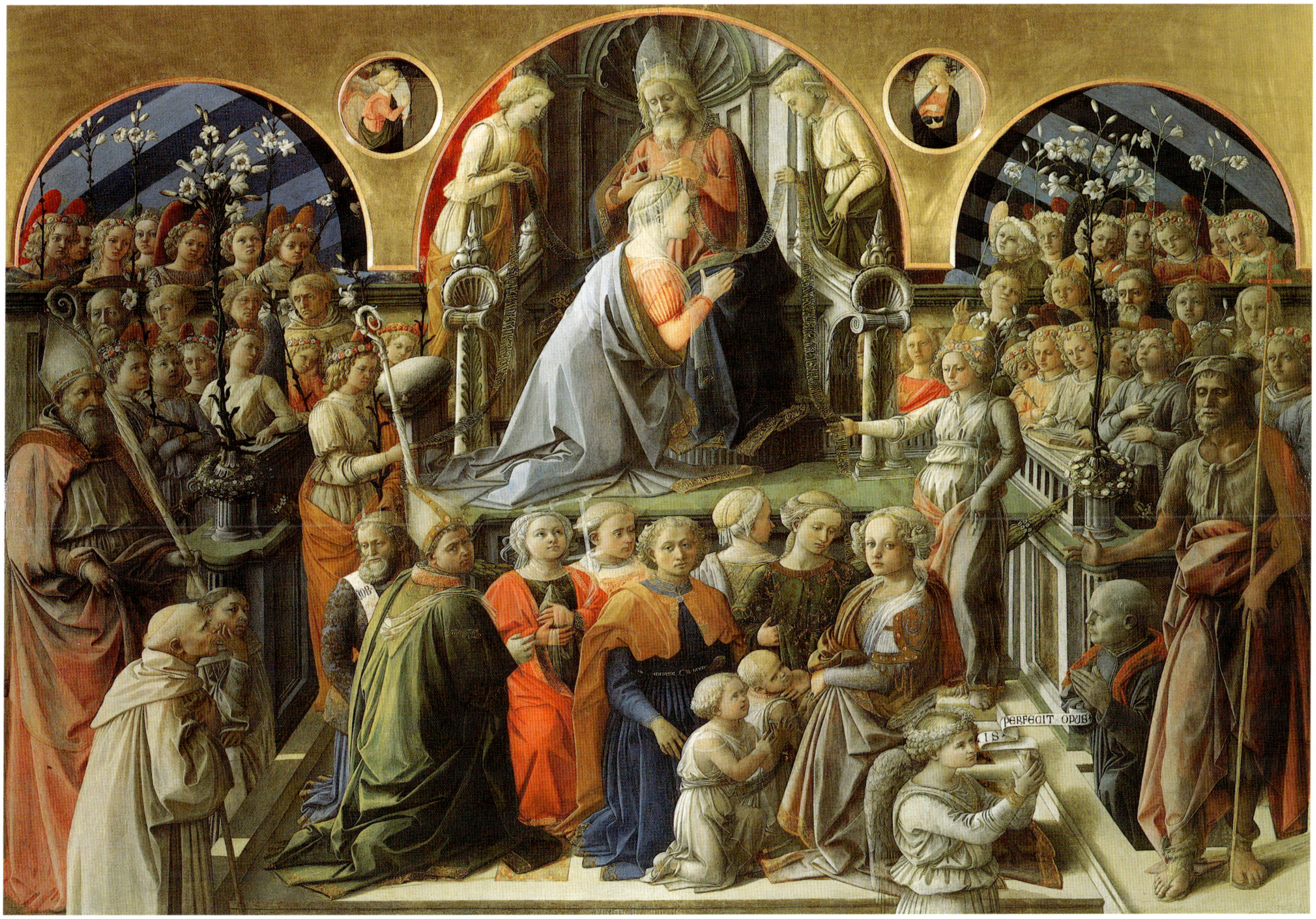

214 Filippo Lippi, *Coronation of the Virgin* from Sant'Ambrogio, 1439–46, Florence, Uffizi.

and Giovanni Benci had played no part in the recent hostilities between the two nunneries and were motivated primarily by personal and familial concerns. Nor were the two abbesses – who sources indicate were involved to varying degrees in the respective altarpiece commissions – historical adversaries. While Abbess Niccolaia Buonaccorsi of Sant'Ambrogio had signed the original agreement between the two colleges of nuns in 1424, and had presided over Sant'Ambrogio during the period of conflict, Abbess Scolastica Rondinelli of Le Murate had arrived since then.[84] Another telling indicator of this rapprochement is Giovanni Benci's decision to place one of his daughters within each convent as a boarder.[85]

Nonetheless, I do not want to bury the hatchet between the two Benedictine nunneries. There were important elements of contrast – competitive contrast – in the different forms of female enclosure that each convent practiced. The two high altar images by Fra Filippo Lippi were called upon, at some level, to reflect these competing forms of female monasticism. I shall turn now to these altarpieces.

THE SANT'AMBROGIO *CORONATION OF THE VIRGIN*

Displayed above the high altar of the church of Sant'Ambrogio, the *Coronation of the Virgin* (fig. 214) serviced a large and diverse group of Florentines in their religious and social practices.[86] It functioned as a focal point in the cult of memory fashioned round the deceased patron, Francesco Maringhi. The Benedictine nuns of Sant'Ambrogio had other needs for the altarpiece, as did the men and women of the parish of Sant'Ambrogio, the members of the confraternities located in the church, and the wider Florentine public that participated in the annual Corpus Christi day celebrations of the Eucharistic relic kept in the church. There have been two studies of the *Coronation of the Virgin* published recently which have probed the relationship between the painting and some of these individuals, communities, and circumstances that laid claims upon the altarpiece's imagery and its subsequent use – what art historians have come to call the "context" of the work of art. Eve Borsook examined the commission and iconography in the light of the important religious cult celebrated in the church, that of Corpus Christi.[87] Jeffrey Ruda explored the patronage of the altarpiece and how it determined the pictorial imagery.[88] Borsook's article, in particular, will be a continual point of reference in my own discussion of the painting.

What interests me here, however, is the nuns' participation in Fra Filippo Lippi's altarpiece. I shall concentrate predominantly on two of the figures in the painting, St. Theopista and the Virgin. I feel that the figure of St. Theopista represents a fragile, unstable point in the altarpiece which reveals the difficulty Fra Filippo had in accommodating the diverse and conflicting claims made upon the imagery, particularly those of the nuns. The Virgin Mary works in opposition to St. Theopista, but only partially resolves the imbalances set in play by the former.

Lippi's abstract Celestial Paradise is packed with sixty figures grouped according to a hierarchy of sacrality and relevance. Under the central arch, on a raised dais, God the Father crowns the Virgin Queen of Heaven. Five angels clad in white vestments officiate – four of them like deacons, assisting the priest during the Mass, and one, acting like the *festaiuolo* on the set of a *sacra rappresentazione*, carrying a banderole before the kneeling patron (fig. 212), telling us that it is Francesco Maringhi's production we are witnessing ("is perfecit opus"). Beneath the smaller lateral arches, a line of angels stand behind a wall. In front of them – and inside the wall, closer to center stage – stand a row of relatively undifferentiated saints, with another tier of angels in front of them. Lippi treats the foreground of the picture like a filmmaker, moving in close on his subject and sharpening the focus. The scale of the figures increases and the space between them widens. They are carefully rendered with distinct expressions, clothing, and attitudes. The two titular saints of the church and chapel, Ambrose and John the Baptist, stand at either side as the two principal intercessors. Next to them, in an ambiguous spatial zone of the picture, are two kneeling figures: the patron Francesco Maringhi[89] at the right and a monk in a white habit resting his chin on his hand at the left (whom many have identified as the Carmelite painter).[90] A second, older, monk in a white habit is probably St. Benedict, the founder of the Order of the congregation of nuns at Sant'Ambrogio. He stands in the left foreground in another indeterminate zone of the picture, seemingly poised somewhere between the viewer's space and the pictorial space.[91]

In the center foreground, a group of saints congregate (fig. 215). They are robustly rendered and without identifying attributes, for the most part. Lippi had recourse to tiny lettering inscribed across their clothing in order to label some of these very human-looking heavenly courtiers as "sacred."[92] Among them is a saintly family, very prominently displayed at the right, disposed outward toward the viewer (fig. 216). This family consists of the Roman cavalry master Eustace, his wife Theopista, and their two children Agapius and Theopistus.[93] Remarkably, in this densely populated picture, with its complexly organized space and orchestrated central drama, St. Theopista calls attention to herself more than any other figure, magnetically drawing the beholder's eye (fig. 217). Lippi achieved this effect through a series of painterly maneuvers. He utilized contemporary portrait conventions to present Theopista directly, at eye level, for scrutiny.[94] Light rakes across Theopista's features, reflecting off the smooth skin of her rounded cheeks and high forehead. But it is her intense gaze out of the picture space that guarantees that the beholder's eye will come to rest upon her. Sts. Eustace and Martin also look out, but they do not hold the attention of the viewer in the same way. Theopista's eyes are larger, deeper set, wide open, and framed by fashionably manicured eyebrows. She has something of the enigmatic expression of Leonardo's *Mona Lisa*, and it is just as difficult to articulate in formal terms what it is about her that attracts one.

What is happening here? Who was St. Theopista and why does she make her way so prominently into the iconography of Lippi's *Coronation of the Virgin*? What are the dynamics of this intense looking? What sort of scopic process is being set into play and why does it concentrate on the figure of St. Theopista?

St. Eustace and his family earned their place within this celestial court on account of the Barducci family's sway at Sant'Ambrogio. Sometime before 1430, Stagio di Giovanni Barducci had endowed the chapel to the right of the high altar at Sant'Ambrogio under the title of his name-saint, Eustace. Following his death, Stagio's sons, Lorenzo and Giovanni, maintained the family chapel, and carried out their father's bequest for memorial masses in the chapel.[95] One of his daughters, Antonia, was a nun at Sant'Ambrogio and eventually became abbess. While it was the cleric Francesco Maringhi who had commissioned the altarpiece, and his nephew Domenico Maringhi who saw the commission through, the Barducci family seems to have played an important role at the juncture where the daily operations of the convent intersected with the altarpiece production. Giovanni di Stagio Barducci – a banker – looked after Lippi's account, acting as the go-between for the convent and the painter. Suora Antonia Barducci herself drew money from the convent *sagrestana* in order to make a final payment on the altarpiece in 1451.[96]

The Barducci chapel was one of the three principal chapels in the church and, hence, St. Eustace was among the most honored saints at Sant'Ambrogio. In so far as the sacred congregation of Celestial Paradise in the altarpiece reflects on the sacred cosmology of the church, one might expect to find Eustace prominently displayed in the image for the high altar. The appearance of Eustace's entire family in such a central position in this non-narrative context, however, is surprising.[97] And,

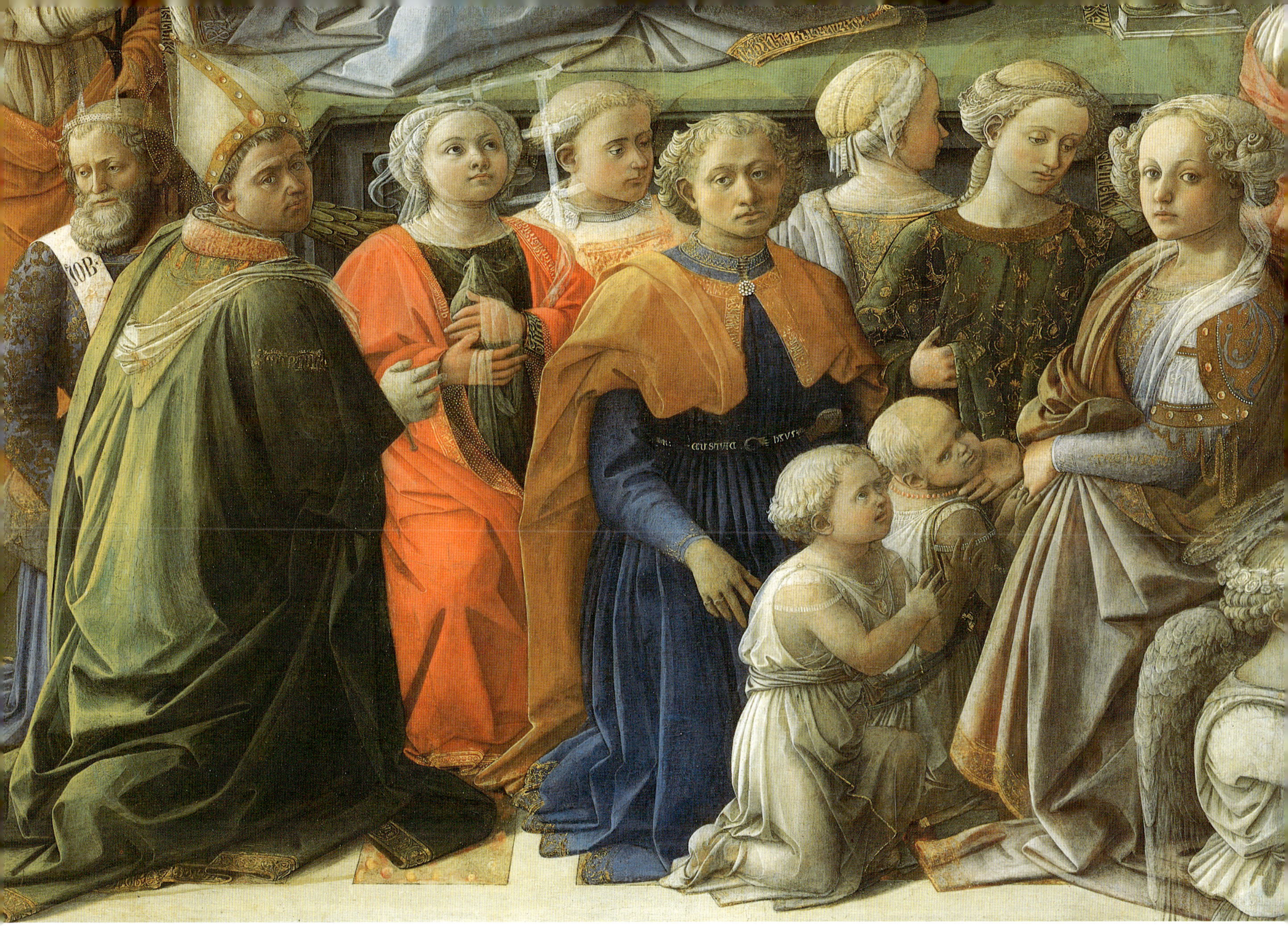

215 Filippo Lippi, *Coronation of the Virgin*, detail of fig. 214.

indeed, for reasons about which one can only speculate, the figures of St. Theopista and the two boys were not part of the original conception.[98] They were added during a later phase of the altarpiece production, superimposed over the painted bodies of the two female saints kneeling at the back of the shelf-like space.[99]

According to the legend, St. Eustace had been a cavalry master named Placidus in the Imperial Roman Army during the reign of Octavian.[100] While out hunting with his men, he beheld the image of the crucified Christ suspended between the antlers of a deer. Christ spoke to him and advised him to have his family baptized. He and his wife and two sons were subsequently baptized and named anew. Now called Eustace, he encountered the crucifix once again and was told that he, like Job, would be made to suffer terrible losses as a test of his faith. His servants and livestock succumbed to disease and his property and position were lost. He decided to leave Rome and boarded a ship with his wife and children for Egypt. Theopista was a very beautiful woman, and the ship's captain became enamored of her. When Eustace was unable to pay the passage fee, the captain had him tossed ashore with his sons, and he sailed away with Theopista. Eustace then proceeded to lose his sons – one snatched by a wolf and the other by a lion. Taking them for dead, he retired to a village and lived for fifteen years as a servant. He was eventually discovered by his old cavalrymen and restored to his former position. Unbeknownst to him, two of the soldiers in his unit happened to be his own sons. They had been saved, one by shepherds and the other by peasants, and had been reared in the same village, without knowing that they were brothers. One day, following a triumphant battle, the Imperial cavalry stopped in a

216 (*following page*) Filippo Lippi, *Coronation of the Virgin*, detail of fig, 214, with St. Eustace and his family.

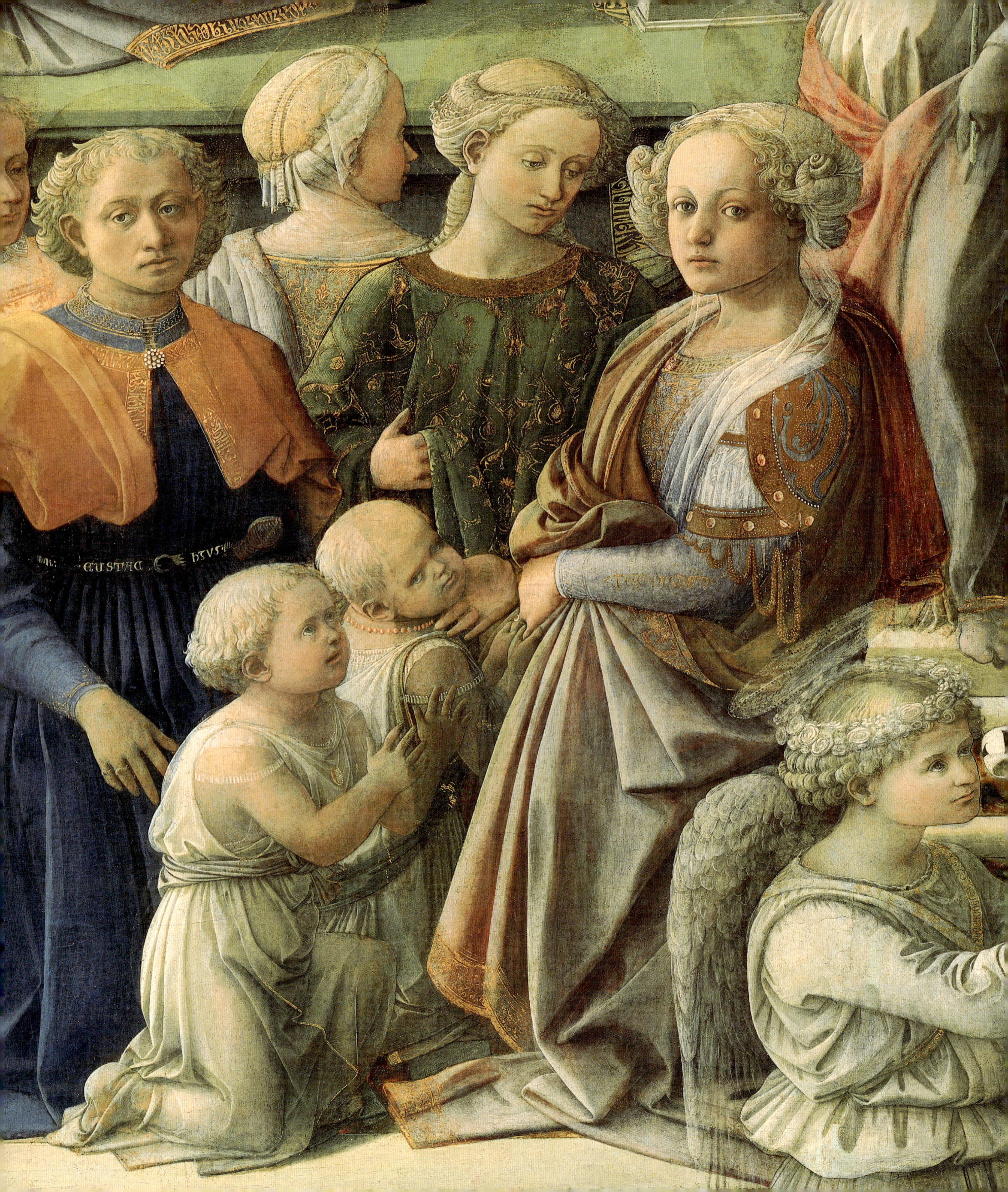

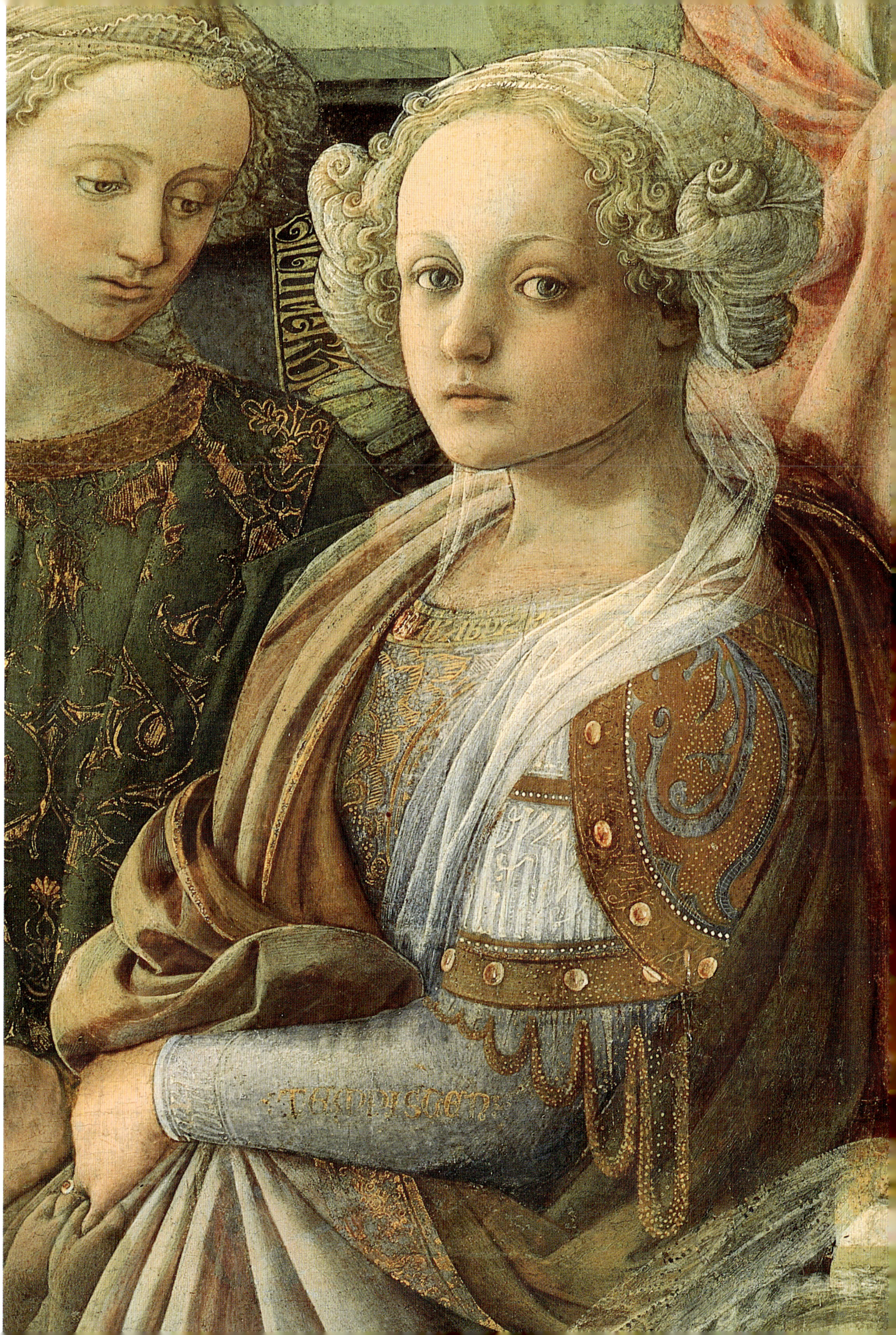

village where Theopista had come to live following the death of the sea captain. She looked after the garden of an inn and, as one might expect, it was to this very inn that the two sons repaired one evening and exchanged stories about their childhood. The coincidences in their stories made them realize that they were brothers. Theopista overheard their conversation, ignorant of their true identity. The next day, however, after she and Eustace had recognized one another and she heard how he had lost each of the boys, she realized that the two soldiers were their sons and that the family was once again reunited in the little village. They returned to Rome with much fanfare. Some time later, however, Eustace refused to participate in a sacrifice in the Temple of Apollo because it was contrary to his Christian beliefs. The family was seized and thrown into an arena with the lions. The wild beasts wouldn't touch them, and they finally met their end burned alive within a bronze bull. Their bodies miraculously remained intact and were recovered by Christians and buried.

The *Vita* of St. Eustace and his family is considered to have no historical basis. The earliest version and model for successive renditions is an anonymous Greek account. The story was very popular in fifteenth-century Italy, circulating in vernacular renditions based on Jacopo da Voragine's *Leggenda Aurea*. Hippolyte Delehaye has demonstrated that the story derives from two different literary genres – the hagiographic legend and the popular romance.[101] Its hybrid genesis accounts for the clashing character of the different parts that make up the tale: the miraculous conversion of Eustace and the heroic martyrdom of his family derive from the tradition of saint literature, while the tumultuous travails of the family members divided and dispersed have their roots in popular romances and tales of misadventure. The image of St. Theopista in particular is rendered inherently unstable by this situation. Certain of her trials are hard to reconcile with the model portrait of the virtuous pious Christian lady that brackets the string of family misfortunes. In the first part of the story, Theopista is represented as a kindly patrician woman who looked after the poor. When she is abducted by the sea captain, the legend assures us that God watched over her at all times, and she was "saved from every corruption." When she is eventually reunited with her husband, she defends her virtue in one quick line, Eustace embraces her, kisses her, and they are once again husband and wife.

This is the material that Fra Filippo Lippi had to work with when contriving a way to represent this holy family. A contemporary Florentine who copied out the legend in Italian made a telling slip that indicates just how difficult it may have been to swallow this story fashioned out of sacred and profane narrative modes. When the two grown-up sons, Agapius and Theopistus, began that evening at the inn to talk about their past and their mother chanced to overhear them, the writer tells us "talking about various things, they began to question one another about the purity [*purita*] of their mother [who] was sitting nearby and heard what they were saying."[102] He evidently meant to write that they spoke of "their childhood [*puerizia*] and their mother was sitting nearby and heard what they were saying" (or even the Latinism "*pueritia*").[103] Instead, the boys touch upon what was evidently on the transcriber's mind – the virtue (*purità*) of their mother.

There is something similar informing Lippi's image of Theopista. He represents the family while the two sons Agapius and Theopistus are still young – hence, before the break-up of the family, the onset of their tribulations, and Theopista's brush with the lusty sea captain. Theopista is thus securely embedded in the bosom of the family. She turns her stunningly beautiful face out toward the viewer, as many an intercessing saint is wont to do. But this direct engagement is problematic. Even in her capacity as saint, this is the face that set the sea captain's heart aflame. It is also problematic because Theopista is so readily readable as "woman," "patrician woman," and through the portrait conventions, even more specifically, as "Florentine patrician woman." But *quattrocento* patrician daughters, wives, and Benedictine nuns were counseled to keep their eyes on the ground and not to meet the eyes of others, particularly men:

> A beautiful face is praised, but unchaste eyes make it ugly through men's scorn. . . . A handsome person is pleasing to see, but a shameless gesture or an act of incontinence in an instant renders her appearance vile. Unchastity angers God, and you know that God punishes nothing so severely in women as he does this lack.[104]

By virtue of her penetrating gaze out of the picture, the figure of Theopista shifts to and from characterizations of saint, patrician lady, and fallen woman. And this makes her a rather curious focus for the nuns of Sant'Ambrogio.[105]

Even Theopista's identity as the patrician lady would potentially have had unsettling associations for the nuns. Theopista is pictured beside her husband. She touches the cheek of one of her sons, presenting him to the viewer, while the other son reaches out to her. She is the consummate mother of the ideal family, one whom *quattrocento* Florentines in particular would have admired. Here was wealth, position, female beauty, and male offspring – all inscribed within a sacred halo. Theopista functions as a generalized image of the ideal Christian mother, an alternative to the humble, uncompromisingly virtuous Virgin represented in a more remote, upper zone of Lippi's painting, who turns away from the viewer. This patrician-mother-saint would have been a representation with which the lay audience at Sant'Ambrogio could readily identify. Theopista offered a familiar face – an idealized mirroring for the patrician female viewer, recognition of somebody's wife, daughter, sister, or neighbor for male viewers. She had other associations for the Sant'Ambrogio *popolo minuto*. But what would this representation have signified to the nuns of Sant'Ambrogio?

It has been noted that during this period in Florence, there was a change in the traditional rhetoric regarding women's social role. In the *trecento*, celibacy was held to be the most honorable and desirable condition for a woman, and the path to the

217 (*previous page*) Filippo Lippi, *Coronation of the Virgin*, detail of fig. 214, with St. Theopista.

nunnery was exalted above all. There was also a lively discourse expounding the important function that nuns fulfilled in preserving the integrity of the community through their religious devotion and virtuous behavior. During the *quattrocento*, however, the model of the married woman came to dominate discourses on women's social vocation and virtuousness.[106] Young patrician girls were raised with both these models before them, but the married woman who was wife and mother was clearly the more valued figure. While the Sant'Ambrogio *Ricordo di monache e doti* would have it that the young women who were committed to the nunnery by their parents or guardians nonetheless were "intelligent" and "conscious" of the decision or "inspired by God,"[107] it is probable that many of them registered disappointment at some level over being denied the opportunity to marry and have children. Widows who entered the convent often had to endure separation from their children, who would remain in the house of their deceased husband's kin. (In one case, one of the Sant'Ambrogio nuns went to the extreme of convincing the nunnery to accept her five-year-old daughter as an oblate so that the two could be together.)[108]

Certain rituals and religious experiences in Sant'Ambrogio were couched in the language of secular nuptial and child-rearing practices and functioned as substitutes. Nuns were the "brides" of Christ and their monastic profession was equated with a marriage ceremony.[109] Some Benedictine abbesses were formally "wed" to local bishops in a ceremony in the convent church complete with the exchange of rings.[110] Young girls bound for the convent frequently brought with them baby Jesus dolls with accompanying sets of clothing. They dressed and cared for these dolls, imitating the Virgin, but also playing out their desires for motherhood.[111] Sexuality and desire figured in the mystical experiences of Italian medieval holy women. Angela of Foligno bared herself before the crucifix and described her love for Christ in erotic language. Agnes of Montepulciano and Margherita of Faenza each had a vision in which the Virgin handed them the Christ Child to look after and when the time came to return the Child, they both refused.[112]

These religious experiences cast in secular terms may have played on latent desires. And when the desires were more overt, as in the case of those nuns who did not take their leave from the *seculum* voluntarily, the symbolic language could become overdetermined, with referents slipping indeterminantly between secular and religious meanings. It is very possible that Lippi's vivid likeness of St. Theopista fed directly into a lack experienced in the lives of many of the cloistered, celibate nuns and had the potential to provoke a longing for the coveted roles of wife and mother.

Some of the problems I have raised regarding the figure of St. Theopista are offset by the dramatic role played by one of the principal figures in the altarpiece, that of the Virgin (fig. 218). The Virgin too is a key focal point in the pictorial imagery. Of all the figures, she is the most illuminated, lit by a strong raking light from the left. She is clearly visible, isolated in the open space of the upper dais. Her rose and light blue garments stand out beside the darker red lake and ultramarine of the robes of God the Father. But in spite of this spotlit place at center stage, the dramatic presence of the Virgin is intentionally undercut by having her turn away from the viewer toward God the Father and by concealing the lines of her body beneath swathes of drapery. Her profile is barely visible.

This rendering of the Virgin was consistent with the image upheld before the Benedictine nuns. The Virgin was the ultimate model of humility, obedience, chastity, and virtue. Just as there was an *imitatio Christi*, so was there an *imitatio Mariae*.[113] More specifically, the Virgin's Coronation was the final moment in the drama of her Assumption into Heaven, a doctrine which the Benedictines had observed since the twelfth century. The Assumption was directly tied into the belief in the Virgin's Immaculate Conception, which was a controversial issue that the Benedictines had accepted as doctrine in the twelfth century.[114] The moment when the Virgin is assumed into Paradise and crowned Queen of Heaven was also symbolically equated with her marriage to Christ.[115] Benedictine nuns, too, were the brides of Christ. It has been pointed out that Lippi's Virgin who kneels down before God the Father resembles a nun at her profession.[116] With her back to the spectator, the Virgin establishes a relationship with God the Father that, in turn, becomes accessible to the viewer. In this way the Virgin acted as a protagonist for the nuns.[117]

There is even the possibility, when considering the question of viewpoint, that the Virgin was the figure most readily visible to the nuns from their position in the church. During church activities that involved both the nuns and the laity, the nuns sat apart, according to the dictates of *clausura*.[118] While the documentation does not allow any definitive conclusions about the location of the nuns' choir, it is possible that they occupied an elevated gallery to the left of the high altar.[119] If this is the case, they would thus have looked down upon Fra Filippo's altarpiece (assuming that the painting were even visible at all). This means that the nuns would have experienced the meaning of the picture in quite a different way from those viewers who stood or knelt at ground level before the image. While the latter would have focused upon the intercessing saints congregating in the foreground, the nuns would have encountered first and foremost the Virgin as she was being crowned Queen of Heaven.

Even if the nuns were unable to meet the eye of St. Theopista from their elevated angle of vision, this does not necessarily resolve the problems raised by her provocative presence. The *Coronation* was the altarpiece for the main altar of the nuns' convent church. They themselves had been involved in its production. When their chaplain, Francesco Maringhi, negotiated the endowment of the high altar, he entered into a contract with the abbess of the convent. During the execution of the altarpiece, the nuns had administered payments from the income derived from Francesco Maringhi's *podere*. There were also occasions when the nuns assembled in the church, such as during

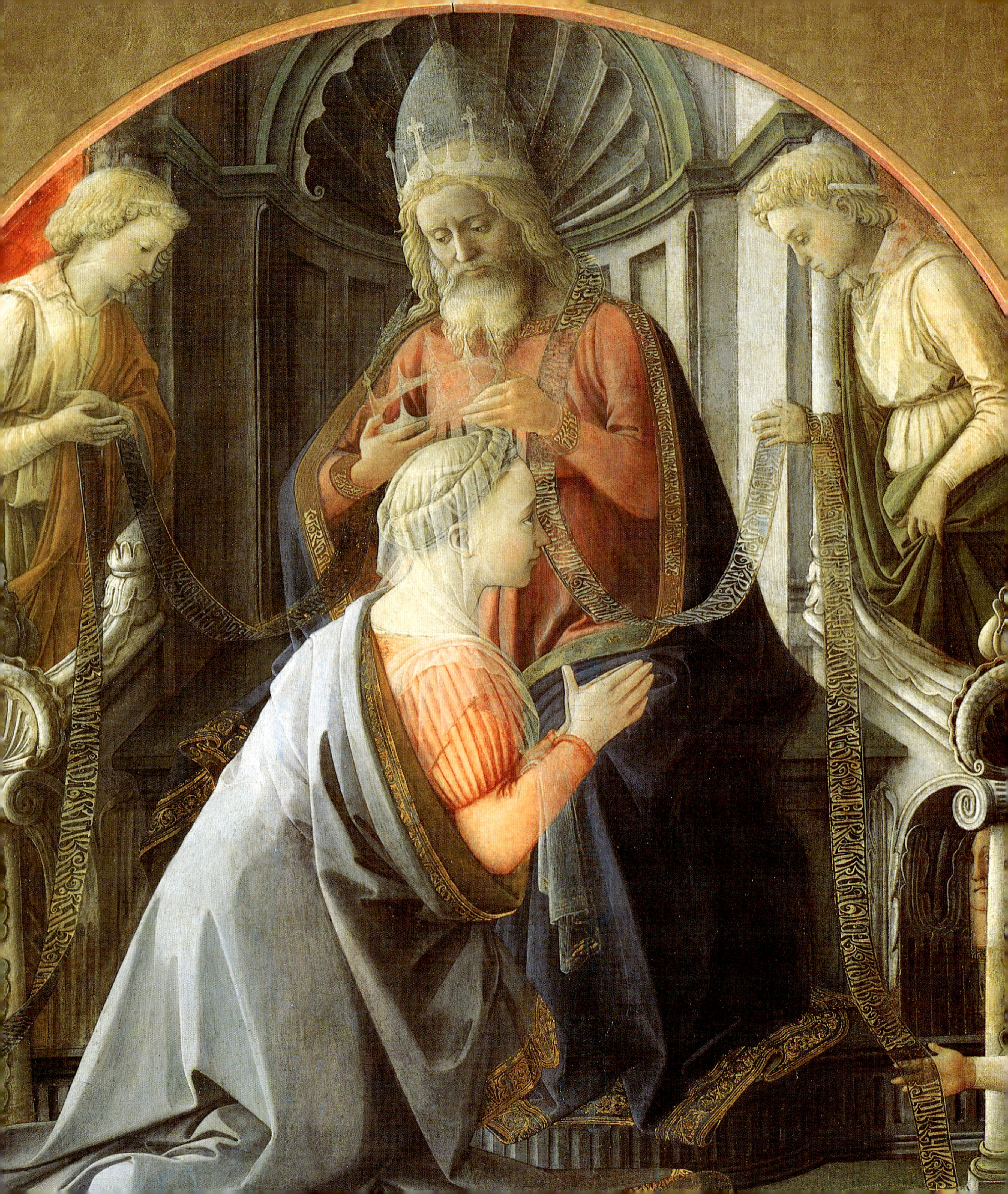

the profession of a nun or during the Corpus Christi celebrations. In these instances, they too would have viewed the image from ground level.[120] Seen from a kneeling position, the Virgin crowned Queen of Heaven stands out at the apex of a triangular composition – but Theopista holds down the right angle of that triangle. Fra Filippo may have addressed his different audiences from alternative viewpoints, but he could not guarantee the fixity of their viewing positions. The nuns circulated round the church, the Maringhi patrons were also convent clerics, and the Barducci family had placed one of their women in the convent.

THE *ANNUNCIATION* FOR LE MURATE

The Chronicle of Le Murate suggests that Abbess Scolastica Rondinelli was actively involved in determining the dedication and the decoration of the three church altars. Scolastica had been acquainted with Giovanni Benci in secular society, before she entered Le Murate in 1438.[121] He had been to visit her several times within the convent, when he announced his intention to found a chapel dedicated to the Virgin Annunciate in the church:

> Hearing this, Madonna Scolastica considered it [an offer] sent from Heaven and entreated him to lend his support. She had already wished to have the high altar [dedicated] to the Annunziata as it was the title of the monastery in imitation of the founding nuns, but she hadn't had the means to do so on her own. Therefore, they joined together and gave orders to build three altars.[122]

Elsewhere in the Chronicle, Giovanni Benci is described as Scolastica's "co-helper in the foundation of the altars of the church."[123]

In dedicating themselves to the Annunciation, the nuns of Le Murate were carrying on the tradition that had begun on the Ponte Rubiconte. By at least 1419, the founding sisters were referred to under the title of the "Annuntiata," and their small church was known as the "Oratory of the Annunciation."[124] The sisters had an image of the Annunciation above the altar in the oratory and when they moved to the new monastery in 1424, they brought the painting with them and presumably placed it above the altar in the small church that they soon built there. In conceiving a new, aggrandized convent church, Scolastica wanted to reinforce the traditional devotional practices of the founders, which were essential to the identity of the nuns and to the positive image the convent conjured up in the minds of contemporary Florentines. The high altar, like that of the original oratory, was dedicated to the Annunziata. One of the two lateral altars was dedicated to the Crucifixion and was adorned with a painted crucifix that the nuns had brought from the Ponte Rubiconte, modeled after the miraculous image of St. Giovanni Gualberto at San Miniato al Monte. The third altar was dedicated to one of the principal reformers of the Benedictine Order, Bernard, reflecting the nuns' continued interest in identifying themselves with religious asceticism.

But the *Annunciation* image from the Ponte Rubiconte was not to adorn the new high altar. Instead, a new painting was ordered from Fra Filippo Lippi.[125] Perhaps the original *Annunciation* was considered lacking in the necessary dimensions and stylistic appeal to render it an efficacious representation for the monastery's public. This public at Le Murate was not made up of parishioners with independent claims on the altarpiece's imagery, as at Sant'Ambrogio, but rather, the patrons of the convent, the relatives of the nuns, and Florentines inspired by the nunnery's reputation. It is also possible that the nuns themselves wished to appropriate the earlier *Annunciation* for their own devotional use. It was placed in the sacristy (to which, unlike the convent church, the nuns had ready access).[126]

How then did Lippi respond to the commission generated by Giovanni Benci, Scolastica Rondinelli, and the nuns of Le Murate? The subject was certainly not new to him, as he had already painted several very successful versions of the Annunciation by the early 1440s.[127] There are certain distinct features particular to the Murate painting that indicate that he was carefully considering the monastic context in which it would be displayed and utilized.

This is the *Annunciation* (fig. 220) in which Lippi emphasized the physical body of the Virgin the least. He gave the Virgin a slight, elongated figure whose contours are concealed beneath the folds of her blue cloak. Having just risen from her seat, she stands passively with her head bowed before Gabriel, in humble acceptance of his message, very much contained within her body. She bears little comparison to the full-figured, dramatic Mary of the somewhat earlier San Lorenzo *Annunciation* (see fig. 221).[128] And here I wonder whether Lippi might have been instructed to reproduce certain features from the original Ponte Rubiconte painting of the *Annunciation*. Unfortunately, this image cannot be identified.[129] However, a painting probably of a slightly earlier date (c. 1380) and larger dimensions, said to have hung on a pillar patronized by the *legnaiuoli* at Orsanmichele, in which the figure of the Virgin has many striking similarities to that in Lippi's work, may reflect an Annunciation formulation similar to the original *Annunciation* at Le Murate (fig. 219).[130]

Two important religious values are communicated through Fra Filippo's presentation of the Virgin (fig. 222) in the *Annunciation* for Le Murate. Obedience is exemplified in the Virgin's humble acceptance of her destiny and abstinence is seen in the emphasis on the spiritual, as opposed to the carnal body.[131] Obedience and abstinence were integral features in traditional Benedictine monasticism and they both figure in the *quattrocento* discourses on Le Murate. In his praise of the nuns, Tommaso Salvetti singled out their obedience ("ses adeo obnoxias faciunt"), while Antonino lauded them for their abstinence ("ieiuniis"), citing it as one of the many manifestations of their extreme observance. Both terms also figure prominently in the sermon that Savonarola preached before the nuns of Le Murate at the end

218 Filippo Lippi, *Coronation of the Virgin*, detail of fig. 214, with the God the Father crowning the Virgin.

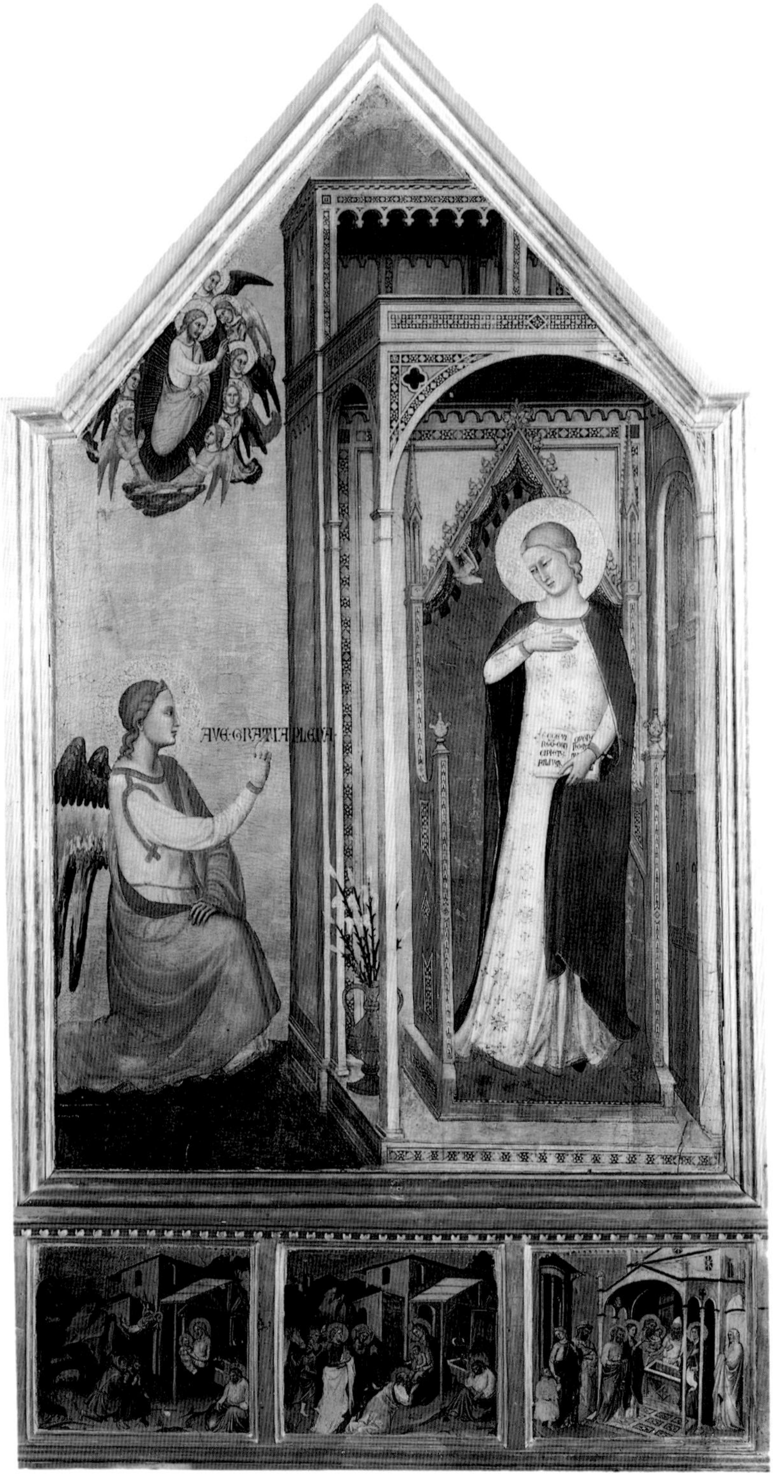

219 Master of the Legnaiuoli Annunciation, *Annunciation*, c. 1380, originally on a column in Orsanmichele, Florence, now in Florence, Uffizi (storage). Predella attributed to Ambrogio di Baldese.

of the century. In encouraging the nuns to return to the true way outlined in Benedict's Rule, he offered metaphors that resonate with Lippi's imagery. He described the "unhappy monk . . . still heavy in body," unable to contemplate divinity because "the *umidità* of his flesh keeps him weighted down." The true believer is like the falcon, "which has feathers fit for flying, with light flesh because it is dry and doesn't feel the pleasures [of the flesh], and is thus fit for contemplation."[132] One thinks of Lippi's disembodied Virgin surrounded by a profusion of wings (angel's wings, dove's wings, the wings adorning the frieze),[133] juxtaposed with the cypress tree which ascends toward the heavens.

In another of Lippi's Annunciation scenes – the lunette painted for the Medici around 1450 (fig. 223) – the painter graphically depicted the miraculous penetration of the Virgin's sacred body and the ensuing fecundity of the body implicit in the Annunciation. The dove of the Holy Spirit is shown in serial images, progressing down toward the Virgin's swollen belly where there is a small opening in her dress emitting golden rays (fig. 225).[134] In the Murate *Annunciation*, the integrity of the Virgin's body is maintained, following the liturgy which emphasized that she was "corporis integritas" and that she was Virgin before and after the incarnation.[135] This representation of the Virgin reflects upon the nuns' vow of chastity, akin to St. Bernard's homily on the Annunciation where he has the Virgin voice a reluctance to "break my vow."[136]

The narrative of miraculous penetration and incarnation is transposed onto subsidiary symbolic elements in the picture, following the medieval exegetical tradition. There is the beautifully rendered transparent glass vase, half full of water, which nourishes the flowers nestled in its neck (fig. 224). The Virgin's womb is contrasted with the empty cavity beneath her lectern and the *hortus conclusus* in the background. Fecundity is implied through the towering cypress in the center of the garden, Gabriel's long-stemmed lilies, the flowers and shells sculpted into the frieze behind the Virgin, and the way in which the dove of the Holy Spirit is suspended in mid-flight along the trunk of the cypress tree (and atop the pediment of the garden portal) – a curious, miraculous germination. A very subtle Incarnation thematics unfolds as a process of divine imprinting. God the Father, wearing a white garment and blue cloak lined with green and hemmed in gold embroidery, dispatches the Holy Spirit to the Virgin whose clothing reproduces the same color schema – with the addition of the gold embroidery on her white gown. The Virgin's ultramarine mantle then loops back up and lies beneath the tassled cushion, much in the same way that her robe is gathered up beneath the Christ Child in the Annalena *Adoration of the Christ Child* (see fig. 169). The cushion, like the Virgin's dress, is white with gold embroidery and the open book which sits upon it is thus a reference to the Word made flesh in the image of God during the Annunciation, which comes to reside in the Virgin's womb – here analogous to the cushion. The shadow cast by the wood of the lectern falls across the cushion – a possible reference to the Passion.

There is restraint and decorum behind this recourse to symbolic, rather than mimetic or narrative, means to recount the mystery of the Annunciation. This is carried through to the setting of the scene. The Murate altarpiece is one of the few Annunciation images by Lippi that is void of all reference to the

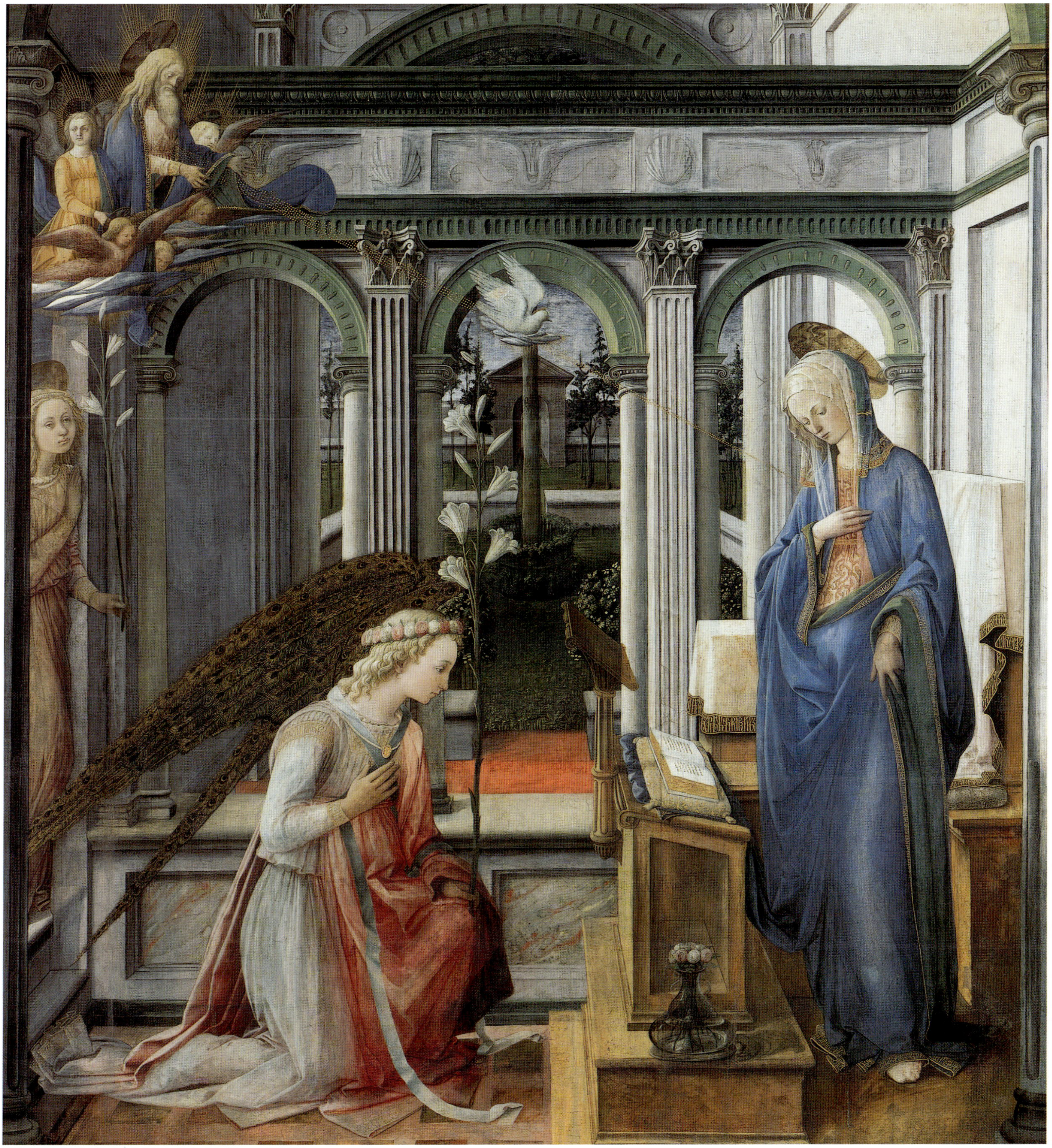

220 Filippo Lippi, *Annunciation* from Le Murate, c. 1443, Munich, Alte Pinakothek.

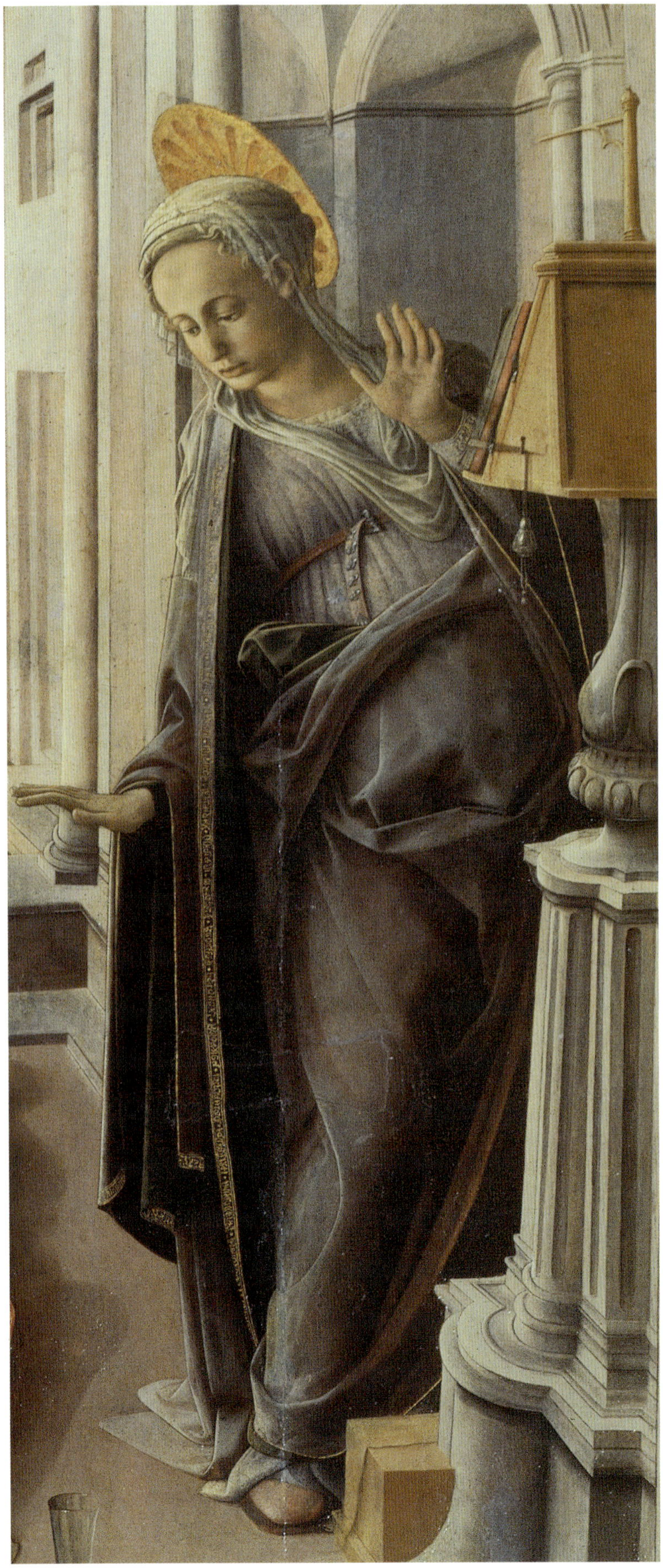

221 Filippo Lippi, *Annunciation*, detail of fig. 104.

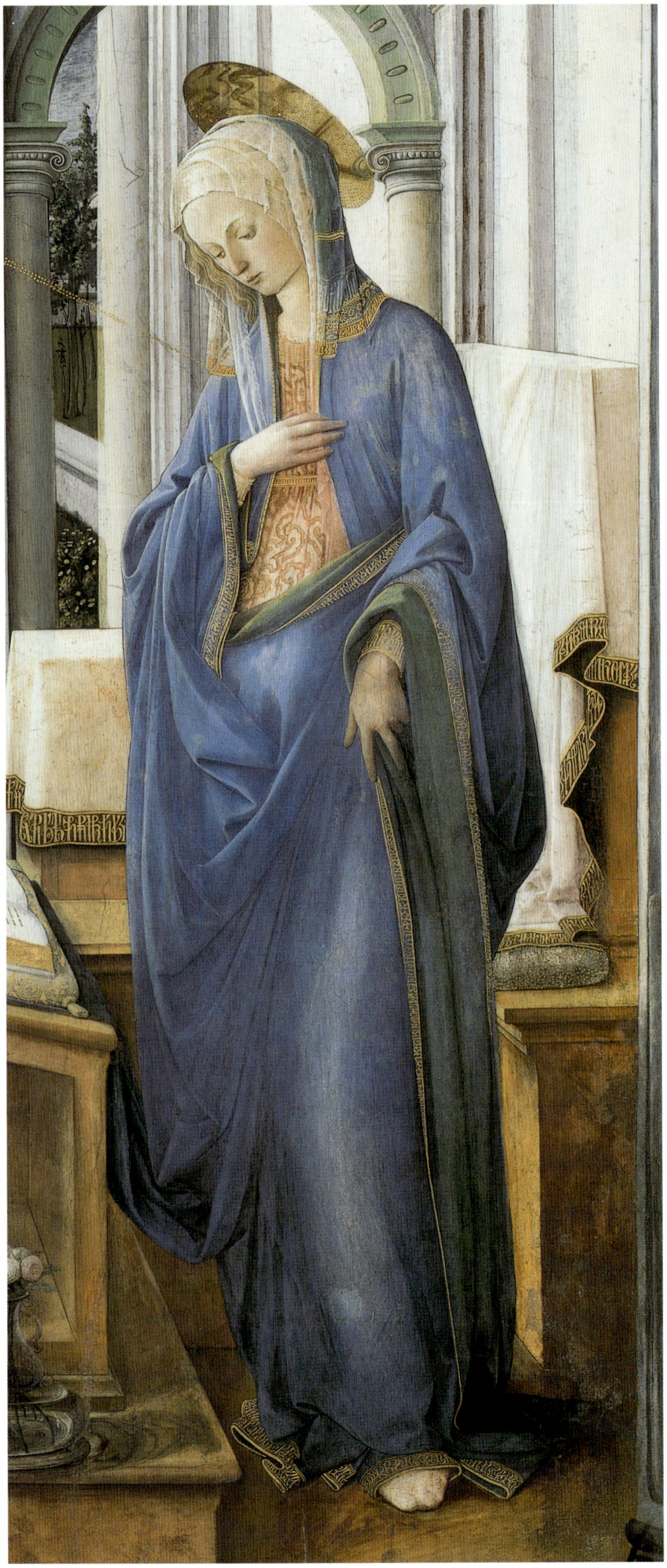

222 Filippo Lippi, *Annunciation*, detail of fig. 220.

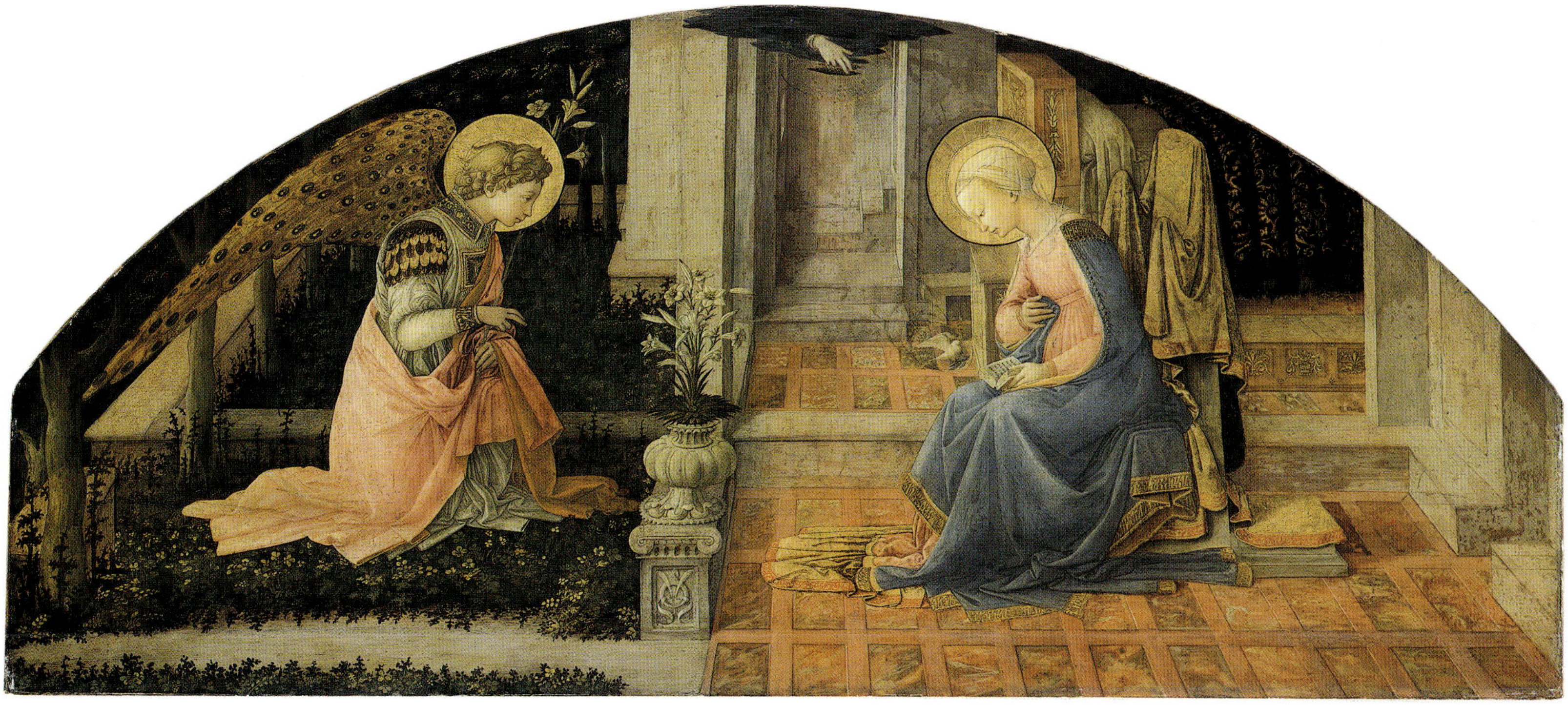

223 Filippo Lippi, *Annunciation*, c. 1450, London, National Gallery.

domestic interior of the Virgin's dwelling – in particular, to her bedroom.[137] In this respect, Fra Filippo followed a tradition reflected in Lorenzo Monaco's Santa Trinita *Annunciation* and Fra Angelico's frescoed *Annunciations* in San Marco.[138] In the Murate *Annunciation* the setting is closer to a church interior, with a rood screen or chapel balustrade cutting through the middle ground, and a cloister beyond. While the traditional literary and pictorial means of revealing the Virgin's humanity, maternity, and her role as *Sponsa* were not at odds with Benedictine orthodoxy and would have been familiar to the nuns and their public, Lippi did not utilize this imagery in his painting. Perhaps he sensed that the robust, descriptive realism that characterized his pictorial idiom in the late 1430s and early 1440s was too vivid a style with which to introduce these themes into an Annunciation in a strict Benedictine context. In Lippi's other paintings of the Annunciation, he indulgently painted in the problematic spaces separating the incommensurate terms out of which a naturalistic rendition of the subject was composed. He shows us what the Virgin's sacred body might look like, how her divine insemination might have happened, and the disposition of the sleeping chamber of Christ's bride. In the *Annunciation* for Le Murate, in contrast, the Virgin is more spirit than body, and the divine insemination is explicated symbolically.

On a more superficial iconographic level, this is one of the few paintings of the Virgin in which Lippi departs from his conventional red and blue color scheme in depicting her clothing. Here Mary is dressed in a white gown with gold brocade beneath her traditional blue robes. These were the colors of the original habit of the nuns of Le Murate (minus the gold) before they switched to the Cassinese Benedictine black robes in 1433. This original habit was chosen in commemoration of the Virgin who was supposed to have dressed in this way.[139] Blue and gold were also the colors of the Benci coat of arms. And, as mentioned before, it is these three colors – blue, gold, and white – that are combined in the picture to articulate the mystery of the Incarnation.

There are other details in Lippi's *Annunciation* for Le Murate that reflect on the devotional practices of the nuns and invoke certain symbols with which the convent was associated. The first of these is the attendant angel who peers in on the Annunciation drama from an open doorway at the left (fig. 226).

Richa, writing in the mid-eighteenth century, considered the second angel "a fanciful thought" as he "watches with amazement from behind the doorway of the room, the Archangel who greets the Virgin."[140] This attendant angel who so struck Richa's post-Tridentine iconographic sensibilities appears occasionally in Annunciation images, including Fra Filippo's own San Lorenzo *Annunciation* (see fig. 104).[141] The figure was also, apparently, a familiar feature within the environment of Le Murate. A trope that appears again and again in the stories recorded in the convent chronicle concerns the virtuous nun of Le Murate who is miraculously guided and protected by an angel.

Among the earliest of these nuns was Sister Benedetta (c. 1393–c. 1479). She was the niece of the first abbess, Agata, and had joined Agata and Apollonia on the Ponte Rubiconte at a very young age, around the year 1400. Benedetta had a guardian angel who kept her constant company. She "was always intently engaged in prayer and contemplation, during which time she

224 and 225 (*following pages*) Filippo Lippi, *Annunciation*, details of figs. 220 and 223, respectively.

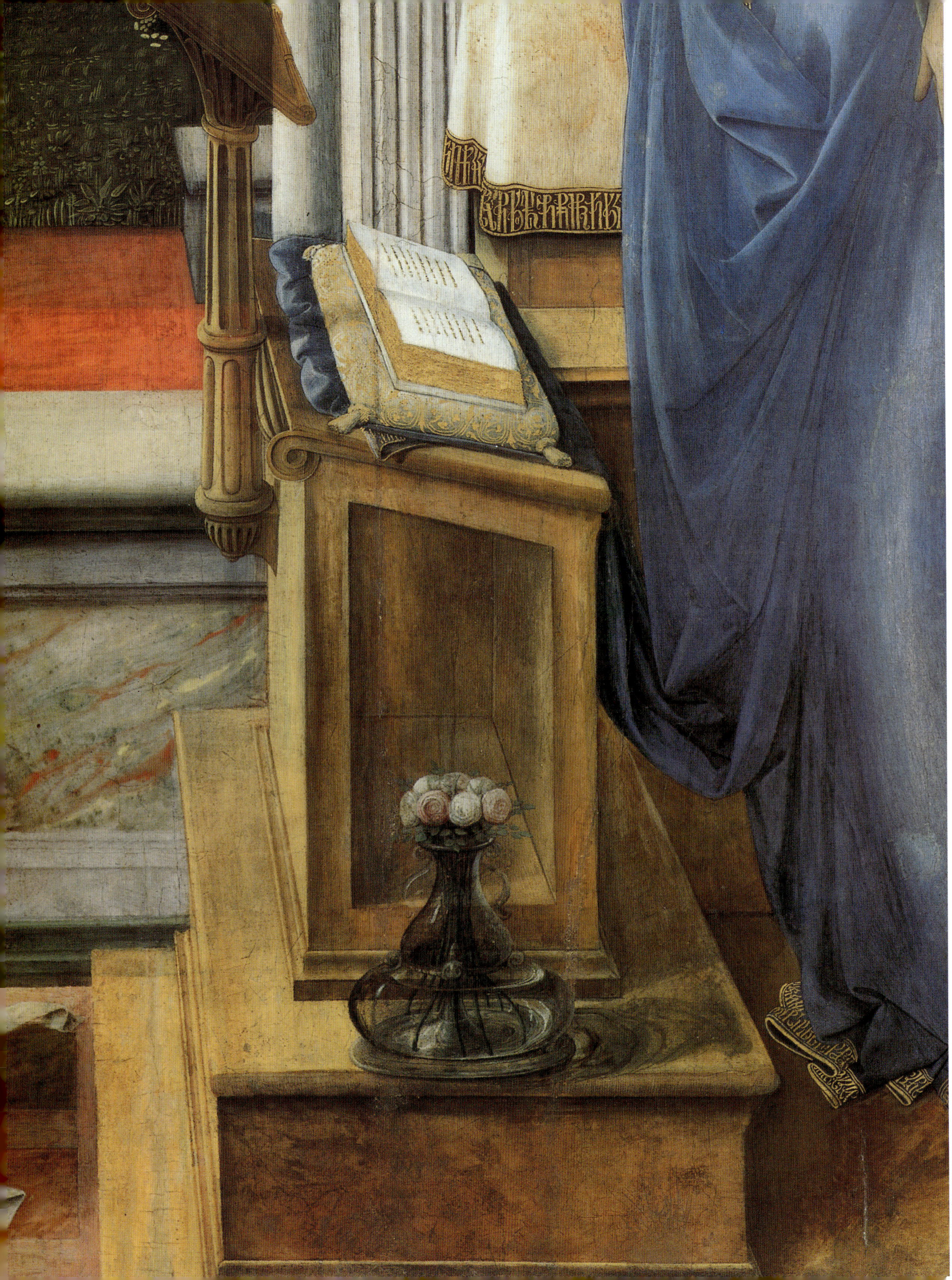

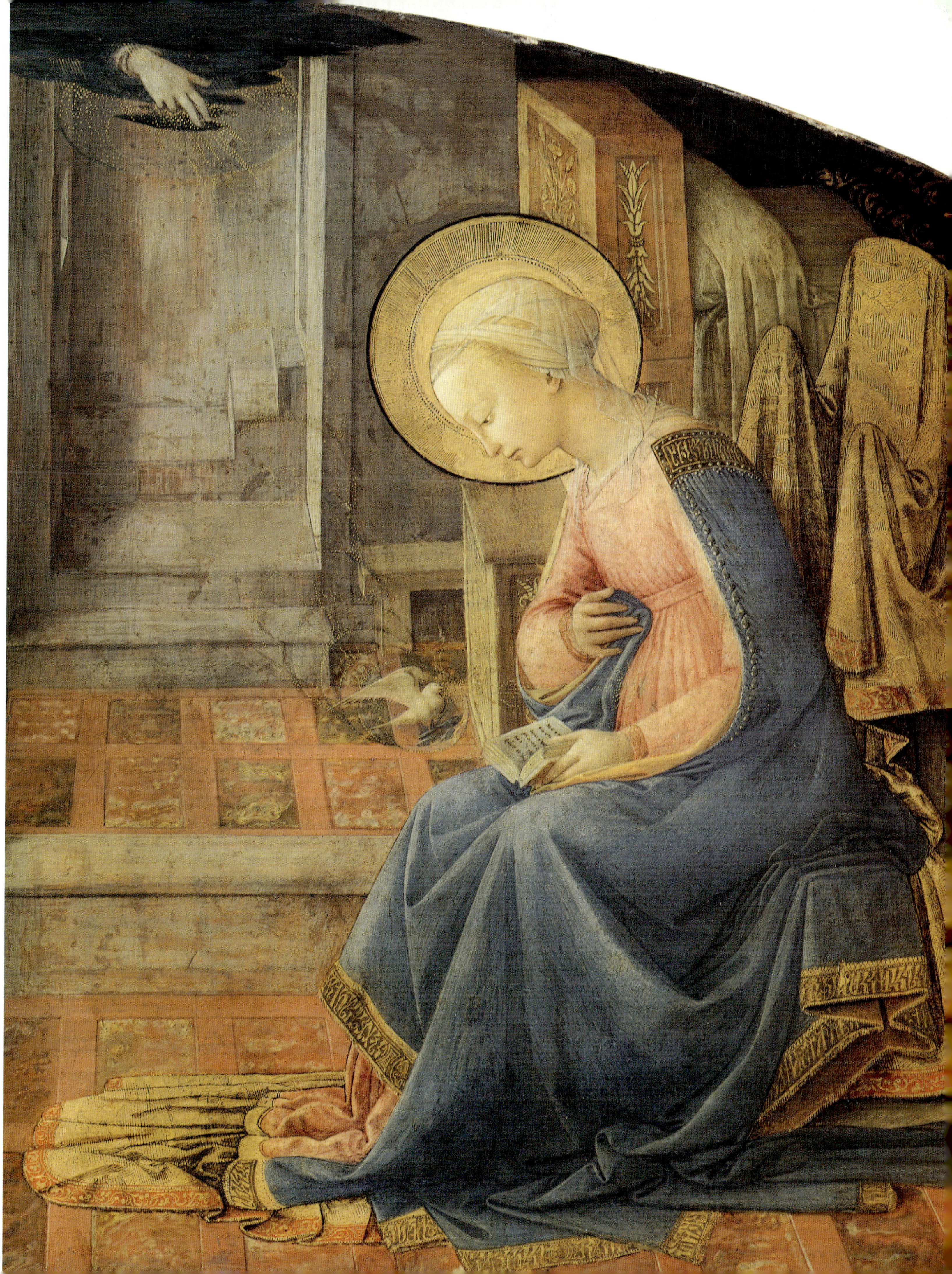

was in continuous conversation with her guardian angel."[142] Visits from her angel were also tied into the festive calendar of the convent where the Annunciation figured prominently:

> During the principal feast [of the Annunciation], she always enjoyed making some sort of new ornament for him through her prayers and he would then please her by appearing and revealing himself in the clothes that she had made him. Once, in particular, she forgot to make him a belt and he appeared with his new clothes but belt-less, and the nun felt no small disgust.[143]

Here, Benedetta literally "dressed up" her vision. It would be most compelling if we could associate this kind of religious image making with Lippi's representation of the *Annunciation* in some way. But Benedetta's life spanned eighty years, and it is not possible to date her many encounters with her guardian angel. In addition, it is unlikely that Benedetta would have had much opportunity to view Lippi's altarpiece, which was located in the convent church – the domain of the convent's public, not its enclosed female population. The nuns recited the Divine Offices in an oratory situated above the church, and after this area was enlarged in the 1460s and provided with an altar, they also attended mass there. Described as a "muraglia," it is unlikely that it provided much of a view of the church interior below.[144]

Be that as it may, I am not arguing for the direct influence of Benedetta's visions on the imagery in Lippi's *Annunciation* (or vice versa). Instead, I am trying to create a picture of confluence between the altarpiece imagery and the mystical experiences, religious practices, and symbolic language that the Florentine urban public would have associated with the nuns of Le Murate. It is very likely that news of the miracles that are recorded in the chronicle would have spread outside the convent, contributing to its reputation as a singularly devout religious house. In fact, one of the later angel miracles occurred before secular witnesses, as a form of public manifestation. The chronicle of Le Murate would have it that Lorenzo de' Medici and another young man, after some friends had voiced skepticism about the nuns' reputation, entered the convent at night, scaled the dormitory walls, and through the windows beheld the nuns asleep in their beds of straw, wearing their coarse woolen tunics, and "at the bedside of each a guardian angel attended."[145] Fra Filippo Lippi was probably familiar with the nuns' public image and may have heard of some of the miracles that had occurred within the touted walls.

In the *Annunciation* for Le Murate, Lippi actively engaged three of the most important features associated with the convent – the Walls, the Portal, and the Sanctuary within. These were key structural components in the actual architecture of the convent and are readily distinguishable in the "Catena" woodcut of the city of Florence from around 1470 (see fig. 207). They were also the essential symbolic elements that defined the nunnery as a spatial metaphor.[146]

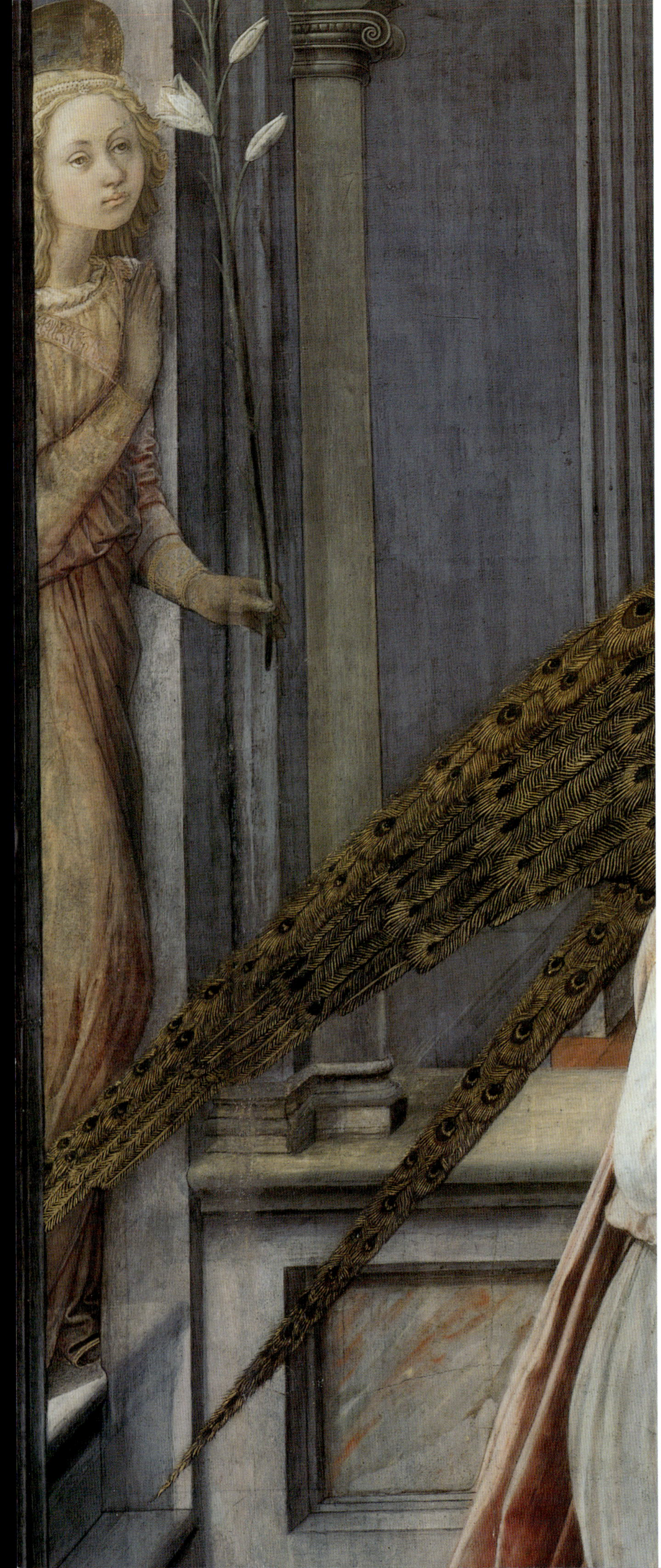

226 Filippo Lippi, *Annunciation*, detail of fig. 220.

The Wall, obviously, was the dominant symbol associated with Le Murate ("if they are 'the Walled Sisters,' they must be as they are named!" cried Savonarola).[147] And the nuns and their patrons and public cultivated the term. As I have mentioned, the nuns closed one of the doorways leading out of the convent in a symbolic reenactment of the original walling-off effected by the founding holy women on the Ponte Rubiconte. The actual walls of the convent had been enlarged by Abbess Scolastica's predecessor, Simona da Panzano. Their girth was expanded once again under Scolastica, with funds provided by Giovanni Benci.

The Portal – or stated more broadly, access – to the convent was no simple affair. According to the Episcopal Constitutions, a nun who left her convent without a license from the bishop was to be excommunicated. Visitors to a convent also required a license, which, from 1430 onward, had to be obtained through the *comune*. There was a special room in a convent known as the *parlatorio* where the nuns could meet and talk to members of the laity from behind a metal grate.[148] Scolastica's Constitutions assigned one of the nuns of Le Murate the task of checking all the windows and doors of the nunnery each evening to make sure that they were closed tight.[149] From Savonarola's sermon quoted above, it is clear that male visitors were permitted in Le Murate, at least by the end of the century.[150] After the Episcopal Constitutions were radically reformed in 1517, only priests, the convent confessor and chaplains, lay persons who worked in the convent, and the closest kin of the nuns were to be allowed contact with the nuns. Perhaps the most telling commentary on the guarded access to Le Murate can be seen in the fate of the building complex after the convent was suppressed in 1808: it was converted into a prison.[151]

The disposition of the Sanctuary within Le Murate was described by Archbishop Antonino in his *Chronica*: "Now they are in a place which is spacious and beautiful in its organization, with workshops, cloisters, and a garden."[152] There was a long tradition of monastic writing allegorizing the interior of the convent. One anonymous writer used a fertile floral imagery trellised upon a framework of ecclesiastical virtues and monastic vows:

> In this paradise grows the tree of life, which is obedience, and the tree of knowledge of good and evil, which is the thoughtful guidance of the abbot. The spiritual brothers are like trees planted along the banks of a river: faith is the sap, hope the flower, and charity the fruit. There flower the lilies of chastity, the tender herbs of humility, the rose of patience, and the virtue of temperance. There every type of fruit matures: the cypress with the spikenard . . .[153]

The sanctuary of a nunnery had the additional association of being a secure environment where the "holy virginity" of the nuns would be protected. This association with security was clearly in the mind of Pope Julius II when, in 1509, he sent the papal tiaras and treasure from Bologna to Florence with instructions that they be stored in Le Murate for safe keeping.[154]

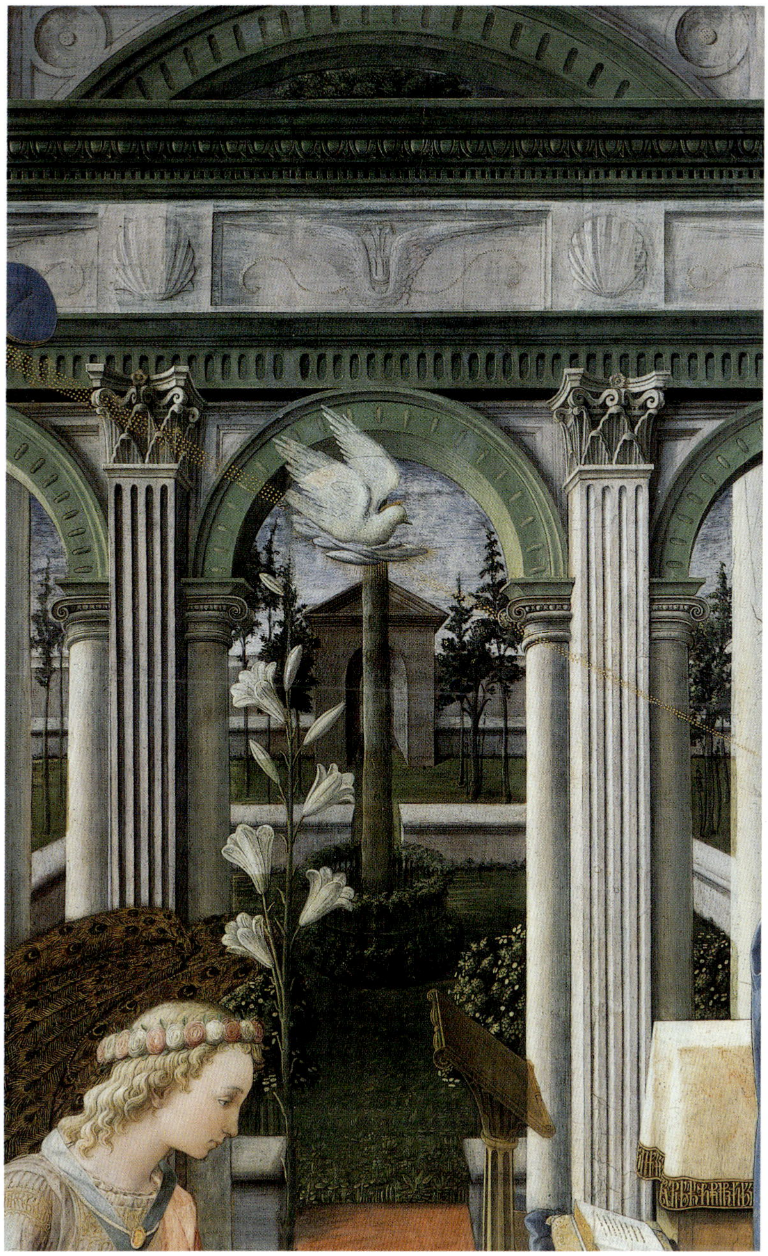

227 Filippo Lippi, *Annunciation,* detail of fig. 220.

The Wall, the Portal, and the Sanctuary were also powerful components in the vocabulary of Annunciation representations. The Annunciation drama involved Gabriel's entry into a closed space and the penetration of the Holy Spirit into a sacred, pure preserve. In the Murate *Annunciation*, Fra Filippo Lippi gave particular emphasis to these potent symbols. The *hortus conclusus* is closed off at the back of the pictorial space by a high outer wall. We see nothing of the world beyond, only the washed-out blue sky above. Within the garden is a second set of lower walls, as in a cloister, which confines an inner verdant space where a monumental cypress tree grows. This cypress is so extraordinarily grand that the viewer is able to see little more than the extensive trunk. The evergreen foliage is just visible within the arch at the top of the picture (fig. 227), with the implication that most of the branches unfurl at heights not visible to the eye.[155] The Annunciation drama occurs before yet another wall, this time a low parapet surmounted by a colonnade resembling a stone roodscreen. This innermost wall closes off the foreground space where the Annunciation drama takes place. Entry into this space is provided by a door at the left where the second angel hovers – a celestial presence mediating access.[156] The walls have carefully plotted openings. The low cloister-like wall is open at the front and back, along the central axis of the picture. In line with this opening is the large Classical portal set within the high outer walls.

There is some ambiguity about whether this outer door is open or closed (fig. 228). The trunk of the cypress passes in front of the opening, obscuring the vanishing point, leaving slight strips of illegible visual information at either side. Lippi literally denies the viewer the satisfaction (and security) of closure.[157] His portal and wall construction invite comparison with Domenico Veneziano's *Annunciation* from the predella of his *St. Lucy* altarpiece (c. 1445; fig. 229). There, the wooden door is locked tight in the vast crenellated wall, offering a clear symbolic reading. In Lippi's *Annunciation*, there is a game of opening and closing going on, a constant play on access and denial. This is one of Lippi's favorite painterly ploys, which appears throughout his work, where he dramatizes the act of viewing – of entering into the pictorial space – by calling attention to points of access, both real (the frame and picture plane) and represented (doorways, paths, windows within the pictorial space). In this way, in the very process of applying a loose Albertian linear perspective, he ruptures the illusion of the discrete "other" pictorial space, posing questions about the relationship between the sacred figures depicted and the contemporary Florentine men and women looking at these religious images. In the Le Murate *Annunciation*, however, this game of opening and closing happens to mimic the real problems accompanying female monastic enclosure, offering a visual analogue.

The high walls of Le Murate erected in the midst of the urban center were not, in fact, designed to keep out all traces of secular life. The nuns negotiated the restrictions of their *clausura* in diverse ways during the *quattrocento*, sometimes allowing for a greater degree of exchange between the convent and the *seculum*. Female relatives of the nuns came to visit. Young boarders were taken on, *converse* and servants lived on the premises. The monastery was also dependent on urban patronage which meant making certain concessions. Male patrons like Giovanni Benci were permitted to enter the convent. Le Murate was dependent on a male clerical and medical staff. Nor, despite its reputation, was it exempt from the scandals that erupted within many of the Florentine convents during the *quattrocento*.[158]

In the end, while Fra Filippo Lippi's *Annunciation* for Le Murate may have been more reflective of the religious values associated with the convent nuns than was his Sant'Ambrogio *Coronation of the Virgin*, it probably figured even less in the devotional exercises of the nuns than did the latter. When the author of the *Cronache* of Le Murate, Giustina Niccolini, described the church decorations, she glossed over the main altarpiece without even naming its celebrated author.[159] Other paintings figured much more prominently in her account and, not surprisingly, they are all images that were displayed within the inner sanctum of the convent. Paintings such as the original *Annunciation* from the Ponte Rubiconte, placed in the sacristy and later in the abbess's cell, a *Madonna lactans* that hung outside the nuns' choir, which had also been brought from the Ponte Rubiconte, and a *Crucifixion* above the altar in the nuns' choir – all emerge as objects of the nuns' intense devotion that inspired many miracles over the years.[160] Lippi's *Annunciation* was situated on the other side of the grate. This image, which was fashioned in the most up-to-date, modern style when the church was built, was intended for public consumption. The Annunciation imagery reflected on the religious practices and tenor of life within the convent as a means of elaborating the public image of the convent for the benefit of the Florentine patriciate.

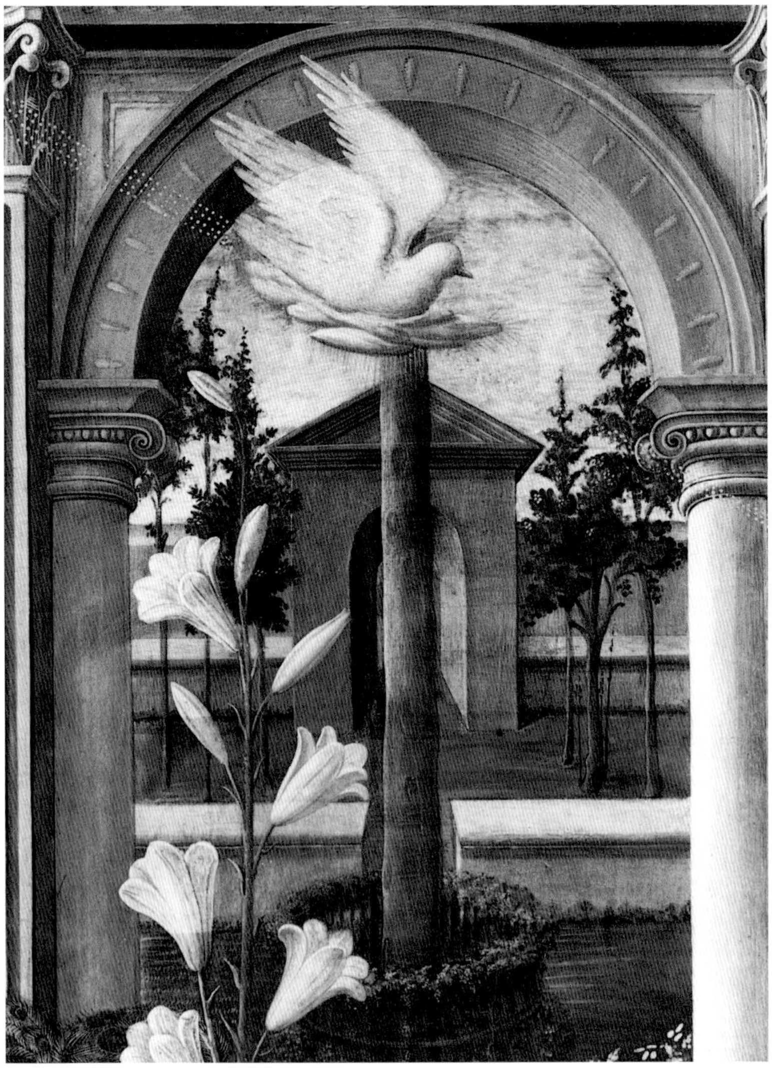

228 Filippo Lippi, *Annunciation*, detail of fig. 220.

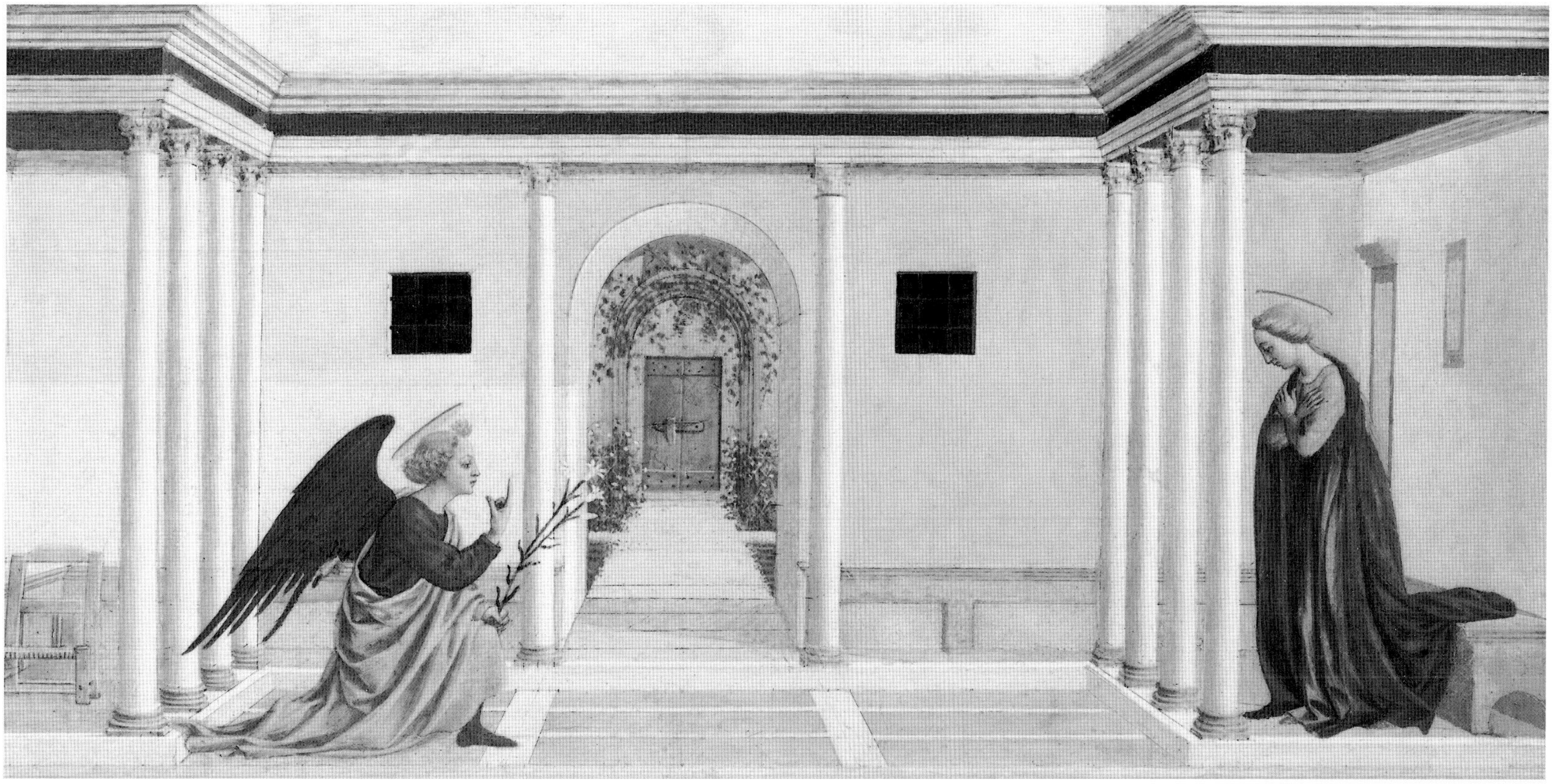

229 Domenico Veneziano, *Annunciation*, c. 1445, predella from the *St. Lucy* altarpiece (fig. 109), Cambridge, Fitzwilliam Museum.

CONCLUSION

The antagonistic relationship between Sant'Ambrogio and Le Murate had become less charged by the late 1430s and early 1440s, on account of the independent circumstances of Le Murate and the sheer demand for places in the city's nunneries. Even so, when Fra Filippo was commissioned to paint the high altarpieces for each of the convent churches, he was indirectly called upon to represent two different, competing varieties of the female monastic experience. The contrasts between the two Benedictine convents and the experiences of the respective groups of nuns are reflected in the two altarpieces. The fact that the Sant'Ambrogio *Coronation of the Virgin* was to serve a diverse viewing public produced certain instabilities within the imagery. The iconography became volatile in trying to secure the likeness of the Holy *Mater-Sponsa*. The Le Murate *Annunciation* was called upon to elaborate a public image of the principal patron of the convent church as devoutly wealthy, and to further the popular perception of the extreme piety of the nuns. Nonetheless, the *Annunciation* for Le Murate, too, has certain areas of ambiguity and overdetermination. The particular attention given to the wall in the painting may have been mandated by the patron Giovanni Benci or the abbess Scolastica Rondinelli, or it may represent the painter's own initiative in elaborating a visual language appropriate for the church of "the Walled Sisters." But the ambiguities evident in the rendering of this potent symbol register – either consciously or not, on the part of the artist – the contradictions attending the practice of enclosure at Le Murate.[161]

The issue of competitiveness between the two convents cannot so easily be put to rest. However secure in its endowment, the convent of Sant'Ambrogio was never to attract the well-to-do women, the lavish gifts, and wealthy, prestigious patrons that Le Murate drew from the late 1430s. Conspicuous artistic display was always a means of redressing this imbalance. Later in the century, Mino da Fiesole was separately commissioned by the nuns of the two convents to sculpt marble tabernacles for their respective churches (figs. 230 and 231). In his *Vita* of Mino, Vasari interjects a note of competitiveness in describing the coincidence:

> Working for the Nuns of the Murate, [Mino] made a marble tabernacle in half-relief to contain the Sacrament. . . . This he had not yet fixed into its place, when the Nuns of Sant'Ambrogio – who desired to have an ornament made, similar in design but richer in ornament, to contain that most holy relic, the Miracle of the Sacrament – hearing of the ability of Mino, commissioned him to execute that work.[162]

There was, in fact, much at stake for the nuns of Sant'Ambrogio in the commission of the marble tabernacle from Mino in 1481. It was intended for a new chapel dedicated to the important Eucharistic relic situated to the left of the *cappella*

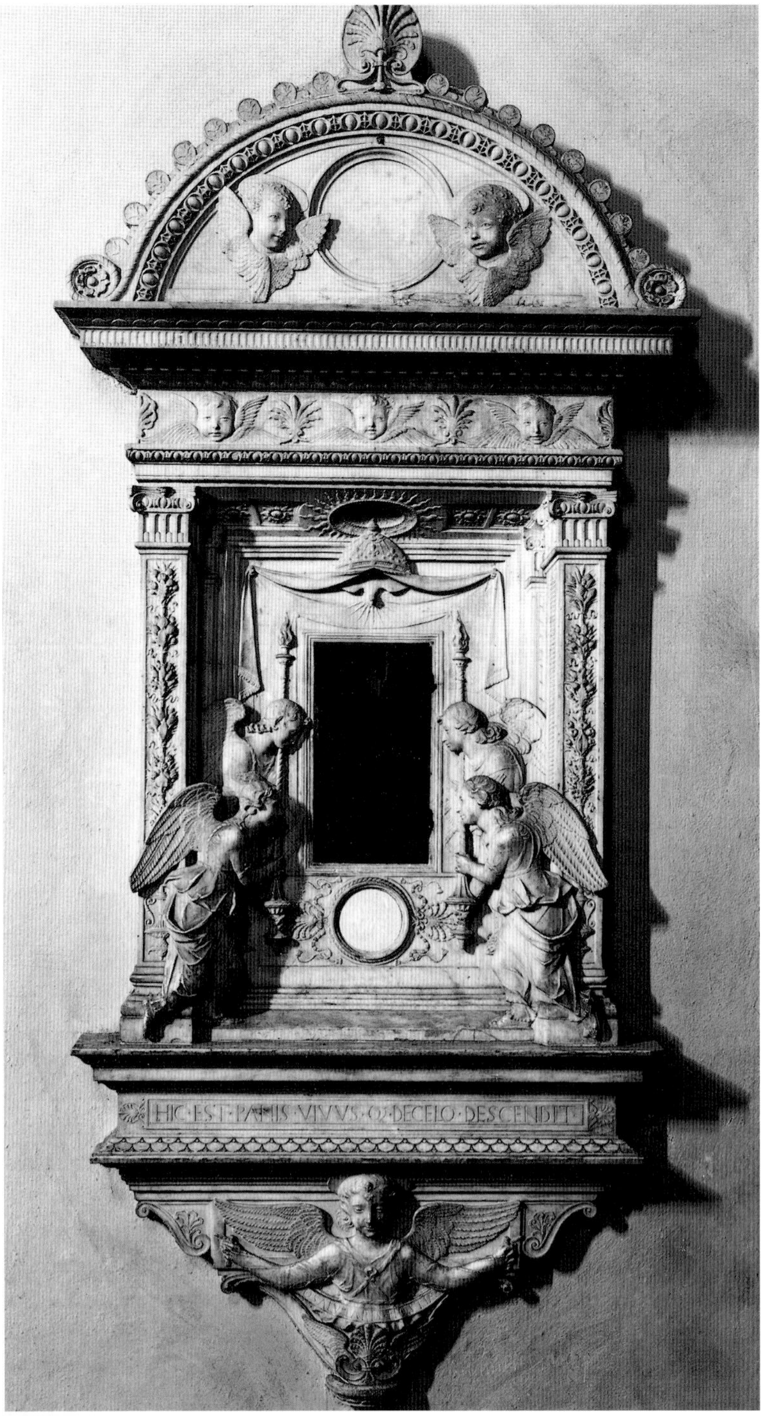

230 Mino da Fiesole, tabernacle of the Sacrament, c. 1473, originally in the church at Le Murate, now in Florence, Santa Croce.

maggiore. The nuns themselves had taken over the patronage of this chapel, wresting the cult of Corpus Christi from the hands of private and corporate patrons and transforming it into the centerpiece of their religious devotion and public appeal. They had Cosimo Rosselli fresco the walls of the chapel between 1484 and 1486, depicting the celebration of the relic in the piazza outside the church.[163]

In these works of art associated with the Eucharistic relic, which the Benedictine nuns commissioned, the nuns themselves appear in the imagery. In Mino's tabernacle relief (fig. 233), eight nuns and a novice are shown on the left side of the composition, kneeling in prayer before the relic, counter-balanced by a separate group of male worshipers on the right. The nuns, however, are presented as the privileged protagonists. The priest offers the relic to one of them – probably the abbess – positioned directly before the altar. In the fresco by Cosimo Rosselli (fig. 232), the nuns play a more reduced role in the celebration of the relic necessitated by the dictates of their *clausura*. The subject may be the historical confirmation of the Eucharistic relic which took place in 1230, or the more current civic celebration of the relic on certain important feast days when it was displayed before the Florentine public. This fresco demonstrates in a much more explicit manner the kind of instabilities that I have argued exist within Fra Filippo Lippi's Sant'Ambrogio *Coronation of the Virgin*, caused by the nuns' exposure to both conventual life and to certain parish activities at Sant'Ambrogio.

Following the convention established by Masaccio in his *Sagra* (see fig. 36) for depicting an ecclesiastical event with important

231 Mino da Fiesole, tabernacle of the Eucharistic Relic, 1481–84, Florence, Sant'Ambrogio, Cappella del Miracolo.

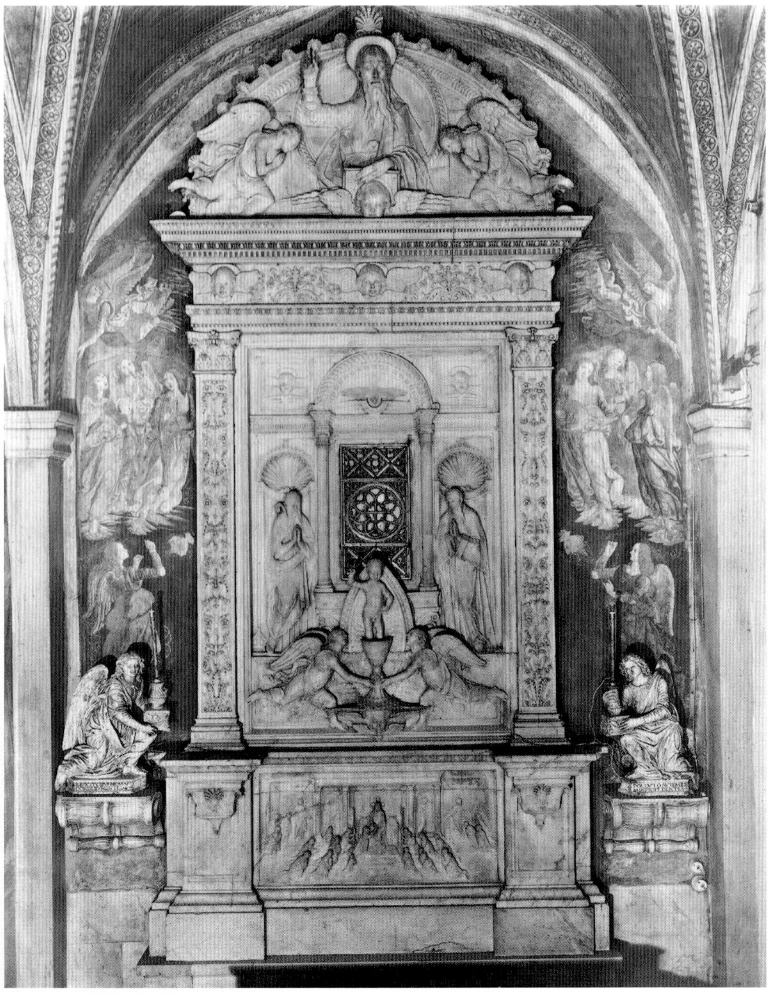

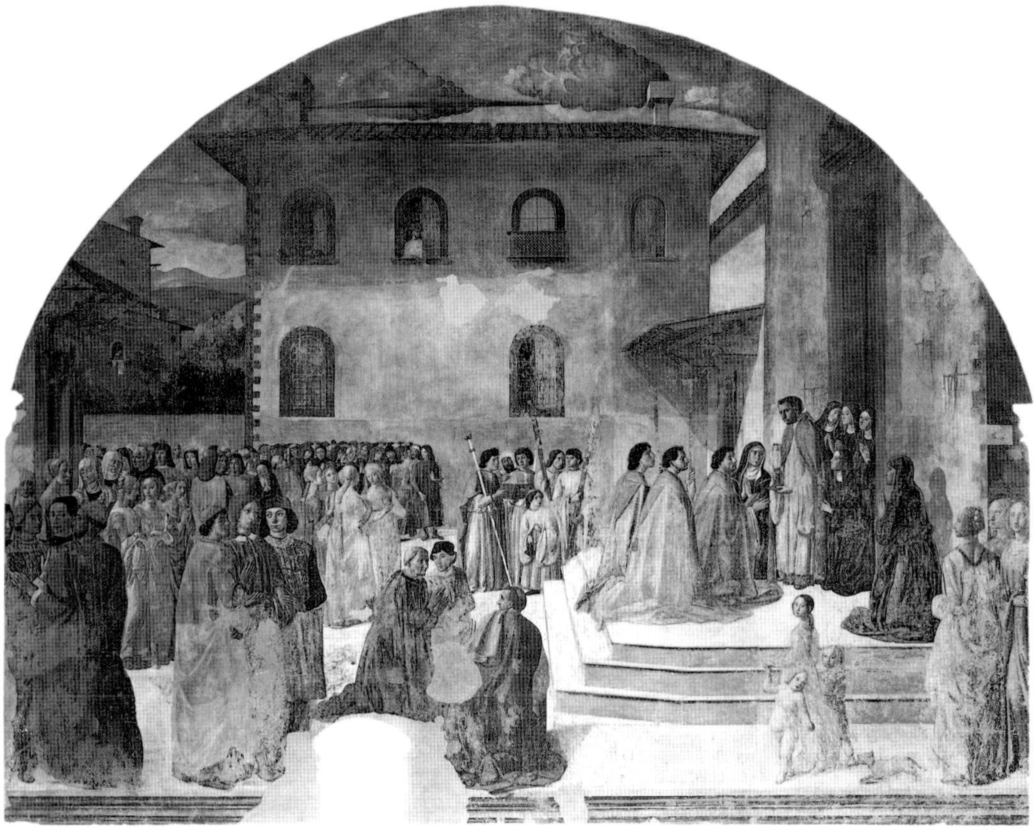

232 Cosimo Rosselli, *Celebration of the Eucharistic Relic in the Piazza Sant'Ambrogio*, 1484–86, Florence, Sant'Ambrogio, Cappella del Miracolo.

233 Mino da Fiesole, tabernacle of the Eucharistic Relic, detail of fig. 231.

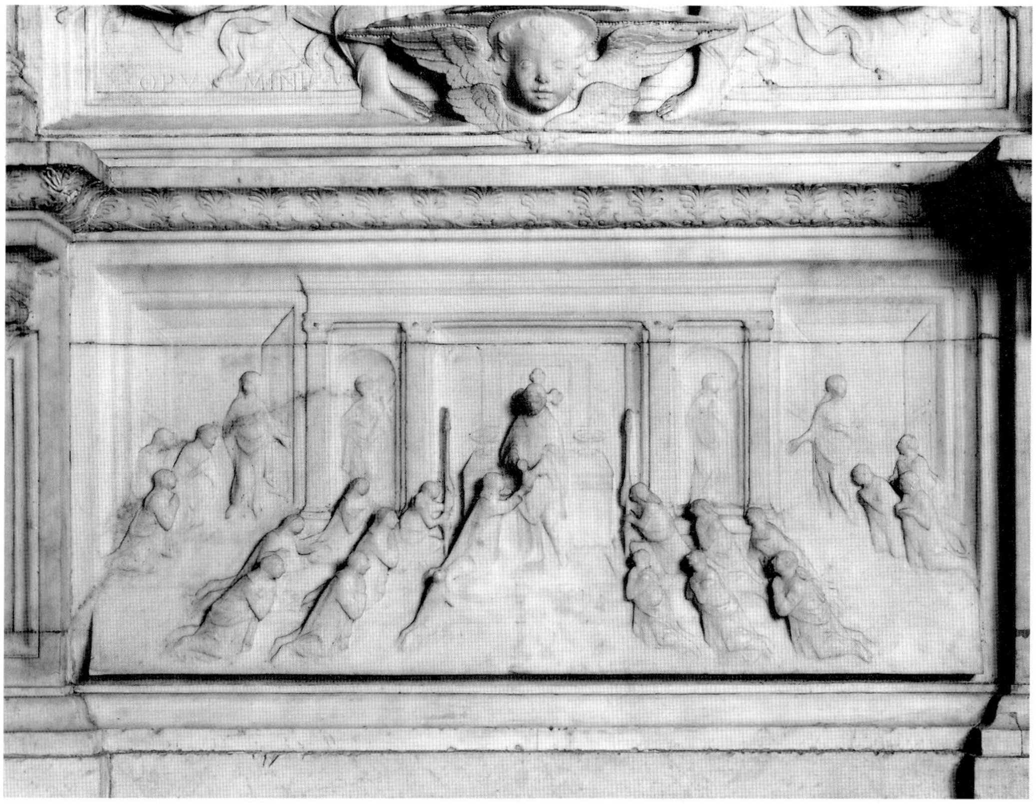

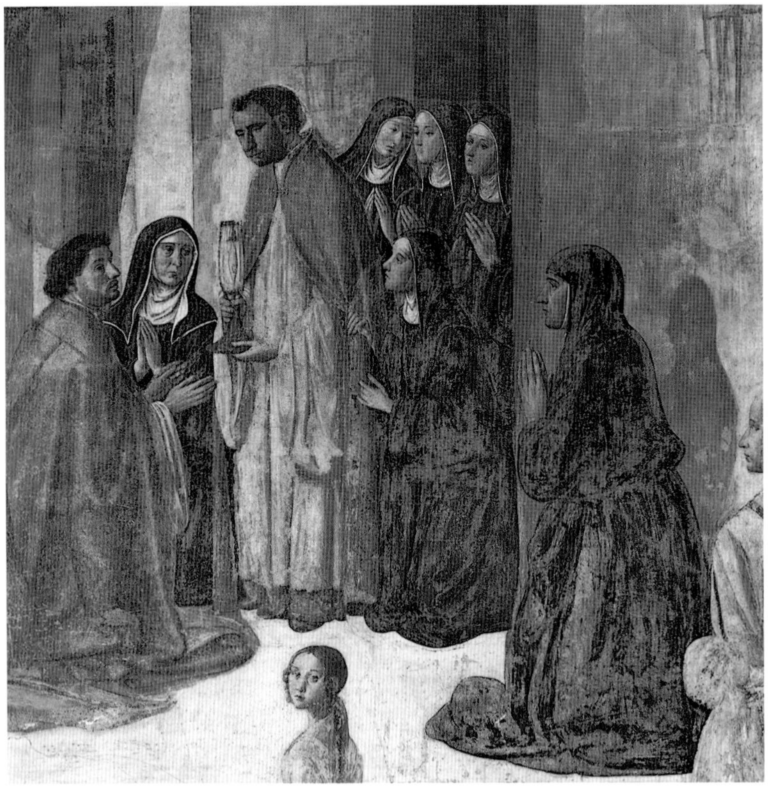

civic dimensions, Rosselli represented the festive ritual taking place outside in the piazza just in front of the church of Sant'Ambrogio. The priest, standing in front of the church – with his back to the congregation of nuns clustered just inside the doorway – holds the relic before the outstretched arms of a kneeling layman. A large crowd of Florentine men and women assemble in the piazza. Three nuns positioned close to the priest establish the Sant'Ambrogio Benedictine nunnery frame for the relic (fig. 234). They are all shown kneeling, with their hands clasped, one slightly behind and to the side of the priest, and two level with him at a short distance to either side. The nun on the right casts what is perhaps the most impressive shadow in the entire fresco against the church facade, making concrete her presence in the ritual celebrations. Behind these three figures, additional members of the enclosed female community of Sant'Ambrogio stand at the threshold of the convent church. The Benedictine nuns' "place" in the fresco is located at the edge of the depicted scene, indeterminantly situated between the closed spaces of monastic *clausura* and the public, civic spaces of the Florentine *seculum*.

234 Cosimo Rosselli, *Celebration of the Eucharistic Relic in the Piazza Sant'Ambrogio*, detail of fig. 232.

NOTES

ABBREVIATIONS

ASF	Archivio di Stato, Florence
BNF	Biblioteca Nazionale, Florence
Con. Sopp.	Conventi Soppressi (Archivio di Stato, Florence)
Cronache del Monastero	Cronache del N.N. Monastero di Santa Maria Annunciata dette Le Murate di Firenze (Biblioteca Nazionale, Florence, II.II.509)
MAP	Mediceo Avanti il Principiato (Archivio di Stato, Florence)
Not. Antecos.	Notarile Antecosimiano (Archivio di Stato, Florence)
Vasari–Barocchi and Bettarini	G. Vasari, *Le vite de' piu eccellenti pittori, scultori ed architettori nelle ridazioni del 1550 e 1568*, eds. P. Barochi and R. Bettarini, 6 vols., Florence, 1966–87.
Vasari–Milanesi	G. Vasari, *Le vite de' piu eccellenti pittori, scultori ed architettori*, ed. G. Milanesi, 9 vols., Florence, 1906.
Vasari–De Vere	G. Vasari, *Lives of the Most Eminent Painters, Sculptors and Architects*, trans. G. De Vere, 10 vols., London 1912–14.

INTRODUCTION

1 "Fra i vicini del Piovano Arlotto c'era un padre con un unico figliolo giovanotto, ben formato e di corpo robusto, a cui da pochi anni era morta la madre. Il padre aveva ripreso per moglie un'altra donna, bella e giovane. . . .

Il padre . . . scoprì il figliolo addosso alla donna; il rumore fu grande e durò molti giorni, e si sentiva per tutto il vicinato; ma non si sapeva ciò per cui litigavano e gridavano ogni giorno. Un giorno gridavano così forte che di nuovo accorsero molti vicini e il Piovano Arlotto. . . . Il Piovano bussò alla porta; vennero giù il padre e il figlio. . . . Il Piovano chiese: – Che avete voi? Ogni giorno non fate altro che gridare da un po' di tempo in qua.

Il padre rispose: – Piovano mio, se voi lo sapeste, direste che io ho ragione.

Essendo in quella situazione, il padre del ragazzo disse: – Piovano, non ve lo posso dire.

Il ragazzo respose: – Piovano, ve lo voglio dire io: mio padre abbracciò forse mille volte mia madre quando era viva, e ora che io ho abbracciato la mia matrigna qualche volta, questo padre mio mette a rumore ogni giorno il vicinato.

Il Piovano disse: – Non fate più rumore. L'abbracciarsi l'uno con l'altro non deriva se non da carità; ognuno di voi prenda ciò che gli fa piacere e d'accordo non litigate più, perché nessuno venga a sapere dei fatti vostri, e nell'avvenire siate savi." *Facezie, Motti e Burle del Piovano Arlotto*, pp. 220–22.

2 On the historical figure Arlotto Mainardi, see *Facezie, Motti e Burle del Piovano Arlotto*, pp. 7–24, and F. W. Kent and A. Lillie, "The Piovano Arlotto: New Documents," in *Florence and Italy: Renaissance Studies in Honour of Nicolai Rubinstein*, ed. P. Denley and C. Elam, London, 1988, pp. 347–67.

3 For this reason, I have tended to shy away from pictures that do not have secure documentation and I have not discussed in any great detail the artist's major frescos in Prato and Spoleto, dating from the last fifteen years of his life.

4 Burckhardt, *The Civilization of the Renaissance in Italy*, p. 303.

5 See the essays collected in Trinkaus and Oberman, *The Pursuit of Holiness in Late Medieval and Renaissance Religion*. See also the work of Roberto Bizzocchi, André Vauchez, Donald Weinstein, and Rudolph Bell.

6 See the work of Natalie Zemon Davis, Richard Trexler, Caroline Walker Bynum, Ronald Weissman, and Carlo Ginzburg.

7 N. Zemon Davis, "Some Tasks and Themes in the Study of Popular Religion," in Trinkaus and Oberman, *The Pursuit of Holiness*, pp. 307–36.

8 See the range of studies presented in C. Atkinson, C. Buchanan, and M. Miles, eds., *Immaculate and Powerful: The Female in Sacred Image and Social Reality*, Boston, 1985; C. Walker Bynum, S. Harrell, and P. Richman, eds., *Gender and Religion: On the Complexity of Symbols*, Boston, 1986; G. Zarri, *Le Sante Vive: Cultura e religiosità femminile nella prima età moderna*, Turin, 1990; C. Monson, ed., *The Crannied Wall: Women, Religion, and the Arts in Early Modern Europe*, Ann Arbor, 1992; G. Zarri, ed., *Donna, disciplina, creanza cristiana dal xv al xvii secolo: Studi e testi a stampa*, Rome, 1996. On gender in Renaissance Italy, see the bibliography in G. Johnson and

S. Matthews Grieco, eds., *Picturing Women in Renaissance and Baroque Italy*, Cambridge, 1997, pp. 247–8, n. 2.

9 "Introduction: The Complexity of Symbols," in Bynum, Harrell, and Richman, *Gender and Religion*, pp. 2 and 9–10.

CHAPTER ONE

1 "Fece in un pilastro in chiesa la figura di San Marziale . . . la quale gli arrecò infinita fama, potendo stare a paragone con le cose che Masaccio aveva dipinte. Per il che sentitosi lodar tanto per il grido d'ognuno, animosamente si cavò l'abito di età d'anni XVII, *ancora che negli ordini sacri fusse già ordinato a Vangelo; di che nulla curandosi o poco, si partì da la religione*." Vasari–Barocchi and Bettarini, *Le vite*, vol. III–text, p. 329. The italicized lines appear in Vasari's 1550 edition, but were cut from the 1568 edition. The translation is from Vasari–De Vere, *Lives*, vol. III, p. 80 (with my translation of the 1550 lines not included in De Vere).

2 "Molti dicevano lo spirito di Masaccio essere entrato nel corpo di Fra Filippo" and "e Michelagnolo l'ha non pur celebrato sempre, ma imitato in molte cose . . ." Vasari–Milanesi, *Le vite*, vol. II, pp. 613 and 626; trans. Vasari–De Vere, *Lives*, vol. III, pp. 80 and 86.

3 See Rubin, *Giorgio Vasari: Art and History*, pp. 75ff. See also D. J. O'Connor, "Artist Friars of the Renaissance in Giorgio Vasari," *Irish Theological Quarterly*, vol. 63, no. 2 (1988), pp. 167–95.

4 "Il priore si risolvette a dargli ogni commodità ed agio d'imparare a dipignere . . ." Vasari–Milanesi, vol. II, p. 612; trans. Vasari–De Vere, vol. III, p. 79.

5 "Esercitandosi del continuo, in compagnia di molti giovani che sempre vi disegnavano, di gran lunga gli altri avanzava di destrezza e di sapere," Vasari–Milanesi, vol. II, p. 613; trans. Vasari–De Vere, vol. III, p. 79. In the *Vita* of Masaccio, Vasari describes Lippi as Masaccio's "discepolo" and includes Lippi in a long list of "tutti i più celebrati scultori e pittori che sono stati da lui in qua, esercitandosi e studiando in questa cappella, sono divenuti eccellenti e chiari," Vasari–Milanesi, vol. II, p. 299. Vasari's esteem for the Brancacci chapel and his views on its influence in the early 16th century are further developed in his life of Perino del Vaga, vol. V, pp. 603–5.

6 See Rubin, *Giorgio Vasari: Art and History*, p. 200.

7 "E d'allora in poi gli diede libertà, che a suo piacere andasse. . . . Per il che, sempre con carezze si ingegnò di tenerlo per l'avvenire: e così da lui fu servito con più prestezza; dicendo egli, che l'eccellenze degli ingegni rari sono forme celesti e non asini vetturini." Vasari–Milanesi, vol. II, p. 617; trans. Vasari–De Vere, vol. III, p. 81.

8 "Dicesi ch'era tanto venereo, che vedendo donne che gli piacessero, se le poteva avere, ogni sua facultà donato le arebbe;" "Ed era tanto perduto dietro a questo appetito, che all'opere prese da lui, quando era in questo umore, poco o nulla attendeva" and "per potere far di sè e dell'appetito suo come gli paresse," Vasari–Milanesi, vol. II, pp. 616 and 629; trans. Vasari–De Vere, vol. III, pp. 81 and 87.

9 "Fu tanto per le sue buone qualità stimato, che molte cose, che di biasimo erano alla vita sua, furono ricoperte mediante il grado di tanta virtù." Vasari–Milanesi, vol. II, p. 624; trans. Vasari–De Vere, vol. III, p. 85.

10 Vasari–Milanesi, vol. II, p. 638 (my translation).

11 Vasari–Milanesi, vol. II, p. 614, n. These "parenti bisognose" refer to the six poor nieces mentioned in Lippi's plaintive letter to Piero de' Medici in 1439: see Ch. 6 below, p. 154.

12 Vasari–Milanesi, vol. II, p. 633.

13 Vasari–Milanesi, vol. II, p. 638. The actual documentation is neither substantial nor explicit and Milanesi's narrative, which continues to dominate the Lippi literature, is highly interpretive.

14 "Egli sviò la Lucrezia dalle monache; e la *menò* via" and "ella, o per paura o per altra cagione, non volle mai ritornare," Vasari–Milanesi, vol. II, p. 621.

15 In my own consultation of the documents – including those cited by Milanesi – I have, in fact, been unable to confirm that Fra Filippo was the *cappellano* of Santa Margherita. In documents from 1459 and 1461 concerning Fra Filippo and the nuns of Santa Margherita, he is simply referred to as "fra Filippo di Tommaso dipintore da Firenze," ASF, Not. Antecos. 19449, c. 391r, and 19450, cc. 98v–101v. The only evidence in support of his being *cappellano* is the anonymous complaint filed in Prato against Lippi in 1461, claiming that he was always to be found at Santa Margherita, "si schusa con essere chappellano," in Caioli, "Un altro sguardo sulla vita di fra Filippo Lippi," pp. 60–61.

16 Vasari–Milanesi, vol. II, p. 635.

17 Vasari had written that it was Eugenius IV who offered to legitimize the union of Fra Filippo and Lucrezia. Milanesi correctly notes that Pope Eugenius was long dead and that it would have had to have been Pius II.

18 Vasari–Milanesi, vol. II, p. 638.

19 Vasari–Milanesi, vol. II, p. 639.

20 On the historiographic tradition, see Marchini, *Filippo Lippi*, pp. 14–17; Fossi, *Filippo Lippi*, pp. 31ff; Ruda, *Fra Filippo Lippi*, pp. 10–13; Mannini and Fagioli, *Filippo Lippi*, pp. 11–15.

21 Caioli, "Un altro sguardo," pp. 30–72.

22 *Ibid.*, pp. 33 and 36 (my translation).

23 *Ibid.*, p. 41.

24 Boskovits, "Fra Filippo Lippi, i carmelitani e il Rinascimento." The question of Lippi's Carmelite status and the influence it had on his art is not a significant concern of Jeffrey Ruda's in his monograph on Lippi, pp. 25 and 47–53.

25 Boskovits, "Fra Filippo Lippi," p. 240 (my translation).

26 Boskovits suggests that Lippi may have encountered northern European painting in a picture or choral manuscript in the possession of a Confraternity member, "Fra Filippo Lippi," pp. 240–41.

27 Boskovits puts together this picture of the Carmine from the documentary research of G. Bacchi, A. Sabatini, L. Saggi, K. W. Humphreys, and L. Perini.

28 *Ibid.*, p. 243.

29 *Ibid.*, pp. 243 and 244.

30 *Ibid.*, p. 240.

31 Among those erudite figures considered humanists, we find two eminent monks – one associated with a reformed Benedictine order and the other a mendicant, the Camaldolese prior general Ambrogio Traversari and the Augustinian prior of Santo Spirito, Luigi Marsili.

32 Vasari–Milanesi, vol. II, pp. 611–12.

33 See Caioli, "Un altro sguardo," p. 31. I have gone through the Carmine *Libro di entrata e uscita* covering 1382 to 1401, ASF, Con. Sopp. 113, n. 83, and found mention of a "Tommaso ortolano" who worked for the convent briefly in 1393 ("item a tomaso ortolano per rachonsciare le pergchole per uno mezzo mese. . . . l.2"; cc. 218r and 222v). Unfortunately, the account book covering 1402–16 is missing.

34 We hear of this house in 1457, when Lippi took the occupant, Mona Lucia, to court, claiming that she owed him 25 fl. in back rent (ASF, Mercanzia 1406, cc. 253r–v, 261r, 353v–355r, 369r–370r, and 391v–392r).

35 Tommaso di Lippo was involved with the Compagnia di San Frediano through 1408 (ASF, Compagnia di San Frediano, n. 32, cc. 3v, 6r, 7r, 31r, 38v; n. 88, c. 43r). His name is recorded as a witness in notarial documents transacted in Santa Maria del Carmine through 1411; see Ruda, *Fra Filippo Lippi*, p. 23.

36 Milanesi cites no documentation to back up this claim, Vasari–Milanesi, vol. II, p. 611, n. 2.

37 ASF, Compagnia di S. Maria delle Laudi detta di S. Agnese, n. 98, cc. 3v and 35r. On the Compagnia di Sant'Agnese and the Compagnia di San Frediano, see Eckstein, *The District of the Green Dragon*, chs. III and IV.

38 See Ruda, *Fra Filippo Lippi*, Doc. 2, pp. 514–15. See also ASF, Catasto 184, c. 191r. Mona Antonia was not without property; she

rented out part of a house located in the parish of San Felice in Piazza at 5 fl. a year: see Ruda, Doc. 9, p. 524. Ruda suggests that the sister mentioned in the *catasto* report may be the same sister recorded in Lippi's house in Florence in 1455, pp. 23 and 535, Doc. 19. IV.

39 See Caioli, "Un altro sguardo," p. 32. Caioli believed that Giovanni was some three years older than Filippo, based on the date of his ordination into the priesthood (1422/23). Giovanni became a Carmelite on Jan. 6, 1419, two and a half years before Lippi: see Ruda, *Fra Filippo Lippi*, Doc. I. I. I, p. 513.

40 Caioli, "Un altro sguardo," p. 32; Ruda, *Fra Filippo Lippi*, p. 348, n. 9, and Doc. I, p. 513. I am not convinced by this argument, which is based solely on the common occurrence of a progenitor "Lippo." Lippo is a diminutive form of Filippo and was a common enough name in 15th-century Florence.

41 The date of Lippi's birth is not documented. Vasari gave two different dates in the two editions (1402 in the 1550 edition and 1412 in 1568). Milanesi suggested a date around 1406, working backward from the date of Lippi's documented profession as a Carmelite in 1421 (Vasari–Milanesi, vol. II, p. 611–12, n. 1). Caioli corrected this to c. 1407, citing the 1369 Carmelite constitution which set the age of profession at fourteen, "Un altro sguardo," p. 34.

42 See Moorman, *A History of the Franciscan Order*, pp. 148–9 and 501–3.

43 There is no guarantee that the *fanciulli* listed in the Carmine books are not in fact novices – although novices are typically referred to as *frati*. I have only found one reference where they are differentiated from the novices – in a payment for cheese: "chacio pe[r] fanciulli novitii," ASF, Con. Sopp. 113, n. 86, c. 24r, Aug. 10, 1440.

44 See, e.g., the record of the return of the *fanciulli* from the annual Corpus Christi procession in 1425 with Fra Arrigo: "item a dì di g[i]ugno [1425] per uova per fanciulli e per fr[at]e ar[r]igho che v[i]ene con esso loro da pistoia in tutto l.0 s.11," ASF, Con. Sopp. 113, n. 85, c. 104r. From these payment records it can be estimated that the *fanciulli* at the Carmine numbered from two to five.

45 There were reportedly 16,000 deaths in the city of Florence: see A. Corradi, *Annali delle epidemie occorse in Italia dalle prime memorie fino al 1850*, Bologna, 1972, vol. I, p. 256.

46 *Necrologium Carmelitanum*, BNF, Con. Sopp., C.5.786 (1593).

47 See *Atti dei capitoli provinciali*, p. 133.

48 It is more likely that the constitution was established in an effort to boost the numbers, and that there were closer to ten novices each year. In 1415, the Tuscan Carmelite provincial statutes refer to the novitiate "de decima in conventu Florentie," *Atti dei capitoli provinciali*, p. 138. A list of the Carmine novices from 1393 includes eight names, ASF, Con. Sopp. 113, n. 83, c. 229v.

49 "Item ordinamus magistrum et informatorem novitiorum in nostro conventu Florentie cum plena auctoritate super ipsos, quem nullus infringere valeat nisi rev. noster provincialis si expediat, fr. Iohannem Dominici lectorem," *Atti dei capitoli provinciali*, p. 146. Giovanni Dominici held the post from 1416 to 1422, excluding 1419–20, pp. 136, 140, 143, 149, 154, and 370.

50 "Tam in divino officio quam in bonis moribus," *Atti dei capitoli provinciali*, p. 134.

51 A 1473 inventory of the library of the novitiate in the Carmine consists primarily of copies of the Rule, Psalters, Bibles, the Divine Offices, and the Gospels and Epistles: see L. Perini, "L'inventario dei codici di S. Maria del Carmine di Firenze del 1461," *Studi Medievali*, 3 Serie X3, 1969, Appendice III, p. 553.

52 The novices' quarters were rebuilt in the 1460s with funds given by Tommaso di Lorenzo Soderini: see Giovannini and Vitolo, *Il Convento del Carmine*, p. 86. The Carmine account books record weekly purchases of cheese for the novices, while the professed friars ate a good deal of meat.

53 See Caioli, "Un altro sguardo," p. 33; Ruda, *Fra Filippo Lippi*, Doc. I. I. 2, p. 513. See Ch. 4 below, p. 81 for a discussion of this ceremony.

54 Lippi's name appears annually on the list of clothing allotments made each January from 1422 to 1432, except for 1423 and 1424 when no lists are provided: see Poggi, "Sulla data dell'affresco di Fra Filippo Lippi," pp. 102–6.

55 Lippi went to Pistoia in July, 1424, on the feast of the patron saint of the city, St. James. He was recorded returning from a procession to Siena on the feast of the Assumption of the Virgin in 1426. In August, 1426, Filippo and his brother Giovanni were among the friars who went to Prato on the feast day of St. Bartholomew, the titular saint of the Pratese Carmelite church: see Caioli, "Un altro sguardo," p. 36; Ruda, *Fra Filippo Lippi*, Doc. I.II, pp. 513–14.

56 Ruda records several occasions where Lippi is cited in notarial documents either as a member of the assembled Carmine chapter or as a witness to a notarial transaction at the Carmine (*Fra Filippo Lippi*, Doc. I.III, p. 514).

57 By the *quattrocento*, it was standard practice for mendicants to assume the priesthood. Lippi is called "presbiter" in the 1440 notarial document recording the miracle of Andrea Corsini (see Ch. 5 below, p. 102), and he was ordained by at least Jan. 19, 1438/39, when he sang a commemorative mass for Forte di Piero da Vico in the Carmine: see Caioli, "Un altro sguardo," p. 42. Caioli makes a complicated case for his ordination on May 6, 1425. On this day the Carmelite account book notes that two unnamed *frati* sang their first masses (p. 44). Lippi would have been about 18 years old at the time – technically too young to be ordained if actual practice followed the regulations set down in the Carmelite statutes (subdeacon at 18, deacon at 20, and priest at 24). See Lickteig, *The German Carmelites at the Medieval Universities*, p. 389.

58 See n. 57 above.

59 "Era nella erudizione delle lettere grosso e male atto ad imparare," Vasari–Milanesi, vol. II, p. 612.

60 The Florentine Carmelite *studium* was founded in 1324. It was later incorporated into the University of Florence (founded in 1349). Initially, the Carmelite *studium* offered only a *baccelliere* degree, but in 1339 a *lettore* degree was added to the curriculum, and in 1420, a full Master of Theology degree. The *studium* also offered a course in the *arti minori*: see Lickteig, *The German Carmelites*, p. 365.

61 See Caioli, "Un altro sguardo," pp. 36–7; *Atti dei capitoli provinciali*, p. 373.

62 There were two provincial chapter meetings in 1428, in May and November. Lippi was designated *sottopriore* at the second meeting, replacing Fra Arrigo d'Arrigo who then replaced him in Aug. 1429. Half of the administrative positions turned over at this meeting, so Lippi's loss of position was not unusual: see *Atti dei capitoli provinciali*, pp. 173 and 176.

63 ASF, Con. Sopp. 113, n. 85, c. 183, published in Ruda, *Fra Filippo Lippi*, Doc. I.II.14, p. 514.

64 On this date, Lippi is recorded receiving 11 oz. of *oltramarino* for the painting of a reliquary tabernacle for the important Franciscan church Il Santo in Padua: See L. Guidaldi, *Il Santo*, Padua, I, 1928, p. 75, and appendix, under 1434; Ruda, *Fra Filippo Lippi*, Doc. 3.I–II, p. 515.

65 On September 28, 1433, Cosimo de' Medici was exiled to Padua for ten years by a Florentine government sympathetic with the Albizzi faction. Cosimo stayed in Padua for two months and then received permission to transfer his place of exile to Venice where his brother Lorenzo had been banished. Cosimo returned to Florence exactly a year later, when he was confident that the prevailing political and popular sentiment was in his favor. The architect Michelozzo followed Cosimo to Venice where he is thought to have executed a design for the library of the Benedictine monastery San Giorgio Maggiore (which was playing host to Cosimo). Mario Salmi has suggested that perhaps Lippi's appearance in Padua at the time had something to do with Cosimo's

presence in the region, "La giovinezza di Fra Filippo Lippi," p. 2.

66 On October 15, 1434, Lippi and the Paduan painter Francesco Squarcione were called before the Episcopal Curia in Padua to value an altarpiece painted by two local artists in the Cathedral: see R. Zanocco, "Un nuovo documento su Fra Filippo Lippi a Padova," *Rivista d'arte*, vol. 18 (1936), pp. 107–9. For an extended treatment of Lippi's Paduan sojourn, see Rowlands, "Filippo Lippi's Stay in Padua and the Impact on his Art," and "Filippo Lippi and his Experience of Painting in the Veneto Region."

67 I do not accept Ruda's claim that Lippi was among the friars of Santa Maria del Carmine on October 24, 1434, *Fra Filippo Lippi*, Doc. I.III.4, p. 514. The "Lippus tomasi" cited in the document is clearly a layman. The date 1437 is on the undocumented, unsigned Tarquinia *Madonna and Child* (fig. 6), which art historians unanimously attribute to Lippi. It originally stood in the church of Santa Maria di Castello in Tarquinia, and is thought to have been commissioned by Giovanni Vitelleschi, the Florentine Archbishop from 1435 to 1437. After serving in the Florentine See, Vitelleschi was transferred to the bishopric of Corneto Tarquinia: see Marchini, *Filippo Lippi*, p. 200; Ruda, *Fra Filippo Lippi*, p. 391.

68 For discussion of the early works of Lippi, see Chapter 3 below.

69 The guild statutes insisted that an apprentice be at least fourteen years old, and that the period of apprenticeship last at least three years: see Fiorilli, "I dipintori a Firenze nell'arte dei medici speziali e merciai," pp. 21 and 26.

70 For a 1991 sensible reassessment of Masolino and Masaccio's activity in the Brancacci chapel, see Christiansen, "Some Observations on the Brancacci Chapel Frescoes after their Cleaning." See also Joannides, *Masaccio and Masolino*, pp. 313–49.

71 An excellent example is the *Madonna and Child* in the National Gallery of Art, Washington (figs. 133 and 134). With the naked eye it is possible to detect the incised lines of a second halo high above the head of the Madonna, indicating a change in the figure orientation. See the more extensive discussion of his painting technique below, Ch. 6, pp. 152–3.

72 This is the case with the male figure seated at the left in *St. John in the Wilderness* in Prato and the female figure seated to the right of the Virgin's bier in the *Dormition of the Virgin*, Duomo, Spoleto.

73 This practice was noticed by Joyce Plesters in her conservation report on the *Madonna and Child*, National Gallery, London, usually attributed to Lippi's workshop (n. 3424).

74 The records for the Compagnia di Sant' Agnese from the late *trecento* and early decades of the *quattrocento* have not survived. As a result, it is not possible to determine at what point the Lippi family associations with the Compagnia began, whether Filippo's father was a member, or whether the Compagnia played a role in the entry of Filippo and his brother Giovanni into Santa Maria del Carmine following their father's death c. 1411. For Antonia, see p. 13 and n. 38 above. Lippi's brother, Fra Giovanni di Tommaso, was the one Carmine friar in the Compagnia from 1432 to 1434 (ASF, Compagnia di S. Maria delle Laudi detta Agnese, n. 98, cc. 37r and 46r). Lippi's name occurs several times in the books of the Compagnia: on May 3, 1431, he made an unspecified payment along with several other friars of s. 5; in Jan. 1440 he donated money to the Ascension Day play; in May 1441 he paid for "chalcine" (*ibid.*, cc. 32v, and 88r, and ASF, Compagnia di S. Maria delle Laudi n. 24, c. 25r).

75 The artist members included Bicci di Lorenzo, Stefano di Lorenzo Pucetti, Stefano di Antonio, Neri di Bicci, Piero del Massaio, Giovanni di Francesco, Jacopo di Cristofano, Bonaiuto di Giovanni, Simone (an engraver apprenticed with Donatello), and Piero di Lorenzo di Pratese: ASF, Compagnia di S. Maria delle Laudi detta S. Agnese, n. 98, annual membership payments; Barr, "Music and Spectacle in Confraternity Drama of Fifteenth-Century Florence," p. 387; see also Bacchi, "La Compagnia di Sta. Maria delle Laudi e di Sant'Agnese nel Carmine di Firenze," pp. 34ff. On the painters who lived in the immediate neighborhood of the Carmine, see Eckstein, *The District of the Green Dragon*, pp. 41–60.

76 This sort of arrangement would, in fact, have violated the statutes of the Arte dei Medici, Speziali e Merciai. The statutes stipulated that a master and a disciple make an official contract that was to be notarized and a copy given to the guild. In addition, both the master and disciple were to pay small sums to the guild's oratory Santa Maria della Tromba: see Fiorilli, "I dipintori a Firenze," pp. 26–7. However, the statutes in effect in the *quattrocento* were designed to protect the interests of the master more than those of the disciple, and were flexibly applied in any case. It is conceivable that the guild would have cast a blind eye on an extra-legal arrangement which neither infringed on the guild's prerogatives nor compromised one of its members.

77 A related example which demonstrates the scope of the Compagnia's interventions pertains to the painter member Jacopo di Cristofano. He died in 1438 and designated the Compagnia di Sant'Agnese guardian of his two small children, Margherita and Francesco. Francesco's tax report of 1457 notes that the eighteen-year-old was then living with Francesco di Stefano, who was his "faciente" during his minority. Francesco di Stefano was the son of the painter Stefano di Lorenzo Pucetti (d. c. 1439), who had been a member of the Compagnia and had a shop on the Corso degli Adimari along with Jacopo di Cristofano. Francesco di Jacopo's guardianship with Stefano di Lorenzo's son could have been established by the Compagnia in response to Jacopo di Cristofano's testament, and could have involved an apprenticeship (Francesco di Stefano is sometimes listed as a painter in his tax reports, although Procacci contends that he practiced as a mercer). See Procacci, "Di Jacopo di Antonio e delle compagnie di pittori del Corso degli Adimari nel XV secolo," pp. 49–50 and 64; and Colnaghi, *Colnaghi's Dictionary of Florentine Painters*, p. 107.

78 The Compagnia's record books cover only the period after 1425 and hence are missing for the relevant years here. The painters listed as members or associates during the second half of the 1420s and the 1430s, who were a generation older than Lippi, are the three mentioned in the text. Here are biographical sketches of each.

Stefano di Lorenzo Pucetti (1377–c. 1439): matriculated into the Arte dei Medici e Speziali c. 1403. He lived on Borgo San Frediano, but had a shop on the Corso degli Adimari, along with Calvano di Cristofano and Jacopo di Cristofano. No extant paintings are associated with him. He apparently made a painted model for the Duomo cupola in 1420, worked on the painted decorations for the Ascension Day play for the Compagnia di Sant'Agnese in 1428, and painted in the Sala del Papa at Santa Maria Novella in 1439. He was active in the Compagnia di San Frediano and the Compagnia di Sant'Agnese. See Procacci, "Di Jacopo di Antonio," p. 49, n. 90, and Colnaghi, *Colnaghi's Dictionary*, p. 258.

Bicci di Lorenzo (1373–1452): son of the painter Lorenzo di Bicci, he matriculated into the Arte dei Medici e Speziali by 1408, and was a member of the Compagnia di San Luca in 1424. He lived in the Santo Spirito *quartiere*, *gonfalone* Drago Verde, and was the father of the painter Neri di Bicci. He was a prolific painter, undertaking major fresco projects at Santa Lucia dei Magnoli, Sant'Egidio, Santa Trinita, and San Marco in Florence, and San Bernardo and San Francesco in Arezzo. He worked for the Barbadori at Santa Felicità, and Antonio Billi claimed that he painted martyrs in the Carmine. He is listed as paying his membership dues to the Compagnia di Sant'Agnese along with his son Neri in 1430. Both he and his wife Benedetta were buried in the Carmine. See Vasari–Milanesi, vol. II, p. 63.

Piero di Chellino Chellini (1383–1459): had matriculated in the Arte dei Medici e

Speziali by 1408 and was a member of the Compagnia di San Luca in 1424. He lived on Borgo San Frediano and had a workshop on the Corso degli Adimari. He collaborated with other painters (Arcangelo di Cola, Piero del Massaio), and worked for numerous corporate bodies and institutions, including the Opera del Duomo and the Archiepiscopacy. His name appears frequently in documents, but there are no extant works that can be associated with him. I have been unable to determine whether Piero was actually a member of the Compagnia di Sant'Agnese. His wife Chosa was a member, and Piero is mentioned as paying for a memorial mass for his deceased son Chellino in 1436: ASF, Compagnia di S. Maria delle Laudi n. 98, cc. 13v and 63r. See Colnaghi, *Colnaghi's Dictionary*, pp. 210–11; U. Thieme and F. Becker, *Allgemeines Lexikon der Bildenden Künstler*, Leipzig, 1933, vol. 27, p. 14.

79 *Il Libro di Antonio Billi*, ed. Fabriczy, p. 28.

80 See Ch. 4, pp. 88 and 93.

81 The suggestion that Lippi may have been influenced by Fra Arrigo d'Arrigo was made by G. Fadalti and M. de Negri in *Fra Filippo Lippi*, Florence, n. d. (after 1970) – a Carmelite publication. They write that Lippi and his Carmelite disciple Fra Diamante "non furono certo indifferenti ai lavori di miniatura che uscivano dalle mani di alcuni loro confratelli, come P. Enrico di Alemagna . . . degno emulo di un altro precedente miniaturista carmelitano, che è stato Frate Francesco di Lambertuccio"(p. 14). They provide no documentation, and I assume their source was the Carmine *Necrologium*.

82 Sabatini claims he was sacristan of the Florentine Carmine in 1411, *Atti dei capitoli provinciali*, p. 119. The Carmine *Libro d'entrata e uscita* is missing for the years 1394 to 1417, and Fra Arrigo first appears in the vestment list of January, 1419, ASF, Con. Sopp. 113, n. 85, c. 13v). For his first mass, see c. 25v: "canto mesa novela frate Arigho Tedescho."

83 *Atti dei capitoli provinciali*, p. 367. There is some confusion in identifying Arrigo d'Arrigo's activities because there was a second German friar in the Tuscan *provincia* during the same period named Arrigo Curradi (d. 1450). Sabatini further confuses things by listing three "Henricus" entries in his index. Modifying Sabatini's entries somewhat, it appears that Arrigo d'Arrigo's official Carmelite career ran as follows: in the convent in Florence he was sacristan in 1411, 1426, 1431, and 1442; sub-prior in 1441 and 1443; and prior in 1455–56. He was sacristan in Pisa in 1415, sub-prior in Siena in 1416, 1426, 1428, and 1429–30, and prior in Pistoia in 1424, and Arezzo in 1427. He seems to have gained recognition and prestige during the mid-1450s when he was prior in Florence, and he served as *socio* for the Florentine convent and for the Tuscan *provincia* in 1454, and *definitore* in 1454 and 1456 (p. 367). The vestment lists of Santa Maria del Carmine in Florence confirm that he was a vested friar in the convent from 1429 through 1437 (after which date there are no more lists): ASF, Con. Sopp. 113, n. 85.

84 "Fr. henrygus henrygi de alamania sacerdos obiit florentie bone famae [continued in a later hand] hic fuit prior et vicar[ius] provincie thuscie qu[i] religare p[lu]res libros feccatus [factus?] et miniis solempnibus et aliis ornamentis decorare et multa alia bona fecit se huic conventui contulit. mortuus et sepultus." *Necrologium Carmelitanum*, BNF, Con. Sopp. F.4.785 (14–16th c.). From this obituary, it seems that Fra Arrigo commissioned the manuscripts rather than illuminated them. Relying on a later edition of the *Necrologium* (16–18th c.), Caioli interpreted "qui iussit compingi seu religari quosdam libros chori" to mean that Fra Arrigo illuminated some of the manuscripts, *Il Beato Angelino*, p. 38. No manuscript associated with Fra Arrigo has been identified.

85 "Item questo dì allettore diede a frate arrigo per panni bianchi s.15;" "Item questo dì a frate arrigo per lengno della croce fece fare di nuovo s.15;" "Item questo dì a frate arrigo per la dipintura del legno della croce s.6": ASF, Con. Sopp. 113, n. 85, c. 243r.

86 As in the obituary quoted above, it is unclear whether Fra Arrigo is doing the work himself, or merely overseeing the production of this crucifix. The expression "fare di nuovo" probably means "to make again from scratch," but could also refer to a restoration. There were a number of painted crucifixes in the Carmine at the time. The "Crocifisso del Chiodo" hung from the second pilaster to the left of the *cappella maggiore*, between the Ferrucci and the Zampalocchi chapels. Its date and provenance are unknown, but it began to accrue miracles from 1440 on and became a cult object: see Richa, *Notizie istoriche delle chiese fiorentine*, vol. x, pp. 46–7. Giovanni Soderini commissioned a crucifix during the mid-14th century – one assumes for the Soderini chapel dedicated to the Crucifix at the end of the left transept arm (transferred to the Serragli in 1390, according to Sabatini, "La Nobile Famiglia Fiorentina del Soderini e il Carmine di Firenze," p. 200). Additional crucifixes were painted in 1420 by Stefano (di Lorenzo?) and his assistants: ASF, Con. Sopp. 113, n. 85, c. 31r (July 6, 1420). All of these images were destroyed in the fire of 1771.

87 See Ch. 6 below, p. 118.

88 Keith Christiansen writes, "The evidence suggests that the order consistently favoured the most progressive style available, whether in Florence, Pisa or Siena." In addition to Masaccio and Masolino, he notes that "in the 1420s and 1430s Filippo Lippi, Sassetta, and Domenico di Bartolo produced works for Carmelite establishments," "Some Observations on the Brancacci Chapel Frescoes after their Cleaning," p. 16.

89 See Ch. 2 below, pp. 42–50.

90 Vasari claimed that Lippi may have painted a bishop saint in the Pisan Carmelite church that was traditionally attributed to Masaccio, Vasari–Milanesi, vol. II, p. 293.

91 On Masaccio's influence on Lippi, see Joannides, *Masaccio and Masolino*, pp. 255ff.

92 H. Janson, *The Sculpture of Donatello*, Princeton, 1963, pp. 103ff. The sixteenth-century sources are *Il Libro di Antonio Billi*, ed. K. Frey, Berlin, 1892, p. 27 and the *Codice Magliabechiano*, p. 97. Vasari, on the other hand, claimed that "Pesello" painted the predella, Vasari–Milanesi, vol. III, p. 37. This predella has recently been associated with a work attributed to Giovanni di Francesco de Cervelliera in the Casa Buonarroti, Florence, showing scenes from the life of St. Nicholas of Bari, M. Tamassia in L. Berti, ed., *Nel Raggio di Piero: La pittura nell'Italia centrale nell'età di Piero della Francesca*, Venice, 1992, pp. 191–2.

93 Carl Strehlke suggests that a fragment of a *Madonna and Child Enthroned* in Princeton from Domenico di Bartolo's early period may have been part of the central panel of the Carmine altarpiece. Strehlke dates the Carmine altarpiece commission to the mid-1430s, explaining the choice of Domenico di Bartolo: "for, during the years immediately following the death of Masaccio in 1428 and the departure of the resident Carmelite artist, Filippo Lippi, for Padua in 1433/34, Domenico was the most prominent exponent of the new, realist style in Tuscany," in Christiansen, Strehlke, and Kanter, *Painting in Renaissance Siena*, p. 254.

94 *Ibid.*, p. 249.

95 John Shearman has pointed out the resemblance of the marbled steps in the Barbadori altarpiece with those in the central panel of Pietro Lorenzetti's polyptych for the Sienese Carmine, San Niccolò, *Only Connect. . . .*, p. 73. This step at the lower edge of the painting, which gives the illusion of breaking into the viewer's space, became a standard feature in Lippi's paintings.

CHAPTER TWO

1 Trexler, *Public Life in Renaissance Florence*, p. 33.

2 Richa, *Notizie istoriche delle chiese fiorentine*, vol. x, p. 7; Giovanni and Vitolo, *Il Convento del Carmine di Firenze*, pp. 41ff; Berti, *La Chiesa di Santa Maria del Carmine*. By at least 1585, the Carmelite myth-making machinery had set the convent foundation date at 743: see de Lezana, *Annales Sacri*, vol. 3, pp. 346, 363, and 393.

3 However, the Carmelite invasion into the

religious territory of the parish church of San Frediano did not go uncontested by its clergy: see Giovannini and Vitolo, *Il Convento del Carmine*, p. 43.

4 The Carmelites' mendicant status was granted in 1229, three years after their Rule was confirmed by Pope Honorius III. However, the Carmelite footing in Western Europe was precarious over the next century. The Carmelites found themselves without friends in high places – up against the well-entrenched competitive mendicant factions and an elaborate apostolic patronage system. They received some support from Pope Alexander IV (1254–61), but they had reached their nadir at the very time the Florentine Carmine was getting under way. In 1275, Pope Gregory X declared all religious orders formed after the fourth Lateran Council (1215) illegitimate, and severely restricted the expansion of mendicant orders, with the exception of the Franciscans and the Dominicans. The Carmelites' status was ambiguous – they had received their Rule prior to the Council, but it had been confirmed afterwards, as had been their petition for reorganization along mendicant lines. However, in 1298, they were granted the same mendicant exemption as the Franciscans and Dominicans, which was confirmed by a strong advocate of the Carmelites', Pope John XXII, in 1317 and 1326. See Saggi, *Santi del Carmelo*, pp. 27ff, and King, *Liturgies of the Religious Orders*, pp. 239ff.

5 Many of the Tuscan Carmelite foundations had distinguished Marian images and relics. Santa Maria delle Selve in Lastra a Signa outside Florence, founded in 1343, had a miracle-working Madonna image known as the "Madonna delle Grazie," ASF, Con. Sopp. 253, n. 14, cc. 72r–v and 74r, and Bacchi, "Santa Maria delle Selve," p. 15. The Sienese Carmine possessed the icon now known as the "Madonna dei Mantellini" (c. 1275/85, Pisan) and a thirteenth-century Byzantine Madonna image: see V. Lusini, *La chiesa di S. Niccolo del Carmine in Siena*, Siena, 1907, pp. 23–4; Belting, *Likeness and Presence*, p. 341. In Lucca, around 1380, a relic of the "sacra frontale della Madonna" (supposed to have been worn by the Virgin when she entered the Temple) was brought to the city from the Holy Land and stored in the Carmelite church: see G. Barsotti, *Lucca sacra*, Lucca, 1923, p. 217. The high altar of the Carmelite church in Prato, San Bartolomeo, was dedicated to the Madonna del Carmine, and there was also a lay Compagnia della Madonna del Carmine there: see G. Pelagatti, *Il Crocifisso del Carmine a S. Bartolommeo in Prato*, Prato, 1899, pp. 72 and 76ff.

6 The Confraternity was founded in 1264, according to a stone inscription destroyed in the 1771 fire. It evolved out of a "compagnia di standardo" that dated back to 1248: see Giovannini and Vitolo, *Il Convento del Carmine*, p. 44, n. 11. The confraternity joined with the Compagnia di Sant'Agnese after 1268, and was thereafter referred to by either that name or as the Compagnia di Santa Maria delle Laudi. It is possible that the Compagnia was directly involved in the worship of the "Madonna del Popolo"; in 1289 the Confraternity's records mention "la tavola de nostra Donna": see Cannon, "Pietro Lorenzetti and the History of the Carmelite Order," pp. 19–20, and Giovannini and Vitolo, *Il Convento del Carmine*, p. 42. See also Newbigin, *Feste d'Oltrarno*, vol. 1, pp. 48ff.

7 Giovannini and Vitolo claim that around sixty friars died in the 1347–48 plague, *Il Convento del Carmine*, pp. 43 and 66, but my own reading of the Carmine *Necrologium*, BNF, Con. Sopp. C. 5.786, puts the figure at thirty-six. The information on the early *quattrocento* friars comes from the Carmine *Libro di entrata e uscita* (1417–36), ASF, Con. Sopp. 113, n. 85, which includes lists of the friars who received vestments from the convent for some of the years.

8 For the Carmelite liturgical calendar, see M. Rickert, *The Reconstructed Carmelite Missal*, Chicago, 1952, esp. pp. 27–35.

9 A procession was made to Prato on the feast day of the patron saint of the Pratese Carmine, Bartholomew. The *frati* journeyed to Pistoia on the feast of St. James, its patron saint. Some of the Carmine *frati* would troop all the way to Siena each year to participate in the Corpus Christi celebrations organized by the Sienese Carmelites. The period around the feast of the Florentine patron saint John the Baptist was frequently chosen for the annual Tuscan Carmelite provincial chapter meeting and the Carmelite friars from the *provincia* joined the other religious groups and civic bodies in the procession through the city.

10 Little of the original structure of the church survives. The *ponte* was torn down in 1568, and many of the nave chapels were rededicated and overhauled during the seventeenth century. In 1771, a fire swept through the church, destroying much of the Gothic interior. The church was consequently renovated in contemporary late Baroque style. Only the crypt, the sacristy, and the Brancacci chapel remained essentially as they had been before the fire: see Procacci, "L'incendio della Chiesa del Carmine del 1771."

11 See Eckstein, *The District of the Green Dragon*, pp. 143–5, 154–5, and 173ff.

12 ASF, Con. Sopp. 113, n. 85, cc. 32v, 46r, 59r, 73v, 81r, 88r, 99v, 107r, and 115v, covering the period 1420–26. The main chapel had originally been endowed by the Nerli family, but patronage rights had fallen to the Serragli at some point during the *trecento*. In 1390, the Serragli and the Soderini seem to have effected a curious patronage swap, whereby the *cappella maggiore* became the province of the Soderini in exchange for the chapel of the Crucifix in the transept and the sacristy chapel: see Richa, *Notizie istoriche delle chiese fiorentine*, vol. x, p. 18 ("un baratto tra le due famiglie"), and Sabatini, "La Nobile Famiglia Fiorentina del Soderini e il Carmine di Firenze," pp. 200ff.

13 Fra Zanobi di Albizzo Soderini served as convent prior during the plague year 1348–49; Fra Bartolomeo di Tommaso ("Maso") Soderini (1400–1490) was a contemporary of Lippi's who studied in the Carmelite *studia* in Florence, Padua, and Montpellier and then served as Florentine prior and regent and Tuscan provincial prior: see *Atti dei capitoli provinciali*, p. 360, and Sabatini, "La Nobile Famiglia," p. 201.

14 See n. 6 above.

15 See G. Piccini, ed., *Libro degli ordinamenti de la Compagnia di Sta. Maria del Carmino scritte nel 1280*, Bologna, 1867; Giovannini and Vitolo, *Il Convento del Carmine*, pp. 42 and 57.

16 ASF, Compagnia di Sta. Maria delle Laudi in Santa Maria del Carmine detta di Sant'Agnese, n. 98, cc. 32r, 35r, and 37r (1431–32). It is evident from this register, the Compagnia's *Libro di entrata e uscita* for 1424–41, that the composition of the confraternity changed significantly over this period, coming to include more men, and among them, members of the patrician class.

17 The confraternities of S. Trinità and SS. Apostoli are mentioned in 1295, but I have found no later references to them: see Mattei, *Ragionamento intorno all'antica chiesa del Carmine di Firenze*, p. 17.

18 Saggi, *Santi del Carmelo*, p. 110; N. Gaegea, *Maria madre e decoro del Carmelo: La pietà dei Carmelitani durante i primi tre secoli della loro storia*, Rome, 1989.

19 See King, *Liturgies of the Religious Orders*, pp. 272–6, and Ch. 6 below, p. 150 and n. 116, for the prayer "Flos Carmeli."

20 This was known as the "Sabbatine Privilege," held to have been revealed to Pope John XXII in a vision and confirmed by him in a bull of 1322. Alexander V confirmed it in 1409. Another tradition, which appears to have been propagated at a later date, ascribed a similar vision to the English Carmelite Simon Stock (d. 1265): see McCaffrey, *The White Friars*, pp. 56ff.

21 Belting, *Likeness and Presence*, p. 341; *Mostra di opere d'arte restaurate nelle provincie de Siena e Grosseto*, Genoa, 1979, p. 104, n. 38; van Os, *Sienese Altarpieces*, vol. 1, p. 37. A documented example of this practice is recounted of William Anesia who carried an image of the Madonna of Carmel from Mount Carmel back to France in 1238, and founded a church outside Toulouse to house it (recorded in a chronicle written around

1320): see Cannon, "Pietro Lorenzetti," p. 21; van Os, *Sienese Altarpieces*, vol. I, ch. VI.

22 Joanna Cannon concludes, "It cannot be proved that all these panels were originally obtained for Carmelite churches, but taken together they may imply an awareness in the Order of its eastern origins," *ibid.*, p. 21.

23 See Paolucci, *Capolavori e Restauri*, p. 425; Cannon, "Pietro Lorenzetti," p. 20, n. 16; Giovannini and Vitolo, *Il Convento del Carmine*, p. 44.

24 The original location of the "Madonna del Popolo" within Santa Maria del Carmine is not known. There is speculation that it was placed above the high altar. It is first documented in the Brancacci chapel in 1460, when a company of women was created to attend to the sacred image. The picture may have been placed there following the banishment of the chapel patron, Felice Brancacci, in 1435. See Paolucci, *Capolavori e Restauri*, p. 424, and Molho, "The Brancacci Chapel," pp. 82–3.

25 Richa, *Notizie istoriche*, vol. X, p. 52.

26 "Et quoniam illo tempore, videlicet anno Domini MCCC. in ecclesia sacri ordinis Carmelitarum, matris Dei icona seu tabula erat, quae a vulgo nuncupabatur Nostra Domina de populo, ad quam populus ex devotione pro gratiis impetrandis confluebat, permaxime mulieres concipere non valentes . . ." *Acta Sanctorum*, Antwerp, 1643, vol. 2 (Jan. 30), p. 1065.

27 See Saggi, *Santi del Carmelo*, pp. 122ff.

28 "Antichissima: scorgendovisi tutta la maniera greca, e la direi portata dal Levante da quei molti Pittori, che a Firenze vennero; o dai Fiorentini, che per ragione di commercio colà andavano," Richa, *Notizie istoriche*, vol. X, p. 40.

29 See Mattei, *Ragionamento intorno*, pp. 40–1.

30 These Elian titles all appear in John of Cheminot's *Speculum Fratrum Ordinis B. Mariae de Monte Carmeli* written in 1337: see Saggi, *Santi del Carmelo*, pp. 32ff.

31 The text is somewhat selective, in the interest of an economy of space and the particular "Elijah" that the Carmelites wished to formulate out of the biblical references. A passage is omitted that demonstrates Elijah's power to destroy as well as to protect and succor. The full text from St. James's Epistle reads "Elijah was a man of like passions with us, and he prayed fervently that it might not rain; and it rained not on the earth for three years and six months. And he prayed again; and the heavens gave rain and the earth brought forth her fruit."

32 Cannon, "Pietro Lorenzetti," pp. 18–28, and Gilbert, "Special Images for Carmelites," pp. 166–80.

33 Cannon, "Pietro Lorenzetti," pp. 24ff.

34 Quoted in *ibid.*, p. 24 (from the preamble to the earliest surviving Constitutions of the Order, written in 1281).

35 Quoted in Gilbert, "Special Images for Carmelites," p. 171.

36 In 1312, Sibert of Beka devised a new Ordinal, which was accepted by the general chapter in 1324: see Cannon, "Pietro Lorenzetti," p. 27; *Ordinaire de L'Ordre de Notre-Dame du Mont-Carmel*. It appears that the earlier Dominicanized liturgy was actively suppressed and copies destroyed: see King, *Liturgies of the Religious Orders*, pp. 254ff.

37 See *Universis christifidelibus* (1300–20), cited in Saggi, *Santi del Carmelo*, p. 127.

38 In his *Viridarium* (c. 1411–35), Fra Giovanni Grossi wrote "Et ob hoc Virgo Maria tamquam suos visitavit sepius ut fratres, et ipsi ad honorem ipsius capellam edificaverunt, eius eligentes titulum," Graziano di S. Teresa, "Viridarium Ioannis Grossi," pp. 263–4.

39 See Ch. 3. n. 34.

40 The Carmelites were given permission by Pope Honorius IV in 1287 to change their dress. The color of the habit worn beneath the white cloak seems to have varied between brown (as decreed in the Constitutions of 1324–69) and black (set forth in the Constitutions of 1396): see King, *Liturgies of the Religious Orders*, p. 243.

41 See Saggi, *Santi del Carmelo*, p. 25.

42 Creighton Gilbert's source is an unpublished MS in the Bodleian Library, "Special Images for Carmelites," pp. 163 and 199, n. 5. See also Koch, "Elijah the Prophet, Founder of the Carmelite Order," p. 548.

43 "Neques in sacra scriptura neques in authentica scriptura reperitur," Antonino Pierozzi, *Historiarum Domini Antonini Archipraesulis Florentini*, Tertia Pars, Tit. XX, Cap. V, c. LXII v. Antonino was referring specifically to the Carmelite claim that their striped habit was modeled on the scorched robe of Elijah.

44 "Il Piovano si trovava una mattina nella chiesa del Carmine e ascoltava la predica da un frate che era giovane e più arioso che dotto.

E predicando su un argomento su chi si era assai ingarbugliato, riguardo a quel passo in cui gli ambasciatori di Giudea domandavano a San Giovanni Battista chi fosse, il frate si voltava verso il Piovano e diceva: – Chi sei tu? Sei tu Elia? Sei tu Geremia? ecc.

E replicate queste parole infinite volte, venne a noia al Piovano, che non poteva trattenere le risa e che rispose forte al frate: – Io non sono nè Elia, nè Geremia, ma sono il Piovano Arlotto; può darsi che tu non mi riconosca!

Questa risposta fece ridere tutti quelli che stavano ad ascoltare la predica." *Facezie, Motti e Burle del Piovano Arlotto*, p. 198. This *facezia* is discussed by Gilbert, "Special Images for Carmelites," p. 164. The translation is taken, with slight modifications, from Gilbert.

45 Mattei, *Ragionamento intorno*, p. 116. The picture now hangs above the door in the sacristy.

46 Elijah was accorded a feast day (20 July) only in the 16th century. Oddly enough, Elisha, Elijah's follower, was celebrated with a feast *duplex vel majus* in late fourteenth and fifteenth-century Carmelite liturgical books, and the general chapter even tried to raise money for the purchase of his body (which they believed was in the church of Sant' Apollinare in Ravenna) by levying a tax in 1369: see King, *Liturgies of the Religious Orders*, p. 282; see also van Os, "Text and Image," p. 165. The following are additional *trecento* examples of Elijah wearing the Carmelite habit: an illustration in a late *trecento* manuscript in Vienna on the origins of the various monastic orders, *De origine, fundatoribus et regulis monachorum et monacharum*, see Koch, "Elijah the Prophet," p. 549; a wing panel of Bartolo di Fredi's 1360 polyptych for the Carmine in Perugia (now in the Galleria Nazionale di Perugia), based on the Lorenzetti Elijah, see van Os, *Sienese Altarpieces*, vol. II, p. 163; a Sienese miniature dating from the second half of the fourteenth century in the Biblioteca Comunale, Siena, representing Elijah and Elisha dressed in Carmelite robes at either side of a blessing bishop in the initial "A;" a small half-length Elijah wearing Carmelite robes in a private collection in Rome published by van Os, which he speculates derives from an altarpiece of Neapolitan origin with strong Tuscan influence, "Text and Image," pp. 163–8. For a discussion of the popular dissemination of Carmelite Elian imagery in the fifteenth century, see Koch, pp. 547–60.

47 "Un trittico con una Annunziata al centro e ai lati due profeti in abito carmelitano" and "[un polittico] con la Vergine nello scomparto centrale e ai lati S. Elia, S. Sebastiano, S. Pietro e S. Paolo," Bacchi, "Santa Maria delle Selve," p. 8. Bacchi does not give a date for the inventory, but includes it in his section describing the church from the date of its foundation in 1343 to the reconstruction of 1525.

48 See Barr, "Music and Spectacle in Confraternity Drama of Fifteenth-Century Florence," pp. 390ff; Boehm in Metropolitan Museum, *Painting and Illumination in Early Renaissance Florence*, pp. 77–80.

49 On St. Angelo and the history of his cult, see Saggi, *Sant'Angelo di Sicilia*.

50 On St. Alberto, see Saggi, *Santi del Carmelo*, pp. 154–5; and Bollandus and Henschenius, *Acta Sanctorum*, vol. 34 (Aug. 2), pp. 215–26.

51 A convent inventory dating predominantly from 1391 lists "item uno forzerino d'avorio con chiave e toppa, con compassi a oro, entrovi reliquie Sancti Alberti" and "item uno tabernacolo tutto di rame orato con smalti con l'arme di Piero del Vagliente, dentrovi reliquie di Santo Alberto da Trapani, fu frate di Santa Maria del Carmino": see Guidotti,

"Fatti, arredi e corredi carmelitani a Firenze," p. 32, nn. 66 and 76.

52 The feast of St. Alberto is first referred to in the Carmine account books in 1418, some seven years after the Office was established by the Carmelite general chapter, ASF, Con. Sopp. 113, n. 85, c. 7r (Aug. 7). The ledger covering the first fifteen years of the century is missing. For the reference to the procession in 1422, see c. 58v.

53 For the documentation regarding these two altars to St. Alberto, see Ch. 3 below, p. 65 and nn. 22, 23, and 25.

54 See Bacchi, "Santa Maria delle Selve," p. 17.

55 The polyptych was obtained in the mid-nineteenth century by James Jarves from Santa Maria delle Selve. It was among the paintings that Jarves sold to Yale University in 1871, and is now on display in the Yale University Art Gallery: see C. Seymour, *Early Italian Paintings in the Yale University Art Gallery*, New Haven, 1970, pp. 112–14, and *Italian Primitives: The Case History of a Collection and its Conservation*, New Haven, 1972, p. 18. Boskovits identifies the "Pseudo Ambrogio di Baldese," to whom the painting was traditionally attributed, with the painter Lippo d'Andrea who is documented painting in Santa Maria del Carmine in 1402, "Il percorso di Masolino: Precisazioni sulla cronologia e sul catalogo," *Arte cristiana*, vol. 75 (1987), p. 51. See n. 60 below.

56 "In omnibus conventibus depingeretur Imago Beati Alberti cum radiis," de Lezana, *Annales Sacri*, vol. 4, p. 801.

57 Another possibility, in addition to the altars dedicated to St. Alberto in the Carmine and at Le Selve, is the chapel in the former dedicated to St. Andrew founded by Forte di Piero da Vico di Val d'Elsa around 1400. Forte died in 1417, leaving the Carmine a healthy endowment of 500 fl. and a *podere* to cover the costs of extensive religious services including special observances for the feasts of Sts. Andrew, Anthony Abbot, and Alberto, ASF, Con. Sopp. 113, n. 13, c. 60.

58 The place of honor accorded Sts. Peter and Paul in the altarpiece may reflect a timely manifestation of Carmelite support for the papacy during the years immediately after the end of the Schism and the return of the pope to Italy with the election of Martin V in 1417. Martin V was residing in Florence in 1420, the year that the altarpiece was painted. On the Carmelite position against the Schism, see Holmes, "'Frate Filippo di Tommaso Dipintore'," p. 148. The Brancacci chapel frescos represent a more elaborate exposition of the strong Carmelite promotion of the newly unified church reestablished in Rome. See A. Debold-von Kritter, *Studien zum Petruszyklus in der Brancacci Kapelle*, Berlin, 1975, pp. 152ff; Molho, "The Brancacci Chapel," pp. 56, 67–9, and 77–8; and Christiansen, "Some Observations on the Brancacci Chapel Frescoes," pp. 8–9.

59 On the decoration of the chapels of Santa Maria del Carmine, see Paatz, *Die Kirchen von Florenz*, vol. III, pp. 188–303; Mattei, *Ragionamento intorno*, pp. 9–78; Procacci, "L'incendio della Chiesa," pp. 141–232.

60 Ugo Procacci and Miklós Boskovits have associated Lippo d'Andrea with the frescoes in the chapel of the Passion in the Carmine (1402), and with the group of paintings now given to the "Pseudo Ambrogio di Baldese." While the association is based on nothing more than convenience, it is an attractive conjecture for my purposes, in the light of the consistent Carmelite link: Procacci, "Lettere a Roberto Salvini," *Scritti di storia dell'arte in onore di R. Salvini*, Florence, 1984, pp. 213–26; for Boskovits, see n. 55 above. See also Procacci, "Rilazione dei lavori eseguiti nella chiesa del Carmine di Firenze per la ricerca di antichi affreschi," pp. 327ff; Berti and Paolucci, *L'età di Masaccio*, pp. 166 and 263–4; Tartuferi, "Le testimonianze superstiti (e le perditi) della decorazione primativa (secoli xiii–xv)," p. 145.

61 ASF, Con. Sopp. 113, n. 85, c. 31r. The crucifixes have not been identified.

62 Regarding Domenico di Bartolo's high altar image, Vasari notes, "Furono l'opere di costui intorno agli anni del Signore 1436; e l'ultime furono, in Santa Trinita di Firenze, una tavola dentrovi la Nunziata; e nella chiesa del Carmine, la tavola dell'altar maggiore," Vasari–Milanesi, vol. II, p. 41. Baldinucci mentions a panel by Domenico di Bartolo in the Carmine in 1681, but it is likely that it had long since been displaced from the high altar, which had been renovated in 1565. Strehlke suggests that a cut-down *Madonna and Child Enthroned* by Domenico di Bartolo (see fig. 34), now in the Art Museum, Princeton, may be a fragment from the original Carmine high altarpiece, Christiansen, Strehlke, and Kanter, *Painting in Renaissance Siena*, pp. 250–4. The fresco fragment of the *Crucifixion* in the chapter house was uncovered in 1970 and has been attributed to Paolo Schiavo. Tartuferi, "Le testimonianze," p. 170; B. Pacciani, "Il complesso di Santa Maria al Carmine. Cenni sui restauri eseguiti dopo l'alluvione del 1966," in Berti, *La Chiesa di Santa Maria del Carmine*, p. 87.

63 James Beck raised some doubt regarding the date of the consecration in his transcription of a copy of an early account of the Sagra where the date was given as Sunday, April 9, 1422, *Masaccio*, pp. 12–13. This must be an error in the copy since the date appears correctly as April 19 in another version of the document, BNF, Con. Sopp. C.5.786, *Necrologium Carmelitanum* (1593), c. 60r. At any rate, in 1422, April 19, and not April 9, fell on a Sunday.

64 While the church had been in use for over a century and the convent even longer, the building program initiated in the late *duecento* was wound down during the early *quattrocento*, when the decoration of the chapels in the transept of the church was completed.

65 "Ad perpetuam rei memoriam. Noverint universi presentes inspecturi, quod Divina gratia ac pietate, Dominca prima post Pascha, die videlicet decimo nono Aprilis, anno Domini millesimo quadringentesimo vigesimo secundo, ex concessione Sanctissimi Martini Papae Quinti, procurata ab honorabili domicello Francisco olim domini Thomae de Soderinis de Florentia (cuius bulla apud nos est) fuit solemnissime, cum magno *gaudio totius civitatis et* concursu populi utriusque sexus, consacrata tota nostra ecclesia convenctus florentini: nec non altare maioris cappellae, altareque Passionis Domini nostri Iesu Christi, in qua requiescunt, ac sepeliuntur corpora fratrum nostrorum: in quorum primo sunt positae haec reliquiae sanctorum, scilicet Bartolomaei apostoli, Thomae apostoli, Marci evangelistae, et Austerii papae et martiris. In secundo vero haec reliquiae sanctorum: Bernarbae apostoli, Laurentii et Pancratii simul, Clementis papae et Sebastiani martiris, à Reverendissimo in Christo patre et domino, Domino Amerigo de Corsini de Florentia benemerito primo archiepiscopo florentino, coassistentibus sibi devote ac solemniter infrascriptis dominis episcopis, videlicet Reverendissimo in Christo Patre et domino, Domino Antonio Fidei de Florentia nostri Ordinis in sacra pagina eximio Doctore, divina gratia benemerito episcopo Suanensi: Reverendissimoque domino et Patre, Domino Benozzo de Federigi de Florentia Dei gratia dignissimo episcopo fesulano. Quorum quilibet trium dictorum dominorum praesulum, de speciali gratia cuilibet devote visitanti confesso et contrito in tali die, scilicet domenica prima post Pascha, et in quolibet die ipsius octavarum indulgentiam suorum peccatorum quadraginta dierum in perpetuam valituram, misericorditer concessit. Gloria Summae Trinitati, unique Deo vero Patri et filio et Spiritui Sancto. apud quam semper pro nobis intercedant Virgo Sanctissima Maria Dei mater, nostri Ordinis matrona et Sancti omnes et Sanctae. Amen." BNF, Con. Sopp. C. 5.786, *Necrologium Carmelitanum* (1593), cc. 60r–v (with the phrase in italics found in a second copy, ASF, Con. Sopp. 113, n. 190, cc. 25v–26r). See Sabatini, "550 Anno della Consacrazione dell'antica chiesa del Carmine di Firenze," pp. 110–15.

66 The descriptions of Masaccio's *Sagra* are not all in agreement regarding the location of the fresco. All maintain that it was above a door in the cloister, but Manetti and the *Libro di*

Antonio Billi indicated that it was the door leading into the church, while Vasari identified it as the door to the convent. See Procacci, "L'incendio della Chiesa," pp. 200–3. The precise location of the door leading from the cloister into the church during the fifteenth century is also subject to debate. Procacci suggested that this door was located in the left corner of the south wall of the cloister, leading directly into the Chapel of the Passion ("Rilazione dei lavori eseguiti nella chiesa del Carmine di Firenze per la ricerca di antichi affreschi," *Bolletino d'arte*, vol. 27 [1934], pp. 332–4 and fig. 7).

67 The effacement of the fresco was chronicled by Stefano Rosselli in his *Sepoltuario* (1657). He described how it was "levata e mandata in terra" in 1612, during the renovation of the large cloister: see Procacci, "L'incendio della Chiesa," p. 203. A second testimony comes from an anonymous annotator of Vasari (c. 1615–30), who wrote in the margins of a 1568 edition, Bibl. Corsiniana, 29.E.4, pp. 298–9, that the *Sagra* "andata giù" and that "questa opera è andata male nell'anno . . . [blank] cioè stata rovinata da chi che sia con poca discretione." (I thank John Shearman for this reference.) The fresco is mentioned by Manetti (1494–97), Albertini (1510), in the *Libro di Antonio Billi* (c. 1516–30), the *Codice Magliabecchiano* (c. 1537–42), and by Vasari (1550, 1568). The drawings are in Folkestone (Florentine, late sixteenth century), an English private collection (attr. Federico Zuccaro), a private collection (style of Bacchiacca), two in the Uffizi (one attr. Andrea Boscoli and the other 20354F), the Casa Buonarroti, Florence (attr. Antonio Mini), the collection of U. Procacci, Florence (Florentine, late sixteenth century), and the Albertina (Michelangelo); see Joannides, *Masaccio and Masolino*, cat. L3, pp. 443–6.

68 Vasari–De Vere, vol. II, pp. 188–9.

69 See n. 67 above.

70 See Gilbert, "The Drawings now associated with Masaccio's Sagra," p. 261.

71 See Joannides's discussion, n. 67 above.

72 The liturgical procedures for the consecration of a church were spelled out in Sibert de Beka's Carmelite Ordinal (c. 1312), *Ordinaire de L'Ordre*, pp. 60–2. These liturgical prescriptions can be compared with contemporary practices reflected in the Carmelite account of the consecration of Santa Maria del Carmine quoted in the text, and the detailed description of the consecration of the Dominican church and convent of Santa Maria Novella in 1420, recorded by Bartolommeo del Corazza in his diary, Corazzini, "Diario Fiorentino di Bartolommeo di Michele del Corazza, anni 1405–38" pp. 270–1.

73 "Totius civitatis et concursu populi" (from the account quoted in full in n. 65 above).

74 A comparison between the two frescos is essential, but problematic. It appears that Bicci di Lorenzo executed his fresco either in 1424–25 or 1440, when he is documented working at Sant'Egidio. The dating of Masaccio's *Sagra* cannot be established with any certainty, and is usually given as c. 1425, preceding his work in the Brancacci chapel. Some scholars feel that Bicci di Lorenzo, as the less talented of the two artists, could not have conceived of such a monumental, complicated composition independently: G. Fiocco, "Dello Delli scultore," *Rivista d'arte*, vol. 11 (1929), pp. 30–5; U. Baldini and L. Berti, *La Mostra di Affreschi Staccati*, Florence, 1958, p. 74; Joannides, *Masaccio and Masolino*, p. 445. Others contend that Bicci's treatment of the subject is grounded in *trecento* artistic conventions and hence is perfectly possible without reference to Masaccio's *Sagra*: Buhler Walsh, "The Fresco Painting of Bicci di Lorenzo," p. 23, and Beck, "Masaccio's Early Career as a Sculptor," p. 181.

75 The consecration proceedings are described in a communal decree of Oct. 16, 1420, published in Richa, *Notizie istoriche*, vol. VIII, p. 198. Martin V came later in the day to confirm the consecration, so it is this confirmation, not the consecration itself, which is represented in Bicci di Lorenzo's fresco: see Beck, "Masaccio's Early Career as a Sculptor," pp. 180 and 195; Buhler Walsh, "The Fresco Painting of Bicci di Lorenzo," pp. 21ff.

76 The 1374 Statutes of Santa Maria Nuova specify that the *spedalingo* and the hospital *conversi* "vadino vestiti di pannobigio romagnuolo, di piccolo prezo e valuta col segnale dello Spedale, cioe una gruccia verde e rossa": see L. Passerini, *Storia degli stabilimenti di beneficenza e d'istruzione elementare gratuita della città di Firenze*, Florence, 1853, p. 840.

77 See Levi Pisetzky, *Storia del costume in Italia*, vol. II, pp. 338–49.

78 Michele di Frusino da Panzano was Rector of Santa Maria Nuova from 1413 to 1443: see Richa, *Notizie istoriche,* vol. VIII, p. 224. He was responsible for the reconstruction and decoration of Sant'Egidio, Vasari–Milanesi, vol. II, p. 55, and commissioned an altarpiece from Lippi in the early 1440s, ASF, Ospedale di Santa Maria Nuova, n. 4490, c. 54v and n. 5818, c. 85v. I thank Jonathan Nelson for this citation; see Holmes, "'Frate Filippo di Tommaso Dipintore'," Appendix, n. 6.

79 Bartolommeo di Michele del Corazza described in his diary this "imbasceria" of eight leading Florentine citizens appointed by the Commune to accompany the pope out of town, Corazzini, "Diario Fiorentino," p. 271.

80 See Bal and Bryson, "Semiotics and Art History," p. 189. Here I am applying a semiotic interpretation based on that of Charles Peirce, which differentiates *icon*, *index*, and *symbol*. According to Peirce, "A symbol is a sign which would lose the character which renders it a sign if there were no interpretant [a mental image of what it stands for]. Such is any utterance of speech which signifies what it does only by virtue of its being understood to have that signification" ("Logic as Semiotic: The Theory of Signs," in R. Innis, *Semiotics: An Anthology*, Bloomington, 1985, p. 5, quoted in Bel and Bryson, *ibid.*).

81 Vasari actually makes the same claim for Bicci di Lorenzo's fresco (which he attributes to Bicci's father, Lorenzo di Bicci): "ritraendovi di naturale quel papa ed alcuni cardinali," Vasari–Milanesi, vol. II, p. 55. On the emergence of portraiture in early *quattrocento* Florentine painting, see Ch. 6 below, pp. 128–9.

82 According to Peirce, an icon is "a sign which would possess the character which renders it significant, even though its object had no existence; such as a lead-pencil streak as representing a geometric line" ("Logic as Semiotic: The Theory of Signs," in R. Innis, *Semiotics: An Anthology*, Bloomington, 1985, pp. 9–10, quoted in Bal and Bryson, "Semiotics and Art History," p. 189). In Bal and Bryson's terms, "Iconicity is . . . a mode of reading, based on a hypothetical similarity between sign and object . . . The decision to suppose that the image refers to something on the basis of likeness is the iconic act, and a sense of specularity is its result," pp. 189–90.

83 Richa, *Notizie istoriche*, vol. VIII, p. 198.

84 The confirmation of the consecration was also depicted in an abbreviated format by Bartolomeo di Fruosino in an illuminated Missal for Sant'Egidio, dating from 1421: see Beck, "Masaccio's Early Career as a Sculptor," p. 180; Levi d'Ancona, *Miniatura e miniatori a Firenze dal xiv al xvi secolo*, pl. 4. The consecration of Sant'Egidio (as distinct from the confirmation of the consecration) was painted on the facade of the church in 1474, supposedly by Gherardo del Fora: see Buhler Walsh, "The Fresco Painting of Bicci di Lorenzo," p. 21; Paatz, *Die Kirchen von Florenz*, vol. IV, p. 13.

85 See L. Pastor, *Storia dei Papi, dalla fine del Medio Evo*, Rome, 1958, vol. I, pp. 216ff. On Martin V's stay in Florence, see Brucker, *The Civic World of Early Renaissance Florence*, pp. 421–5, and Trexler, *Public Life in Renaissance Florence*, pp. 304–5. Two contemporary accounts record his stay: Corazza's diary (Corazzini, "Diario Fiorentino") and Paolo Petribuoni's *Priorista Fiorentina*, cc. 98v–103r.

86 See Corazzini, "Diario Fiorentino," p. 274.

87 An entry in the convent account book in April 1419 reads: "item avemo piatanza dal

nostro cardinale," ASF, Con. Sopp. 113, n. 85, c. 15v.

88 On the feast of the Conception of the Virgin in December 1419, expenses are recorded in the convent account book "per fare honore a chantori del papa che vengono a chantare a la festa," ASF, Con. Sopp. 113, n. 85, c. 24r. In 1419, 150 place-settings were rented from Matteo Scodellaio to accommodate the "signori, cardinali, veschovi" and "secolari" who came to the Carmine for the festive meal. Vast sums were spent on food and entertainment, cc. 16r–17r. The outlay was even greater the following year, and the invitation list as impressive, cc. 29r–v.

89 Corazza noted that "Andarongli incontro tutte le Regole de' frati con loro reliquie e parati" (Feb. 26, 1418), Corazzini, "Diario Fiorentino," p. 256. See also Petribuoni, *Priorista Fiorentina*, c. 98v. The Carmelite's presence is confirmed in the Carmine account books, where it is noted in late February 1418 that the priors from Prato, Pistoia, and Montecatini had come for "la procisione quando ci vene il papa," ASF, Con. Sopp. 113, n. 85, c. 14r.

90 Petribuoni, *Priorista Fiorentina*, c. 101v.

91 The consecration ceremonies are described in great detail in Corazza's diary, Corazzini, "Diario Fiorentino," pp. 270–1.

92 Santa Maria Novella was founded in 1221 and completed in the mid-*trecento*: see R. Lunardi, *Arte e storia in Santa Maria Novella*, Florence, 1983.

93 See *Bullarium Carmelitarum*, vol. I, p. 172. The timing of Martin's *breve* is curious. It was issued three days after an ominous clash between the Pope and the Florentine Republic – the most serious manifestation of the differences that lay beneath the surface of the public homages. During Martin's stay in Florence, he had been negotiating with the "Republic of Bologna," which had declared itself independent from the Papal States. Florence sought amicable relations with Bologna and thus when ambassadors arrived from Bologna seeking Florentine recognition of the Bolognese republic, they were admitted to the city. The Pope was outraged and on April 10, 1420, placed the city under interdict. The Florentines requested that the Pope remove the interdict within at most four days, and that the Bolognese ambassadors should leave the city within the same period. The Pope backed down and lifted the interdict the next evening, while the Bolognese ambassadors withdrew on their own initiative, easing the tension: see Brucker, *The Civic World of Early Renaissance Florence*, pp. 423ff; Petribuoni, *Priorista Fiorentina*, c. 101v. The pope's *breve* issued on April 13 may thus have been a propitiatory measure intended to appease the angered Florentine patriciate.

94 Creighton Gilbert is thus incorrect when he claims that Masaccio's *Sagra* showed "the consecration of the church of the Carmine itself in the presence of Pope Martin V, whose stay in the city at that time no doubt led to the decision to schedule the ceremony," "Special Images for Carmelites," p. 192.

95 Sibert de Beka's Carmelite Ordinal (c. 1312) indicates that Advent, the octave of Epiphany, and the first Sunday in the octave of Easter were standard occasions for the consecration of a church, *Ordinaire de L'Ordre*, p. 60.

96 See Mallett, *The Florentine Galleys in the Fifteenth Century*, pp. 36–8; Molho, *Florentine Public Finances in the Early Renaissance, 1400–1433*, Cambridge, 1971, pp. 129–30.

97 "A dì xvii et diciotto e xx d'Aprile 1422 cioe Venerdi e Sabato e lunedi . . . si fecie solenne processione per tutta la terra et massimamente Lunedi a dì xx d'Aprile con tutte le r[e]lique e reghole di frati e preti colle crocie delle chiese. . . . Et questo perchè Lunedi . . . dovea partire di Pisa la prima ghalea sottile armata che debbe andare inn Allessandria. E questo dì si incomincio a provare in Corsicha." Petribuoni, *Priorista Fiorentina*, c. 106v; see Mallett, *Florentine Galleys*, pp. 36–7.

98 In the 1550 edition of *Le vite*, Vasari identified only Donatello and Brunelleschi. All the other identifications were added in the 1568 edition; Gilbert, "The Drawings now associated with Masaccio's *Sagra*," p. 261.

99 On the inclusion of artists' portraits in in fifteenth-century Florentine frescos, see Ch. 6 below, p. 156.

100 On the question of the Brancacci chapel patronage, see Molho, "The Brancacci Chapel," pp. 70ff; Pandimiglio, *Felice di Michele vir clarissimus e una consorteria*, pp. 45–51; Joannides, *Masaccio and Masolino*, pp. 318ff.

101 Felice Brancacci's pious donations to the Carmine are chronicled in the convent account books. He contributed toward the Easter feast in 1421, a festive meal at Corpus Christi in 1422, and another meal during the octave of the Annunciation in 1423, ASF, Con. Sopp. 113, n. 85, cc. 41r, 57r, and 67v. In addition, "uno de Branchacci" donated a meal on the third Sunday in September, 1421, c. 47v; see also Guidotti, "Fatti, arredi e corredi," p. 26. Felice's public offices to date included one of the 16 *gonfalonieri* in 1412, one of the 12 *buonuomini* and ambassador to Lunigiana in 1418, and the captain representing the town of Anghiari in a dispute with Città di Castello in 1420: see *Dizionario biografico degli Italiani*, Rome, 1971, vol. 3, pp. 764–6; see also Pandimiglio, *Felice di Michele*.

102 Corazza, recording the departure of the first galley on April 20, 1422, from Pisa in his diary, claimed that the two ambassadors themselves were on board. Mallett refutes this, citing other contemporary accounts, *Florentine Galleys*, p. 36.

103 Lorenzo Ridolfi, Niccolò da Uzzano, Giovanni di Bicci de' Medici, and Bartolomeo Valori were all active in the city government during the first two decades of the *quattrocento*, and were respected, established statesmen: see Brucker, *The Civic World*, p. 265; Litta, *Famiglie Celebri di Italia*, Ser. I, vol. v, Valori tav. I., and Ser. 2, vol. VII, Uzzano tav. II; Martines, *Lawyers and Statecraft in Renaissance Florence*, p. 483; Pope-Hennessy, *The Portrait in the Renaissance*, p. 10. Giovanni de' Medici is perhaps the odd man out, as the other three were core members of a governmental faction that resisted the consolidation of Medici power. In fact, the year before the consecration of Santa Maria del Carmine, Niccolò da Uzzano had fought against a move to elevate Giovanni de' Medici to *gonfaloniere*.

104 For a discussion of the Sea Consuls, see Mallett, *Florentine Galleys*, p. 23. Litta notes that Niccolò da Uzzano and Francesco Soderini were on friendly terms, *Famiglie Celebri*, Ser. 2, vol. VII, Soderini tav. III.

105 The most active patron of the Carmine during the early 1420s was Francesco Soderini, followed by Felice Brancacci, Andrea di Giusto Coverelli, Fra Albizzo de' Nerli, and the Compagnia di Sant'Agnese, ASF, Con. Sopp. 113, n. 85, cc. 25v–113r.

106 Both Francesco Soderini and Felice Brancacci were members of the political faction dominated by Palla Strozzi, Lorenzo Ridolfi, and Niccolò da Uzzano that ran afoul of the ascendant Cosimo de' Medici in the mid-1430s. (They were also Strozzi's sons-in-law.) Francesco suffered repercussions after Cosimo's return to Florence, ending in his imprisonment in 1438, accused of conspiracy. He had a brief return to political life in the early 1450s, and died in 1457: see Litta, *Famiglie Celebri*, Soderini tav. III. Felice Brancacci was accused in 1431 of embezzling 2,900 fl. from the communal exchequer during his tenure as cashier in 1425, but was disciplined very lightly. In 1434, however, he was exiled from Florence following Cosimo's return and died in exile around 1450: see Molho, "The Brancacci Chapel," pp. 76–8.

107 Christiansen, "New Light on the Early Work of Filippo Lippi," p. 342.

108 The Carmelite historian Andrea Sabatini made the suggestion that Francesco Soderini paid for the fresco, "550 Anno della Consacrazione," p. 113.

109 "Altare maius tuus Genitor de Bonis sibi a Deo collatis fundavit, altiusque desuper elevatam testudinem construi, & sumptibus non mediocribus laudabiliter depingi fecit," *Bullarium Carmelitanum*, vol. I, p. 172.

110 According to Sibert de Beka's Ordinal, the anniversary of the consecration of the church was to follow a similar format and liturgy as the original consecration, also being accorded a *totum duplex*, *Ordinaire de L'Ordre*, p. 60.

111 "Spese facte per la Sagra" and "la piatanza del

convento fu pella consecratione," ASF, Con. Sopp. 113, n. 85, cc. 68v and 82r. In subsequent years, the "Sagra" is not mentioned by name in the account books and it is impossible to determine whether the anniversary continued to be celebrated on a lavish scale because the Easter period was a time of heavy expenditure and "Sagra" payments cannot be distinguished from those for the Easter feasting. There is mention of the "Sagra" once again in 1441, a festive year for the Carmelites following Beato Andrea Corsini's prediction of the Florentine victory at Anghiari in June of the previous year, ASF, Con. Sopp. 113, n. 86, cc. 34r–v.

112 The consecration of the collegiate church at San Gimignano was commemorated in a fresco on the inside facade wall: see L. Pecori, *Storia della Terra di San Gimignano*, Florence, 1853, p. 390. I thank Deborah Krohn for this information.

113 Newbigin, *Feste d'Oltrarno*, vol. I, pp. 60–3. Newbigin's translation into English is taken from the Russian text published by N. S. Tichonravov, "Novyj otryvok iz putevych zapisok Suzdal'skago episkopa Avraamija (1439 g.)," *Vestnik obscestva dreve-russkago iskusstva pri Moskovskom publicnom muzee*, 1–12, 1874–76, III, pp. 37–42, and IV, pp. 22–6. Abraham of Suzdal's unit of measurement, the *sagene*, is roughly equivalent to the English yard or 0.9 meters: see Newbigin, p. 63. Newbigin makes an interesting case that a short fifteenth-century Ascension Day play by Feo Belcari was in fact written for the Carmine, pp. 98ff. For a reconstruction of the staging of the play based on Abraham's description, see Ventrone, *Le tems revient 'l tempo si rinuova*, p. 217.

114 The ascension of Elijah is described in 2 Kings 2:11–12 and is in fact the source for the description of the Ascension of Christ found in Acts 1:9–11: see Barr, "Music and Spectacle in Confraternity Drama of Fifteenth-Century Florence," p. 379.

115 The Rite of the Holy Sepulcher has a distinct liturgy for the celebration of Christmas, Easter, the Ascension, the Birth of the Virgin, the feasts of the Patriarchs Abraham, Isaac, and Jacob, and of the Bishops of Jerusalem St. Lazarus and Cleophas: see King, *Liturgies of the Religious Orders*, pp. 248–9.

116 See *Ordinaire de L'Ordre*, pp. 185 and 241.

117 The annual *sacra rappresentazione* is usually considered to have started around 1422. Cyrilla Barr corrects this misapprehension, pointing to the testimony of Franco Sacchetti who refers to the Ascension drama in one of his *Trecento novelle*, dating from the last decades of the fourteenth century, "Music and Spectacle," p. 378. In addition, there is a reference to "le tavole chon che si fece il palcho del'aciensione" in a Carmine account book entry made on Oct. 11, 1420, ASF, Con. Sopp. 113, n. 85, c. 34r.

118 Vasari's description is found in his life of Francesco d'Agnolo, known as "Il Cecca" (1447–88), a Florentine engineer who was engaged to work on the Ascension Day machinery later in the century, Vasari–Milanesi, vol. III, pp. 197ff; Newbigin, *Feste d'Oltrarno*, vol. I, pp. 64–5.

119 Vasari does not describe Brunelleschi's particular contributions to the Carmine *sacra rappresentazione*. He devotes much attention, instead, to Brunelleschi's staging of the Annunciation play in the church of San Felice in Piazza, Vasari–Milanesi, vol. II, pp. 375–8; see also A. Blumenthal, "A Newly Identified Drawing of Brunelleschi's Stage Machinery," *Marsyas*, vol. 13 (1966–67), pp. 20–32, and Pochat, "Brunelleschi and the 'Ascension' of 1422," pp. 232–4.

120 See U. Procacci, "Sulla cronologia delle opere di Masaccio e di Masolino tra il 1425 e il 1428," *Rivista d'arte*, 1953, pp. 39–40; Barr, "Music and Spectacle," p. 399, n. 24.

121 ASF, Con. Sopp. 113, n. 85, cc. 16r–17r. The Compagnia di Sant'Agnese also hosted two meals of lesser magnitude during the Ascension festivities – one on Wednesday evening prior to the Ascension and a second for the *festaiuoli* of the Ascension play on Friday: see Newbigin, "*Cene* and *Cenacoli* in the Ascension and Pentecost Companies of Fifteenth-Century Florence," p. 98.

122 See Newbigin, *Feste d'Oltrarno*, vol. I, pp. 45–155, and vol. II, pp. 283–657; Eckstein, *The District of the Green Dragon*, pp. 55–8.

123 See Barr, "Music and Spectacle," p. 378. She refers to the Communal *Provvisioni Registri*, where allocations were recorded in 1435, 1445, and 1465, ASF, Provv. n. 126, cc. 195v–196v; n. 136, cc. 212v-213v and 255v–256v.

124 "Entrata di gientia channo fatto aiuto alla festa dello escensione 1440," ASF, Compagnia di S. Maria delle Laudi detta di S. Agnese, n. 98, c. 78; Eckstein, *The District of the Green Dragon*, p. 55. Both Lippi and Paolo di Lorenzo gave the Confraternity s. 11.

125 The performance witnessed by Bishop Abraham in 1439 was probably a more lavish production on account of the Council of Florence.

126 I am obviously at a disadvantage here, working from Nerida Newbigin's English translation of Abraham's Russian text.

127 Patriarch Gregory Melissenos, quoted by Belting, *Likeness and Presence*, p. 1.

128 Barr, "Music and Spectacle," pp. 383 and 386; Newbigin, *Feste d'Oltrarno*, vol. I, pp. 72 and 80.

129 Petribuoni, *Priorista Fiorentina*, c. 107r. See also Pochat, "Brunelleschi and the 'Ascension' of 1422," pp. 232–4.

130 The language used in the account books of the Compagnia di Sant'Agnese regarding preparations for the *sacra rappresentazione* is similarly ambiguous: money is taken out in 1447, "per dare mangiare agli angioli" and "per . . . chollezione degli apostoli la mattina dell'Asensione": see Barr, "Music and Spectacle," p. 399, n. 16.

131 "Uno mio amico veggendo il dì dell'Ascensione all'ordine de' frati del Carmine di Firenze, che ne faceano festa, il nostro Signore su per una corda andare in su verso il tetto, e andando molto adagio, dicendo uno: – E' va sì adagio che non giugnerà oggi al tetto. – E quel disse: – Se non andò più ratto, egli è ancor tra via." F. Sacchetti, *Il Trecento novelle*, Florence, 1946, p. 160. See Barr, "Music and Spectacle," pp. 377–8.

132 "Lo venerabile frate Angiolo, fu visto da una grande moltitudine di homini [sic?] digni di fede, li quali predicando cum grande fiducia et infiamato et aceso di carità e di amor, fè una excelente predicatione, predicando dello martirio et della gloria et delle corone, le quale sono incoronati li martiri in vita eterna. Et sopra questo passo si infiamò lo servo di Dio tanto, che fu uno stupore a tuta la plebe; essendo così infiamato, che fu veduto visibilmente, che dua angioli stavano dinanzi a lui, l'uno dala parte dextra e l'altro dala parte sinistra, e teneano in mani dui bacini d'oro. E dalla boca del preditto padre uscivano rose et fiori, et cadevano dentro li ditti bacini. Et li ditti angioli li pigliavano di quelle rose e faciono corone e sì li ponevano sopra lo capo del beato frate Angiolo. E di sopra la sua capa biancha fu visto uno palio di sotta violato. E questo fu veduto da una [gran]de moltitudine di gente." Graziano di S. Teresa, "'Vita fratrum del Sancto Monte Carmelo'," pp. 409–10 (my translation).

133 G. M. Brocchi claims that the painting was executed "poco dopo la . . . morte" of Fra Angelo Mazzinghi, *Vite de' Santi e Beati Fiorentini*, vol. II, part. 2, p. 229. The painting is first documented in 1689, when it is described as "una tavola antica . . . incassata in un pilastro" by Fra Girolamo Castaldi in his description of the Carmine: see Procacci, "L'incendio della Chiesa," pp. 153–4.

134 "Si vede l'effigie di . . . [Beato Angelo Mazzinghi] in una misteriosa Imagine . . . il predetto Padre dipinto tutto intiero da' raggi celesti circondato nel capo, con la faccia rivolta verso del Cielo, con un libro nella destra mano, e nella sinistra uno scettro rosso, circondato da sette candide Colombe, col rostro, e piedi rossi, tre per parte, ed un piede loro appogia sopra una Croce rossa, un'altra poi è senza croce in atto di volare con l'ali distese, e con i raggi al capo, che denota lo Spirito Santo, con i suoi sette doni, e pronunzia per aria queste parole: *Exultet iustus in conspectu Dei*. Sotto a' piedi di questo benedetto Padre vi è un agnello mansuetissimo disteso, e due Angioli celesti coronano questo terrestre con ghirlanda di rose, con vasi poi tessuti di salci, o di vimini ricolgono d'avanti al suo petto le rose, che dalla bocca

gli cadono, perchè . . . invece delle parole, invisibili furono veduti talvolta uscire dalla sua bocca predicante mazzetti sensibili di rose, e di gigli bellissimi." Brocchi, *Vite de' Santi*, vol. II, part. 2, p. 230 (my translation). See also the descriptions in BNF, Con. Sopp. F.5.4, *Acta Processus Translationis Corporis B. Angeli de Mazzinghis*, 1739, particularly 19r–v and 30v–31r, where the painting is described as 2 *braccia* high and 1 *braccia* wide, with a kneeling woman and her young son painted to the left of the figure of Beato Angelo. In the early eighteenth-century *Ricordanze del Beato Angiolo Mazzinghi per la riconoscenza del suo culto*, the painting is described as "dipinta in tela con cornice" with an inscription: "B. Angelinus Mazzinghi Florentinus Ord: Carmelitanum ex cuius ore visi sunt rosarum et liliorum pulcherrimi erumpere manipuli floruit 1438." ASF, Con. Sopp. 133, n. 217, c. 32.

135 On Fra Angelo Mazzinghi, see D. M. Manni, *Angelo Mazzinghi*, Florence, 1739 and 1761 (also his manuscript notes in the Biblioteca Moreniana, Florence); M. Couret de Villeneuve, *Biblioteca Carmelitana*, Rome, 1752 (republished in 1927), vol. I, p. 105; Brocchi, *Vite de' Santi*, vol. II, part. 2, pp. 226–39; Caioli, *Il Beato Angelino*; Saggi, *La Congregazione Mantovana dei Carmelitani*, pp. 31–6; and *Atti dei capitoli provinciali*, p. 357.

136 We know very little about the initial reforms instituted by Fra Jacopo Alberti because his Constitutions have not survived. However, one can speculate on the basis of the primitive Carmelite Rule presented to the Carmelites by Albert Patriarch of Jerusalem at the beginning of the thirteenth century and on the Observant reforms that were codified in 1442, when Le Selve became part of the reformed Mantua Congregation: see Saggi, *La Congregazione Mantovana*, pp. 6ff.

137 "Item confirmaverunt omnes et singulas gratias conventuy nostro observantie scil. sancte Marie de Silvis, quas concessit insuper et confirmavit R. M. Ordinis," *Atti dei capitoli provinciali*, p. 133; see Saggi, *La Congregazione Mantovana*, pp. 29–30.

138 See Ruda, *Fra Filippo Lippi*, Doc. 1.II.7, p. 514.

139 This position did not prevent him from serving as prior of the Florentine convent in 1435–36. He served as prior at Le Selve once again in 1437, and was also elected *custode* of Santa Lucia, an ex-Augustinian convent on the Via San Gallo that Pope Eugenius had placed under the jurisdiction of the friars of Le Selve in 1435.

140 "Vir venerabililis, maxime virtuosus, optime doctrine, magister consilii, alte fame sanctissimeque vite et predicator famosissimus, qui primus fuit filius in inceptione observantie Silvarum," quoted in Saggi, *La Congregazione Mantovana*, p. 35.

141 Among the thirty or so professed friars in the Carmine from 1417 to 1431, I have been able to identify only around 17% at any given time from patrician families, the majority of which were from the neighborhood of the Carmine.

142 He used his influence to assist the German weavers in establishing a confraternity dedicated to St. Catherine in the Carmine. Mona Betta Abbadinghi left all of her goods to Fra Angelo, who was to oversee the foundation of a chapel dedicated to St. Michael and the celebration of the annual feast of the saint. See Brocchi, *Vite de' Santi*, vol. II, part. 2, p. 231, and D. M. Manni, manuscript notes for the *Vita del Beato Angelo*, Biblioteca Moreniana, Florence, c. 16v.

143 The primitive Carmelite Rule had been mitigated in 1247, when the friars began to establish themselves in urban convents in the Holy Land and in Western Europe. Restrictions regarding separate cells, silence to be maintained throughout the day, and eating in isolation were lifted at that time: see Saggi, *La Congregazione Mantovana*, pp. 6ff.

144 The Carmelite general chapter ordered that the bull be observed by all chapters at the general meeting of 1440, and again in 1456 and 1469. And yet, in 1442, as the mitigated Rule was being implemented throughout the Order, a separate "Congregation of Mantua" was approved, incorporating the three reformed Carmelite convents that observed the early Carmelite Rule. These convents – Le Selve, Gironda, and Mantua – were placed outside of the jurisdiction of the provincial priors and came under the direct authority of the general prior.

145 "Ò tolto a dipigniere e metere d'oro . . . uno tabernacholo a sportegli . . . nel quale ò a fare uno quadretto . . . drentovi una Nostra Donna e chol Banbino, meno asai che dal mezo in su, dipinta alla grecha molto anticha; negli sportegli ò farere [sic] nel'uno lato drento Santo Elia e Santo Alberto e nel'altro Santo Eliseo e Santo Agniolo di Gierusalem e di sopra a detto quadretto di Nostra Donna uno Dio Padre cho molti serafini . . . e negli sportegli di fuori una Nunziata e l'angelo . . ." (Sept. 8, 1454). Neri di Bicci, *Le Ricordanze*, p. 19. The commission was from the "frati e chapitolo e chonvento di Santa Maria delle Selve," through their *procuratore* Agniolo di Nicholò, with the stipulation that the completed work be evaluated by Tommaso di Lorenzo Soderini. When the friars were unable to come up with the final payment, they agreed to give the tabernacle to Soderini, who covered the cost and saw that the tabernacle was installed in the church, p. 35. Payments for the tabernacle were completed by Sept. 13, 1455, while the predella was commissioned afterwards and was paid for on the very date (April 8, 1456) painted on the predella, *ibid.*, p. 54.

146 Guido Carocci described a "Madonna, del secolo XII di carattere bizantino, entro un tabernacolo dipinto da Neri di Bicci" in *Comune di Lastra a Signa*, Florence, 1895, p. 13; Giovanni Poggi also saw the tabernacle, and recorded that the date, "8 aprile 1456," was inscribed on the predella, "Le ricordanze de Neri di Bicci," *Il Vasari*, vol. I (1927), p. 334. It has been suggested that the Marian image at the center of Neri di Bicci's tabernacle was the venerated votive image of Le Selve, known in the fifteenth century as "Nostra Donna" and later as the "Madonna delle Grazie": see Hoeniger, *The Renovation of Paintings in Tuscany*, pp. 49–51.

147 The other religious images at Le Selve during the early years of the reform also reinforced the religious traditions of the Order. Two of the nave chapels housed important Madonna images – the "Madonna delle Grazie" and the "Madonna del Carmine." The former may have been the "alla grecha" panel later incorporated into the Neri di Bicci tabernacle, while the "Madonna del Carmine" was inserted into a second tabernacle by Neri di Bicci in 1482 for Filippo Strozzi's chapel in the church: see E. Borsook, "Documenti relativi alle Cappelle di Lecceto e delle Selve di Filippo Strozzi," *Antichità viva*, vol. IX, no. 3 (1970), pp. 6–8; Hoeniger, *Renovation of Paintings*, pp. 49–51. There was an altarpiece with the Virgin Annunciate flanked by Elijah and Elisha, and another image of the Madonna with Elijah among the lateral saints. There were at least three images of St. Alberto of Trapani at Le Selve during the *quattrocento*: see Bacchi, from an undated inventory, "Santa Maria delle Selve," pp. 8, 14–15. The Jarves polyptych described earlier in this chapter, which included an image of St. Alberto, may also have been at Le Selve.

148 The Florentine Carmelite's orchestration of events and their promotion of a particular public image must be seen in direct relation to developments within other religious orders. As mentioned above, the Dominican church of Santa Maria Novella was consecrated in 1420, in the presence of Pope Martin V. The figure of the popular Observant Franciscan preacher Bernardino looms large in the account of the preaching miracle of Angelo Mazzinghi and the description of the commemorative painting. Soon after Bernardino's death in 1444, Sano di Pietro depicted him preaching the Lenten sermons of 1425 and 1427, in addition to several versions of him elevated by angels, the earliest dating from 1450: see Christiansen, Strehlke, and Kanter, *Painting in Renaissance Siena*, pp. 41–2 and 268.

149 Fra Albizzo de' Nerli was a member of one of the wealthiest and most prominent families in the *gonfalone* Drago Verde where the Carmine stood. He had an illustrious academic career, studying in France and England, teaching in the Florentine Carmelite *studium*,

and eventually serving as the regent in Pisa and Florence. He also served as prior of the Florentine Carmine and provincial prior of the Tuscan province. He appears to have fallen from grace for a brief period in 1410, when he kept the provincial Carmelite seal and books for personal use, but was pardoned and later re-elected provincial prior: see *Atti dei capitoli provinciali*, pp. 114 and 355. He was a patron of his own monastery, contributing to annual feasts and "variis atque sumptuosis ornamentis ecclesiasticis ab eodem conventui huic acquisitis," BNF, *Necrologium*, Con. Sopp. C. 5.786, under Dec. 12. See also P. Caioli, "Vita del B. Angelo Mazzinghi," *Rivista storica Carmelitana*, Anno III, nos. 3–4 (1931–2), pp. 85–7.

150 "In vita sua sempre si levava al Mattutino e di poi stava in chiesa due ore, e quando se n'andava alla Camera sua, molti frati affirmano aver veduto in lume innanzigli, il quale l'accompagnava insino alla Camera, e domandato da i Frati che cosa fusse quella, egli facendosi promettere di non dir cosa alcuna durante sua vita, disse che quello era l'Angel Raffaello che l'accompagnava. . . . Quattro giorni avanti la sua morte, essendo un Frate in chiesa vedde da lungi un gran razzo, e un bellissimo giovane parlare col maestro, e preso animo seguì innanzi, e quando gli fu appresso sentì dirli 'Sempre sii tu ringraziato iddio, poiche ti piace chiamarmj a te.' E domandandogli il Frate che cosa era questa, rispose 'Io presto mj morirò, e andrommi a riposare. . . .' quando che cantandosi la messa della Madonna . . . e star ginocchioni, e cantare insieme con li Novizi, e con gran devozione . . . si sentò dire da lui 'In Manus tuas Domine commendo Spiritum meum,' e spirò. Cosi si crede l'anima sua sia andata in Paradiso. Da più persone fû veduto un grandissimo razzo sopra la chiesa intorno alle 12 ore, e starvi tanto quanto il detto Padre morì, e da tutti si crede l'anima sua accompagnata da quel razzo essere andata in Paradiso." This letter exists in an eighteenth-century transcription in the Biblioteca Moreniana, Florence (Manuscriti Moreni n. 8); my translation. The transcription does not provide specific information about the date of the letter or the correspondents, noting simply that it is a "Lettera della morte del Rev. P. Maestro Albizo de Nerli scritta da uno de suoi Padri [del Carmine] a una delle nostre Monache [di San Felice in Piazza]." Maestro Albizzo had been confessor to the nuns of San Felice.

151 This general reference was made by D. M. Manni in his manuscript notes for his *Vita del B. Angelo*, Biblioteca Moreniana, Florence.

152 See Brocchi, *Vite de' Santi*, vol. II, part. 2, p. 232.

153 Brocchi cites G. M. Fornari's *Anno memorablile de' Carmelitani*, Milan, 1688, vol. II, p. 270 in *Vite de' Santi*, vol. II, part. 2, pp. 233ff. I have been unable to locate this source or determine where Fornari came by his information.

154 In the tradition of Tuscan images of *beati* and newly canonized saints, the narrative details were explicated symbolically in an iconic full-figure image of Fra Angelo. Extant examples that date from the mid-*quattrocento* include the many images of St. Bernardino and Giovanni di Paolo's rendition of St. Niccolò da Tolentino in Montepulciano, painted ten years after his canonization: see Christiansen, Strehlke, and Kanter, *Paintings in Renaissance Siena*, pp. 41–42 and 211. Regarding Giovanni di Paolo's *S. Niccolò da Tolentino*, H. van Os claims that "images of this type were mostly put on pillars in the church for popular veneration," *Sienese Altarpieces*, vol. II, p. 50, fig. 26.

CHAPTER THREE

1 Berenson, "Fra Angelico, Fra Filippo e la cronologia."

2 Salmi, *Masaccio*, pp. 82 and 104, and "La giovinezza di Fra Filippo Lippi."

3 Berenson, *Italian Pictures of the Renaissance*, p. 172, and *Pitture italiane del Rinascimento*, p. 380.

4 Berenson gave the Empoli *Madonna and Child with Saints and Angels* to Pesellino in *Italian Pictures of the Renaissance*, but changed the attribution to Lippi in the index of the Italian version, *Pitture italiane del Rinascimento*: see also Marchini, *Filippo Lippi*, p. 199.

5 See Pittaluga, *Filippo Lippi*, p. 201; L. Ragghianti-Collobi, *Lorenzo il Magnifico e le arti*, ex. cat., Florence, 1949, p. 24; Marchini, *Filippo Lippi*, pp. 199–200.

6 See Christiansen, "New Light on the Early Work of Filippo Lippi," pp. 338–43; Ruda, *Fra Filippo Lippi*, cat. 7, pp. 63–4 and 572–3. I do not accept Boskovits's suggestion that a double portrait in a private collection is stylistically consistent with the second group of paintings, "Fra Filippo Lippi, i carmelitani e il Rinascimento," pp. 239 and 250, fig. 14.

7 Marchini, *Filippo Lippi*, cat. 3–7, pp. 198–200; Boskovits, "Fra Filippo Lippi," pp. 235ff; Berti and Paolucci, *L'età di Masaccio*, pp. 186ff; Fossi, *Filippo Lippi*, pp. 36ff.

8 Shell, "The Early Style of Fra Filippo Lippi."

9 Christiansen, "New Light," p. 342.

10 Ruda, *Fra Filippo Lippi*, p. 64.

11 *Ibid.*, pp. 47–88, 365–80. Ruda expands the body of works immediately pre-dating the Tarquinia *Madonna and Child* (1437) by pushing back the traditional dating of a number of paintings (the Verona *Man of Sorrows*, the Poldi Pezzoli *Pietà*, the Washington National Gallery of Art *Nativity*, the Frick *Annunciation*, the Altenburg *St. Jerome in the Wilderness*, and the Metropolitan Museum *Double Portrait*) and upgrading to autograph two others (the *Dead Christ with Saints*, Palazzo del Arcivescovado, Florence, and a small *Cardinal Saint* in Bern). He also dates to this period the interesting *Madonna and Child*, Utah Museum of Fine Arts.

12 See Marchini, *Filippo Lippi*, p. 199; A. Paolucci, *Il Museo della Collegiata di S. Andrea in Empoli*, Florence, 1985, no. 33, pp. 94–6; Berti and Paolucci, *L'età di Masaccio*, no. 64, p. 188; Ruda, *Fra Filippo Lippi*, pp. 52, 367–8.

13 See White, *The Birth and Rebirth of Pictorial Space*, pp. 170ff.

14 Ruda considers the canopy to be a later addition, *Fra Filippo Lippi*, p. 367.

15 Keith Christiansen identifies the right foreground saint as the Carmelite St. Angelo (whose attribute of martyrdom was a knife), "New Light," p. 343. I accept the traditional identification of the Apostle Bartholomew because the figure is not tonsured and his loose white cape does not resemble the tailored Carmelite hooded mantle. However, the similarity between his dress and the Carmelite habit seems to be intentional.

16 See Caioli, "Un altro sguardo sulla vita di Fra Filippo Lippi," p. 72; Boskovits, "Fra Filippo Lippi," p. 237; Christiansen, "New Light," p. 343.

17 See Ch. 2 above, pp. 38–9 for more on St. Alberto and for the celebration of his cult at Santa Maria del Carmine.

18 Boskovits hypothesizes that the picture could have been painted for one of the Carmelites at Le Selve, "Fra Filippo Lippi," pp. 237 and 247, n. 20.

19 John Shearman has pointed out to me that there is a similar dynamic in the Barbadori altarpiece (see fig. 103), where the Christ Child looks at the crozier which St. Frediano proffers.

20 I thank John Shearman for pointing this out to me.

21 See Salmi, *Masaccio*, pp. 82 and 104; Marchini, *Filippo Lippi*, p. 198; Ruda, *Fra Filippo Lippi*, pp. 52–3 and 366–7.

22 The oratory was built in the cemetery "nel chanto di due muri dietro alluogo ove si ragiuna la compagnia di santa agnesa," in the area outside the left nave wall of the church, ASF, Con. Sopp. 113, n. 16 (Oct. 13, 1419), n.p. The documentation for the Compagnia di Sant'Alberto is very fragmentary for the *quattrocento*: see ASF, Con. Sopp. 113, n. 85, cc. 58v, 76r, and 107r; ASF, Catasto 185, c. 739r. Later in the century, the Compagnia combined with the Compagnia del Chiodo, and by at least 1499, it had the distinction of being composed of both "fanciulli" and "huomini," ASF, Compagnia della Dottrina dell'Assunta e S. Alberto fanciulli n. 13, n.p.

23 A note annotating an agreement made on Feb. 17, 1495 between the friars and the Compagnia, regarding a new space for the latter in the cemetery, reads: "Procura a poter'vendere per murare dov'era il quadro

di S. Alberto," ASF, Compagnia della Dottrina dell'Assunta e S. Alberto fanciulli n. 13, n.p.

24 Dieciaiuti was a Florentine notary who lived in the Drago Verde *gonfalone*. He was also a member of the Compagnia di Sant'Agnese. Given his date of birth, the altar foundation could not have been earlier than the 1430s.

25 "Nello altare poi di dietro a detto ponte intitolato a S. to Alberto della famiglia Diociaiuti se prelevò la tavola," ASF, Con. Sopp. 113, n. 19, c. 75r, published in M. Fabbri, E. Garbero-Zorzi, and A. M. Petrioli Tofani, eds., *Il Luogo Teatrale a Firenze*, Florence, 1975, p. 59; ASF, Con. Sopp. 113, n. 13, c. 7 – a description of the chapels and *oblighi* of the church written in 1689; Richa, *Notizie istoriche delle chiese fiorentine*, vol. x, p. 58.

26 ASF, Con. Sopp. 113, n. 13, c. 7. The foundation of the chapel dedicated to St. Angelo must have occurred between the time when the cult of St. Angelo began to gain ground in the early *quattrocento* and the dismantling of the *ponte* in 1568. It may have coincided with the official recognition of the cult of Angelo by Pope Pius II in 1459.

27 P. Caioli, "Un'opera dimenticata di Fra Filippo Lippi," *Il Monte Carmelo*, vol. 25 (1939), pp. 230ff.

28 Bishop Abraham of Suzdal's *Journey*, 1439. See Newbigin's translation above, Ch. 2, pp. 50–51.

29 "[con tanta] Giocundità e humilità, . . . modestia et obedientia, che non parevano homini, ma angioli," Graziano di S. Teresa, "'Vita fratrum del sancto Monte Carmelo' del P. Nicola Calciuri," p. 393.

30 See McCaffrey, *The White Friars*, pp. 56ff; Saggi, *Santi del Carmelo*, pp. 130ff.

31 Calciuri's scheme and floral imagery also derived from St. Francis's *Fioriti*, Graziano di S. Teresa, "'Vita fratrum del Sancto Monte Carmelo'," pp. 304–5 and 429ff.

32 Kaftal identified this figure as Beata Angela, the daughter of the King of Bohemia, who died on July 6, 1253, *Iconography of the Saints in Tuscan Painting*, Florence, 1952, pp. 57–8.

33 See Kaftal, *Iconography of the Saints*, p. 14; M. Pfeiffer, *Einzel-Formschnitte des fünfzeznten Jahrhunderts in der Königl. Bibliothek Bamberg*, Strassburg, 1911, vol. 2, pp. 12–13, n. 8; W. L. Schreiber, *Handbuch der Holz- und Metallschnitte des XV. Jahrhunderts*, Leipzig, 1927, vol. 3, p. 4, n. 1184 (I thank Dr. Werner Taegert of the Staatsbibliothek in Bamberg for the last two references).

34 The altarpiece depicting scenes from the Carmelite legend of St. Anne was commissioned by the Confraternity of Saint Anne for their chapel in the Frankfurt Carmelite church around 1490; it is now in the Kunsthistorisches Museum in Frankfurt. See Ashley and Sheingorn, *Interpreting Cultural Symbols*, pp. 27ff; G. Tervarent, "Le Rétable de Sainte Anne au Musée de Francfort," in *Les Enigmes de l'art du moyen âge*, 2 ser., Paris, 1941, pp. 35–46; *Gemälde des Historischen Museums*, Frankfurt am Main, 1957, pp. 26–9.

35 See Ch. 7 below, pp. 169–71.

36 See King, *Liturgies of the Religious Orders*, p. 280.

37 I thank John Shearman for pointing this out to me.

38 "Lavorò di verde terra, nel chiostro vicino alla Sagra di Masaccio, un Papa che conferma la regola dei Carmelitani," Vasari–Milanesi, vol. II, p. 613; Eng. trans. Vasari–De Vere, *Lives*, vol. III, p. 80.

39 This fresco was first mistaken for Masaccio's *Sagra*, and even after the association with Lippi's *Confirmation of the Carmelite Rule* was made in 1896, some scholars protested that it was not painted in terra verde as Vasari had written: see Marchini, *Filippo Lippi*, p. 198.

40 The detached fresco is on display at Santa Maria del Carmine. See A. de Witt, "Un affresco di Fra Filippo Lippi nel Chiostro del Carmine," *Dedalo*, 1932, pp. 585–93; Poggi, "Sulla data dell'affresco di Fra Filippo Lippi nel chiostro del Carmine;" Marchini, *Filippo Lippi*, p. 198, cat. no. 3; Boskovits, "Fra Filippo Lippi," pp. 235ff; Berti and Paolucci, *L'età di Masaccio*, pp. 186–7; Hood, *Fra Angelico at San Marco*, pp. 126–9; Ruda, *Fra Filippo Lippi*, pp. 49–52 and 365–6.

41 Poggi, "Sulla data dell'affresco," p. 98.

42 Ruda noted that the bull was issued not in 1432 but in 1435, and then back-dated to the year that the Carmelites had made their request for official papal sanction for the mitigation of their Rule, "The National Gallery Tondo of the Adoration of the Magi and the Early Style of Filippo Lippi," pp. 35ff. Both Ruda and Boskovits argue that the style of the fresco is too early for a date as late as 1435, and Boskovits also demonstrates that this particular mitigation – coming in the midst of a period of Observant reform in the monastic orders – would not necessarily have been a subject that the Carmelites would have wanted to commemorate: see Boskovits, "Fra Filippo Lippi," pp. 235ff.

43 Salmi, "La giovinezza di Fra Filippo Lippi," p. 3. "Tebaide" refers to the early Christian hermits who lived in the Egyptian desert around Thebes, described in a collection of writings known as the *Vitae Patrum*, translated into *vulgare* by the Dominican Fra Domenico Cavalca in the fourteenth century.

44 Boskovits, "Fra Filippo Lippi," p. 236 (my translation).

45 Published by Graziano di S. Teresa, "Viridarium Ioannis Grossi."

46 Published by Graziano di S. Teresa, "'Vita fratrum del sancto monte Carmelo'."

47 Giovanni Grossi was a Frenchman from the convent of Appamiarus in Toulouse. He renounced the general priorship of the Order in 1430, and died five years later. Fra Nicola Calciuri, on the other hand, Lippi probably would have known, although somewhat later, in 1441, when Calciuri was the sacristan of the Florentine Carmine.

48 "In isto monte multa mirabilia fecit ipse Elias. . . . Assumens igitur in socios Elyseum, Abdiam, Jonam et multos alios prophetas, eos docuit vivere in virginitate ad honorem . . . Virginis. . . .

Ipse igitur Elyseus, transacto Elia, cum prophetarum filijs propter vitam insignem multos traxit ad ipsius montis Carmeli habitacionem et devocionem." Graziano di S. Teresa, "Viridarium Ioannis Grossi," pp. 264 and 266; my translation.

49 Calciuri had to reconcile the actual history of the Order whereby Mount Carmel was the first and principal Carmelite establishment, with the Carmelite "Doctrine of Origin" based on the Book of Kings which makes no mention of a hermitage on Mount Carmel. He did so by elaborating an ideal monasticism founded by Elijah and Elisha along the banks of the River Jordan as described in Kings, and then affixing it to the potent symbol of Mount Carmel: see Graziano di S. Teresa, "'Vita fratrum del sancto monte Carmelo'," pp. 266 and 375.

50 *Ibid.*, p. 382.

51 "Dove è lo sancto monte Carmelo;" "Come edificato è lo convento et in che forma;" "Del modo et forma dell'officio divino;" "Del loro modo et forma del loro mangiare;" "Dello exerticio [sic] manuale."

52 "Questo santissimo luogo era di una grande santità, in tanto che cum licentia del priore facevano ogni penitentia che li frati . . . voleano," *ibid.*, p. 387.

53 "Tuti li vedeti stare alegri e contento [*sic*], vivendo in santa penitentia," *ibid.*

54 "A dua a dua uscendo della chiesa" and "in chiesa et per le citade, sempre portavano lo mantello," *ibid.*, pp. 389 and 391.

55 Cannon, "Pietro Lorenzetti and the History of the Carmelite Order," p. 25. See also Ch. 2 above, pp. 35–6.

56 See this and other images of Elisha described in Ch. 2 above, pp. 36–8 and n. 46.

57 See Gilbert, "Special Images for Carmelites," p. 193.

58 "Una cum apostolis in quibuscumque regionibus fidem Christi predicaverunt," Graziano di S. Teresa, "Viridarium Ioannis Grossi," p. 267. Creighton Gilbert suggests that the Carmelites were included in this particular scene from the life of Peter because it commemorates the institution of the clerical tonsure, "Special Images for Carmelites," pp. 193ff. A more likely explanation is that the Carmelites make their appearance in the two Brancacci chapel scenes that most unequivocally represent the apostolic functions of Peter – his preaching and his founding of churches. One of the major transformations that the Carmelite Order underwent after relocating to the West was

to follow the Dominicans and Franciscans in pursuing the apostolic mission of preaching, teaching, and administering the sacraments.

59 I have described the Carmelite Observant movement and the relationship between the reformed house Le Selve and the Florentine Carmine in Ch. 2. Calciuri was himself involved in the Observant movement at Le Selve and at Santa Lucia (a dependent of Le Selve) from the mid-1430s on. He is mentioned in relation to Le Selve in 1434, Santa Lucia in 1440, and in 1459 he is documented going to Mantua, which was the center of the newly formed Observant Mantuan Congregation. He also held various positions in the Florentine Carmine, and during the last five years of his life, he was the *governatore* of a company of Carmelite tertiaries. Graziano di S. Teresa suggests that the *Vita fratrum del sancto monte Carmelo* may have been written as a spiritual guide for the latter. In his notes to Calciuri's second book "Paradiso," he suggests that among various literary sources, the author may have referred to "usi forse dell'Osservanza delle Selve," "'Vita fratrum del sancto monte Carmelo'," pp. 260ff and 287.

60 St. Basil (c. 330–79) was the author of one of the first monastic rules which became the standard for Eastern monasticism and was later utilized by Saint Benedict in composing his Rule. Grossi represents Basil as one of the hermits of Mount Carmel, Graziano di S. Teresa, "Viridarium Ioannis Grossi," p. 267.

61 "Tempore Allexandri pape tercij nacione Tuscij, pontificatus sui anno 5," *ibid.*, p. 271.

62 "Tempore huius Innocencius papa 3. confirmavit Regulam Ordinis, pontificatus sui anno primo," *ibid.*, p. 272.

63 See *Bullarium Carmelitanum*, vol. I, p. 1; Canon, "Pietro Lorenzetti," pp. 22–3.

64 See Saggi, *Santi del Carmelo*, pp. 27ff; King, *Liturgies of the Religious Orders*, pp. 239ff.

65 Graziano di S. Teresa, "Viridarium Ioannis Grossi," p. 273.

66 Francis had made his first trip to Rome seeking the authorization of his brotherhood in 1210. Innocent III approved the Order verbally, while a more comprehensive version of the Rule was approved by Pope Honorius III in 1223. Dominic had petitioned Pope Innocent III for the official recognition of his Order in 1215. His petition coincided with the Fourth Lateran Council which was attempting to curb the multiplication of religious orders. Innocent encouraged Dominic to follow one of the existing rules, and he chose that of Augustine. A year later, after the death of Innocent, the Dominican Order was confirmed by the new Pope, Honorius III. The source for the supposed meeting between Sts. Francis and Dominic in Rome in 1215 is *Vitae Fratrum* (c. 1260), written by the Dominican Gerardo di Frachet: see Moorman, *A History of the Franciscan Order*, pp. 27ff.

67 "Come testifica Vincentio, Historiale. Dice in questa forma a libri xxxi, capitoli xxiii: '*In tempo di Federico imperador, che incominciò nelli anni del Signor M.cc.xi.* Dice queste parole: "*Questi dui preditti padri, principiatori delli novelli ordini, Francesco e Domenico, incominciorono nel tempo di Innocentio tertio; et morto Innocentio, sucesso Honorio papa. Et questo Honorio . . . aprovò la regola deli frati [heremiti] habitanti nel monte sancto Carmelo. . . .*"' Graziano di S. Teresa, "'Vita fratrum del sancto monte Carmelo'," p. 397; my translation.

68 Joanna Cannon suggests that these figures refer generically to the many popes who confirmed the original and the amended Carmelite Rule. She cites the preamble of the Carmelite constitutions of 1281, which states that Albert's Rule was "confirmed by Honorius III, his successor Innocent, and many of their successors," "Pietro Lorenzetti," p. 23.

69 See M. Maccarrone, *Studi su Innocenzo III*, 1972, Padua, pp. 279ff.

70 See n. 42 above.

71 The Carmelites of Santa Maria del Carmine were the first among many Florentine monastic establishments in the fifteenth century to decorate their cloisters with a frescoed program rooted in the history, traditions, and customs of their Order. See Hood, "Ritual Sites: Florentine Painted Cloisters and the Representation of History," *Fra Angelico at San Marco*, pp. 123–45.

CHAPTER FOUR

1 ASF, Con. Sopp. 113, n. 85, c. 183, published by Poggi in "Sulla data dell'affresco di Fra Filippo Lippi nel chiostro del Carmine," p. 106.

2 The name "Fra Angelico" was in fact first used during the fifteenth century. Fra Domenico da Corella referred to the friar artist as "Angelicus pictor" in his *Theotocon* (1469) and a decade later Cristoforo Landino sang his well-known praises to "Fra Giovanni angelico": see Cardile, "Fra Angelico and his Workshop at San Domenico," pp. 9–10.

3 "Io che vengo a quest' Arte e compagnia giuro alle sante di Dio evangelia fare l'arte mia bene e lealmente e dirittamente, e ubbidire a' Consoli presenti e che saranno e a' loro comandamenti leciti e onesti, dummodo non sieno contro al Comune e Popolo di Firenze e alla pubblica utilità, e osservare tutti gli statuti e ordinamenti della detta Arte, e ogni altra cosa fare che fare sono tenuti gli artefici della detta Arte nei fatti della detta Arte." Fiorilli, "I dipintori a Firenze nell'arte dei medici speziali e merciai," p. 21 (Rubric 55 of the 1349 guild statutes); my translation.

4 Some 70–80 percent of the painters known to have been working in Florence during the *quattrocento* matriculated into either the Arte dei Medici e Speziali (which included the painters and illuminators, the latter under the *cartolai*) or one of the other guilds that included practitioners of the visual arts, such as the Arte della Seta. See Frey, *Die Loggia dei Lanzi*, pp. 312–69; Wackernagel, *The World of the Florentine Renaissance Artist*, p. 302.

5 "Chiedo la misericordia di Dio e della Vergine Maria, e l'abito della religione Carmelitana, e che sia fatto degno di essere ammesso alla professione." The passage is reconstructed by Paolo Caioli, based on the outlines given for the investiture ceremony in the Carmelite Constitutions of 1324, *S. Andrea Corsini*, p. 24.

6 "Fecit professionem etc. in manu dicti prioris, presentis stipulantis et recipientis pro dicta regula et Ordine et pro reverendo patre fratre Johanne Grosso, generale totius dicti Ordinis etc. et promisit castitatem, paupertatem et obedientiam iuxta morem regule predicte, et se et sua bona presentia et futura dicto Ordini et capitulo et conventui dedicavit etc." ASF, Not. Antecos. 7384 (June 18, 1421), n.p., reproduced in Caioli, "Un altro sguardo sulla vita di fra Filippo Lippi," p. 34.

7 For the Dominican profession, see Hood, *Fra Angelico at San Marco*, p. 293, n. 35.

8 See Fiorilli, "I dipintori a Firenze;" F. Ziccardi, "Gli statuti dei pittori fiorentini e senesi nel secolo xiv," *Rivista di diritto industriale*, 1966, pp. 116–21 (section 6).

9 See Herlihy and Klapisch-Zuber, *Tuscans and their Families*, ch. 1. For a fourteenth-century list of the *gabelle* levied on materials relevant to painting, see R. Ciasca, *L'Arte dei Medici e Speziali nella storia e nel commercio fiorentino dal secolo XII al XV*, Florence, 1927, Doc. XIX, pp. 759ff.

10 See Fiorilli, "I dipintori a Firenze," pp. 16ff; Brucker, *Renaissance Florence*, p. 147.

11 For Lippi's litigation in the Florentine courts, see Ch. 5 below, pp. 106–11.

12 Ordained monks were valuable members of confraternities because they were able to officiate at masses at the confraternity altars. Lippi and his brother were active in the Compagnia di Sant'Agnese at Santa Maria del Carmine. A few of the monastic painters also belonged to the painters' Compagnia di San Luca: Fra Giovanni di Duccio da Sant'Ambrogio is listed in 1368 and the Vallombrosian Fra Diamante in 1472: see Frey, *Die Loggia dei Lanzi*, p. 319, n. 1; Vasari–Milanesi, vol. II, p. 640. Lorenzo Monaco too may have remained a member of the same confraternity after his profession in 1391: see Eisenberg, *Lorenzo Monaco*, pp. 209–11.

13 See Bizzocchi, *Chiesa e potere nella Toscana del quattrocento*, p. 145; Trexler, *Synodal Law in*

Florence and Fiesole, pp. 87ff. For attempts by Pope Nicholas V and Eugenius IV to readdress the problem, see *Bullarium Carmelitanum*, vol. I, pp. 234 and 243.

14 See Hay, *The Church in Italy in the Fifteenth Century*, pp. 59ff; Brucker, *Renaissance Florence*, pp. 190ff; Moorman, *A History of the Franciscan Order*, pp. 354ff.

15 *The Rule of St. Benedict*, p. 93.

16 *Ibid.*, p. 87.

17 See Cannon, "Dominican Patronage of the Arts in Central Italy," pp. 74–108; Hood, *Fra Angelico at San Marco*, p. 295, n. 52.

18 The Carmelite Rule stated: "You must give yourselves to work of some kind, so that the devil may always find you busy; no idleness on your part must give him a chance to pierce the defenses of your souls. . . . whoever is not willing to work should not be allowed to eat either": see Clarke and Edwards, *The Rule of Saint Albert*, pp. 89–91.

19 See Ch. I above, pp. 13–14, for a more detailed description of the routine religious obligations of a Carmelite friar.

20 See Goldthwaite, *Wealth and the Demand for Art in Italy*.

21 See M. Wackernagel, *Der Lebensraum des Künstlers in der florentinischen Renaissance*, Leipzig, 1938 (trans. *The World of the Florentine Renaissance Artist*, 1981); H. Lerner-Lehmkuhl, *Zur Struktur und Geschichte des Florentinischen Kunstmarktes im 15. Jahrhundert*, Wattenscheid, 1936; Procacci, "Di Jacopo di Antonio e delle compagnie di pittori del Corso degli Adimari nel XV secolo;" Baxandall, *Painting and Experience in Fifteenth Century Italy*; Glasser, *Artists' Contracts of the Early Renaissance*; E. Borsook's review of B. Santi's edition of Neri di Bicci's *Le Ricordanze* (Pisa, 1976) in *Art Bulletin*, 1979, pp. 313–18; Thomas, *The Painter's Practice in Renaissance Tuscany*.

22 William Hood's study, *Fra Angelico at San Marco*, is the most thoroughgoing and satisfactory treatment of this subject. See also Martindale, *The Rise of the Artist in the Middle Ages and Early Renaissance*, ch. 3: "The Artist in the Cloister," pp. 65–77; Orlandi, *Beato Angelico*; Boskovits, "Su Don Silvestro, Don Simone e la 'Scuola degli Angeli';" Even, "Artistic Collaboration in Florentine Workshops," ch. 5: "Monastic Enterprises: Fra Filippo Lippi;" Bent, "Santa Maria degli Angeli and the Arts."

23 See J. Baudrillard, *For a Critique of the Political Economy of the Sign*, St. Louis, 1981, pp. 112–13.

24 See Boskovits's critical discussion in "Su Don Silvestro," pp. 35ff, and Bent, "Santa Maria degli Angeli," vol. I, pp. 242–326. On Fra Angelico's workshop, see Cardile, "Fra Angelico," pp. 52, 56 and 390; Pope-Hennessy, *Fra Angelico*, p. 8; Orlandi, *Beato Angelico*, pp. 152–6.

25 The monastery of Monte Oliveto hired the illuminator Venturino d'Andrea Mercati da Milano in 1472 to come and live in the monastery with his *garzone* and illuminate the convent manuscripts. While at Monte Oliveto, he was referred to in the monastery books as "our illuminator": see Borghesi and Banchi, *Nuovi documenti per la storia dell'arte senese*, p. 207.

26 "don Lorenzo dipintore da siene del nostro ordine," O. Siren, *Lorenzo Monaco*, Strassburg, 1905, p. 179.

27 See Borghesi and Banchi, *Nuovi documenti per la storia dell'arte senese*, p. 211.

28 "Nel detto monasterio degli Angeli . . . vi fiorirono ancora per lungo spazio di molti anni, e prima e poi, uomini eccellenti nelle cose del disegno," Vasari–Milanesi, vol. II, pp. 21–2.

29 "Sempre per addietro attesero i monaci alla pittura e al disegno," Vasari–Milanesi, vol. II, p. 21; trans. Vasari–De Vere, vol. II, p. 56.

30 The term *scriptorium* was first applied to Benedictine monastic complexes during the tenth century. It was typically staffed by a librarian, an archivist, a copyist, and a "pergamenarius": see M. Rotto, "Lo Scriptorium monastico," *Codici liturgici miniati dei Benedettini in Toscana*, ed. M. Ciardi Dupré Dal Poggetto, Florence, 1982, pp. 47–73.

31 *Officina* was the term used to identify a work space in medieval plans and descriptions of Benedictine monasteries (notably, the famous St. Gall plan): see Swartwout, *The Monastic Craftsman*, pp. 28ff. For a bibliography on the fifteenth-century Florentine monastic painter's workplace, see Even, "Artistic Collaboration in Florentine Workshops," pp. 112ff.

32 Don Niccolò di Rossello went to live in the Florentine Badia in 1443 to illuminate a Grand Psalter for the Benedictines. He agreed to work every day excluding Sundays and feast days, receiving a daily salary of s. 5, and was accommodated in the refectory: see Levi d'Ancona, *Miniatura e miniatori a Firenze*, pp. 216–17. Another Camaldolese monk, Don Simone, worked under similar conditions in the Florentine Carmine in 1388, pp. 239ff.

33 Placido Lugano provides a chronological chart of the documented activities of each Olivetan illuminator and scribe in his *Memorie dei più antichi miniatori e calligrafi Olivetani*. These tables reveal that the monks moved frequently from one convent to another, usually within the same province.

34 These include the Camaldolesi Don Simone and Don Lorenzo Monaco (see Levi d'Ancona, *Miniatura e miniatori*, p. 240, and below n. 37), Fra Angelico (see below n. 35), and Fra Filippo Lippi.

35 The *garzoni* working with Fra Angelico were his nephew Giovanni d'Antonio, Carlo di Lazzaro da Narni, Jacopo d'Antonio da Poli, and Piero Jacomo da Forlì: see Orlandi, *Beato Angelico*, p. 95.

36 See Borgo, *The Works of Mariotto Albertinelli*, pp. 122–52.

37 Boskovits, "Su Don Silvestro," p. 49 (my translation). See also Metropolitan Museum of Art, *Painting and Illumination in Early Renaissance Florence*, pp. 124–6; 195–217. Bent, perhaps too reductively, concludes that with the exception of Lorenzo Monaco, the pictorial decoration of manuscripts at Santa Maria degli Angeli was contracted out to professional secular painters, "Santa Maria degli Angeli and the Arts," vol. I, pp. 279–302.

38 See the list of manuscripts produced by these three monasteries in Levi d'Ancona, *Miniatura e miniatori*, pp. 397–400 and 407–10.

39 On Battista di Biagio Sanguigni, see Levi d'Ancona, *Miniatura e miniatori*, p. 59 (while there is no record of his matriculation into the guild, his death is given in the guild's *Necrologium*). On Fra Angelico's training, see D. Cole, *Fra Angelico: His Role in Quattrocento Painting*, Ph.D. dissertation, University of Virginia, New York, 1977, p. 67ff. On Zanobi Strozzi, see Cardile, "Fra Angelico," p. 390, and Levi d'Ancona, pp. 261–8.

40 While the guild did not have much control over those painters who chose not to join, it was able to prevent its members from collaborating with them: see Fiorilli, "I dipintori a Firenze," pp. 20, 22 and 26.

41 "Abitazioni ad uso di bottega . . . da far colori" (from a description dating c. 1529 after the destruction of the convent): see P. Bensi, "Gli Arnesi dell'Arte: I Gesuati di San Giusto alle mura e la pittura del Rinascimento a Firenze," *Studi di Storia delle arti*, 1980, p. 39.

42 The richest source of apprentice contracts is Neri di Bicci's *Ricordanze* where he records contracts and transactions with some twenty apprentices from 1453 to 1475, *Le Ricordanze*, p. XXIX.

43 See Fiorilli, "I dipintori a Firenze," p. 26.

44 Andrew Martindale arrives at the same conclusion for the medieval period, *The Rise of the Artist*, p. 70.

45 See nn. 34 and 37 above.

46 Vasari–Milanesi, vol. IV, p. 200. Milanesi noted that Fra Paolino (c. 1490–1547) was the son of a painter and probably learned the rudiments of painting from his father before becoming a Dominican, p. 212. As a friar, he continued to paint under the influence of Fra Bartolomeo and later, according to Vasari, was the teacher of the Dominican painter nun Suor Plautilla Nelli (1523–87/88), vol. V, pp. 79–80; see also Sutherland Harris and Nochlin, *Women Artists*, pp. 20–1.

47 See Lugano, *Di Fra Giovanni da Verona*. Fra Sebastiano de Istria, who professed in 1460 in his 40s, brought his craft to the monastery and his principal follower was Fra Giovanni da Verona (d. 1537). A handful of Olivetan friars of the subsequent generation appear

to have trained under Fra Sebastiano and Fra Giovanni, becoming accomplished woodworkers in their own right: Fra Antonio da Venezia (oblate, d. 1548), Fra Raffaello da Brescia (*converso*, professed 1502, d. 1531), and Fra Vincenzo de Vachi (professed 1498, d. 1531). By the next generation, the Olivetan "school" of woodworkers had begun to atrophy.

48 See Lugano, *Memorie*, p. 24, and Levi d'Ancona, *Miniatura e miniatori*, p. 8.

49 See Lugano, *Memorie*, p. 47.

50 "Restandogli in mano danari per colori e per le cose necessarie del dipignere," Vasari–Milanesi, vol. IV, p. 200; Vasari–De Vere, vol. IV, p. 162.

51 See Ch. 1 above, pp. 16–18.

52 "Per una soma di legnie per fare colla per dipigniere la chassa del beato Andrea" (Jan. 11, 1440/41); some days later, he was paid again for wood. See Ch. 5 below, pp. 102–3.

53 "Era dispensato ne'frati, che in coro a ufficio nessuno non andasse," Vasari–Milanesi, vol. IV, p. 200; Vasari–De Vere, vol. IV, p. 162. Vasari claimed that initially, after professing, Fra Bartolomeo ceased to paint for four years, but that he was "pregato molto dal priore e dagli amici suoi più cari che e' facesse qualche cosa di pittura," vol. IV, p. 182.

54 From "nostro miniatore" to "loro miniatore," Borghesi and Banchi, *Nuovi documenti*, p. 207. It was particularly in reformed orders like the Olivetans that a friar who was assigned to a new monastery became a member of the new chapter. This was designed to prevent stagnation and corruption in individual monasteries: see Hay, *The Church in Italy*, p. 77. In contrast, the Carmelite Lippi was listed as a vested friar in Santa Maria del Carmine even when he was serving as the sacristan in the Siena Carmelite monastery San Niccolò from November, 1428 to August, 1429, ASF, Con. Sopp. 113, n. 85, c. 152.

55 Orlandi, *Beato Angelico*, pp. 194–5.

56 "Die 3 Julii concessum est fratri Johanni de lavezolis de ferraria quod possit stare extra conventus ordinis cum honesta societate donec perficiat summi pontificis fenestras vitreas, et quod possit acceptare beneficium curatum vel non curatum interveniente auctoritate sedis apostolice. Valeat eciam eligere confessorem ordinis et idoneum qui quater in anno absolvat eum ab his de quibus potest magister ordinis. possit eciam elimosinas recipere et eas infra ordinem dispensare." Orlandi, *Beato Angelico*, p. 190, n. 14.

57 The story is from the *Cronaca* of P. Girolamo Borselli (d. 1497). My translation is derived from Orlandi's Italian translation in *Fra Angelico*, p. 149.

58 See Orlandi, *Beato Angelico*, p. 111.

59 See Eisenberg, *Lorenzo Monaco*, pp. 4–5, 211–15. San Bartolomeo, where Lorenzo Monaco first resided, was the parish where the Corso degli Adimari (lined with painters' *botteghe*) was located: see Procacci, "Di Jacopo di Antonio," pp. 3–70. Lorenzo bought the house beside Santa Maria degli Angeli in 1414, with the stipulation that it would devolve to the monastery upon his death. According to the contract, when Don Lorenzo was out of town, the monks of Santa Maria degli Angeli were to rent out the house, and turn over the income to the painter. Lorenzo's lay assistants when he was painting an altarpiece for the church of Sant'Egidio in 1421–22 were Giovannino di Francesco and Franceschino di Giovanni.

60 The Observant Franciscan Jacopo di Filippo di Matteo Torelli, who came from a prominent family of miniaturists, was paid for his work on a gradual for SS. Annunziata in 1472 by the illuminated letter: "Frate Jacopo di Filippo miniatore de avere l.32 s.2 d.8 sono per miniatura di 268 lettere di penna a s.2 d.4 l'una e 2 di pennello," Levi d'Ancona, *Miniatura e miniatori*, p. 165. Don Simone, from Santa Maria degli Angeli, was paid "3 soldi a day, according to his rate, not including meals and Sundays" when he contracted to work for the *frati* of Santa Maria del Carmine in 1388, while a year later, working again for the Carmelites, he was paid by the letter (thirty initials in brush at 26 *soldi* a piece), Levi d'Ancona, *Miniatura e miniatori*, p. 239. The Dominican glazier Fra Bernadino di Stefano was paid by the Florentine Opera del Duomo in 1415, at the rate of fl.3 l.3 for each square *braccia* of glass: see Marchese, *Memorie dei più insigni pittori, sculturi e architetti Domenicani*, 1869, vol. I, p. 498; *Necrologio di S. Maria Novella*, vol. II, pp. 215–16.

61 See Orlandi, *Beato Angelico*, p. 173; *Necrologio*, vol. II, pp. 535 and 577.

62 See Moorman, *A History of the Franciscan Order*, p. 356; *Necrologio*, vol. I, p. xxviii. The Carmelite Fra Angelo Mazzinghi is an example of a mendicant who held personal patrimony in the form of Monte shares which his brother administered for him. His brother turned over the annual interest to the Carmelite for his personal expenses, with the agreement that the shares would be passed to the heirs of his uncle upon Fra Angelo's death (which technically was in violation of the Carmelite Constitutions; see below n. 71). See the notes of Domenico Maria Manni in the Biblioteca Moreniana, Florence, *Vita del Beato Angelo Mazzinghi*, 1739, cc. 2r and 5r.

63 *Necrologio*, vol. I, p. 355, n. 29.

64 "Non dipinse maj per prezo et se l'ebbe di cosa alcuna tutto era del convento" (c. 1472), quoted in Orlandi, *Beato Angelico*, p. 196.

65 "Non mihi sit laudi quod eram velut alter Apelles sed quod lucra tuis omnia Christe dabam." These are the first two lines of the second inscription on Fra Angelico's tomb, which Girolamo Borselli, *Cronaca* (written before 1497), says that Pope Nicholas V had added to the original inscription the same year of Fra Angelico's death (1455): see Orlandi, *Beato Angelico*, pp. 146 and 196; trans. of text from Pope-Hennessy, *Fra Angelico*, p. 8.

66 "Ducati sette ci lascia per parte di pagamento d'una tavola la quale debbe dipingere Giovanni," quoted by Even, "Artistic Collaboration in Florentine Workshops," p. 117.

67 Working for the Operai of the Cathedral of Orvieto, Fra Angelico was paid at a rate of 200 fl. for the year, Gozzoli received 84 fl. and each *garzone*, 12 fl., Orlandi, *Beato Angelico*, pp. 188–9.

68 See Ch. 6 below, p. 152.

69 "Quel più siano mezzi di Frati, a mezi di Mariotto [Albertinelli]," Marchese, *Memorie dei più insigni pittori*, 1879, vol. II, pp. 606–9; Borgo, *The Works of Mariotto Albertinelli*, p. 123; Even, "Artistic Collaboration," pp. 116–17.

70 In 1335 he used some of this money to help finance the new dormitory in the convent ("Fra Giovanni da Campi reca fior. 30 del suo onorario del Ponte"): see *Necrologio*, vol. I, pp. 354–5.

71 For Lorenzo Monaco, see n. 59 above. Carmelite regulations regarding private possessions were defined in the Constitutions of 1369. A friar was required to reveal all private property to his superiors, but could keep "money, gifts, books, and other imperishable objects of notable value." These possessions reverted to the friar's convent upon his death: see Smet, *The Carmelites*, p. 81.

72 "Non exerceant artes ad proprium comodum," mentioned in Lugano, *Di Fra Giovanni da Verona*, p. 5.

73 This was Don Giuliano Amidei, Abbot of Santa Maria di Agnano in the Aretine, who received this permission from Pope Innocent VIII in 1491: see Levi d'Ancona, *Miniatura e miniatori*, p. 158; Vasari–Milanesi, vol. III, p. 229.

74 "Partissi adi 2 di settembre 1443 perche lo mando il generale suo a Vinegia [Venice] con animo di tornare adi 6 del detto mese la mattina incomincio a lavorare," Levi d'Ancona, *Miniatura e miniatori*, p. 216.

75 See Marchese, *Memorie dei più insigni pittori*, 1869, vol. I, p. 497, and *Necrologio*, vol. II, p. 216.

76 When Lippi left Florence for Prato to undertake the frescos in the *cappella maggiore* in Santo Stefano, he was still under contract to finish a painting for Lionardo Bartolini. Lippi's patrons in Prato agreed to pay a fine were the artist to fail to complete the painting on time (which indeed came to pass, and the Pratesi paid Bartolini accordingly, debiting Lippi's account): see Borsook, "Fra Filippo Lippi and the Murals for Prato Cathedral," docs. 55, 64, 65, and 113. When Giovanni de' Medici sought to engage Lippi to paint an altarpiece for King Alfonso of

Naples, he first obtained formal permission from the Pratesi who already had Lippi under contract, p. 51 and doc. 261.

77 See K. Lowe, "Rainha D. Leonor of Portugal's Patronage in Renaissance Florence and Cultural Exchange," in K. Lowe, ed., *Cultural Links between Portugal and Italy in the Renaissance*, Oxford, 1999; J. Vichi Imberciadori and P. and M. Torriti, *La Collegiata di San Gimignano e il suo Museo d'Arte Sacra*, Siena, 1988, p. 67. I thank Kate Lowe for bringing this embroidery to my attention. On the artistic production at Le Murate, see Ch. 9 below, p. 219.

78 Vasari–Milanesi, vol. II, p. 217, n. 3. Milanesi gives no reference.

79 S. Cohn, *Death and Property in Siena, 1205–1800*, Baltimore, 1988, p. 35.

80 See Borghesi and Banchi, *Nuovi documenti*, p. 210; they document the activity of the nuns from 1446 to 1475. In 1475, the Hospital of S. Maria della Scalla paid the nuns l.36 s.16 "per dugiento dodici lettere miniate a penna." This rate of about s.3 d.7 per penned initial was considerably higher than the rate of s.2 d.4 paid to the Observant Franciscan Jacopo di Filippo Torelli in 1472–73 by the Servites of SS. Annunziata in Florence.

81 See Lowe, "Women's Work at the Benedictine Convent of Le Murate in Florence."

82 See Sutherland Harris in *Women Artists*, p. 21.

83 See G. Milanesi, in Vasari–Milanesi, vol. II, p. 640. The glazier Fra Guglielmo da Marcillat left the Dominicans to become either a Benedictine or an Augustinian canon regular, Vasari–Milanesi, vol. IV, pp. 418–19, and Marchese, *Memorie dei più insigni pittori*, 1869, vol. I, p. 522. Another Dominican glazier, Fra Ambrogio di Bindo of San Domenico in Siena, joined the Camaldolesi in 1416, vol. I, p. 500.

84 See the monastic artisans and artists listed in Marchese, *ibid.*, vol. I; Lugano, *Memorie* and *Di Fra Giovanni da Verona*.

85 Boskovits, "Su Don Silvestro," pp. 41–2.

86 The two portraits by Lippi in New York and Berlin (see below pp. 129–35) are thus important exceptions. These works are manifestations of how Lippi's established artistic practice exceeded the limits characteristic of the other monastic artists of the period.

87 This is confirmed by Marchese, *Memorie dei più insigni pittori*, 1869, vol. I, p. 226, and M. Escobar, ed., *Ordini e congregazioni religiosi*, Turin, 1951, vol. I, pp. 217–18.

88 "Fra Domenico" is recorded as one of the two painters (along with Giovanni Toscani) of the frescos depicting St. Nicholas in the Ardinghelli chapel at Santa Trinita in 1424: see Paatz, *Die Kirchen von Florenz*, vol. V, p. 291. He has been associated with "Fra Domenico maestro di mini" (1404), Levi d'Ancona, *Miniatura e miniatori*, p. 82.

89 See Moorman, *History of the Franciscan Order*, p. 353; Brucker, *Renaissance Florence*, pp. 176 and 189ff.

90 See Hood, *Fra Angelico at San Marco*. See also I. M. Strunk, *Fra Angelico aus dem Dominikanerorden*, Gladbach, 1927; Cardile, "Fra Angelico;" Bent, "Santa Maria degli Angeli and the Arts."

91 See Goldthwaite, *Wealth and the Demand for Art*, pp. 69–148.

92 No one has adequately documented this tradition. Examples of medieval monastic artists who were accredited with a special relationship to the sacred subjects they represented are recorded by Swartwout, *The Monastic Craftsman*, 60–2; Martindale, *The Rise of the Artist*, pp. 67–8; V. Wylie Egbert, *The Medieval Artist at Work*, Princeton, 1967, pp. 68–9.

93 Baxandall, *Painting and Experience*, pp. 149–50.

94 "Huic data prae reliquis merito pictoribus, illi Gratia fingendae Virginis una fuit," Domenico da Corella, *Theotocon*, Book III, p. 111; trans. C. Gilbert, *Italian Art, 1400–1500: Sources and Documents*, Englewood Cliffs, 1980, p. 152.

95 "Quella tavola di San Bernardo che scrive . . . sta tanto contemplativo, che bene si conosce in lui un non so che di celeste, che resplende in quella opera a chi la considera attentamente; dove molta diligenza ed amor pose insieme," Vasari–Milanesi, vol. IV, p. 183; Vasari–De Vere, vol. IV, p. 155.

96 See Brucker, *Renaissance Florence*, p. 191, and Herlihy and Klapisch-Zuber, *Tuscans and their Families*, pp. 85–6.

97 See Hay, *The Church in Italy*, pp. 59ff, and Brucker, *Renaissance Florence*, pp. 190ff. See also Ambrogio Traversari's *Hodoeporicon* (1431–4), Florence, 1985.

98 See Borgo, *The Works of Mariotto Albertinelli*, p. 124. The friars of San Marco also presented Cardinal Giovanni de' Medici (later Leo X) with a *Nativity* by Fra Bartolomeo: see C. Fischer, *Fra Bartolommeo: Master Draughtsman of the High Renaissance*, Rotterdam, 1990, p. 292. One can also see how the Signoria itself utilized Fra Bartolomeo in its international diplomacy. In 1512, Piero Soderini gave Fra Bartolomeo's *Madonna and Child with Saints* (then in the church of San Marco) to the French ambassador as a gift, pp. 187–90. A second altarpiece from the Fra Bartolomeo–Albertinelli shop was commissioned by the French procurator of Margaret of Austria, Ferry Carondelet, in 1511, for the cathedral at Besançon, p. 235.

99 Eleven of the twenty confraternities founded in Florence between 1224 and 1400 were established in mendicant churches: see R. Weissman, *Ritual Brotherhood in Renaissance Florence*, New York, 1982, pp. 41ff.

100 J. Henderson, "Society and Religion in Renaissance Florence," *The Historical Journal*, vol. 29.1 (1986), p. 218.

101 See Hay, *The Church in Italy*, p. 66.

102 C. Walker Bynum defines the concept of *imitatio* in use by the mid-*trecento* as "shaping oneself to," "'becoming' or 'being' (not merely feeling or understanding)," *Holy Feast and Holy Fast*, p. 256.

103 My ideas on this subject are somewhat influenced by Richard Trexler. For Trexler, the *quattrocento* inaugurated what he terms "the Medicean challenge to traditional social and ritual organization" in Florence. Before this time, "the urban laity [had] shared with its clergy the task of maintaining life through ritual," joining "in prayer and procession to preserve their communities because they were sovereigns of their destinies." The Medici provided the Florentine Republic with "an incontrovertibly charismatic center" which prefigured the local potentates of the absolutist states to come. This was part of a broader transformation within Western Europe which eventually led to "the decline of local sovereignties, the integration of urban economies into world and national ones, and the outside regulation of civil precedence and order. As a result, the court assumed responsibility for maintaining life through ritual. . . . The city in the meantime turned from processions to theater," *Public Life in Renaissance Florence*, pp. xx–xxi.

104 The *Adoration of the Magi* at San Marco is considered to have been painted by the young Benozzo Gozzoli, who assisted Fra Angelico at San Marco.

CHAPTER FIVE

1 Lippi is last mentioned in the Carmine account books during this period in the vestment list of January 1432. He is next documented in Padua, on July 1, 1434, and then in Florence again on March 8, 1437, working on the Barbadori altarpiece: see Ruda, *Fra Filippo Lippi*, Doc. 1.II.15, p. 514; Doc. 3.I.1–2, p. 515; Doc. 4.II.15, p. 518. I do not accept Ruda's documentary citation of Lippi among the Carmelites of Santa Maria del Carmine in Florence on October 24, 1434. The "Lippus tomasi" listed in this notarial document is clearly a layman, Doc. 1.III.4, p. 514.

2 Fra Giovanni di Tommaso was sub-prior of the Florentine convent from June 24, 1440, to June 15, 1441. He later assisted Lippi in his curative duties at San Quirico at Legnaia, acting as his proxy in his absence (see n. 36 below).

3 See Ch. 6 below, p. 154.

4 In 1439, he completed the Barbadori altarpiece, worked for the Medici, and began the Sant'Ambrogio *Coronation of the Virgin*. His undocumented San Lorenzo *Annunciation* dates from about this time, too.

5 See Caioli, "Un altro sguardo sulla vita di Fra Filippo Lippi," p. 45; Ruda, *Fra Filippo Lippi*, Doc. 5.I, p. 519.

6 ASF, Compagnia di S. Maria delle Laudi detta di S. Agnese 98, c. 78r (Jan. 1439/40).

7 See Bayley, *War and Society in Renaissance Florence*, pp. 163ff.

8 The account of the series of visions of Giovanni Dazzi is contained in two near-contemporary sources. The earliest is the *Ricordanza* of Giovanni Dazzi. There are two existing editions – a short paragraph in the Strozziana and a longer version in the Riccardiana, Codex Chartaces, Scanzia O III, which gives day-by-day coverage and is reproduced in Richa, *Notizie istoriche delle chiese fiorentine*, vol. X, pp. 72ff. This longer version was supposedly written by Dazzi on July 6, 1440, and then transcribed on July 1, 1448. However, there is a section at the end which appears to have been added around 1463, and it is impossible to ascertain the extent to which the original text was altered. The second account of Dazzi's visions appears in the *Vita* of Andrea Corsini written by the Carmelite friar Pietro da Castagna some time between 1440 and 1459, and published by the Bollandists in 1643, *Acta Sanctorum*, vol. 2, Jan. 30.

9 The Carmelites of Santa Maria del Carmine responded to these initial prophecies recounted by Dazzi by modifying the tomb of Andrea Corsini, possibly to accommodate the growing number of people who were drawn to this site of sacred manifestation. An entry in the convent account book on June 23, 1440 reads, "Item pagai a maestri che lavorarono lo edifice del beato Andrea per parte di loro pagamento lire quatro soldi dodici l.iiii s.12," ASF, Con. Sopp. 113, n. 86, c. 22v, published by Caioli, *S. Andrea Corsini*, p. 164.

10 See Bayley, *War and Society*, pp. 167ff.

11 Each year during the 1440s, the city magistrates, the Six of the Mercanzia, and the Capitani of the guilds, joined the public in paying homage to Beato Andrea. In following decades, however, participation ebbed: see Caioli, *S. Andrea Corsini*, pp. 155–6.

12 See *ibid.*, pp. 155ff. The cult even spread to other countries. When the English Carmelite provincial Nicholas Kenton became ill in Florence, he was cured of a debilitating headache by rubbing the head and face of the image of Beato Andrea in the Carmine. When he left for England, he carried with him an image of Beato Andrea and propagated his cult there, p. 166. While the pope had officially sanctioned the cult, the Carmelites evidently had higher hopes for this exalted member of their Order. In 1464, six Florentine citizens petitioned the pope on behalf of the Carmelites for his sanctification, but Corsini was not to be canonized until the seventeenth century, pp. 171ff.

13 ASF, Not. Antecos. 16201, c. 50r. This testimony, contained in the notarial *filze* (registers) of Paolo di Lorenzo Dieciaiuti, was summarized by Fra Pietro da Castagna in his life of Beato Andrea Corsini, written between 1440 and 1459 and published in the *Acta Sanctorum*, vol. 2, p. 1073. The Carmelite scholar Andrea Sabatini made the connection between the "fratre Philippo di Thomasij" mentioned in Fra Pietro da Castagna's life of Beato Andrea, and the painter Lippi, "Fra Filippo Lippi," *Roseti del Carmelo*, 1973, pp. 227–32. The actual notarial document is presented, with a more extended discussion, in Holmes, "'Frate Filippo di Tommaso Dipintore'," pp. 331–3 and Appendix 3.

14 "Honesto et religioso probo viro frate Filippo Tomasi," ASF, Not. Antecos. 16201, c. 50r. A similar formulaic notarial language is used in the papal bull appointing Lippi rector of San Quirico at Legnaia, ASF, Not. Antecos. 14193, c. 252r.

15 "Item adì 11 [di Gennaio, 1440/41] a frate filippo per una soma di lengnie per fare colla per dipigniere la chassa del beato Andrea, soldi xi" and "Item a frate filippo adì 13 [I read 17] di gennaio per lengne per la chassa del beato Andrea, soldi 9," ASF, Con. Sopp. 113, n. 86, cc. 29r–v, cited by Caioli, "Un altro sguardo," p. 46–7; see also Ruda, *Fra Filippo Lippi*, Doc. 5.II.1, p. 519.

16 Caioli, "Un altro sguardo," p. 46.

17 Among the new Carmine patrons were "la Contessa dal Borgo alla Collina" and "Guido ispenditore de nostri magnifici signori" who "misse uno suo figliuolo nell'ordine nostro," ASF, Con. Sopp. 113, n. 86, cc. 23v and 30r.

18 ASF, Compagnia di S. Maria delle Laudi n. 98, cc. 25r and 88, and Ruda, *Fra Filippo Lippi*, Doc. 5.II.2, p. 519.

19 "Casse che lascio in camera dove abitava dinfermeria," ASF, Con. Sopp. 113, n. 86, cc. 37v and 41v, cited by Caioli, "Un altro sguardo," p. 47, and Ruda, *Fra Filippo Lippi*, Doc. 5.II.3, p. 519.

20 "La chiesa di frate iohanni di tommaso e di frate filippo," Caioli, "Un altro sguardo," p. 49; Ruda, *Fra Filippo Lippi*, Doc. 5.III. 2, p. 519; see n. 35 below for the full quote.

21 See n. 46 below.

22 See Ruda, *Fra Filippo Lippi*, Doc. 5.IV, pp. 519–20.

23 See Holmes, "'Frate Filippo di Tommaso Dipintore'," Appendix 9, and ASF, Mercanzia 1406, cc. 353v–355r; cc. 389r–391r. For Fra Bartolomeo Soderini, see Ch. 2 above, n. 13.

24 "Ad preti et a frati et vicini per lo exequio de frate Filippo" and "ad frate giovanni quando venne a spoleti lultima volta," Fausti, "Le pitture di Fra Filippo Lippi nel Duomo di Spoleto," pp. 26 and 30; Ruda, *Fra Filippo Lippi*, Doc. 27.I.43, p. 544, without the reference to *frate* Giovanni.

25 The last clear reference to Fra Giovanni di Tommaso is found in a notarial document of Jan. 22, 1454, recording that he had rented out property acting as Lippi's chaplain and procurator at San Quirico, ASF, Not. Antecos. 16202, c. 100r.

26 I thank William Hood for his helpful comments on the relationship between the *claustrum* and the *seculum* in Italy prior to the Council of Trent. See the discussion above in Ch. 4 on how monastic artists may have benefited their religious orders.

27 It is, of course, quite possible that Lippi was taken to task by his Carmelite superiors in private sessions that were not recorded. Instances of Carmelite punitive measures taken against their own members can be found in the acts of the Tuscan provincial chapter meetings: see *Atti dei capitoli provinciali*. Fra Diamante, Lippi's assistant, was imprisoned by the Carmelites in 1464 (after he had already left the Carmelites for the Vallombrosan Order) for an unrecorded transgression.

28 This information is presented without documentation by Milanesi in Vasari–Milanesi, vol. II, pp. 614 and 645. The bull is contained in the notarial register of Piero Migliorelli, ASF, Not. Antecos. 14193, cc. 252r–254r. I thank Gino Corti for his assistance with this document.

29 See G. Carocci, *Dintorni di Firenze*, Florence, 1907, vol. II, pp. 395–6. Carocci claims that the dei Bostichi were superseded by the Pucci at the end of the fourteenth century, but the proceedings from the court case involving Lippi's loss of the rectorship in the 1450s indicate that the dei Bostichi were still in control of the benefice, ASF, Not. Antecos. 13505, cc. 29r–30r. See Bizzocchi, *Chiesa e potere nella Toscana del quattrocento*, pp. 37–53, for a discussion of the relationships of rural parishes, their traditional patrons, and the Florentine episcopacy.

30 Lippi's responsibilities as rector of San Quirico are not described in the papal bull. For a detailed discussion of the responsibilities of the parish rector and priest as spelled out in the Florentine episcopal statutes, see Trexler, *Synodal Law in Florence and Fiesole*, pp. 36ff. Another source of information regarding the activities of the country priest during the *quattrocento* are the comic tales told about the Piovano Arlotto, *Facezie, Motti e Burle del Piovano Arlotto*.

31 E. Conti, *La formazione della struttura agraria moderna nel contado Fiorentino*, Rome, 1965, vol. III, part 2, pp. 248–9.

32 ASF, Not. Antecos. 14193, c. 252r.

33 During the *quattrocento*, the ecclesiastical careerists from the Florentine patrician class were drawn to the papal curia more than to local ecclesiastical institutions: see Bizzocchi, *Chiesa e potere*, pp. 13–53.

34 See *ibid.*, pp. 37–9 and n. 54 for a bibliography. See also *Facezie, Motti e Burle*. There were several papal bulls promulgated during the 1450s by Nicholas V and Callistus III treating the allocation of ecclesiastical benefices to mendicants, *Bullarium Carmelitanum*, vol. I, pp. 234 and 243. These bulls

were designed to force the generals of the various orders to take greater responsibility for the conduct of beneficed friars.

35 ASF, Con. Sopp. 113, n. 81, c. 143: "Domenicha VI post Trinitatem adj 10 di luglio. Item non facemo offerta alla messa questa mattina per rispetto della processione che si fece per andare a San Chiricho cioe alla chiesa di frate iohanni di tommaso e di frate filippo," cited in Caioli, "Un altro sguardo," pp. 48–9, and Ruda, *Fra Filippo Lippi*, Doc. 5.III.2, p. 519.

36 ASF, Diplomatico, Badia a Ripoli, 1451, 14 Ott. (the parchment fine copy) and Not. Antecos. 16202, c. 21r (the rough copy). We see an example of the affairs Fra Giovanni was transacting in his brother's name in a notarial document of 1454. Fra Giovanni, acting as "procuratore nomine frat[r]is Filippi Tommasi," rented a vineyard located on the San Quirico lands to one Andrea d'Orlando Bartolommei for 27 lire for five years, ASF, Not. Antecos. 16202, c. 100r.

37 The documents are reviewed by Ruda, *Fra Filippo Lippi*, Docs. 7 and 19, pp. 520–3 and 534–6; see also Holmes, "'Frate Filippo di Tommaso Dipintore'," Appendix 4 and 10.

38 Initially, a Dominican, Tommaso di Bernardo de Quercetani, had been nominated to the position, but it appears that this appointment did not go through, for reasons unknown: see Ruda, Doc. 19.VIII, p. 535; Holmes, "'Frate Filippo di Tommaso Dipintore'," Appendix 10, under Aug. 2 and Aug. 27.

39 ASF, Mercanzia 1406, c. 253r.

40 The information regarding Lippi's receipt of the benefice of San Niccolò de' Frieri is found without references in Vasari–Milanesi, vol. II, p. 614, n. 1. The documentation for this position is in the account book, *Libro dei debitori e creditori dal 1423 al 1461*, of San Niccolò: ASF, Con. Sopp. n. 133, n. 39, cc. 108r, 111v–112r, 115v–116r, 133v–134r. On San Niccolò de' Frieri (later known as San Giovanni de' Cavalieri), see Paatz, *Die Kirchen von Florenz*, vol. II, pp. 272ff; Richa, *Notizie istoriche*, vol. IX, pp. 97–8.

41 "honeste conversationis et fame," cited in Trexler, *Synodal Law*, pp. 215–16.

42 On June 21, 1421, the Florentine Commune established the Ufficiali de' Monasteri composed of nine married men over the age of fifty who were responsible for checking the moral conduct within the city's nunneries. The commission was later amalgamated with the Ufficiali di Notte in 1433: see Brucker, *Renaissance Florence*, pp. 192–3; M. Rocke, *Forbidden Friendships: Homosexuality and Male Culture in Renaissance Florence*, New York, 1996, pp. 46ff.

43 See R. Trexler, "The Episcopal Constitutions of Antoninus of Florence," *Quellen und Forschungen aus italienischen Archiven und Bibliotheken*, vol. 59 (1979), p. 270, no. 48.

44 No documentation has come to light regarding the official appointment of Lippi as chaplain of San Niccolò. Milanesi claims that it was through the episcopal vicar Ugolino Giungi that Lippi obtained both this position and his subsequent chaplaincy at Santa Margherita in Prato, without providing documentary references, Vasari–Milanesi, vol. II, p. 614, n. 1.

45 "Frate filippo di tommaso di frati del Carmino de' avere che sta chon cioe chon noi per nostro chappellano a dì 20 di febraio 1449 et a dire messa ogni domenicha et poi 2 della settemana et l'altre chose che ci anno fatto gli altri nostri chappellani . . . et Noi gli debiamo dare per suo salario lemosina fl.nove di lire 4 a fiorino l'anno." ASF, Con. Sopp. 133, n. 39, c. 112r.

46 This practice is in fact only documented during Feb. 1450, prior to Lippi's official appointment as chaplain (after which he was given a salary and payments for individual masses were no longer recorded), and then again on July 2, 1452. The friars filling in for Lippi were Fra Francesco di Giovanni (Feb. 3, 1450), Maestro Piero [d'Andrea da Castagna?](Feb. 15, 1450), and Fra Leonardo (around July 2, 1452), ASF, Con. Sopp. 133, n. 39, cc. 108r and 133v.

47 ASF, Con. Sopp. 133, n. 39, cc. 108r, 111v–112r, 113v, 133v–134r. The nunnery's *Libro dei debitori e creditori* provides interesting insight into Fra Filippo's expenditures during the period. He kept a running account for expenditures roughly equivalent to his salary as chaplain. He purchased wine and oil, paid the annual *decima* tax for San Quirico at Legnaia, and was involved in two separate unspecified business transactions, one with Domenico di Buonachasa Ferretti of Legnaia, and the other with Antonio di Mona Lucia, cc. 111v and 135v.

48 ASF, Con. Sopp. 133, n. 39, cc. 115v–116r. The documentation for this incident was published by C. Fabriczy, "Michelozzo di Bartolomeo." It is consequently noted in the Michelozzo literature, but never in studies on Lippi: see Caplow, *Michelozzo*, vol. I, p. 439, n. 39.

49 "La cittorono 2 volte e la prima volta venne fatta moza per manchamento di Michelozo che chosi buono maestro dj fare champane; la sechonda pure per lui che la chorona non era asciutta chel metallo quando sentj l'umido ne schizzo fuori monta." ASF, Con. Sopp. 133, n. 39, cc. 116r; Fabriczy, "Michelozzo di Bartolomeo," Doc. 18, p. 66.

50 "Frate Filippo nostro chappellano . . . fa mezano tra loro e Noi afarci fare la detta champana," ASF, Con. Sopp. 133, n. 39, c. 115v.

51 Lippi's first recorded involvement in the fresco project at Prato is dated May 6, 1452, when he was invited there to discuss the project. He received his first payment on July 11, 1452, indicating that he had begun to paint by this time: see Borsook, "Fra Filippo and the Murals for Prato Cathedral," pp. 75–7; Ruda, *Fra Filippo Lippi*, Docs. 13.I.2 and 4, p. 527.

52 Milanesi claimed that Lippi became the *cappellano* of Santa Margherita at the beginning of 1456, Vasari–Milanesi, vol. II, p. 635. The only documented confirmation of this title is the *tamburazione* of 1461 (see p. 106 below).

53 Vasari, in fact, was not aware that Lippi was the *cappellano* of the nunnery and he thus used the occasion of Lippi's painting the altarpiece to unite Lucrezia Buti with the artist, Vasari–Milanesi, vol. II, p. 620.

54 See M. Mannini, ed., *Il Museo Civico di Prato*, Florence, 1990, pp. 79–80.

55 The documents inform us that Lucrezia Buti and her sister Spinetta were placed in Santa Margherita in 1451, at the ages of sixteen and seventeen, by their brother Antonio, following the death of their father Francesco. They had both professed by April 8, 1454, when they are mentioned in a deliberation regarding the sale of a piece of land by the convent, Vasari–Milanesi, vol. II, p. 634.

56 This is the sequence of events related by Milanesi, *ibid.*, p. 636. The only document which he cites is the notarial protocol recording the retaking of the nuns' vows on Dec. 23, 1459, ASF, Not. Antecos. 19449 (Dietaiuti di Lapo Spighi da Prato 1457–59), cc. 405r–v. The document is a dry, formulaic description of the profession of the five nuns with no mention of a scandal or the fact that the nuns were taking their vows anew. It is not clear how Milanesi came about his information regarding the flight of the five nuns from Santa Margherita, and Lucrezia and Spinetta taking up residence in Lippi's house. A review of Dietaiuti di Lapo's notarial registers has revealed nothing further.

57 ASF, Not. Antecos. 19450, cc. 98v–101v. See Holmes, "'Frate Filippo di Tommaso Dipintore'," Appendix 11, under 1461. The property, located in Villa Coiano alla Colombaia (northeast of Prato), consisted of half of an undivided house with an orchard and accompanying land. It is possible that Lucrezia Buti could have been behind this property transaction, being the unnamed disciple in the sales agreement. A country residence would have provided Lucrezia and Filippino with a permanent abode and quelled the scandal to some extent.

58 For the full text of the *tamburazione*, see Milanesi's transcription in Vasari–Milanesi, vol. II, p. 637, n. 4; see also Ruda, *Fra Filippo Lippi*, Doc. 24, p. 540.

59 "E 'l detto frate Filippo à avuto uno figliuolo maschio d'una che si chiama Spinetta. E detto fanciullo à in casa: è grande, e à nome Filippino," Vasari–Milanesi, *ibid.* See also Ruda, *Fra Filippo Lippi*, Doc. 24, p. 540. Lippi's son, the painter Filippino Lippi, pro-

vides the confirmation of the relationship between Lucrezia and Lippi, naming Lucrezia as his mother in his will: see Nelson, "Aggiunte alla cronologia di Filippino Lippi," pp. 55–7.

60 "Detto ser Piero à usato e usa al Munisterio di Sancta Margherita di Prato . . . quando lo volete trovare, ogni dì ve lo troverete lui e un altro che si chiama Frate Filippo: e lui si schusa con essere chappellano, e l'altro con essere procuratore," Vasari–Milanesi, *ibid.*

61 Lippi was well connected in Prato, falling into the protective patronage nets of many of the high ecclesiastic and civil officials. The Podestà of Prato (until his death on Sept. 9, 1458) was Piero Corsini, a relative of the Carmelite Beato Andrea Corsini. Piero had himself commissioned Lippi to paint his arms in the Palazzo del Podestà along with other small commissions. The provost of the Pieve, Gemignano Inghirami (d. 1460), commissioned Lippi to fresco his burial chapel in the church of San Francesco in Prato, while his successor, Carlo de' Medici, was the natural son of Lippi's principal patron, Cosimo de' Medici. In addition, Prato was in the diocese of Pistoia, presided over by another Medici, Bishop Donato de' Medici.

62 "Dello errore di Fra Filippo naviamo riso un pezzo" (May 27, 1458, in a letter from Giovanni de' Medici to Bartolomeo Serragli), reproduced in Ruda, *Fra Filippo Lippi*, Doc. 21.III.1, p. 537. It is assumed that this refers to Lippi's scandalous relationship with the nuns of Santa Margherita. The birth of his illegitimate son is thought to have occurred around this time.

63 In his will of Sept. 21, 1488, Filippino Lippi left a house in Prato to his sister Alessandra as part of her dowry. Filippino had arranged her marriage with Ciardo di Giuliano Ciardi da Tavola around 1487, Vasari–Milanesi, vol. II, p. 638.

64 Wittkower, *Born Under Saturn*, p. 157.

65 *Ibid.*, pp. 181ff.

66 Ruda, *Fra Filippo Lippi*, Doc. 10. I, p. 524.

67 See Bombe, "Urkunden über ein verschollenes Altarbild Filippo Lippis." While the determinations of the court are not known, Bombe concluded that the case was decided in Lippi's favor because payments were made to the painter and to those who supplied him with his materials on Sept. 24, by the prior of San Marco who was acting as a go-between or facilitator.

68 ASF, Not. Antecos. 9170, c. 20r.

69 See Borsook, "Fra Filippo Lippi and the Murals for Prato Cathedral," docs. 55, 64, 65, and 113; Ruda, *Fra Filippo Lippi*, Doc. 14, pp. 531–2.

70 See Mendelsohn, *Fra Filippo Lippi*, pp. 233–4; Glasser, *Artists' Contracts of the Early Renaissance*, p. 191; Ruda, *Fra Filippo Lippi*, Doc. 16, pp. 532–3.

71 See Ruda, *Fra Filippo Lippi*, Doc. 19, pp. 534–6; Holmes, "'Frate Filippo di Tommaso Dipintore'," Appendix, 4 and 10.

72 Ruda, *Fra Filippo Lippi*, Doc. 20.I–III, p. 536.

73 See nn. 37–8 above.

74 ASF, Mercanzia 1406, cc. 253r–v, 261r, 353v–355r, 369r–370r, and 391v–392r; Holmes, "'Frate Filippo di Tommaso Dipintore'," Appendix 9.

75 Vasari–Milanesi, vol. II, p. 637, n. 4; Ruda, *Fra Filippo Lippi*, Doc. 24, p. 540.

76 See Borsook, "Fra Filippo Lippi and the Murals for Prato Cathedral," pp. 124–5, n. 241 and doc. 416.

77 See *ibid.*, pp. 65ff; Ruda, *Fra Filippo Lippi*, Doc. 13.II.9–11, pp. 529–31.

78 Giuseppe Marchini has characterized Lippi's writing as "diritta, rotonda, chiara, con poche abbreviazioni e invece certi nessi eseguiti con un tratto scorrevole senza soluzione di continuità." He identifies it as a "scrittura mercantesca," acquired in the pragmatic workplace rather than in the convent, "Una curiosità sul Lippi," *Archivio storico pratese*, vol. 51, ser. II (1975), p. 174. See the discussion of Lippi's two letters to his Medici patrons below, ch. 6, pp. 154–5.

79 "Obscura, inepta et malfatta, et non procede et non conchiude et mancha delli suoi debiti requisiti, et le cose in quella contenute et nominate furono et non sono vere," Bombe, "Urkunden," p. 118; trans. D. S. Chambers, *Patrons and Artists in the Italian Renaissance*, Glasgow, 1970, p. 203.

CHAPTER SIX

1 See the proposed chronology of the paintings and catalogue entries in the three most recent monographs, Marchini, *Filippo Lippi*, Ruda, *Fra Filippo Lippi*, and Mannini and Fagioli, *Filippo Lippi*. While the notion of "artistic style" was arguably vague and undefined during the first half of the fifteenth century, pictorial qualities and artistic innovations were increasingly discernible, commodified features of works of art, which figured in their valuation as inspired artistic expression and as material goods in the marketplace. In discussing Lippi's paintings, I shall draw upon a lexicon of pictorial style provided by Baxandall in *Painting and Experience in Fifteenth-Century Italy*, pp. 128–39ff. Baxandall uses, as a point of departure, Cristoforo Landino's descriptions of the outstanding Florentine artists of the century in the Preface of his "Commentary" on Dante's *Divine Comedy* (1481). Landino wrote about Lippi: "Fu fra Philippo gratioso et ornato et artificioso sopra modo: valse molto nelle compositioni et varieta, nel colorire, nel rilievo, negli ornamenti d'ogni sorte, maxime o imitati dal vero o ficti," quoted by Baxandall, p. 118.

Cennino Cennini used the terms "maniera" and "aria" to define the characteristics of a good master that should be emulated by one learning to draw ("guarda di pigliar sempre il migliore [maestro] e quello che ha maggior fama; e, seguitando di dì in dì, contra natura sarà che a te non venga preso di suo' maniera i di suo' aria"), *Il Libro dell'arte*, Cap. XXVII, ed. M. Serchi, Florence, 1991, p. 36. On the development of the concept of *maniera* in Italian Renaissance art, see J. Shearman, "Mannerism as an Aesthetic Ideal," in *Renaissance Art*, ed. C. Gilbert, New York, 1970, pp. 184ff. Stephen Campbell has recently defined artistic style in a fifteenth-century court culture as "a set of gestures or signs, through which an artist performs his distinctiveness and virtuosity. Quality and individuality become inter-dependent, to the extent that individuality becomes a conventionalized version of quality," "Pictura and Scriptura," p. 273.

2 See Ch. 1 above, p. 14.

3 See Ruda, *Fra Filippo Lippi*, p. 26 and n. 11.

4 Fra Filippo's name does not occur among the lists of friars of Santa Maria del Carmine after 1432. It is not until 1442 that we have any record of his whereabouts in Florence, when he received the benefice of San Quirico at Legnaia, which must have served as an occasional residence. In 1450, he was living on Via Chiara, near the Carmine, ASF, Con. Sopp. 133, n. 39, cc. 108r and 133v. In 1451, he came into the possession of half of a house that had belonged to his father on Borgo San Frediano, and it is possible that he set up residence there, ASF, Mercanzia 1406, cc. 253r–v, 261r, 353v–355r, 369r–370r, and 391–392r; see also Ruda, *Fra Filippo Lippi*, Doc. 9, p. 524, for his possible co-ownership of a house in the parish of San Felice in Piazza in 1451. See also n. 13 below.

5 See the discussion of his early style and painting technique in Ch. 1 above, pp. 14–20.

6 See Baxandall, *Painting and Experience*, pp. 135–7.

7 See John Shearman's discussion of Lippi in *Only Connect . . .*, pp. 70–8.

8 Fra Angelico offers an interesting contrast here. Just as Fra Angelico effected a more mediated relationship between the sacred figures in his painting and the viewer than did Fra Filippo, so the Dominican painter's experience of secular society was a more mediated one than Lippi's, given the former's choice to live and work within the convent.

9 In his *Memoriale di molte statue et picture sono nella inclypta cipta di Florentia* (1510), Albertini mentioned two altarpieces by Lippi located in Santa Maria Nuova: see Marchini, *Filippo Lippi*, p. 216. Jonathan Nelson has recently found documentary confirmation for one of these paintings. In 1443, there is a record in an account book of the hospital for the purchase of gold leaf for an altarpiece that the rector of the hospital, Michele di Frusino,

had commissioned from Lippi, ASF, Ospedale di Santa Maria Nuova, n. 4490, c. 54v. Two years later, on Feb. 17, 1445, another account book recorded a debt owed by Lippi pertaining to "una tavola daltare che ser Michele di Frusino gli dette a dipingere piu tempo fa," ASF, Ospedale di Santa Maria Nuova, n. 5818, c. 85v. I thank Jonathan Nelson for these references. See also Holmes, "'Frate Filippo di Tommaso Dipintore'," Appendix, 6.

10 Baxandall, *Painting and Experience*, pp. 128–39ff.

11 Ruda also made this observation, *Fra Filippo Lippi*, p. 151. The only painting in this group of works exhibiting the influence of Fra Angelico that is securely dated is the *Vision of St. Bernard* (1447). For this reason, it is difficult to date these works with any certainty, although following Bernard Berenson's "Fra Angelico, Fra Filippo e la cronologia," most scholars place them in the late 1440s and early 1450s.

12 Interestingly, both Fra Angelico and Donatello were away from Florence during much of this period. Fra Angelico was in Orvieto and Rome from 1445 to 1448, while Donatello was working in Padua, Mantua, Modena, and Ferrara from 1444 to 1453. The absence of these two significant figures in the Florentine artistic scene could have provoked a crisis of style in Lippi, or perhaps challenged him to pick up the mantle of the Dominican *frate dipintore* and work in a stylistic mode potentially more readily associated with a religious painter.

13 Lippi clearly had a residence in Florence in 1455, when the archiepiscopal nuncio sought him at his house (location not given), only to be informed by his sister that he was in Prato: Ruda, *Fra Filippo Lippi*, Doc. 19. IV, p. 535. In 1455, he bought a house in Prato from the Opera del Sacro Cingolo where he lived during his stay in Prato. He purchased a second property in Prato in 1468 (after he had gone to Spoleto): see Borsook, "Fra Filippo Lippi and the Murals for Prato Cathedral," p. 48; Ruda, *Fra Filippo Lippi*, Doc. 27. I. 25, p. 543. For a reference to payments to the Hospital of Santa Maria Nuova in Florence for a house in Prato in 1457, see Nelson, "Aggiunte alla cronologia di Filippino Lippi," pp. 37–8. See n. 4 above for his earlier Florentine residences and properties.

14 I am making the assumption that the frescos in the cloister at the Dominican convent Santa Maria Novella and in the more "public" of the monastic buildings in the Observant Dominican convent San Marco would have been accessible to the Carmelite friar painter. Andrea del Castagno's frescos executed in 1447, in the refectory and cloister of the Benedictine nunnery Sant'Apollonia, which obviously would have been of interest to Lippi, may not have been accessible.

15 See Borsook, "Fra Filippo Lippi and the Murals for Prato Cathedral," pp. 21 and 28.

16 See n. 1 above.

17 Most scholars agree that Lippi's pictorial style was significantly influenced by Netherlandish painting, particularly in the works dating from the late 1430s and 40s: see Oertel, *Fra Filippo Lippi*, pp. 16–22; M. Meiss, "Jan van Eyck and the Italian Renaissance" (1956) in *The Painter's Choice: Problems in the Interpretation of Renaissance Art*, New York, 1976, pp. 24–6; Ames-Lewis, "Fra Filippo Lippi and Flanders," who has even gone so far as to posit a trip to northern Europe during the mid-1430s when Lippi appears to have been absent from Florence; Rowlands, "Fra Filippo Lippi's Stay in Padua and its Impact on his Art," pp. 87–130. Ruda, however, has systematically refuted the arguments for Flemish influence, pointing instead to local Italian precedents for most of these features that appear in the painter's work. He also argues that Lippi would have had limited access to the works of his Flemish contemporaries, particularly during the late 1430s and 40s, when the supposed Flemish influence on his painting was most pronounced, "Flemish Painting and the Early Renaissance in Florence: Questions of Influence," *Zeitschrift für Kunstgeschichte*, vol. 47 (1984), pp. 210–36; *Fra Filippo Lippi*, pp. 126–33. See also Pittaluga, *Filippo Lippi*, p. 52.

18 While the documented examples of Flemish paintings and painters in Italy during the first half of the fifteenth century are very scanty, there is nonetheless evidence to suggest that Netherlandish painting was known and valued in Italy at an early date. Van Eyck painted the portrait of the Italian Cardinal of Santa Croce, Niccolò Albergati (fig. 111), probably during 1431 when Albergati was in the Burgundian court as papal legate: see L. Baldass, *Jan van Eyck*, London, 1952, p. 280. The Cardinal is presumed to have brought the portrait back to Italy with him. A painting by van Eyck of St. Jerome in his study was in the possession of Alfonso of Naples by 1456 and may be the work dated 1442 now in Detroit, *ibid.*, p. 276. In 1449, the Venetian Marco Barbarigo had his portrait painted by a follower of van Eyck in London and he returned to Venice with the work: see L. Campbell, "Notes on Netherlandish Pictures in the Veneto in the Fifteenth and Sixteenth Centuries," *Burlington Magazine*, vol. 123 (1981), p. 468. Ciriaco d'Ancona saw a Deposition by Rogier van der Weyden in Ferrara in 1449, and there are payments made by Lionello d'Este to him in 1450, the same year that he traveled to Rome for the Jubilee: see M. Davies, *Rogier van der Weyden*, London, 1972, p. 212. These isolated documented examples suggest a greater degree of incidence of Flemish painting circulating in Italy c. 1430–50, the crucial years for Lippi. By the 1460s, during the final decade of Lippi's life, documented examples are more plentiful. In 1460, Alessandra Strozzi received a cache of Flemish paintings from her son Niccolò, which she resold in Florence at a profit, while in 1466, the Medici ordered Flemish pictures from their Bruges agent to decorate their Florentine palace: see L. Campbell, "The Art Market in the Southern Netherlands in the Fifteenth Century," *Burlington Magazine*, vol. 118 (1976), pp. 196–7.

19 On the emergence of the *tavola quadrata*, see Gardner von Teuffel, "Lorenzo Monaco, Filippo Lippi und Filippo Brunelleschi" and "From Polyptych to Pala;" Hills, "The Renaissance Altarpiece;" Miller, "Major Florentine Altarpieces from 1430 to 1450." Discussions about the development of the *sacra conversazione* often cover similar ground.

20 Alberti, *On Painting and On Sculpture*, pp. 48–9 and 54–5.

21 For a general discussion of mathematical perspective in early *quattrocento* Florence, see M. Kemp, *The Science of Art*, New Haven and London, 1992, pp. 11–26. See also Shearman's interesting discussion of the implications of this "shared space" in early *quattrocento* Florentine religious representation in *Only Connect . . .*, pp. 59–78.

22 On medieval image theory, see Belting, *Likeness and Presence*; Camille, *The Gothic Idol*. On medieval image theory in a fifteenth-century Florentine context, see R. Trexler, "Florentine Religious Experience: The Sacred Image," *Studies in the Renaissance*, vol. 19 (1972), pp. 7–41, and *Public Life in Renaissance Florence*, pp. 61–73; Didi-Huberman, *Fra Angelico*.

23 Didi-Huberman, *Fra Angelico*, p. 45.

24 Eliade, *The Sacred and the Profane*, pp. 20–4.

25 Camille, *Gothic Idol*, p. 230.

26 Shearman pointed to Masaccio's Pisa polyptych (1426) as a key transitional work in the development of the *tavola quadrata*, "Masaccio's Pisa Altar-piece: An Alternative Reconstruction," *Burlington Magazine*, vol. 108 (1966), pp. 449–55. In his reconstruction of the dismantled and fragmentary work, Shearman proposed a wide rectangular central panel incorporating the London National Gallery *Madonna and Child* at its center surrounded by (now lost) saints, surmounted with gabled moldings, in which the sacred figures all congregated within a well defined continual pictorial space. While there is no doubt that Masaccio provided an important impetus in the evolution of the *tavola quadrata*, Shearman's reconstruction effectively downplays the role of Lippi's Barbadori altarpiece by suggesting that Masaccio in-

vented the innovative spatial configuration found in Lippi's altarpiece.

27 For a discussion and bibliography, see Ruda, *Fra Filippo Lippi*, pp. 101–15 and 392–6. See also Shearman, *Only Connect . . .*, pp. 70–3. The main panel of the altarpiece is now in the Louvre and the predella in the Uffizi.

28 White, *The Birth and Rebirth of Pictorial Space*, p. 172.

29 Shearman, *Only Connect . . .*, p. 73.

30 See Ruda, "A 1434 Building Programme," pp. 358–61.

31 The painting measures 175 × 183 cm. For a discussion and bibliography, see Ruda, *Fra Filippo Lippi*, pp. 115–26 and 399–403; Marchini, *Filippo Lippi*, p. 203.

32 See Ames-Lewis, "Fra Filippo Lippi's S. Lorenzo *Annunciation*," p. 160.

33 White, *Birth and Rebirth*, p. 176.

34 On the dating, see Ruda, *Fra Filippo Lippi*, p. 402.

35 On its physical structure, see Gardner von Teuffel, "Lorenzo Monaco," pp. 18–19 and Abb. 18; Ames-Lewis, "Fra Filippo Lippi's S. Lorenzo *Annunciation*," pp. 155–6 and fig. 2.

36 Giovanni di Francesco de Cervelliera, who was working in Lippi's shop in 1440, has been suggested as the artist responsible for the predella: see Bellosi, *Pittura di Luce*, pp. 31–7.

37 This position is held by Shearman, who suggests that the panels originally constituted organ shutters: see Gardner von Teuffel, "Lorenzo Monaco," p. 18, and Ames-Lewis, who speculates that they formed the doors of a reliquary cabinet in the Medici chapel at the end of the left transept of San Lorenzo, "Fra Filippo Lippi's S. Lorenzo *Annunciation*," pp. 155–63.

38 Hood, *Fra Angelico at San Marco*, pp. 102–7 and pp. 310–11, n. 34. Christa Gardner von Teuffel argues for Lippi, "Lorenzo Monaco," pp. 17–24; "From Polyptych to Pala," pp. 327–8. She is supported by Ruda, *Fra Filippo Lippi*, pp. 117 and 399–401. William Hood makes the case for Fra Angelico's Annalena altarpiece in *Fra Angelico at San Marco*, p. 107. Two transitional works that need mentioning here are Fra Angelico's *Annunciation* (mid-1420s) for San Domenico in Cortona and Bicci di Lorenzo's rectangular *Nativity* altarpiece (1435) in San Giovannino de' Cavalieri. While set within square framing elements, these narrative altarpieces are not considered fully realized *tavole quadrate* on account of their archaic frame designs: see Gardner von Teuffel, "Lorenzo Monaco," p. 22; Ruda, "A 1434 Building Programme for San Lorenzo in Florence," p. 358, n. 5. The dating of the Annalena work has swung between the mid-1430s to the mid-1450s: see Pope-Hennessy, *Fra Angelico*, p. 211. The later date is tied to the founding of the Florentine convent of San Vincenzo d'Annalena where the painting was housed at the time of the convent's suppression in 1810. Most scholars, however, have recognized the earlier style of the painting, and Mario Salmi identified the altarpiece as the "prima unitaria tavola rinascimentale" in his 1958 monograph on Fra Angelico, cited by Orlandi, *Beato Angelico*, p. 45.

39 See Pope-Hennessy, *Fra Angelico*, pp. 211–12. The painting, now in the Museo di San Marco, is lacking its original frame.

40 Hood, *Fra Angelico at San Marco*, p. 102.

41 See Orlandi, *Beato Angelico*, pp. 71–4, Pope-Hennessy, *Fra Angelico*, pp. 199–202; Hood, *Fra Angelico at San Marco*, pp. 107–21.

42 See Pope-Hennessy, *Fra Angelico*, p. 199; on the original frame design, see p. 201.

43 See Didi-Huberman's reflections on the impact of Albertian and Brunelleschian perspective on the temporal and spatial dimensions of religious representation in *Fra Angelico*, pp. 132ff. See also my discussion of Lippi's *pala* for the novitiate chapel of Santa Croce in Ch. 8 below. Lippi's other *tavole quadrate* dating from the 1440s are his Annunciations in Rome and Munich. Fra Angelico's rectangular altarpiece for Bosco ai Frati is dated by Pope-Hennessy c. 1450–52, *Fra Angelico*, p. 215.

44 Gardner von Teuffel has discussed how Neri di Bicci's recorded contracts in the *Ricordanze* define the structural components of the *all'antica*-framed *tavola quadrata*. She cites a 1455 collaboration with Giuliano da Maiano: "una tavola d'altare . . . quadra, al'anticha, chon predella da pie', cholonne a chanali da lato e architrave, fregio, chornicione e foglia di sopra," "From Polyptych to Pala," p. 325.

45 See C. Filippini, "Il recupero del fondo d'oro e altre tendenze," in Gregori, Paolucci, and Acidini Luchinat, *Maestri e Botteghe*, pp. 181–98; Jacob Burckhardt's chapter "The Survival of the Polyptych in the Renaissance," in his *The Altarpiece in Renaissance Italy*, trans. and ed. P. Humfrey, Oxford, 1988, pp. 56–63.

46 The painting was later cut up, so that the original framing and the disposition of the lateral saints cannot be determined: see Ruda, *Fra Filippo Lippi*, pp. 429–32.

47 See M. Kemp, "Introduction: The altarpiece in the Renaissance: a taxonomic approach," and P. Hills, "The Renaissance altarpiece: a valid category?" both in Humfrey and Kemp, *The Altarpiece in the Renaissance*, pp. 1–20 and 34–48. See also the essays in Borsook and Superbi Gioffredi, *Italian Altarpieces*.

48 These portrait categories are my own. Lorne Campbell discusses the Renaissance nomenclature ("ritratto", "effigies") in *Renaissance Portraits*, p. 1.

49 See Pope-Hennessy, *The Portrait in the Renaissance*; E. Castelnuovo, "Il significato del ritratto pittorico nella società," in *Storia d'Italia*, vol. 5, *I documenti*, ed. R. Romano and C. Vivanti, Turin, 1973, pp. 1035–94; Campbell, *Renaissance Portraits*.

50 The record of Simone Martini's lost portraits of Petrarch's beloved Laura and of Cardinal Orsini, however, suggest that a more complex and diversified practice may have existed alongside that of dynastic declaration during the fourteenth century: see Martindale, *Simone Martini*, pp. 49–50 and 183–4.

51 The earliest extant Florentine portrait panel may be the curious triple portrait of the artist members of the Gaddi family in the Uffizi, once attributed to Agnolo Gaddi and dated to the last decade of the fourteenth century: see L. Marcucci, *I dipinti toscani del secolo XIV*, Florence, 1965, pp. 142–4. More recently, however, Luciano Bellosi has reattributed the panel to Domenico di Michelino, placing it in the context of *quattrocento* portraiture and relating it to the panel in the Louvre representing five Florentine artists attributed to Uccello, *Gli Uffizi: Catalogo Generale*, Florence, 1979, p. 861.

52 See Hatfield, "Five Early Renaissance Portraits;" Joannides, *Masaccio and Masolino*, pp. 456, 458, and 460; Wohl, *The Paintings of Domenico Veneziano*, pp. 138–40. On Lippi's two portraits, see Ruda, *Fra Filippo Lippi*, pp. 385 and 413. Ruda's date of c. 1435–36 seems too early for the Metropolitan double portrait and the date of mid-1440s too late for the Berlin portrait. I date both works to the early 1440s.

53 See Hatfield, "Five Early Renaissance Portraits," p. 317.

54 Hatfield argues that the profile view and generalized features communicate the "regularity of human countenance" and convey that the sitter is a "'balanced' person, in whom reason rules over emotion," tying these characterizations to Alberti's portrayal of *virtù*, *ibid.*, pp. 222–3.

55 Alberti, in his well-known comment on portraiture in *De pictura*, wrote "Painting possesses a truly divine power in that not only does it make the absent present (as they say of friendship), but it also represents the dead to the living many centuries later, so that they are recognized by spectators with pleasure and deep admiration for the artist," *On Painting and On Sculpture*, p. 61.

56 See Hatfield, "Five Early Renaissance Portraits," pp. 325–6. A documented portrait commission from around this time demonstrates another variety of portrait commemoration. In 1444, Andrea del Castagno was commissioned to paint a portrait of the recently deceased Leonardo Bruni to be hung alongside an image of Coluccio Salutati in the palace of the Arte dei Giudici e Notai: see Horster, *Andrea del Castagno*, p. 204. Both chancellors had been members of the guild. The portrait does not survive.

57 See Ruda, *Fra Filippo Lippi*, pp. 85–8 and 385–6.

58 See *ibid.*, pp. 182 and 412–13.

59 Ruda notes that Lippi's *Double Portrait* and Pisanello's *Portrait of Ginevra d'Este*(?) are the two earliest surviving Italian independent portrait panels of women, *ibid.*, p. 85. On Simone Martini's *Portrait of Laura*, see Martindale, *Simone Martini*, pp. 49–50 and 183–4. I do not accept Miklòs Boskovits's attribution to the young Lippi (or his early dating of c. 1435) of a double portrait sold at Sotheby's, London, in 1955, "Fra Filippo Lippi, i carmelitani e il Rinascimento," p. 239, fig. 14.

60 See Simons, "Women in Frames," pp. 42ff. Kent Lydecker refutes this association between female portraiture and marriage, "The Domestic Setting of the Arts in Renaissance Florence," pp. 159–61. Ruda suggests that the *Double Portrait* may commemorate the death of the female subject, rather than a marriage (see n. 70 below).

61 Ruda, *Fra Filippo Lippi*, pp. 385–6.

62 See Patricia Simons's interesting observations regarding the profile convention in fifteenth-century Florentine female portraits, "Women in Frames," pp. 45–52.

63 These qualities are upheld in a variety of discourses, including poetry, conduct literature, sermons, epistolary exchange, and civil court proceedings: see M. de Matteis, ed., *Idee sulla donna del Medioevo*, Bologna, 1981; Simons, "Women in Frames," pp. 42–5; Molho, *Marriage Alliance in Late Medieval Florence*, pp. 138–43; P. Tanagli, *Women in Italian Renaissance Art*, Manchester, 1997, pp. 47–83.

64 See Ruda, *Fra Filippo Lippi*, p. 384, for a discussion of the woman's clothing.

65 See Simons, "Women in Frames," pp. 43 and 45.

66 Simons provides an interesting analysis of this process of objectification in fifteenth-century Florentine female portraits, *ibid.*, pp. 41–52.

67 An example of paired portraits are the companion panels by the Master of Flémalle in the London National Gallery, dated c. 1430. On the manuscript tradition, see S. Ringbom, "Filippo Lippis New Yorker Doppelporträt: Eine Deutung der Fenstersymbolik," *Zeitschrift für Kunstgeschichte*, vol. 48 (1985), pp. 133–7. On double portraits, see Campbell, *Renaissance Portraits*, pp. 53–4, and Wackernagel, *The World of the Florentine Renaissance Artist*, p. 170, n. 148.

68 See R. Baldwin, "A Window from the Song of Songs in Conjugal Portraits by Fra Filippo Lippi and Bartholomäus Zeitlom," in *Source: Notes in the History of Art*, vol. 5, no. 2 (1986), pp. 7–14. On the discourse about women, beauty, and art, see E. Cropper, "The Beauty of Woman: Problems in the Rhetoric of Renaissance Portraiture," in *Rewriting the Renaissance: The Discourses of Sexual Difference in Early Modern Europe*, ed. M. W. Ferguson, M. Quilligan, and N. Vickers, Chicago, 1986, pp. 175–90.

69 A. Wright, "The Memory of Faces: Representational Choices in Fifteenth-Century Florentine Portraiture," chapter in G. Ciappelli and P. Rubin, eds., *Family and Memory in Renaissance Florence*, Cambridge, forthcoming. Wright notes that Alberti refers to this passage from Pliny in *De pictura*.

70 The central position of the woman and the "spatial and psychological independence" of the two figures has prompted Ruda to conclude that the picture may have commemorated the woman's death rather than the couple's marriage, *Fra Filippo Lippi*, p. 385.

71 Keith Christiansen in discussion. D. Jansen, "Fra Filippo Lippis Doppelbildnis im New Yorker Metropolitan Museum," *Wallraf-Richartz Jahrbuch*, vols. 48–49 (1987–88), pp. 97–121.

72 See Camille, *Gothic Idol*, pp. 314ff.

73 The practice of including secular donors in religious images is found throughout medieval art. It represents the prevalent form of "portraiture" in *trecento* Italian painting prior to the development of the individual portrait panel. On Masaccio's *Trinity*, see Joannides, *Masaccio and Masolino*, pp. 356–68.

74 Lippi's panel paintings that include donor portraits are the Fitzwilliam Triptych, the Cini *Madonna and Child with Saints*, the Palazzo Barberini *Annunciation*, the Marsuppini *Coronation of the Virgin*, the Sant'Ambrogio *Coronation of the Virgin*, the Alessandri *St. Lawrence Enthroned*, the *Madonna del Ceppo*, the Inghirami *Death of St. Jerome*, the Santa Margherita *Madonna giving her Girdle to St. Thomas with Saints*, and the Corsham Court *Annunciation*.

75 Pope-Hennessy, *The Portrait in the Renaissance*, p. 258. He claims that "some lingering memory of the realistic aspiration of the first generation of Florentine Renaissance artists can still be felt" in the portrait of Francesco Maringhi in the *Coronation of the Virgin*, while the donor portraits of Gemignano Inghirami, and Alessandro Alessandri and his sons are considered a "return to medieval practice."

76 A documented example of Lippi providing such services is the commemorative mass that he performed on Jan. 19, 1439, with twenty other Carmelites in the chapel of Forte di Piero da Vico in Santa Maria del Carmine: see Caioli, "Un altro sguardo," p. 45; Ruda, *Fra Filippo Lippi*, Doc. 5.1, p. 519.

77 The exceptions are the *Madonna del Ceppo* tabernacle and the Alessandri *St. Lawrence* altarpiece.

78 John Shearman has compared this wooden structure to prayer stalls in a private oratory, *Only Connect . . .*, p. 77.

79 See *ibid.*, p. 75.

80 See n. 74 above for the list of panel paintings with donor portraits. Two of these altarpieces have been associated with private chapels, although in both cases there is no firm documentation. Vasari claimed that the *St. Lawrence Enthroned* was commissioned for the altar in the private chapel attached to the Alessandri villa in Vincigliata, Vasari–Milanesi, vol. II, pp. 626–7; Ruda, *Fra Filippo Lippi*, pp. 429; while it has been suggested that the Palazzo Barberini *Annunciation* came from the Larioni family oratory in Pian di Ripoli: see I. B. Supino, *Fra Filippo Lippi*, Florence, 1902, p. 53; Ruda, *Fra Filippo Lippi*, p. 403.

81 For Alberti's comment, see n. 55 above.

82 See P. Meller, "La Cappella Brancacci: Problemi ritrattistici ed iconografici," *Acropoli*, 1960–61, fasc. III, pp. 195–6. See also Ch. 3 above, pp. 73–4.

83 Vasari wrote that Domenico Veneziano included portraits in his fresco of the *Marriage of the Virgin* in Sant'Egidio, Vasari–Milanesi, vol. II, p. 677. Alberti had encouraged painters to include his portrait in their *istorie* in acknowledgment of his contribution to the art of painting (see n. 182 below).

84 Borsook, "Fra Filippo Lippi and the Murals for Prato Cathedral," pp. 23–4.

85 Vasari–Milanesi, vol. II, p. 624.

86 See C. Gilbert's review of J. Pope-Hennessy's *The Renaissance Portrait* in *Burlington Magazine*, vol. 110 (1968), p. 282, n. 5; Borsook, "Fra Filippo Lippi and the Murals for Prato Cathedral," pp. 28 and 56–7; Ruda, *Fra Filippo Lippi*, p. 463. Scholars disagree over whether Mantegna's panel served as a model for Lippi's fresco or vice versa: see R. Lightbown, *Andrea Mantegna*, Oxford, 1986, p. 415.

87 Borsook, "Fra Filippo Lippi and the Murals for Prato Cathedral," pp. 58–60.

88 See the suggested identifications in Ruda's catalogue entry, *Fra Filippo Lippi*, pp. 463–4. Pope-Hennessy makes the sweeping statement that the fresco is "filled with more than twenty portraits, of Carlo de' Medici, the provost of the church, and past and present members of the governing body of the Opera Pia del Ceppo," *The Portrait in the Renaissance*, p. 12.

89 See Savonarola's *Sermons on Amos*, 1496, quoted in C. Gilbert, *Italian Art, 1400–1500: Sources and Documents*, Englewood Cliffs, 1980, pp. 157–8.

90 The Florentine artists commissioned to paint the lower walls of the Sistine Chapel in the Vatican in 1481–3 integrated portraits into their narrative frescos.

91 See Goldthwaite, *Wealth and the Demand for Art*, pp. 224–55; Lydecker, "The Domestic Setting of the Arts;" Thornton, *The Italian Renaissance Interior*, 1991; Wackernagel, *The World of the Florentine Renaissance Artist*, pp. 153–80.

92 See Hauptmann, *Der Tondo*; Kecks, *Madonna und Kind*, pp. 43–50; Wackernagel, *The World of the Florentine Renaissance Artist*, p. 175; Lydecker, "The Domestic Setting of the

Arts," pp. 65–6. Hauptmann provides examples of tondi used as altarpieces and in civic display sites, *Der Tondo*, pp. 18ff; I thank Kim Butler for bringing this to my attention.

93 Lydecker, *ibid.* Kim Butler, in her dissertation work on Raphael's Madonnas for Johns Hopkins University, has associated tondi with the Classical *clipeus* tradition and suggests that these images may have accommodated a range of devotional activities that took place within the townhouse bedroom, which included providing contemplative objects for the dying.

94 See Hauptmann, *Der Tondo*, pp. 11–38.

95 On *deschi da parto*, see J. Pope-Hennessy and K. Christiansen, "Secular Painting in 15th-Century Tuscany: Birth Trays, Cassone Panels, and Portraits," *The Metropolitan Museum Art Bulletin*, 1980, pp. 6–11; C. de Carli, *I Deschi da Parto e la pittura del primo rinascimento toscano*, Turin, 1997; and J. M. Musacchio, *The Art and Ritual of Childbirth*, New Haven and London, 1999.

96 J. Ruda, "The National Gallery Tondo of the Adoration of the Magi and the Early Style of Filippo Lippi," *Studies in the History of Art* (The National Gallery of Art, Washington), vol. 7, 1977, pp. 7–39; Ruda, *Fra Filippo Lippi*, pp. 316–25 and 437–41.

97 "Un certo tondo di legniame" with "certa storia . . . della Vergine Maria," in Ruda, *Fra Filippo Lippi*, p. 531. See Hauptmann, *Der Tondo*, pp. 187ff; Marchini, *Filippo Lippi*, p. 209, and Ruda, *Fra Filippo Lippi*, pp. 240–4, 453–5, and 531–2. Ruda opposes the standard view that the tondo now in the Pitti Palace is the painting documented in 1452 as commissioned by Lionardo Bartolini. I don't accept Ruda's position because the description of the painting in the document is too close to the most unusual iconography of the tondo to leave room for doubt. For Bartolini himself, see n. 100 below.

98 See Ruda, *Fra Filippo Lippi*, pp. 437 and 453.

99 Ruda has convincingly argued that the arms blocked out on the reverse pertain not to the Bartolini family, but to the Martelli, *ibid.*, p. 454. In addition, the fact that the design is off-axis with the Madonna and Child represented on the verso suggests that the arms were not intended as a finished backing for the tondo, and may be an unrelated design similar to the other drawings found on the reverse of a number of panels by Lippi.

100 Lionardo di Bartolomeo Bartolini and his wife Maddelena di Giovanni Baroncelli had six children: Bernardo (b. 1442), Bartolomeo (b. 1444), Cosimo (b. 1448), Marco (b. 1451), Damiano (b. Aug. 21, 1453), and Andrea (b. 1455). The painting was under way by April 13, 1452 and to be completed by Dec. 8 (a deadline that, true to form, Lippi did not meet, resulting in a fine). The tondo may thus have been commissioned to commemorate the birth of Marco in 1451: see *Raccolta di tutte le prose fiorentine pubblicate, e di osservazioni storiche e critiche accresciute dagli Accademici Fiorentini*, Florence, 1786, vol. XXV, pp. 327–9.

101 Lydecker has found evidence in one inventory dating from 1510 to confirm the practice of displaying tondi high on the wall of the *camera*: "Una Nostra Donna tonda, di sopra, dorata intorno cho'l figliuolo e Santo Giovanni," "The Domestic Setting of the Arts," p. 66, n. 87.

102 Lydecker concludes that tondi were among the most prized possessions displayed in the *camera* and *antecamera* on account of their being listed first among the furnishings in inventories, *ibid.*, p. 65.

103 On Domenico Veneziano's tondo, see Wohl, *The Paintings of Domenico Veneziano*, pp. 70–4 and 120–3.

104 See Wohl's diagram, *ibid.*, fig. 9.

105 See S. Ringbom, *Icon to Narrative: The Rise of the Dramatic Close-up in Fifteenth-Century Devotional Painting*, Abo, Finland, 1965, pp. 58–61. On the increase in the demand for devotional paintings, see Goldthwaite, *Wealth and the Demand for Art*, pp. 140ff.

106 See Kecks, *Madonna und Kind*, pp. 37–41.

107 See Lydecker, "The Domestic Setting of the Arts," pp. 175–82. Using visual evidence from painted narratives dating from the second half of the *quattrocento* and the *cinquecento*, Kecks provides examples of how these images were displayed in both public and private settings, *Madonna und Kind*, figs. 1–33.

108 Neri di Bicci, *Le Ricordanze*, pp. 118 and 126 (July 25 and Oct. 11, 1459). See also the Madonna images listed in the inventories of fifteenth- and sixteenth-century Florentine palazzi furnishings collected by Lydecker, *ibid.*, pp. 61, n. 82, 63, n. 84, 91, n. 16, 175–80.

109 The nine paintings are listed below chronologically, with the page references to Ruda's catalogue entries in *Fra Filippo Lippi*: Turini Collection (early 1430s, Ruda, p. 373); Utah (mid-1430s, Ruda, p. 380); Washington (early 1440s, Ruda, p. 408); Denver (1440s, Ruda, p. 404); London (c. 1445–early 1450s, Ruda, p. 434); Rau Collection, Switzerland (early 1450s, Ruda, p. 435); Florence, Uffizi (1460s, Ruda, p. 468); Munich (1460s, Ruda, p. 469); Florence, Palazzo Medici–Riccardi (*c.*1465, Ruda, p. 470). Four half-length Madonna and Child panels often given to Lippi, which are in my opinion of questionable attribution, are: Manila (Ruda, p. 406); Botinaccio, Montespertoli (Ruda, p. 433); Baltimore (Ruda, p. 433); Fondazione Magnani–Rocca, Parma (Ruda, p. 436). For a discussion of the iconography of Lippi's later Madonna and Child panels, see Ruda, pp. 244–52.

110 See Ruda, *Fra Filippo Lippi*, pp. 373–4.

111 Marchini, *Filippo Lippi*, pp. 19–20.

112 See Ruda, *Fra Filippo Lippi*, pp. 408–9. I do not accept Ruda's position that the Denver *Madonna and Child* pre-dates the Washington panel. The painting in Denver (which Ruda dates c. 1440, pp. 404–6) appears to be a much more mature work from later in the decade.

113 *Ibid.*, pp. 470–1.

114 See *ibid.*, pp. 468–9, and Shearman, *Only Connect . . .*, pp. 73–5.

115 See Ch. 2 above, pp. 29–30, and Ch. 7 below, pp. 169–72.

116 Taken from Nicola Calciuri's version of St. Simon Stock's prayer to the Virgin *Flos Carmeli*: "Fiore carmelita et vita fiorita, splendore dello ciello, et virgine parturisti, singulare . . . alli tuoi Carmeliti dà alcuno previlegio, stella del mare," Graziano di S. Teresa, "'Vita fratrum del sancto monte Carmelo' di P. Nicola Calciuri," p. 404. Calciuri's *Vita fratrum del sancto Monte Carmelo* was written in 1461, but his account of Simon Stock follows very closely a manuscript now in the Vatican of Florentine provenance, p. 270.

117 See n. 135 below.

118 Giovanni di Francesco was involved in the litigation which led to Lippi's loss of the San Quirico benefice in 1455, described in Ch. 5 above. The apprenticeship contract is one of the documents that was assembled by the archiepiscopal notary as evidence in the case. See Ruda, *Fra Filippo Lippi*, Docs. 7 and 19, pp. 520–3 and 534–6. On Giovanni di Francesco, see Bellosi, *Pittura di Luce.*

119 "Ihs adì primo di giugnio MCCCCXXXX Sia noto a ciascheduna persona chome questo dì primo di giugnio millesimo di sopra viene asstare Giovanni di Franciescho chonesso me cho cio – e frate Philippo di Tommaso dipintore che questi modi e patti cio – e chel detto Giovanni sia e debba fare tutte quelle chose che pel detto fra FFilippo li fussono chomandante a uso buono diciepolo. E io li debba essia tenuto di quello sapessi circha allarte del dipingniere, sia tenuto a insegnialli e a mostralli di quello sapessi circha allarte della dipintura. E ppiu Io sopra detto mobrigho a dalli per sua faticha assalaro faciendo cio che detto di sopra a uso di buona disciepolo fiorini quaranta." ASF, Not. Antecos. 19112, c. 342r, and Ruda, *Fra Filippo Lippi*, Doc. 7.1, pp. 520–1, from whom my translation is in part derived.

120 Salaries varied according to the age and expertise of the apprentice. Neri di Bicci paid his apprentice Cosimo Rosselli (who had been with him for three years) 18 fl. for the year 1456, while Giovanni d'Antonio, after six years in Neri's service, received 36 fl. for the year 1466, Neri di Bicci, *Le Ricordanze*, pp. 51 and 283–4; see also Thomas, *The Painter's Practice in Renaissance Tuscany*, p. 85. Contracts could also be negotiated for two or three years at a time, Neri di Bicci, *ibid.*, p. 192, and while the duration of the contract between Fra Filippo and Giovanni di

Francesco is not stated, it is possible that it was intended to cover two years.

121 "Io frate Philippo, dipintore, rettore di San Chiricho a Llegniaria, fo oggi questo dì xvi di novembre m[illesim]o 442 di chonchordia insieme chon Giovanni di Franciescho, dipintore, che d'ongni e ciascheduna chosa avessimo fatto insieme o in rag[i]onamento o per isscritura in nome di chompangnia, questo dì detto di sopra detto s'intenda e volgliamo sia anullata e chosì facciamo l'uno e ll'a[l]tro e ll'a[l]tro e ll'uno chon questi patti, cio.e: che 'l detto Giovanni à rice[v]uto a rachonciare uno quadro grande di Giotto a quale lui debbe finire di tutto, chon chornicie d'oro intorno, e champo azzuro, e adornamenti ne' panni e cielate e altre armadure, chome a uso di ben lavorio finito. E' ssuo paghamento sia fiorini se' immediate che quello di qui e' verra per esso, allora sia e intenda essere suo pachamento. E se 'l detto di qui è i' detto quadro non venisse per esso, li si farà uno protesto. E udita sua intenzione, chon licienzi[a] di chi ci puo fare ragione che ssi possa vendere, si venda e quello se n'avesse di più, si renderà a vuello di qui è, cioe a me frate Filippo. E più sono contento che i' detto Giovanni abbia lire sette e soldi quindici, e chosì fini[s]cie lui me ed io lui d'ongni e ciascheduna chosa che da il dì di settembre nel quarantadue in qua addì xvi detto di sopra e milesimo. E per chiarezza di ciò, io frate Philippo pernominato di sopra, per chiarezza di ciò ò ffatta questa scritta di mia propia mano, e il detto Giovanni si soscriverrà di sua mano a essere chontento a ciò che adì sopra si chontiene." ASF, Not. Antecos. 19112, c. 342r; Ruda, *Fra Filippo Lippi*, Doc. 7.III, p. 522, my translation. It is difficult to determine from the text exactly what arrangements were made regarding the payment for the restoration of the painting by Giotto. I have translated the text as literally as possible, intentionally leaving the wording vague in order to give room for interpretation. Ruda considers the 6 fl. an advance payment subject to adjustment depending upon the eventual price received for the panel. He also speculates that this price may represent only the anticipated profit following the restoration, rather than Lippi's investment in the painting, considering 6 fl. to be too low a price for a work by Giotto in the fifteenth century, p. 522.

122 "Io Giovanni di Franceschо mi chiamo chontento e pagato per i[n]fino questo dì sedici di febraio 1450 [Florentine style]," Ruda, *Fra Filippo Lippi*, Doc. 7.II, p. 522. He had written out a near verbatim copy of the accord.

123 Ruda, *Fra Filippo Lippi*, Doc. 19, pp. 534–6. The documents related to the business transactions and subsequent court case between the two painters are extremely confusing. See *ibid.*, p. 34 for an analysis, and Doc. 19, pp. 534–6 for a partial presentation of the documents.

124 See Borsook, "Cults and Imagery at Sant' Ambrogio in Florence," pp. 163–4 and n. 113. Chiara Lachi considers Piero di Lorenzo di Pratese to have been a member of Lippi's workshop, "Il problema della bottega di Filippo Lippi," p. 36. That Lippi seems also to have collaborated with Pesellino on occasion is evident in Pesellino's execution of the predella for Lippi's altarpiece for the novitiate chapel in Santa Croce.

125 See Borsook, "Cults and Imagery," p. 163 and n. 113.

126 There are no extant paintings signed by Fra Diamante, but he is credited with a number of works that are very close in style to Lippi, suggesting that they were products of Lippi's workshop. He is also associated with those autograph paintings that reveal a collaboration between Lippi and a second artist working on lesser features of the composition. Attributed to Fra Diamante are the *St. Jerome in Penitence with the Baptist and St. Ansanus(?)* (Fogg Museum, Cambridge, Mass.) and the *Madonna giving her Girdle to St. Thomas with Saints* (Galleria Comunale, Prato). Works considered to be designed and partially executed by Lippi with the assistance of Fra Diamante include the *Madonna del Ceppo* (Galleria Comunale, Prato), the *Death of St. Jerome* (Santo Stefano, Prato), the *Circumcision* (Spirito Santo, Prato), and the *Adoration of the Christ Child with Sts. George and Vincent Ferrer* (Galleria Comunale, Prato). On Fra Diamante, see Eve Borsook's entry in the *Dizionario biografico degli Italiani*, Rome, 1991, vol. 39, pp. 634–6.

127 "Don Diamante de [blank] garzone de frate Filippo pentore fiorentino," Ruda, *Fra Filippo Lippi*, Doc. 27.I.53, p. 544.

128 There are payments for his goods which arrived from Urbino in May and June, ASF, Con. Sopp. 79, n. 155, c. 82r. A payment made on May 10 informs us that "Bartolomeo sta chol lui [Fra Filippo]," while on Nov. 28 of the same year, he is referred to as "dipintore e disciepolo di Frate Philippo," c. 51v. The documents are discussed in de Angelis and Conti, "Un libro antico della sagrestia di Sant'Ambrogio," p. 105.

129 See Ruda, *Fra Filippo Lippi*, Doc. 27.I.29, p. 543.

130 Botticelli is described as Lippi's disciple in the *Libro di Antonio Billi* (c. 1516–30), the *Codice dell'Anonimo Magliabechiano* (c. 1542–48), and by Vasari (1550): see H. Horne, *Sandro Botticelli*, London, 1908, pp. 6 and 343–4.

131 "Lo Spanguolo" is mentioned on May 22 and June 19, 1445, as a member of Lippi's household when the artist was working on the Sant'Ambrogio altarpiece, ASF, Con. Sopp. 79, n. 155, c. 82r. He is not, however, referred to as a *discepolo* or *garzone*.

132 A "Jacopo" is documented collecting gold leaf for Lippi on April 29, 1454, when the painter was working on the frescos in Prato: See Borsook, "Fra Filippo Lippi and the Murals for Prato Cathedral," pp. 44–5, and Lachi, "Il problema della bottega," p. 34.

133 When Lippi was working on the *Trinity* for the Compagnia della SS. Trinità in Pistoia in 1460, there is reference in the documents to "Domenico suo gharzone" (July 26, 1460) and "Domenicho suo discepolo" (August? 1460), Ruda, *Fra Filippo Lippi*, Docs. 22.V.1–2, p. 539. This painter has been associated with Domenico di Zanobi; Lachi, "Il problema della bottega," p. 34.

134 In 1460, when Lippi was completing the *Trinity* altarpiece in Pistoia, a payment was made "a frate Filippo . . . e a gharzoni suoi," Ruda, *Fra Filippo Lippi*, Doc. 22.III.1, p. 538. After Lippi moved to Spoleto to undertake the frescos in the Duomo, he sent 15 fl. on April 26, 1467 to "suo garzoni" in Florence, *ibid.*, Doc. 27.I.14, p. 542.

135 In addition to the documented workshop participation described above, art historians working from a connoisseurial perspective have populated the shop with two painters known as the "Master of the Castello Nativity" and "Pseudo-Pier Francesco Fiorentino." Piero di Lorenzo di Pratese – who, in fact, collaborated with Lippi as an independent master – is also placed within the shop. See Lachi, "Il problema della bottega," who identifies the "Master of the Castello Nativity" with Piero di Lorenzo di Pratese. The paintings grouped under these names demonstrate a strong influence by Lippi but, in my opinion, need not have been executed within the immediate workshop environment.

136 "Et adì 21 di gennaio [1446] a fra Filipo per portatura della tavola da cha(sa) al munistero di santa apollonia": see Borsook, "Cults and Imagery at Sant'Ambrogio," n. 121.

137 Francesco wrote to Giovanni de' Medici that he had stayed with the artist late one Saturday evening, urging him to work on the altarpiece. While Francesco does not state that he was in the artist's workshop, this becomes implicit when he adds that after he left Lippi, the latter "e andone a casa." See n. 151 below.

138 These include the restoration of the painting by Giotto described above. On April 19, 1451, Lippi was paid for touching up the figure of Dante "et alios famosos viros" in a cycle of *Uomini Famosi* in the Palazzo della Signoria in Florence, Ruda, *Fra Filippo Lippi*, Doc. 12, p. 526. In 1454, while in Prato working on the frescos in Santo Stefano, Lippi restored the frescos by Agnolo Gaddi in the Chapel of the Virgin's Girdle in the same church following the installation of a new organ: see Borsook, "Fra Filippo Lippi

and the Murals for Prato Cathedral," p. 90, n. 75.

139 See J. Levenson, K. Oberhuber, and J. Sheehan, *Early Italian Engravings from the National Gallery of Art*, Washington, DC, 1973, p. 3, fig. 1–1.

140 On the visual evidence for shop assistance in the Barbadori and Sant'Ambrogio altarpieces, see Ruda, *Fra Filippo Lippi*, p. 426. On the Prato frescos, see L. Bellosi, "Tre note in margine a uno studio sull'arte in Prato," *Prospettiva*, vols. 33–6 (1983–4), pp. 44–55; on the Spoleto frescos, see Benazzi and Virilli, *Filippo Lippi nel Duomo di Spoleto*, pp. 13ff.

141 An example of a secondary commission allocated to another artist is the restoration of the painting by Giotto assigned to Lippi's partner Giovanni di Francesco in 1442, mentioned above. A situation where perhaps Lippi thought he could get away with delegating the work to an assistant is the painting commissioned by the Perugian Antonio del Branca, in 1451. The latter refused to pay Lippi the promised 70 fl., claiming that "non fece la detta tavola" and "l'a fatta fare ad altri." The matter went before the Florentine Tribunale della Mercanzia where the Perugian was apparently unsuccessful in his case: see Bombe, "Urkunden über ein verschollenes Altarbild Filippo Lippis," pp. 115–18. Shop assistance is also evident in a number of the secondary projects that Lippi undertook in Prato. The *Madonna del Ceppo* painted for the Ceppo Nuovo is considered to have been executed in part by Fra Diamante. The *Death of St. Jerome* painted for Gemignano Inghirami is meticulously painted in the foreground, while the background (fig. 140) is carelessly worked in some areas and static in others, indicating the hand of assistants and a relative lack of interest on the part of Lippi. The *Madonna giving her Girdle to St. Thomas with Saints* in the Galleria Comunale in Prato is usually attributed to Fra Diamante.

142 Lippi was fined in 1453 for not completing the tondo for Lionardo Bartolini on time, Ruda, *Fra Filippo Lippi*, pp. 531–2.

143 See n. 163 below.

144 See Ruda, *Fra Filippo Lippi*, pp. 524–6.

145 See *ibid.*, p. 437.

146 See n. 161 below.

147 See Ruda, *Fra Filippo Lippi*, p. 451.

148 See *ibid.*, pp. 457 and 475.

149 Martin Wackernagel noted the great discrepancy in the prices of panel paintings during the period 1400–70, citing 20–40 fl. as the common range, *The World of the Florentine Renaissance Artist*, pp. 338–9. Prices, of course, were related to the size of a panel or fresco, the complexity of design (often calculated according to the number of figures), and the cost of materials. These factors must be taken into consideration when comparing prices. Here are some comparative figures for the paintings of Lippi's contemporaries:

Fra Angelico: 12 fl. for the lost altarpiece painted for the chapel of Giovanni de' Gherardini in S. Stefano a Ponte, Florence, in 1418; 10 lire for the lost crucifix for Santa Maria Nuova in 1423; 11 fl. for a lost *Annunciation* for the Servites of Sant' Alessandro in Brescia in 1432; 190 fl. for the Linaiuoli Tabernacle in 1433; 250 fl. for the *Deposition* for Santa Trinita in c. 1435; 15 ducats for the *Lamentation over the Dead Christ* for the Confraternity of Santa Maria della Croce al Tempio in 1436: see Orlandi, *Beato Angelico*, pp. 32, 42, 47, 169, 179, 181, 187–8.

Andrea del Castagno: 10 fl. for a lost portrait of Leonardo Bruni (1444–45); 104 lire (c. 22 fl.) for the altarpiece of the *Assumption of the Virgin* (1449) for San Miniato al Torri (now in Berlin); fl.58 l.35 s.2 (out of an anticipated 100 fl.) for the three frescoed scenes from the life of the Virgin in the *cappella maggiore* of Sant'Egidio in 1451–53; 11 fl. for frescos of "tre figure" and "uno angelo" in the funerary chapel of Orlando de' Medici in SS. Annunziata in 1455; 24 fl. for the frescoed Tolentino Monument (1456): see Horster, *Andrea del Castagno*, pp. 189, 204–6.

Paolo Uccello: 15 fl. for his two versions of the Hawkwood monument in 1436: see Borsook, *The Mural Painters of Tuscany*, p. 75.

Domenico Veneziano: 100 fl. for one fresco at Sant'Egidio (The *Meeting at the Golden Gate*) in 1439.

Neri di Bicci: between 1453 and 1475, his altarpieces averaged between 25 and 50 fl.: see *Le Ricordanze*.

Piero Pollaiuolo: 100 fl. for the altarpiece for the Chapel of the Cardinal of Portugal at San Miniato al Monte in 1467; 20 fl. for each of the Virtue panels for the Mercanzia in 1469: see L. Ettlinger, *Antonio and Piero Pollaiuolo*, Oxford and New York, 1978, pp. 139 and 142–4.

Benozzo Gozzoli: 7 fl. a month salary as Fra Angelico's assistant, for the painting of the Chapel of St. Peter at St. Peter's in Rome in 1447 (as compared to Fra Angelico's salary of 200 fl. a year and the three *garzoni* who received 1 fl. a month); the same salary at Orvieto in 1447, when frescoing the vault of the San Brizio chapel in the Duomo; 300 lire (c. 60 fl.) for the altarpiece for the Compagnia della Purificazione, Pisa, in 1461; 10 fl. for the fresco of St. Sebastian in the Collegiata in San Gimignano in 1465; $66\frac{2}{3}$ fl. for each frescoed scene in the Campo Santo in Pisa, 1469–85: see D. Cole Ahl, *Benozzo Gozzoli*, New Haven and London, 1996, pp. 275–80.

Domenico Ghirlandaio: 1,000 fl. for the frescos in the *cappella maggiore* of Santa Maria Novella, 1485–90.

150 The 1983–90 restoration of the frescos in the Duomo at Spoleto has revealed much about Lippi's execution and technique. I had the opportunity to go up on the scaffolding twice while work was in progress, and talk with the restorers Paolo Virilli and Sergio Fusetti, and with Giordana Benazzi, the director of the restoration from the Soprintendenza ai Beni Ambientali, Architettonici, Artistici e Storici dell'Umbria. They were most generous with their time and observations. According to their assessment, published in the pamphlet by Benazzi and Virilli, *Filippo Lippi nel Duomo di Spoleto 1467–1469*, pp. 13–17 and 19–20, work went along simultaneously on both sides of the giant apse, with Lippi responsible for most of the figures on the left-hand side and Fra Diamante and Piermatteo d'Amelia executing much of the fresco work on the right side. Lippi then went over the figures blocked out by his assistants, painting in *a secco* the details, drapery modeling, and ornament.

Carmen Bambach Cappel has demonstrated that a number of painters working in Florence began to use cartoons during the 1430s and 40s, "Piero della Francesca, the Study of Perspective and the Development of the Cartoon in the Quattrocento," in *Piero della Francesca tra arte e scienza: Atti del Convegno Internazionale di Studi*, ed. M. Dalai Emiliani and V. Curzi, Venice, 1996, pp. 143–66. While Lippi was so often on the cutting edge in technical and compositional experimentation, this was not the case with cartoons, which he used in his fresco painting only in the repetitive ornamental decorations, Benazzi and Virilli, *ibid.*, pp. 13 and 20.

151 "Fra Filippo de' amettere d'oro quelli civori della tavola a un debitore stava a' Buondelmonti et io l'ò solleciatato ogni dì insino a sabato sera ste' con lui un'ora a farlo lavorare. Restavali a fare per un dì. Come mi parti' da llui gli prese quel fatto et andone a casa et hiersera si spacciò. Quelle cose sono restate pegno per la pigione. Io lascio questa trama sbrigare al Serragl[i]o, se nno alla tornata ne trarrò le mani io. Ma vedete a che pericolo l'uomo va!" Ruda, *Fra Filippo Lippi*, pp. 38 and 537, Doc. 21.II.2; trans. adapted from Ruda. The letter was sent from Florence on Aug. 31, 1457. See Ruda's discussion, pp. 38–40.

152 "Io mi sto perchè io non ò più oro ne' ddanari per chi llo mette. Io vi priegcho ch'io non mi stia, è tre dì ch'io non fo niente

e aspetto ci siate," *ibid.*, pp. 38 and 537, Doc. 21.II.1.

153 Yael Even, in her study "Artistic Collaboration in Florentine Workshops," devotes a chapter to Lippi entitled "Monastic Enterprises." She contends that Lippi was "a free trader without a base," with an "itinerant" shop, working out of monastic facilities or private quarters. She concludes that "Lippi's connections in ecclesiastical circles guaranteed him the economic security that his lay contemporaries maintained through the upkeep of a stable workshop," pp. 119–20 and 123. I put a greater emphasis on Lippi's lay patronage after he left Santa Maria del Carmine.

154 Two of the principal Carmine patrons, Felice Brancacci and Francesco Soderini, opposed the Medici in 1434 and suffered for it following Cosimo's return to Florence: see Ch. 2, p. 49 above and n. 106.

155 "Ihs addì xiii d'aghosto ccccxxxviiij
Per risposta d'una vi mandai o rricieuta da voi, ch'è penata tredici dì àvella, che nn'ò auto danno assai. Voi mi rispondete in concrusione che ddella tavola ne altro partito ne potete pigliare – e ch'io vela chonservi, che perdio ò male, el modo s'io mi parto, e ppiù non mi potete dare uno quatrino. Io di questo ò auto gra[n]de dolore per più rispetti e questo è uno di quelli: ed è chiaro essere uno de' più poveri frati che sia in firenze sono Io. Ed à mmi la[s]ciato Dio chon sei nipoti fa[n]c[i]ulle da marito e infermi ed inutili e quello pocho e assai di bene a lloro sono io. Se potessi farmi dare a chasa vostra uno pocho di grano e di vino che mi è vendete mi sarà gra[n]de letizia, ponedolo a mio chonto. Io ve ne gravo cholle lagrime alli ochi, che s'io mi parto lo lasci a questi poveri fanc[i]ulli. Io v'aviso ch'io sono suto chon Ser Antonio del marchese e voluto sapere da llui quello mi volesse fare, dicie che a[n]dando a servire el marchese ci presterrà cinque fiorini perr uno e pparte[n]doci da chasa vegcho non mi potrei fare uno paio di chalze. Io vi priegcho, non vi sia grave, due versi a llui a Ser Antonio, ch'io li sia rachomandato, e lla risposta vostra fia subito, partirmi l'altro dì, che sono chiaro s'io ci sto otto dì io sono morto tanto è lla paura. Per Dio respondete a chasa vostra che chosì la do, a cciò non intervengcha chome dell'altra.
Frate Filippo dipintore in Firenze
Piero di Chosimo altrebbio in mugello," Ruda, *Fra Filippo Lippi*, pp. 27 and 520, Doc. 6; trans. adapted from Ruda. See Ruda's discussion pp. 27–30.

156 See *ibid.*, p. 29. There is evidence that Lippi did work for the Marchese of Mantua. Mario Equicola, in his *Dell'istoria di Mantova libri cinque* (1521), noted that Ludovico Gonzaga gave Lippi many gifts (presumably in return for the painter's services): see Warnke, *The Court Artist*, p. 49.

157 See Trexler on the conventions of social address used in Renaissance Florence between associates of unequal social footing, *Public Life in Renaissance Florence*, pp. 131ff.

158 Ruda provides the relevant passages from the letters, *Fra Filippo Lippi*, pp. 536–8, and translations, pp. 36–40. In a letter written much later, in 1468, by Lippi to the young Lorenzo de' Medici, the friar responds to Lorenzo's request that he use his influence to promote a candidate for an ecclesiastical benefice, *ibid.*, p. 41 and Doc. 29, p. 545. Ruda argues that this letter demonstrates that Lippi could assume a deferential attitude on occasion (or else that he had "mellowed" considerably in his old age).

159 "Retta ne fui chon Bartolomeo Martelli, disse . . . ch'io al tutto faciessi quanto era di vostra volontà, e molto mi riprese mostrando io avere el torto contro di voi," *ibid.*, pp. 36 and 537, Doc. 21.II.1.

160 "Io feci quanto m'imponesti della tavola et missimi in punto d'ongni chosa." "Ora Giovanni io sono qui al tutto esservi schiavo, e ffarò chon effetto," *ibid.*, pp. 36–8 and 537, Doc. 21.II.1.

161 "Volglio per amore di voi non [togliere?] più che . . . ciento fiorini," *ibid.*, pp. 38 and 537.

162 "Ss'io fussi presuntuoso inn avervi scritto perdonatemi e ffarò senpre quell più e quell meno piacerà alla reverenza vostra," *ibid.*

163 "Io ho hauto adi passati più tue lettere, per le quali ho inteso che havevi presentato la tavola alla Mtà. del Re, et che glera assi piaciuta" (27 May, 1458). "Vegho quanto scrivi la Mtà havere stimata la tavola che m'è grato. Et il signor Cont'd'Ariano ne vuole un'altra, tornando tu in qua puoi pigliare il disegno et esserne sollicitatore. Et se lui non harà pressa, credo la potrà havere" (10 June, 1458), *ibid.*, pp. 40 and 537–8, Docs. 21.III.1,2.

164 Baxandall, *Painting and Experience*, p. 3. See also Martin Warnke's discussion of Cosimo de' Medici's diplomatic use of art in his negotiations with various courts in Italy, *The Court Artist*, pp. 46–53.

165 Francis Ames-Lewis suggests that this unidentified painting is the San Lorenzo *Annunciation*, "Fra Filippo Lippi's San Lorenzo *Annunciation*," while Ruda points to the *St. Jerome in Penitence* in Altenburg, *Fra Filippo Lippi*, p. 383.

166 See Ch. 8 below.

167 Sources: Vasari; 1591 Medici inventory. The painting is now in Berlin. See Ch. 7 below.

168 Sources: Vasari; the 1492 and 1560 Medici inventories. This painting has been associated with the panel in the Altenburg collection: Ruda, *Fra Filippo Lippi*, pp. 382–4, dated to 1436–38, which I consider too early.

169 These panels were sold shortly before 1848, from the Palazzo Medici–Riccardi. They are now in the National Gallery, London.

170 Source: the correspondence with Giovanni de' Medici, Lippi, and Medici agents: see Ruda, *Fra Filippo Lippi*, Doc. 21, pp. 536–8.

171 Sources: Vasari, who misidentified the patron of the cell as the wife of Cosimo de' Medici, and a 1710 Camaldoli chronicle: see Ruda, *Fra Filippo Lippi*, pp. 465–6 and Doc. 26, p. 541.

172 Alessandri's daughter Ginevra was married to Giovanni di Cosimo de' Medici. For information about his political activities, see *Dizionario biografico degli Italiani*, vol. 2, pp. 161–2. See also his correspondence with Giovanni di Cosimo de' Medici in ASF, Mediceo Avanti il Principato.
Lippi painted the *St. Lawrence Enthroned* altarpiece for him, with Sts. Cosmas, Damian, Anthony Abbott and a bishop-monk, and the donor and his two sons (see fig. 97). See n. 80 above. Vasari wrote that Alessandri was one of Lippi's friends ("amico suo"). The only documentary evidence of any kind of relationship existing between Alessandri and Lippi is a record of a series of payments made by the artist in the early 1440s, ASF, Con. Sopp. 79, n. 155, c. 81r.

173 Lionardo Bartolini seems to have acted as an agent for the Medici during the late 1450s and 60s, involved in both economic and political dealings: see his correspondence with Giovanni and Piero di Cosimo de' Medici in ASF, Mediceo Avanti il Principato, filza 6, nos. 323 and 371; filza 9, n. 356; filza 17, nos. 209, 222, and 419. Over this period, he held the positions of one of the "Cinque di Pisa," the *vicario* of San Giovanni, and the Gonfaloniere di Giustizia in Florence. In an obvious homage to the Medici, he named his son born in 1448, "Cosimo," and another son born in 1453, "Damiano." See the biographical sketch in *Raccolta di tutte le prose fiorentine pubblicate e di osservazioni storiche, e critiche accresciute dagli Accademici Fiorentini*, Florence, 1786, vol. XXV, p. 327–8; see also A. Butterfield, *The Sculptures of Andrea Verrocchio*, New Haven and London, 1997, pp. 60–1, for his participation in the commission for Verrocchio's *Doubting Thomas*.

174 Vasari–Milanesi, vol. II, p. 616.

175 Orlandi, *Beata Angelico*, p. 80.

176 I have explored the patronage strategies of a Medici supporter in my article "Giovanni Benci's Patronage of the Nunnery Le Murate."

177 See the classic study by R. and M. Wittkower, *Born Under Saturn*; also Baxandall, *Giotto and the Orators*; Kemp, "From 'Mimesis' to 'Fantasia';" Warnke, *The Court Artist*; P. Burke, *The Italian Renaissance: Culture and Society*, Cambridge, 1986; Wackernagel, *The World of the Florentine Renaissance Artist*.

178 I wish to emphasize that these new conceptions about art and the artist that emerged during the Renaissance, and the transformations within artists' practices, coexisted in interesting and complex ways with traditional

attitudes and practices. See Gregori, Paolucci, and Acidini Luchinat, *Maestri e botteghe*; the introduction to D. S. Chambers, *Patrons and Artists in the Italian Renaissance*, London, 1970, pp. xxiii–xxxv; Thomas, *The Painter's Practice in Renaissance Tuscany*.

179 "Ritrasse allo specchio sè stesso, vestito di nero in abito da prelato, ed il suo discepolo Fra Diamante; dove si piange Santo Stefano," Vasari–Milanesi, vol. II, p. 624. Vasari's portrait of Lippi that opens the 1568 edition of *The Lives*, however, appears to derive from the Francesco Maringhi donor portrait in the *Coronation of the Virgin*, Vasari–Barocchi and Bettarini, *Le vite*, vol. III, Testo, pp. 327.

180 See Ruda, *Fra Filippo Lippi*, p. 464. There is some disagreement regarding which of the two figures in black represents Lippi, with Giuseppe Marchini arguing for the figure at the right, and Eve Borsook suggesting the figure at the left, directly behind the portrait head identified as Carlo de' Medici: Marchini, *Filippo Lippi*, p. 10; Borsook, *Mural Painters of Tuscany*, p. 103. Ruda, however, does not accept that there is a self-portrait in this fresco.

181 Marchini, *Filippo Lippi*, p. 215. See also J. Woods-Marsden, *Renaissance Self-Portraiture: The Visual Constructions of Identity and the Social Status of the Artist*, New Haven and London, 1998, pp. 57–60. Art historians have identified two other self-portraits in Lippi's panel paintings: the figure at the extreme left behind the wall wearing a hooded white mantel in the Barbadori altarpiece (see fig. 103) and the tonsured figure in the left foreground in a similar mantel in the Sant'Ambrogio *Coronation of the Virgin* (see fig. 214): see U. Mengin, *Les deux Lippi*, Paris, 1932, pp. 11 and 14; Oertel, *Fra Filippo Lippi*, pp. 20 and 65; Marchini, *Filippo Lippi*, p. 201–2; Ruda, *Fra Filippo Lippi*, pp. 141 and 396. The tell-tale "self-portrait indicators" are considered to be features in common with the Prato and Spoleto images (snub nose, round face, eyes close together, small, full mouth that turns down at the sides), a self-conscious, engaging gaze out of the picture, and the gesture of the chin resting on the hand – these two became conventions of self-portraiture in the early sixteenth-century. Not all scholars are in agreement over these self-portrait designations. Vasari's portrait identifications for *trecento* and *quattrocento* paintings must be considered with caution, as he tended to project a mid-sixteenth-century sensibility about portraiture back onto these earlier works. Borsook refutes the self-portrait identification in the two panel paintings, claiming that the figure in the Sant'Ambrogio *Coronation* is not wearing Carmelite robes and that the designated self-portraits bear little likeness to one another, "Cults and Imagery at Sant'Ambrogio," p. 170 and n. 161. I find the Prato and Spoleto self-portrait identifications convincing, particularly in the light of Lippi's practice of integrating portraits within his narrative frescos.

182 "Faciem meam in suis historiis pingant, quo illos memores beneficii et gratos esse ac me artis studiosum fuisse posteris praedicent," Alberti, *On Painting and On Sculpture*, pp. 106–7. Lorenzo Ghiberti included his sculpted self-portrait among the *clipei* adorning the frames of the North (1403–24) and East (1425–52) Doors of the Florentine Baptistery.

183 Borsook has suggested that this cleric in red robes is Pius II, "Fra Filippo and the Murals for Prato Cathedral," pp. 58–60. If this identification is correct, the repetition of the pose could function as a form of emulation.

184 See Ch. 7 below, p. 185.

185 Curiously, the pointing left hand is partly obscured by the candle, painted *a secco*, held by the young boy (considered to be a portrait of Lippi's son, Filippino). Perhaps even more odd is the "painter's hand" itself. The friar's right hand clutches his white Carmelite mantle, but this gesture can also be read as an inverted two-finger sign of the "corna." Is this a chance occurrence, or an intentional play undermining the rhetoric celebrating artistic invention, setting it against another order of potent power – *magia*?

186 The sculpted portrait of Lippi on the tomb appears to have been copied from the Spoleto self-portrait, with the pointing gesture here assumed by the right hand that is praised in the verses by Poliziano. The tomb was commissioned by Lorenzo de' Medici in 1488 after a design by Filippino Lippi. I wish to thank Antoinette Roesler-Friedenthal, who is currently finishing her dissertation on *quattrocentro* self-portraiture, for pointing out to me the relationship between the fresco and the tomb effigy and verses. The epitaph reads: "CONDITUS HIC EGO SUM PICTURAE FAMA PHILIPPUS/NULLI IGNOTA MEE EST GRATIA MIRA MANUS/ARTIFICIS POTUI DIGITIS ANIMARE COLORES/SPERATAQUE ANIMOS FALLERE VOCE DIU/IPSA MEIS STUPUIT NATURA EXPRESSA FIGURIS/MEQUE SUIS FASSA EST ARTIBUS ESSE PAREM," Ruda, *Fra Filippo Lippi*, with a prose trans., p. 43.

187 For an interpretation of the signed axe handle, see Ch. 7 below, pp. 178–80.

188 In this regard, Lippi's practice can be contrasted with that of Fra Angelico, who, while also patronized by the Medici and important Florentine patricians and corporations, developed a pictorial style that was placed more directly in the service of religious devotion, with less emphasis on innovation and *invenzioni* for their own sake.

189 Michael Baxandall defines *ingenium* as used within Renaissance humanist rhetoric on the arts as "innate talent that could not be learnt," "particularly associated with invention," Baxandall, *Giotto and the Orators*, p. 15. Martin Kemp notes "I have taken the advice of Michael Baxandall and avoided translating *ingegno*, *ingenium* etc. as 'genius' which carries too many later associations. Perhaps 'innate brilliance' would be the best rendering. 'Talent,' itself, does not convey adequately the intellectual importance of the faculty in the classical tradition," "From 'Mimesis' to 'Fantasia'," p. 351, n. 14. Kemp provides an example of a learned Florentine viewer's response to artistic *ingenium* in Poggio Bracciolini's remark (c. 1429) that he was "moved by the *ingenium* of the artist" and "forced to admire [the ancient sculptors'] . . . *ingenium* and art, since they render a mute and lifeless thing as if it breathed and spoke," p. 391.

190 For Landino's assessment of Lippi's pictorial style, see n. 1 above.

191 Ghiberti wrote "Lo ingegnio sança disciplina o la disciplina sança ingegnio non puo perfetto artefice," quoted by Kemp, "From 'Mimesis' to 'Fantasia'," p. 389.

192 See Baxandall, *Giotto and the Orators*, pp. 15–17; Kemp, *ibid.*, pp. 387–93.

193 "Ma poi che io dal lungo essilio in quale siamo noi Alberti invecchiati, qui fui in questa nostra sopra l'altre ornatissima patria ridutto, compresi in molti ma prima in te, Filippo, e in quel nostro amicissimo Donato scultore, e in quegli altri Nencio e Luca e Masaccio, essere a ogni lodata cosa ingegno da non posporli a qual si sia stato antiquo e famoso in queste arti," Alberti, *On Painting and On Sculpture*, p. 32, cited in Kemp, *ibid.*, p. 388.

194 Campbell, "Pictura and Scriptura," p. 273, who describes "a recognition of distinguishable artistic identity, but one based on quality or superior performance, the possession of certain properties which distinguish the master artist from the common herd. In documents of commission or payment this quality might be referred to as *ingegno*, or *difficultà*, or *magistero*. . . . For rank and file artists, however, especially for those working in collaboration or in subordination to a master, individualizing tendencies are viewed pejoratively in the assessment of quality," p. 273.

195 See Kemp's discussion of the *quattrocento* conceptions of *inventio*, "From 'Mimesis' to 'Fantasia'," pp. 348–61.

196 For a discussion of these altarpieces, see Ch. 7 below, pp. 172–82.

197 Kemp, "From 'Mimesis' to 'Fantasia'," pp. 361–84.

198 Kemp notes that *fantasia*, while mentioned by Cennino Cennini, is not a critical term in Alberti's *De pictura* or *De re aedificatoria*, and it is not until the second half of the fifteenth century in the writings of Filarete and Leonardo da Vinci that the concept is given further elaboration in the visual arts, *ibid.*, pp. 368–9. Regarding Filarete's use of *fantasia*,

Kemp observes "*fantasia* is not wildly irrational; it acts in conjunction with thought, deliberation, investigation, research and discovery, extending the boundaries of rational intellect," p. 370.

199 See Ruda, *Fra Filippo Lippi*, pp. 421–2.

200 "Conviene avere fantasia e operazione di mano, di trovare cose non vedute, cacciandosi sotto ombra di naturali, e fermarle con la mano, dando a dimostrare quello che non è, sia," Cennino, Cennini, *Il Libro dell'Arte*, ed. M. Serchi, p. 17, cited in Kemp, "From 'Mimesis' to 'Fantasia'," p. 368.

CHAPTER SEVEN

1 According to *Il Libro di Antonio Billi* (c. 1516–30), "e al Carmino dipinse . . . sulla piaza sopra la porta del chiostro la Nunziata," cited in Procacci, "L'incendio della Chiesa del Carmine del 1771," p. 199, n. 1.

2 Borsook, "Fra Filippo Lippi and the Murals for Prato Cathedral," p. 60.

3 See Ch. 2 above for an analysis of the Ascension Day enactment. While the religious play was not necessarily a "Carmelite" production, I am including it because it was a major event at Santa Maria del Carmine, and hence, was a Carmine if not a Carmelite presentation.

4 See Barr, "Music and Spectacle in Confraternity Drama," p. 386; Newbigin, *Feste d'Oltrarno*, vol. I, pp. 80 and 94.

5 Barr, "Music and Spectacle," p. 383, from Neri di Bicci's 1466 inventory of the props used in the play.

6 "Di charta pechora, tinto di rosso, chon una lucernuza dirieto," *ibid.*, p. 400, n. 38.

7 *Ibid.*, pp. 383ff (Barr's translation). See also Pochat, "Brunelleschi and the 'Ascension' of 1422," pp. 232–4.

8 Baxandall, *Painting and Experience in Fifteenth Century Italy*, pp. 72ff. Baxandall uses Lippi's young John the Baptist in the Camaldoli *Adoration of the Christ Child* (Uffizi) as an example of such a figure.

9 See Barr, "Music and Spectacle," pp. 380–1 and 399, n. 19.

10 See the model of the play setting constructed by Cesare Lisi in Ventrone, *Le tems revient 'l tempo si rinuova*, p. 217.

11 See Benazzi and Virilli, *Filippo Lippi nel Duomo di Spoleto*, p. 7.

12 For a discussion of the many religious dramas performed in the city, see N. Newbigin, "The Word Made Flesh: The *Rappresentazioni* of Mysteries and Miracles in Fifteenth Century Florence," in Verdon and Henderson, *Christianity and the Renaissance*, pp. 361–75; Ventrone, *Le tems revient*, pp. 207–19.

13 See d'Ancona, *Origini del Teatro Italiano*, vol. I, pp. 249ff, and *Il luogo teatrale a Firenze*, ed. M. Fabbri, E. Garbero-Zorzi, and A. M. Petrioli Tofani, Florence, 1975, pp. 55–7.

14 Vasari–Milanesi, *Le vite*, vol. II, pp. 375–8. See also Newbigin, *Feste d'Oltrarno*, vol. I, pp. 1–43. For a model of the stage setting of the San Felice play, see Ventrone, *Le tems revient*, p. 218.

15 Newbigin, *Feste d'Oltrarno*, vols. I and II; *Sacre Rappresentazioni fiorentine del Quattrocento*, ed. G. Ponte, Milan, 1974, and *Sacre Rappresentazioni fiorentine del Quattrocento*, ed. N. Newbigin, Bologna, 1983.

16 See the discussion in Ch. 6 above, pp. 141–5.

17 J. Pope-Hennessy, *The Study and Criticism of Italian Sculpture*, New York, 1980, p. 69; Rowlands, "Filippo Lippi and his Experience of Painting in the Veneto Region," p. 75.

18 Surely this is the significance of the odd little piglet that follows behind the mother and child, just visible at the lower right of the picture.

19 "[Il] convento di Santa Anna in Ierusalem, di rimpetto allo tempio di Salomone, in giù per la via che si va alla Porta di sancto Stefano, a mano a manca. E questo è quelo luogo, dove naque la Vergine Maria, lo quale luogo fu dato ali nostri fratri heremiti 30 anni di poi la morte di sancto Jacopo," Graziano di S. Teresa, "'Vita fratrum del Sancto Monte Carmelo' del P. Nicola Calciuri," p. 416. Calciuri wrote that the convent "fu casa della Vergine Maria," p. 422. Calciuri's source was one of the early *Vite* of Fra Angelo of Sicily, who was said to have been a friar in this convent.

20 "Apud Jerusalem in Porta Aurea, ubi Anna et Joachim, Virginis Marie progenitores, se mutuo obviaverunt, religiose concedunt et ibi ad honorem Virginis, ubi concepta fuit, ecclesiam fabricaverunt," Graziano di S. Teresa, "Viridarium Ioannis Grossi," p. 267, written c. 1411–35. This claim was first made in the *Universis christifidelibus* of 1300–20: see Saggi, *Santi del Carmelo*, p. 126.

21 Saggi, *ibid.* (my translation).

22 See *ibid.*, pp. 109–30. For visual representations, see C. Emond, *L'Iconographie Carmélitaine dans les anciens Pays-Bas méridionaux*, Brussels, 1961, figs. 26–7.

23 Given this privileged view into a predominantly female space, it is interesting to consider the gendered viewer in the domestic sphere – Bartolini family, kin, friends, associates, and servants. On the gendering of the domestic interior, see R. San Juan, "Mythology, Women and Renaissance Private Life: The Myth of Eurydice in Italian Furniture Painting," *Art History*, vol. 15 (1992), pp. 127–45. On the themes of lineage and domestic concerns within the Renaissance tondo, see A. Hayum, "Michelangelo's Doni Tondo: Holy Family and Myth," *Studies in Iconography*, vols. 7–8 (1981–82), pp. 211–51.

24 Lippi painted this scene on another occasion in the predella panel in the Ashmolean Museum, Oxford. In this rendition, the couple meets outside the city gate in a landscape setting. It is once again a private encounter, with only an angel above and a figure like a *festaiuolo* attending. This contrasts with most representations of the Meeting of the Golden Gate that include a crowd of onlookers (Giotto's fresco in the Arena chapel is a well-known example).

25 See, e.g., Neri di Bicci, *Le Ricordanze*, pp. 111–12.

26 See Ruda, *Fra Filippo Lippi*, the chapter called "The Wilderness Adoration," pp. 218–35.

27 See *ibid.*, pp. 441–4 and 447–8. On the Medici chapel *Adoration*, see also Acidini Luchinat, *Benozzo Gozzoli*, pp. 10 and 15; and Hatfield, "Cosimo de' Medici and the Chapel of his Palace."

28 Ruda, "Style and Patronage in the 1440s," pp. 364–5.

29 See *ibid.*, pp. 218–35.

30 Acidini Luchinat, *Benozzo Gozzoli*, pp. 12–14.

31 F. Cardini, *La Cavalcata d'Oriente: I Magi di Benozzo a Palazzo Medici*, Rome, 1991, pp. 145–51; Acidini Luchinat, *ibid.*

32 See Hatfield, "The Compagnia de' Magi": according to Paolo di Matteo Petribuoni, in 1429, the Epiphany Day procession included "seven hundred costumed men on horseback, among whom were the three Magi and their retinue, honorably dressed," p. 112.

33 *Ibid.*, pp. 135ff, referring to the 1451 procession, in a letter written by Cosimo's wife to his son Giovanni.

34 "Ad Cosmianum sacellum in cuius prima p[ar]te Magi in 2a Angeli canentes in 3a Maria partum adorans, ut corde, v[er]bo et op[er]e adeuntes sacrificarent pingebatur. Regum dona, preces sup[er]um, Mens Virginis ar[a]e sunt sacra Siste procul turba p[ro]fana pedem," Acidini Luchinat, *Benozzo Gozzoli*, p. 13; trans. from C. Acidini Luchinat, "Benozzo Gozzoli's Chapel of the Magi Restored and Rediscovered," in Ames-Lewis, *The Early Medici and their Artists*, p. 132. Acidini Luchinat argues that while the verses were recorded around 1465, they were composed earlier and that the second verse may have been inscribed in the chapel on the step leading to the *scarsella*.

35 The altarpiece was set within an *all'antica* frame of red marble described in the 1492 Medici inventory, Acidini Lucinat, *Benozzo Gozzoli*, p. 10.

36 Paolo Petribuoni described a platform in the Piazza San Marco upon which the manger was set, used in the celebrations of 1429, Hatfield, "The Compagnia de' Magi," p. 112.

37 See Ruda, *Fra Filippo Lippi*, p. 227.

38 Sermon 62, discussed by G. B. Burch in his Introduction to Bernard's *The Steps of Humility*, Cambridge, 1950, pp. 78–80. See Hatfield, "Cosimo de' Medici," p. 230. On St. Bernard's presence in the altarpiece imagery, see Ames-Lewis, *The Early Medici*, pp. 119–20.

39 Art historians working on northern European early Renaissance landscape painting have explored the function of the painted landscape in religious devotion. Two recent examples are R. L. Falkenburg, *Joachim Patinir: Landscape as an Image of the Pilgrimage of Life*, Amsterdam–Philadelphia, 1988, and C. Wood, *Albrecht Altdorfer and the Origins of Landscape*, London, 1993. There was also a well-established tradition in late medieval Europe of the "imaginary pilgrimage" to the Holy Land, effected through religious contemplation. See also M. Botvinick, "The Painting as Pilgrimage: Traces of a Subtext in the Work of Campin and his Contemporaries," *Art History*, vol. 15 (1992), pp. 1–18.

40 See Ruda, *Fra Filippo Lippi*, pp. 224–6.

41 Nicola Calciuri wrote in his *Vita fratrum del sancto Monte Carmelo* (1461): "Legessi nella Sancta Scriptura dello nostro padre Elya e lo nostro padre Eliseo, feciono congregatione e conventi, secondo che scripto è nello libro delli Re.4 Regum ca.vi. dice queste parole: 'Dissono li fratelli nostri figliuoli delli propheti allo nostro padre Eliseo: 'Echo lo luogo lo quale noi habitiamo con esso teco et è aostero a nnoi. Noi ti pregiamo, che ti piaccia di andare al fiumo Iordano, e ciascuno di noi piglerà le legne del boscho per aconciare uno luocho per potersi abitare.' Et ecco come li nostri antichi padri Elia e Eliseo furono primi inventori e trovatori che edificassino conventi," Graiziano di S. Teresa, "'Vita fratrum del sancto monte Carmelo'," pp. 374–5.

42 One could argue that the *Seven Saints* lunette (in the National Gallery, London, painted for the Medici around the late 1440s or early 50s) also belongs with this group of images representing hermetic retreats. The seven saints are seated upon a stone bench placed in the middle of a wooded landscape.

43 In addition to the Medici Palace chapel and the Medici cell in the Camaldoli hermitage mentioned above, there were other sites where the Medici family conceptualized and enacted the religious retreat during the mid-*quattrocento*. Cosimo had a cell built for himself in the Observant Dominican convent San Marco just down the street from his palace on the Via Larga. The Medici villas at Careggi, Trebbio, and Cafaggiolo all had chapels where the Medici could worship during their country sojourns. Cosimo de' Medici's patronage of the Observant Franciscan convent Bosco ai Frati in the Mugello near Trebbio and Cafaggiolo is another example, and there is an interesting description of Bosco by Alberto Avogadro in *De Religione et Magnificentia Illustris Cosmi Medices Florentini* (c. 1465), full of classical references to the sylvan environment, pp. 124–6.

44 I thank John Shearman for pointing out the probable likeness between the landscape in the Adoration paintings and the Medici Mugello lands, and how this visual reference might have functioned for the Medici.

45 Eliade, *The Sacred and the Profane*, pp. 37ff.

46 "E per le singulare gratie e previlegii li quali Dio à concesso a questo sancto monte Carmelo, [è] monte di dolcezza e di mele, monte di suavità, monte di fructi corporali e spirituali," Graziano di S. Teresa, "'Vita fratrum del Sancto Monte Carmelo'," p. 341.

47 Quoted in McCaffrey, *The White Friars*, p. 59.

48 Alexander V was one of the schismatic popes. He was supported by the Carmelites who lobbied hard to end the Schism. There is a copy of Alexander's 1409 bull transcribed in Santa Maria del Carmine in 1422, now in the Florentine archives, ASF, Diplomatico, Santa Maria del Carmine, Jan. 2, 1422. A version of the bull also occurs in Nicola Calciuri's *Vita fratrum del sancto monte Carmelo*, Graziano di S. Teresa, "'Vita fratrum del sancto monte Carmelo'," pp. 405–6. Calciuri also describes the rather similar "Vision of St. Simon Stock" where the Virgin presents Simon with the Carmelite scapular and declares "Questo sarà a te et a tuti li Carmeliti previlegio. Et con questo scapularo moren[do], '*in eternum*' non sentirà pena di fuoco; et con questo morendo sarà salvo," p. 404.

CHAPTER EIGHT

1 The construction of the novitiate at Santa Croce is not documented. There had been a fire in the convent in 1423 followed by a rebuilding of the dormitory, library, cloister, and chapter house, undertaken by different patrons. References to Cosimo de' Medici's patronage at Santa Croce are found in a letter written by the Franciscan minister general Giacomo da Mozzanica in 1457 (quoted in the text), in Vespasiano da Bisticci's *Renaissance Princes, Popes, and Prelates* (quoted in the text), in Domenico da Corella's *Theotocon* (1469), in Timoteo Maffei's *In magnificentiae Cosmi Medicei Florentini detractores* (c. 1454–6), and Avogadro's *De Religione et Magnificentia Illustris Cosmi Medices Florentini* (c. 1465). Vasari wrote that Cosimo built the novitiate dormitory, chapel, stairway, and the passage leading from the church to the sacristy, Vasari–Milanesi, *Le Vite*, vol. II, p. 442, and this seems to be confirmed by the presence of the Medici arms throughout these structures. On the novitiate, see Caplow, *Michelozzo*, vol. II, pp. 577ff; Paatz, *Die Kirchen von Florenz*, vol. I, pp. 508ff; Saalman, "Michelozzo Studies"; Richa, *Notizie Istoriche delle Chiese Fiorentine*, vol. I, pp. 104ff; S. Cabassi and R. Tani, "Il Noviziato di Michelozzo a S. Croce," *Città di Vita*, Florence, 1982, pp. 277–306.

2 The novitiate chapel is listed in a 1439 inventory of the chapels of Santa Croce: see Hall, *Renovation and Counter-Reformation*, p. 166. A bell formerly in the chapel bore an inscription and foundry date of 1445, and this is often accepted as a *terminus ante quem* for the chapel construction: see Moisé, *S. Croce di Firenze*, pp. 162–3; Paatz, *Die Kirchen von Florenz*, vol. I, p. 508; Caplow, *Michelozzo*, vol. 2, pp. 577 and 581; Miller, "Major Florentine Altarpieces from 1430 to 1450," p. 189.

3 The altarpiece was removed from the novitiate chapel in the early nineteenth century and is now in the Uffizi. Two of the predella panels are in the Louvre, while the other three are in the Uffizi. The painting measures 196 × 196 cm, without the original frame. See Ruda, *Fra Filippo Lippi*, pp. 163–8 and 414–16, and Miller, "Major Florentine Altarpieces," pp. 180–202 for a good general discussion, and pp. 188–9 on the predella (attributed to Pesellino). Ruda dates the altarpiece to 1445, while I place it somewhat earlier, c. 1440–5.

4 See Lasareff, "Studies in the Iconography of the Virgin."

5 See Holmes, "Disrobing the Virgin."

6 Vespasiano da Bisticci, *Renaissance Princes*, pp. 218–22.

7 Gombrich, "The Early Medici as Patrons of Art," p. 53.

8 Trexler, *Public Life in Renaissance Florence*, pp. 422–3. On Cosimo's patronage, see also Paoletti, "Strategies and Structures of Medici Artistic Patronage in the 15th Century" and "Fraternal Piety and Family Power;" Robinson, "The Early Medici and Architecture."

9 See D. Kent, *The Rise of the Medici Faction in Florence*, pp. 151–3 and 335–7.

10 Howard Saalman believes that the Pazzi chapel construction at Santa Croce may have been motivated by similar interests. The Pazzi at this date were Medici allies, and he sees their patronage of the conspicuous new chapter house as Medici cultural politicking by proxy. Cited by D. Kent, "The Dynamic of Power in Cosimo de' Medici's Florence," in *Patronage, Art, and Society in Renaissance Italy*, ed. F. W. Kent and P. Simons, Oxford, 1987, p. 70. See also Paoletti, "Strategies and Structures," p. 30.

11 There do not appear to have been any pre-existing Medici links with the church of Santa Croce. It is telling that Cosimo's patronage was directed toward the convent, rather than in the more public church space that was dominated by families associated with the anti-Medici faction.

12 For the chapel dedications at Santa Croce during the *quattrocento*, see the "Inventory of 1439" published by Hall, *Renovation and Counter-Reformation*, Appendix. See also Paatz, *Die Kirchen von Florenz*, vol. I, pp. 414–15, for a ground plan of the church and pp. 544ff for information about the chapel dedications and patronage.

13 See n. 10 above.

14 See H. W. Janson, *The Sculpture of Donatello*, Princeton, 1963, pp. 105–6.

15 Santa Maria del Carmine had an "Oratorio del Noviziato" by 1589, ASF, Con. Sopp. 113, n. 13, c. 85. San Marco, too, had a novitiate chapel built in 1504–6 with an altarpiece of the Purification by Fra Bartolomeo: see H. Teubner, "San Marco in Florenz: Umbauten vor 1500 Ein Beitrag zum Werk des Michelozzo," *Mitteilungen des Kunsthistorischen Institutes in Florenz*, vol. 23 (1979), p. 269; Vasari–Milanesi, vol. IV, p. 161.

16 There is an undated letter written by the novices of Santa Croce to Lorenzo de' Medici, ASF, MAP, filza VII, n. 436. The novices wrote "Noi novitii di Santa Croce et figliuoli di vostra magestia a quella supplichiamo Come nostro signore et padrone die Li sia dispiacere di fare provisione alla casa sua cioe al Novitiato di Sancta Croce di Un buono et optimo reggimento." It is clear from the letter that Lucrezia Tornabuoni had been involved in selecting the master of novices at Santa Croce, and that the novices desired Lorenzo to intervene in the selection of a new master: "sia in nostro utile, si in costumi, come in virtu, cioe d'un maestro come siamo soliti di havere et maximo questo anno preferito che havendo noi havuto Un maestro secondo el nostro bisognio, de qual provedimento ne fu mezzo La Magestia di Madonna Lucretia Vostra zia, desidereremo non mutare altro governo."

17 In a convent ledger recording the annual masses and chapel services over 1581–1611, there is a reference to "la cappella di Cosimo di Giovanni Piccarda de Medici Vecchio posta nel nostro Noviziato li fratini ci hanno a cantare ogni sabato una Messa della Vergine Maria per l'anima di detto Cosimo come per il Breve appare nella nostra Opera d'Archivio," ASF, Con. Sopp. 92, n. 362, c. 61r; Ruda, *Fra Filippo Lippi*, p. 415.

18 "Cum acceperim a fide dignis qualiter completo, et ad finem deducto loco gratissimo pro conservatione et tutela novitiorum dicti nostri Florentini conventus, grata convenientia [facta] fuit inter fratres et virum clarissimum Cosmam de Medicis pro aliquali satisfactione, seu retributione tanti beneficii et domicilii erectione, ut omni mane in aurora cantetur missa in capella sanctorum martyrum Cosmae et Damiani ob reverentiam Virginis gloriosae Mariae, Matris Christi, per ipsos novitios; et quod deberet poni in tabula in qualibet hebdomada unus frater sacerdos, qui praefatam missam debeat cantare sine defectu, et commemorationem facere de SS. martyribus iam dictis Cosma et Damiano," Mencherini, *S. Croce*, pp. 7–8.

19 ASF, Con. Sopp. 92, n. 362, c. 61r; Ruda, *Fra Filippo Lippi*, p. 415.

20 That Lippi was considered among the most accomplished painters of the day – at least from the Medici point of view – is established by Domenico Veneziano's letter to Piero de' Medici of 1438, in which he discourages Piero from giving an altarpiece commission to Lippi or Fra Angelico, suggesting that he would be the artist most suitable to take on the project. Domenico actually mentions the Barbadori altarpiece (then in progress), "una tavola che va in Santo Spirito, la quale lavorando lui dì e note, non la farà in cinqu'ani, sì è gran lavorio": see Wohl, *The Paintings of Domenico Veneziano*, p. 340.

21 See P. Rubin, "Magnificence and the Medici," in Ames-Lewis, *The Early Medici and their Artists*, p. 45.

22 See Miller, "Major Florentine Altarpieces," p. 190. See also Ames-Lewis, "Early Medicean Devices," p. 127, n. 24.

23 See Brown, "A Humanist Portrait of Cosimo de' Medici, Pater Patriae," pp. 190ff.

24 "Pater ille patronus ille perpetuus fautor et adiutor," Donato Acciaiuoli, in the preface to his translation of Plutarch's *Life of Hannibal*, which was dedicated to Piero de' Medici (written by 1467): see *ibid.*, p. 198.

25 "Quam vir magnanimus Cosmas aetate recenti gente satus Medica condidit aere suo," Domenico da Corella, *Theotocon*, p. 105.

26 "La moltitudine delle basse genti sopra tutte le cose Cosimo amavano," Giovanni Cavalcanti, in his *Istorie fiorentine* (1420–40), quoted by D. Kent, "The Importance of Being Eccentric: Giovanni Cavalcanti's View of Cosimo de' Medici's Florence," *The Journal of Medieval and Renaissance Studies*, vol. 9 (1979), p. 119; see also Vespasiano da Bisticci, *Renaissance Princes*, p. 215.

27 Avogadro, *De Religione*, pp. 122–4. This text was written by 1465, which is considered to be the year of Avogadro's death: see E. Gombrich, "Alberto Avogadro's Descriptions of the Badia of Fiesole and of the Villa of Careggi," *Italia medioevale e umanistica*, vol. 5, 1962, pp. 217–29.

28 "Perchè fate porre tante palle in tutti i lati del monistero?", Bizzocchi, *Chiesa e potere nella Toscana del Quattrocento*, p. 95.

29 "In clericorum religiosorumque structuris insignia sua et picta et variis in locis exsculpta cernerentur; quae res gloriae magis, quam divini cultus, cupiditatem quamdam prae se ferre videtur. Nec umquam existimabo illum tot tantasque structuras excitasse, nisi ad quamdam sui nominis immortalitatem, et inanem gloriam adsequendam," Maffei, *In Magnificentiae Cosmi Medicei*, p. 157. See also Bizzocchi, *Chiesa e potere*, p. 95; Gombrich, "The Early Medici," p. 39; A. Fraser Jenkins, "Cosimo de' Medici's Patronage of Architecture and the Theory of Magnificence," *Journal of the Warburg and Courtauld Institutes*, vol. 33 (1970), pp. 162–70; Ames-Lewis, "Early Medici Devices," pp. 127ff.

30 We can see how permission for this was negotiated in the notarized agreement between Cosimo de' Medici and the prior of San Lorenzo in 1442. Cosimo was given the exclusive rights to display his arms in the main chapel and central nave of the church in exchange for funding the completion of the church: see A. Molho, "Cosimo de' Medici: *Pater Patriae* or *Padrino*?," *Stanford Italian Review*, vol. 1 (1979), p. 28.

31 It is telling that Giuseppe Richa, the first commentator to describe the altarpiece, mentions only "Gesù e Maria, e . . . Santi Cosimo e Damiano," omitting altogether the Franciscan saints, *Notizie istoriche*, vol. 1, p. 104.

32 Francesco Benoffi, *Custodia Fiorentina*, 1597, in the Oliveriana di Pesaro MS. 1687 in the Santa Croce Archive, published in Mencherini, *S. Croce*, p. 1. This contrasts with Vespasiano's account, which put Cosimo de' Medici's contribution at 8,000 fl. Cosimo's donation at Santa Croce can be compared with those of Tommaso Spinelli who financed a new cloister (17,859), the heirs of Michele di Guardino who underwrote the library construction (7,948), and the Florentine *comune* which contributed toward the new dormitory (2,000).

33 Bonaventura, *Life of Saint Francis*, pp. 640 and 681.

34 See W. Braunfels, *Abendländische Klosterbaukunst*, Cologne, 1969, pp. 307–8; G. Villetti, "Legislazione e prassi edilizia degli Ordini mendicanti nei secoli XIII e XIV," in *San Francesco d'Assisi: conventi e chiese*, Milan, 1982, pp. 23–31; see also Joanna Cannon's discussion of the influence of Dominican legislation on art on the Franciscans in "Dominican Patronage of the Arts in Central Italy."

35 "Frate Iovenale de Aliss da Fiorenza, lo quale fo uno de li più principali frati che edificasse et fondasse lo convento de Santa Croce de Fiorenza. Quisto, secondo che recita maestro Bartholomeo da Pisa, ha questa pena nel purgatorio: Che sempre, per fine al dì del iudicio, sonno doi martelli sopra lo capo suo, li quali continuamente li percoteno la testa. Et questo lo revelò esso medesimo aparendo ad uno frate, dechiarandoli la pena e lo dolore che sosteneva per questo peccato de fare contra la santa povertà," Oddi, *Franceschina* (c. 1474), vol. II, p. 380. Oddi's source was Bartolomeo da Pisa's *De Conformitate Vitae Beati Francisci*, written in the late fourteenth century, *Analecta Franciscana*, vol. V (1912), p. 108.

36 On the Franciscan Observant movement, see Moorman, *A History of the Franciscan Order from its Origins to 1517*, p. 373ff.

37 See Moorman, *A History of the Franciscan Order*, pp. 375–448; Pulinari, *Cronache dei Frati Minori della Provincia di Toscana* (1580).

38 See Iriarte, *Storia del Francescanismo*, pp. 132ff,

and Moorman, *A History of the Franciscan Order*, pp. 569–85.

39 *Ibid.*, p. 445.

40 See Pulinari, *Cronache dei Frati Minori*, pp. 147–264, 317ff, and 352ff.

41 On Santa Croce, see Moisé, *Santa Croce di Firenze*; Mencherini, *S. Croce*; Benoffi, *Custodia Fiorentina*; and Bartolomeo da Pisa, *De Conformitate Vitae Beati Francisci*, vol. IV, pp. 517–18.

42 Santa Croce ranks fourteenth on Gene Brucker's list of eighteen Florentine monasteries listed according to their wealth in property holdings, based on the 1427 *catasto*. The Benedictine Badia tops the list, with property equal to nearly 20,000 fl., followed by the Umiliati of Ognissanti (13,028) and the Dominican Santa Maria Novella (7,345). The Santa Croce property was valued at 2,370 fl., Brucker, "Monasteries, Friaries, and Nunneries in Quattrocento Florence," p. 45, Table 1.1.

43 Lesnick claims that 86 percent of the friars were from families of low economic means, *Preaching in Medieval Florence*, pp. 48ff.

44 Bizzocchi, *Chiesa e potere*, pp. 28–9.

45 The Alberti were the patrons of the *cappella maggiore*: see Lesnick, *Preaching in Medieval Florence*, Appendix 6; D. Kent, *The Rise of the Medici Faction*, pp. 151 and 335–7.

46 See Brucker, "Monasteries, Friaries and Nunneries," pp. 52ff; and Rubinstein, "Lay Patronage and Observant Reform in Fifteenth-century Florence."

47 The date of Cosimo's building at Bosco ai Frati is not documented and it is difficult to establish the relationship between that and the novitiate at Santa Croce. Michelozzo's work at Bosco ai Frati is usually dated to the mid-1430s following Cosimo's return from exile. A documented visit by Eugenius IV to the nearby Medici villa at Cafaggiolo in 1436 is associated with the consecration of the convent church: see Robinson, "Cosimo de' Medici and the Franciscan Observants at Bosco ai Frati," in Ames-Lewis, *Cosimo "il Vecchio" de' Medici*, pp. 181–94; C. Nottolini, *Bosco ai Frati*, 1989, San Piero a Sieve, pp. 11ff.

48 See Pulinari, *Cronache dei Frati Minori*, pp. 186–7.

49 Brucker lists a series of communal interventions on behalf of the Observant Franciscans from 1431 through 1451, "Monasteries, Friaries and Nunneries," p. 51.

50 San Francesco in Fiesole was established with a land grant from Guido del Palagio in the late fourteenth century. Niccolò da Uzzano gave the land upon which San Salvatore al Monte was built and also supported the Observant Ospizio dello Spedale del Ceppo. Castello Quaratesi's offer to finance the building of the new Observant convent at San Salvatore al Monte was supposedly rejected by the friars at first: see Pulinari, *Cronache dei Frati Minori*, pp. 186 and 319ff; and Rubinstein, "Lay Patronage and Observant Reform," pp. 65 and 68.

51 See D. Kent, *The Rise of the Medici Faction*, pp. 151 and 335–7.

52 See Moisé, *S. Croce di Firenze*, pp. 90 and 491–8.

53 See Paatz, *Die Kirchen von Florenz*, vol. I, p. 591; Seymour, *Early Italian Paintings in the Yale University Art Gallery*, pp. 116–17.

54 There is very little information on the Franciscans of Santa Croce during the *quattrocento* because nearly all of the convent records dating from this epoch were destroyed over the centuries by the periodic flooding of the nearby Arno. The *catasto* of 1427 contains a declaration of the convent's property, ASF, Catasto 194, cc. 368v–369v. There are no complete lists of the friars from the convent or accounts of their activities. Benoffi's *Custodia Fiorentina* provides an incomplete *necrologium* for Santa Croce during the *quattrocento*.

55 In 1300, there were 123 friars in Santa Croce: see Lesnick, *Preaching in Medieval Florence*, p. 45.

56 See Brucker, "Monasteries, Friaries, and Nunneries," p. 44.

57 Of the friars listed in a 1446 notarial document, ASF, Diplomatico, S. Croce, 1446, July 15, the only Florentines among the ministers were the Tuscan provincial minister, Jacopo Biada, and the Tuscan Franciscan inquisitor, Fra Niccolò de Spinelli. The *magister studii* was from Arezzo, the master of the novices from Reggiuolo, the vicar of the convent from Montalcino, and one of the students in the *studium* from France.

58 Benoffi, *Custodia Fiorentina*, "Necrologium." In a notarial document of July 15, 1446, a "Romulus de Medicis" is listed among the friars of Santa Croce.

59 See Burckhardt, *The Civilization of the Renaissance in Italy*, pp. 283–4; Moorman, *History of the Franciscan Order*, pp. 514ff; Hay, *The Church in Italy in the Fifteenth Century*, p. 59.

60 Of course, it was Michelozzo who had designed the Observant Franciscan church at Bosco ai Frati, and the Observant Dominican church and convent of San Marco. Perhaps the new architectural style with the somber *pietra serena* supporting elements and unadorned white walls was associated with a religious asceticism, in contrast with the earlier style in Franciscan churches where the lofty height, elaborate vaulting, and frescoed walls were contrary to the early Franciscan building legislation.

61 On Franciscan novices, see Moorman, *History of the Franciscan Order*, pp. 148–9, 501–3, and 507; Iriarte, *Storia del Francescanismo*, pp. 167ff.

62 Francis of Assisi, *Writings and Early Biographies*, p. 32.

63 For the Constitutions of Narbonne, see *Archivum Francescanum Historicum*, vol. 34 (1941), pp. 39–40. For the Martinae, see L. Wadding, *Scriptores Ordinis Minorum* (Annales), 1906, Rome, vol. X, p. 154.

64 See Iriarte, *Storia del Francescanismo*, p. 169. These texts were influenced by Hugh of St. Victor's *De Institutione Novitiorum*. See also Bynum, *Jesus as Mother*, pp. 268–9, for a bibliography on monastic and canonical treatises for novices (11th–13th centuries).

65 "Discant . . . una saltem diei vel noctis hora tempus et otium vindicare, quando, ad se reversi mentisque cubiculum introgressi, *orent Patrem suum in abscondito* [Matt. 6:6] et in corde contrito et humiliato [Psalm 50:19] universorum Domino familiariter astent," Bernardo da Bess (attr.), *Speculum disciplinae*, Pars II, Cap. I, "De ordinatione respectu Dei," p. 394.

66 "Magister saepenumero hortetur novitios suos doceatque meditari passionem Christi, propriam miseriam, diem mortis, infernales poenas, propria peccata perpetrata et gloriam eis promissam. . . . singulis diebus faciant coronam Virginis Mariae cum VII meditationibus, sicut VII sunt partes ipsius coronae. . . . Prima meditatio est, quando Angelus Gabriel salutavit Virginem Mariam; secunda, quando Christus natus est; tertia, quando praesentavit Virgo Maria eum in templum; quarta, quando Christus discessit a Matre et accessit ad celebrandam coenam cum discipulis; quinta, quando Virgo Maria ploravit Filium suum ante crucem; sexta, quando Christus fuit positus in sepulcro; septima, quando Christus surrexit a mortuis et apparuit Matri suae," *Analecta Franciscana*, vol. II, 1887, p. 342. The letter was written on Nov. 15, 1452, to Albertus Puchelbach, the *guardianus* of the Observant Franciscan convent in Nuremberg.

67 Bartolomeo da Pisa, *De Conformitate*, vol. IV, p. 433; Oddi, *Franceschina*, vol. I, p. 137, and vol. II, pp. 370–1 and 393–4; Pulinari, *Chronache dei Frati Minori*, p. 438, no. 4, and pp. 444–6, no. 8.

68 "Per chi ti sei tu deliberato di lasciarmi!", Pulinari, *Chronache dei Frati Minori*, p. 438, no. 4.

69 Oddi, *Franceschina*, vol. II, p. 371.

70 *Ibid.*, vol. II, p. 393.

71 "Allora vidde chiaramente uscire Yhesu Christo de quella casetta dove se conserva el Sacramento, et andare in verso lui," *ibid.*

72 "Anche foro doi ioveni cari compagni che usciero del seculo et fecerse frati Menori con maximo fervore. Ma uno de loro temptato dal demonio dixe a l'altro: 'Tu me prometteste de tornarte al seculo, si non me piaceva essere frate. Io te dico mo ch'io non voglio essere più frate.' Et lo compagno lo preghò multo, che volesse provare ancora uno poco più; ma quello per alcuni dì consentì,

ma pure stava forte nella sua mala volontà. Al quale dixe lo compagno: 'Io te prego che nante che noi usciamo dell'Ordene, che noi entriamo in chiesia et facciamo alquanto oratione a la Vergene Maria, che ci aiute a pigliare el megliore partito.' Et quillo consentendo, se n'andaro insieme denante a la imagine de la Madonna. Et facendo tutti e doi oratione, quillo che non se ne voleva uscire faceva cum lacrime molto affettuosamente prece per lo compagno. Et in quisto pianto così cordiale, quillo che se ne voleva uscire vidde santo Francesco venire lì, et coglire quelle lacrime del suo compagno in uno vasello d'oro, et presentavale a la Vergene Maria, pregandola che per sua benignità li piacesse exaudire le lacrime del frate caritativo e devoto. Vedendo questa meravigliosa cosa quillo frate temptato, tutto tramortito se recò in sè, et sentisse totalmente essere liberato da quella temptatione diabolica, et visse et finì santamente nella religione," *ibid.*, p. 394; my translation.

73 I am assuming that the Franciscan novices attended the Divine Offices in the choir of the church with the other friars, and used the novitiate chapel for daily masses.

74 See Hood's discussion of the frescos in the novitiate, *Fra Angelico at San Marco*, pp. 195–207.

75 On the pillar in scriptural exegesis, see Didi-Huberman, *Fra Angelico*, Eng. ed., pp. 145–7.

76 "Filius spiritualis beati Francisci; bonus et optimus, quia in omnibus imitatus est patrem suum beatum Franciscum," Gamboso, "L'immagine di S. Antonio nei panegirici dei secoli XIII–XIV," p. 302.

77 The master–disciple relationship between Francis and Anthony was emphasized in the sermons of Jacopo di Pietro di Santo, Corrado di Sassonia, and Roberto d'Angio, in addition to anonymous sermons and panegyrics dating from the thirteenth and fourteenth centuries, *ibid.*, pp. 303ff.

78 "Illorum de primo fuit beatus Franciscus absolute loquendo, quia, inter cetera dona Dei, amoris fervor in eo splenduit. . . . De ordine secundo extitit beatus Antonius, quia inter cetera dona Dei, splendor scientie et cognitionis in ipso primatum tenuit," *ibid.*, p. 302.

79 See Hood's discussion of the Dominican devotional attitudes represented in the frescos by Fra Angelico and his assistants in the convent of San Marco, "Saint Dominic's Manners of Praying: Gestures in Fra Angelico's Cell Frescoes at S. Marco," *Art Bulletin*, vol. 68 (1986), pp. 195–206; "Fra Angelico at San Marco: Art and the Liturgy of Cloistered Life," in Verdon and Henderson, *Christianity and the Renaissance*, pp. 108–31; *Fra Angelico at San Marco*, pp. 200–7.

80 Julia Miller points out how unusual it is to find seated attendant saints in an altarpiece, "Major Florentine Altarpieces," p. 193. She too suggests that this odd feature may derive from the painting's function as an altarpiece for Franciscan novices. She maintains that the seated position represents an ideal, reverentially low position, which a devotee should assume before the Virgin. John Shearman has suggested to me that the arrangement evokes a chapter-house ambience, with the prior's elevated seat flanked by benches – an instruction in hierarchy and discipline.

81 "Et semper ad totum officium sis erectus . . . hoc tantum excepto, quod in nocte, dicto Matutino beatae Virginis, liceat tibi appodiare. . . . Et quamdiu stas in officio, taliter sis honestus, ut nunquam respicias circumstantes nec cum aliquo loquaris ibidem, sed capite aliquantulum inclinato, oculis demissis, manus habeas ante te aut in modum crucis, aut manum in manu ante pectus positam." This passage is from Bonaventura, *Regola novitiorum*, under the chapter "De divino officio," p. 193. There are similar elaborations in other sections of the *Regola*, and throughout Bernardo da Bess, *Speculum disciplinae*. The guides also instruct the novices when and how to move from a seated to a standing or kneeling position, and how to avoid making too much noise manipulating the folding seats of the wooden choir stalls: "Sedilia vero debent non passim cum pede, sed cum manu elevari et caute deponi," Bernardo da Bess, *Speculum disciplinae*, Pars I, Cap. XV, p. 322.

82 Miller, "Major Florentine Altarpieces," p. 194.

83 See Bynum, *Jesus as Mother*, pp. 113–25.

84 Francis of Assisi, *Writings and Early Biographies*, p. 143.

85 Quoted in Miles, "The Virgin's One Bare Breast," p. 202.

86 From the 1223 Franciscan Rule, Francis of Assisi, *Writings and Early Biographies*, p. 73. Caroline Walker Bynum has emphasized the role reversal underlying St. Francis's frequent reference to himself as "mother," *Holy Feast and Holy Fast*, pp. 95ff.

87 "Quidquid superior vel praepositus eis vel instructor iniunxerit, quasi divinitus imperatum, statim ut veri obedientiae filii devote adimpleant," Bernardo da Bess, *Speculum disciplinae*, Pars II, Cap. III, p. 405.

88 See the Franciscan Rules of 1221 and 1223 in Francis of Assisi, *Writings and Early Biographies*, pp. 34–7.

89 *Ibid.*, p. 637.

90 "Matrem se illis in lenitatis dulcedine, patrem in correctionis censura exhibeat," Bernardo da Bess, *Speculum disciplinae*, Pars I, Cap. X, p. 309. See Bynum, *Holy Feast and Holy Fast*, pp. 101ff.

91 Steinberg, *The Sexuality of Christ in Renaissance Art and in Modern Oblivion*; Bynum, *Jesus as Mother*; *Holy Feast and Holy Fast*, and "The Body of Christ in the Later Middle Ages: A Reply to Leo Steinberg," *Renaissance Quarterly*, vol. 39 (1986), pp. 399–439; and Miles, "The Virgin's One Bare Breast." See also Holmes, "Disrobing the Virgin."

92 Steinberg, *Sexuality of Christ*, pp. 14–15, fig. 144.

93 Miles, "The Virgin's One Bare Breast," pp. 200ff.

94 Francis of Assisi, *Writings and Early Biographies*, pp. 78 and 93.

95 "*Delectabile . . . et suave videre Matrem clementiae et audire, quae omnibus delectabilis est, quae filiis suis propinat lac et mel in sua Prole*, ut sit mel in gustu Deitatis, et lac in gustu humanitatis," from Bonaventura's Sermon on the Nativity (Op. 9, 708a), excerpted in Laurentius di Fonzo, *Doctrina Sancti Bonaventurae de Universali Meditatione B. Virginis Mariae*, Rome, 1938, pp. 186–7.

96 John O'Malley speculates on this possibility in his "Postscript" to Steinberg's *Sexuality of Christ*, p. 202: "The poverty issue that racked the Franciscan order was still very much alive in the 15th and 16th centuries. Could there, at least in some instances, be a vague allusion to the prophetic, radical impulse articulated in the evocative slogan so popular in the late Middle Ages – 'Nudum sequi nudum Christum?' In other words, might there be an ascetical and reform overtone even to the seemingly comfortable scenes of nude infancy?"

97 Bynum, *Holy Feast and Holy Fast*, p. 98.

98 In a letter to Francesco Barbaro of 1428, Poggio Bracciolini noted "Sum tamen satis apertus et ore, et calamo, quamvis non ut frater ille de Observantia, qui nuper Anagniae nudus ad populum concionatus est," T. Tonelli, *Poggii Florentini epistolae*, Florence, 1832, vol. I, epist. XXVI, p. 262, referred to in Hay, *The Church in Italy*, p. 70.

99 Bonaventura does not make any references to the Virgin's maternity in these chapters. In fact, the Virgin and St. Francis are rarely mentioned as *exempla* in the *Regula novitiorum* and *Speculum disciplinae*. It is Christ who is invoked directly, in the spirit of Francis's advocacy of the *imitatio Christi*.

100 Millard Meiss was able to associate only two of the *trecento Madonna lactans* images he collected with the Franciscans (one in Naples and one in Palermo), as opposed to nine images with Dominican ties, *Painting in Florence and Siena after the Black Death*, p. 144. To Meiss's Franciscan *Madonna lactans* images can be added two frescos from Santa Croce in Florence: a half-length version from a vault in the first cloister (now detached and in the Museo S. Croce), attributed to the circle of Orcagna, and an early fifteenth-century fresco (see fig. 196) from the nave of the church (also detached and in the Museo): see L. Becherucci, ed., *I Musei di Santa Croce e di Santo Spirito a Firenze*, Florence, 1983, pp. 167 and 171, figs. 116 and 126; a panel by Taddeo di Bartolo (c. 1397) in Budapest from San Francesco in Pisa: see S. Symeonides,

Taddeo di Bartolo, Siena, 1965, pp. 51 and 205–6, pl. XIa; a late fifteenth-century Sienese half-length version of unknown provenance with Sts. Bernardino and Anthony of Padua flanking the Virgin at the Walters Gallery in Baltimore: see F. Zeri, *Italian Paintings in the Walters Art Gallery*, 1976, Baltimore, vol. I, pp. 130–1, fig. 88; and an early sixteenth-century della Robbia shop terracotta from San Francesco in Foiano: see A. Marquand, *Andrea della Robbia and his Atelier*, Princeton, 1922, vol. II, pp. 215–16. There is a narrative illustration of the Madonna nursing the Christ Child in the manger in a fourteenth-century Italian manuscript of the Franciscan *Meditations on the Life of Christ*, Bibliothèque Nationale, Paris, MS. Ital. 115, reproduced in I. Ragusa and R. Green, eds., *Meditations on the Life of Christ*, Princeton, 1961, p. 53. There is no evidence, however, that this particular copy of the popular and widely disseminated text was used in a Franciscan context.

101 This painting has recently been associated with Observant Franciscanism in Siena: see Christiansen, Strehlke, and Kanter, *Painting in Renaissance Siena 1420–1500*, p. 249; and C. Strehlke, "La *Madonna dell'Umiltà* di Domenico di Bartolo e San Bernardino," *Arte cristiana*, vol. 72 (1984), pp. 381–90.

102 Perhaps the only concession made to a Franciscan iconography of poverty can be seen in the headdress, which, uncharacteristically for Lippi, consists of a simple white veil that covers the Virgin's long blond hair. This arrangement is somewhat similar to that of "Lady Poverty" in the painting *St. Francis Marrying Lady Poverty* ascribed to the circle of the Sienese artist Vecchietta in the Alte Pinakothek in Munich, *Alte Pinakothek München*, Munich, 1983, p. 542.

103 See Ch. 6, n. 1 above.

104 See Hood, *Fra Angelico at San Marco*, pp. 195–207.

105 From Bonaventura's *Life of St. Francis*, pp. 642–3.

106 Francis of Assisi, *Writings and Early Biographies*, p. 669.

107 "Turpe est enim religiosis personis carnium nuditate occurrere cavet omnis honestus, ne eius umquam appareat caro nuda, nisi quantum compulerit necessitas manifesta," Bernardo da Bess, *Speculum disciplinae*, Pars I, Cap. XXV, p. 367.

108 "Piero, perchè tu sei stato giovane mondano e lascivo, però questi frati dubitano del tuo fervore: onde vogliamo provare, se tu sei morto al mondo totalmente in verità; onde io voglio menarti nudo al refettorio e batterti avanti ai frati," Pulinari, *Chronache dei Frati Minori*, p. 170.

109 Richa, *Notizie istoriche*, vol. I, p. 72.

110 "Sed nec facile matrem propriam osculentur," Bernardo da Bess, *Speculum disciplinae*, Pars I, Cap. XXX, p. 381.

111 Bonaventura, *Life of Saint Francis*, p. 666.

112 St. Anthony of Padua's experience was the prototype for subsequent Franciscan miracles of this type. A story included in the *Speculum disciplinae* for its instructional value tells of one superior's vision that took place in the choir of the church while the friars were reciting the Divine Office. The Virgin appeared and offered the Christ Child to each of the friars assembled, with the exception of those who weren't kneeling in the proper devotional stance, Bernardo da Bess, *Speculum disciplinae*, Pars I, Cap. XV, "De disciplina circa divinum officium in choro," pp. 324–5.

113 Bonaventura, *Life of St. Francis*, pp. 783–4.

114 See Bynum, *Holy Feast and Holy Fast*, p. 101.

115 "How readily she nursed Him, feeling a great and unknown sweetness in nursing this Child, such as could never be felt by other women!," Ragusa and Green, *Meditations on the Life of Christ*, p. 55. See also n. 100 above.

116 I have explored the polysemic character of the *Madonna lactans* in fifteenth-century Florentine art in my article "Disrobing the Virgin."

117 See Meiss, *Painting in Florence and Siena*, pp. 133ff; Lasareff, "Studies in the Iconography of the Virgin;" F. Antal, *Florentine Painting and its Social Background*, London, 1948, pp. 334–45.

118 See Meiss, *Painting in Florence and Siena*, pp. 137ff.

119 Miles, "The Virgin's One Bare Breast," pp. 203–4.

120 See E. Sanders, "Realism in Florentine Painting, 1400–1465: Practice and Theory," Ph.D. dissertation, Columbia University, 1984, Abstract.

121 These include a street tabernacle by Bicci di Lorenzo (c. 1420s) near San Salvi, now in storage at San Salvi, Florence; a panel close in style to Bicci di Lorenzo (c. 1425–50) from the Ospedale di S. Maria Nuova, now in the Palazzo Davanzati, Florence; a panel attributed to Niccolò di Pietro Gerini in the Acton Collection, Florence.

122 See P. L. Roberts, *Masolino da Panicale*, London, 1993, pp. 181–2 and 208–9 (dated 1425), and Joannides, *Masaccio and Masolino*, p. 379 (dated c. 1420–5).

123 The wet nurse's gown seems to have had either two laced or buttoned slits or a single laced opening up the front: see Levi Pisetzky, *Storia del costume in Italia*, vol. II, p. 230, fig. 99. My argument may be somewhat circular here, as the evidence for the appearance of Renaissance nursing attire is found in artistic representations of the allegorical figure Charity, the *Madonna lactans*, and the *balie* attending in scenes of the Birth of the Virgin and the Birth of the Baptist.

124 Meiss (writing more specifically about the *Madonna lactans* of the Madonna of Humility variety) observed that during the *quattrocento* there was a tendency to "monumentalize and ennoble the representation" by raising the Virgin on a dais with a rich cloth and elaborate architectural backdrop behind and rarely showing the Child in the act of nursing, *Painting in Florence and Siena*, pp. 139–40.

125 In all fairness, Vasari, in his life of Lippi, noted that when the painter was commissioned to execute an altarpiece for Carlo Marsuppini, the patron encouraged him "che egli avvertisse alle mani che dipigneva, perchè molto le sue cose erano biasimate," Vasari–Milanesi, vol. II, p. 618. And indeed, one often finds *pentimenti* in Lippi's pictures around the hands and feet of his figures.

126 The notable exception is Benozzo Gozzoli's interesting St. Sebastian fresco in San Gimignano, where the Madonna, with both breasts bared, appears kneeling alongside the mature Christ who points to his bleeding wound (1464, Sant'Agostino): See D. Cole Ahl, *Benozzo Gozzoli*, New Haven and London, 1996, pp. 142–5 and fig. 174 and p. 303, n. 71. The *Madonna lactans* does appear on occasion in the work of Neri di Bicci, and in a group of paintings attributed to Masaccio's brother Giovanni di Giovanni "Lo Scheggia." The majority of these images were not displayed in the city of Florence, however, but rather in the provinces and subject towns.

127 Examples include paintings by Cosimo Rosselli: from 1471, in Santa Maria, Lungtuono, Castelfiorentino; in the Uffizi (1492); and in the Kress Collection, Rolins College, Winter Park, Florida; by Botticelli: the Bardi altarpiece, 1485, Berlin; the Raczinsky tondo, Berlin; a tondo in the Ambrosiana, Milan, and two paintings after Botticelli in Avignon and in the National Gallery, London; by Filippino Lippi: a "double intercession" (c. 1490) in the Alte Pinakothek, Munich, and the *Madonna and Child with Sts. Jerome and Dominic* (1490s) for the Rucellai chapel in San Pancrazio, now in the National Gallery, London; and by the Ghirlandaio shop.

128 For a more extensive discussion of the *Madonna lactans* in fifteenth-century Florentine art and culture, see Holmes, "'Frate Filippo di Tommaso Dipintore'," pp. 423–38, and "Disrobing the Virgin."

129 Fra Angelico's polyptych for San Domenico in Perugia is dated anywhere from 1437 to 1450.

130 Neri di Bicci's pictorial output (1453–80) includes many gold-ground altarpieces and many examples of the rectangular single-field altarpiece in which an illusionistic framing is contrived to separate the lateral saints into their own compartments.

131 Examples include Botticelli's Bardi altarpiece for the Bardi chapel in Santo Spirito (1485, now in Berlin); the Verrocchio shop *Madonna and Child with the Baptist and St. Donato* (1478/85) in the Duomo in Pistoia, and Cosimo Rosselli's *Madonna and Child with*

Sts. James and Peter (1492) currently in storage at San Salvi, Florence.

132 Humfrey and Kemp, *The Altarpiece in the Renaissance*, pp. 4–5.

133 See M. Righetti, *Storia Liturgica*, Milan, 1964, vol. I, pp. 85–6 and pp. 354–5, and vol. II, pp. 663–4.

134 I am by no means suggesting any direct relationship between the writings of Rudolph de Tongres and this innovation in Florentine altarpiece design.

CHAPTER NINE

1 According to the concessions, the construction of any monastery, church, oratory, hospital, or religious house in the parish of Sant'Ambrogio was prohibited without a license from the nuns, ASF, Con. Sopp. 79, n. 169, #36.

2 The agreement was drawn up by the Florentine notary Tommaso di Bartolomeo di Francesco and exists in a parchment copy, ASF, Diplomatico, Sant'Ambrogio, 1424, Dec. 2, and a rough version among Tommaso di Bartolomeo's notarial protocols, ASF, Not. Antecos. 20293, cc. 101v–102r and 105r.

3 My account is based in part on primary documentation but also relies heavily on a chronicle written in 1598 by one of the nuns of Le Murate, Suora Giustina Niccolini, *Cronache del N. N. Monastero di Santa Maria Annunciata dette le Murate di Firenze* – hereafter, *Cronache del Monastero* – now in the Biblioteca Nazionale, Florence, II.II.509. Suora Giustina consulted many primary sources retained in the monastery, including "le antiche cronache," a "Libro di Vita et Morte," copies of papal bulls, and notarial documents. Her account was evidently consulted by Giuseppe Richa who reproduces some of the information in his chapters on Le Murate, Richa, *Notizie istoriche delle chiese fiorentine*, vol. II, pp. 79–112. I wish to thank Kate Lowe for informing me about this invaluable source.

4 *Cronache del Monastero*, cc. 13r–14r.

5 This bull is published by Eduardo Nunes, *Dom Frey Gomez*, pp. 309–10. The terms of the bull and its implementation are spelled out in a notarial document written a year later, which exists in two copies in the Florentine State Archives: ASF, Diplomatico, Sant'Ambrogio, 1435, June 3 (the original) and ASF, Con. Sopp. 81, n. 104, #4 (n.p; a considerably more legible copy dating from the eighteenth century, which also contains a copy of the bull).

6 *Cronache del Monastero*, cc. 9v–10r. The church is described as "un poco di Chiesina," while the *Cronache* explains that the nuns were prohibited from having a bell unless it were "di pochissimo peso."

7 *Cronache del Monastero*, c. 17r.

8 Lippi's painting of St. Bernard (which Vasari described as representing "storie di San Benedetto e San Bernardo") was destroyed in a flood in 1547, *Cronache del Monastero*, c. 17r: "andò in pezzi nella piena che fù l'anno 1547;" Vasari–Milanesi, *Le vite*, vol. II, p. 617. For the identification of the *Annunciation* for the main altar, see n. 125 below.

9 See Julian Gardner's article "Nuns and Altarpieces." For a discussion of Lippi's *Annunciation* for Le Murate from the perspective of the patron Giovanni Benci's interests, see Holmes, "Giovanni Benci's Patronage of the Nunnery Le Murate."

10 For the history of Sant'Ambrogio, see Richa, *Notizie istoriche*, vol. II, pp. 236–50, and G. Anichini, "Sant'Ambrogio e la chiesa di Firenze," in *Ambrosiana: scritti di storia, archeologia e arte pubblicati nel XVI centenario della nascita di Sant'Ambrogio*, Milan, 1942, pp. 339–47. Anichini claimed that the nuns were already at Sant'Ambrogio by c. 988, p. 346. The first documentary reference attesting their presence is a papal bull of Innocent II dated May 4, 1141, which places the nuns of Sant'Ambrogio under the protection of the Holy See, ASF, Diplomatico, Sant'Ambrogio, 1141, May 4.

11 The early convent documents are few and provide little information regarding the social background of the nuns: see Richa, *Notizie istoriche*, vol. II, pp. 238 and 244–5, and ASF, Diplomatico, Sant'Ambrogio 1268, March 1, and 1351, Dec. 1.

12 In my archival research, I have focused primarily on the fifteenth-century material and can make only tentative suggestions about the earlier congregations of nuns. Sharon Strocchia is undertaking a study of Sant'Ambrogio in conjunction with four other Benedictine convents in Florence, and we must await the publication of her research for more specific information on the early history of the convent. On the parish of Sant'Ambrogio, see S. Cohn, *The Laboring Classes in Renaissance Florence*, New York, 1980, pp. 29 and 175ff.

13 On Aug. 6, 1368, the bishop of Florence reconfirmed the nuns' traditional rights in the parish, with the explanation that the nuns' income was much reduced and that they could not afford to lose alms to competing religious institutions, ASF, Con. Sopp. 79, n. 169, no. 36.

14 ASF, Diplomatico, Sant'Ambrogio, 1305, Sept. 2 and 3. The ceiling was established because the papal legate felt that the convent could not physically house a larger number.

15 In 1424, the nuns of Sant'Ambrogio were Abbess Niccolaia di Stefano Buonaccorsi, her sister Caterina, Francesca di Niccolò Bartolini, Antonia di Stagio Barducci, and Giovanna d'Antonio del Cane. A year later, Leonarda d'Antonio di Tano joined them, ASF, Diplomatico, Sant'Ambrogio, 1424, Dec. 2, and ASF, Not. Antecos. 20293, cc. 105r and 135v. A decade later, the core group of professed nuns continued to number around six, with an additional three to five women who were either boarders or novices, ASF, Con. Sopp. 79, n. 451, n.p. – the nuns are listed in entries made in July and Sept. 1431, in Nov. 1433, and Nov. 1434.

16 There were other nunneries in the area: San Pier Maggiore (Benedictine), Santa Verdiana (Vallombrosan), Santa Maria di Candeli (Augustinian), and Santa Maria Maddalena (Benedictine *convertite*). Le Murate and Santa Verdiana, however, were the only nunneries in the immediate parish of Sant'Ambrogio.

17 R. Trexler, "Le célibat à la fin du Moyen Age." See also Brucker, "Monasteries, Friaries, and Nunneries in Quattrocento Florence," and Molho, "Tamquam vere mortua: Le professioni religiose femminili nella Firenze del tardo medioevo." On the causes of the increase in female enclosure, see Zarri, "Monasteri femminili e città," pp. 360ff; Herlihy and Klapisch-Zuber, *Tuscans and their Families*, pp. 223–6; Molho, *ibid.*, p. 9.

18 Trexler, "Le célibat," p. 1333.

19 *Ibid.*, p. 1334, tab. II.

20 Trexler's figures can be compared with Molho's tabulations based on the percentage of women with investments in the dowry fund (*Monte delle doti*) who became nuns, increasing from 3.6 percent in 1425–99 to 15.5 percent in 1500–29, "Tamquam vere mortua," p. 7, tab. 2.

21 Trexler calculated 75%, based on the number of nuns with family names listed in the ecclesiastical *catasto* of 1427, "Le célibat," p. 1339. Unfortunately, there are only a handful of convent lists in the *catasto*, accounting for only 122 of the estimated c. 900 nuns and *converse* in the city. Many religious institutions did not file *catasto* reports and those which did provided very uneven information. David Herlihy and Christiane Klapisch-Zuber pared Trexler's percentage down to 66%, looking at the taxable income declared by the nuns' families in the *catasto*, using an income of 1,600 fl. as the lower cut-off point, *Tuscans and their Families*, pp. 136 and 152–3.

22 In 1456, there were fifteen nuns, ASF, Con. Sopp. 79, n. 169, nos. 114 and 115.

23 *Ricordo di Monache e doti dal 1447 al 1468*, ASF, Con. Sopp. 79, n. 455.

24 Twenty of the twenty-three nuns, or 87 percent, are given patronyms. If this is used as an indicator of patrician status, then the patrician percentage of nuns at Sant'Ambrogio was considerably higher than the Florentine average of 75 percent calculated by Trexler and the 66 percent calculated by Herlihy and Klapisch-Zuber: see n. 21 above.

25 Lisa d'Antonio di Michele, widow of Betto Peruzzi, was in the convent by 1451. Margherita di Giovanni di Jacopo di Bertino Strozzi entered the convent in 1449 with a

dowry of 100 fl. and Lisabetta di Chierico degli Strozzi entered the convent at the end of 1459, ASF, Con. Sopp. 79, n. 455, cc. 7r, 9r, and n.p. at end of register. In 1468, two daughters of Barillo di Palla Novello Strozzi entered the convent, along with one of his brother Agnolo's daughters, ASF, Con. Sopp. 79, n. 455, cc. 39v and 40r.

26 Gabriella Zarri writes that the convent dowries during the Renaissance were from $\frac{1}{10}$ to $\frac{1}{3}$ the amount of marriage dowries, "Monasteri femminili," p. 367. By the mid-*quattrocento*, marriage dowries ranged from 300 to 1,000 fl., with 600 fl. as the average: see Trexler, "Le célibat," p. 1340; Herlihy and Klapisch-Zuber, *Tuscans and their Families*, p. 224; see also Molho, "Tamquam vere mortua," pp. 18–19.

27 The sisters were Ginevra (1443) and Agnola (1447) di Francesco Bagnesi; Maria (1443) and Alessandra (1452) di Antonio di Giovanni Barbadori; Giuliana (1446) and Maddalena di Nofri del Caccia, ASF, Con. Sopp. 79, n. 455, c. 2v, 3r, 3v, 12r, and 23r, and n. 155, c. 50v. A stipulation in the Episcopal Constitutions of Florence limited the number of members from the same family in a nunnery to two. The 1517 Statutes explained that "experience shows that sects and divisions are generated by a multitude of relatives": see Trexler, *Synodal Law in Florence and Fiesole*, p. 92.

28 In early 1456, a five-year-old was permitted to enter the convent as a *pupilla* with the intention of following the religious life, but the wording of the *Ricordo di Monache* makes it clear that this was an exception made on account of the fact that her mother was already in the convent, ASF, Con. Sopp. 79, n. 455, cc. 18v–19r. The situation at Sant'Ambrogio can be compared with that of the general population of Florentine nunneries. While the age of religious profession was set at sixteen, many girls entered the nunneries as *fanciulle* and lived most of their lives within the convent walls. A second group entered at around age sixteen, after whatever possibilities of marriage had fallen through. Widows joined nunneries in large numbers and Florentines also placed their young daughters destined for marriage in convents as boarders. Working with the scanty information contained in the ecclesiastical *catasto* of 1427, Herlihy and Klapisch-Zuber estimated that one-fifth of the women in convents were between the ages of five and eighteen, *Tuscans and their Families*, p. 137, while Molho, using the data from the *Monte delle doti*, calculates that the average age of profession before 1480 was 17.6 years, "Tamquam vere mortua," pp. 13–14.

29 Niccolaia Buonaccorsi was the abbess by 1422 when the Florentine archbishop Amerigo Corsini reviewed the nunnery during his episcopal visitations, Archivio Arcivescovile (Florence), Visite Pastorali, Amerigo Corsini 1422, c. 42v. The last reference I have found that describes her as abbess dates from March 12, 1465, ASF, Con. Sopp. 79, n. 455, c. 27r.

30 See the entry on Buonaccorsi in the *Dizionario biografico degli italiani*, vol. 15, pp. 97–100. Lauro Martines also gives a rough biographical sketch of him in *Lawyers and Statecraft in Renaissance Florence*, p. 483.

31 Buonaccorsi was not himself a resident of the Sant'Ambrogio parish, living in the parish of San Ruffillo, *Dizionario biografico*, vol. 15, p. 100. His involvement with Sant'Ambrogio probably came as a result of his membership in the Arte dei Giudici e Notai, which was very active in the Corpus Christi celebrations at Sant'Ambrogio. He served as a witness to numerous contracts negotiated in the convent, in addition to transacting some of his own business on the premises. He placed two of his daughters in the convent, Caterina and Niccolaia. See ASF, Con. Sopp. 79, n. 169, no. 52, and ASF, Diplomatico, Sant' Ambrogio, 1426, Aug. 8; AFS, Diplomatico, Sant'Ambrogio, 1426 (Florentine Style), Feb. 9; and AFS, Diplomatico, Sant'Ambrogio, 1429, June 15.

32 Antonia Barducci became abbess after the death of Niccolaia Buonaccorsi, after March 12, 1465. She held the position until July 4, 1469. She was succeeded by Maria d'Antonio Barbadori: see Borsook, "Cults and Imagery at Sant'Ambrogio in Florence," p. 198, n. 170; ASF, Con. Sopp. 79, n. 169, no. 148.

33 In 1427, Lorenzo and Giovanni di Stagio Barducci lived together in a house in the Sant'Ambrogio parish on Borgo Allegri. Their combined taxable income in the *catasto* is given as 2,833 fl., ASF, Catasto 80, c. 99. Nicolai Rubinstein classifies Lorenzo's son Stagio among the candidates belonging to the "new families" who qualified for the first time in the 1466 draw for the gonfaloniership, *The Government of Florence under the Medici*, p. 154. Giovanni's son Lorenzo made a similar leap into the ranks of the grander patriciate through his employment by the Medici in the London branch of their bank: see R. de Roover, *The Rise and Decline of the Medici Bank (1397–1494)*, p. 331.

34 See Borsook, "Cults and Imagery," p. 169 and n. 96. There is a curious early reference to Giovanni Barducci in the documents of the Arte dei Medici e Speziali, as the "camerario" of the guild who received Masaccio's inscription fee when the latter entered the guild on Jan. 7, 1422: see Beck, *Masaccio*, p. 11.

35 Apollonia had been given the house by the *comune*, through the agency of a wealthy, influential woman who was impressed by her extreme piety, *Cronache del Monastero*, c. 4r.

36 In late 1419, when Martin V conferred indulgences upon the nuns, there were ten of them living on the Ponte Rubiconte: see Nunes, *Dom Frey Gomez*, p. 307, n. 61.

37 *Cronache del Monastero*, c. 11r.

38 *Ibid.*

39 Eduardo Nunes described the gradual introduction of the title "Le Murate" during the 1430s, *Dom Frey Gomez*, p. 309.

40 According to the *Cronache del Monastero*, they began to "occuparsi non solo nella vita contemplativa et mortificatione del corpo ma ancora all'opere manuale con che si aiutavano et acquistavano assai tenendo ogni cosa in comune," c. 10r.

41 *Ibid.*, cc. 10r, 15r, and 45r ("arretavono, e grani di Profumo, et gittavono in forma le Pitture di gesso"). Nunes has found evidence of some of these activities at Le Murate during the 1430s and 40s in the account books of the Badia, *Dom Frey Gomez*, p. 309. Kate Lowe records a number of manuscripts presented by the nuns of Le Murate on ceremonial occasions, dating from the late fifteenth and early sixteenth centuries, "Female Strategies for Success in a Male-ordered World," p. 217, nn. 43 and 44. These included a gift received by the Duchess of Ferrara in 1490; a prayer book sent to the Queen of Portugal; a missal given to Leo X in 1515; and a manuscript copied by Suora Battista Carducci of Le Murate (but considered to have been illuminated by a layman) with Julius II's arms: see Lowe, "Women's Work at the Benedictine Convent of Le Murate in Florence."

42 In the *Cronache del Monastero*, this change is presented in a reforming context, as a switch to the primitive Benedictine habit that had been used by Benedict's followers at Monte Cassino, c.11v.

43 Lowe, "Female Strategies," pp. 213ff.

44 "Non furono Nobile di Sangue eccetto che una delli Ubaldini," *Cronache del Monastero*, c. 13. This was Caterina d'Antonio Ubaldini who joined the nuns by 1424, and became the fourth abbess in 1475.

45 None of the thirteen nuns mentioned in 1424 is given a patronym, although this is characteristic of notarial records pertaining to nunneries. Twelve of the thirteen nuns who moved from the Ponte Rubiconte to the new monastery on Via Ghibellina are named in the 1424 accord as Abbess Agata di Domenico, Apollonia di Venturo, Antonia di Bernardo, Filippa di Giovanni, Benedetta di Bartoldo, Piera di Nanno, Maddalena d'Antonio, Margherita di Cecco, Barbara di Nori, Maria di Niccola, Jacopa di Domenico, and Caterina d'Antonio, ASF, Con. Sopp. 81, n. 104, no. 4 (n.p.). Caterina is elsewhere identified as the only patrician nun, belonging to the Ubaldini family: see n. 44 above.

46 The *Cronache del Monastero* gives her age as forty-two when she became abbess. However, the inscription on her tomb in the convent church indicates that she was eighty-

one when she died in 1475, and this would set her birth date in 1394, and her age in 1439 at forty-five, *Cronache del Monastero*, c. 16v.

47 F. W. Kent, "Lorenzo de' Medici, Madonna Scolastica Rondinelli," p. 365. Kent misidentifies Scolastica's father as Rinaldo Rondinelli: see *Cronache del Monastero*, c. 16v, and ASF, Catasto 614, cc. 134r–135r (1442, S. Croce, Carro).

48 Scolastica placed one daughter in the convent three years before she herself entered, while a second daughter, age eight, accompanied her when she entered Le Murate in 1438, *Cronache del Monastero*, c. 16v; see also ASF, Catasto 614, *ibid.* The members of the Strozzi family were Cecilia di Pagorro Strozzi who professed in 1445 at age nineteen, Raffaella di Carlo Strozzi who professed in 1452 at age sixteen, and Teodosia di Carlo Strozzi who professed in 1453 at age eight, ASF, Carte Strozzi, ser. 3, n. 93, c. 395.

49 Caterina was born in 1438. After spending some time at Le Murate as a boarder, she married Piero Vespucci, *Cronache del Monastero*, cc. 22r and 25v; see also ASF, Catasto 608, c. 512r.

50 *Cronache del Monastero*, cc. 22r–v.

51 *Ibid.*, cc. 47r–49v.

52 "Le complessione cominciavono a indebolire, et dificilmente harebbon potuto in progresso di tempo vivere con tanta rigorosita et strettezza da loro incominciate," *ibid.*, c. 41r.

53 Bartolomeo Lenzi, one of the convent's patrons, offered to finance the building of separate rooms for each of the nuns around 1460, but his offer was refused on the grounds that the version of the Benedictine Rule followed by the nuns stipulated that they share a common dormitory, *ibid.*, c. 24r.

54 *Ibid.*, c. 45r.

55 "Venerabiles ipse moniales, que in presentiarum sunt numero copioso, sese adeo obnoxias faciunt, quin meritis ipsius nunquam arbitrantur satisfacere posse." The passage is from the Latin *Vita* of Abbot Gomez written by Tommaso Salvetti, now in the Biblioteca Laurenziana, Florence (Ashburnham 885, cc. 9r–10r). It is reproduced in Nunes, *Dom Frey Gomez*, pp. 306ff.

56 "Quae nunc transcendunt numerum centenarium, in magnis observantiis, ieiuniis, silentiis, exercitiis, tenuitate victus et vestitus.

Divinis officiis omnes concurrentes; extra canonicas horas continuo, die noctuque, duae ex singulis choris in ecclesia vicissim aliae aliis succedentes, psalterium perlegunt. . . .

Nedum autem proprietas apud aliquam reperitur, sed nec possessiones aut reditus in communi habent monacis concessos. Victum sibi parcum labore manuum et eleemosynis eis largitis procurant. In summa charitate unum cor et unam animam in Domino habentes." Antonino, *Chronica domini*, Lyon, 1543, vol. III, c. 526, reproduced in Nunes, *Dom Frey Gomez*, pp. 304–5. For other fifteenth-century accounts of Le Murate, see the brief history of the convent offered in the 1448 papal bull of Nicholas V, ASF, Diplomatico, Strozziane-Ugoccioni, 1448, June 8; I thank Brenda Preyer for this reference; Giovanni Rucellai's description in his *Zibaldone* recorded in 1469, *Giovanni Rucellai ed il suo zibaldone*, London, 1960, p. 65; Domenico da Corella, *Theotocon* (1469), p. 114.

57 Antonino's remark, "scandalum populorum," was recorded in his *Chronica domini* quoted in Bizzocchi, *Chiesa e potere nella Toscana del Quattrocento*, p. 32. On the critical discourse on female enclosure in fifteenth-century Florence, see Bizzocchi; Brucker, *The Society of Renaissance Florence*, pp. 206–12 and *Renaissance Florence*, pp. 192–4; Trexler, *Synodal Law*, pp. 91–102, and "The Episcopal Constitutions of Antoninus of Florence," *Quellen und Forschungen aus italienischen Archiven und Bibliotheken*, vol. 59 (1979), p. 270, no. 48.

58 "Io fui alle Murate venerdì passato. . . . Io gli ho predicato . . . che le lascino le zachere e rete e reticelle e ulivi che fanno d'oro e d'argento e loro libriccini. Secondo, se sono Murate, debbono stare come hanno il nome. E dico che questa è una cosa pessima ad aprire a'Signori che vi vadino; io so ancora, io, chi sono e cortigiani che sono come una galla leggieri; e ho detto loro che quello canto figurato l'ha trovato Satanasso e che le giettino via questi libri di canti e organi. E se la prima che ha el governo non può provedere, che la renunci a l'officio," Savonarola, *Prediche Italiane ai Fiorentini*, vol. II, p. 156. The sermon was given on Sunday, May 10, 1495. See Lowe, "Female Strategies," p. 216. Savonarola dedicated his *Operette sopra i dieci comandamenti* (1495) to the abbess and nuns of Le Murate.

59 "Ma perchè, oh frate, hai tu detto questo? Non perchè io dica che le sieno cattive, chè dico sono buone, ma bisogna che tornino a questa simplicità," Savonarola, *ibid.*, p. 216.

60 Savonarola was apparently not the first cleric to take on the nuns of Le Murate. The Abbot of Monte Cassino and papal secretary, Don Gratia, apparently visited and advised Abbess Scolastica that her wards required more than the Rule to guide them, on account of their feminine frailty. He recommended very strict measures regarding diet, dress, and bedding, *Cronache del Monastero*, c. 41r.

61 These documents are presented in two articles: de Angelis and Conti, "Un libro antico della sagrestia di Sant'Ambrogio," and Borsook, "Cults and Imagery."

62 For the contemporary reference, see n. 67 below. The painting is mentioned by Manetti in his *Uomini singolari dal MCCCC* (c. 1480), in *Operette istoriche edite ed inedite di Antonio Manetti*, ed. G. Milanesi, Florence, 1887, p. 167; by Albertini in his *Memoriale di molte statue et picture sono nella inclypta cipta di Florentia* (1510), Florence, p. 15; in *Il Codice Magliabechiano* p. 97; and by Vasari, Vasari–Milanesi, vol. II, p. 617. Vasari's reference is the most extensive: "Fece alle monache delle Murate due tavole; una della Annunziata, posta allo altar maggiore: l'altra nella medesima chiesa a un altare, dentrovi storie di San Benedetto e di San Bernardo."

63 In 1438, Domenico Veneziano wrote to Piero de' Medici "fra' Felipo à una tavola che va in Santo Spirito, la quale lavorando lui dì e note, non la farà in cinqu' ani, sì è gran lavorio": see Wohl, *The Paintings of Domenico Veneziano*, p. 340. In 1439, Lippi wrote to Piero de' Medici, referring to a painting on which he was working for him (see Ch. 6 above, p. 154).

64 See Borsook, "Cults and Imagery," pp. 159 and 164, n. 121. The 1440s were productive years for Lippi: see Ruda, *Fra Filippo Lippi*, pp. 135–87. In addition to the works discussed by Ruda, Jonathan Nelson has found documentary evidence for one of the two altarpieces for Santa Maria Nuova mentioned by Albertini: see Ch. 6, n. 9 above.

65 My calculations are based on the total payments made to Lippi tabulated by Laura de Angelis from the convent account book, "Un libro antico," p. 100. She came up with 1716 lire 18 soldi for the altarpiece and predella, and I converted this into florins, using a rate of l.4 s.6 to the florin (the same rate used by the bookkeeper of Sant'Ambrogio when tabulating Lippi's account). I came up with a total of 399 florins 6 soldi. Ruda's calculation is "slightly more than 400 florins," *Fra Filippo Lippi*, p. 423.

66 *Cronache del Monastero*, cc. 16v and 17r: "Terminando questi Altari et Pitture nel MCCCCXXXXIII con edificatione di tutte."

67 In the account book from Sant'Ambrogio covering the expenditures on the high altar decoration one entry reads: "Et a dì 16 daprile 1445 a fra filipo per lui a giovanni di stagio Barducci et compagnia furono per resto di ragione di detto fra filipo per ragione tenuto per la tavola di giovanni benci l.xi x.v," ASF, Con. Sopp. 79, n. 155, c. 81v.

68 "Disse il sudetto Benci havere speso nella [altare] maggiore fl. 200 e tanti in fra li altri dua compresovi le Altari con tutte le loro appartenente," *Cronache del Monastero*, c. 17r.

69 It could be argued that I am setting up the relationship between the two commissions unfairly by not including in my tabulations the second altarpiece painted by Lippi for the altar of St. Bernard at Le Murate (which no longer survives). On the other hand, according to *quattrocento* payment conventions, which were often based on the number of

figures in a painting and the amount of gold leaf used, Lippi got a very good price for the Murate *Annunciation*, and a lower price, in comparison, for the *Coronation*.

70 See Borsook, "Cults and Imagery," p. 158 and n. 84.

71 Eve Borsook notes that "By 1435, if not earlier, the Baldesi may have lost their rights of patronage to the main chapel because a member of their family was involved in an anti-papal plot and this provoked the confiscation of many of their properties," *ibid.*, p. 158. About that time, Francesco Maringhi began to establish the financial base for endowing a chapel dedicated to St. John the Baptist "Decollato." It was only in 1439 that the chapel was designated in the documents as the *cappella maggiore* of Sant'Ambrogio.

72 The relic dated back to 1230, when a blood and flesh substance was discovered in a chalice that a priest had failed to clean following the Mass. It was initially stored in a stone tabernacle in the *cappella maggiore* of the church and the Guild of Judges and Notaries took an active interest in promoting the Corpus Christi cult. In 1468, the relic was appropriated by Domenico Maringhi, nephew of Francesco Maringhi, and removed to a chapel dedicated to St Lawrence along the right wall of the nave. It was placed in 1471 in a tabernacle set within a painting by Baldovinetti and stood in this new location for only a decade before it was moved in the mid-1480s to a new chapel situated to the left of the main altar, patronized by the nuns of Sant'Ambrogio: see the detailed discussion in Borsook, "Cults and Imagery," pp. 170–83.

73 *Ibid.*, p. 163. Ruda disagrees, considering the Coronation subject "the result of careful planning, rather than a last-minute change," *Fra Filippo Lippi*, p. 139.

74 See Holmes, "Giovanni Benci's Patronage of the Nunnery Le Murate."

75 See the entry on Giovanni d'Amerigo Benci in *Dizionario biografico*, vol. 8, pp. 194–6. See also de Roover, *The Rise and Decline of the Medici Bank*, pp. 56–7ff.

76 In notarial documents of 1454, Giovanni Benci is described as "olim populi Sta Lucia de Magnoli de Flor. et hodie populi Sto Jacopo tra Fossis," ASF, Not. Antecos. 3530, cc. 2v, 14v, and 80v; I thank Brenda Preyer for this reference. He may have been living in a house in that parish on the Piazza dei Peruzzi where his sons were residing by 1457, rented from the heirs of Ridolfo Peruzzi, ASF, Catasto 82, c. 217r. In the 1460s, his sons established a grand new family palace on the street leading from the Ponte Rubiconte to the Piazza Santa Croce, a street that became known as the Via de' Benci: see E. Möller, "Leonardos Bildnis der Ginevra dei Benci," *Münchner Jahrbuch der Bildenden Kunst*, vol. XII (1937–38), p. 196; ASF, Catasto 929, c. 280r.

77 *Cronache del Monastero*, c. 16v. See also n. 121 below.

78 *Ibid.*, c. 26v; D. Schlossman Pines, "The Tomb Slabs of Santa Croce: A New 'Sepoltuario'," Ph.D. dissertation, Columbia University, 1985, pp. 390–5, I thank Andrew Butterfield for this reference; S. Rosselli, *Sepoltuario Fiorentino* (1657), ASF, Manoscritti 624, cc. 320 and 464.

79 For the disposition of the nuns' oratory in the church, see n. 144 below.

80 Giovanni Benci appears to have been intimate with the Barducci family: he had an illegitimate son, Damiano, with a slave named Anna who belonged to Lorenzo di Stagio Barducci in 1430, ASF, Catasto 832, c. 217r, and he placed one of his daughters in the nunnery of Sant'Ambrogio as a boarder in c. 1446: see n. 85 below.

81 *Cronache del Monastero*, cc. 25v–27r.

82 This sum is given in a papal bull issued by Nicholas V on June 8, 1448, ASF, Diplomatico, Strozziane-Uguccioni, 1448, June 8; I thank Brenda Preyer for this reference. Giovanni Benci and his heirs together spent around 40,000 fl. at Le Murate, *Cronache del Monastero*, c. 27r.

83 "Quod monasterium per Iohannem de Bencis constructum a principio, usque in finem per eum consummatum est," Antonino, *Chronica Domini*, vol. III, c. 526, quoted in Nunes, *Dom Frey Gomez*, p. 305. Domenico da Corella wrote in his *Theotocon* on Le Murate: "Vir locuples multo cui Bencius aere Iohannes, obtulit insignem religione locum," p. 114.

84 Abbess Scolastica convinced the prior of the parish of Sant'Ambrogio, Giovanni Battista Bonciani Pieriano di Giogoli, to leave Sant'Ambrogio in order to become the confessor at Le Murate, *Cronache del Monastero*, c. 63v. This seems to have taken place shortly after she became abbess in 1439.

85 Caterina, born in 1438, joined the women of Le Murate some time in the 1440s, and lived in the convent until her marriage to Piero Vespucci. In the *Cronache del Monastero*, she is described as "in serbo" and treated like a daughter by the Abbess Scolastica, cc. 22v and 25v; ASF, Catasto 608, c. 512r. Giovanni's younger daughter Alessandra entered Sant'Ambrogio around 1446, when she was seven years old, and probably remained there until her marriage to Tommaso Antinori in 1453, ASF, Con. Sopp. 79, n. 455, c. 6r; ASF, Catasto 608, c. 512r; see also P. Schubring, *Cassoni*, Leipzig, 1923, p. 447, n. 46. It seems that both girls entered the convents following the death of their mother, Genevra de' Peruzzi, in 1444. Giovanni Benci was left with nine young children (two of whom were illegitimate) and, although he eventually remarried, the convent was a convenient and immediate solution for this large family without a mother, ASF, Catasto 832, c. 217r.

86 The *Coronation of the Virgin* no longer has its original frame and only one of the predella panels survives, depicting a miracle of Sant'Ambrogio, now in the Berlin Staatliche Museen. The *Coronation* was cleaned in the early 1970s. For the bibliography on the painting, see Ruda, *Fra Filippo Lippi*, pp. 422–6, and Marchini, *Filippo Lippi*, pp. 201–3. I discuss only the central image of the altarpiece. The altarpiece ensemble also included a predella with at least one scene from the life of Sant'Ambrogio. There is also an Annunciation, badly abraded but still visible, set in roundels in the spandrels on either side of the central arch of the Uffizi panel.

87 Borsook, "Cults and Imagery," pp. 147–202.

88 J. Ruda, "Style and Patronage in the 1440s: Two Altarpieces of the Coronation of the Virgin by Filippo Lippi," *Mitteilungen des Kunsthistorischen Institutes in Florenz*, 1984, pp. 363–84. See also Ruda, *Fra Filippo Lippi*, pp. 139–47.

89 Marchini maintained that this figure is Domenico Maringhi, interpreting the phrase "is perfecit opus" to mean that this is he who brought the picture to conclusion, *Filippo Lippi*, p. 202. Borsook refutes this, pointing out that it is Francesco rather than Domenico who is treated as the donor in all of the documents related to the altarpiece. She also notes that the figure in the painting is shown kneeling in a cavity that resembles a tomb, "Cults and Imagery," p. 170 and nn. 163 and 164.

90 See Ch. 6 above, n. 181.

91 Giuseppe Marchini, who took the kneeling donor figure at the right to be Domenico Maringhi, identified this tonsured monk as St. Bernard, painted in the likeness of Francesco Maringhi, *Filippo Lippi*, p. 202. Ruda identified this figure as St. Anthony Abbot, *Fra Filippo Lippi*, p. 141.

92 These include "Job," "Martinus," "Eustachyus," and "Tempisten." Fra Angelico uses a similar technique in his contemporary *Coronation of the Virgin* (now in the Uffizi) for the nuns' choir of Sant'Egidio, the hospital church of Santa Maria Nuova.

93 Sts. Eustace and Theopista are identified by the labels "Eustachyus" and "Tempisten" on their clothing, and it follows that the two children kneeling between them are their sons Agapius and Theopistus, described in the *Leggenda Aurea*.

94 The three-quarters view was a contemporary Flemish portrait convention (see, e.g., the *Portrait of a Woman* attributed to the Master of Flémalle in the National Gallery, London). However, I do not want to open the Lippi–Northern painting can of worms here

by insisting that Lippi was necessarily referring to a Northern prototype.

95 Borsook, "Cults and Imagery," p. 193, n. 96. Stagio Barducci is not listed in the 1427 *catasto* and it is likely that he was already dead by this date. The chapel was probably endowed as a bequest, and carried out by his sons. Lorenzo (1376–1442/46) and Giovanni (1391–after 1446) lived together in a house in the parish of Sant'Ambrogio on Borgo degli Albizi. Lorenzo died between 1442 and 1446, and Giovanni took over the position of head of house, ASF, Catasto 420, c. 32v, and Catasto 681, c. 227. In Giovanni's *catasto* declaration of 1446, under "incarichi" there is a share in the Monte worth 300 fl., the interest on which was to be used to pay the chaplain of the family chapel at Sant'Ambrogio, ASF, Catasto 681, c. 227.

96 "A di xviiii di Septenbre 1451, redette mona Anbruogia sagrestana a mona Antonia de Barducci lire xvii s.5, i quali danari sono per resto de danari presso per la tavola et i detti danari sarebbe di queghli del podere di messer Francesco s.xvii s.v," ASF, Con. Sopp. 79, n. 155, c. 61r.

97 In most *quattrocento* Florentine depictions of St. Eustace, the saint is represented individually (e.g., Pollaiuolo's altarpiece for the Chapel of the Cardinal of Portugal). In a fresco at Sant'Apollonia attributed to a follower of Andrea del Castagno, narrative scenes from the saint's life surround the standing figure. An exception is the side panel of an altarpiece by Giovanni del Ponte (S. Andrea, Brozzi), where St. Eustace is shown kneeling with his two sons, holding a deer.

98 Borsook suggests that the St. Eustace figure may be a portrait, "Cults and Imagery," p. 169, and I have already alluded to the portrait conventions used to represent St. Theopista. It is possible that the couple represents two members of the Barducci family – idealized portraits of the founder of the chapel, Stagio, and his wife; or his eldest son Lorenzo (who died during the production of the altarpiece) and his wife Maria, or the surviving children of the chapel founder, Giovanni and Antonia.

99 This was pointed out to Borsook by Barbara Schleicher who assisted in the restoration of the painting, "Cults and Imagery," p. 168 and n. 156.

100 My rendering of the legend is taken from Jacopo da Voragine's *Leggenda Aurea*, vol. III, pp. 1344–54, embellished by two versions derived from the *Leggenda Aurea*, copied out by unidentified fifteenth-century Florentines, in the BNF, Panciatichi 41, cc. 27–31, and Panciatichi 42, cc. 132–8.

101 H. Delehaye, "La Légende de S. Eustache," in *Mélanges d'hagiographie grecque et latine (Subsidia Hagiographica)*, vol. 42 (1966), pp. 212–39. See also G. Gerauld, "Forerunners, Congeners and Derivatives of the Eustace Legend," *Publications of the Modern Language Association of America*, 1904, pp. 335–448.

102 "Ragionando di certe chose inchominciaronsi a dimandare insieme della loro purita della madere loro sedeva qui presso e udiva quello che dicevano," BNF, Panciatichi 42, c. 30v. This Life of Eustace is found in a collection of saints' *Vite* written in the vernacular around the middle of the fifteenth century. The same passage in the vulgarized *trecento* version of the *Leggenda Aurea* reads "ragionando insieme, diceva l'uno al'altro di quelle cose ch'erano avvenute ne la fanciullezza loro; e la madre loro, seggendo loro presso, udiva attentamente quelle cose che ellino si raccontavano insieme," Jacopo da Voragine, *Leggenda Aurea*, vol. III, p. 1352.

103 In fact, later on when Theopista is recounting the exchange she overheard between the two boys to Eustace, she uses the word "puerizia": "Ieri di dietro nell'orto della casa vidi due giovani di questa tua gente che vi sono alberghati parlare insieme della loro puerizia," BNF, Panciatichi 42, c. 31v.

104 Leon Battista Alberti, *I libri della famiglia*, trans. *The Family in Renaissance Florence*, ed. R. Watkins, Columbia, 1969, p. 213. Scolastica Rondinelli's Constitutions for Le Murate demanded that the nuns keep "li Occhi fissi in su" when in the refectory, *Cronache del Monastero*, c. 47v.

105 Attempts to historicize the psychoanalytic concept of "the gaze" within Western medieval and Renaissance visual culture include Camille, *The Gothic Idol*, pp. 303–4; R. Stefaniak, "Correggio's Camera di San Paolo: An Archaeology of the Gaze," *Art History*, vol. 16 (1993), pp. 203–38; and M. Garrard, "Here's Looking at Me: Sofonisba Anguissola and the Problem of the Woman Artist," *Renaissance Quarterly*, vol. 47 (1994), pp. 556–622.

106 Herlihy and Klapisch-Zuber, *Tuscans and their Families*, pp. 228–31. They explain: "But the society of late trecento Florence, slipping radically in numbers, could ill afford to recommend celibacy to its citizens. Amid the devastating epidemics of the late Middle Ages, a new and more affirmative attitude toward marriage emerged at Florence," p. 229. They point to St. Bernardino as a strong proponent of the traditional position on celibacy in his "De laudibus virginitatis." For a discussion of the history and development of this traditional attitude toward celibacy, see Tibbetts Schulenburg, "The Heroics of Virginity."

107 One entry reads: "inspirata da dio entrro nel monistero" and another, referring to a five-year-old girl, "intelligentia che conoscesse in quella anni tenessi questo essere al bisogno della sua salute et redendo lei disposta udire esse privata del mondo et rinchiusa in luogo di religiose," ASF, Con. Sopp. 79, n. 455, cc. 12r and 18v.

108 ASF, Con. Sopp. 79, n. 455, c. 18v.

109 See K. Lowe, "'A Marriage of Sorts': Interpreting the Parallels between the Wedding Ceremonies of Nuns and Secular Brides in Italy during the Renaissance and Counter-Reformation," in *Marriage in Late Medieval and Early Modern Italy*, ed. T. Dean and K. Lowe, Cambridge, forthcoming.

110 The bishops of Florence wedded the abbesses of San Piero Maggiore: see Orlandi, "S. Antonino: I Primi 5 Anni di Episcopato di S. Antonino," *Memorie Domenicane*, 1959, p. 123. The bishops of Fiesole were married to the abbesses of San Martino a Maiano. This fascinating ritual is described in detail by Caioli in *S. Andrea Corsini*, pp. 78–9.

111 C. Klapisch-Zuber, "Holy Dolls: Play and Piety in Florence in the Quattrocento," in *Women, Family, and Ritual in Renaissance Italy*, Chicago, 1985, pp. 311ff.

112 See Bynum, *Holy Feast and Holy Fast*, pp. 246ff.

113 Bynum makes an interesting point regarding the *imitatio Mariae*. While it was readily invoked in the Lives of female saints and holy women written by men, in women's writing and devotional practices, there was a stronger identification with the figure of Christ, *Holy Feast and Holy Fast*, p. 269.

114 See Borsook, "Cults and Imagery," p. 167.

115 See P. Verdier, *Le Couronnement de la Vierge: Les origines et les premiers développements d'un thème iconographique*, Paris, 1980, pp. 81ff; and M. Warner, *Alone of All Her Sex: The Myth and the Cult of the Virgin Mary*, London, 1976, Part Three: "The Bride," pp. 121–74. Warner gives an example of a Tuscan *trecento* representation of the Mystical Marriage of the Virgin and Christ that utilizes the typical Coronation of the Virgin format but, instead of crowning the Virgin, Christ places a ring upon her finger, p. 132 and fig. 17, in the gable of a diptych, Boston Museum of Fine Arts.

116 A. Venturi, *Storia dell'Arte Italiana*, Milan, 1911 (1967 reprint, Nendeln), vol. 7, part 1, p. 373.

117 I thank John Shearman for this observation.

118 See Gardner, "Nuns and Altarpieces," pp. 29–31 and 52ff.

119 The existence of an elevated gallery is documented only in the mid-seventeenth century. Borsook tentatively suggests that this loggia was built during the reconstruction of the high altar directed by Francesco Maringhi. She suggests that the nuns may have originally congregated in the area at the back of the *cappella maggiore*, before the ciborium which housed the miraculous relic. This area had become a choir for the male clergy of Sant'Ambrogio by 1454, "Cults and Imagery," pp. 167 and 196, nn. 132–4.

120 In Mino da Fiesole's relief carving on the tabernacle which contained the Eucharistic relic made in the 1480s, the nuns are shown at ground level in prayer before the relic –

which, until that time, had been kept in the *cappella maggiore*.

121 Scolastica was known in secular society as Cecilia, wife of Piero di Nofri dell'Antella, *Cronache del Monastero*, c. 16v; ASF, Catasto 68, c. 144r. Giovanni Benci and Piero dell'-Antella owned neighboring farms in the countryside south of Florence in Antella, ASF, Catasto 608, c. 510.

122 "Il che sentendo Madonna Scolastica lo prese come cosa che li venissi da Cielo, et lo supplicò a darli aiuto, che ancor lei voleva fare l'Altare grande della Sta Nuntiata per essere il Titolo del Monasterio e per immitare l'antiche Monache, Ma non haveva comodo da per se. Però si unirono insieme et detton ordine a farvi tre Altari," *Cronache del Monastero*, c. 17r.

123 "Coaiutore nell'edificatione delli Altari della chiesa," *ibid.*, c. 25v.

124 Nunes, *Dom Frey Gomez*, p. 307, n. 61.

125 The Murate *Annunciation* has been identified with the *Annunciation* in the Munich Alte Pinakothek. The strongest supportive evidence for this claim is Richa's description of the painting which he saw in situ in the mid-eighteenth century (the convent was suppressed in 1808), which corresponds in important details to the Munich *Annunciation*: see Richa, *Notizie istoriche*, vol. II, p. 109.

There have been no extended discussions of this altarpiece. The bibliography contains only passing references or catalogue entries: Vasari–Milanesi, vol. II, p. 617; Pittaluga, *Filippo Lippi*, pp. 68ff; Marchini, *Filippo Lippi*, p. 207; Ruda, *Fra Filippo Lippi*, pp. 157–9, 411–12; *Alte Pinakothek München*, Munich, 1983, p. 294; White, *The Birth and Rebirth of Pictorial Space*, pp. 180–2; F. Ames-Lewis, "Art in the Service of the Family: The Taste and Patronage of Piero di Cosimo de' Medici," in *Piero de' Medici "il Gottoso" (1416–1469): Art in the Service of the Medici*, ed. A. Beyer and B. Boucher, Berlin, 1993, pp. 209–10; Cornelia Syre, "Filippo Lippi: *Die Verkündigung Maria* in der Alten Pinakothek, Beobachtungen zur Maltechnik," in *Bayerische Staatsgemäldesammlungen Jahresbericht, 1977*, Munich, 1998, pp. 19–24. The question of dating remains problematic. On the basis of style, art historians have pushed for a date around 1450, while Ruda and those following the *Cronache del Monastero* have argued for the mid-1440s. I place the picture c. 1443–45, after the convent church was completed. I do not find the style inconsistent with other pictures dating from the early to mid-1440s, such as the Sant'Ambrogio and Santa Croce altarpieces. There is a fifteenth-century copy of the picture in the Accademia, Florence.

126 *Cronache del Monastero*, c. 30r. The picture was later placed in the cell of the abbess, where it was to be found in 1598 when the *Cronache* was written, c. 8v. I have been unable to track down this painting (see n. 129 below).

127 The San Lorenzo *Annunciation* for the chapel of Niccolò Martelli was painted in the late 1430s or early '40s (see fig. 104). Ruda argues – rightly, I think – for an earlier dating (in the early 1440s) than is usually given for the *Annunciation* in the Palazzo Barberini and, less convincingly, for a late 1430s date for the uneven *Annunciation* in the Washington National Gallery of Art, *Fra Filippo Lippi*, pp. 403 and 397.

128 In this respect, the Murate *Annunciation* is much closer to Fra Angelico's renditions of the subject than to Lippi's San Lorenzo *Annunciation*. There, the presentation – by virtue of the original divided format – is implicitly dramatic. The two wing panels would have come together, signifying the arrival of the Holy Spirit. The Virgin demonstrates "conturbatio." See Michael Baxandall's description of the dramatic moments within the Annunciation narrative derived from Fra Roberto Carraciolo's sermon on the subject, *Painting and Experience in Fifteenth Century Italy*, pp. 49–56.

129 The *Annunciation* from the Ponte Rubiconte does not seem to be listed in inventories of images recorded at Le Murate following the suppression of the convent in 1808. There is only one painting of the Annunciation mentioned – a very small work measuring $1\frac{1}{3} \times \frac{1}{6}$ braccia (76 × 10 cm), which is not distinguished as an "opera antica," Archivio dell'Accademia delle Belle Arti, n. 17, c. 12, and n. 18, no. 9.

130 On the *Annunciation* from Orsanmichele, see *Gli Uffizi: Catalogo Generale*, ed. L. Berti, Florence, 1979, p. 353; L. Marcucci, *I dipinti toscani del secolo XIV*, Rome, 1965, n. 57.

131 One could also argue that the refined features and bearing of the Virgin reflect the social ambitions of the patron and the abbess. Giovanni Benci was climbing into the ranks of the upper patriciate, while Scolastica Rondinelli wished to transform the convent into a house of patrician women.

132 "Tristo religioso, il quale ha lo abito di religione, . . . è ancora grave di corpo, però dice che non vola mai, però che la umidità della sua carne lo tiene giù grave." In contrast, the falcon "ha le penne atte a volare con la carne leggieri, perchè è asciutto, non sente diletto di quella e cosi è atto a contemplazione," Savonarola, *Prediche Italiane*, vol. II, pp. 116–17. The sermon is dated 1494, but it is probable that this was the sermon that Savonarola refers to in his address of May 10, 1495, where he claims that after not visiting Le Murate for three years, he had been to the convent two days earlier and spoken to the nuns.

133 It is likely that this design of three flowers between open bird wings refers more specifically to the patron's *imprese*. I have not been able to find any information on the personal devices of Giovanni Benci. The Benci arms which appear in the convent church were composed of two lions rampant flanking a mountain, while the Rondinelli arms consisted of a series of robins in profile beneath a bar.

134 See Leo Steinberg's interesting and provocative article on this painting, "'How Shall This Be?' Reflections on Filippo Lippi's *Annunciation* in London." In a conversation, Charles Dempsey made the valid point that because the iconography of this *Annunciation* is so extraordinary and unprecedented (if not downright heretical), it is more likely that it was determined by Lippi's Medici patrons than by the artist himself, and that the painting was intended for their private use.

135 See F. Cabrol, *Dictionnaire D'Archéologie Chrétienne et de Liturgie*, Paris, 1907, vol. 2, pp. 2251–4.

136 "If it behooves me to break my vow in order to bear such a son, I both rejoice in the son and grieve at the disposition. His will be done. But if I may conceive virginally and virginally give birth, which, if it please Him shall not be impossible, than shall I know that He has truly regarded the low estate of His handmaid," *Super missus est*, in Steinberg, "'How Shall this Be?'," p. 42, n. 1.

137 Lippi's San Lorenzo *Annunciation* is the only other where there is no reference to the Virgin's bedroom.

138 For a discussion of the evolution of the iconographic variations of the Annunciation, see D. Robb, "The Iconography of the Annunciation in the Fourteenth and Fifteenth Centuries," *Art Bulletin*, vol. 18 (1936), pp. 480–526. One of the variants which he discusses is the Annunciation in an ecclesiastical setting, popularized in northern Europe in the early fifteenth century. See also Didi-Huberman's fascinating *Fra Angelico: Dissemblance et Figuration*, where the second half of the book is structured around the Annunciation mystery and metaphor.

139 *Cronache del Monastero*, cc. 10v and 11v. "Le camice heron d'lana bianca et azzura il che dicono che usarono in memoria detto panni che portava la Gloriosa Vergine che si dice heron di tal colore di quale furno devotissima," c. 10v. A white gown with gold brocade covered by a blue cloak were also characteristic of the Virgin's dress in Sienese paintings from the fourteenth and fifteenth centuries.

140 "Vedesi la Tavola vaghissima di Fra Filippo Lippi, il quale rappresentò in essa il mistero della Nunziata, con un capriccioso pensiero avendo effigiato un altr'Angiolo, che dietro l'uscio della stanza attonito osserva l'Arcangiolo, che saluta la Vergine," Richa, *Notizie Istoriche*, vol. II, p. 109.

141 The history of the iconography is discussed by D. Denny, *The Annunciation from the Right*

from Early Christian Times to the Sixteenth Century, New York, 1977, addendum entitled "The Annunciation with Many Angels," pp. 148–60.

142 "Hera intentissima sempre all'Oratione et Contemplatione, Onde che haveva continuo colloquio col suo Angel custode," *Cronache del Monastero*, c. 18v.

143 "Nella Festività principale si dilettava di farli sempre qualche nuovo ornamento con le sue Oratione, et Laudi poi la compiaceva di apparirli, et mostrase li conquella Veste che lei li haveva fatte. Et una volta in particulare sendosi scordata di farli il Cinto, quello li appari con nuove veste ma bene senza Cinto, di che senti la monaca non piccol' disgusto," *ibid.*, c. 19r.

144 The raised oratory originally spanned the first bay of the church. It was enlarged by an additional bay in 1460 with money donated by Bartolomeo Lenzi and an altar dedicated to the Crucifixion was set up there, *ibid.*, cc. 23v–24r. In the chronicle there is a description, c. 30v, of a miracle which occurred in the area of the nuns choir (after its enlargement) that gives some idea of the relationship between nuns and the laity in the church below. The lay public had come to hear Vespers sung and when the nuns ceased their song in reaction to a miraculous healing in their midst, the people below had no inkling of what had happened. Saundra Weddle discusses the orientation and features of the church in her doctoral dissertation "Enclosing Le Murate: The Ideology of Enclosure and the Architecture of a Florentine Convent," Cornell University, 1997.

145 "Al capezzale di ciascuna assisteva l'Angel' custode," *Cronache del Monastero*, c. 43r.

146 See Puccetti, "Note sulla simbologia del Monastero," and the broader study by Leclercq, *La Vita perfetta.*

147 See n. 58 above.

148 In the Florentine Constitutions, much attention was devoted to the physical layout of the nunnery, and in particular, to the *parlatorio*. The grate was to be a double-lattice affair, with the two screens separated by a hand's length and the holes so small that nothing could be passed through them. When a nun spoke with a male who was not a relative, a veil was to cover the grate: see Trexler, *Synodal Law in Florence*, p. 93.

149 *Cronache del Monastero*, c. 48v.

150 This is confirmed in the chronicle. It appears as though there were periods when the enclosure was somewhat relaxed, followed by a tightening. There is evidence that the situation had become relatively lax by the end of Scolastica's life. Scolastica's successor, Caterina Ubaldini, for some years prohibited any laymen from entering the convent, "ne Benci, ne Parenti, ne altri Benefattori," and even restricted the access of the male clerical staff and convent doctors, *ibid.*, cc. 41r and 52r.

151 "La carcera," in fact, is invoked metaphorically in one sixteenth-century convent drama to reflect upon the conditions of the enclosed nuns: see E. Weaver, "Spiritual Fun: A Study of Sixteenth-Century Tuscan Convent Theater," in *Women in the Middle Ages and the Renaissance*, ed. M. B. Rose, Syracuse, 1988, p. 192.

152 "Nunc degunt in spatioso loco et pulcherrimo in structuris, officinis, claustris et horto," Antonino Pierozzi, *Chronica Domini*, vol. III, c. 526, reproduced in Nunes, *Dom Frey Gomez*, p. 304.

153 "In questo paradiso germoglia l'albero di vita che è l'obbedienza e l'albero della conoscenza del bene e del male che sono i premurosi suggerimenti dell'abate. I fratelli nello spirito sono come alberi piantati in riva ad un fiume: la fede è linfa, la speranza fiore e la carità frutto. Ivi fioriscono i gigli della castità, l'erbetta dell'umilità, la rosa della pazienza e la virtù della temperanza. In esso matura ogni specie di frutto, il cipro col nardo," Leclercq, *La Vita perfetta*, pp. 167–8, partially quoted in Puccetti, "Note sulla simbologia," p. 397.

154 See D. Moreni, *Continuazione delle memorie istoriche dell'Ambrosiana imperial Basilica di San Lorenzo di Firenze*, Florence, 1816, vol. I, p. 177: I thank Kate Lowe for this reference.

155 The tree defies the proportional logic governing much of the perspectival scheme. What is more, it is placed along the central axis of the painting, obscuring the vanishing point, which should lie at the top of the arch of the portal. Thus, it functions something like an axis of the unfathomable, exposing the limits of vision and reason when cast upon the Mystery of the Incarnation.

156 There is an interesting parallel between the attendant angel in the Murate *Annunciation* and the two angels in the left panel of the San Lorenzo *Annunciation* (the only other Annunciation by Lippi that has these attendant angels): in the latter the principal access to the Annunciation drama itself is through the picture plane. The attendant angel who looks out at the beholder, like the angel in the Murate *Annunciation*, is mediating access.

157 It is interesting that in a copy of the Murate *Annunciation* made a few decades later, now in the Accademia, Florence, the artist disposed of this ambiguity in the original by showing strips of brown on either side of the cypress trunk to represent a closed door.

158 A case in point is the extraordinary Sister Eugenia di Tommaso da Treviso. She entered Le Murate in 1450 at age thirty-three and quickly ran afoul. She was denounced by a cleric who claimed she was a corrupting influence on the other nuns. She was thrown out of the convent and made her way to Rome, where she cleared her name, insisting that she had been violated by the very priest who denounced her. Many years later, after colorful adventures, she returned to Le Murate: see K. Lowe, "Female Strategies," pp. 215–16; *Cronache del Monastero*, cc. 53r–56v.

159 *Cronache del Monastero*, c. 17r. There is a note in the margin written in another hand referring to Vasari's passage ascribing authorship to Lippi.

160 *Ibid.*, cc. 9r, 24r, 30r, 31r–v and 34v. An interesting note regarding the *Crucifixion* demonstrates how one patron tried to maintain some control over a pious donation situated within the convent. The painting was commissioned by Bartolomeo Lenzi from Neri di Bicci in 1461 for the nuns' choir – with the condition that Abbess Scolastica promise him that each nun, upon entering the choir, would say an Ave Maria for him, *ibid.*, c. 24r; ASF, Con. Sopp. 81, n. 89, no. 3 (n.p.); Neri di Bicci, *Le Ricordanze*, p. 166.

161 While Lippi's *Annunciation* for Le Murate remained in place until at least the middle of the eighteenth century, the Sant'Ambrogio *Coronation of the Virgin* was displaced from the high altar in 1585, when it was reframed by the nuns and set up elsewhere in the church. Stefano Rosselli saw it beside the door leading to the convent along the left wall of the nave just before the chancel. He assumed that it was removed from the high altar in 1585 because there was an inscription bearing this date along the lower edge of the new frame: "Ab huius Ecclesie Priore Francesco Maringhio anno 1441 facta, et a Monialibus ornata fuit anno 1585," *Sepoltuario*, ASF, Manoscritti 624, cc. 471–2.

162 "[Mino], per servigio delle donne delle Murate, fece un tabernacolo di marmo, di mezzo rilievo, per tenervi il Sacramento; . . . il qual non aveva ancora murato, quando inteso le monache di Sant'Ambruogio (le quali erano desiderose di far fare un ornamento simile nell'invenzione, ma più ricco d'ornamento, per tenervi dentro la santissima reliquia del miracolo del Sacramento) la sufficienza di Mino, gli diedero a fare quell'-opera," Vasari–Milanesi, vol. III, pp. 119–20; trans. Vasari–De Vere, *Lives*, vol. III, p. 155. Mino's tabernacle for Le Murate, usually dated c. 1473 on the basis of style, is now in the Castellani chapel in Santa Croce: see G. Sciolla, *La Scultura di Mino da Fiesole*, Turin, 1970, p. 73. The tabernacle for Sant'Ambrogio is still in place in the Cappella del Miracolo in the church: see D. Francioni, *Storia del Santissimo miracolo seguito in Firenze nel 1230 di Sant'Ambrogio*, Florence, 1875, p. 133; Borsook, "Cults and Imagery," pp. 178–81.

163 See Borsook, "Cults and Imagery," pp. 170–83.

BIBLIOGRAPHY

I ARCHIVAL AND MANUSCRIPT SOURCES

Benoffi, Francesco, *Custodia Fiorentina*, 1597, in the Oliveriana di Pesaro MS. 1687, Santa Croce Archive, Florence (a copy is on microfilm at the Kunsthistorisches Institut, Florence).

Cronache del Monastero, see Niccolini, Giustina

Florence, Archivio di Stato (ASF)

—, Compagnia di Santa Maria delle Laudi detta di Santa Agnese, n. 98, *Libro di entrata e uscita segnato B, 1421–1441*.

—, Conventi Soppressi 79 (Sant'Ambrogio), n. 455, *Ricordo di monache e doti dal 1447 al 1468*.

—, Conventi Soppressi 79 (Sant'Ambrogio), n. 155, *Libro di entrata e uscita, 1442–1457*.

—, Conventi Soppressi 113 (Santa Maria del Carmine), n. 83, *Libro di entrata e uscita, 1382–1401*.

—, Conventi Soppressi 113 (Santa Maria del Carmine), n. 85, *Libro di entrata e uscita, 1417–36*.

—, Conventi Soppressi 113 (Santa Maria del Carmine), n. 86, *Libro di entrata e uscita, 1437–1452*.

—, Conventi Soppressi 133 (San Niccolò de' Frieri), n. 39, *Libro dei debitori e creditori dal 1423 al 1461*.

—, Mercanzia 1406, *Libro d'atti in cause ordinarie 1457 19 Aug.–14 Nov.*

—, Notarile Antecosimiano, 14193 (Piero Migliorelli), 1434–1443.

—, Notarile Antecosimiano, 16201 (Paolo Dieciauti), 1439–1450.

—, Notarile Antecosimiano, 16201 (Paolo Dieciauti), 1451–1461.

Necrologium Carmelitanum, Biblioteca Nazionale, Florence, Conventi Soppressi, C. 5.786 (1593).

—, Biblioteca Nazionale, Florence, Conventi Soppressi, F. 4.785 (14–16th centuries).

Niccolini, Giustina, *Cronache del N. N. Monastero di Santa Maria Annunciata detto le Murate di Firenze*, 1598, Biblioteca Nazionale, Florence, II.II.509.

Petribuoni, Paolo di Matteo, *Priorista Fiorentina*, Biblioteca Nazionale, Florence, Conventi Soppressi, C. 4.895.

II PUBLISHED PRIMARY SOURCES

Alberti, L. B., *On Painting and On Sculpture*, ed. C. Grayson, London, 1972.

Albertini, F., *Memoriale di molte statue et picture sono nella cipta di Florentia*, Florence, 1510.

Antonino Pierozzi, *Historiarum Domini Antonini Archipraesulis Florentini*, 3 vols., Lyon, 1543.

Arlotto, see *Facezie, Motti e Burle del Piovano Arlotto*

Atti dei capitoli provinciali di Toscana dei Carmelitani, 1375–1491, ed. A. Sabatini, Rome, 1975.

Avogadro, Alberto, *De Religione et Magnificentia Illustris Cosmi Medices Florentini* (c. 1465) in G. Lami, *Deliciae eruditorum*, Florence, 1742, vol. XII, pp. 117–49.

Bartolomeo da Pisa, *De Conformitate Vitae Beati Francisci*, in *Analecta Franciscana*, vols. IV (1906) and V (1912).

Bernardo da Bess (attr.), *Speculum disciplinae*, in *Selecta Scripta S. Bonaventurae*, Florence, 1942, pp. 274–422.

Billi, Antonio, see *Il Libro di Antonio Billi*.

Bollandus J., and Henschenius, G., *Acta Sanctorum*, 68 vols., Antwerp, 1643–1845.

Bonaventure, *Regula novitiorum*, in *Selecta Scripta S. Bonaventurae*, Florence, 1942, pp. 189–233.

—, *Selecta Scripta S. Bonaventurae*, Florence, 1942.

—, *Life of Saint Francis*, in Francis of Assisi, *Writings and Early Biographies*, ed. M. A. Habig, Chicago, 1983, pp. 627–787.

Borghesi, S., and Banchi, L., eds., *Nuovi documenti per la storia dell'arte senese* (Appendix), Siena, 1898.

Bullarium Carmelitanum, ed. E. Monsignani and I. A. Ximenez, 2 vols., Rome, 1715.

Calciuri, Nicola, see Graziano di S. Teresa, "'Vita fratrum'"

Clarke, H., and Edwards, B., eds., *The Rule of Saint Albert*, Aylesford and Kensington, 1973.

Il Codice dell'Anonimo Magliabechiano (1537–42), ed. K. Frey, Berlin, 1892.

Corazza, Bartolommeo di Michele del, see Corazzini, G.

Corazzini, G., "Diario Fiorentino di Bartolommeo di Michele del Corazza, anni 1405–38," *Archivio storico italiano*, 5th ser., vol. 14 (1894), pp. 233–98.

Domenico da Corella, *Theotocon* (1469), in G. Lami, *Deliciae eruditorum*, Florence, 1742, vol. XII, pp. 49–116.

Facezie, Motti e Burle del Piovano Arlotto, ed. Chiara Amerighi, Florence, 1982.

Francis of Assisi, *Writings and Early Biographies*, ed. M. A. Habig, Chicago, 1983.

Gaye, G., ed., *Carteggio inedito d'artisti dei secoli xiv, xv, xvi*, 2 vols., Florence, 1839.

Graziano di S. Teresa, "'Vita fratrum del Sancto Monte Carmelo' del P. Nicola Calciuri O.C. (d. 1466)," *Ephemerides Carmeliticae*, vol. 6 (1955), pp. 241–531.

—, "Viridarium Ioannis Grossi," *Ephemerides Carmeliticae*, vol. 7 (1956), pp. 240–84.

Grossi, Giovanni, see Graziano di S. Teresa, "Viridarium"

Jacopo da Voragine, *Leggenda Aurea*, 3 vols., Florence, 1926.

Lami, G., *Deliciae eruditorum*, Florence, 17 vols., 1736–45.

de Lezana, I. B., *Annales Sacri, Prophetici, et Eliani Ordinis Beatiss. Virginis Mariae de Monte Carmeli*, 4 vols., Rome, 1645–59.

Il Libro di Antonio Billi (c. 1516–30), ed. C. Fabriczy, Florence, 1891.

—, ed. K. Frey, Berlin, 1892.

Maffei, Timoteo, *In magnificentiae Cosmi Medicei Florentini detractores* (c. 1454–56), in G. Lami, *Deliciae eruditorum*, Florence, 1742, vol. XII, pp. 150–68.

Necrologio di S. Maria Novella, ed. S. Orlandi, 2 vols., Florence, 1954–55.

Neri di Bicci, *Le Ricordanze*, ed. B. Santi, Pisa, 1976.

Oddi, Giocomo da Perugia, *Franceschina*, see Oddi, Giocomo da Perugia, *Specchio*

—, *Specchio del'ordine Minore o Franceschina* (c. 1474), 2 vols., Assisi, 1929 (republished 1981).

Ordinaire de L'Ordre de Notre-Dame du Mont-Carmel par Sibert de Beka (vers 1312), ed. B. Zimmerman, Bibliothèque Liturgique, Paris, 1910.

Pulinari, Dionisio da Firenze, *Cronache dei Frati Minori della Provincia di Toscana* (1580), ed. S. Mencherini, Arezzo, 1913.

Richa, G., *Notizie istoriche delle chiese fiorentine*, 10 vols., Florence, 1754–62; reprint Rome, 1989.

The Rule of St. Benedict, ed. A. Meisel and M. del Mastro, Garden City, 1975.

Savonarola, *Prediche Italiane ai Fiorentini*, 2 vols., Perugia/Venice, 1930.

Vasari, G., *Le vite de' più eccellenti pittori, scultori ed architettori* (1568), ed. G. Milanesi, 9 vols., Florence, 1906.

—, *Le vite de' più eccellenti pittori, scultori e architettori nelle redazioni del 1550 e 1568*, ed. P. Barocchi and R. Bettarini, 6 vols., Florence, 1966–87.

—, *Lives of the Most Eminent Painters, Sculptors and Architects*, trans. G. De Vere, 10 vols., London, 1912–14 (reissued New York, 1976).

Vespasiano da Bisticci, *Renaissance Princes, Popes, and Prelates*, ed. M. Gilmore, New York, 1963.

III SECONDARY SOURCES

Acidini Luchinat, C., ed., *Benozzo Gozzoli: La Cappella dei Magi*, Milan, 1993; Eng. ed., *The Chapel of the Magi: Benozzo Gozzoli's Frescoes in the Palazzo Medici-Riccardi, Florence*, London and New York, 1994.

Ames-Lewis, F., "Early Medicean Devices," *Journal of the Warburg and Courtauld Institutes*, vol. 42 (1979), pp. 122–43.

—, "Fra Filippo Lippi and Flanders," *Zeitschrift für Kunstgeschichte*, vol. 42 (1979), pp. 255–73.

—, "Fra Filippo Lippi's S. Lorenzo *Annunciation*," *Storia dell'arte*, vol. 69 (1990), pp. 155–63.

—, ed., *Cosimo "il Vecchio" de' Medici, 1389–1464*, Oxford, 1992.

—, ed., *The Early Medici and their Artists*, London, 1995.

d'Ancona, A., *Origini del teatro italiano*, 2 vols., Turin, 1891.

de Angelis, L., and Conti, A., "Un libro antico della sagrestia di Sant'Ambrogio," *Annali della Scuola Normale Superiore di Pisa*, serie III, vol. VI, 1 (1976), pp. 97–109.

Ashley, K., and Sheingorn, P., eds., *Interpreting Cultural Symbols: Saint Anne in late Medieval Society*, Athens, Georgia, 1990.

Bacchi, G., "Santa Maria delle Selve," offprint from *Rose del Carmelo*, Florence, 1926.

—, "La Compagnia di Sta. Maria delle laudi e di Sant'Agnese nel Carmine di Firenze," *Rivista storica carmelitana*, vol. 3 (1931), pp. 12–39.

Bal, M., and Bryson, N., "Semiotics and Art History," *Art Bulletin*, vol. 73 (1991), pp. 174–208.

Barr, M. C. "Music and Spectacle in Confraternity Drama of Fifteenth-Century Florence," in *Christianity and the Renaissance*, ed. T. Verdon and J. Henderson, pp. 376–404.

Baxandall, M., *Giotto and the Orators*, Oxford, 1971.

—, *Painting and Experience in Fifteenth Century Italy*, Oxford, 1972.

Bayley, C. C., *War and Society in Renaissance Florence: The "De Militia" of Leonardo Bruni*, Toronto, 1961.

Beck, J., "Masaccio's Early Career as a Sculptor," *Art Bulletin*, vol. 53 (1971), pp. 177–95.

—, *Masaccio: The Documents*, Locust Valley (New York), 1978.

Bellosi, L., ed., *Pittura di Luce: Giovanni di Francesco e l'arte fiorentina di metà Quattrocento*, ex. cat., Milan, 1990.

Belting, H., *Likeness and Presence: A History of the Image before the Era of Art*, Chicago, 1994.

Benazzi, G., and Virilli, P., *Filippo Lippi nel Duomo di Spoleto 1467–1469: Notizie dopo il restauro*, Spoleto, 1990.

Bent, G., "Santa Maria degli Angeli and the Arts: Patronage, Production and Practice in a Trecento Florentine Monastery," 2 vols., Ph.D. dissertation, Stanford University, 1993.

Berenson, B., *Italian Pictures of the Renaissance*, Oxford, 1932.

—, "Fra Angelico, Fra Filippo e la cronologia," *Bollettino d'arte*, vol. 26 (1932–33), pp. 1–22, 49–66.

—, *Pitture italiane del rinascimento*, Milan, 1936.

Berti, L., ed., *La Chiesa di Santa Maria del Carmine a Firenze*, Florence, 1992.

—, and Paolucci, A., eds., *L'età di Masaccio: Il primo Quattrocento a Firenze*, ex. cat., Milan, 1990.

Bizzocchi, R., *Chiesa e potere nella Toscana del Quattrocento*, Bologna, 1987.

Bombe, W., "Urkunden über ein verschollenes Altarbild Filippo Lippis," *Repertorium für Kunstwissenschaft*, vol. 34 (1911), pp. 115–18.

Borgo, L., *The Works of Mariotto Albertinelli*, New York, 1976.

Borsook, E., "Fra Filippo and the Murals for Prato Cathedral," *Mitteilungen des Kunsthistorischen Institutes in Florenz*, vol. 19 (1975), pp. 1–148.

—, *The Mural Painters of Tuscany*, 2nd ed., Oxford, 1980.

—, "Cults and Imagery at Sant'Ambrogio in Florence," *Mitteilungen des Kunsthistorischen Institutes in Florenz*, vol. 25 (1981), pp. 147–202.

—, and Superbi Gioffredi, F., *Italian Altarpieces 1250–1550: Function and Design*, Oxford, 1994.

Boskovits, M., "Su Don Silvestro, Don Simone e la 'Scuola degli Angeli'," *Paragone*, Anno XXXIII (1972), 1, vol. 265, pp. 35–62.

—, "Fra Filippo Lippi, i carmelitani e il Rinascimento," *Arte cristiana*, vol. 74 (1986), pp. 235–52.

Brocchi, G. M., *Vite de' Santi e Beati Fiorentini*, 3 vols., Florence, 1742–61.

Brown, A., "A Humanist Portrait of Cosimo de' Medici, Pater Patriae," *The Journal of the Warburg and Courtauld Institutes*, vol. 24 (1961), pp. 186–221.

Brucker, G., *Renaissance Florence*, New York, 1969.

—, *The Society of Renaissance Florence: A Documentary Study*, New York, 1971.

—, *The Civic World of Early Renaissance Florence*, Princeton, 1977.

—, "Monasteries, Friaries, and Nunneries in Quattrocento Florence," in *Christianity and the Renaissance*, ed. T. Verdon and J. Henderson, pp. 41–62.

Buhler Walsh, B., "The Fresco Painting of Bicci di Lorenzo," Ph.D. dissertation, Indiana University, 1981.

Burckhardt, J., *The Civilization of the Renaissance in Italy* (1860), London and New York, 1944.

Bynum, C. Walker, *Jesus as Mother: Studies in the Spirituality of the High Middle Ages*, Berkeley, 1982.

—, *Holy Feast and Holy Fast: The Religious Significance of Food to Medieval Women*, Berkeley, 1987.

Caioli, P., *S. Andrea Corsini*, Florence, 1929.

—, *Il Beato Angelino*, Florence, 1938.

—, "Un altro sguardo sulla vita di fra Filippo Lippi," *Carmelus*, vol. 5 (1958), pp. 30–72.

Camille, M., *The Gothic Idol: Ideology and Image-making in Medieval Art*, Cambridge, 1989.

Campbell, L., *Renaissance Portraits: European Portrait-Painting in the 14th, 15th and 16th Centuries*, New Haven and London, 1990.

Campbell, S., "Pictura and Scriptura: Cosmè Tura and Style as Courtly Performance," *Art History*, vol. 19 (1996), pp. 267–95.

Cannon, J., "Dominican Patronage of the Arts in Central Italy: The Provincia Romana, c. 1220–1320," Ph.D. dissertation, London University, 1980.

—, "Pietro Lorenzetti and the History of the Carmelite Order," *The Journal of the Warburg and Courtauld Institutes*, vol. 50 (1987), pp. 18–28.

Caplow, H. McNeal, *Michelozzo*, 2 vols., New York, 1977.

Cardile, P., "Fra Angelico and his Workshop at San Domenico (1420–35)," Ph.D. dissertation, Yale University, 1977.

Christiansen, K., "New Light on the Early Work of Filippo Lippi," *Apollo*, vol. 122 (1985), pp. 338–43.

—, "Some Observations on the Brancacci Chapel Frescoes after their Cleaning," *Burlington Magazine*, vol. 133 (1991), pp. 5–20.

—, Strehlke, C., and Kanter, L., *Painting in Renaissance Siena, 1420–1500*, ex. cat., New York, 1988.

Colnaghi, D., *Colnaghi's Dictionary of Florentine Painters*, Florence, 1986.

Didi-Huberman, G., *Fra Angelico: Dissemblance et Figuration*, Paris, 1990; Eng. ed., *Dissemblance and Figuration*, Chicago, 1995.

Dizionario biografico degli italiani, vols. 1–49, Rome, 1960–97.

Eckstein, N., *The District of the Green Dragon: Neighborhood Life and Social Change in Renaissance Florence*, Florence, 1995.

Eisenberg, M., *Lorenzo Monaco*, Princeton, 1989.

Eliade, M., *The Sacred and the Profane: The Nature of Religion*, New York, 1959.

Even, Y., "Artistic Collaboration in Florentine Workshops: Quattrocento," Ph.D. dissertation, Columbia University, 1988.

Fabriczy, C., "Michelozzo di Bartolomeo," *Jahrbuch der Königlich Preuszischen Kunstsammlungen*, vol. 25 (1904), pp. 34–110.

Fausti, L., "Le pitture di Fra Filippo Lippi nel Duomo di Spoleto," *Archivio per la storia ecclesiastica dell'Umbria*, vol. 2 (1915), pp. 1–36.

Fiorilli, C., "I dipintori a Firenze nell'arte dei medici speziali e merciai," *Archivio storico italiano*, vol. 78 (1920), II, pp. 5–74.

Fossi, G., *Filippo Lippi* (Eng. ed.), Florence, 1989.

Frey, C., *Die Loggia dei Lanzi zu Florenz*, Berlin, 1885.

Gamboso, V., "L'immagine di S. Antonio nei panegirici dei secoli XIII–XIV," in *I Volti antichi e attuali del Santo di Padova: Colloquio interdisciplinare su "l'immagine di S. Antonio"*, in *Il Santo*, Anno XIX, Serie II, fasc. 2–3, May–Dec. 1979, pp. 263–314.

Gardner, J., "Nuns and Altarpieces: Agendas for Research," *Römisches Jahrbuch der Biblioteca Hertziana*, vol. 30 (1995), pp. 27–57.

Gardner von Teuffel, C., "Lorenzo Monaco, Filippo Lippi and Filippo Brunelleschi: die Erfindung der Renaissancepala," *Zeitschrift für Kunstgeschichte*, vol. 45 (1982), pp. 1–30.

—, "From Polyptych to Pala: Some Structural Considerations," in *La pittura nel xiv e xv secolo: il contributo dell'analisi tecnica alla storia dell'arte*, ed. H. van Os and J. van Asperen de Boer, Bologna, 1983, pp. 323–30.

Gilbert, C., "The Drawings now associated with Masaccio's Sagra," *Storia dell'arte*, vol. 3 (1969), pp. 260–78.

—, "Special Images for Carmelites," in *Christianity and the Renaissance*, ed. T. Verdon and J. Henderson, pp. 166–80.

Giovannini, P., and Vitolo, S., eds., *Il Convento del Carmine di Firenze: Caratteri e documenti*, Florence, 1981.

Glasser, H., *Artists' Contracts of the Early Renaissance*, New York, 1977.

Goldthwaite, R., *Wealth and the Demand for Art in Italy 1300–1600*, Baltimore, 1993.

Gombrich, E., "The Early Medici as Patrons of Art," *Norm and Form*, New York, 1978, pp. 35–57.

Gregori, M., Paolucci, A., and Acidini Luchinat, C., eds., *Maestri e Botteghe: Pittura a Firenze alla fine del quattrocento*, Milan, ex. cat., 1992.

Guidotti, A., "Fatti, arredi e corredi carmelitani a Firenze," in *La Chiesa di Santa Maria del Carmine a Firenze*, ed. L. Berti, pp. 21–53.

Hall, M., *Renovation and Counter-Reformation*, Oxford and New York, 1979.

Hatfield, R., "Five Early Renaissance Portraits," *Art Bulletin*, vol. 47 (1965), pp. 315–34.

—, "The Compagnia de' Magi," *The Journal of the Warburg and Courtauld Institutes*, vol. 33 (1970), pp. 107–61.

—, "Cosimo de' Medici and the Chapel of his Palace," in *Cosimo "il Vecchio" de' Medici, 1389–1464*, ed. F. Ames-Lewis, Oxford, 1992, pp. 221–44.

Hauptmann, M., *Der Tondo*, Frankfurt, 1936.

Hay, D., *The Church in Italy in the Fifteenth Century*, Cambridge and New York, 1977.

Herlihy, D., and Klapisch-Zuber, C., *Tuscans and their Families: A Study of the Florentine Catasto of 1427*, New Haven, 1985.

Hills, P., "The Renaissance Altarpiece: A Valid Category?" in *The Altarpiece in the Renaissance*, ed. P. Humfrey and M. Kemp, pp. 34–48.

Hoeniger, C., *The Renovation of Paintings in Tuscany, 1250–1500*, Cambridge, 1995.

Holmes, M., "'Frate Filippo di Tommaso Dipintore': Fra Filippo Lippi and Florentine Renaissance Religious Practices," Ph.D. dissertation, Harvard University, 1993.

—, "Disrobing the Virgin: The *Madonna lactans* in Fifteenth-Century Florentine Art," in *Picturing Women in Renaissance and Baroque Italy*, ed. G. Johnson and S. Matthews Grieco, Cambridge, 1997, pp. 167–95.

—, "Giovanni Benci's Patronage of the Nunnery Le Murate," in *Family and Memory in Renaissance Florence*, ed. G. Ciappelli and P. Rubin, Cambridge, forthcoming.

Hood, W., *Fra Angelico at San Marco*, New Haven and London, 1993.

Horster, M., *Andrea del Castagno*, Oxford, 1980.

Humfrey, P., and Kemp, M., eds., *The Altarpiece in the Renaissance*, Cambridge and New York, 1990.

Iriarte, L., *Storia del Francescanismo*, Naples, 1982.

Joannides, P., *Masaccio and Masolino: A Complete Catalogue*, London and New York, 1993.

Kecks, R., *Madonna und Kind: Das häusliche Andachtsbild im Florenz des 15. Jahrhunderts*, Berlin, 1988.

Kemp, M., "From 'Mimesis' to 'Fantasia': The Quattrocento Vocabulary of Creation, Inspiration and Genius in the Visual Arts," *Viator*, vol. 8 (1977), pp. 347–98.

Kent, D., *The Rise of the Medici Faction in Florence 1426–1434*, Oxford and New York, 1978.

Kent, F. W., "Lorenzo de' Medici, Madonna Scolastica Rondinelli e la politica di mecenatismo architettonico nel convento delle Murate (1471–72)," in *Arte, committenza ed economia a Roma e nelle corti del Rinascimento 1420–1530*, ed. A. Esch and C. L. Frommel, Turin, 1995, pp. 353–82.

King, A., *Liturgies of the Religious Orders*, London, 1955.

Klapisch-Zuber, C., "The 'Cruel Mother': Maternity, Widowhood, and Dowry in Florence in the Fourteenth and Fifteenth Centuries," *Women, Family, and Ritual in Renaissance Italy*, Chicago, 1985, pp. 117–31.

Koch, R., "Elijah the Prophet, Founder of the Carmelite Order," *Speculum*, vol. 34 (1959), pp. 547–60.

Lachi, C., "Il problema della bottega di Filippo Lippi: Nuove scoperte," in *La Natività di Filippo Lippi: Restauro, saggi e ricerche*, ed. M. Pia Mannini, Prato, 1995, pp. 33–9.

Lasareff, V., "Studies in the Iconography of the Virgin," *Art Bulletin*, vol. 20 (1938), pp. 26–65.

Leclercq, J., *La Vita perfetta*, Milan, 1961.

Lesnick, D., *Preaching in Medieval Florence: The Social World of Franciscan and Dominican Spirituality*, Athens, Georgia, 1989.

Levi d'Ancona, M., *Miniatura e miniatori a Firenze dal XIV al XVI secolo*, Florence, 1962.

Levi Pisetzky, R., *Storia del costume at Italia*, 5 vols., Milan, 1964–69.

Lickteig, F., *The German Carmelites at the Medieval Universities*, Rome, 1981.

Litta, P., *Famiglie Celebri di Italia*, 2 series, 13 vols., Milan, 1819–85; 1902.

Lowe, K., "Female Strategies for Success in a Male-ordered World: The Benedictine convent of Le Murate in Florence in the Fifteenth and Early Sixteenth Centuries," *Studies in Church History*, vol. 27 (1990), pp. 209–21.

—, "Women's Work at the Benedictine Convent of Le Murate in Florence: Suora Battista Carducci's Roman Missal of 1509," in *Women and the Book: Assessing the Visual Evidence*, ed. L. Smith and J. Taylor, London, 1997, pp. 133–46.

Lugano, P., *Memorie dei più antichi miniatori e calligrafi Olivetani*, Florence, 1903.

—, *Di Fra Giovanni da Verona: Maestro d'Intaglio e di Tarsio e della sua Scuola*, Siena, 1905.

Il luogo teatrale, ed. M. Fabbri, E. G. Zorzi, and A. M. Petrioli Tofani, Milan, 1975.

Lydecker, J. K., "The Domestic Setting of the Arts in Renaissance Florence," Ph.D. dissertation, Johns Hopkins University, 1987.

Mallett, M., *The Florentine Galleys in the Fifteenth Century*, Oxford, 1967.

Mannini, M. Pia, and Fagioli, M., *Filippo Lippi: Catalogo completo,* Florence, 1997.

Marchese, V., *Memorie dei più insigni pittori, scultori e architetti domenicani*, 2 vols., Genoa, 1869 and 1879 eds.

Marchini, G., *Filippo Lippi*, Milan, 1975.

Martindale, A., *The Rise of the Artist in the Middle Ages and Early Renaissance*, London, 1972.

—, *Simone Martini*, Oxford, 1988.

Martines, L., *Lawyers and Statecraft in Renaissance Florence*, Princeton, 1968.

Mattei, S., *Ragionamento intorno all'antica chiesa del Carmine di Firenze*, Florence, 1869.

McCaffrey, P. R., *The White Friars*, Dublin, 1926.

Meiss, M., *Painting in Florence and Siena after the Black Death*, Princeton, 1951.

Mencherini, S., *S. Croce*, Florence, 1929.

Mendelsohn, H., *Fra Filippo Lippi*, Berlin, 1909.

Metropolitan Museum of Art, *Painting and Illumination in Early Renaissance Florence 1300–1450*, ed. L. Kanter, B. Boehm, C. Strehlke, G. Freuler, C. Mayer Thurman, P. Palladino, New York, ex. cat., 1994.

Miles, M., "The Virgin's One Bare Breast," in *The Female Body in Western Culture*, ed. S. Suleiman, Cambridge, Mass., 1986, pp. 193–208.

Miller, J., "Major Florentine Altarpieces from 1430 to 1450," Ph.D. dissertation, Columbia University, 1983.

Moisé, F., *Santa Croce di Firenze, Illustrazione storico-artistica*, Florence, 1845.

Molho, A., "The Brancacci Chapel: Studies in its Iconography and History," *The Journal of the Warburg and Courtauld Institutes*, vol. 40 (1977), pp. 50–98.

—, "Tamquam vere mortua: Le professioni religiose femminili nella Firenze del tardo medioevo," *Società e storia*, vol. 43 (1989), pp. 1–44.

—, *Marriage Alliance in Late Medieval Florence*, Cambridge, Mass., 1994.

Moorman, J., *A History of the Franciscan Order from its Origins to the Year 1517*, Oxford, 1968.

Nelson, J., "Aggiunte alla cronologia di Filippino Lippi," *Rivista d'arte*, vol. 43 (1991), pp. 3–57.

Newbigin, N., "*Cene* and *Cenacoli* in the Ascension and Pentecost Companies of Fifteenth-Century Florence," in *Crossing the Boundaries: Christian Piety and the Arts in Italian Medieval and Renaissance Confraternities*, ed. K. Eisenbichler, Kalamazoo, 1991, pp. 90–107.

—, *Feste d'Oltrarno: Plays in Churches in Fifteenth-Century Florence*, 2 vols., Florence, 1996.

Nunes, E., *Dom Frey Gomez Abade de Florença, 1420–1440*, vol. 1, Braga, 1963.

Oertel, R., *Fra Filippo Lippi*, Vienna, 1942.

Orlandi, S., *Beato Angelico*, Florence, 1964.

van Os, H., "Text and Image: The Case of a Jewish Prophet in Carmelite Disguise," in *Non Nova sed Nove: Mélanges de civilisation médiévale dédiés à Willem Noomen*, Groningen, 1984, pp. 163–8.

—, *Sienese Altarpieces 1215–1460*, 2 vols., Groningen, 1984 and 1990.

Paatz, E. and W., *Die Kirchen von Florenz*, 5 vols., Frankfurt, 1940–54.

Pandimiglio, L., *Felice di Michele vir clarissimus e una consorteria: I Brancacci di Firenze*, Milan, 1987.

Paoletti, J., "Fraternal Piety and Family Power: The Artistic Patronage of Cosimo and Lorenzo de' Medici," in *Cosimo "il Vecchio" de' Medici, 1389–1464*, ed. F. Ames-Lewis, pp. 195–219.

—, "Strategies and Structures of Medici Artistic Patronage in the 15th Century," in *The Early Medici and Their Artists*, ed. F. Ames-Lewis, pp. 19–36.

Paolucci, A., *Capolavori e Restauri*, ex. cat., Florence, 1986.

Pittaluga, M., *Filippo Lippi*, Florence, 1949.

Pochat, G., "Brunelleschi and the 'Ascension' of 1422," *Art Bulletin*, vol. 60 (1978), pp. 232–4.
Poggi, G., "Sulla data dell'affresco di Fra Filippo Lippi nel chiostro del Carmine," *Rivista d'arte*, vol. 18 (1936), pp. 95–106.
Pope-Hennessy, J., *The Portrait in the Renaissance*, New York, 1966.
—, *Fra Angelico*, London, 1974.
Procacci, U., "L'incendio della Chiesa del Carmine del 1771," *Rivista d'arte*, vol. 14 (1932), pp. 141–232.
—, "Relazione dei lavori eseguiti nella chiesa del Carmine di Firenze per la ricerca di antichi affreschi," *Bollettino d'arte*, vol. 27 (1933–4), pp. 327–34.
—, "Di Jacopo di Antonio e delle compagnie di pittori del Corso degli Adimari nel XV secolo," *Rivista d'arte*, vol. 35 (1960), pp. 3–70.
Puccetti, S., "Note sulla simbologia del Monastero," in *Iconografia di San Benedetto nella pittura della Toscana*, ed. G. Viti, Florence, 1982, pp. 391–8.
Robinson, C., "The Early Medici and Architecture," in *The Early Medici and their Artists*, ed. F. Ames-Lewis, pp. 51–69.
de Roover, R., *The Rise and Decline of the Medici Bank (1397–1494)*, Cambridge, Mass., 1963.
Ricostruzione grafica delle fasi storiche della chiesa del Carmine, Florence, 1974.
Rowlands, E., "Fra Filippo Lippi's Stay in Padua and its Impact on his Art," Ph.D. dissertation, Rutgers University, 1983.
—, "Filippo Lippi and his Experience of Painting in the Veneto Region," *Artibus et Historiae*, vol. 19/X (1989), pp. 53–83.
Rubin, P., *Giorgio Vasari: Art and History*, New Haven and London, 1995.
Rubinstein, N., *The Government of Florence under the Medici 1434–1494*, Oxford, 1966.
—, "Lay Patronage and Observant Reform in Fifteenth-century Florence," in *Christianity and the Renaissance*, ed. T. Verdon and J. Henderson, pp. 64–82.
Ruda, J., "The National Gallery Tondo of the Adoration of the Magi and the Early Style of Filippo Lippi," *Studies in the History of Art* (National Gallery, Washington), no. 7 (1975), pp. 6–39.
—, "A 1434 Building Programme for San Lorenzo in Florence," *Burlington Magazine*, vol. 120 (1978), pp. 358–61.
—, "Style and Patronage in the 1440s: Two Altarpieces of the Coronation of the Virgin by Filippo Lippi," *Mitteilungen des Kunsthistorischen Institutes in Florenz*, vol. 28 (1984), pp. 363–84.
—, *Fra Filippo Lippi*, New York and London, 1993.
Saalman, H., "Michelozzo Studies," *Burlington Magazine*, vol. 108 (1966), pp. 242–50.
Sabatini, A., "La Nobile Famiglia Fiorentina del Soderini e il Carmine di Firenze," *Roseti del Carmelo*, vol. 24 (1971), pp. 197–205.
—, "550 Anno della Consacrazione dell'antica chiesa del Carmine di Firenze: La 'Sagra' del Masaccio," *Roseti del Carmelo*, vol. 25 (1972), pp. 110–15.
Saggi, L., *La Congregazione Mantovana dei Carmelitani*, Rome, 1954.
—, *Sant'Angelo di Sicilia: Studio sulla vita, devozione, folklore*, Rome, 1962.
—, ed., *Santi del Carmelo*, Rome, 1972.
Salmi, M., *Masaccio* (French ed.), Rome, 1932.
—, "La giovinezza di Fra Filippo Lippi," *Rivista d'arte*, vol. 18 (1936), pp. 1–24.
Seymour, C., *Early Italian Paintings in the Yale University Art Gallery*, New Haven, 1970.
Shearman, J., *Only Connect.... Art and the Spectator in the Italian Renaissance*, Princeton, 1992.
Shell, C., "The Early Style of Fra Filippo Lippi and the Prato Master," *Art Bulletin*, vol. 43 (1961), pp. 197–209.
Simons, P., "Women in Frames: The Gaze, the Eye, the Profile in Renaissance Portraiture," in *The Expanding Discourse*, ed. N. Broude and M. Garrard, New York, 1992, pp. 38–57.
Smet, J., *The History of the Brothers of Our Lady of Mount Carmel*, Rome, 1975.
Steinberg, L., *The Sexuality of Christ in Renaissance Art and in Modern Oblivion*, New York, 1983.
—, "'How Shall This Be?' Reflections on Filippo Lippi's *Annunciation* in London," *Artibus et Historiae*, vol. 16/VIII (1987), pp. 25–44.
Sutherland Harris, A., and Nochlin, L., *Women Artists: 1550–1950*, Los Angeles, 1976.
Swartwout, S. E., *The Monastic Craftsman*, Cambridge, 1932.
Tartuferi, A., "Le testimonianze superstiti (e le perdite) della decorazione primitiva (secoli XIII–XV)," in *La Chiesa di Santa Maria del Carmine a Firenze*, ed. L. Berti, pp. 143–71.
Thomas, A., *The Painter's Practice in Renaissance Tuscany*, Cambridge, 1995.
Thornton, P., *The Italian Renaissance Interior 1400–1600*, London, 1991.
Tibbetts Schulenburg, J., "The Heroics of Virginity: Brides of Christ and Sacrificial Mutilation," in *Women in the Middle Ages and the Renaissance*, ed. M. B. Rose, Syracuse, New York, 1986, pp. 29–72.
Trexler, R., *Synodal Law in Florence and Fiesole, 1306–1518*, Vatican City, 1971.
—, "Le célibat à la fin du Moyen Age: Les religieuses de Florence," *Annales*, vol. 27 (1972), pp. 1329–50.
—, *Public Life in Renaissance Florence*, New York, 1980.
Trinkaus, C., and Oberman, H., eds., *The Pursuit of Holiness in Late Medieval and Renaissance Religion*, Leiden, 1974.
Ventrone, P., ed., *Le tems revient 'l tempo si rinuova: Feste e spettacoli nella Firenze di Lorenzo il Magnifico*, Milan, 1992.
Verdon, T., and Henderson, J., eds., *Christianity and the Renaissance*, Syracuse, New York, 1990.
Wackernagel, M., *The World of the Florentine Renaissance Artist* (1938), ed. A. Luchs, Princeton, 1981.
Warnke, M., *The Court Artist: On the Ancestry of the Modern Artist*, Cambridge, 1993.
White, J., *The Birth and Rebirth of Pictorial Space*, London, 1987.
Wittkower, M. and R., *Born Under Saturn*, New York, 1963.
Wohl, H., *The Paintings of Domenico Veneziano*, New York and London, 1980.
Zarri, G., "Monasteri femminili e città (secoli xv–xviii)," in *Storia d'Italia, Annali 9: La Chiesa e il potere politico dal Medioevo all'età contemporanea,* Turin, 1986, pp. 359–429.

PHOTOGRAPH CREDITS

Many of the illustrations have been made from photographs or transparencies provided by the owners or custodians of the works. Those plates for which further credit is due are listed below.

Alinari: 58, 85, 147, 230

Art Resource: 47 (Alinari), 75, 121, 126, 204 (Scala)

Artothek, Peissenberg: 3, 96, 220, 222, 224, 226–8

Nicolò Orsi Battaglini: 107

Biblioteca Nazionale, Florence: 127, 157–8, 181

Biblioteca Moreniana, Florence: 153

Joanna Cannon: 20

Courtauld Institute of Art, London: 122; 185 and 233 (Conway Library)

Gabinetto fotografico, Soprintendenza per i Beni Ambientali e Architettonici, Florence: 187, 209

Gabinetto fotografico, Soprintendenza per i Beni Artistici e Storici, Florence: 33, 35, 37, 41, 52, 64, 81–2, 94, 99, 109, 117, 136–7, 141, 146, 149, 162, 166–7, 169, 196, 198, 219, 231, 232, 234

Gabinetto fotografico, Soprintendenza per i Beni Artistici e Storici, Siena: 17, 79–80

Kent County Council, Folkestone, Kent: 36, 38

Kunsthistorisches Institut, Florence: 106, 191, 206–7,

K. J. P. Lowe and Megan Holmes: 213a and b

The Pierpont Morgan Library, New York: 72, 77

Antonio Quattrone: 2, 8–10, 12, 18, 40, 45, 49–51, 59–63, 65–71, 89, 93, 98, 104–5, 123–5, 130, 142, 144–5, 148, 152, 156, 160, 163, 168, 174–6, 179, 182-3, 221

Réunion des Musées Nationaux: 103

Eve Sanders: 43–4

Scala: 1, 5–7, 11, 14, 19, 21–7, 29, 53–5, 78, 83–4, 86–8, 90–2, 100, 102, 108, 110, 118, 120, 135, 138, 140, 143, 154–5, 159, 161, 164–5, 170–1, 180, 184, 186, 188–90, 192–5, 197, 205, 212, 214–18

INDEX